PENGUIN MODERN CLASSICS

The Orwell Diaries

George Orwell (whose real name was Eric Arthur Blair) was born in 1903 in India and then went to Eton when his family moved back to England. From 1922 to 1927 he served with the Indian Imperial Police in Burma, an experience that inspired his first novel, *Burmese Days* (1934). He lived in Paris before returning to England, and *Down and Out in Paris and London* was published in 1936. After writing *The Road to Wigan Pier* and *Homage to Catalonia* (his account of fighting for the Republicans in the Spanish Civil War), Orwell was admitted to a sanatorium in 1938 and from then on was never fully fit. He spent six months in Morocco where he wrote *Coming Up for Air*. During the Second World War Orwell served in the Home Guard and worked for the BBC. His political allegory *Animal Farm* was published in 1945 and it was this novel, together with *Nineteen Eighty-Four* (1949), which brought him worldwide fame. George Orwell was taken seriously ill in the winter of 1948–9 and died in London in 1950.

Peter Davison is Research Professor of English at De Montfort University, Leicester. He was born in Newcastle upon Tyne in 1926 and studied for a London External BA (1954) by correspondence course. He edited an Elizabethan text for a London MA (1957) and then taught at Sydney University, where he gained a Ph.D. He was awarded a D.Litt and an Hon. D. Arts by De Montfort University in 1999. He has written and edited twenty-three books as well as the facsimile edition of the manuscript of *Nineteen Eighty-Four* and the twenty volumes of Orwell's *Complete Works* (with Ian Angus and Sheila Davison). He is a past president of the Bibliographical Society, whose journal he edited for twelve years. He was made an OBE in 1999 for services to literature. He was awarded the Gold Medal of the Bibliographical Society in 2003 and appointed a Professor Emeritus of Glyndŵr University in 2009.

GEORGE ORWELL

The Orwell Diaries

Edited by Peter Davison

PENGUIN BOOKS

PENGUIN CLASSICS

Published by the Penguin Group
Penguin Books Ltd, 80 Strand, London WC2R ORL, England
Penguin Group (USA) Inc., 375 Hudson Street, New York, New York 10014, USA
Penguin Group (Canada), 90 Eglinton Avenue East, Suite 700, Toronto, Ontario, Canada M4P 2Y3
(a division of Pearson Penguin Canada Inc.)
Penguin Ireland, 25 St Stephen's Green, Dublin 2, Ireland (a division of Penguin Books Ltd)
Penguin Group (Australia), 250 Camberwell Road, Camberwell, Victoria 3124, Australia
(a division of Pearson Australia Group Pty Ltd)
Penguin Books India Pvt Ltd, 11 Community Centre, Panchsheel Park, New Delhi – 110 017, India
Penguin Group (NZ), 67 Apollo Drive, Rosedale, North Shore 0632, New Zealand
(a division of Pearson New Zealand Ltd)
Penguin Books (South Africa) (Pty) Ltd, 24 Sturdee Avenue, Rosebank, Johannesburg 2196, South Africa

Penguin Books Ltd, Registered Offices: 80 Strand, London WC2R ORL, England

www.penguin.com

First published by Harvill Secker 2009
Published in Penguin Classics 2010
004

Diaries collected from *The Complete Works of George Orwell*, edited by Peter Davison, OBE, published in Great Britain in 1998 by Secker & Warburg

Printed in England by Clays Ltd, St Ives plc

978–0–141–19154–6

www.greenpenguin.co.uk

Penguin Books is committed to a sustainable future for our business, our readers and our planet. This book is made from Forest Stewardship Council™ certified paper.

ALWAYS LEARNING PEARSON

CONTENTS

Introduction

George Orwell was an inveterate writer of diaries and lists, he filled notebooks with his ideas, and into them sketched drafts of poems – ''Twas on a Tuesday morning' and 'Joseph Higgs, late of this parish' – and copied and pasted items of information from newspapers, recipes, garden hints, and so forth. He made lists of nationalist leaders, popular songs, words and phrases in Latin, French and other languages. He famously made a list of those he regarded as crypto-communists and fellow-travellers and he noted his extensive reading in the last year of his life. For many years he collected pamphlets (now in the British Library) and started to catalogue them. And he carefully noted what he had been paid for his writings to aid in the declaration of his earnings for his income tax return. Unfortunately, only his earnings from July 1943 to December 1945 survive; ironically, those payments are listed in a notebook that Eileen had used when working in Whitehall in the Censorship Department. Although he usually gave no thought to the preservation of the manuscripts of his published work – what survive (for example, the typescripts of *Animal Farm* and *Nineteen Eighty-Four*) probably do so simply because he did not live long enough to destroy them. His diaries, however, he kept and they were often typed up. Eleven survive. They were not Pepysian-like private diaries written in a code but, in the main, straightforward records of his life, his observations of Nature, and the political events of his time. When he was away from Wallington in September 1939, Eileen filled in his Domestic Diary and in the winter of 1947–48, when he was in hospital, his sister Avril noted on his behalf such basic information as the state of the weather and work undertaken around Barnhill.

It is as certain as things can be that a twelfth, and possibly a thirteenth diary, are secreted away in the NKVD Archive in Moscow. In March 1996, Professor Miklos Kun, grandson of the Hungarian Communist leader, Béla Kun, told me that the NKVD had targeted Orwell and he knew of a file in its Archive devoted to him. (Béla Kun, having fallen out with the Soviet authorities, was probably shot in a Soviet Gulag on 29 August 1938, although an earlier Soviet account states that he died in one of its prisons on 30 November 1939.) Unfortunately the archive was closed to the public before it could be examined. Orwell wrote to Charles Doran on 2 August 1937 (*CW*, XI, p. 386) that documents had been seized from his wife's room at the Continental Hotel in Barcelona. In *Homage to Catalonia* he states that six plainsclothes policemen took 'my diaries' (p. 164). Given Orwell's addiction to writing diaries, it is at least possible that he also wrote a diary when he was serving with the police in Burma but it is unlikely that such a diary will surface. In his Domestic Diary for 1 June 1946, Orwell refers to a rabbit-skin recipe 'in the other diary' – but that diary has not been identified. Despite evident losses, these eleven diaries, and the diary entries in two notebooks, provide, with some gaps, a personal record of Orwell's life from his venture into hop-picking in 1931 until his final days in hospital.

Orwell's diary entries from 9 August 1938, accompanied by excellent maps of Orwell's travels at the time of the diary entries, have been posted day by day precisely seventy years later on the Orwell Prize website, www.orwelldiaries.wordpress.com.

In presenting Orwell's diaries here I have endeavoured to retain characteristics typical of Orwell as a diarist rather than as Orwell the perfectionist author whilst ensuring the text is easily readable. Trivial errors and misspellings such as 'actualy' for 'actually' have been corrected silently and his habit of writing 'i.e.' and e.g.' as 'ie.' and 'eg.' are retained, but, for example, names of journals are italicized. Significant changes are noted. Orwell's capitalization was often erratic (so one has 'Canterbury bells' and 'Canterbury Bells' an entry or two later) and frequently omitted. Words are only capitalized if (as in this example) not to do so might cause confusion. It is noticeable that Eileen's spelling, when she writes up the diary, is more accurate than is her husband's. Thus, she has 'scabious' and he has 'scabius'. Both spellings are retained. I have identified as many individuals noted only by initials as I can and have tended to spell out (using square brackets) names frequently mentioned – e.g. A[vril] and B[ill]. If Orwell typed up his diaries from their handwritten originals only a few interesting variants are noted. Most of Orwell's handwritten corrections in typewritten final versions are taken in silently. Full details can be found in the *Complete Works of George Orwell.* References in footnotes to *Complete Works* are indicated by the letters *CW* and by volume and page. The notes here, whilst omitting the minor variants noted above, are considerably amplified from those in *The Complete Works.*

Grateful thanks are due to The Orwell Estate, in particular Richard Blair and Bill Hamilton, and to Gill Furlong, Archivist, UCL Special Collections Library, for allowing these Diaries to be published in this edition. I am also very grateful to Myra Jones for casting such an acute eye over the proofs.

Finally: given that Orwell was so averse to his biography being written, it is ironic that these diaries offer a virtual autobiography of his life and opinions for so much of his life.

*Orwell's own footnotes are indicated (as was his practice) by symbols (e.g. *, †, §). The superior degree sign (°) is used selectively to indicate one of his idiosyncratic spellings but most are left unnoticed. Editorial footnotes are placed as close as is practicably convenient to their references.*

Hop-Picking Diary

25 August 1931 – 8 October 1931

George Orwell was born on 25 June 1903 in Motihari, Bengal, to Richard Walmesley Blair, then a sub-deputy agent in the Opium Department of the Indian Civil Service, and his wife, Ida. He was christened Eric Arthur. He had an older sister, Marjorie, and the children returned to England in 1904 and settled at Henley-on-Thames. He saw his father again in the summer of 1907 when he returned on leave. A younger sister, Avril, was born on 6 April 1908. When Mr Blair retired in 1912 the family moved to Shiplake, Oxfordshire, where Orwell made friends with the Buddicom family, especially their eldest child, Jacintha. A useful map of the neighbourhood where they both lived and played will be found in Jacintha Buddicom's *Eric & Us* (and see especially second edition for the postscript by Dione Venables, 2006). Orwell was educated first by Anglican nuns, then at St Cyprian's Preparatory School, Eastbourne (the subject of a famous but one-sided essay, 'Such, Such Were the Joys' and where he wrote two patriotic poems published in the *Henley and South Oxfordshire Standard*). Then, having won a scholarship, he went for a term to Wellington College and after that to Eton as a King's Scholar. After the First World War, the Blairs moved to Southwold on the Suffolk coast.

Orwell served in Burma in the Indian Imperial Police from October 1922 to December 1927, a period of his life that gave rise to his novel, *Burmese Days*, and two of his most important early essays, 'Shooting an Elephant' and 'A Hanging'. When back in England on leave, he resigned his commission and gave up his relatively well-paid job in order to scratch a living as he sought to become a writer. He tramped and made a number of expeditions to the East End of London to examine the way the poor lived and to share that experience with them. From spring 1928 until late in 1929 he lived in a working-class district of Paris, at first surviving on his savings from his time in Burma, and wrote – and had published – a number of articles. He also wrote one or two novels (his own accounts conflict) but destroyed them, something he later regretted. His first articles, all but one published by minor Parisian journals, foreshadow his later literary interests: censorship, unemployment, the poor, imperialist exploitation, literature (an essay on John Galsworthy), and popular culture. Having had his last savings stolen, he worked for a while in the disgusting kitchen of an outwardly luxurious hotel and then returned to England. He lived with his parents at Southwold, writing the first draft of what would become *Down and Out in Paris and London*, reviewing for *The Adelphi* magazine, and continuing to tramp and live with down-and-outs. In the autumn of 1931 he went hop-picking in Kent and this first diary records that experience. The entries are printed from Orwell's typescript, which he made on 10 October 1931. He sent a carbon copy to his friend Dennis Collings in Southwold. Collings (1905–2001) was an anthropologist; he became assistant curator of the Raffles Museum in Singapore in 1934. When Singapore fell he escaped to Java but was captured by the Japanese and imprisoned. Writing on 22 January 1946, Orwell said he had seen him on his return and he 'appeared not to have had absolutely too bad a time, having been a camp interpreter' (*CW*, XVIII, p. 53). Orwell suggested the typescript might be shown to Collett Cresswell Pulleyne, a barrister from Yorkshire and a friend they had in common, and also to Eleanor Jaques, to whom Orwell was romantically inclined but who would marry Collings in 1934. Orwell also wrote an article, 'Hop-Picking' which was published by *The New Statesman and Nation* on 17 October 1931 over the name Eric Blair (*CW*, X, pp. 233–5); a section of the diary was used for that article. Dorothy Hare, in *A Clergyman's Daughter*, spends time hop-picking (Chapter II, sections iii–vi; pp. 108–41).

Orwell's own 'Notes' at the end of this diary give his definitions (e.g., of 'drum'); such words in the text are indicated here by a superior degree sign (°).

HOP-PICKING DIARY

25.8.31: On the night of the 25th I started off from Chelsea with about 14/– in hand, and went to Lew Levy's kip[1] in Westminster Bridge Road. It is much the same as it was three years ago, except that nearly all the beds are now a shilling instead of ninepence. This is owing to interference by the L.C.C. who have enacted (in the interests of hygiene, as usual) that beds in lodging houses must be further apart. There is a whole string of laws of this type relating to lodging houses,* but there is not and never will be a law to say that the beds must be reasonably comfortable. The net result of this law is that one's bed is now three feet from the next instead of two feet, and threepence dearer.

1. *kip:* originally a brothel; then a common lodging-house (as here) and by extension, a bed; today a sleep.

*For instance, Dick's café in Billingsgate. Dick's was one of the few places where you could get a cup of tea for 1d, and there were fires there so that anyone who had a penny could warm himself for hours in the early mornings. Only this last week the L.C.C. closed it on the ground that it was unhygienic [Orwell's note]. L.C.C. was the London County Council.

26.8.31: The next day I went to Trafalgar Square and camped by the north wall, which is one of the recognized rendezvous of down and out people in London. At this time of year the square has a floating population of 100 or 200 people (about ten per cent of them women), some of whom actually look on it as their home. They get their food by regular begging rounds (Covent Garden[2] at 4 am. for damaged fruit, various convents during the morning, restaurants and dustbins late at night etc.) and they manage to 'tap' likely-looking passers by for enough to keep them in tea. Tea is going on the square at all hours, one person supplying a 'drum',° another sugar and so on. The milk is condensed milk at 2½d a tin. You jab two holes in the tin with a knife, apply your mouth to one of them and blow, whereupon a sticky greyish stream dribbles from the other. The holes are then plugged with chewed paper, and the tin is kept for days, becoming coated with dust and filth. Hot water is cadged at coffee shops, or at night boiled over watchmen's fires, but this has to be done on the sly, as the police won't allow it. Some of the people I met on the square had been there without a break for six weeks, and did not seem much the worse, except that they are all fantastically dirty. As always among the destitute, a large proportion of them are Irishmen. From time to time these men go home on visits, and it appears that they never think of paying their passage, but always stow away on small cargo boats, the crews conniving.

I had meant to sleep in St Martin's Church,[3] but from what the others said it appeared that when you go in you are asked searching questions by some woman known as the Madonna, so I decided to stay the night in the square. It was not so bad as I expected, but between the cold and the police it was impossible to get a wink of sleep, and no one except a few hardened old tramps even tried to do so. There are seats enough for about fifty people, and the rest have to sit on the ground, which of course is forbidden by law. Every few minutes there would be a shout of 'Look out, boys, here comes the flattie!' and a policeman would come round and shake those who were asleep, and make the people on the ground get up. We used to kip down again the instant he had passed, and this went on like a kind of game from eight at night till three or four in the morning. After midnight it was so cold that I had to go for long walks to keep warm. The streets are somehow rather horrible at that hour; all silent and deserted, and yet lighted almost as bright as day with those garish lamps, which give everything a deathly air, as though London were the corpse of a town. About three o'clock another man and I went down to the patch of grass behind the Guards' parade ground, and saw prostitutes and men lying in couples there in the bitter cold mist and dew. There are always a number of prostitutes in the square; they are the unsuccessful ones, who can't earn enough for their night's kip. Overnight one of these women had been lying on the ground crying bitterly, because a man had gone off without paying her fee, which was sixpence. Towards morning they do not even get sixpence, but only a cup of tea or a cigarette. About four somebody got hold of a number of newspaper posters,[4] and we sat down six or eight on a bench and packed ourselves in enormous paper parcels, which kept us fairly warm till Stewart's café in St Martin's Lane opened. At Stewart's you can sit from five till nine for a cup of tea (or sometimes three or four people even share a cup between them) and you are allowed to sleep with your head on the table till seven; after that the proprietor wakes you. One meets a very mixed crowd there – tramps, Covent Garden porters, early business people, prostitutes – and there are constant quarrels and fights. On this occasion an old, very ugly woman, wife of a porter, was violently abusing two prostitutes, because they could afford a better breakfast than she could. As each dish was brought to them she would point at it and shout accusingly, 'There goes the price of another fuck! We don't get kippers for breakfast, do we, girls? 'Ow do you think she paid for them doughnuts? That's that there negro that 'as 'er for a tanner' etc. etc., but the prostitutes did not mind much.

2. *Covent Garden:* in Orwell's time (and for some three hundred years before) the central fruit and vegetable market serving London. The market moved to Nine Elms, Battersea, in 1974.
3. *St Martin-in-the-Fields Church:* faces on to the North-East corner of Trafalgar Square. Its crypt provided shelter for down-and-outs. Shelter is still provided today.
4. *posters:* handwritten substitution for *parcels*.

27.8.31: At about eight in the morning we all had a shave in the Trafalgar Square fountains, and I spent most of the day reading *Eugenie Grandet*,[5] which was the only book I had brought with me. The sight of a French book produced the usual remarks – 'Ah, French? That'll be something pretty warm, eh?' etc. Evidently most English people have no idea that there are French books which are not pornographic. Down and out people seem to read exclusively books of the Buffalo Bill type. Every tramp carries one of these, and they have a kind of circulating library, all swapping books when they get to the spike.[6]

That night, as we were starting for Kent the next morning, I decided to sleep in bed and went to a lodging house in the Southwark Bridge Road. This is a sevenpenny kip, one of the few in London, and looks it. The beds are five feet long, with no pillows (you use your coat rolled up), and infested by fleas, besides a few bugs. The kitchen is a small, stinking cellar where the deputy sits with a table of flyblown jam tarts etc. for sale a few feet from the door of the lavatory. The rats are so bad that several cats have to be kept exclusively to deal with them. The lodgers were dock workers, I think, and they did not seem a bad crowd. There was a youth among them, pale and consumptive looking but evidently a labourer, who was devoted to poetry. He repeated

> 'A voice so thrilling ne'er was 'eard
> In Ipril from the cuckoo bird,
> Briking the silence of the seas
> Beyond the furthest 'Ebrides'[7]

with genuine feeling. The others did not laugh at him much.

5. *Eugénie Grandet:* novel by Honoré de Balzac (1834) in the series 'Scenes from Provincial Life' of his *Comédie Humaine.*
6. *spike:* workhouse
7. *'A voice so thrilling . . . furthest 'Ebrides':* a corrupted form of a verse from Wordsworth's poem, 'The Solitary Reaper': 'A voice so thrilling ne'er was heard / In spring-time from the Cuckoo-bird, / Breaking the silence of the seas / Amongst the farthest Hebrides' (1805).

28.8.31: The next day in the afternoon four of us started out for the hop-fields. The most interesting of the men with me was a youth named Ginger, who is still my mate when I write this. He is a strong, athletic youth of twenty six, almost illiterate and quite brainless, but daring enough for anything. Except when in prison, he has probably broken the law every day for the last five years. As a boy he did three years in Borstal,[8] came out, married at eighteen on the strength of a successful burglary, and shortly afterwards enlisted in the artillery. His wife died, and a little while afterwards he had an accident to his left eye and was invalided out of the service. They offered him a pension or a lump sum, and of course he chose the lump sum and blued it in about a week. After that he took to burglary again, and has been in prison six times, but never for a long sentence, as they have only caught him for small jobs; he has done one or two jobs which brought him over £500. He has always been perfectly honest towards me, as his partner, but in a general way he will steal anything that is not tied down. I doubt his ever being a successful burglar, though, for he is too stupid to be able to foresee risks. It is all a great pity, for he could earn a decent living if he chose. He has a gift for street selling, and has had a lot of jobs at selling on commission, but when he has had a good day he bolts instantly with the takings. He is a marvellous hand at picking up bargains and can always, for instance, persuade the butcher to give him a pound of eatable meat for twopence, yet at the same time he is an absolute fool about money, and never saves a halfpenny. He is given to singing songs of the

Little Grey Home in the West type,[9] and he speaks of his dead wife and mother in terms of the most viscid sentimentality. I should think he is a fairly typical petty criminal.

Of the other two, one was a boy of twenty named Young Ginger, who seemed rather a likely lad, but he was an orphan and had had no kind of upbringing, and lived the last year chiefly on Trafalgar Square. The other was a little Liverpool Jew of eighteen, a thorough guttersnipe. I do not know when I have seen anyone who disgusted me so much as this boy. He was as greedy as a pig about food, perpetually scrounging round dustbins, and he had a face that recalled some low-down carrion-eating beast. His manner of talking about women, and the expression of his face when he did so, were so loathsomely obscene as to make me feel almost sick. We could never persuade him to wash more of himself than his nose and a small circle round it, and he mentioned quite casually that he had several different kinds of louse on him. He too was an orphan, and had been 'on the toby' almost from infancy.

I had now about 6/–,[10] and before starting we bought a so-called blanket for 1/6d and cadged several tins for 'drums'. The only reliable tin for a drum° is a two-pound snuff tin, which is not very easy to come by. We had also a supply of bread and margarine and tea, and a number of knives and forks etc., all stolen at different times from Woolworth's. We took the twopenny tram as far as Bromley, and there 'drummed up'° on a rubbish dump, waiting for two others who were to have joined us, but who never turned up. It was dark when we finally stopped waiting for them, so we had no chance to look for a good camping place, and had to spend the night in long wet grass at the edge of a recreation ground. The cold was bitter. We had only two thin blankets between the four of us, and it was not safe to light a fire, as there were houses all round; we were also lying on a slope, so that one rolled into the ditch from time to time. It was rather humiliating to see the others, all younger than I, sleeping quite soundly in these conditions, whereas I did not close my eyes all night. To avoid being caught we had to be on the road before dawn, and it was several hours before we managed to get hot water and have our breakfast.

8. *Borstal:* a town in Kent which developed a system designed to reform young offenders through punishment, education, and job training. It was applied more widely to a series of such institutions but was abolished by the Criminal Justice Act, 1982, and replaced by youth custody centres.
9. *Little Grey Home in the West:* sentimental song, composed 1911, words by D. Eardley-Wilmot; music by Hermann Lohr. It was popularised in the First World War by the Australian baritone, Peter Dawson, whose fine voice readily overcame the disadvantages of acoustic recording and shellac discs.

10. *6/– :* six shillings and, later in the sentence, *1/6* = one shilling and sixpence or 18 pence. In pre-metric currency, one pound sterling (£1) was divided into twenty shillings and each shilling into twelve pennies – so £1 = 240 pence. It is difficult to give precise equivalents of value with today's prices because individual items vary considerably. However, a rough approximation can be gained if prices in the 1930s are multiplied by forty to suggest current values. Thus, six shilling is equivalent (roughly) to £12 today.

29.8.31: When we had gone a mile or two we came to an orchard, and the others at once went in and began stealing apples. I had not been prepared for this when we started out, but I saw that I must either do as the others did or leave them, so I shared the apples; I did not however take any part in the thefts for the first day, except to keep guard. We were going more or less in the direction of Sevenoaks, and by dinner time we had stolen about a dozen apples and plums and fifteen pounds of potatoes. The others also went in and tapped[11] whenever we passed a baker's or a teashop, and we got quite a quantity of broken bread and meat. When we stopped to light a fire for dinner we fell in with two Scotch tramps who had been stealing apples from an orchard nearby, and stayed talking with them for a long time. The others all talked about sexual subjects, in a revolting manner. Tramps are disgusting when on this subject, because their poverty cuts them off entirely from women, and their minds consequently fester with obscenity. Merely lecherous people are all right, but people who would like to be lecherous, but don't get the chance, are horribly degraded by it. They remind me of the dogs that hang enviously round while two other dogs are copulating. During the conversation Young Ginger related how he and some others on Trafalgar Square had discovered one of their number to be a 'Poof', or Nancy Boy. Whereupon they had instantly fallen upon him, robbed him of 12/6d, which was all he had, and spent it on themselves. Evidently they thought it quite fair to rob him, as he was a Nancy Boy.

We had been making very poor progress, chiefly because Young Ginger and the Jew were not used to walking and wanted to stop and search for scraps of food all the time. On one occasion the Jew even picked up some chipped potatoes that had been trodden on, and ate them. As it was getting on in the afternoon we decided to make not for Sevenoaks but for Ide Hill spike, which the Scotchmen had told us was better than it is usually represented. We halted about a mile from the spike for tea, and I remember that a gentleman in a car nearby helped us in the kindest manner to find wood for our fire, and gave us a cigarette each. Then we went on to the spike, and on the way picked a bunch of honeysuckle to give to the Tramp

Major.[12] We thought this might put him in a good temper and induce him to let us out next morning, for it is not usual to let tramps out of the spike on Sundays. When we got there however the Tramp Major said that he would have to keep us in till Tuesday morning. It appeared that the Workhouse Master was very keen on making every casual do a day's work, and at the same time would not hear of their working on Sunday; so we should have to be idle all Sunday and work on Monday. Young Ginger and the Jew elected to stay till Tuesday, but Ginger and I went and kipped on the edge of a park near the church. It was beastly cold, but a little better than the night before, for we had plenty of wood and could make a fire. For our supper, Ginger tapped the local butcher, who gave us the best part of two pounds of sausages. Butchers are always very generous on Saturday nights.

11. *tapped:* obtained – in effect, begged.
12. *Tramp Major:* official in charge of day-to-day organisation and discipline of the tramps in the workhouse.

30.8.31: Next morning the clergyman coming to early service caught us and turned us out, though not very disagreeably. We went on through Sevenoaks to Seal, and a man we met advised us to try for a job at Mitchell's farm, about three miles further on. We went there, but the farmer told us that he could not give us a job, as he had nowhere where we could live, and the Government inspectors had been snouting round to see that all hop-pickers had 'proper accommodation'. (These inspectors,* by the way, managed to prevent some hundreds of unemployed from getting jobs in the hop-fields this year. Not having 'proper accommodation' to offer to pickers, the farmers could only employ local people, who lived in their own houses.) We stole about a pound of raspberries from one of Mitchell's fields, and then went and applied to another farmer called Kronk, who gave us the same answer; we had five or ten pounds of potatoes from his fields, however. We were starting off in the direction of Maidstone when we fell in with an old Irishwoman, who had been given a job by Mitchell on the understanding that she had a lodging in Seal, which she had not. (Actually she was sleeping in a toolshed in somebody's garden. She used to slip in after dark and out before daylight.) We got some hot water from a cottage and the Irish woman had tea with us, and gave us a lot of food that she had begged and did not want; we were glad of this, for we had now only 2½d left, and none too much food. It had now come on to rain, so we went to a farmhouse beside the church and asked leave

* Appointed by the Labour Government [Orwell's note].

to shelter in one of their cowsheds. The farmer and family were just starting out for evening service, and they said in a scandalised manner that of course they could not give us shelter. We sheltered instead in the lych-gate of the church, hoping that by looking draggled and tired we might get a few coppers from the congregation as they went in. We did not get anything, but after the service Ginger managed to tap a fairly good pair of flannel trousers from the clergyman. It was very uncomfortable in the lych-gate, and we were wet through and out of tobacco, and Ginger and I had walked twelve miles; yet I remember that we were quite happy and laughing all the time. The Irishwoman (she was sixty, and had been on the road all her life, evidently) was an extraordinarily cheerful old girl, and full of stories. Talking of places to 'skipper'° in, she told us that one cold night she had crept into a pigsty and snuggled up to an old sow, for warmth.

When night came on it was still raining, so we decided to find an empty house to sleep in, but we went first to buy half a pound of sugar and two candles at the grocer's. While I was buying them Ginger stole three apples off the counter, and the Irishwoman a packet of cigarettes. They had plotted this beforehand, deliberately not telling me, so as to use my innocent appearance as a shield. After a good deal of searching we found an unfinished house and slipped in by a window the builders had left open. The bare floor was beastly hard, but it was warmer than outside, and I managed to get two or three hours' sleep. We got out before dawn, and by appointment met the Irishwoman in a wood nearby. It was raining, but Ginger could get a fire going in almost any circumstances, and we managed to make tea and roast some potatoes. When it was light the Irishwoman *1.9.31:* ° went off to work, and Ginger and I went down to Chambers' farm, a mile or two away, to ask for work. When we got to the farm they had just been hanging a cat, a thing I never heard of anyone doing before. The bailiff said that he thought he could give us a job, and told us to wait; we waited from eight in the morning till one, when the bailiff said that he had no work for us after all. We made off, stealing a large quantity of apples and damsons, and started along the Maidstone road. At about three we halted to have our dinner and make some jam out of the raspberries we had stolen the day before. Near here, I remember, they refused at two houses to give me cold water, because 'the mistress doesn't allow us to give anything to tramps.' Ginger saw a gentleman in a car picnicking nearby, and went up to tap him for matches, for he said, that it always pays to tap from picnickers, who usually have some food left over when they are going home. Sure enough the gentleman presently came across with some butter he had not used, and began talking to us. His manner was so friendly that I forgot to put on my cockney accent, and he looked closely at me, and said how painful it must be for a man of my stamp etc. Then he said, 'I say, you won't be offended, will you? Do you mind taking this?' 'This' was a shilling, with which we bought some tobacco and had our first smoke that day. This was the only time in the whole journey when we managed to tap money.

We went on in the direction of Maidstone, but when we had gone a few miles it began to pour with rain, and my left boot was pinching me badly. I had not had my boots off for three days and had only had about eight hours sleep in the last five nights, and I did not feel equal to another night in the open. We decided to make for West Malling spike, which was about eight miles distant, and if possible to get a lift part of the way. I think we hailed forty lorries before we got a lift. The lorry drivers will not give lifts nowadays, because they are not insured for third party risks and they get the sack if they have an accident. Finally we did get a lift, and were set down about two miles from the spike, getting there at eight in the evening. Outside the gates we met an old deaf tramp who was going to skipper in the pouring rain, as he had been in the spike the night before, and they would confine him for a week if he came again. He told us that Blest's farm nearby would probably give us a job, and that they would let us out of the spike early in the morning if we told them we had already got a job. Otherwise we should be confined all day, unless we went out 'over the wall' – i.e. bolted when the Tramp Major was not looking. Tramps often do this, but you have to cache your possessions outside, which we could not in the heavy rain. We went in, and I found that (if West Malling is typical) spikes have improved a lot since I was last in.* The bathroom was clean and decent, and we were actually given a clean towel each. The food was the same old bread and marg, though, and the Tramp Major got angry when we asked in good faith whether the stuff they gave us to drink was tea or cocoa.† We had beds with straw palliasses and plenty of blankets, and both slept like logs.

In the morning they told us we must work till eleven, and set us to scrubbing out one of the dormitories. As usual, the work was a mere formality. (I have never done a stroke of real work in the spike, and I have never met anybody who has.) The dormitory was a room of fifty beds, close together, with that warm, faecal stink that you never seem to get away from in the workhouse. There was an imbecile pauper there, a great lump of about sixteen stone, with a tiny, snouty face and a sidelong grin. He was at work very slowly emptying chamberpots. These workhouses seem all alike, and there is something intensely disgusting in the atmosphere

* No: a bit worse if anything [Orwell's note].

† To this day I don't know which it was [Orwell's note].

of them. The thought of all those grey-faced, ageing men living a very quiet, withdrawn life in a smell of W. Cs, and practising homosexuality, makes me feel sick. But it is not easy to convey what I mean, because it is all bound up with the smell of the workhouse.

At eleven they let us out with the usual hunk of bread and cheese, and we went on to Blest's farm, about three miles away; but we did not get there till one, because we stopped on the way and got a big haul of damsons. When we arrived at the farm the foreman told us that he wanted pickers and sent us up to the field at once. We had now only about 3d left, and that evening I wrote home asking them to send me 10/–; it came two days later, and in the mean time we should have had practically nothing to eat if the other pickers had not fed us. For nearly three weeks after this we were at work hop-picking, and I had better describe the different aspects of this individually.

X2.9.31 to 19.9.31:* Hops are trained up poles or over wires about 10 feet high, and grown in rows a yard or two apart. All the pickers have to do is to tear them down and strip the hops into a bin, keeping them as clean as possible of leaves. In practice, of course, it is impossible to keep all the leaves out, and the experienced pickers swell the bulk of their hops by putting in just as many leaves as the farmer will stand for. One soon gets the knack of the work, and the only hardships are the standing (we were generally on our feet ten hours a day), the plagues of plant lice, and the damage to one's hands. One's hands get stained as black as a negro's with the hop-juice, which only mud will remove,† and after a day or two they crack and are cut to bits by the stems of the vines, which are spiny. In the mornings, before the cuts had reopened, my hands used to give me perfect agony, and even at the time of typing this (October 10th) they show the marks. Most of the people who go down hopping have done it every year since they were children, and they pick like lightning and know all the tricks, such as shaking the hops up to make them lie loose in the bin etc. The most successful pickers are families, who have two or three adults to strip the vines, and a couple of children to pick up the fallen hops and clear the odd strands. The laws about child labour are disregarded utterly, and some of the people drive their children pretty hard. The woman in the next bin to us, a regular old-fashioned East Ender, kept her grandchildren at it like slaves. – 'Go on, Rose, you lazy little cat, pick

* The passage between crosses (at least the substance of it) has been used for an article in the *Nation* [Orwell's note]. The second X is six paragraphs later. For the article, see *CW*, X, pp. 233–5.

† Or hop-juice, funnily enough [Orwell's note].

them 'ops up. I'll warm your arse if I get up to you' etc. until the children, aged from 6 to 10, used to drop down and fall asleep on the ground. But they liked the work, and I don't suppose it did them more harm than school.

As to what one can earn, the system of payment is this. Two or three times a day the hops are measured, and you are due a certain sum (in our case twopence) for each bushel you have picked. A good vine yields about half a bushel of hops, and a good picker can strip a vine in about 10 minutes, so that theoretically one might earn about 30/– by a sixty hour week. But in practice this is quite impossible. To begin with, the hops vary enormously. On some vines they are as large as small pears, and on others hardly bigger than peas; the bad vines take rather longer to strip than the good ones – they are generally more tangled – and sometimes it needs five or six of them to make a bushel. Then there are all kinds of delays, and the pickers get no compensation for lost time. Sometimes it rains (if it rains hard the hops get too slippery to pick), and one is always kept waiting when changing from field to field, so that an hour or two is wasted every day. And above all there is the question of measurement. Hops are soft things like sponges, and it is quite easy for the measurer to crush a bushel of them into a quart if he chooses. Some days he merely scoops the hops out, but on other days he has orders from the farmer to 'take them heavy', and then he crams them tight into the basket, so that instead of getting 20 bushels for a full bin one gets only 12 or 14 – i. e. a shilling or so less. There was a song about this, which the old East End woman and her grandchildren were always singing:

'Our lousy hops!
Our lousy hops!
When the measurer he comes round,
Pick 'em up, pick 'em up off the ground!
When he comes to measure
He never knows where to stop;
Ay, ay, get in the bin
And take the fucking lot!'

From the bin the hops are put into 10-bushel pokes[13] which are supposed to weigh a hundredweight and are normally carried by one man. It used to take two men to hoist a full poke when the measurer had been taking them heavy.

With all these difficulties one can't earn 30/– a week or anything near it. It is a curious fact, though, that very few of the pickers were aware how little they really earned, because the piece-work system disguises the low rate of payment. The best pickers in our gang were a family of gypsies, five adults and a child, all of whom, of course, had picked hops every year since they could walk.[14] In a little under three weeks these people earned exactly £10 between them – i.e., leaving out the child, about 14/– a week each. Ginger and I earned about 9/– a week each,[15] and I doubt if any individual picker made over 15/– a week. A family working together can make their keep and their fare back to London at these rates, but a single picker can hardly do even that. On some of the farms nearby the tally, instead of being 6 bushels to the shilling, was 8 or 9, at which one would have a hard job to earn 10/– a week.

When one starts work the farm gives one a printed copy of rules, which are designed to reduce a picker more or less to a slave. According to these rules the farmer can sack a picker without notice and on any pretext whatever, and pay him off at 8 bushels a shilling instead of six – i.e. confiscate a quarter of his earnings. If a picker leaves his job before the picking is finished, his earnings are docked the same amount. You cannot draw what you have earned and then clear off, because the farm will never pay you more than two thirds of your earnings in advance, and so are in your debt till the last day. The binmen (i. e. foremen of gangs) get wages instead of being paid on the piecework system, and these wages cease if there is a strike, so naturally they will raise Heaven and earth to prevent one. Altogether the farmers have the hop-pickers in a cleft stick, and always will have until there is a pickers' union. It is not much use to try and form a union, though, for about half the pickers are women and gypsies, and are too stupid to see the advantages of it.

As to our living accommodation, the best quarters on the farm, ironically enough, were disused stables. Most of us slept in round tin huts about 10 feet across, with no glass in the windows, and all kinds of holes to let in the wind and rain. The furniture of these huts consisted of a heap of straw and hop-vines, and nothing else. There were four of us in our hut, but in some of them there were seven or eight – rather an advantage, really, for it kept the hut warm. Straw is rotten stuff to sleep in (it is much more draughty than hay) and Ginger and I had only a blanket each, so we suffered agonies of cold for the first week; after that we stole enough pokes to keep us warm. The farm gave us free firewood, though not as much as we needed. The water tap was 200 yards away, and the latrine the same distance, but it was so filthy that one would have walked a mile sooner than use it. There was a stream where one could do some laundering, but getting a bath in the village would have been about as easy as buying a tame whale.

X The hop-pickers seemed to be of three types: East Enders, mostly costermongers, gypsies, and itinerant agricultural labourers with a sprinkling of tramps. The fact that Ginger and I were tramps got us a great deal of sympathy, especially among the fairly well-to-do people. There was one couple, a coster and his wife, who were like a father and mother to us. They were the kind of people who are generally drunk on Saturday nights and who tack a 'fucking' on to every noun, yet I have never seen anything that exceeded their kindness and delicacy. They gave us food over and over again. A child would come to the hut with a saucepan: 'Eric, mother was going to throw this stew away, but she said it was a pity to waste it. Would you like it?' Of course they were not really going to have thrown it away, but said this to avoid the suggestion of charity. One day they gave us a whole pig's head, ready cooked. These people had been on the road several years themselves, and it made them sympathetic. – 'Ah, I know what it's like. Skippering° in the fucking wet grass, and then got to tap the milkman in the morning before you can get a cup of tea. Two of my boys were born on the road' etc. Another man who was very decent to us was an employee in a paper factory. Before this he had been vermin-man to Lyons, and he told me that the dirt and vermin in Lyons' kitchens, even Cadby Hall, passed belief. When he worked at Lyons' branch in Throgmorton Street, the rats were so numerous that it was not safe to go into the kitchens at night unarmed; you had to carry a revolver.[16] After I had mixed with these people for a few days it was too much fag to go on putting on my cockney accent, and they noticed that I talked 'different'. As usual, this made them still more friendly, for these people seem to think that it is especially dreadful to 'come down in the world'.

Out of about 200 pickers at Blest's farm, 50 or 60 were gypsies. They are curiously like oriental peasants – the same heavy faces, at once dull and sly, and the same sharpness in their own line and startling ignorance outside it. Most of them could not read even a word, and none of their children seemed ever to have gone to school. One gypsy, aged about 40, used to ask me such questions as, 'How far is Paris from France?' 'How many days' journey by caravan to Paris?' etc. A youth, aged twenty, used to ask this riddle half a dozen times a day. – 'I'll tell you something you can't do?' – 'What?' – 'Tickle a gnat's arse with a telegraph pole.' (At this, never-failing yells of laughter.) The gypsies seem to be quite rich, owning caravans, horses etc. yet they go on all the year round working as itinerant labourers and saving money. They used to say that our way of life (living in houses etc.) seemed disgusting to them, and to explain how clever they had been in dodging the army during the war. Talking to them, you had the feeling of talking to people from another century. I often heard a gypsy say, 'If I knew where so and so was, I'd ride my horse till it hadn't a shoe left to catch him' – not a 20th century metaphor at all. One day some gypsies were talking about a noted horse-thief called

George Bigland, and one man, defending him, said: 'I don't think George is as bad as you make out. I've known him to steal Gorgias' (Gentiles') horses, but he wouldn't go so far as to steal from one of us.'

The gypsies call us Gorgias and themselves Romanies, but they are nicknamed Didecais (not certain of spelling). They all knew Romany, and occasionally used a word or two when they didn't want to be understood. A curious thing I noticed about the gypsies – I don't know whether it is the same everywhere – was that you would often see a whole family who were totally unlike one another. It almost seems to countenance the stories about gypsies stealing children; more likely, though, it is because it's a wise child etc.

One of the men in our hut was the old deaf tramp we had met outside West Malling pike – Deafie, he was always called. He was rather a Mr F.'s aunt[17] in conversation, and he looked just like a drawing by George Belcher,[18] but he was an intelligent, decently educated man, and no doubt would not have been on the road if he could hear. He was not strong enough for heavy work, and he had done nothing for years past except odd jobs like hopping. He calculated that he had been in over 400 different spikes. The other man, named Barrett, and a man in our gang named George, were good specimens of the itinerant agricultural labourer. For years past they had worked on a regular round: Lambing in early spring, then pea-picking, strawberries, various other fruits, hops, 'spud-grabbing', turnips and sugar beet. They were seldom out of work for more than a week or two, yet even this was enough to swallow up anything they could earn. They were both penniless when they arrived at Blest's farm, and I saw Barrett work certainly one day without a bite to eat. The proceeds of all their work were the clothes they stood up in, straw to sleep on all the year round, meals of bread and cheese and bacon, and I suppose one or two good drunks a year. George was a dismal devil, and took a sort of worm-like pride in being underfed and overworked, and always tobying from job to job. His line was, 'It doesn't do for people like us to have fine ideas'. (He could not read or write, and seemed to think even literacy a kind of extravagance.) I know this philosophy well, having often met it among the dishwashers in Paris.[19] Barrett, who was 63, used to complain a lot about the badness of food nowadays, compared with what you could get when he was a boy. – 'In them days we didn't live on this fucking bread and marg, we 'ad good solid tommy. Bullock's 'eart. Bacon dumpling. Black pudden. Pig's 'ead.' The glutinous, reminiscent tone in which he said 'pig's 'ead' suggested decades of underfeeding.

Besides all these regular pickers there were what are called 'home-dwellers'; i.e. local people who pick at odd times, chiefly for the fun of it. They are mostly farmers' wives and the like, and as a rule they and the regular pickers loathe one another. One of them, however, was a very decent woman, who gave Ginger a pair of shoes and me an excellent coat and waistcoat and two shirts. Most of the local people seemed to look on us as dirt, and the shopkeepers were very insolent, though between us we must have spent several hundred pounds in the village.

One day at hop-picking was very much like another. At about a quarter to six in the morning we crawled out of the straw, put on our coats and boots (we slept in everything else) and went out to get a fire going – rather a job this September, when it rained all the time. By half past six we had made tea and fried some bread for breakfast, and then we started off for work, with bacon sandwiches and a drum° of cold tea for our dinner. If it didn't rain we were working pretty steadily till about one, and then we would start a fire between the vines, heat up our tea and knock off for half an hour. After that we were at it again till half past five, and by the time we had got home, cleaned the hop juice off our hands and had tea, it was already dark and we were dropping with sleep. A good many nights, though, we used to go out and steal apples. There was a big orchard nearby, and three or four of us used to rob it systematically, carrying a sack and getting half a hundredweight of apples at a time, besides several pounds of cobnuts. On Sundays we used to wash our shirts and socks in the stream, and sleep the rest of the day. As far as I remember I never undressed completely all the time we were down there, nor washed my teeth, and I only shaved twice a week. Between working and getting meals (and that meant fetching everlasting cans of water, struggling with wet faggots, frying in tin-lids etc.) one seemed to have not an instant to spare. I only read one book all the time I was down there, and that was a Buffalo Bill. Counting up what we spent I find that Ginger and I fed ourselves on about 5/– a week each, so it is not surprising that we were constantly short of tobacco and constantly hungry, in spite of the apples and what the others gave us. We seemed to be forever doing sums in farthings to find out whether we could afford another half ounce of shag or another two-pennorth of bacon. It wasn't a bad life, but what with standing all day, sleeping rough and getting my hands cut to bits, I felt a wreck at the end of it. It was humiliating to see that most of the people there looked on it as a holiday – in fact, it is because hopping is regarded as a holiday that the pickers will take such starvation wages. It gives one an insight into the lives of farm labourers, too, to realise that according to their standards hop-picking is hardly work at all.

One night a youth knocked at our door and said that he was a new picker and had been told to sleep in our hut. We let him in and fed him in the morning, after which he vanished. It appeared that he was not a picker at all, but a tramp, and that tramps often work this dodge in the hopping season, in order to get a kip under shelter. Another night a woman who was going home asked me to help her get her luggage to Wateringbury station. As she was leaving early they had paid her off at eight bushels a shilling, and her total earnings were only just enough to get herself and family home. I had to push a perambulator, with one eccentric wheel and loaded with huge packages, two and a half miles through the dark, followed by a retinue of yelling children. When we got to the station the last train was just coming in, and in rushing the pram across the level crossing I upset it. I shall never forget that moment – the train bearing down on us, and the porter and I chasing a tin chamber-pot that was rolling up the track. On several nights Ginger tried to persuade me to come and rob the church with him, and he would have done it alone if I had not managed to get it into his head that suspicion was bound to fall on him, as a known criminal. He had robbed churches before, and he said, what surprised me, that there is generally something worth having in the Poor box. We had one or two jolly nights, on Saturdays, sitting round a huge fire till midnight and roasting apples. One night, I remember, it came out that of about fifteen people round the fire, everyone except myself had been in prison. There were uproarious scenes in the village on Saturdays, for the people who had money used to get well drunk, and it needed the police to get them out of the pub. I have no doubt the residents thought us a nasty vulgar lot, but I could not help feeling that it was rather good for a dull village to have this invasion of cockneys once a year.

13. *pokes:* sacks (compare 'a pig in a poke').
14. *walk:* Orwell originally wrote *work*.
15. *9/- a week each:* £18 at today's values – far less than the theoretical earnings of 30/- (thirty shillings, say £60 today) referred to earlier.
16. Names omitted when first printed in 1968.
17. *Mr F.'s aunt:* the aunt of Flora Finching's deceased husband in Dickens's *Little Dorrit*. Left in Flora's care, she was simply known as 'Mr F.'s Aunt'. Her major characteristics are described as 'extreme severity and grim taciturnity; sometimes interrupted by a propensity to offer remarks in a deep warning voice, which, being totally uncalled for by anything said by anybody, and traceable to no association of ideas, confounded and terrified the mind'. One interjection might have had a special appeal for Orwell, who lived at Henley-on-Thames as a child: 'Mr F.'s Aunt, after regarding the company for ten minutes with a malevolent gaze, delivered the following fearful remark: "When we lived at Henley, Barnes's gander was stole by tinkers"' (ch. 13).
18. *George Belcher* (1875–1947), a Royal Academician whose books of drawings included *Characters* (1922), *Taken from Life* (1929), and *Potted Char* (1933).
19. *the dishwashers in Paris:* Orwell worked as a dishwasher – a *plongeur* – in 1929; see *Down and Out in Paris and London*, published in 1933, two years after his hop-picking experiences.

19.9.31: On the last morning, when we had picked the last field, there was a queer game of catching the women and putting them in the bins. Very likely there will be something about this in the *Golden Bough*.[20] It is evidently an old custom, and all harvests have some custom of this kind attached to them. The people who were illiterate or thereabouts brought their tally books to me and other 'scholars' to have them reckoned up, and some of them paid a copper or two to have it done. I found that in quite a number of cases the farm cashiers had made a mistake in the addition, and invariably the mistake was in favour of the farm. Of course the pickers got the sum due when they complained, but they would not have if they had accepted the farm cashier's reckoning. Moreover, the farm had a mean little rule that anyone who was going to complain about his tally book had to wait till all the other pickers had been paid off. This meant waiting till the afternoon, so that some people who had buses to catch had to go home without claiming the sum due to them. (Of course it was only a few coppers in most cases. One woman's book, however, was added up over £1 wrong.)

Ginger and I packed our things and walked over to Wateringbury to catch the hoppickers' train. On the way we stopped to buy tobacco, and as a sort of farewell to Kent, Ginger cheated the tobacconist's girl of fourpence, by a very cunning dodge. When we got to Wateringbury station about fifty hoppers were waiting for the train, and the first person we saw was old Deafie, sitting on the grass with a newspaper in front of him. He lifted it aside, and we saw that he had his trousers undone and was exhibiting his penis to the women and children as they passed. I was surprised – such a decent old man, really; but there is hardly a tramp who has not some sexual abnormality. The Hoppers' train was ninepence cheaper than the ordinary fare, and it took nearly five hours to get us to London – 30 miles. At about 10 at night the hop-pickers poured out at London Bridge station, a number of them drunk and all carrying bunches of hops; people in the street readily bought these bunches of hops, I don't know why. Deafie, who had travelled in our carriage, asked us into the nearest pub and stood us each a pint, the first beer I had had in three weeks. Then he went off to Hammersmith, and no doubt he will be on the bum till next year's fruit-picking begins.

On adding up our tally book, Ginger and I found that we had made just 26/– each by eighteen days' work. We had drawn 8/– each in advances (or 'subs' as they are called), and we had made another 6/– between us by selling stolen apples. After paying our fares we got to London with about 16/– each. So we had, after all, kept ourselves while we were in Kent and come back with a little in pocket; but we had only done it by living on the very minimum of everything.

20. *The Golden Bough: A Study in Magic and Religion*, 2 volumes, 1890; 12 volumes, 1906–15, by Sir James George Frazer (1854–1941).

19.9.31 to 8.10.31: Ginger and I went to a kip in Tooley Street, owned by Lew Levy who owns the one in Westminster Bridge Road. It is only sevenpence a night, and it is probably the best sevenpenny one in London. There are bugs in the beds, but not many, and the kitchens, though dark and dirty, are convenient, with abundant fires and hot water. The lodgers are a pretty low lot – mostly Irish unskilled labourers, and out of work at that. We met some queer types among them. There was one man, aged 68, who worked carrying crates of fish (they weigh a hundredweight each) in Billingsgate market. He was interested in politics, and he told me that on Bloody Sunday in '88 [21] he had taken part in the rioting and been sworn in as a special constable on the same day. Another old man, a flower seller, was mad. Most of the time he behaved quite normally, but when his fits were on he would walk up and down the kitchen uttering dreadful beast-like yells, with an expression of agony on his face. Curiously enough, the fits only came on in wet weather. Another man was a thief. He stole from shop counters and vacant motor cars, especially commercial travellers' cars, and sold the stuff to a Jew in Lambeth Cut. Every evening you would see him smartening himself up to go 'up West'. He told me that he could count on £2 a week, with a big haul from time to time. He managed to swoop the till of a public house almost every Christmas, generally getting £40 or £50 by this. He had been stealing for years and only been caught once, and then was bound over. As always seems the case with thieves, his work brought him no good, for when he got a large sum he blued it instantly. He had one of the ignoblest faces I ever saw, just like a hyena's; yet he was likeable, and decent about sharing food and paying debts.

Several mornings Ginger and I worked helping the porters at Billingsgate.[22] You go there at about five and stand at the corner of one of the streets which lead up from Billingsgate into Eastcheap. When a porter is having trouble to get his barrow up, he shouts 'Up the 'ill!' and you spring forward (there is fierce competition for the jobs, of course) and shove the barrow behind. The payment is 'twopence an up'. They take on about one shover-up for four hundredweight, and the work knocks it out of your thighs and elbows, but you don't get enough jobs to tire you out. Standing there from five till nearly midday, I never made more than 1/6d. If you are very lucky a porter takes you on as his regular assistant, and then you make about 4/6d a morning. The porters themselves seem to make about £4 or £5 a week. There are several things worth noticing about Billingsgate. One is that vast quantities of the work done there are quite unnecessary, being due to the complete lack of any centralised transport system. What with porters, barrowmen, shovers-up etc, it now costs round about £1 to get a ton of fish from Billingsgate to one of the London railway termini. If it were done in an orderly manner, by lorries, I suppose it would cost a few shillings. Another thing is that the pubs in Billingsgate are open at the hours when other pubs are shut. And another is that the barrowmen at Billingsgate do a regular traffic in stolen fish, and you can get fish dirt cheap if you know one of them.

After about a fortnight in the lodging house I found that I was writing nothing, and the place itself was beginning to get on my nerves, with its noise and lack of privacy, and the stifling heat of the kitchen, and above all the dirt. The kitchen had a permanent sweetish reek of fish, and all the sinks were blocked with rotting fish guts which stank horribly. You had to store your food in dark corners which were infested by black beetles and cockroaches, and there were clouds of horrible languid flies everywhere. The dormitory was also disgusting, with the perpetual din of coughing and spitting – everyone in a lodging house has a chronic cough, no doubt from the foul air. I had got to write some articles, which could not be done in such surroundings, so I wrote home for money and took a room in Windsor Street near the Harrow Road. Ginger has gone off on the road again. Most of this narrative was written in the Bermondsey public library, which has a good reading room and was convenient for the lodging house.

21. *Bloody Sunday:* this took place in London on 13 November 1887 (not 1888). Some 10,000 protesters marched to Trafalgar Square where a number of speakers (including George Bernard Shaw) were to address them. They were protesting about conditions in Ireland and demanded the release from prison of an MP, William O'Brien. Some two thousand police and four hundred soldiers opposed them (although the latter did not resort to the use of their bayonets or firing rifles).
22. *Billingsgate:* Billingsgate Fish Market (Trafalgar Way, London, E14) has over fifty traders mainly selling fish but some poultry and other products (e.g. potatoes) are sold. Nowadays it is open from Tuesday to Saturday, from 5.00am to 8.00am; one trader sells shellfish on Sundays from 6.00am to 8.00am.

Orwell's notes

New words (i.e. words new to me) discovered this time.

Shackles . . . broth or gravy.

Drum, a a billy can. (With verb to drum up meaning to light a fire.)

Toby, on the . . . on the tramp. (Also to toby, and a toby, meaning a tramp. Slang Dictionary gives the toby as the highroad.)

Chat, a . . . .a louse. (Also chatty, lousy. S.D. gives this but not a chat.)

Get, a ? (Word of abuse, meaning unknown.)[23]

Didecai, a a gypsy.

Sprowsie, a ... .a sixpence.

Hard-up tobacco made from fag ends. (S.D. gives a hard-up as a man who collects fag ends.)

Skipper, to . . . to sleep out. (S.D. gives a skipper as a barn.)

Scrump, to . . . to steal.

Knock off, to . . . to arrest.

Jack off, to . . . to go away.

Jack, on his . . . on his own.

Clods coppers

Burglars' slang.

A stick, or a cane a jemmy. (S.D. gives stick.)

Peter a . . . . . . a safe. (In S.D.)

Bly,* a . . . . . .an oxy-acetylene blowlamp

Use of the word 'tart' among the East Enders. This word now seems absolutely interchangeable with 'girl', with no implication of 'prostitute'. People will speak of their daughter or sister as a tart.

Rhyming slang. I thought this was extinct, but it is far from it. The hop-pickers used these expressions freely: A dig in the grave, meaning a shave. The hot cross bun, meaning the sun. Greengages, meaning wages. They also used the abbreviated rhyming slang, e.g. 'Use your twopenny' for 'Use your head.' This is arrived at like this: Head, loaf of bread, loaf, twopenny loaf, twopenny.

Homosexual vice in London. It appears that one of the great rendezvous is Charing Cross underground station. It appeared to be taken for

* I forgot to mention that these lamps are hired out to burglars. Ginger said that he had paid £3.10.0 a night for the use of one. So also with other burglars' tools of the more elaborate kinds. When opening a puzzle-lock, clever safe-breakers use a stethoscope to listen to the click of the tumblers [Orwell's note].

granted by the people on Trafalgar Square that youths could earn a bit this way, and several said to me, 'I need never sleep out if I choose to go down to Charing Cross.' They added that the usual fee is a shilling.

23. *a Get:* presumably the contemptuous 'git' as in 'you git', an ignorant fool. Compare the Scots 'gyte' (pronounced 'git'), formerly used for a child.

The Road to Wigan Pier Diary

31 January 1936 – 25 March 1936

On 2 December 1943 Orwell took part in a transatlantic radio programme, *Your Questions Answered*. He was asked about Wigan Pier. This is his answer:

> 'Well, I am afraid I must tell you that Wigan Pier doesn't exist. I made a journey especially to see it in 1936, and I couldn't find it. It did exist once, however, and to judge from the photographs it must have been about twenty feet long.
>
> Wigan is in the middle of the mining areas, and though it's a very pleasant place in some ways its scenery is not its strong point. The landscape is mostly slag-heaps, looking like the mountains of the moon, and mud and soot and so forth. For some reason, though it's not worse than fifty other places, Wigan has always been picked on as a symbol of the ugliness of the industrial areas. At one time, on one of the little muddy canals that run round the town, there used to be a tumble-down wooden jetty; and by way of a joke someone nicknamed this Wigan Pier. The joke caught on locally, and then the music-hall comedians get° hold of it, and they are the ones who have succeeded in keeping Wigan Pier alive as a byword, long after the place itself had been demolished'. (*CW*, XVI, p. 11)

THE DIARY

31 January 1936 – 25 March 1936

After Orwell had completed several drafts of what would become *Down and Out in Paris and London*, and had changed the order of events (originally, those in London preceded his Parisian experiences), the book was rejected by Jonathan Cape and by T.S. Eliot on behalf of Faber & Faber (just as later on both would reject *Animal Farm*). Orwell then gave up. However, a friend, Mrs Sinclair Fierz, sent the typescript to the man who would become Orwell's literary agent, Leonard Moore of Christy & Moore. Moore persuaded Victor Gollancz to publish it. Orwell wished to publish anonymously, first because he thought his low-life slumming might upset his parents, and secondly because, as he told his friend, Sir Richard Rees (an editor of *The Adelphi* for which he wrote), he had a curious fear – a superstition – that if one's real name appeared in print it might enable an enemy to 'work some kind of magic on it'. However, Gollancz was keen to have a name and eventually Orwell suggested, among several others, George Orwell. He would still be Eric Blair in some contexts and to old friends, but his writing thereafter, except for some at the BBC, was under the name 'George Orwell'. On 9 January 1933, *Down and Out in London and Paris* was published by Gollancz and, six months later, in New York.

From April 1932 to July 1933 he taught at The Hawthorns, a private school for boys aged 10–16, in Hayes, Middlesex. He wrote a play for the boys, *Charles II*, for Christmas 1932. In autumn 1933 he taught at a slightly better school, Fray's College, Uxbridge, and whilst there finished writing *Burmese Days*. However, in December he was taken ill with pneumonia and he gave up teaching. From January until October 1934 he lived with his parents at Southwold. *Burmese Days* was first published in New York on 25 October 1934 and then, following changes to ensure that no one could claim libel, by Victor Gollancz on 24 June 1935. Whilst living at Southwold he wrote *A Clergyman's Daughter* (published 11 March 1935 and on 17 August 1936 in New York). From October 1934 until January 1936 he worked part-time as an assistant in a bookshop in Hampstead. Whilst there he wrote *Keep the Aspidistra Flying* – which features a young man attempting to become a poet whilst working in a bookshop.

On 31 January 1936, the day Orwell started his journey to Wigan – and made his first entry in this diary – he also wrote to Victor Gollancz. Gollancz's lawyer, Harold Rubinstein (himself an author, dramatist, and critic) wanted to be assured that an advertisement Orwell had referred to in *Keep the Aspidistra Flying* was 'not based on any identifiable advert. or any real advert. whatever'. Having given that assurance, Orwell thought, wrongly, he had resolved all the libel and defamation queries that might arise before his typescript was sent to the printer and he could concentrate on his next project: studying, at Gollancz's suggestion, conditions in what were called 'the Distressed Areas' of the north of England. A misunderstanding has led to the impression that Orwell was given an advance of £500 to travel north. This has now been shown to be erroneous. Further, it does not stand up to the well attested fact that Gollancz

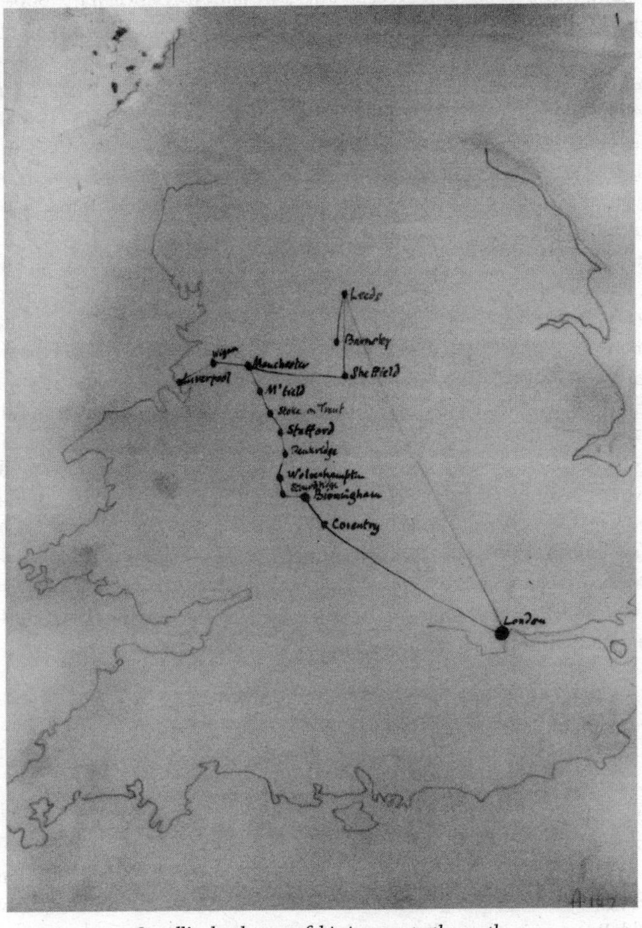

Orwell's sketch map of his journey to the north.

never advanced large sums of money to his authors. As can be seen from his dire penury on his journey, he had very little financial backing for his expedition. Quite recently it was discovered by D.J. Taylor that as late as 29 October 1936, Victor Gollancz, in a letter to Orwell's agent, Leonard Moore, did not even know what Orwell was writing (Taylor, p. 175). By this time he had nearly completed *The Road to Wigan Pier*.

Orwell used his diary entries when writing *The Road to Wigan Pier* but he also did a considerable amount of research and many of the documents he worked from have survived. For reprints of much of this material and further details, see *CW*, X, pp. 538–584. It is possible that Orwell typed his diary whilst in the north using the typewriter he had with him which he used for typing letters. However, the typescript is in two separately paginated sections (1–36 for 31 January to 5 March inclusive; 1–25, headed 'Diary', for the remainder), so later typing for at least the second section seems probable and Eileen may have typed some of the original handwritten diary – see headnote, *CW*, X, p. 417, for full analysis. The typescript has manuscript changes but only the most significant are noted here. Full details are given in *Complete Works*. Minor slips are corrected silently.

Orwell gives details of the costs he incurred on his journey north and his stay there. These, of course, are in 'old money' and when costs and prices were far lower than today. For convenience – there were 12 pence in a shilling and twenty shillings to the £ (so a £ was equivalent to 240 pennies). A penny could be divided into two – a halfpenny or ha'penny – and four (a farthing). It is difficult to give modern equivalents of prices in 1936 and seventy years later but, multiplying by 40 will give a rough approximation. It is important to understand that this is an average: whereas some items may have increased by many times more than 40, some have increased less sharply.

Annotations either follow the days to which they refer or are included at a convenient point within that day. Orwell's annotations are indicated by symbols (as was his practice); editorial annotations are numbered. The superior degree sign (°) is used sparingly where one of Orwell's idiosyncratic spellings is retained.

31.1.36: To Coventry by train as arranged, arriving about 4 pm. Bed and Breakfast house, very lousy, 3/6. Framed certificate in hall setting forth that (John Smith) had been elected to the rank of Primo Buffo.[1] Two beds in room – charge for room to yourself 5/–. Smell as in common lodging houses. Half-witted servant girl with huge body, tiny head and rolls of fat at back of neck curiously recalling ham-fat.

1. *Primo Buffo:* chief comic singer

1.2.36: Lousy breakfast with Yorkshire commercial traveller. Walked 12 miles to outskirts of Birmingham, took bus to Bull Ring (very like Norwich Market) and arrived 1 pm. Lunch in Birmingham and bus to Stourbridge. Walked 4–5 miles to Clent Youth Hostel. Red soil everywhere. Birds courting a little, cock chaffinches and bullfinches very bright and cock partridge making mating call. Except for village of Meriden,[2] hardly a decent house between Coventry and Birmingham. West of Birmingham the usual villa-civilization creeping out over the hills. Raining all day, on and off.

Distance walked, 16 miles. Spent on conveyances, 1/4. On food, 2/3.

2. *Meriden:* traditional centre of England and site of First World War memorial to cyclists.

2.2.36: Comfortable night in hostel, which I had to myself. One-storey wooden building with huge coke stove which kept it very hot. You pay 1/– for bed, 2d for the stove and put pennies in the gas for cooking. Bread, milk etc. on sale at hostel. You have to have your own sleeping bag but get blankets, mattress and pillows. Tiring evening because the warden's son, I suppose out of kindness, came across and played ping-pong with me till I could hardly stand on my feet. In the morning long talk with the warden who keeps poultry and collects glass and pewter. He told me how in France in 1918, on the heels of the retreating Germans, he looted some priceless glass which was discovered and looted from him in turn by his divisional general. Also showed me some nice pieces of pewter and some very curious Japanese pictures, showing clear traces of European influence, looted by his father in some naval expedition about 1860.

Left 10 am., walked to Stourbridge, took bus to Wolverhampton, wandered about slummy parts of Wolverhampton for a while, then had lunch and walked 10 miles to Penkridge. Wolverhampton seems frightful place. Everywhere vistas of mean little houses still enveloped in drifting smoke, though this was Sunday, and along the railway line huge banks of clay and conical chimneys ("pot-banks").[3] Walk from W'ton to Penkridge very dull and raining all the way. Villa-civilization stretches almost unbroken between the two towns. In Penkridge about 4.30 halted for cup of tea. A tiny frouzy° parlour with a nice fire, a little wizened oldish man and an enormous woman about 45, with tow-coloured bobbed hair and no front teeth. Both of them thought me a hero to be walking on such a day. Had tea with them *en famille*. About 5.15 left and walked another couple of miles, then caught bus the remaining 4 miles to Stafford. Went to Temperance Hotel thinking this would be cheap, but bed and breakfast 5/–. The usual dreadful room and twill sheets greyish and smelly as usual. Went to bathroom and found commercial traveller developing snapshots in bath. Persuaded him to remove them and had bath, after which I find myself very footsore.

Distance walked, about 16 miles. Spent on conveyances, 1/5. On food, 2/8½.

3. *conical chimneys ("pot-banks"):* for the manufacture of pottery.

3.2.36: Left 9 am. and took bus to Hanley. Walked round Hanley and part of Burslem. Frightfully cold, bitter wind, and it had been snowing in the night; blackened snow lying about everywhere. Hanley and Burslem about the most dreadful places I have seen. Labyrinths of tiny blackened houses and among them the pot-banks like monstrous burgundy bottles half buried in the soil, belching forth smoke. Signs of poverty everywhere and very poor shops. In places enormous chasms delved out, one of them about 200 yards wide and about as deep, with rusty iron trucks on a chain railway crawling up one side, and here and there on the almost perpendicular face of the other, a few workmen hanging like samphire-gatherers, cutting into the face with their picks apparently aimlessly, but I suppose digging out clay. Walked on to Eldon and lunch at pub there. Frightfully cold. Hilly country, splendid views, especially when one gets further east and hedges give way to stone walls. Lambs here seem much more backward than down south. Walked on to Rudyard Lake.[4]

4. *Rudyard Lake:* Orwell had to make a detour to walk by Rudyard Lake. Dr Robert Fyson has shown why Orwell did this. In 1863, Lockwood Kipling and Alice Macdonald had a picnic here. They married two years later and when their first child was born they gave him the name Rudyard. Rudyard Kipling died on 18 January 1936 and Orwell had written an appreciation of him published on 23 January in *New English Weekly* (*CW*, X, pp. 409–10). In this he wrote 'now that he is dead, I for one cannot help wishing that I could offer some kind of tribute – a salute of guns, if such a thing were available – to the story-teller who was so important to my childhood'. This detour, in the bitter cold, was his tribute.

Rudyard Lake (really a reservoir, supplying the pottery towns) very depressing. In the summer it is a pleasure resort. Cafés, houseboats and pleasure-boats every ten yards, all deserted and flyblown, this being the offseason. Notices relating to fishing, but I examined the water and it did not look to me as though it had any fish in it. Not a soul anywhere and bitter wind blowing. All the broken ice had been blown up to the south end, and the waves were rocking it up and down, making a clank-clank, clank-clank – the most melancholy noise I ever heard. (Mem. to use in novel some time and to have an empty Craven A packet bobbing up and down among the ice.)

The hostel (now Cliffe Park Hall, a private house overlooking Rudyard Lake) where Orwell stayed on 3 February 1936. It was built about 1811 and served as a youth hostel from 1933–1969. It could accommodate forty-six men and twenty women.

Found hostel, about 1 mile further on, with difficulty. Alone again. A most peculiar place this time. A great draughty barrack of a house, built in the sham-castle style – somebody's Folly – about 1860. All but three or four of the rooms quite empty. Miles of echoing stone passages, no lighting except candles and only smoky little oilstoves to cook on. Terribly cold.

Only 2/8d left, so tomorrow must go into Manchester (walk to Macclesfield, then bus) and cash cheque.

Distance walked, 12 miles. Spent on conveyances 1/8. On food, 2/8.

4.2.36: Got out of bed so cold that I could not do up any buttons and had to [go] down and thaw my hands before I could dress. Left about 10.30 am. A marvellous morning. Earth frozen hard as iron, not a breath of wind and the sun shining brightly. Not a soul stirring. Rudyard lake (about 1½ miles long) had frozen over during the night. Wild ducks walking about disconsolately on the ice. The sun coming up and the light slanting along the ice the most wonderful red-gold colour I have ever seen. Spent a long time throwing stones over the ice. A jagged stone skimming across ice makes exactly the same sound as a redshank whistling.

Walked to Macclesfield, 10 or 11 miles, then bus to Manchester. Went and collected letters, then to bank to cash cheque but found they were shut – they shut at 3 pm here. Very awkward as I had only 3d in hand. Went to Youth Hostel headquarters and asked them to cash cheque, but they refused, then to Police Station to ask them to introduce me to a solicitor who would cash a cheque, but they also refused. Frightfully cold. Streets encrusted with mounds of dreadful black stuff which was really snow frozen hard and blackened by smoke. Did not want to spend night in streets. Found my way to poor quarter (Chester Street), went to pawnshop and tried to pawn raincoat but they said they did not take them any longer. Then it occurred to me my scarf was pawnable, and they gave me 1/11d on it. Went to common lodging house, of which there were three close together in Chester Street.

Long letter from Rees advising me about people to go and see, one of them, luckily, in Manchester.

Distance walked, about 13 miles. Spent on conveyances, 2/–. On food, 10d.

5.2.36: Went and tried to see Meade[5] but he was out. Spent day in common lodging house. Much as in London, 11d for bed, cubicles not dormitories. The "deputy" a cripple as they seem so often to be. Dreadful method here of making tea in tin bowls. Cashed cheque in morning but shall stay tonight in lodging house and go and see Meade tomorrow.

5. *Frank Meade:* an official of the Amalgamated Society of Woodworkers. He ran the Manchester office of *The Adelphi* (which, from 1930, had published some of Orwell's reviews), and was business manager of *Labour's Northern Voice*, an organ of the Independent Socialist Party.

6–10.2.36: Staying with the Meades at 49 Brynton Rd., Longsight, Manchester. Brynton Rd. is in one of the new building estates. Very decent houses with bathrooms and electric light, rent I suppose about 12/– or 14/–. Meade is some kind of Trade Union Official and has something to do with the editing of *Labour's Northern Voice* – these are the people who do the publishing side of the *Adelphi*. The M.s have been very decent to me. Both are working-class people, speak with Lancashire accents and have worn the clogs in their childhood, but the atmosphere in a place like this is entirely middle-class. Both the M.s were faintly scandalised to hear I had been in the common lodging house in Manchester. I am struck again by the fact that as soon as a working man gets an official post in the Trade Union or goes into Labour politics, he becomes middle-class whether he will or no. ie. by fighting against the bourgeoisie he becomes a bourgeois. The fact is that you cannot help living in the manner appropriate and developing the ideology appropriate to your income (in M's case I suppose about £4 a week.) The only quarrel I have with the M.s is that they call me "comrade." Mrs M., as usual, does not understand much about politics but has adopted her husband's views as a wife ought to; she pronounces the word "comrade" with manifest discomfort. Am struck by the difference of manners even as far north as this. Mrs M. is surprised and not altogether approving when I get up when she enters the room, offer to help with the washing-up, etc. She says, "Lads up here expect to be waited on."

M. sent me across to Wigan to see Joe Kennan,[6] an electrician who takes a prominent part in the Socialist movement. Kennan also lives in a decent Corporation house (Beech Hill Building Estate) but is more definitely a working man. A very short, stout, powerful man with an extraordinarily gentle, hospitable manner and very anxious to help. His elder child was upstairs in bed (scarlet fever suspected) the younger on the floor playing with soldiers and a toy cannon. Kennan smiles and says, "You see – and I'm supposed to be a pacifist." He sent me to the N. U. W. M.[7] shelter with a letter to the secretary asking him to find me a lodging in Wigan. The shelter is a dreadful ramshackle little place but a godsend to these unemployed men as it is warm and there are newspapers etc. there. The secretary, Paddy Grady, an unemployed miner. A tall lean man about 35, intelligent and well-informed and very anxious to help. He is a single man getting 17/– bob° [= shillings] a week and is in a dreadful state physically from years of underfeeding and idleness. His front teeth are almost entirely rotted away. All the men at the N. U. W. M. very friendly and anxious to supply me with information as soon as they heard I was a writer and collecting facts about working-class conditions. I cannot get them to treat me precisely as an equal, however. They call me either "Sir" or "Comrade."

6. *Joe Kennan*: at the time an unemployed coal miner and activist in the Independent Labour Party. He found Orwell lodgings with John and Lily Anderton (Mr and Mrs Hornby in this diary). For a valuable interview with Joe Kennan, see *Orwell Remembered* (pp. 130–3). See also n. 19 below.
7. *N. U. W. M.*: National Unemployed Workers' Movement.

11.2.36: Staying at 72 Warrington Lane, Wigan.[8] Board and lodging 25/– a week. Share room with another lodger (unemployed railwayman), meals in kitchen and wash at scullery sink. Food all right but indigestible and in monstrous quantities. Lancashire method of eating tripe (cold with vinegar) horrible.

The family. Mr Hornby, aged 39, has worked in the pit since he was 13. Now out of work for nine months. A largish, fair, slow-moving, very mild and nice-mannered man who considers carefully before he answers when you ask him a question, and begins, "In my estimation." Has not much accent. Ten years ago he got a spurt of coal dust in his left eye and practically lost the sight of it. Was put to work "on top" for a while but went back to the pit as he could earn more there. Nine months ago his other eye went wrong (there is something called "nyastygmus"[9] or some such name that miners suffer from) and he can only see a few yards. Is on "compensation" of 29/– a week, but they are talking of putting him on "partial compensation" of 14/– a week. It all depends whether the doctor passes him as fit for work, though of course there would not be any work, except perhaps a job "on top," but there are very few of these. If he is put on partial compensation he can draw the dole until his stamps are exhausted.

Mrs Hornby. Four years older than her husband. Less than 5 feet tall. Toby-jug figure. Merry disposition. Very ignorant – adds up 27 and 10 and makes it 31. Very broad accent. There seem to be 2 ways of dealing with the "the" here. Before consonants it is often omitted altogether ("Put joog on table," etc.) before vowels it is often incorporated with the word. eg. "My sister's in thospital" – th as in thin.

The son "our Joe," just turned 15 and has been working in the pit a year. At present is on night shift. Goes to work about 9 pm returns between 7 and 8 am, has breakfast and promptly goes to bed in bed vacated by another lodger. Usually sleeps till 5 or 6pm. He started work on 2/8 a day, was raised to 3/4, ie. £ a week. Out of this 1/8 a week comes off for stoppages (insurance etc.) and 4d a day for his tram fares to and from the pit. So his net wage, working full time, is 16/4 a week. In summer, however, he will only be working short-time. A tallish, frail, deadly pale youth, obviously much exhausted by his work, but seems fairly happy.

Tom, Mrs Hornby's cousin, unmarried and lodging there – paying 25/– a week. A very hairy man with a hare-lip, mild disposition and very simple. Also on night shift.

Joe, another lodger, single. Unemployed on 17/– a week. Pays 6/– a week for his room and sees to his own food. Gets up about 8 to give his bed up to "our Joe" and remains out of doors, in Public Library etc., most of day. A bit of an ass but has some education and enjoys a resounding phrase. Explaining why he never married, he says portentously, "Matrimonial chains is a big item." Repeated this sentence a number of times, evidently having an affection for it. Has been totally unemployed for 7 years. Drinks when he gets the chance, which of course he never does nowadays.

The house has two rooms and scullery downstairs, 3 rooms upstairs, tiny back yard and outside lavatory. No hot water laid on. Is in bad repair

– front wall is bulging. Rent 12/– and with rates 14/–. The total income of the Hornbys is:

Mr Hornby's compensation	29/–	a week
Joe's wages	16/4	"
Tom's weekly payment	25/–	"
Joe's ditto.......................................	6/–	"
Total..	£3-16-4.	[10]

Payment of rent and rates leaves £3-2-4. This has to feed 4 people and clothe and otherwise provide for 3.* Of course at present there is my own contribution as well but that is an abnormality.

Wigan in the centre does not seem as bad as it has been represented – distinctly less depressing than Manchester. Wigan Pier said to have been demolished. Clogs commonly worn here and general in the smaller places outside such as Hindley. Shawl over head commonly worn by older women, but girls evidently only do it under pressure of dire poverty. Nearly everyone one sees very badly dressed and youths on the corners markedly less smart and rowdy than in London, but no very obvious signs of poverty except the number of empty shops. One in three of registered workers said to be unemployed.

Last night to Co-Op hall with various people from the N.U.W.M. to hear Wal Hannington[11] speak. A poor speaker, using all the padding and cliches of the Socialist orator, and with the wrong kind of cockney accent (once again, though a Communist entirely a bourgeois), but he got the people well worked up. Was surprised by the amount of Communist feeling here. Loud cheers when Hannington announced that if England and U.S.S.R went to war U.S.S.R would win. Audience very rough and all obviously unemployed (about 1 in 10 of them women) but very attentive. After the address a collection taken for expenses – hire of hall and H.'s train-fare from London. £1-6-0 raised – not bad from about 200 unemployed people.

You can always tell a miner by the blue tattooing of coal dust on the bridge of his nose. Some of the older men have their foreheads veined with it like Roquefort cheese.

8. *Warrington Lane:* illustrated in Peter Lewis, *George Orwell: The Road to 1984* (1981, p. 50. Wigan Pier is illustrated on the same page.)
9. *nyastygmus* = nystagmus, continual rapid oscillation of the eyeballs.
10. The total income of the Hornbys is *roughly* equivalent to £150 today.
11. *Wal Hannington:* (1896–1996), a leader of the NUWM and author of *Unemployed Struggles 1919–1936* and *The Problem of the Distressed Areas*, published by the Left

* The H.s are well-off by local standards [Orwell's handwritten footnote].

Book Club in November 1937. Like *The Road to Wigan Pier*, which preceded it, it had a centre section of thirty-two plates. Reg Reynolds, one of Orwell's pacifist friends, writing of his sympathy with the Hunger Marchers, observed that when they arrived at Hyde Park Corner, London, they 'did not look at all hungry – least of all that stout Communist, Wal Hannington, who led them' (*My Life and Crimes*, 1956, p. 106). Hannington also wrote the useful *Mr Chairman! A Short Guide to the Conduct and Procedure of Meetings* (1950). The £1-6-0 raised is equivalent to 312 pence – by an audience of about 200, so about a penny-ha'penny from each person on average.

12.2.36: Terribly cold. Long walk along the canal (one-time site of Wigan Pier) towards some slag-heaps in the distance. Frightful landscape of slag-heaps and belching chimneys. Some of the slag-heaps almost like mountains – one just like Stromboli. Bitter wind. They had had to send a steamer to break the ice in front of the coal barges on the canal. The bargemen were muffled to the eyes in sacks. All the "flashes" (stagnant pools made by the subsidence of disused pits) covered with ice the colour of raw umber. Beards of ice on the lock gates. A few rats running slowly through the snow, very tame, presumably weak with hunger.

13.2.36: Housing conditions in Wigan terrible. Mrs H. tells me that at her brother's house (he is only 25, so I think he must be her half brother, but he has already a child of 8), 11 people, 5 of them adults, belonging to 3 different families, live in 4 rooms, "2 up 2 down. "

All the miners I meet have either had serious accidents themselves or have friends or relatives who have. Mrs Hornby's cousin had his back broken by a fall of rock – "And he lingered seven year afore he died and it were a-punishing of him all the while" – and her brother in law fell 1200 feet down the shaft of a new pit. Apparently he bounced from side to side, so was presumably dead before he got to the bottom. Mrs H. adds: "They wouldn't never have collected t'pieces only he were wearing a new suit of oilskins."

15.2.36: Went with N.U.W.M. collectors on their rounds with a view to collecting facts about housing conditions, especially in the caravans. Have made notes on these, Q.V.[12] What chiefly struck me was the expression on some of the women's faces, especially those in the more crowded caravans. One woman had a face like a death's head. She had a look of absolutely intolerable misery and degradation. I gathered that she felt as I would feel if I were coated all over with dung. All the people however seemed to take these conditions quite for granted. They have been promised houses over and over again but nothing has come of it and they have got into the way of thinking that a livable house is something absolutely unattainable.

12. *Q.V.* = *quod vide* = which see (in this case Orwell's notes, some of which are reproduced in *Complete Works*; see X, 546; also plate 31 of *The Road to Wigan Pier* (where the caravans are in Durham, not Wigan).

Passing up a horrible squalid side-alley, saw a woman, youngish but very pale and with the usual draggled exhausted look, kneeling by the gutter outside a house and poking a stick up the leaden waste-pipe, which was blocked. I thought how dreadful a destiny it was to be kneeling in the gutter in a back-alley in Wigan, in the bitter cold, prodding a stick up a blocked drain. At that moment she looked up and caught my eye, and her expression was as desolate as I have ever seen; it struck me that she was thinking just the same thing as I was.

Orwell developed this entry in *The Road to Wigan Pier*

The train bore me away, through the monstrous scenery of slag-heaps, chimneys, piled scrap-iron, foul canals, paths of cindery mud criss-crossed by the prints of clogs. This was March, but the weather had been horribly cold and everywhere there were mounds of blackened snow. As we moved slowly through the outskirts of the town we passed row after row of little grey slum houses running at right angles to the embankment. At the back of one of the houses a young woman was kneeling on the stones, poking a stick up the leaden waste-pipe which ran from the sink inside and which I suppose was blocked. I had time to see everything about her – her sacking apron, her clumsy clogs, her arms reddened by the cold. She looked up as the train passed, and I was almost near enough to catch her eye. She had a round pale face, the usual exhausted face of the slum girl who is twenty-five and looks forty, thanks to miscarriages and drudgery; and it wore, for the second in which I saw it, the most desolate, hopeless expression I have ever seen. It struck me then that we are mistaken when we say that 'It isn't the same for them as it would be for us', and that people bred in the slums can imagine nothing but the slums. For what I saw in her face was not the ignorant suffering of an animal. She knew well enough what was happening to her – understood as well as I did how dreadful a destiny it was to be kneeling there in the bitter cold, on the slimy stones of a slum backyard, poking a stick up a foul drain-pipe.

But quite soon the train drew away into open country, and that seemed strange, almost unnatural, as though the open country had been a kind of park . . . [13]

13. The contrast between the two passages will be apparent. In the Diary, Orwell is on foot when passing the squalid side-alley. When the young women looks up and catches Orwell's eye there is an obvious immediacy.

In the book, Orwell is at a distance, in a train, looking through a window and being drawn away from the young women at the waste-pipe: there is a distancing effect emphasised by Orwell's 'I was almost near enough to catch her eye'.

Changing lodgings as Mrs H. is ill with some mysterious malady and ordered into hospital. They have found lodgings for me at 22 Darlington Rd., over a tripe shop where they take in lodgers.[14] The husband an ex-miner (age 58) the wife ill with a weak heart, in bed on sofa in kitchen. Social atmosphere much as at the H.s but house appreciably dirtier and very smelly. A number of other lodgers. An old ex-miner, age about 75, on old age pension plus half a crown weekly from parish (12/6 in all.) Another, said to be of superior type and "come down in the world," more or less bedridden. An Irish ex-miner who had shoulder blade and several ribs crushed by a fall of stone a few years ago and lives on disability pension of about 25/– a week. Of distinctly superior type and started off as a clerk but went "down pit" because he was big and strong and could earn more as a miner (this was before the War.) Also some newspaper canvassers. Two for *John Bull,*[15] distinctly moth eaten, ages about 40 and 55, one quite young and was for four years in rubber firm in Calcutta. Cannot quite make this lad out. He puts on Lancashire accent when talking to the others (he belongs locally) but to me talks in the usual "educated" accent. The family apart from the Forrests themselves consists of a fat son who is at work somewhere and lives nearby, his wife Maggie who is in the shop nearly all day, their two kids, and Annie, fiancée of the other son who is in London. Also a daughter in Canada (Mrs F. says "at Canada.") Maggie and Annie do practically the whole work of the house and shop. Annie very thin, overworked (she also works in a dress-sewing place) and obviously unhappy. I gather that the marriage is by no means certain to take place but that Mrs F. treats Annie as a relative all the same and that Annie groans under her tyranny. Number of rooms in the house exclusive of shop premises, 5 or six and a bathroom-W.C. Nine people sleeping here. Three in my room besides myself.

Struck by the astonishing ignorance about and wastefulness of food among the working class people here – more even than in the south, I think. One morning when washing in the H.s' scullery made an inventory of the following food: A piece of bacon about 5 pounds. About 2 pounds of shin of beef. About a pound and a half of liver (all of these uncooked.) The wreck of a monstrous meat pie (Mrs H. when making a pie always made it in an enamelled basin such as is used for washing up in. Ditto with puddings.) A dish containing 15 or 20 eggs. A number of small cakes. A flat fruit pie and a "cake-a-pie" (pastry with currants in it.) Various fragments of earlier pies. 6 large loaves and 12 small ones (I had seen Mrs H. cook these the night before.) Various odds and ends of butter, tomatoes, opened tins of milk etc. There was also more food keeping warm in the oven in the kitchen. Everything except bread habitually left about uncovered and shelves filthy. Food here consists almost entirely of bread and starch. A typical day's meals at the H.s'. Breakfast (about 8 am): Two fried eggs and bacon, bread (no butter) and tea. Dinner (about 12.30 pm): A monstrous plate of stewed beef, dumplings and boiled potatoes (equal to about 3 Lyons[16] portions) and a big helping of rice pudding or suet pudding. Tea (about 5 pm): A plate of cold meat, bread and butter, sweet pastries and tea. Supper (about 11 pm): fish and chips, bread and butter and tea.

14. *22 Darlington Rd.:* ('Rd.' typed in error for Street). Orwell left 72 Warrington Lane when Mrs Hornby was taken ill and had to be admitted to hospital. Lodgings were found for him over the infamous tripe shop described in chapter 1 of *The Road to Wigan Pier*. This is usually taken to be 22 Darlington Street (see Crick, p. 282) but Sydney Smith (b. 1909) argues it was 35 Sovereign Street, lodgers living next door at no. 33. See *Orwell Remembered*, pp. 136–9. Orwell certainly addressed his letters from 22 Darlington Street.
15. *John Bull:* founded 1906 and initially edited by Horatio Bottomley (1860–1933). The journal specialised in sensationalism and competitions for relatively large prizes. Bottomley, described himself in World War One as 'The Soldier's Friend', and campaigned for Ramsay MacDonald (later Labour Prime Minister) to be imprisoned, but it was Bottomley who ended up in prison for fraud.
16. *Lyons:* at this time, a chain of popular teashops and restaurants.

16.2.36: Great excitement because a couple who stayed here for a month about Xmas have been arrested (at Preston) as coiners and it is believed they were making their false coins while here. The police inspector here for about an hour asking questions. Mrs F. tells of snooping round their room while they were out and finding a lump of something like solder under the mattress and some little pots like egg-cups only larger. Mrs F. agreed instantly to everything the police inspector suggested, and when he was upstairs searching the room I made two suggestions and she agreed to those too. I could see she had made up her mind they were guilty on hearing they were unmarried. When the inspector had written out her statement it came out that she could not read or write (except her signature), though her husband can read a little.

One of the canvassers' beds is jammed across the foot of mine. Impossible to stretch my legs out straight as if I do so my feet are in the small of his back. It seems a long time since I slept between linen sheets. Twill sheets even at the M[eade]s. Theirs (the M.s') was the only house I have been in since leaving London that did not smell.

17.2.36: The newspaper-canvassers are rather pathetic. Of course it is a quite desperate job. I fancy what *John Bull* do is to take on people who make frantic efforts and work up a little more or less spurious business for a while, then sack them and take on more, and so on. I should judge these men each make £2 or £3 a week. Both have families and one is a grandfather. They are so hard up that they cannot pay for full board but pay something for their rooms and have a squalid little cupboard of food in the kitchen, from which they take out bread, packets of marg. etc and cook themselves meals in a shamefaced manner. They are allocated so many houses each day and have to knock at every door and book a minimum number of orders. They are at present working some swindle on behalf of John Bull by which you get a "free" tea set by sending two shillings worth of stamps and twenty four coupons. As soon as they have had their food they start filling up blank forms for the next day, and presently the older one falls asleep in his chair and begins snoring loudly.

Am struck, though, by their knowledge of working-class conditions. They can tell you all about housing, rents, rates, state of trade etc. in every town in the north of England.

18.2.36: In the early morning the mill girls clumping down the cobbled street, all in clogs, make a curiously formidable sound, like an army hurrying into battle. I suppose this is the typical sound of Lancashire. And the typical imprint in the mud the outline of a clog-iron, like one half of a cow's hoof. Clogs are very cheap. They cost about 5/– a pair and need not wear out for years because all they need is new irons costing a few pence.

As always and everywhere, the dress peculiar to the locality is considered plebeian. A very down in the mouth respectable woman, at one of the houses I visited with the N.U.W.M. collectors, said:

"I've always kept myself decent-like. I've never worn a shawl over my head – I wouldn't be seen in such a thing. I've worn a hat since I was a girl. But it don't do you much good. At Christmas time we was that hard put to it that I thought I'd go up and try for a well-wisher. (Hamper given away by some charitable organization.) When I got up there the clergyman says to me, '*You* don't want no well-wisher;' he says. 'There's plenty worse than you. We knows many a one that's living on bread and jam,' he says. 'And how do you know what *we're* living on?' I says. He says, 'You can't be so bad if you can dress as well as that,' he says – meaning my hat. I didn't get no well-wisher. If I'd ha' gone up with a shawl over my head I'd ha' got it. That's what you get for keeping yourself respectable."

On 18 February Orwell responded to the first of a number of letters from Victor Gollancz Ltd, requesting more changes to *Keep the Aspidistra Flying* to settle Mr Rubinstein's anxieties about libel and defamation. Orwell became increasingly upset by these requests. Some must have seemed especially trivial after he had had a day crawling painfully through mine workings and seen the conditions that colliers worked in. On 24 February he wrote to his agent, Leonard Moore: 'Why I was annoyed was because they had not demanded these alterations earlier. The book was looked over and O.K.'d by the solicitor as usual . . . I would have entirely rewritten the first chapter and modified several others. But they asked me to make alterations when the book was in type and asked me to equalise the letters, which of course could not be done without spoiling whole passages and in one case a whole chapter'. (Before computer setting, type was set in lead and adjustments to equalise the lengths of lines were a tedious and time-consuming business: hence the request to replace words with those of the same number of letters.)

19.2.36: When a "dirt-heap" sinks, as it does ultimately, it leaves a hummocky surface which is made more so by the fact that in times of strikes the miners dig into some of these places in search of small coals. One which is used as a playground looks like a choppy sea suddenly frozen. It is called locally "the flock mattress." The soil over them is grey and cindery and only an evil-looking brownish grass grows on them.

This evening to a social the N.U.W.M had got up in aid of Thaelmann's[17] defence-fund. Admission and refreshments (cup of tea and meat pie) 6d. About 200 people, preponderantly women, largely members of the Co-Op,° in one of whose rooms it was held, and I suppose for the most part living directly or indirectly on the dole. Round the back a few aged miners sitting looking on benevolently, a lot of very young girls in front. Some dancing to the concertina (many of the girls confessed that they could not dance, which struck me as rather pathetic) and some excruciating singing. I suppose these people represented a fair cross-section of the more revolutionary element in Wigan. If so, God help us. Exactly the same sheep-like crowd – gaping girls and shapeless middle-aged women dozing over their knitting – that you see everywhere else. There is no *turbulence* left in England. One good song, however, by an old woman, I think a cockney, who draws the old age pension and makes a bit by singing at pubs, with the refrain:

"For you can't do that there 'ere,
"No, you can't do that there 'ere;
"Anywhere else you can do that there,
"But you can't do that there 'ere." [18]

17. *Ernst Thaelmann:* (1886–1944), a transport worker and Chairman of the German Communist Party from 1925. He was a member of the Reichstag, 1924–33, and ran for the Presidency against Hindenburg in 1932, attracting five million votes. He was arrested in 1933; his trial was postponed several times and in October 1936 it was announced that he would be detained for life without trial. He was officially reported killed in an air raid but was in fact shot by the Nazis at Buchenwald in August 1944. Germans fighting for the Republic in Spain formed themselves into the Thaelmann Centuria (later, Brigade).
18. *For you can't do that there 'ere*: Orwell mentions this song in 'Songs We used to Sing', 19 January 1946 (*CW,* XVIII, p. 51) and suggests it seems to be 'a reflection of the existing political situation . . . perhaps a half-conscious response to Hitler'.

20.2.36: This afternoon with Paddy Grady to see the unemployed miners robbing the "dirt-train," or, as they call it, "scrambling for the coal." A most astonishing sight. We went by the usual frightful routes along the colliery railway line to fir-tree sidings, on our way meeting various men and women with sacks of stolen coal which they had slung over bicycles. I would like to know where they got these bicycles – perhaps made of odd parts picked off rubbish dumps. None had mudguards, few had saddles and some had not even tyres. When we got to the big dirt-heap where the trainloads of shale from that pit are discharged, we found about 50 men picking over the dirt, and they directed us to the place further up the line where the men board the train. When we got there we found not less than 100 men, a few boys, waiting, each with a sack and coal hammer strapped under his coat tails. Presently the train hove in sight, coming round the bend at about 20 mph. 50 or 70 men rushed for it, seized hold of the bumpers etc. and hoisted themselves onto the trucks. It appears that each truck is regarded as the property of the men who have succeeded in getting onto it while it is moving. The engine ran the trucks up onto the dirt-heap, uncoupled them and came back for the remaining trucks. There was the same wild rush and the second train was boarded in the same manner, only a few men failing to get on to it. As soon as the trucks had been uncoupled the men on top began shovelling the stuff out to their women and other supporters below, who rapidly sorted out the dirt and put all the coal (a considerable amount but all small, in lumps about the size of eggs) into their sacks. Further down the "broo" were the people who had failed to get onto either train and were collecting the tiny fragments of coal that came sliding down from above. You do not, of course, when you are boarding the train, know whether you are getting onto a good truck or not, and what kind of truck you get is entirely luck. Thus some of the trucks, instead of being loaded with the dirt from the floor of the mine, which of course contains a fair quantity of coal, were loaded entirely with shale. But it appears, what I had never heard of before, that among the shale, at any rate in some mines, there occurs an inflammable rock called "cannel" (not certain of spelling) which makes fairly good fuel. It is not commercially valuable because it is hard to work and burns too fast, but for ordinary purposes is good enough. Those who were on the shale trucks were picking out the "cannel," which is almost exactly like the shale except that it is a little darker and is known by splitting horizontally, almost like slate. I watched the people working until they had almost emptied the trucks. There were twenty trucks and something over 100 people were at work on them. Each, so far as I could judge, got about ½ cwt. of either coal or "cannel." This performance sometimes happens more than once a day when several dirt-trains are sent out, so it is evident that several tons of fuel are stolen every day.

The economics and ethics of the whole business are rather interesting. In the first place, robbing the dirt-train is of course illegal, and one is technically trespassing by being on the dirt-heap at all. Periodically people are prosecuted – in fact in this morning's *Examiner* there was a report of 3 men being fined for it. But no notice is taken of the prosecutions, and in fact one of the men fined was there this afternoon. But at the same time the coal company have no intention of using the coal etc. that is thrown out among the dirt, because it would not repay the cost of sorting. If not stolen, therefore, it would be wasted. Moreover, this business saves the company the expense of emptying the trucks, because by the time the coal-pickers have done with them they are empty. Therefore they connive at the raiding of the train – I noticed that the engine-driver took no notice of the men clambering onto the trucks. The reason for the periodical prosecutions is said to be that there are so many accidents. Only recently a man slipped under the train and had both legs cut off. Considering the speed the train goes at, it is remarkable that accidents do not happen oftener.

The most curious vehicle I saw used for carrying away coal was a cart made of a packing case and the wheels from two kitchen mangles.

Some of this coal that is stolen is said to be on sale in the town at 1/6 a bag.

21.2.36: The squalor of this house is beginning to get on my nerves. Nothing is ever cleaned or dusted, the rooms not done out till 5 in the afternoon, and the cloth never even removed from the kitchen table. At supper you still see the crumbs from breakfast. The most revolting feature is Mrs F. being always in bed on the kitchen sofa. She has a terrible habit of tearing off strips of newspaper, wiping her mouth with them and then throwing them onto the floor. Unemptied chamberpot under the table at breakfast this morning. The food is dreadful, too. We are given those little twopenny readymade steak and kidney pies out of stock. I hear horrible stories, too, about the cellars where the tripe is kept and which are said to swarm with black beetles. Apparently they only get in fresh supplies of tripe at long intervals. Mrs F. dates events by this. "Let me see, now. I've had in three lots of froze (frozen tripe) since then," etc. I judge they get in a consignment of "froze" about once in a fortnight. Also it is very tiring being unable to stretch my legs straight out at night.

24.2.36: Yesterday went down Crippen's mine with Jerry Kennan,[19] another electrician friend of his, two small sons of the latter, two other electricians and an engineer belonging to the pit, who showed us round. The depth to the cage bottom was 300 yards. We went down at 10.30 and came up at 1.30, having covered, according to the engineer who showed us round, about 2 miles.

19. *Jerry (Joe) Kennan:* an unemployed collier at the time and an activist in the Independent Labour Party. He maintained that the lodgings at 72 Warrington Lane were spotlessly clean, despite Orwell's strictures, and 'that Orwell left it for the tripe shop in order to find something worse'. Whether hurried or not, Orwell's departure tallies with Mrs Hornby's illness (see n. 14 above). Kennan, understandably, may have resented not being sent an autographed copy of *The Road to Wigan Pier;* on the other hand he was gracious in stating that 'the book was a fair book. I don't think it exaggerated the situation at all. And I think it gives a clear picture of what conditions were like in industrial areas in 1936' (*Orwell Remembered,* pp. 130 and 133).

As the cage goes down you have the usual momentary qualm in your belly, then a curious stuffed-up feeling in your ears. In the middle of its run the cage works up a tremendous speed (in some of the deeper mines they are said to touch 60 mph. or more) then slows down so abruptly that it is difficult to believe you are not going upwards again. The cages are tiny – about 8 feet long by 3½ wide by 6 high. They are supposed to hold 10 men or (I think) about a ton and a half of coal. There were only six of us and two boys, but we had difficulty in packing in and it is important to face in the direction you are going to get out the other end.

Down below it was lighter than I expected, because apart from the lamps we all carried there were electric lights in the main roads. But what I had not expected, and what for me was the most important feature all through, was the lowness of the roof. I had vaguely imagined wandering about in places rather like the tunnels of the Underground; but as a matter of fact there were very few places where you could stand upright. In general the roof was about 4 ft. or 4 ft. 6 ins high, sometimes much lower, with every now and again a beam larger than the others under which you had to duck especially low. In places the walls were quite neatly built up, almost like the stone walls in Derbyshire, with slabs of shale. There were pit-props, almost all of wood, every yard or so overhead. They are made of small larch trees sawn to the appropriate length (from the quantity used I see now why people laying down plantations almost always plant larch) and are simply laid on the ends of the upright props, which are laid on slabs of wood, thus:

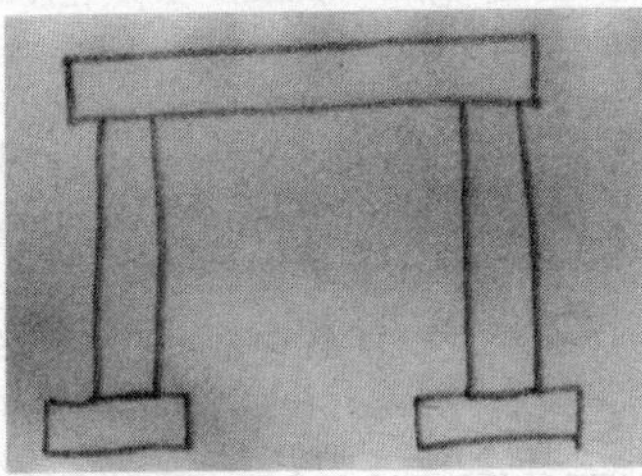

and not fixed in any way. The bottom slabs gradually sink into the floor, or, as the miners put it, "the floor comes up," but the weight overhead keeps the whole thing in place. By the way the steel girders used here and there instead of wooden props had buckled, you got an idea of the weight of the roof. Underfoot is thick stone dust and the rails, about 2½ ft. wide, for the trolleys. When the path is down hill miners often slide down these on their clogs, which, being hollow underneath, more or less fit onto the rails.

After a few hundred yards of walking doubled up and once or twice having to crawl, I began to feel the effects in a violent pain all down my thighs. One also gets a bad crick in the neck, because though stooping one has to look up for fear of knocking into the beams, but the pain in the thighs is the worst. Of course as we got nearer the coal face the roads tended to get lower. Once we crawled through a temporary tunnel which was like an enlarged rat hole, with no props, and in one place there had been a fall of stone during the night – 3 or 4* tons of stuff, I should judge. It had blocked up the entire road except for a tiny aperture near the roof which we had to crawl through without touching any timber. Presently I had to stop for a minute to rest my knees, which were giving way, and then after a few hundred yards more we came to the first working. This was only a small working with a machine worked by two men, much like an enlarged version of the electric drills[20] used for street mending. Nearby was the dynamo (or whatever it is called) which supplied the power through cables to this and the other machines; also the comparatively small drills (but they weigh 50 lbs. each and have to be hoisted onto the shoulder) for drilling holes for blasting charges; also bundles of miners' tools locked together on wires like bundles of keys, which is always done for fear of losing them.

20. Orwell presumably meant pneumatic drills.

* Jerry Kennan said 20 or 30. I don't know which of us would be best judge [Orwell's handwritten footnote].

We went a few hundred yards further and came to one of the main workings. The men were not actually working here, but a shift was just coming down to start work about 250 yards further on. Here there was one of the larger machines which have a crew of 5 men to work them. This machine has a revolving wheel on which there are teeth about a couple of inches long set at various angles; in principle it is rather like an immensely thickened circular saw with the teeth much further apart, and running horizontally instead of vertically. The machine is dragged into position by the crew and the front part of it can be swivelled round in any direction and pressed against the coal face by the man working it. Two men called "scufters" shovel the coal onto a rubberbelt conveyor which carries it through a tunnel to the tubs on the main road, where it is hauled by steam haulage to the cages. I had not realised before that the men operating the coal-cutter are working in a place rather less than a yard high. When we crawled in under the roof to the coal face we could at best kneel, and then not kneel upright, and I fancy the men must do most of their work lying on their bellies. The heat also was frightful – round about 100 degrees F. so far as I could judge. The crew keep burrowing into the coal face, cutting a semi-circular track, periodically hauling the machine forward and propping as they go. I was puzzled to know how that monstrous machine – flat in shape, of course, but 6 or 8 feet long and weighing several tons, and only fitted with skids, not wheels – could have been got into position through that mile or so of passages. Even to drag the thing forward as the seam advances must be a frightful labour, seeing that the men have to do it practically lying down. Up near the coal face we saw a number of mice, which are said to abound there. They are said to be commonest in pits where there are or have been horses. I don't know how they get down into the mine in the first place. Probably in the cages, but possibly by falling down the shaft, as it is said that a mouse (owing to its surface area being large relative to its weight) can drop any distance uninjured.

On the way back my exhaustion grew so great that I could hardly keep going at all, and towards the end I had to stop and rest every fifty yards. The periodical effort of bending and raising oneself at each successive beam was fearful, and the relief when one could stand upright, usually owing to a hole in the roof, was enormous. At times my knees simply refused to lift me after I had knelt down. It was made worse by the fact that at the lowest parts the roof is usually on a slope, so that besides bending you have to walk more or less sideways. We were all pretty distressed except the engineer taking us round, who was used to it, and the two small boys, who did not have to bend to any extent; but I was by a good deal the worst, being the tallest. I would like to know whether any miners are as tall as I am, and if so, whether they suffer for it. The few miners whom we met down the pit could move with extraordinary agility, running about on all fours among the props almost like dogs.

After we had at last emerged and washed off the more obtrusive dirt and had some beer, I went home and had dinner and then soaked myself for a long time in a hot bath. I was surprised at the quantity of dirt and the difficulty of getting it off. It had penetrated to every inch of my body in spite of my overalls and my clothes underneath those. Of course very few miners have baths in their homes – only a tub of water in front of the kitchen fire. I should say it would be quite impossible to keep clean without a proper bathtub.

In the room where we changed our clothes there were several cages of canaries. These have to be kept there by law, to test the air in case of explosion. They are sent down in the cage, and, if they do not faint, the air is all right.

The Davy lamps give out a fair amount of light. There is an air intake at the top but the flame is cut off from this by a fine gauze. Flame cannot pass through holes of less than a certain diameter. The gauze therefore lets the air in to sustain the flame but will not let the flame out to explode dangerous gases. Each lamp when full will burn for 8–12 hours, and they are locked, so that if they go out down the pit they cannot be relighted. Miners are searched for matches before going down the pit.

27.2.36: On Wednesday (25th) went over to Liverpool to see the Deiners[21] and Garrett.[22] I was to have come back the same night, but almost as soon as I got to Liverpool I felt unwell and was ignominiously sick, so the Deiners insisted on putting me to bed and then on my staying the night.[23] I came back yesterday evening.

21. *May and John Deiner* ran the Liverpool branch of *The Adelphi* circle. Orwell was introduced to them either by Middleton Murray or Richard Rees of *The Adelphi*. John was a telephone engineer. Orwell arrived very ill and because of this he saw less of Liverpool than he had hoped. He spoke to them of wishing to return to London by ship in order to experience conditions at sea. There is a charming memoir of Orwell by May Deiner in *Orwell Remembered*, pp. 134–6. She concludes: 'He was such a real man . . . We didn't feel any embarrassment at all with him. Just that he hadn't much to say unless he was talking about his books or the things that interested him, about the depression . . . And yet you felt the warmth there; you felt the concern if you like'.
22. *George Garrett* (1896–1966) was an unemployed seaman with whom Orwell got on very well. He wrote for *The Adelphi* and short stories under the pseudonym 'Matt Lowe' (i.e. *matelot*). He had spent much of the 1920s in the USA and was a member of 'the Wobblies', the Industrial Workers of the World, a revolutionary industrial union. His ability to imitate an American accent won him small parts at the Merseyside Unity Theatre.
23. Of the four or five days Orwell stayed with the Deiners, Orwell was, at their insistence, kept in bed for three days (Crick, p. 285).

I was very greatly impressed by Garrett. Had I known before that it is he who writes under the pseudonym of Matt Lowe in the *Adelphi* and one or two other places, I would have taken steps to meet him earlier. He is a biggish hefty chap of about 36, Liverpool-Irish, brought up a Catholic but now a Communist. He says he has had about 9 months' work in (I think) about the last 6 years. He went to sea as a lad and was at sea about 10 years, then worked as a docker. During the War he was torpedoed on a ship that sank in 7 minutes, but they had expected to be torpedoed and had got their boats ready, and were all saved except the wireless operator, who refused to leave his post until he had got an answer. He also worked in an illicit brewery in Chicago during Prohibition, saw various hold-ups, saw Battling Siki[24] immediately after he had been shot in a street brawl, etc. etc. All this however interests him much less than Communist politics. I urged him to write his autobiography, but as usual, living in about 2 rooms on the dole with a wife (who I gather objects to his writing) and a number of kids, he finds it impossible to settle to any long work and can only do short stories. Apart from the enormous unemployment in Liverpool it is almost impossible for him to get work because he is blacklisted everywhere as a Communist.

24. *Battling Siki* (1897–1925; born Amadou M'Barick Fall) a Senegalese boxer who had fought with a French Colonial regiment in World War One. He unexpectedly knocked out the great French champion Georges Carpentier early in 1922 to take the light heavyweight championship of the world. He lost the title shortly afterwards to the Irishman, Mike McTigue. Siki's attempt to make his name as a boxer in the USA was unsuccessful and one morning he was found shot dead in a back street of New York. The Siki-Carpentier fight was filmed and shown widely; Orwell may well have seen it before leaving for Burma.

He took me down to the docks to see dockers being taken on for an unloading job. When we got there we found about 200 men waiting in a ring and police holding them back. It appeared that there was a fruit ship which needed unloading and on the news that there were jobs going there had been a fight between the dockers which the police had to intervene to stop. After a while the agent of the company (known as the stevedore, I think) emerged from a shed and began calling out the names or rather numbers of gangs whom he had engaged earlier in the day. Then he needed about 10 men more, and walked round the ring picking out a man here and there. He would pause, select a man, take him by the shoulder and haul him foreward,° exactly as at a sale of cattle. Presently he announced that that was all. A sort of groan went up from the remaining dockers, and they trailed off, about 50 men having been engaged out of 200. It appears that unemployed dockers have to sign on twice a day, otherwise they are presumed to have been working (as their work is mainly casual labour, by the day) and their dole docked for that day.

I was impressed by the fact that Liverpool is doing much more in the way of slum-clearance than most towns. The slums are still very bad but there are great quantities of Corporation houses and flats at low rents. Just outside Liverpool there are quite considerable towns consisting entirely of Corporation houses, which are really quite livable and decent to look at, but having as usual the objection that they take people a long way from their work. In the centre of the town there are huge blocks of workers' flats imitated from those in Vienna. They are built in the form of an immense ring, five stories high, round a central courtyard about 60 yards across, which forms a playground for children. Round the inner side run balconies, and there are wide windows on each side so that everyone gets some sunlight. I was not able to get inside any of these flats, but I gather each has either 2 or 3 rooms,* kitchenette and bathroom with hot water. The rents vary from about 7/– at the top to 10/– at the bottom. (No lifts, of course.) It is noteworthy that the people in Liverpool have got used to the idea of flats (or tenements, as they call them) whereas in a place like Wigan the people, though realising that flats solve the problem of letting people live near their work, all say they would rather have a house of their own, however bad it was.

There are one or two interesting points here. The re-housing is almost entirely the work of the Corporation, which is said to be entirely ruthless towards private ownership and to be even too ready to condemn slum houses without compensation. Here therefore you have what is in effect Socialist legislation, though it is done by a local authority. But the Corporation of Liverpool is almost entirely Conservative. Moreover, though the re-housing from the public funds is, as I say, in effect a Socialist measure, the actual work is done by private contractors, and one may assume that here as elsewhere the contractors tend to be the friends, brothers, nephews etc. of those on the Corporation. Beyond a certain point therefore Socialism and Capitalism are not easy to distinguish, the State and the capitalist tending to merge into one. On the other side of the river, the Birkenhead side (we went through the Mersey tunnel) you have Port Sunlight, a city within a city, all built and owned by the Leverhulme soap works. Here again are excellent houses at fairly low rents, but, as with publicly-owned property, burdened by restrictions. Looking at the Corporation buildings on the one side, and Lord Leverhulme's buildings on the other, you would find it hard to say which was which.

* presumably 3 – living room & 2 bedrooms [Orwell's handwritten footnote].

Another point is this. Liverpool is practically governed by Roman Catholics. The Roman Catholic ideal, at any rate as put forward by the Chesterton-Beachcomber[25] type of writer, is always in favour of private ownership and against Socialist legislation and "progress" generally. The Chesterton type of writer wants to see a free peasant or other small-owner living in his own privately owned and probably insanitary cottage; not a wage-slave living in an excellently appointed Corporation flat and tied down by restrictions as to sanitation etc. The R.Cs in Liverpool, therefore, are going against the supposed implications of their own religion. But I suppose that if the Chestertons *et hoc genus* grasped that it is possible for the R.Cs to capture the machinery of local and other government, even when it is called Socialist, they would change their tune.

No clogs or shawl over head in Liverpool. Returning by car, noticed how abruptly this custom stops a little west of Wigan.*

Am trying to arrange to return to London by sea if G. can get me a passage on a cargo boat.

Bought two brass candlesticks and a ship in a bottle. Paid 9/– for the candlesticks. G. considered I was swindled but they are quite nice brass.

25. *Chesterton-Beachcomber:* G.K. Chesterton (1897–1925), Roman Catholic apologist, editor, and prolific writer, creator of the priest-detective, Father Brown. He had published Orwell's first professional article in English ('A Farthing Newspaper', 1928, *CW,* X, pp. 119–21). The 'Beachcomber' column in the *Daily Express* was started in 1924 by J. B. Morton (1893–1979), also a Roman Catholic. The column was mildly satiric and the object of frequent pejorative reference by Orwell. For a more considered comparison of Chesterton and Morton by Orwell, see 'As I Please', no 30 (23 June 1944, *CW,* XVI, pp. 262–5).

2.3.36: At 154 Wallace Road, Sheffield.

Thick snow everywhere on the hills as I came along. Stone boundaries between the fields running across the snow like black piping across a white dress. Warm and sunny, however. For the first time in my life saw rooks copulating.[26] On the ground, not in a tree. The manner of courtship was peculiar. The female stood with her beak open and the male walked round her and it appeared as though he was feeding her.

Memories of Wigan: Slagheaps like mountains, smoke, rows of blackened houses, sticky mud criss-crossed by imprints of clogs, heavy-set young women standing at street corners with their babies wrapped in their

* It is said by everyone in Wigan that clogs are going out. Yet in the poorer quarters 1 person in 2 seems to me to wear clogs, & there are (I think) 10 shops which sell nothing else [Orwell's footnote].

shawls, immense piles of broken chocolate in cut-price confectioners' windows.

26. *rooks copulating:* All editions of *Road to Wigan Pier* until *CW*, V, 16, line 16 have 'rooks treading'. The second proof has 'rooks courting', but even that was regarded by the publisher as too explicit. According to Eileen Blair's letter to Gollancz of 17 January 1937, Orwell had originally written 'copulating', as here in his diary.

3.3.36: This house: Two up two down, living room about 14′ by 12′, parlour rather smaller. Sink and copper in living room, no gas fire, outside W.C. Rent with rates about 8/6. 2 cellars as well. Husband is out of work (P.A.C.[27] – was previously store-keeper at a factory which closed down and discharged its whole staff), wife works as a char at 6d an hour. One kid aged 5.

27. *P.A.C.:* The local authority's Public Assistance Committee to whom those out of benefit could apply for financial assistance.

James Brown: age 45 but looks less. Has malformed right hand, also one foot. This was inherited and he fears it is transmissible, so will not marry. Owing to this has never had much in the way of regular work. Was with a circus for some years as groom, clown and "Wild West" rider – he could apparently handle the bridle with his damaged hand. Now lives alone and for some reason gets no dole, only something from the parish and help from his brother. Has a single room with only an open fireplace, no oven, to cook on. Is terribly embittered and declares that feeling of actual hatred for the bourgeoisie, even personal hatred of individuals, is necessary to any genuine Socialist. Is nevertheless a good fellow and very anxious to help. Mixed up with his political feelings is the usual local patriotism of the Yorkshireman and much of his conversation consists of comparison between London and Sheffield to the detriment of the former. Sheffield is held to lead London in everything, eg. on the one hand the new housing schemes in Sheffield are immensely superior, and on the other hand the Sheffield slums are more squalid than anything London can show. I notice that apart from the usual hatred between the Northerner and the Southerner, there is also hatred between the Yorkshireman and the Lancashireman, and also internecine hatred between the various Yorkshire towns. No one up here seems to have heard of any place in the south of England except London. If you come from the south you are assumed to be a cockney however often you deny it. At the same time as the Northerner despises the Southerner he has an uneasy feeling that the latter knows more of the arts of life and is very anxious to impress him.

Had a very long and exhausting day (I am now continuing this March

4th) being shown every quarter of Sheffield on foot and by tram. I have now traversed almost the whole city. It seems to me, by daylight, one of the most appalling places I have ever seen. In whichever direction you look you see the same landscape of monstrous chimneys pouring forth smoke which is sometimes black and sometimes of a rosy tint said to be due to sulphur. You can smell the sulphur in the air all the while. All buildings are blackened within a year or two of being put up. Halting at one place I counted the factory chimneys I could see and there were 33. But it was very misty as well as smoky – there would have been many more visible on a clear day. I doubt whether there are any architecturally decent buildings in the town. The town is very hilly (said to be built on seven hills, like Rome) and everywhere streets of mean little houses blackened by smoke run up at sharp angles, paved with cobbles which are purposely set unevenly to give horses etc. a grip. At night the hilliness creates fine effects because you look across from one hillside to the other and see the lamps twinkling like stars. Huge jets of flame shoot periodically out of the rooves of the foundries (many working night shifts at present) and show a splendid rosy colour through the smoke and steam. When you get a glimpse inside you see enormous fiery serpents of red-hot and white-hot (really lemon-coloured) iron being rolled out into rails. In the central slummy part of the town are the small workshops of the "little bosses," ie, smaller employers who are making chiefly cutlery. I don't think I ever in my life saw so many broken windows. Some of these workshops have hardly a pane of glass in their windows and you would not believe they were inhabitable if you did not see the employees, mostly girls, at work inside.

The town is being torn down and rebuilt at an immense speed. Everywhere among the slums are gaps with squalid mounds of bricks where condemned houses have been demolished and on all the outskirts of the town new estates of Corporation houses are going up. These are much inferior, at any rate in appearance, to those at Liverpool. They are in terribly bleak situations, too. One estate just behind where I am living now, at the very summit of a hill, on horrible sticky clay soil and swept by icy winds. Notice that the people going into these new houses from the slums will always be paying higher rents, and also will have to spend much more on fuel to keep themselves warm. Also, in many cases, will be further from their work and therefore spend more on conveyances.

In the evening was taken to a Methodist Church where some kind of men's association (they call it a Brotherhood)[28] meet once a week to listen to a lecture and have discussions. Next week a Communist is speaking, to the evident dismay of the clergyman who made the announcements. This week a clergyman who spoke on "Clean and Dirty Water." His lecture consisted of incredibly silly and disconnected ramblings about Shaw's *Adventures of a Black Girl*[29] etc. Most of the audience did not understand a word of it and in fact hardly listened, and the talk and the questions afterwards were so unbearable that Brown and I slipped out with his friend Binns to see the latter's back to back house, on which I took notes. B. says that most of the members of this Brotherhood are unemployed men who will put up with almost anything in order to have a warm place where they can sit for a few hours.

Accent in Sheffield not so broad as in Lancashire. A very few people, mostly miners I think, wear clogs.

28. *Brotherhood:* in *Nineteen Eighty-Four*, O'Brien explains that those who have read Goldstein's Testament 'will be full members of the Brotherhood', which opposes the State (*CW*, IX, p. 182).
29. *Adventures of a Black Girl: The Adventures of the Black Girl in Her Search for God* by George Bernard Shaw, 1932, in which the author, posing as an innocent but intelligent and inquisitive black girl, makes an allegorical philosophical journey asking such questions as why God is male. In the Preface, Shaw explains that he was inspired to write 'this tale' when held up in Knysna, South Africa, for five weeks 'in the African summer and English winter of 1932'. He had intended to write a play 'but found myself writing the story of the black girl instead'. Having written it, 'I proceed to speculate on what it means'.

5.3.36: At 21 Estcourt Avenue, Headingley, Leeds.[30]

30. *21 Estcourt Avenue:* Home of Orwell's older sister, Marjorie (1898–1946), and her husband, Humphrey Dakin (1896–1970). They had married in July 1920. He worked for the National Savings Committee. Orwell visited them from time to time 'to get some writing done and be looked after by his sister. Humphrey seemed to resent this', considering Orwell as a work-shy drop-out (see *Orwell Remembered*, pp. 127–30). Orwell stayed with the Dakins from 5–11 and 26–30 March 1936.

I left Sheffield at 10.30 this morning, and in spite of its being such a frightful place and of the relief of getting back into a comfortable house, I was quite sorry to leave the Searles. I have seldom met people with more natural decency. They were as kind to me as anyone could possibly be, and I hope and trust they liked me. Of course I got their whole life-history from them by degrees. Searle is 33 and was an only child. When a youth he joined the Army and was in the Ordnance Corps (or whatever it is called) with the army of occupation in Palestine and in Egypt. He has vivid memories of Egypt and wishes he was back there. Since then he has only had short-lived jobs, eg. as store-keeper and check-weighman at various works, also as railway (outside) porter. Mrs. S. comes from a somewhat more prosperous family, as her father till only a few weeks ago* was in a good job at £5 a week and also made something on the side by making fishing rods. But it was a very large family (11) and she went into service. She married S. when he was on the dole, against the opposition of her family. At first they could not get a house, and lived in a single room, in which two children were born and one died. They told me they had only one bed for the family and had to "lay out" the dead baby in the perambulator. Finally, after frightful difficulty (one reason for this is that private landlords are not too keen on letting to people on the dole and there is a certain amount of bribery of agents) they got this house, of which the rent is about 8/6. Mrs. S. earns about 9/– a week from her charring. Exactly what deduction is made for this from S's dole I don't know, but their total income is 32/6. In spite of which I had great difficulty in getting them to accept enough for my keep while there – they wanted to charge only 6/– for full board and lodging from Monday night to Thursday morning. They keep the house very clean and decent, have a bit of garden, though they can't do much with it, as it has factory chimneys on one side and the gas works on the other, besides being poor soil, and are very fond of one another. I was surprised by Mrs S's grasp of the economic situation and also of abstract ideas – quite unlike most working-class women in this, though she is I think not far from illiterate. She does not seem resentful against the people who employ her – indeed she says they are kind to her – but sees quite clearly the essential facts about domestic service. She told me how the other day as she waited at the lunch table she calculated the price of the food on the table (for 5 persons for one meal) and it came to 6/3 – as much as the P.A.C. allows her child for a fortnight.

Brown was very good and took my request to "show me over Sheffield" even too seriously, so that from morning to night I was being rushed from place to place, largely on foot, to see public buildings, slums, housing estates etc. But he is a tiresome person to be with, being definitely disgruntled and too conscious of his Communist convictions. In Rotherham we had to have lunch at a slightly expensive restaurant because there didn't seem to be any others except pubs (B. is TT.), and when in there he was sweating and groaning about the "bourgeois atmosphere" and saying he could not eat this kind of food. As he declares that it is necessary to literally hate the bourgeoisie, I wondered what he thought of me, because he told me at the very start I was a bourgeois and remarked on my "public school twang." However, I think he was disposed to treat me as a sort of

* He died very suddenly & his wife has now no resources except the old age pension & an insurance policy [Orwell's handwritten footnote].

honorary proletarian, partly because I had no objection to washing in the sink etc., but more because I seemed interested in Sheffield. He was very generous and though I had told him at the start that I was going to pay for his meals etc. while we were together, he would always go out of his way to spare me expense. It seems that he lives on 10/– a week – I had this from Searle: exactly where B's 10/– comes from I don't know – and the rent of his room is 6/–. Of course it would not be possible to subsist on the remainder, allowing for fuel. You could only keep alive on 4/– a week (see attached)[31] if you spent nothing on fuel and nothing on tobacco or clothes. I gather B. gets meals from time to time from the S's and other friends, also from his brother who is in comparatively good employ. His room is decent and even cultured-looking, as it has bits of "antique" furniture which he has made himself, and some crude but not disagreeable pictures, mostly of circuses, which he has painted. Much of his bitterness obviously comes from sexual starvation. His deformity handicaps him with women, his fear of transmitting it has stopped him from marrying (he says he would only marry a woman past the childbearing age), and his inability to earn money makes it more impossible still. However, at one of the Adelphi summer schools he picked up with some schoolmistress (aged 43) who I gather is his mistress when opportunities permit and who is willing to marry him, only her parents oppose it. The Searles say he has improved greatly since taking up with this woman – before that he used to have fits occasionally.

31. *attached:* the item attached was a cutting from the *News of the World*, 1 March 1936, showing how a W. Leach of Lilford Road, London, S.E., needed to spend only 3s 11½d a week on food (20p in decimal currency). When, in November 1993, I costed the items he listed the total came to about £8.80. Mr Leach stated that though he preferred to boil the carrots he bought, he ate them raw because 'to boil water would cost too much'. This remark prompts one to wonder how genuine was Mr Leach's claim. For further details see *The Road to Wigan Pier*, pp. 87–8.

We had an argument one evening in the Searles' house because I helped Mrs S. with the washing-up. Both of the men disapproved of this, of course. Mrs S. seemed doubtful. She said that in the North working-class men never offered any courtesies to women (women are allowed to do all the housework unaided, even when the man is unemployed, and it is always the man who sits in the comfortable chair), and she took this state of things for granted, but did not see why it should not be changed. She said that she thought the women now-a-days, especially the younger women, would like it if men opened doors for them etc. The position now-a-days is anomalous. The man is practically always out of work, whereas the woman occasionally is working. Yet the woman continues to do all the housework and the man not a handsturn, except carpentering and gardening. Yet I think it is instinctively felt by both sexes that the man would lose his manhood if, merely because he was out of work, he became a "Mary Ann."

One particular picture of Sheffield stays by me. A frightful piece of waste ground (somehow, up here a piece of waste ground attains a squalor that would be impossible even in London), trampled quite bare of grass and littered with newspaper, old saucepans etc. To the right, an isolated row of gaunt four-room houses, dark red blackened by smoke. To the left an interminable vista of factory chimneys, chimney behind chimney, fading away into a dim blackish haze. Behind me a railway embankment made from the slag of furnaces. In front, across the piece of waste ground, a cubical building of dingy red and yellow brick, with the sign, "John Grocock, Haulage Contractor."

Other memories of Sheffield: stone walls blackened by smoke, a shallow river yellow with chemicals, serrated flames, like circular saws, coming out from the cowls of the foundry chimneys, thump and scream of steam hammers (the iron seems to scream under the blow), smell of sulphur, yellow clay, backsides of women wagging laboriously from side to side as they shove their perambulators up the hills.

Mrs Searle's recipe for fruit loaf (very good with butter) which I will write down here before I lose it:

1 lb flour. 1 egg. 4 oz. treacle. 4 oz. mixed fruit (or currants). 8 oz. sugar. 6 oz. margarine or lard.

Cream the sugar and margarine, beat the egg and add it, add the treacle and then the flour, put in greased tins and bake about ½ to ¾ hour in a moderate oven.

Also her '54321' recipe for sponge cake:

5 oz. flour, 4 oz. sugar, 3 oz. grease (butter best), 2 eggs, 1 teaspoonful baking powder. Mix as above and bake.

7.3.36: Staying till next Wed. with M[arjorie] and H[umphrey] at 21 Estcourt Avenue, Headingley. Conscious all the while of difference in atmosphere between middle-class home even of this kind and working-class home. The essential difference is that here there is *elbow-room,* in spite of there being 5 adults and 3 children, besides animals, at present in the house. The children make peace and quiet difficult, but if you definitely want to be alone you can be so – in a working-class house never, either by night or day.

One of the kinds of discomfort inseparable from a working-man's life is *waiting about.* If you receive a salary it is paid into your bank and you draw it out when you want it. If you receive wages, you have to go and get them in somebody else's time and are probably kept hanging about and probably expected to behave as though being paid your wages at all was a favour. When Mr Hornby at Wigan went to the mine to draw his compensation, he had to go, for some reason I did not understand, on two separate days each week, and was kept waiting in the cold for about an hour before he was paid. In addition the four tram journeys to and from the mine cost him 1/–, reducing his compensation from 29/– weekly to 28/–. He took this for granted, of course. The result of long training in this kind of thing is that whereas the bourgeois goes through life expecting to get what he wants, within limits, the working-man always feels himself the slave of a more or less mysterious authority. I was impressed by the fact that when I went to Sheffield Town Hall to ask for certain statistics,[32] both Brown and Searle – both of them people of much more forcible character than myself – were nervous, would not come into the office with me, and assumed that the Town Clerk would refuse information. They said, "He might give it to you, but he wouldn't to us." Actually the Town Clerk was snooty and I did not get all the information I asked for. But the point was that I assumed my questions would be answered, and the other two assumed the contrary.

32. See *CW*, X, pp. 571–5, for Statistical Information provided by Sheffield Medical Officer of Health.

It is for this reason that in countries where the class hierarchy exists, people of the higher class always tend to come to the front in times of stress, though not really more gifted than the others. That they will do so seems to be taken for granted always and everywhere. NB. to look up the passage in Lissagaray's *History of the Commune* describing the shootings after the Commune had been suppressed. They were shooting the ringleaders without trial, and as they did not know who the ringleaders were, they were picking them out on the principle that those of better class than the others would be the ringleaders. One man was shot because he was wearing a watch, another because he 'had an intelligent face.' NB. to look up this passage.

Yesterday with H. and M. to Haworth Parsonage, home of the Brontes and now a museum. Was chiefly impressed by a pair of Charlotte Bronte's cloth-topped boots, very small, with square toes and lacing up at the sides.

9.3.36: Yesterday with H and M. to their cottage at Middlesmoor, high up on the edge of the moors. Perhaps it is only the time of year, but even up there, miles from any industrial towns, the smoky look peculiar to this part of the country seems to hang about anything. Grass dull-coloured, streams muddy, houses all blackened as though by smoke. There was snow everywhere, but thawing and slushy. Sheep very dirty – no lambs, apparently. The palm was out and primroses putting out new shoots: otherwise nothing moving.

11.3.36: On the last two evenings to "discussion groups" – societies of people who meet once a week, listen-in to some talk on the radio and then discuss it. Those at the one on Monday were chiefly unemployed men and I believe these "discussion groups" were started or at any rate suggested by the Social Welfare people who run the unemployed occupational centres. That on Monday was decorous and rather dull. Thirteen people including ourselves (one woman besides M[arjorie]), and we met in a room adjoining a public library. The talk was on Galsworthy's play *The Skin Game*[33] and the discussion kept to the subject until most of us adjoined° to a pub for bread and cheese and beer afterwards. Two people dominated the assembly, one a huge bull-headed man named Rowe who contradicted whatever the last speaker had said and involved himself in the most appalling contradictions, the other a youngish, very intelligent and extremely well-informed man named Creed. From his refined accent, quiet voice and apparent omniscience, I took him for a librarian. I find he keeps a tobacconist's shop and was previously a commercial traveller. During the War he was imprisoned as a conscientious objector. The other meeting was at a pub and the people were of higher standing. The arrangement is that M[arjorie] and H[umphrey] go there taking the portable radio, and the publican, who is a member of the group, lets them have a room for the evening. On this occasion the talk was called "If Plato lived Today," but actually no one listened-in except M. and myself – H. has gone to Bedford. When the talk was over the publican, a Canadian with a very bald head, a market gardener who was already the worse for drink, and another man, rolled in and there began an orgy of drinking from which we escaped with difficulty about an hour later. Much talk on both nights about the European situation and most people saying (some of them with ill-dissembled hope) that war is certain. With two exceptions all pro-German.

33. *The Skin Game:* tragicomedy in three acts by John Galsworthy, 1920. It dramatises a feud between two families, one long-established and upper-class and the other a lower-class family who had become wealthy. In 1931 Alfred Hitchcock made it into a film (not one of his best). Galsworthy had died fairly recently (1933).

Today to Barnsley to fix up about a place to stay. Wilde, secretary of the South Yorkshire Branch of the Working Men's Club & Institute Union, has fixed it all up for me. The address is 4 Agnes Avenue. The usual 2 up 2 down house, with sink in living room, as at Sheffield. The husband is a miner and was away at work when we got there. House very disorganised as it was washing day, but seemed clean. Wilde, though kind and helpful, was a very vague person. He was a working miner till 1924 but as usual has been bourgeois-ified. Smartly dressed with gloves and umbrella and very little accent – I would have taken him for a solicitor from his appearance.

Barnsley is slightly smaller than Wigan – about 70,000 inhabitants – but distinctly less poverty-stricken, at any rate in appearance. Much better shops and more appearance of business being done. Many miners coming home from the morning shift. Mostly wearing clogs but of a square-toed pattern different from the Lancashire ones.

13.3.36: At 4 Agnes Terrace,[34] Barnsley.

This house is bigger than I had imagined. Two rooms and tiny larder under the stairs downstairs, 3 or 4* rooms upstairs. 8 people in the house – 5 adults and 3 children. Front room which should be parlour is used as bedroom. Living room, about 14 by 12, has the usual kitchener, sink and copper. No gas stove. Electric light in all rooms save one. Outside W. C.

34. *Terrace:* Orwell wrote 'Terrace' rather than 'Avenue' of a dozen or so lines earlier.

The family. Mr Grey, a short powerful man, age about 43, with coarse features, enlarged nose and a very fatigued, pale look. He is rather bald, has his own teeth (unusual in a working class person of that age) but they are very discoloured. A bit deaf, but very ready to talk, especially about technicalities of mining. Has worked in the pit ever since a small boy. On one occasion was buried by a fall of earth or stone – no bones broken, but it took ten minutes to dig him out and two hours to drag him to the cage. He tells me no machinery (stretchers etc.) exists for conveying injured men away from the scene of accidents. Obviously some kind of stretcher running on the trolley rails could be contrived, but this would involve stopping all the haulage of coal while it was being done. So injured men have to be carried to the cage by helpers who are themselves bending double and can only get them along very slowly. Mr G. works at removing the coal onto the trucks after it is cut – "scufting" I think it is called. He and his mate are paid piece-work 2/2 per ton – 1/1 each. On full time his wages average £2-10-0 a week. His stoppages amount to 6/11. He works at Darton, about 4 miles away and goes there by bus.[35] Journeys cost 6d a day. So his net wages on full time are about £2-0-0 a week.

* 3 [Orwell's handwritten footnote].

Mrs G. is about 10 years younger,* motherly type, always cooking and cleaning, accent less broad than her husband's. Two little girls, Doreen and Ireen (spelling?) aged 11 and 10. The other lodgers are a widowed joiner, employed on the woodwork at the new dog-track, and his son aged about 11, and a professional singer who is going to sing at one of the pubs. All the larger pubs in Barnsley employ singers and dancers (some of these very immoral according to Mrs G.) more or less constantly.

The house is very clean and decent and my room the best I have had in lodgings up here. Flanelette sheets this time.

35. *bus:* Orwell's handwritten emendation for the original 'tram'.

14.3.36: Much talk last night with Mr G. about his War experiences. Especially about the malingering he saw going on when he was invalided with some injury to his leg, and the astute ways the doctors had of detecting it. One man feigned complete deafness and successfully kept it up during tests lasting two hours. Finally he was told by signs that he would be discharged and could go, and just as he was passing through the door the doctor said casually "Shut that door after you, would you?" The man turned and shut it, and was passed for active service. Another man feigned insanity and got away with it. For days he was going round with a bent pin on a bit of string, pretending to be catching fish. Finally he was discharged, and on parting with G. he held up his discharge papers and said "This is what I was fishing for." I was reminded of the malingering I saw in the Hôpital Cochin[36] in Paris, where unemployed men used to remain for months together on pretence of being ill.

Beastly cold again. Sleet this morning. But yesterday as I came on the train they were ploughing and the earth looked much more spring-like; especially in one field where the earth was very black, not like the usual clay soil hereabouts, and as the ploughshare turned it over it looked like chocolate fudge being sliced up with a knife.

I am very comfortable in this house but do not think I shall pick up much of interest in Barnsley. I know no one here except Wilde, who is thoroughly vague. Cannot discover whether there is a branch of the N.U.W.M. here. The public library is no good. There is no proper reference library and it seems no separate directory of Barnsley is published.

36. *Hôpital Cochin:* Orwell was admitted for 'une grippe' to this Parisian hospital from 7th to 22nd March 1929. He wrote about the experience in 'How the Poor Die', 6 November 1946, *CW*, XVIII, pp. 459–67.

* Actually their ages are 50 & 38 [Orwell's handwritten footnote].

15.3.36: Last night with Wilde and others to the general meeting of the South Yorkshire Branch of the Working Men's Club & Institute Union, held at one of the clubs in Barnsley. About 200 people there, all busily tucking into beer and sandwiches, though it was only 4.30 pm – they had got an extension for the day. The club was a big building, really an enlarged pub with one big hall which could be used for concerts etc., and in which the meeting was held. It was a bit stormy in parts, but Wilde and the chairman had them pretty well in hand and were complete masters of all the usual platform phraseology and procedure. I notice from the balance sheet that W.'s salary is £260 per annum. Before this I had never realised the number and importance of these working men's clubs, especially in the North and especially in Yorkshire. These at this meeting consisted of pairs of delegates sent by all the clubs in South Yorkshire. There would have been I should say 150 delegates, representing therefore 75 clubs and probably about 10,000 members. That is in South Yorkshire alone. After the meeting I was taken to have tea in the committee room with about 30 of what were, I gathered, some of the more important delegates. We had cold ham, bread and butter, cakes and whisky which everyone poured into their tea. After that with W. and the others went down to the Radical and Liberal Club in the middle of the town, where I have been before. There was a sort of smoking concert going on, as these clubs, like the pubs, all engaged singers etc. for the weekends. There was quite a good knockabout comedian whose jokes were of the usual twins-mother-in-law-kippers type, and pretty steady boozing. Wilde's accent becomes much broader when he is in these surroundings. It appears that these clubs were first started as a kind of charitable concern in the mid-nineteenth century, and were, of course, Temperance. But they escaped by becoming financially self-supporting and have developed, as I say, into sort of glorified co-operative pubs. Grey, who belongs to the Radical and Liberal Club, tells me his subscription is 1/6d a quarter and all drinks are 1d or 2d a pint cheaper than at the pubs. Youths under 21 are not admitted and (I think) women cannot be members but can go there with their husbands. Most of the clubs are avowedly non-political, and in this and in the fact that the members are mostly of the more prosperous working-class type – comparatively few unemployed – one can foresee the germs of a danger that they will be politically mobilised for anti-socialist purposes.

Talking with a man who was previously a miner but now works as a labourer for the Corporation. He was telling me about the housing conditions in Barnsley in his childhood. He grew up in a back to back house in which there were 11 people (two bedrooms, I suppose) and you not only had to walk 200 yards to get to the lavatory, but shared it with, in all, 36 people.

Have arranged to go down the Grimethorpe pit next Saturday. This is a very up-to-date pit and possesses certain machinery that does not exist anywhere else in England. Also to go down a "day hole" pit on Thursday afternoon. The man I spoke to told me it was a mile to the coal face, so if the "travelling" is bad I shan't go the whole way – I only want to see what a "day hole" is like and am not going to incapacitate myself like last time.

When G. comes back from the pit he washes before having his food. I don't know whether this is usual, but I have often seen miners sitting down to eat with Christy Minstrel faces – completely black except very red lips which become clean by eating. When G. arrives he is as black as ink, especially his scalp – for this reason miners usually wear their hair short. He pours out a large basin of hot water, strips to the waist and washes himself very methodically, first his hands, then his upper arms, then his forearms, then his chest and shoulders, then his face and head. Then he dries himself and his wife washes his back. His navel is still a nest of coal-dust. I suppose from the waist down he must normally be quite black. There are public baths and the miners go to them but as a rule not more than once a week – one cannot be surprised at this, as a miner has not much time between working and sleeping. Miners' houses with bathrooms, other than the new Corporation ones, are practically unknown. Only a few colliery companies have baths at the pit-heads.

I notice that G. does not eat very much. At present, working on the afternoon shift, he has the same breakfast as I have (an egg and bacon, bread – no butter – and tea) and has a light lunch, such as bread and cheese, about half past twelve. He says he cannot do his work if he has eaten too much. All he takes with him to the pit is some bread and dripping and cold tea. This is the usual thing. The men do not want much in the stifling air down there, and besides, they are not allowed any time off for eating. He gets home between 10 and 11 pm, and it is then that he has his only heavy meal of the day.

16.3.36: Last night to hear Mosley[37] speak at the Public Hall, which is in structure a theatre. It was quite full – about 700 people I should say. About 100 Blackshirts on duty, with two or three exceptions weedy-looking specimens, and girls selling *Action*[38] etc. Mosley spoke for an hour and a half and to my dismay seemed to have the meeting mainly with him. He was booed at the start but loudly clapped at the end. Several men who tried at the beginning to interject questions were thrown out, one of them – who as far as I could see was only trying to get a question answered –

with quite unnecessary violence, several Blackshirts throwing themselves upon him and raining blows on him while he was still sitting down and had not attempted any violence. M. is a very good speaker. His speech was the usual claptrap – Empire free trade, down with the Jew and the foreigner, higher wages and shorter hours all round etc. etc. After the preliminary booing the (mainly) working-class audience was easily bamboozled by M. speaking from as it were a Socialist angle, condemning the treachery of successive governments towards the workers. The blame for everything was put upon mysterious international gangs of Jews who are said to be financing, among other things, the British Labour Party and the Soviet. M.'s statement re. the international situation: "We fought Germany before in a British quarrel; we are not going to fight them now in a Jewish one"[39] was received with loud applause. Afterwards there were questions as usual, and it struck me how easy it is to bamboozle an uneducated audience if you have prepared beforehand a set of repartees with which to evade awkward questions, eg. M. kept extolling Italy and Germany, but when questioned about concentration camps etc. always replied "We have no foreign models; what happens in Germany need not happen here." To the question, "How do you know that your own money is not used to finance cheap foreign labour?" (M. having denounced the Jewish financiers who are supposed to do this), M. replied, "All my money is invested in England," and I suppose comparatively few of the audience realised that this means nothing.

At the beginning M. said that anyone ejected would be charged under the public meetings act. I don't know whether this was actually done, but presumably the power to do so exists. In connection with this the fact that there are no police on duty *inside the building* is of great importance. Anyone who interrupts can be assaulted and thrown out and then charged into the bargain, and of course the stewards, ie. M. himself, are the judges of what constitutes an interruption. Therefore one is liable to get both a hammering and a fine for asking a question which M. finds it difficult to answer.

At the end of the meeting a great crowd collected outside, as there was some public indignation about the men who had been thrown out. I waited for a long time in the crowd to see what would happen, but M. and party did not emerge. Then the police managed to split the crowd and I found myself at the front, whereupon a policeman ordered me away, but quite civilly. I went round to the back of the crowd and waited again, but still M. did not appear and I concluded he had been sneaked out by a back door, so went home. In the morning at the *Chronicle* office, however, I was told that there had been some stone-throwing and two men had been arrested and remanded.

G. changed this morning onto the early morning shift. He gets up at 3.45 am and has to be at work, ie. at the coal face, at 6. He gets home about 2.30 pm. His wife does not get up to get his breakfast and he says few miners will allow their wives to do so. Also that there are still some miners who if they meet a woman on their way to work will turn back and go home. It is considered bad luck to see a woman before going to work. I presume this only applies to the early morning shift.

37. *Mosley:* Sir Oswald Mosley, Bt. (1896–1980), fought in First World War, which left him with a permanent limp. He was first elected to Parliament (as a Conservative) in 1918 and then after sitting as an Independent, joined the ILP in 1924 but became a Labour MP in 1929. Founded the New Party and then, in 1932, the British Union of Fascists. He married Diana, one of the Mitford sisters, in the home of Dr Josef Goebbels in 1936. They were interned during the war.
38. *Action:* journal of the British Union of Fascists. On 9 July 1936 Orwell was asked by Mrs Hastings Bonara if she could quote from the Trafalgar Square scene of *A Clergyman's Daughter* in a review she was writing for *Action*. She wrote that she hoped he was not violently anti-Fascist and would 'consequently say CERTAINLY NOT'. Evidently Orwell did. In later correspondence she claimed that at least the BUF had a programme 'for ameliorating the lot of our "Misérables".'
39. *in a Jewish one:* seven months later, in October, Mosley attempted to force the BUF through the East End of London in an anti-Jewish protest march. The ensuing violent opposition led to what became known as the Battle of Cable Street.

18.3.36: The Barnsley public baths are very bad. Old-fashioned bathtubs, none too clean, and not nearly enough of them. I judged by the appearance of the place there were at most 50 baths* – this in a town of 70–80 thousand inhabitants, largely miners, not one of whom has a bath in his own house, except in the new Corporation houses.

Some curious coincidences. When I went to see Len Kaye he recommended me to see Tommy Degnan, to whom I had also been recommended by Paddy Grady at Wigan. But what was more curious still, D. was one of the men who were thrown out at Mosley's meeting, though not the one I actually saw thrown out. I went round to see D. last night and had some difficulty in finding him. He lives in a dreadful barn of a place called Garden House, which is an old almost ruinous house which half a dozen unemployed men have taken and made a sort of lodging house of. D. himself is not unemployed, though at the moment "playing" because a few days before the hammering he got at M.'s meeting he was slightly crushed by a fall of stone in the mine. We went out to look for

* Actually 19! [Orwell's handwritten footnote].

the man whom I actually saw thrown out, as I want to get particulars and see his bruises before writing to the papers about it, but couldn't find him, and I am to see him today. Then in the street we ran across another man whom I saw thrown out. The latter's ejection was an interesting instance of the way any upset can be misrepresented and turned to advantage by a demagogue of the type of Mosley. At the time of the uproar at the back of the hall, this last man – name Hennesy,* I think – was seen to rush on to the stage, and everyone thought he had gone there to shout something out and interrupt M.'s speech. It struck me at the time as curious that though on the stage he didn't shout anything out, and the next moment, of course, the Blackshirts on the platform seized him and bundled him out. M. shouted out, "A typical example of Red tactics!" It now appears what happened was this. Hennesey° saw the Blackshirts at the back of the hall bashing D., and couldn't get to him to help him because there is no aisle up the middle; but there was an aisle up the right hand side, and the only way he could get to this was over the stage. D. after being thrown out was charged under the Public Meetings Act, but H not. I don't know yet whether the other man, Marshall, was. The woman who was thrown out – this was somewhere at the back and I didn't see it – was hit on the head with a trumpet and was a day in hospital. D. and H. were in the Army together and H. was wounded in the leg and D. taken prisoner when the Vth Army[40] was defeated in 1918. D., being a miner, was sent to work in the Polish mines. He said all of them had pit-head baths. H. says the French ones have them too.

40. *Vth Army:* presumably D. was taken prisoner during the German spring offensive south of the River Somme launched by Erich Ludendorff on 21 March 1918. The Fifth Army was forced to retreat and suffered very heavy casualties.

G. told me a dreadful story of how a friend of his, a "dataller", was buried alive. He was buried under a fall of small stone, and they rushed to him and, though they could not get him out completely, they got his head and shoulders free so that he could breathe. He was alive and spoke to them. At this moment they saw that the roof was coming down again and had to take to flight themselves. Once again he was buried, and once again they managed to get to him and uncover his head, and again he was alive and spoke to them. Then the roof came down again, and this time they did not get him out for some hours, after which, of course, he

* His name is Firth, I got it as Hennessey because he was introduced to me as Hellis Firth. (Ellis Firth – people here very capricious about their H's.) [Orwell's handwritten footnote]. The variations in spelling Hennessey are Orwell's. For Ellis Firth's weekly budget, see *CW*, X, pp. 365–67.

was dead. But the real point of the story, from G.'s point of view, was that this man had known beforehand that this part of the mine was unsafe and likely to bury him: "And it worked on his mind to that extent that he kissed his wife before he went to work. And she told me afterwards that it was the first time in years he'd kissed her."

There is a very old woman – a Lancashire woman – living near here who in her day has worked down the pit, dragging tubs of coal with a harness and chain. She is 83, so I suppose this would be in the seventies.

19.3.36: In frightful exhaustion after going down the "day hole," as, of course, when the time came I had not the strength of mind to say I did not want to go as far as the coal face.

I went down with the "deputy" (Mr Lawson) about 3 pm. and came up about 6.30 pm. L. said we had covered not quite 2 miles. I must say that I got on perceptibly better than at Wigan, either because the going was a little better, as I think it was – probably one could stand upright about one third of the way – or because L., who is an old man, moderated his pace to mine. The chief feature of this pit, apart from its being a "day hole," is that it is infernally wet in most places. There were quite considerable streams running here and there, and two enormous pumps have to be kept running all day and most of the night. The water is pumped up to ground level and has made a considerable pool, but curiously enough it is clear clean water – even drinkable, L. said – and the pool was quite ornamental with waterhens swimming about on it. We went down when the morning shift came up, and there are comparatively few men on the afternoon shift for some reason I did not understand. When we got to the coal face the men were there with the coal-cutter, which was not running at the moment, but they set it running to show me. The teeth on a revolving chain – in principle it is an enormously tough and powerful band-saw – cut in underneath the coal face, after which huge boulders of coal can be easily tumbled out and broken up with picks before being loaded onto the tubs. Some of these boulders of coal, not yet broken up, were about 8 feet long by two thick by four high – the seam is four feet six, I think – and must have weighed many tons.* As it cuts the machine travels backwards or forwards, as desired, along the coalface, on its own power. The place where these men, and those loading the broken coal onto the tubs, were working, was like hell. I had never thought of it before, but of course as the machine works it sends forth clouds of coal dust which almost stifle one and make it impossible

* A cubic yard of coal said to weight 27 cwt [1,372 kg. Orwell's handwritten footnote].

to see more than a few feet. No lamps except Davy lamps of an old-fashioned pattern, not more than two or three candle-power, and it puzzled one to see how these men can see to work, except when there are a number of them together. To get from one part of the coal face to another you had to crawl along awful tunnels cut through the coal, a yard high by two feet wide, and then to work yourself on your bottom over mountainous boulders of coal. Of course in doing this I dropped my lamp and it went out. L. called to one of the men working and he gave me his lamp. Then L. said "You'd better cut yourself a bit of coal as a memento" (visitors always do this), and while I was cutting out a piece of coal with the pick, I knocked my second lamp between the two of us, which was disconcerting and brought it home to me how easily you could lose yourself down there if you didn't happen to know the roads.

We passed tubs, carrying props etc., going to and fro on the endless belt, which is worked by electricity. The tubs only move at 1½ miles an hour. All the miners at this pit seem to carry sticks, and they gave me one which was a great help. They are about two foot six long and hollowed out just below the knob. At moderate heights (4 ft to 5 ft) you keep your hand on the knob, and when you have to bend really low you grip the stick by the hollow. The ground underfoot was as mucky as a farm yard in many places. They say the best way to go is to keep one foot on the trolley-rail and the other on the sleepers, if you can find them. The miners going down the roads run, bent double of course, in places where I could barely stagger. They say it is easier to run than walk when you have the hang of it. It was rather humiliating that coming back, which we did by the most direct route, took me three-quarters of an hour and only takes the miners a quarter of an hour. But we had gone to the nearest working, only about halfway to the end. Those who work at the furthest working take nearly an hour to get to their work. This time I was given one of the new crash helmets which many, though not all miners, now wear. To look at they are very like a French or Italian tin hat, and I had always imagined they were made of metal. Actually they are of a kind of compressed fibre and very light. Mine was a bore because it was too small and fell off when I bent very low. But how glad of it I was! Coming back when I was tired and could not bend much I must have bashed my head twenty times – once hard enough to bring down a huge chunk of stone – but felt absolutely nothing.

Walked home with L. to Dodworth as I could get the bus more easily there. He has a two-mile walk with some pretty stiff hills going to and from work, in addition to the walk inside the mine when he gets there. But I suppose as "deputy" he doesn't do much manual work. He has worked in this mine 22 years and says he knows it so well that he never even needs to look up [to] see when there is a beam coming.

Birds all singing. Tiny pink buds on the elms that I had never noticed before. Many female flowers on the hazels. But I suppose as usual the old maids will be cutting them all off for Easter decorations.

When I sit typing the family, especially Mrs G. and the kids, all gather round to watch absorbedly, and appear to admire my prowess almost as much as I admire that of the miners.

20.3.36: Talking with Firth (see notes on his house.[41]) He gets 32/– a week from the U.A.B.[42] Mrs F. is a Derbyshire woman. Two kids, ages 2 years 5 months and 10 months. They are fairly sturdy as yet and it is evidently the case that these kids do much better in infancy than later, as for about their first three years they get help from the Infants' Welfare Clinic. Mrs F. gets three packets of baby's food (dried milk) a week and also a little Nestle's milk. On one occasion she got an allowance of 2/– a week for a month to buy eggs for the elder child. While there we sent out for some beer. I noted both the F. s let the children drink a little beer out of their glasses. Another kid was in and out of the house mothering the F. baby. Her father was murdered four years ago. The widowed mother gets an allowance of 22/– a week, I do not know from what source, on which she has to keep herself and 4 children.

41. See *CW*, X, p. 558 (12 Albert Street East).
42. *U.A.B.*: Unemployment Assistance Board. For details see *Road to Wigan Pier*, pp. 85–6.

I did not know before, what F. told me, that when the mines have baths at the pithead these are built not by the company but by the miners themselves, out of the Welfare Fund to which every miner subscribes. This is the case at any rate round here – must try and find out if it is so everywhere. It is by the way another argument against the statement that miners do not want or appreciate baths. One reason why not all pits have baths is that when a pit is anywhere near being worked out it is not considered worth while to build baths.

I forgot to mention that in the day-hole at Wentworth the pit props, owing to the damp, had strange fungi exactly like cotton wool growing on them. If you touched them they went all to nothing, leaving a nasty smell. It appears that a Lancashire miner, instead of slinging his lamp round his neck, has a band above the elbow and hangs the lamp from that.

Today G. earned little or nothing. The coal-cutter had broken down so there was no coal for him to fill into the tubs. When this happens those on piece-work get no compensation, except a shilling or two for odd jobs called bye-work.

I see the *Manchester Guardian* has not printed my letter re. Mosley and

I suppose they never will. I hardly expected the *Times* to print it, but I think the *M. G.* might, considering their reputation.

21.3.36: This morning went down the Grimethorpe pit. Not exhausting this time, because in order not to clash with the visit of some students from the Technical College we went to the nearest working, only about ¼ mile and little bending.

The depth of the mine, at least at the part we went to, is a little over 400 yards. The young engineer who took me thought the cages *average* 60 mph. when going down, in which case they must touch 80 or more at their fastest. I think this must be an exaggeration, but they certainly travel faster than the average railway train. The especial feature of this pit is the "skip wagon," by which the coal is sent straight up in special cages instead of being sent up, much more laboriously, in tubs. The full tubs come slowly along an inclined rail and are controlled by men at the sides with brakes. Each tub halts for a moment on a weighing machine and its weight is entered up, then the tubs move on and move two at a time into a kind of container which grips them underneath. The container then turns right over, spilling the coal down a shute° into the cage below. When the cage has got 8 tons, ie. about 16 tubs, in it, it goes out and the coal is spilt down a similar chute on the surface. Then it goes along conveyor belts and over screens which automatically sort it, and is washed as well. The coal which is being sold to factories etc. is shot straight into goods trucks on the railway line below and then weighed truck and all, the weight of the truck being known. This is the only pit in England which works this system – all others send the coal up in the tubs, which takes much more time and needs more tubs. The system has been worked for a long time in Germany and U. S.A. The Grimethorpe pit turns out about 5000 tons of coal a day.

This time I saw the fillers actually working at the coal face, and now having seen the different operations of coal-getting, except blasting, in progress separately, I understand more or less how it is done. The coal-cutter travels along the face cutting into the bottom of the ledge of coal to the depth of 5 feet. Then the coal can be tumbled out in boulders with picks, or – as here, the Grimethorpe coal being very hard – is first loosened with blasting charges and then extracted. Then the fillers (who have also extracted it) load it onto the conveyor belt which runs behind them and carries it to a chute from which it runs into the tubs. Thus:

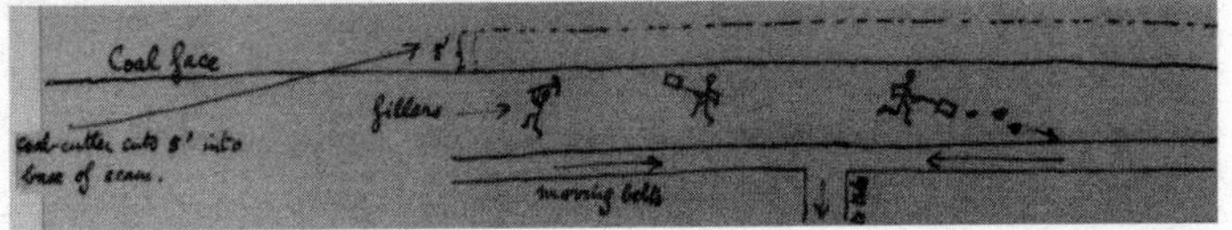

As far as possible the three operations are done in three separate shifts. The coal-cutter works on the afternoon shift, the blasting is done on the night shift (when the minimum number of people are in the pit), and the fillers extract the coal on the morning shift. Each man has to clear a space 4 or 5 yards wide. So, as the seam of coal is about a yard high and the cutter has undermined it to a depth of 5 feet, each man has to extract and load onto the belt (say) 14 x 5 x 3 cubic feet of coal, equals 210 cubic feet, equals nearly 8 cubic yards of coal. If it is really the case that a cubic yard of coal weighs 27 cwt, this would be well over 10 tons – ie. each man has to shift nearly a ton and a half an hour. When the job is done the coal face has advanced 5 feet, so during the next shift the conveyor belt is taken to pieces, moved 5 feet forward and reassembled, and fresh props are put in.

The place where the fillers were working was fearful beyond description. The only thing one could say was that, as conditions underground go, it was not particularly hot. But as the seam of coal is only a yard high or a bit more, the men can only kneel or crawl to their work, never stand up. The effort of constantly shovelling coal over your left shoulder and flinging it a yard or two beyond, while in a kneeling position, must be very great even to men who are used to it. Added to this there are the clouds of coal dust which are flying down your throat all the time and which make it difficult to see any distance. The men were all naked except for trousers and knee-pads. It was difficult to get through the conveyor belt to the coal face. You had to pick your moment and wriggle through quickly when the belt stopped for a moment. Coming back we crawled onto the belt while it was moving; I had not been warned of the difficulty of doing this and immediately fell down and had to be hauled off before the belt dashed me against the props etc. which were littered about further down. Added to the other discomforts of the men working there, there is the fearful din of the belt which never stops for more than a minute or so.

Electric lights this time – no Davy lamps used in the pit except for testing for gas. They can detect the presence of gas by the flame turning blue. By the height to which the flame can be turned while still remaining blue, they have a rough test of the percentage of gas in the atmosphere. All the roads we went through, except one or two galleries used for short cuts, were high and well-built and even paved underfoot in places. I have at last grasped the reason for the doors one passes through from time to time. The air is sucked out of one entry by fans and goes in of its own accord at another entry. But if not prevented it will come back by the shortest route instead of going all round the mine. Hence the doors, which stop it from taking short cuts.

Excellent baths at the pit. They have no less than 1000 h. & c. shower baths. Each miner has two lockers, one for his pit clothes and one for his ordinary clothes (so that the pit clothes shall not dirty the others.) Thus he can come and go clean and decent. According to the engineer, the baths were built partly by the Miners' Welfare, partly by the royalty owners, and the company also contributed.

During this week G. has had two narrow escapes from falls of stone, one of which actually grazed him on its way down. These men would not last long if it were not that they are used to the conditions and know when to stand from under. I am struck by the difference between the miners when you see them underground and when you see them in the street etc. Above ground, in their thick ill-fitting clothes, they are ordinary-looking men, usually small and not at all impressive and indeed not distinguishable from other people except by their distinctive walk (clumping tread, shoulders very square) and the blue scars on their noses. Below, when you see them stripped, all, old and young, have splendid bodies, with every muscle defined and wonderfully small waists. I saw some miners going into their baths. As I thought, they are quite black from head to foot. So the ordinary miner, who has not access to a bath, must be black from the waist down six days a week at least.

I have been wondering about what people like the Firths have to eat. Their total income is 32/– a week. Rent 9/0½d. Gas say 1/3. Coal (say 3 cwt. @ 9d)) 2/3. Other minor expenses (eg. F. keeps up his Union payments) say 1/–. That leaves 18/6. But Mrs F. gets a certain amount of baby-food free from the Clinic, so say the baby only costs 1/– a week beyond this. That leaves 17/6. F. smokes at any rate some cigarettes, say 1/– (6 packets of Woodbines a week.) That leaves 16/6 a week to feed 2 adults and a girl aged 2 years, or about 5/6 per week per head. And this takes no account of clothes, soap, matches etc. etc. Mrs F. said they fed chiefly on bread and jam. If I can do so delicately I must ask F. to give me a fairly exact account of their meals for one day.

22.3.36: Kaye says his father, a collier (now too old for work), always washed the top half of his body and his feet and legs to above the knees. The rest of his body was only washed at very long intervals, the old man believing that washing all over led to lumbago.

Communist meeting in the Market Place disappointing. The trouble with all these Communist speakers is that instead of using the popular idiom they employ immensely long sentences full of "despite" and "notwithstanding" and "be that as it may" etc. in the Garvin[43] strain – and this in spite of always speaking with broad provincial or cockney accents – Yorkshire in this case. I suppose they are given set speeches which they learn by heart. After the visiting speaker Degnan got up to speak and was a much more effective speaker – he speaks very broad Lancashire and though he can talk like a leading article if he wants to he doesn't choose. The usual crowd of men of all ages gaping with entirely expressionless faces and the usual handful of women a little more animated than the men – I suppose because no woman would go to a political meeting unless exceptionally interested in politics. About 150 people. Collection taken for the defence of the young men arrested in the Mosley affair and realised 6/–.

43. *J. L. Garvin:* (1868–1947) the right-wing editor of *The Observer* from 1908–42.

Wandering round Barnsley Main Colliery and the glassworks along the canal with F. and another man whose name I did not get. The latter's mother had just died and was lying dead at home. She was 89 and had been a midwife for 50 years. I noted the lack of hypocrisy with which he was laughing and joking and came into the pub to have a drink etc. The monstrous slag-heaps round Barnsley Main are all more or less on fire under the surface. In the darkness you can see long serpentine fires creeping all over them, not only red but very sinister blue flames (from sulphur) which always seem on the point of going out and then flicker up again.

I notice that the word "spink" (for a great tit, I think, but at any rate some small bird) is in use here as well as in Suffolk.

23.3.36: At Mapplewell. Houses about the worst I have seen, though we did not manage to get into the very worst ones, which were one-roomed or two-roomed cabins of stone, about 20′ by 15′ by 15′ high, or even less, and practically ruinous. Rent of these, some of which are property of colliery, said to be about 3/–. In the row called Spring Gardens we found public indignation because the landlords have served about half the row with notices to quit for arrears of, in some cases, only a few shillings. (Firth, in Barnsley, has a notice to quit though only about 5/– in arrear and paying this off at 3d per week.) The people took us in and insisted on our seeing their houses. Frightful interiors. In the first one (see notes[44]) old father, out of work of course, obviously horribly bewildered by his notice to quit after 22 years tenancy and turning anxiously to F. and me with some idea that we could help him. The mother rather more self-possessed. Two sons aged about 24, fine big men with powerful well-shaped bodies, narrow faces and red hair, but thin and listless from obvious undernourishment and with dull brutalised expressions. Their sister, a little older and very like them, with prematurely lined face, glancing from F. to me, again with the idea that perhaps we might help. One of the sons, taking no notice of our presence, all the while slowly peeling off his socks in front of the fire; his feet almost black with sticky dirt. The other son was at work. The house terribly bare – no bedclothes except overcoats etc. – but fairly clean and tidy. At the back children playing about in the muck, some of them, aged 5 or 6, barefoot and naked except for a sort of shift. F. told the tenants if the notice to quit was persisted with to come into Barnsley and see him and Degnan. I told them the landlord was only bluffing and to hold their ground and if he threatened taking it to court to threaten in return to sue him for lack of repairs. Hope I did the right thing.

I have glanced at Brown's novel.[45] It is b—s.

44. See *CW*, X, p. 544.
45. *Brown's novel*: *Daughters of Albion* (1935) by Alec Brown. In Orwell's review of *The Novel Today* by Philip Henderson, he described it as 'a huge wad of mediocre stuff' (*CW*, X, p. 534). The dash between 'b' and 's' is Orwell's.

25.3.36: Men along the private line leading to Gauber pit unloading trucks of slack. They say the mine "can't get shut o' t'slack" and are laying it by. This is regarded as a sinister sign. If the pits are storing slack already they will soon be running short time. The men get 4d a ton for unloading the slack. A truck holds about 10 tons, so they have to unload 3 trucks to make a day's wage.

I think the dirtiest interiors I see, more than any of the various kinds of squalor – the piles of unwashed crocks, the scraps of miscellaneous food all over the lino-topped table, the dreadful rag mats with the crumbs of years trodden into them – the things that oppress me most are the scraps of newspaper that are scattered all over the floor.

G. is quite badly ill with bronchitis. He stayed away from work yesterday, then this morning, when still obviously ill, insisted on going to work.

Returning to Leeds tomorrow, then on to London on Monday [30 March].

Domestic Diary Volume 1

9 August 1938 – 28 March 1939

INTERCALATED WITH

Morocco Diary

7 September 1938 – 28 March 1939

On his return from Wigan, Orwell rented The Stores, Wallington, Hertfordshire, for 7s 6d a week (equivalent to about £15 today). The house was primitive, especially by current standards, but it had enough land for him to engage in two of his passions: growing food and keeping goats and chickens. His first goat (with which he was photographed: see Crick, plate 19), was called Muriel – the name of the goat in *Animal Farm*. He ran this small shop until the outbreak of war and it seems to have brought him enough to pay his modest rent. On 9 June 1936 he married Eileen O'Shaugnessy. He set about writing *The Road to Wigan Pier* and delivered the manuscript to Victor Gollancz on Monday, 21 December 1936. It so happened that the founder of Portmeirion, Clough Williams Ellis, visited Gollancz about the time that the manuscript was delivered and suggested that it should be illustrated. A scrap of paper survives torn from Gollancz's blotter giving some of the names suggested (illustrated in *CW*, I, p. xxxiii and X, p. 530). The book was not commissioned by The Left Book Club (as is sometimes assumed) but early in 1937 it was decided that the book should be issued by the Club. This ensured that it had a wide sale and Orwell received royalties, after commission, up until 28 November 1939 of £604.57 – far exceeding the highest amount he had received for any of his earlier books, for example, £127.50 for *Down and Out in Paris and London*.

At Christmas Orwell left for Spain, calling on Henry Miller whilst passing through Paris where he picked up his travel documents. Initially he intended to report on the Spanish Civil War but quickly joined the POUM Militia (the Workers' Party of Marxist Unification) to fight for the Republicans on the Aragón front. Jennie Lee, the wife of Aneurin Bevan and who served in Labour governments from 1964–70, who later became the first Minister for the Arts, wrote in a letter that Orwell arrived in Barcelona without credentials, had paid his own way out, and won her over by pointing to his boots, slung over one shoulder: 'He knew he could not get boots big enough for he was over six feet. This was George Orwell and his boots arriving to fight in Spain' (*CW*, XI, p. 5). After serving in the front line, whilst on leave in Barcelona, he became involved with the POUM in the attempt by the Communists to suppress all revolutionary parties, including the POUM. He returned to the front, was wounded in the throat, narrowly escaping death, and whilst convalescent had to hide in Barcelona until he and his wife, with John McNair, leader of the Independent Labour Party, and the youngest member of Orwell's unit, Stafford Cottman, could escape from Spain on 23 June 1937. A document was later discovered, forming part of an official judiciary record of the trial against the POUM, asserting they were 'confirmed Trotskyists' and thus anathema to the Communist regime. Orwell never knew of the existence of this document. Sir Richard Rees met Eileen in Barcelona when she was working in the ILP Office and wrote 'In Eileen Blair I had seen for the first time the symptoms of a human being living under a political Terror'. On 8 March 1937, whilst Orwell was serving at the front, *The Road to Wigan Pier* was published and the following weekend Eileen spent two days at the front. As explained in the Introduction, Orwell's diary or diaries written when he was in Spain are probably still locked away in the NKVD Archive in Moscow.

When the Orwells returned to The Stores early in July, Orwell wrote articles and reviews trying to give a true account of what was happening in Spain and he set about writing *Homage to Catalonia,* despite receiving a letter from Victor Gollancz dated 5 July 1937 that he would be unlikely to publish it because it might 'harm the fight against fascism'. On the very next day a letter came from Roger Senhouse of Martin Secker & Warburg informing him that they would be interested in Orwell's account for it 'would not only be of great interest but of considerable political importance'. So began the break with Gollancz and, in due time, Secker & Warburg becoming Orwell's publishers.

On 15 March 1938 Orwell was admitted to Preston Hall Sanatorium, Aylesford (near Maidstone), Kent, following a heavy discharge of blood from the lungs. He was suspected to be suffering from tuberculosis but it was decided that in all probability it was bronchiectasis of the left lung (see Shelden, pp. 316–19). He remained in hospital throughout the summer and on 25 April *Homage to Catalonia* was published in a small edition of 1,500 copies. Despite now being regarded as one of Orwell's finest books (and a very important personal account of the Spanish Civil War) it would not sell even this small number of copies by the time a second edition was published in 1951 after Orwell's death. Whilst at Preston Hall, Orwell joined the Independent Labour Party on 13 June 1938 and on the 24th his article 'Why I Join the I.L.P.' was published (*CW*, XI, pp. 167–9). He would leave the party at the start of the war because of its pacifist stance and because he 'considered they were talking nonsense' which would 'make things easier for Hitler'. He described himself as definitely 'left' but as a writer he was better 'free of party labels' (*CW*, XII, p. 148). He did not leave hospital until the very end of August. He was recommended to spend the winter in a warm climate and he and Eileen chose to go to Morocco (not, as it happens, the best choice), on the basis of a gift or loan of £300 from an anonymous donor. Orwell never knew that this was provided by the novelist, L.H. Myers, because it was arranged through an intermediary, Dorothy Plowman (see *CW*, XI, p. 452). He was later able to repay this generous gesture from the proceeds of *Animal Farm* but after Myers's death. After a short visit to see his father, who was gravely ill, in Southwold, they left on 2 September from Tilbury on the S.S. *Stratheden*.

Orwell kept two diaries in 1938: a domestic diary and a diary devoted to his and Eileen's time in Morocco, including the journeys there and back. His Domestic Diary begins on 9 August 1938; his Morocco Diary, on 7 September. The Domestic Diary is handwritten, the Morocco Diary mainly typed (see headnote to 12.3.39). Slight errors have been silently corrected. Orwell stuck newspaper cuttings into the Domestic Diary. These are not reproduced, but a heading or brief descriptive note is given within square brackets indicating what had attracted his attention. The texts of these cuttings can be consulted at the Orwell Archive, University College London. Orwell also drew illustrations for certain entries, usually on otherwise blank verso pages. These have been incorporated into the entries they illustrate. Notes are placed after the relevant dates. Dates of entries and paragraphing (in the manuscript, variably indented) have been regularized.

The Diaries are intercalated in datal order. Quite often Orwell wrote in both diaries on the same day. When entries to both diaries are given for the same day, those for the Domestic Diary are given first and indicated by **D**; Morocco Diary entries are indicated by **M.** Footnotes are numbered in a single series for both diaries.

DOMESTIC DIARY VOLUME I

D

August 9, 1938: Caught a large snake in the herbaceous border beside the drive. About 2′ 6″ long, grey colour, black markings on belly but none on back except, on back of neck, a mark resembling an arrow-head (⌂) Not certain whether an adder, as these I think usually have a sort of broad arrow mark (⩓) all down the back. Did not care to handle it too recklessly, so only picked it up by extreme tip of tail. Held thus it could nearly turn far enough to bite my hand, but not quite. Marx[1] interested at first, but after smelling it was frightened & ran away. The people here normally kill all snakes. As usual, the tongue referred to as the "fangs."[2]

1. *Marx:* the Orwells' dog, a black poodle. Whether it was named after Groucho or Karl Marx is a matter of dispute.
2. *fangs:* it was an ancient belief that a poisonous snake injects its venom by means of its forked tongue and not, as in this case, through two fangs. In *Richard II* Shakespeare has 'a lurking adder / Whose double tongue may with a mortal touch / Throw death upon thy sovereign's enemies' (3.2.20-22). See also diary entry for 11 August.

D

August 10: Drizzly. Dense mist in evening. Yellow moon.

D

August 11: This morning all surfaces, even indoors, damp as result of mist. A curious deposit all over my snuff-box, evidently result of moisture acting on lacquer.

Very hot, but rain in afternoon.

Am told the men caught another snake this morning – definitely a grass snake this time. The man who saw them said they had tied a string round its neck & were trying to cut out its tongue with a knife, the idea being that after this it could not "sting."

The first Beauty of Bath apples today.

D

August 12: Very hot in the morning. In the afternoon sudden thunderstorm & very heavy rain. About 50 yards from the gate the road & pavement flooded a foot deep after only 1½ hours rain.

Blackberries beginning to redden.

D

August 16: Several days past uncertain weather, rainy & sometimes hot. Most of the wheat & barley now cut & stacked. Children picking more or less ripe blackberries two days ago. Saw a white owl two nights ago – the first in about two years. Also in the distance another bird probably a little owl. Horse-chestnuts full-size but not ripe yet. Hops about the size of hazelnuts. Yesterday went to the Zoo* again. Another litter of lion-cubs, which are a bit bigger than a domestic cat & spotted all over. Those born just a year ago are about the size of a St Bernard dog. The ration of meat for a lion – I suppose its only meal in the day – seems to be about 6 or 7 lbs.

The Sardinian mouflon sheep[3] has a large udder like a goat & would probably yield a pint or more. I notice that the zebra's hooves, at least the front ones, are quite perpendicular, but those of the ass-zebra hybrid are like those of a horse. The hybrid has very slightly larger ears, otherwise so far as shape goes almost exactly like the zebra.

3. *Sardinian mouflon sheep:* a wild sheep found in the mountains of Sardinia and Corsica and, by extension, any large, wild, big-horned sheep.

D

August 17: Warm & fine, rather windy.

The barley from the 22-acre field is not stacked yet, but the wheat is stacked & makes two stacks measuring so far as I can judge it 30′ by 18′ x 24′ (high) & 18′ x 15′ x 20′ (high). If these estimates are correct, this works out at 14,040 cubic feet of stack for about 14 acres of ground. Allowing 1 ton

* ie. near Maidstone [Orwell's note].

per acre, it seems 1000 cubic feet of stack represent a ton of grain. NB. to check when the whole field is stacked.

Catmint, peppermint & tansies full out. Ragwort & willow-herb going to seed. A few ripe blackberries. Elderberries beginning to turn purple.

Oak planks etc. made from the boughs instead of the trunk is known as bastard oak & is somewhat cheaper.

Disused railway sleepers here sold off at £1=1=0 10cwt. This probably works out at about 1/- each, ie. 2d a foot.

[*Newspaper cutting*: short article on greenheart timber]

D

August 19: Ref. the stacks in the cornfield. Actually the area under wheat & barley was about the same, & the crop makes 4 stacks, 2 of 30′ x 18′x 24′ (high) & 2 of 18′ x 15′ x 20′ (high.) This works out at about 28,000 cubic feet of stack for 22 acres. Yesterday fine & rather windy. A fair number of ripe blackberries. Elderberries changing colour rapidly. Hazel nuts almost fully formed. Valerian & mulleins over. For improving finish of cement:

[*Newspaper cutting* describing method to be adopted]

Weather today cold, blowy & rather wet. Haws getting quite red. Some rain in the afternoon.

D

August 21: Yesterday fine & fairly warm. Went in afternoon & saw Kit's Coty,[4] a druidical altar or something of the kind. It consists of four stones arranged more or less thus:

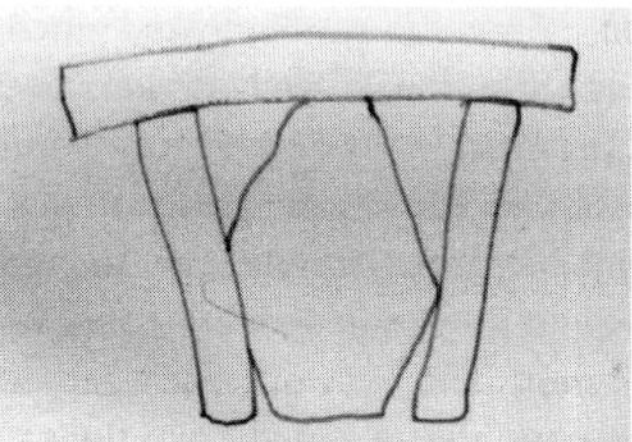

The whole about 8′ high & the stone on top approximately 8′ square by something over a foot thick. This makes about 70 cubic feet of stone. A cubic yard (27 cubic feet) of coal is supposed to weigh 27 cwt., so the top stone if of coal would weigh about 3½ tons. Probably more if I have estimated the dimensions rightly. The stones are on top of a high hill & it appears they belong to quite another part of the country.

4. *Kit's Coty*: Kit's Coty House is the chamber of a long barrow – an ancient grave mound – on Blue Bell Hill a little to the north of Aylesford. Orwell's sketch, coupled with his description, gives a good approximation of the standing stones.

[*Newspaper cutting*: 'Fruit Bottling Without Sugar, Old-Time Country Method'; see 29.8.38]

D

August 22: Warmish day, with showers. Nights are getting colder & more like autumn. A few oaks beginning to yellow very slightly. After the rain enormous slugs crawling about, one measuring about 3″ long. Large holes, presumably ear-holes, some distance behind head. They were of two distinct colours, some light fawn & others white, but both have a band of bright orange round the edge of the belly, which makes one think they are of the same species & vary individually in colour. On the tip of their tails they had blobs of gelatinous stuff like the casing of water-snails' eggs. A large beetle, about the size of a female stag-beetle but not the same, extruding from her hindquarters a yellow tube about the length of herself. Possibly some sort of tube through which eggs are laid?

[*Newspaper cutting* on how to make sloe gin]

D

August 22:[5] *Southwold*: Cool this morning & raining most of the day.

Most of the crops in & stacked. Blackberries in Suffolk much less forward than Kent, otherwise little difference in the vegetation.

When clipping fowls' wings, clip only one wing, preferably the right (left wing keeps the ovaries warm.)

Cold tea is good fertiliser for geraniums.

5. *August 22:* As the preceding entry is also dated 22nd August, this was probably the 23rd. Orwell had gone to Southwold to see his parents before leaving for North Africa.

D

August 25: *Preston Hall*: Everything in Suffolk is much more dried-up than in Kent. Until the day we arrived there had been no rain for many weeks & various crops had failed. Near S'wold saw several fields of oats & barley being harvested which had grown only 1′ or 18″ high. Ears nevertheless seemed normal. Wheat crop all over the world said to be heavy.

A bedstraw hawk-moth found in our back garden & mounted by Dr Collings.[6] Evidently a straggler from the continent. Said to be the first seen in that locality for 50 years.

Little owl very common round here. Brown owl does not seem to exist.

Dr C. says the snake I caught was the "smooth snake", non-poisonous & not very common.

Today hot again.

Gipsies beginning to arrive for the hop-picking. As soon as they have pitched their caravans the chickens are let loose & apparently can be depended on not to stray. The strips of tin for clothes-pegs are cut out of biscuit boxes. Three people were on the job, one shaping the sticks, one cutting out the tin & another nailing it on. I should say one person doing all these jobs (also splitting the pegs after nailing) could make 10–15 pegs an hour

Another white owl this evening.

6. *Dr Collings:* The Blairs' family doctor. His son, Dennis, was one of Orwell's friends: see Introduction to 'Hop-Picking Diary'.

D

August 26: Hot. Dense ground-mist early this morning. Many blackberries now ripe, very large & fairly sweet. Also fair number of dew-berries. Walnuts now nearly full-sized. Plenty of English apples in the shops.

D

August 28: Night before last an hour's rain. Yesterday hot & overcast. Today ditto, with a few drops of rain in the afternoon. The hop-picking due to start in about a week.

D

August 29: Overcast & very chilly. Heavy rain last night. Dahlias now in full bloom.

[*Newspaper cutting:* response to cutting on fruit bottling (see 21.8.38), which was 'bound to give unsatisfactory results in many cases'].

D

August 30: Warmer.

Leaves of the tulip tree beginning to yellow. Sunflowers & gladioli in full bloom. Godetias getting past their best. Montbretias coming into bloom. Elderberries now ripe & bird-shit everywhere deep purple. Purple stains on logs etc. where they have been. Seems difficult to believe that birds digest much of what they eat. The man who keeps the guinea pigs here seems uncertain whether or not they sleep. Says they close their eyes sometimes, but it is uncertain whether they are asleep. First English eating pears today.

D

August 31: Morning very cold, warm & fine later.

D

September 1: Fine & fairly warm.

D

September 2: Fine & fairly warm.

D

September 3: Writing on P.& O. ss. *Stratheden*, 22,500 tons. No of passenger berths 1063.[7] Left Tilbury dock 6 pm yesterday. Position marked this morning (not certain whether 8 am or noon) as 49.25 N, 3.34 W, run being 288 miles. Distance to go 1007 miles. Passed Ushant, about 5–10 miles on port side, about 5 pm. Now entering Bay of Biscay & travelling about due South. Should sight land again tomorrow night. Sea at present calm. Once or twice small shoal of fish, pilchards or sardines, leaping out of the water as though something was after them. Small land-bird, bunting or some such thing, came on board this morning when out of sight of land. Also pigeons perching on rigging.

7. The *Stratheden* was built at Barrow for P & O and commissioned in 1938. She was 664 feet long, 23,722 tons, and carried 448 first class and 563 tourist class passengers. She made fifty-five round trips to Australia returning from the last in September 1963. During the war she served as a troopship. After six years with a Greek owner she was broken up in 1969.

D

September 4: Today crossing mouth of Bay of Biscay. Sea a little rougher, ship rolling somewhat. Not sick (seasickness remedy "Vasano" evidently efficacious.) Passing C. Finisterre about 5 pm but invisible owing to mist. Run of the ship (12–12) 403 miles. Gibraltar is about 5° west of Greenwich. Clocks will be retarded ½ hour on Monday & Tuesday, then put forward again at Marseilles. We are due in at Tangier 7 am on Tuesday (6th) & Gibraltar at 1.30 pm. Run of 1007 miles to Tangier takes about 89 hours. Today a few porpoises passing the ship. Yesterday saw a gull I did not know, dark brown with white bands on wings. Otherwise no life.

Length of ship is about 250 yards, width at widest about 25 yards. There are 7 decks above water-level. Do not yet know number of crew, who including stewards are mainly lascars.

D

September 5: Last night much fog, syren° sounding continually. This morning the sea much smoother, grey & oily, about the colour of lead. Later in the day very hot, & the sea bright blue. Passed Cape Roca about 10 am, but invisible in mist. Passed Cape St. Vincent quite close in, about 2–3 miles, at 6 pm. Run of the ship (noon to noon) 342 miles. Due at Tangier early tomorrow.

Gulls here of a breed I do not know, dark brown or black on top, white below, hawking over the water only a few inches above the surface, just like an owl over grass. Clumps of seaweed as we got nearer land. Some swallows or martins (different from the English) following the ship when still far from land. Two whales said to have been seen yesterday, but I missed them.

This is not, as I had thought, a steam turbine ship, but an oil turbine. Crew thought to be about 600. The tourist class (really midway between 2nd & 3rd class) has three lounges apart from the dining saloon, two decks where games are played, a small swimming bath & a rather primitive cinematograph. R. C. mass & Anglican H. C. held every day. Tourist fare London–Gibralter £6-10.[8]

Later. Number of crew 543. Ship carries 8 or 9 thousand tons cargo.

8. *£6-10:* Six pounds and ten shillings – perhaps about £250 today.

The Domestic Diary is now intercalated with the Morocco Diary

MOROCCO DIARY

7 September 1938 – 28 March 1939

M

GIBRALTAR 7.9.38:

English newspapers reach Gibraltar by P & O four days late. Local English daily *Gibraltar Chronicle & Official Gazette*, 8 pages of which about 2½ advertisements, 1d. Current number 31,251. More or less pro-Fascist. Local Spanish papers *El Annunciador* and *El Campanse*, each four pages largely adverts, 1d. daily. No very definite standpoint politically, perhaps slightly pro-Franco. Ten or eleven Franco papers sold here, also three Government papers including *Solidaridad Obrera*. The latter at least six days old when obtainable here, and much less in evidence. Also two pro-Government Spanish papers published in Tangier, *El Porvenir* and *Democracia*. Prices of these stated in Franco exchange.

Impossible to discover sentiments of local Spanish population. Only signs on walls are Viva Franco and Phalangist symbol, but very few of these.

Population of town about 20,000, largely Italian origin but nearly all bilingual English-Spanish. Many Spaniards work here and return into Spain every night. At least 3000 refugees from Franco territory. Authorities now trying to get rid of these on pretext of overcrowding. Impossible to discover wages and food prices. Standard of living apparently not very low, no barefooted adults and few children. Fruit and vegetables cheap, wine and tobacco evidently untaxed or taxed very little (English cigarettes 3/– a hundred, Spanish 10d. a hundred), silk very cheap. No English sugar or matches, all Belgian. Cows' milk 6d. a pint. Some of the shopkeepers are Indians and Parsees.

Spanish destroyer *Jose Luis Diez* lying in Harbour. A huge shell-hole, probably four or five feet across, in her side, just above water-level, on port side about fifteen to twenty feet behind bow. Flying Spanish Republican flag. The men were at first apparently prevented from going ashore, now allowed at certain hours to naval recreation grounds (i.e. not to mix with local population). No attempt being made to mend the ship.

Overheard local English resident: "It's coming right enough. Hitler's going to have Czechoslovakia all right. If he doesn't get it now he'll go on and on till he does. Better let him have it at once. We shall be ready by 1941."

D

September 8: *Gibraltar:* Weather mostly hot & nights sometimes uncomfortably so. Sea variable mostly rather choppy. When no wind fish visible at least 10 feet below surface.

The Barbary Ape is said to be now very rare at Gibraltar & the authorities are trying to exterminate them as they are a nuisance. At a certain season of the year (owing to shortage of food I suppose) they come down from the rock & invade people's houses & gardens. They are described as large doglike ape with only a short stump of tail. The same species found on the African coast just opposite.

The breed of goat here is the Maltese, or at any rate is chiefly Maltese. The goat is rather small, & has the top half of its body covered with long & rather shaggy hair which overhangs it to about the knees, giving the impression that it has very short legs. Ears are set low & drooping. Most of the goats are hornless, those having horns have ones that curve back so sharply that they lie against the head, & usually continue round in a semicircle, the point of the horn being beside the eye. Udders are very pendulous & in many cases simply a bag with practically no teats, or teats barely ½ inch long. Colours black, white & (especially) reddish brown. Yield said to be about a litre a day. Goats apparently will graze on almost anything, eg. the flock I watched had grazed the wild fennel plants right to the ground.

Breed of donkeys here small, like the English. The conveyance peculiar to the place a little partly closed in carriage rather like the Indian gharry with the sides taken out.

Hills steep & animals on the whole badly treated. No cows. Cows' milk 6d a pint. Fruits now in season, apples, oranges, figs, grapes, melon, prickly pear, brinjals & various English vegetables. Prickly pear grows very plentifully on poor soil. Few hens here & eggs small. "Moorish eggs" advertised as though a superior kind.

Cats of Maltese type. Dogs all muzzled.

D

September 10: *Tangier:* Temperature here said never to rise above about 85°. Sea is fairly warm, water extremely clear, objects 20 & 30 feet below being visible when there is no wind. There is a tide rise of about a foot. Sea & harbour full of fish, but for some reason only the smaller kinds seem to be caught. There is a largish fish, generally about 6″ to a foot long, brown-coloured & somewhat resembling a pollock, which haunts the stones of the jetties in great numbers, swimming in shoals of 5–20, but all the fishermen say that these cannot be taken on a hook. The method of fishing with rod & line for the smaller fish seems to be foul-hooking. A contrivance made of about half a dozen small hooks set back to back, with a bait of bread or meat just above it, is lowered into the shoal & drawn rapidly up as the fish gather round it. Long-shore fishing with a net is done as follows. A net about 150 feet long & 6' deep, finely meshed in the middle but coarse towards the end, is carried out to sea by boats & placed in position, being held up by floats. Attached to each end of the net is an immensely long rope, probably half a mile or more. This is gradually hauled in, the men on each rope converging gradually then bring the net into a curve. There is a team of 6 or 8 men & boys on each rope. They do not pull with their hands but have a string round the waist & on the end of it a knot that can be attached immediately to the rope. They then pull with the body, leaning backwards & doing most of the work with the right leg. As the rope comes in it is coiled, & as each man reaches the coils he detaches his string, runs forward & hooks on to the seaward end of the rope. Hauling in takes at least an hour. Of the one I saw hauled in, the bag was about 30 lbs of sardines (or some similar small fish) & about 5 lb. of sundries, including squids, red mullet, long-nosed eels etc., etc. Probable value (to the fishermen) about 5/–, & representing about 2 hours work-time to 15 men & boys, say 20 adult work-hours, or 3d an hour.

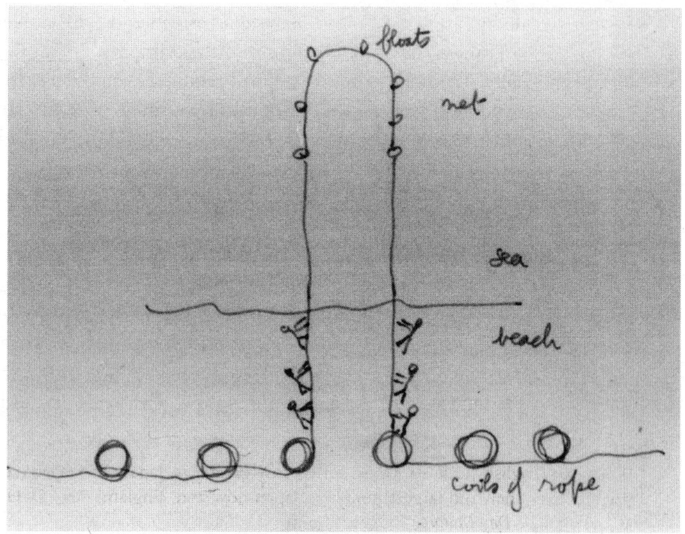

Donkeys here overworked to a terrible degree. They stand about 9–10 hands & carry loads which must often be well over 200 lbs. After putting a considerable load on the donkey's back the driver then perches himself in the middle. Hills here extremely steep, 1 in 5 or 6 in many places, but donkeys go up carrying loads so immense that they are sometimes almost invisible underneath. They are nevertheless extremely patient & willing, usually wear no bridle or halter & do not have to be driven or even led. They follow or walk just in front of their master like a dog, stopping when he stops & waiting outside any house while he is inside. The majority seem to be uncastrated, ditto with many of the horses (all small & in poor condition.)

Smells here not bad, in spite of the heat & labyrinthine bazaars.

Fruits in season, prickly pear, melons of many kinds, grapes, brinjals, otherwise all European. Water carried in goatskins & sold. Large fig-tree here has both green & purple figs on it, a thing I did not know happened. A sort of convolvulus creeper very common here has blue flowers & pinkish flowers on same plant & sometimes on same stem. Flowers now out, cannas, bourgainvillea, geraniums; peculiar coarse grass for lawns.

Two kinds of swallow or martin here. No gulls in harbour.

Gets dark here well before 7 pm (ie. really 7, summer time not being in operation.)

Butter here all right, but fresh milk apparently almost unobtainable.

M

TANGIER 10.9.38:

Papers on sale in Tangier: *La Presse Marocaine* (morning daily Casablanca), strongly pro-Franco; *Le Petit Marocain* (ditto), impartial; *La Dépêche Marocaine* (daily Tangier), somewhat pro-Franco; *Le Journal de Tanger*° (apparently weekly), seemingly non-political, business announcements etc.; *Tangier Gazette & Morocco Mail* (English weekly Tangier, Fridays), corresponds to above, seems slightly anti-Fascist and strongly anti-Japanese;* also various others, French and Spanish, but seemingly no local Spanish pro-Franco paper.

Two buildings here flying Spanish Republican flag, including one called La Casa de Espana, some sort of club, displaying the usual Government posters. Some shops display Franco posters (the Arriba Espana poster almost exactly like a Government one). Writings on wall not common and pro-Franco and pro-Government ones about equally common, the latter perhaps slightly more so. Generally simply Viva or Muera Franco,

* N.B. That English trade to Morocco has lost greatly to Japanese since 1934. England was then 2nd largest importer. Japan now 2nd, England 6th. (D. H. Warre, *Present Day Morocco*) [Orwell's note].

or U.H.P., or C.N.T., F.A.I., or very rarely U.G.T. No initials of political parties except the F.A.I., the Phalange and once the J.S.U. All these inscriptions invariably Spanish. No clue to attitude of Moors. (See newspaper cutting *Petit Marocain* of 15.9.36.)*[9]

Poverty here not extreme for an oriental city. Nevertheless an immense development of mendicancy, the whole town living on the tourist trade. Not many actual beggars but countless touts for curio-shops, brothels etc. Most people speak Spanish, many French and all those connected with the tourist racket speak some English. Local physique very good, especially the young men both Moors and Spaniards etc. In spite of Europeanisation almost all Moors wear the burnous and fez and most of the younger women are veiled. Estimated earnings of longshore fishermen about 3d. an hour.

There are four post offices, one French, one British, and two Spanish, Franco and Government. Stamps are British surcharged Tangier. Coinage as in French Morocco.[10]

9. In 1940, when France fell, Spain took control of the whole of Tangier. After the war it was returned to its international status, until it became part of the Kingdom of Morocco in 1956. CNT was the Anarcho-Syndicalist Trade Union; FAI, the Anarchist Doctrinal Vanguard; UGT, the Socialist Trade Union; JSU, the United Youth Movement; and UHP stood for '!Uníos, Hermanos Proletarios!' – 'Unite, proletarian brothers', a call first used during the miners' rising in Asturias, 1934. See Thomas, p. xiii.

10. The Orwells arrived in Morocco on 11 September 1938, as the deposition before Robert Parr, the British Consul at Marrakech shows; see *CW*, XI, p. 196. Orwell's date of birth is given as 1902, not 1903. In his letter to A. H. Joyce of 12 February 1938 (see *CW*, XI, pp. 120–2), he said that by mistake his date of birth had been incorrectly entered as 1902 in his passport. They were to stay for a little over six months, sailing from Casablanca for England on 26 March 1939. On 18 September, signing as Eric Blair, Orwell accepted the lease of 'une villa et une piece de domestique, route de casa, apartenant° a Monsieur Simont, Boucher a Marrakech' ('casa' means Casablanca) for a minimum period of six months at 550 francs per month, running from 15 October 1938. The villa was about five kilometres from Marrakech. R. L. Bidwell records the French franc as being at 165 to the pound (31 to the dollar) in March 1938, and by January 1939 the rate had become 176.5 to the pound (39.8 to the dollar), a rate maintained at the following January *(Currency Conversion Tables*, 1970, 20). Thus, 550 francs was about £3.25 ($15.50) during these six months. The rent of the cottage at Wallington was 7s 6d per week or £1.50 (in today's coinage, if not value) for four weeks.

Until they could take up residence in M. Simont's villa, the Orwells stayed at Madame Vellat's house, rue Edmond Doutte, Marrakech.

* *Le Temps* of 23.1.39 said to have leading article (which I have not seen) seriously suggesting the French might take over Sp. Morocco on the conclusion of the Spanish War [Orwell's note].

MARRAKECH 13.9.38:

Summer Time observed in Spanish Morocco, not in French. Franco soldiers at the stations dressed almost exactly like those of the Spanish Government. Luggage searched on the train, but very carelessly, by typical Spanish official. Another official entered and impounded all French newspapers, even those favourable to Franco. French travellers much amused by this and ditto the official, who evidently realised the absurdity of it.

Spanish Morocco evidently less developed than French, possibly owing to the barrenness of that particular area. Further South, in French Morocco, great contrast between the areas cultivated by Moors and Europeans. The latter have enormous areas given over to wheat (1,000,000 acres said to be cultivated by 3000 French with coloured labour), fields so vast that they reach the horizon on each side of the railway track. Great contrast in fertility. Soil in places is rich and very black, in others almost like broken-up brick. South of Casablanca the land generally poorer, most of it uncultivated and giving barely any pasture for animals. For about 50–100 km. North of Marrakech actual desert, ground and hills of sand and chipped rock, utterly bare of vegetation. *Animals:* about the end of Spanish Morocco camels begin to appear, getting commoner until near Marrakech they are almost as common as donkeys. Sheep and goats about equally numerous. Horses not many, mules hardly any. Cows in the better parts. Oxen ploughing near Marrakech but none further north. All animals almost without exception in wretched condition. (This said to be one to two successive famine years.) Casablanca is in appearance a completely French town (of about 150,000–200,000 inhabitants, a third of these Europeans). Evidently considerable tendency for both races to keep themselves to themselves. Europeans doing manual and menial work of all kinds, but evidently better paid than the Moors. (In the cinematograph only Moors in the cheapest seats, in buses many white people unwilling to sit next to a Moor.) Standard of living seems not exceptionally low. Mendicancy noticeably less than at Tangier or Marrakech.

Marrakech has large European quarters but is more typically a Moorish town. Europeans not doing actual menial work except in restaurants etc.* Cab-drivers Europeans in Casablanca, Moors in Marrakech. Mendicancy so bad as to make it intolerable to walk through the streets. Poverty without any doubt very severe. Children beg for bread and when given it eat it greedily. In the bazaar quarter great numbers of people sleeping in the street, literally a family in every doorway. Blindness extremely common, some ringworm and a certain number of deformities. Large

* A lot of waiters etc. who look like Europeans speak to each other in Arabic & are probably Eurasians [Orwell's note].

number of refugees camping outside the town. Said to be some of the people who fled north from the famine districts further south. It is said here to be punishable by law to grow tobacco plants in the garden.*

D

September 14: *Marrakesh:* Birds seen on railway journey Tangier–Casablanca–Marrakech.[11] Ibis extremely numerous, Kestrels fairly common & also two larger kinds of hawk or kite, a few solitary crows very similar to the English bird. No storks, tho' said to exist here. A very few partridges.

Goldfinches, apparently identical with English bird, common in Marrakech. Saw a man carrying a hare, otherwise no wild quadrupeds at all. There are said to be literally none, except a few hares & jackals, in Fr. Morrocco.° A few camels in Sp. Morocco, but not common till south of Casablanca. In general a camel seems to stand about 18 hands high. All are extremely lean & have calloused patches on all joints. Most are muzzled. Donkies° in Marrakech slightly less overloaded & slightly less docile than in Tangier.

Dates are now almost ripe. The partially ripe dates are bright yellow & hang in thick clusters on stems of their own just where the crown of the palm joins the trunk. There are generally about 6 clusters per tree & the whole would weigh about ½ hundredweight. The fallen date looks just like an acorn without its cup. Apparently there are several varieties of date palm including a dwarf one.

The peppercorns on the pepper trees just about ripe. Apparently these are known as "false pepper", although it can be used in the ordinary way. Walnuts, evidently local, just ripe. Pears & peaches rather under-ripe. Lemons here are round & green, more like the Indian lime, only larger & thicker-skinned. Wine grapes in great profusion & very cheap.

The marine life at Casablanca seemed almost exactly the same as in England. Winkles, limpets, barnacles, land-crabs & one kind of anenome apparently identical. Saw no gulls, however. Forgot to mention that at Tangier there were catches of very large mackerel.

Rosemary grows well in Marrakech. Roses do well, petunias grow into huge bushes, as in India. Zinnias also thrive. Apparently good grass can be grown if there is sufficient water.

11. *Marrakesh – Marrakech:* Orwell uses both forms and sometimes it is not clear whether 's' or 'c' is intended. It is given as 'Marrakech' hereafter.

D

September 15: Caught a water-tortoise, about 8″ long, outside the small zoological gardens here (evidently it had *not* escaped from within, though of the same kind as those kept inside.) It was in an irrigation ditch,

* i.e. more than a certain specific area [Orwell's note].

swimming against the current & only succeeding in remaining about stationary. When turned onto its back it was unable to turn over. It smelt abominably, though active & apparently in good condition.

No ordinary sparrows here, but a small bird of the finch family, with brown body, bluish head & long tail, very common.

A few Michaelmas daisies in flower in the Z[oological] gardens, which surprised me. Olives almost ripe. Some turning bluish-red, which is perhaps their ripe colour. Oranges still green. These trees evidently need a lot of manure. Runner beans in pod, much as at home. Grapes here are poor, rather dry & tasteless.

Large ants here, half red & half black, enlarging their hole in the ground. One carrying out a bean-shaped stone about ¼″ long by ½″ thick. Flies here very trying, mosquitoes fairly numerous, but as yet no plagues of flying insects.

Tonight dark by 7 pm.

M

MARRAKECH 16.9.38: The two papers normally read here are the Casablanca dailies, *Le Petit Marocain*, obtainable about midday, and *La Vigie Marocaine*, not obtainable till evening. Both are patriotic, more or less anti-Fascist, but neutral as to Spanish Civil War and anti-Communist. The local paper, *L'Atlas*, weekly, seems utterly insignificant. Yesterday (15th) in spite of sensational news of Chamberlain flying to Berlin, with which the papers made great play, there was utter lack of interest here and evidently no belief in war being imminent. Nevertheless there have been large transfers of troops to Morocco. Two of the French liners which run Marseilles–Tangier–Casablanca were more or less completely filled with troops. There has been a large increase recently in the local Air Force and 125 new officers are said to have arrived.

D

September 19: For sale along with the bright orange half-ripe dates are others equally bright purple, about the colour of brinjals. Pomegranates for sale in large piles everywhere. Some oranges beginning to yellow. Immense vegetable marrows for sale, probably weighing 20–30 lbs. each. Also a kind of smooth pale green extremely elongated marrow – possibly a species of cucumber. Black bread made & sold here in the bazaar; presumably barley but looks like rye.

Goldfinches extremely common here. Storks it appears are migratory & do not appear here till mid-winter. Great variations in temperature. Today & yesterday fairly cool, the day before unbearable, temperature even at 6 pm being 25°C. (ie. 77°F.) & probably about 40°C at midday. Is said to reach 45°C. (ie. 113°F.) as hottest indoor temperature here. After cooling off about 4 pm it generally seems to get hotter again about 6, perhaps owing to the prevailing warm wind. At night a sheet over one is sufficient, but in the early morning one generally pulls up the blanket.

A donkey is said to cost about Fr. 100 (about 12/6d.) Lettuces said to be very difficult to grow here.

D

September 20: Lathes used by Jewish carpenters who make the string-seated chairs etc. are of extremely primitive type. There are two clamps, the left hand one fixed, the right sliding upon a metal rod, with a metal point in each. The bar of wood to be turned is fixed upon the two points & turns itself, the points being stationary. Before it is put on the string of a bow is looped once round it. The carpenter holds the movable clamp in place with his right foot & works the bow with his right hand, holding the chisel in his left hand & steadying it with his left foot. In this way he can turn a piece of wood apparently as accurately as on a proper lathe, judging by eye to about 1/100 inch. Working the bow makes the wood revolve at an astounding speed.

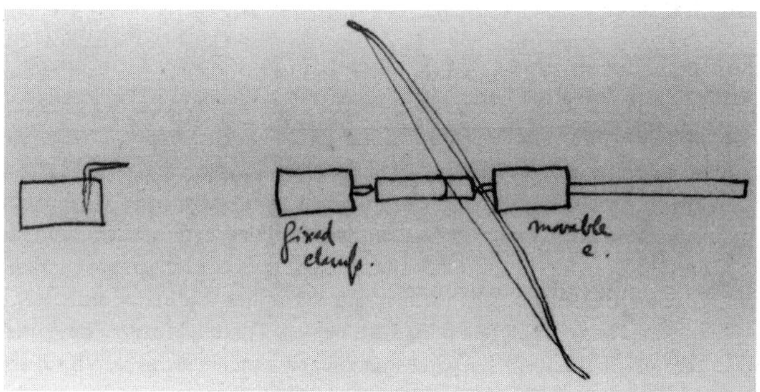

The earth walls here are made out of earth which is dug out at a depth of 4–6 feet, either because this is different earth or because at this depth it is easier to find it damp enough to be workable. It is a peculiar chocolate colour & it dries into the light pink distinctive of this town. Having been dug out it is mixed with rubble & a little water, then cast in sections in a wooden frame, just like cement, but when in the frame it has to be packed together very hard with heavy rammers. When one section is hard enough to stand unsupported the next is made, & the joins do not show, the mud setting almost like cement. These mud walls are said to stand many years in spite of torrential rains.

The orange trees which grow in the street here are of an inedible bitter kind. This kind is used as a stock for grafting the sweet orange on.

Some of the olive trees here have, among the ordinary green olives, a certain number which are bluish red, though apparently ordinary in every other respect.

The superstition that it is lucky to touch a hunchback apparently obtains among the Arabs as well.

Today stifling hot about midday, otherwise somewhat cooler, though we did not want a coat till about 6-30 pm. We have not yet had a day when it was clear enough to see whether the Atlas mountains have snow on them or not.

D

September 25: Yesterday morning blowy & overcast, then some fairly heavy showers of rain. Today no rain, but cooler & still windy.

The reason for the galls always present on camels joints is that these are what they kneel down on, usually on stones etc. Nearly all camels here also have galled backs. It is said that a camel can often only be managed by one man whom it knows, & that one must at all costs avoid beating them. Relative to size they carry a much smaller load than a donkey. Some of them have flies & maggots burrowing into the galls on their backs, without appearing to notice it. Children also pay very little attention to flies, which are sometimes crusted in sores all round their eyes.

Hollyhocks just over & sunflowers coming to an end. The former grow 10 or 12 feet high.

Chrysanthemums in the public gardens budding. Cannas are very fine, in 4 colours.

There is no snow at present on the Atlas mountains. At sunset when it is clear they take on a remarkable purplish-red colour.

The bow which is used for a lathe is also used for a drill. A drill with a cylindrical wooden handle in the base of which there is a hole is fitted against a steel point & rotated with the bow. It is kept firm by the other end being in contact with the wood that is drilled. It seems to work as exactly as an ordinary drill & very rapidly.

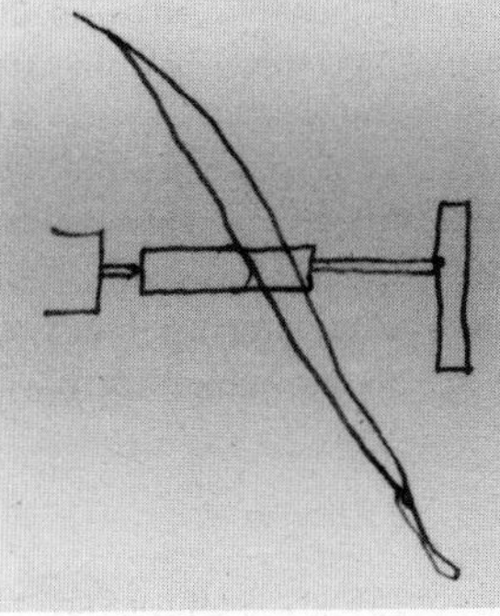

Bought two turtle doves this morning. Two doves 10 Fr. (an overcharge), bamboo cage about 20″ by 15″ by 20″ , 15 Fr. Total cost about 3/–. These birds seem to domesticate very easily.

Ordinary blackbird, or some bird extremely similar, is common here. Also the little owl or some very similar owl. Bats here are large, about twice the size of English bat.

It gets dark now at about 6.45 pm.

D

September 27: Yesterday cooler. Some thunder in afternoon, then an hour's steady rain in the evening. Have not worn dark glasses for several days past.

M

MARRAKECH 27.9.38:

The other local daily paper read here is *La Presse Marocaine*, which is somewhat more right-wing (at any rate more anti-Russian and more pro-Franco) than the *Petit Marocain*.

There are said to be about 15,000 troops in Marrakech. Apart from officers and N.C.Os, these will all be Arab or negro troops, except for a detachment of the foreign legion.* The latter are evidently looked on as dangerous ruffians, though good troops, and are debarred from visiting certain parts of the town except with a special permit. The Arab cavalry (from their badges apparently the 2nd Spahis) look pretty good, the Arab infantry less good, probably about equal to a second-rate Indian regiment. There is a large number of Senegalese infantry (called tirailleurs – presumably rifles – the badge is an anchor†) here. They are of admirable physique and said to be good marchers. They are used for picket duty at certain parts of the town. In addition the local detachment of artillery (do not know how much, but recently saw a battery of largish field guns, probably larger than 75 mm., on the march) is manned by negroes. They only act as drivers etc. under white N.C.Os and are not taught to aim the guns. Arabs are not used for this purpose, obviously because they could not be prevented from learning too much. All the troops here are said to be standing by and ready to move at a moment's notice. On the fortified hill immediately west of the town there are guns which command the Arab quarter "in case of trouble". Nevertheless the local French show an utter lack of interest in the European crisis, so much so as to make it impossible to think that they believe war will break out. There is no scramble for papers, no one broaches the subject of war unless prompted and one

* Apparently there were some white troops as well as the N.C.Os. [Orwell's note].

† The anchor is the artillery [Orwell's note].

overhears no conversations on the subjects in the cafés. A Frenchman, questioned on the subject, says that people here are well aware that in case of war "it will be more comfortable here than in France." Everyone will be mobilised, but only the younger classes will be sent to Europe. The re-opening of schools has not, as in France, been postponed. It is not easy to be absolutely certain about the volume of poverty here. The province has undoubtedly passed through a very bad period owing to two years drought, and on all sides fields which have obviously been under cultivation recently have reverted to almost desert condition, utterly dried up and bare even of weeds. As a result many products, eg. potatoes, are very scarce. There has been a great to and fro of refugees from the dried up areas, for whom the French have made at any rate some provision. The great French wheat estates are said to be worked largely with female labour, and in bad times the unemployed women flock into the towns, which is said to lead to a great increase in prostitution. There is no doubt that poverty in the town itself is very severe by European standards. People sleep in the streets by hundreds and thousands, and beggars, especially children, swarm everywhere. It is noticeable that this is so not only in quarters normally frequented by tourists, but also in the purely native quarters, where any European is promptly followed by a retinue of children. Most beggars are quite satisfied with a sou (twenty sous equal a penny halfpenny). Two illustrative incidents: I asked a boy of about 10 to call a cab for me, and when he returned with the cab gave him 50 centimes (three farthings, but by local standards an overpayment.) Meanwhile about a dozen other boys had collected, and when they saw me take a handful of small change out of my pocket they flung themselves on it with such violence as to draw blood from my hand. When I had managed to extricate myself and give the boy his 50 centimes a number of others flung themselves on him, forced his hand open and robbed him of the money. Another day I was feeding the gazelles in the public gardens with bread when an Arab employee of the local authorities who was doing navvy work nearby came up to me and asked for a piece of the bread. I gave it him and he pocketed it gratefully. The only doubt raised in one's mind about all this is that in certain quarters the population, at any rate the younger ones, have been hopelessly debauched by tourism and led to think of Europeans as immensely rich and easily swindled. Numbers of young men make a living ostensibly as guides and interpreters, actually by a species of blackmail.

When one works out the earnings of the various kinds of petty craftsmen and pieceworkers here, carpenters, metal-workers, porters etc., it generally comes to about 1d or 2d an hour. As a result many products are very cheap, but certain staple ones are not, eg. bread, which is eaten by all Arabs when they can get it, is very expensive. ¾lb of inferior white bread (the European bread is dearer) costs 1 franc or 1½d. It is habitually sold in half cakes. The lowest sum on which an Arab, living in the streets with no home, can exist is said to be 2 francs a day. The poorer French residents regard 10 francs or even 8 francs a day as a suitable wage for an Arab servant (out of this wage he has to provide his own food).*

The poverty in the Jewish quarter is worse, or at any rate more obtrusive than in the Arab quarters. Apart from the main streets, which are themselves very narrow, the alleys where the people live are 6 feet or less across and most of the houses have no windows at all. Overcrowding evidently goes on to an unbelievable extent and the stench is utterly insupportable, people in the narrowest alleys habitually urinating in the street and against the wall. Nevertheless it is evident that there are often quite rich people living among this general filth. There are about 10,000† Jews in the town. They do most of the metal work and much of the woodwork. Among them are a few who are extremely wealthy. The Arabs are said to feel much more hostility towards the Jews than towards the Europeans. The Jews are noticeably more dirty in their clothes and bodies than the Arabs. Impossible to say to what extent they are orthodox, but all evidently observe the Jewish festivals and almost all, at any rate of those over 30, wear the Jewish costume (black robe and skull-cap.) In spite of poverty, begging in the Jewish quarters not worse than in the Arab quarters.

Here in Marrakech the attitude of the French towards the Arabs is noticeably more like the Anglo-Indian attitude than, eg., in Casablanca. "Indigene" exactly corresponds to "native" and is freely used in the newspapers. The French here do not, as in Casablanca, do menial jobs such as cab-driving, though there are French waiters in the cafés. In the Jewish quarter there is a very poor French population some of whom appear to have "gone native", but these are not altogether distinguishable from the Jews, most of whom are quite white. There is an immensely higher proportion of French-speaking Arabs than of English-speaking Indians, indeed every Arab who is much in contact with Europeans speaks a certain amount of French. The French almost always tu-toi the Arabs in speaking to them, and the Arabs do so in return whether or not understanding the implication (2nd person in Arabic has not this implication). Most French people of long standing here speak some Arabic, but probably not a great deal. A French officer speaking to his N.C.O. speaks in French, at any rate some of the time.

* Female servants receive 3–5 Fr. a day [Orwell's note].

† 13000 [Orwell's note].

D

September 28: Distinctly cooler at night. Last night used a blanket all night. Red hibiscus in flower.

D

October 1: Snow on the Atlas today. Evidently it fell last night.

Camels vary greatly in size, also in colour, some being almost black. Ditto donkeys, which range from reddish fawn to almost black, the latter the commonest colour. Saw yesterday a donkey, evidently full grown, less than 3′ high. The man riding it had one foot on the ground.

The Atlas said to go up to 3200 metres (about 10,000 feet.) (Actually about 13,500.)

D

October 2: Nightjars here, much as in England. Female donkey today, very heavily in foal, carrying respectable load of wood, & its master. Load something over 200 lb., plus the foal.

The Spahis ride stallions. Arab saddles, but not blinkers. Horses of different colours. Donkeys here, when male, are always uncastrated.

D

October 4: Still very hot in the middle of the day. Huge lumps of camel-fat (presumably from the hump), very white, like pork-fat, on sale in the bazaar. Said to be only eaten by "people from the mountains."

Wooden spoons here are cut out with a small adze, which is used with great skill until the spoon is almost entirely hollowed out, after which a gouge-like tool (but with the edge at the side) is used, & then sandpaper. Some of these spoons are 2′ or 3′ feet long & the head as large as a breakfast cup. This work done mainly by children, ditto the work of making wooden ploughs (very primitive, & sold in such numbers as to suggest they have to be renewed every year.)

D

October 6: Yesterday insufferably hot, & this continued till about 6 am this morning, when I felt the need of a blanket on the bed. Flies & mosquitoes still very bad.

Unbearably hot all day. Apparently this is very unusual for the time of year. Camel cub supposed to be about 6 months old is already about 5′ high. They are still sucking when quite a considerable size. Contrary to what I had been told, camels appear to be fairly tractable, as after changing owners they behave quite normally, only the young ones having a tendency to take fright. They vary not only in size & colour (white to almost black, the latter being usually small), but also in the nature of their coats, which are sometimes curly, sometimes smooth, a few camels having a sort of beard all down the neck. They have very little smell.

Horses are sometimes excellent in appearance, always uncastrated.

Arab saddle like Mexican, but the Arabs ride with rather short stirrups. The stirrup is a long flat piece of steel with sharp corners which serve as spurs. The Arabs do not sit very gracefully in the saddle, but have

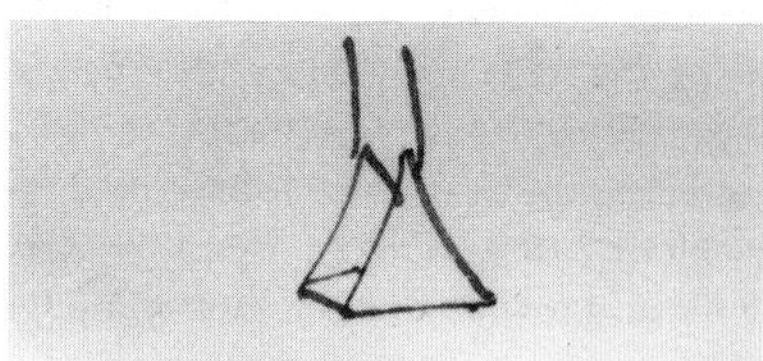

complete mastery of the horse, which goes forward, changes pace & stops all with a loose rein & apparently mostly from the man's voice. The mule is always ridden on the hindquarters. It is evident that the tractability of animals here is due to their being constantly handled from childhood.

D

October 9: Day before yesterday still unbearably hot, yesterday cooler but night very stuffy. Very hot today at midday, in the afternoon a violent dust-storm, much thunder & then fairly heavy rain for about an hour. Fearful mud in the bazaar in consequence. Air much fresher after the rain.

Primitive drill used by the Arabs – not certain whether merely drill for wood or used for stone & earthenware – constructed as follows. The drill is attached to an upright which passes through a heavy round stone of 5–10 lb. Above this is a cross-piece which fits round the upright but is movable. From the ends of the cross-piece strings go to the top of the upright. These are twisted round the upright & the cross-piece worked up & down, causing the upright & therefore the drill to rotate. The stone serves merely as a weight.

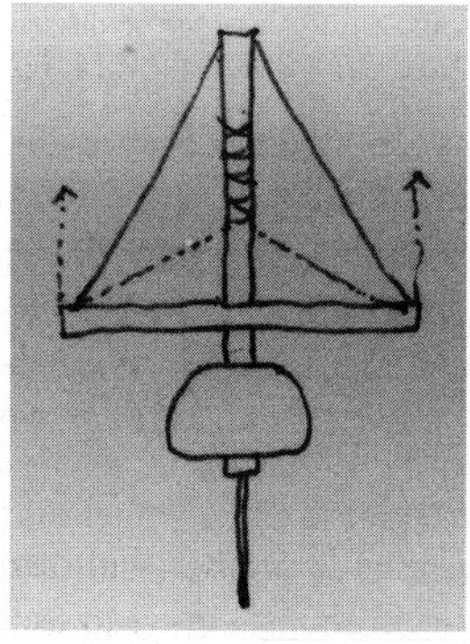

Arab drug kiff,[12] said to have some kind of intoxicating effect, smoked in long bamboo pipe with earthenware head about the size of a cigarette holder. The drug resembles chopped grass. Unpleasant taste & – so far as I am concerned – no effect. Sale said to be illegal, though it can be acquired everywhere for 1 Fr. for about a tablespoonful.

The one smell one rarely encounters here is garlic, which apparently the Arabs do not use much. Almost a majority of the ripe olives now on sale are purple. Possibly these are the ones black olives are made from. Dates getting very ripe. They seem to be a rather dry & inferior kind.

12. *kiff:* Indian hemp, marijuana, from the Arabic, 'kaif', meaning enjoyment, well-being, state of dreamy intoxication. Also as kef, keef, kif.

M

MARRAKECH 9.10.38 :

The other daily paper sometimes obtainable is *Maroc Matin*, illustrated, Casablanca. Much more left wing than the others. Poor paper and print, evidently not prosperous and not much in evidence, in fact seldom obtainable.

After the crisis was over everyone here showed great relief and was much less stolid about it than they had been during the trouble itself. Educated Frenchwoman in official position, known to us personally, writes letter of congratulation to Daladier.[13] It is perfectly evident from the tone of the press that even in the big towns where there is a white proletariat there was not the smallest enthusiasm for the idea of going to war for the sake of Czechoslovakia.

13. *Edouard Daladier* (1884–1970): Socialist Premier of France, 1938–40. He signed the Munich Pact with Chamberlain, Hitler, and Mussolini, surrendering the Sudetenland to Germany on 30 September 1938. For Churchill's account of Daladier's visit to London on 18 September to discuss Hitler's demands with Chamberlain, see his *The Second World War*, vol 1, pp. 270–72.

I was wrong in thinking the brass-work etc. was done exclusively by Jews. Actually Jews and Arabs seem to do much the same class of work. Much of the work of making wooden ploughs, wooden spoons, brass and copper utensils, and even some classes of blacksmithing, is done by very young children. Children certainly not older than 6 work at some of the simpler parts of these jobs. Children of about 8–10 work with adze and chisel, very diligently and with great skill. Children almost too young to stand are set to such jobs as keeping flies off piles of fruit. Arab woodwork, though rather rough and done with extremely primitive tools, is quite good, but they seem almost always to use unseasoned wood, which of course is liable to warp. Shafts for ploughs are cut straight out of green boughs. This is presumably due to lack of capital and storage space. It is also evident that peasants have to buy a new plough every year.

Women servants receive less than men. Madame V[ellat] pays her cook-general Aicha Frs. 6.50 a day, but it appears that Frs. 5 is more usual, and in some cases Frs. 3.50 or even 3. In no case would the servant getting these wages receive any food or lodging. A[icha] is an extremely good plain cook who in England would be considered worth £50 a year and her keep.[14]

14. If she worked a seven-day week, she would be paid Frs. 45 a week; £50 a year was about Frs. 170 a week.

Most riding and baggage animals here are exceedingly cheap. The following prices quoted at the Bab el Khemis animal fair (some of these subject to reduction if one bargained). Full-grown but smallish camel Frs. 300. Riding horse, 15–16 hands, apparently good, Frs. 275. Donkeys Frs. 75–150. Cow in milk Frs. 650. Mules Frs. 250-1000.* High price of mules is due to their being ridden by rich men, the mule being in fact the badge of wealth. Goats (very poor) 30–50 Frs.

Immense prevalence of blindness here. In some of the poorest quarters it is possible to pass three or four blind people in 50 yards. A few of the blind beggars are probably impostors, but the main cause is no doubt the flies with which every child's eyes are constantly crusted. Curiously enough children below a certain age, say 5, appear not to notice the flies.

The Arab women, though almost invariably veiled, are anything but shy, do not object to going about alone and in quarrels, bargaining etc. do not seem at all inhibited by their veils. Arabs seem to attach less importance than most orientals to touching and being touched. Arab men often go about hand in hand, and sometimes hand in hand with a woman (unthinkable in some oriental races.) In the buses mild flirtations between Arab women and European men. The Mahometan rules about not drinking seem to be strictly kept and drunkenness unheard of. On the other hand there is much smoking of a sort of drug called kiff, which is at any rate supposed to have narcotic effects. It is said to [be] illegal but is obtainable every where. No Europeans are admitted to the mosques here.

The French authorities enrol a sort of special constables, a force known as the sûreté, who are armed with truncheons and called out when criminals are to be rounded up. I have not yet got reliable particulars but it appears that either these or the regular police can summarily order flogging of thieves etc. and that savage floggings are administered without trial.

* 10% tax paid by purchaser on each sale [Orwell's note].

Have seen a good many of the Foreign Legion. Do not look very dangerous ruffians. Almost universally poor physique. Uniforms even worse than those of the conscripts.

Official advertisement of post for girl teacher of native girls in state school, teacher evidently expected to be daughter of army officer or something of the kind, wage to be Frs. 900 a month (about 25/– a week.)

French film *Légion d'Honneur*, propaganda film corresponding to *Bengal Lancer*, dealing with the French Sahara. Certain social differences interesting. French officer speaks to Touareg tribesmen largely through interpreter. Calling for two men for special duty he refers to them by their numbers instead of their names. Officers (represented as more or less aristocratic) smoke cigars with bands on and wear uniform off duty, eg. on ship going home.

On getting the English newspapers of the period of the crisis, it was evident that the local French press had systematically minimised the whole thing, for obvious reasons.

In the bazaar a tiny screw of tea (green China tea, of which the Arabs drink a great deal), perhaps ¼ to ½ oz., and about 1oz. of sugar, can be bought for 25 centimes. Utterly impossible to buy things in such quantities in most European countries. Price of a cup of water 1 sou. This may be taken as meaning that the sou has no other purchasing power.

Have not yet seen a single sign of any hostility towards Europeans as such, of the kind one is constantly seeing in an Indian city.

D

10.10.38: Midday temperature (indoors) today 26°, ie. about 78°F. This is much cooler than the last few days. This evening cool enough to wear a coat.

D

12.10.38: A lot cooler. No snow now visible on the Atlas, but perhaps obscured by clouds.

Have installed the hens & goats. Hens about the size of the Indian fowl, but of all colours, some with a species of topknot, white ones very pretty. These are supposed to be laying pullets but have not laid yet. Twelve brought crammed together in two small baskets, then sent on donkey back about 5 miles, at the end of which one fowl was dead, apparently pecked to death by others. They appear not to like maize, probably not used to it, or possibly when unbroken it is too big for them. Arabs always keep them in completely grassless runs. Tried giving them some green stuff at which they pecked not very enthusiastically. Hope they may take to it later.

Goats are tiny. Searching all over the market could not find any of decent size or with large bags, though one does see some not actually bad goats in the flocks that graze on the hillsides. The breed here is very shaggy & tends to get its coat dirty. Of ours one, a tiny red goat, is evidently about to kid soon. The other, somewhat larger, supposed to be in milk, but doubt whether she will give more than ½ pint a day at first. After feeding up for 10 days probably a pint. Arabs all scandalised at the idea of giving grain of any kind to goats. Said we should only give them grass. If given grain they drink enormously & swell up. Quite good chopped fodder (lucerne I think) sold in the bazaar for 10c. a bunch. One franc's worth should be enough for 2 goats for a day so far as green food goes. Gave them for their first meal mixture of barley & bran. They had perhaps not seen such a thing before & took no notice of it. Then later smelt it & got to work on it. Goats here do not object to eating off the ground. They are very shy but being so small are easy to handle & do not try to use their horns. They are gentle with each other & do not quarrel over food. Were taken to the house in paniers° one on each side of a donkey, the donkey's owner sitting in the middle.

The only form of mash given to fowls here is bran. Grocers here, & apparently everyone else, have never heard of suet – ie. for use in puddings etc.

M. Simont's[15] oranges just beginning to ripen. Dates now ripe, but rather dry & poor. Walnuts very good. Pomegranates exquisite colour inside. The reason why so many dates are gathered when bright yellow is said to be that they are a kind which are used for cooking.

Curiously enough, among the general misery of the animals here, the sheep are very good. They are a long-tailed kind, fairly large, apparently fat (the mutton is quite good & tender) & with very thick, firm coats. They are very docile & tend to huddle all together in a bunch, which makes them easy to manage. When buying a sheep a man carries it across his shoulders, where it lies completely docile like a large slug. A man will ride a bicycle carrying a sheep like this.

15. *M. Simont:* Orwell's landlord, a butcher in Marrakech. The villa was set in an orange grove.

D

13.10.38: Today fairly cool, & up to about 10 am almost chilly in the shade. This evening another violent dust-storm followed by rain.

D

14.10.38: Stuffy, but not very hot. Today milked the small goat (which is probably *not* in kid) for the first time. For a long time could get no milk at all, though the udder was large & obviously contained milk. Finally discovered that if instead of running my hand down the teat in the ordinary way, I took hold of the whole quarter & squeezed as if squeezing out a sponge, the milk came quite easily. Apparently a different configuration of udder. Wretched yield, about ½ pint from two goats combined. But they are eating well & should improve soon.

Ripe pepper falling from the trees. No eggs.

D

16.10.38: *Villa Simont, route de Casablanca:* Yesterday intolerably hot. In the evening thunderstorm & torrential rain, flooding the ground some inches deep.

This morning a disaster. One hen dead, another evidently dying. Forget the name of the disease, which has something to do with the throat. The hen is unable to stand & head droops forward. The dead one had evidently perched for the night & then fallen off the perch. May have something to do with perching in the rain, as they all did so, though I put up another perch for them under cover.

Goats a little tamer. The wife of the Arab who works in the orange plantation & looks after the sheep says that the brown goat *is* in kid.

D

18.10.38: We have now lost 3 fowls in addition to the one which was presumably pecked to death. Symptoms all the same – loss of power of legs & head drooping. Evidently paralysis, tho' attributed by the Arabs to a black parasite infesting the birds. Cause & effect uncertain here. The Arabs' treatment is rubbing with a mixture of charcoal ash, salt & water. Seems effective, at any rate two which were slightly affected seem better today & able to run about. The remaining 8 fowls seem now in good condition, but their appetite is very small even allowing for small size. They will never eat maize unless boiled, & do not care greatly for mash.

Goats tamer. Am milking the small one only once a day, & getting about ½ pint a day from the two. Even this is more than a few days back. The small one had slight diarrhea yesterday, probably caused by too much wet green fodder, so am now drying the lucerne into a kind of hay. About the same time one of M. Simont's sheep mysteriously died – attributed to eating too much of the herbage which sprang up after the rain. Goats will eat almost anything, eg. orange peel, & a certain amount of maize can be given them if boiled & mixed with mash. Flaked maize not obtainable here. The goats already follow & know the way to their shed.

Saw a lizard this morning, walking up the window pane. About 4″ long, rather stumpy, resembling an alligator, prickly tail. The first lizard seen in Morocco.

A little cooler, & today very still.

Large ant can drag two peppercorns & the twig connecting them. Ants of various sizes drag a grain of wheat each.

The fowls perched on the new perch for the first time last night.

D

20.10.38: The turtle doves after about 2 days plucked up courage to leave their house, flew off & presently disappeared. The Arabs said that they would not return. However, they come every day for corn, & sleep in the pepper tree behind the house.

M. Simont's sheep are allowed to browse among the orange trees. Apparently the idea is that they will not eat the leaves of the trees (presumably bitter) but will keep the weeds down. Actually they do nibble at a leaf occasionally.

Cooler. Nice autumnal feeling in the early mornings. Goats giving distinctly more milk. More than ½ pint, though am only milking the brown one once daily.

Hens all well, but no eggs. These hens, even allowing for size, have extraordinarily small appetites.

Arabs round here growing practically all English vegetables (carrots, radishes, lettuces, cabbages, tomatoes, runner beans, crown artichokes, marrows) besides large green chillis which are extremely hot. Most of the vegetables rather poor quality. Dates very dry & poor. Sheep here eat half-ripe dates.

The charcoal braziers generally used here are quite satisfactory for cooking. They are generally about 1′ across by 8″ deep & either have very many holes in sides or a double bottom with holes in the top one. The charcoal can be started with very little paper & wood & smoulders for hours. A few strokes with the bellows gets it into a fierce heat. A small tin oven is placed on top & bakes fairly satisfactorily.

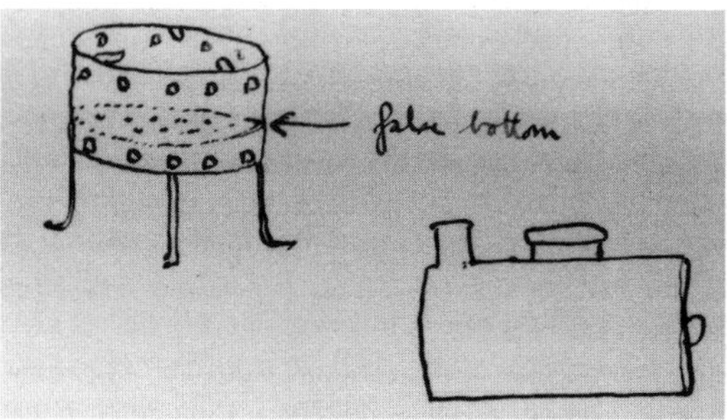

D

21.10.38: Yesterday went to the Oued Tensift, about 2 Km. from here, the principal river of these parts. About 5 yards wide & 1–3′ deep, but lies in a considerable valley & probably rises at some times of the year. Poor water, but said to have small fish in it. Muddy banks & bottom. Fresh water mussels, very similar to those in the Thames, moving to & fro in the mud leaving deep track behind them. Red shank & ringed plover, or extremely similar birds, live on the mud. Feathery shrub which in England is used for making hedges in gardens, arbutus[16] I think, growing everywhere. Patches of grass almost like English grass.

Still very hot. Last night unbearably so till quite late at night.

The water here is almost undrinkable, not only tasting of mud but also distinctly salty.

The bitter oranges grown here as grafting stocks said to be good for marmalade, so presumably the same as Seville oranges.

Some of the goats round here a bright silvery-grey colour. First-class Spanish goat said to cost Frs. 500.

16. *arbutus:* It is not certain what Orwell is describing here because arbutus has leathery, rather than feathery, leaves. The most likely possibility is a tamarisk, which could grow in the situation Orwell describes.

D

23.10.38: The water here evidently has some mineral in it which is the cause of the almost continuous belly-ache we have had since coming here.

Near the Oued Tensift noticed that where the water had receded it had left some white deposit behind. Possibly something akin to Epsom salts – at any rate not an organism as it is not affected by boiling. Arranging to get Marrakech tap water (which is all right & said to come from the Atlas.)

Various bottled table-waters impossibly expensive, actually dearer than the cheapest wine.

Soil here is extremely deep, at least 4′ without any change of substance. Rather light & reddish, though it dries into a kind of brick, & said to need a lot of manure.

Some of the small oranges ("mandarins") are yellowing. Some lemons almost ripe, others only in blossom – different kinds,[17] perhaps.

Today the first day we have had when it was cool all the time. Overcast, windy & some rain rather like a damp day in September in England. The day before yesterday a little rain with much thunder.

The doves come to the house from time to time & are very tame, eating from one's hand with a little persuasion. Saw a partridge in the grounds yesterday.

Today sowed seeds of nasturtiums, phlox D.[18] & pansies.

Flytox very good & kills flies by the thousand. Otherwise they are utterly intolerable.

Red chillis spread out to dry in the fields, like huge red carpets.

17. *lemons . . . different kinds:* Orwell was evidently unaware that in the lemon all stages of flowering and fruiting occur at the same time on a single tree. However, he comes to this conclusion later: see Domestic Diary, 4.3.39.

18. *Phlox D.:* perhaps the annual, phlox drummondii, found in several varieties.

D

25.10.38: Much cooler. Yesterday overcast & cool all day, with occasional sharp showers. Violent wind & storms of rain in the night. Fire last night & this morning, not absolutely necessary but acceptable.

The brown goat, besides being very difficult to milk, gives little or nothing. Perhaps she is really going off preparatory to kidding, in which case she would probably kid in some weeks' time.

The pigeons this morning of their own accord went into the pigeon-house in which we put them for our first day here. They are now very tame.

Goats eat boiled wheat & maize readily.

D

27.10.38: On Tuesday afternoon (25th) tremendous rain, much as in the tropics except that it was very cold rain. Everything flooded feet deep, the earth not dry yet. The Oued Tensift is now quite a considerable stream & low ground all round it has turned into marsh. Today near the Oued Tensift came upon a sort of large pool where there were a flight of wild duck swimming about. Managed to scare them onto the wing, & after much circling round they came straight overhead. Sixteen in number, & evidently mallards, same as in England, or very similar. Saw another larger flight in the distance afterwards. Almost the first game birds seen here.

Ordinary sparrows fairly common in the garden here. In Marrakech itself one used not to see them.

Large numbers of black beetles, about 1″ long, crawling everywhere, evidently brought out by the rain. Have sowed sunflowers, sweet peas & marigolds. The other seeds not up yet, as it has been much cooler (we are having fires every evening.) The ground here is lumpy & unpleasant to work, but at present not many weeds – more when this rain has taken effect, perhaps. Some weeds as in England, eg. bindweed & twitch grass, but not growing very strongly. Silver poplar or some very similar tree grows here. Tomatoes here are grown in large patches without sticks. Very poor floppy plants & smallish tomatoes, but plenty of them.

Yesterday on milking the brown goat found her milk had gone sour & came out quite thick. This is because she is only being milked once a day & had not been fully milked for two days owing to her restiveness. Squeezed the bad milk onto the ground & tonight her milk was all right again. Another hen bad in the legs this evening. Examined & found enormous black lice. Hope treatment will be effective as before. The stripey goat's milk increases, but very slightly, still not much over ½ pint a day. She is very thin, though she eats well. The present ration of hard food is 2 handfuls of barley & 2 of bran morning & evening, with a mash of boiled maize & bran about once a week. The doves readily eat maize if it is broken.

Today saw some doves in an aviary which had eggs.

The fountain in front of the house filled up after the rain & mosquito larvae are multiplying rapidly.

One egg (the first) yesterday, none today.

D

28.10.38: One egg. Many black beetles squashed in the road. Inside they are brilliant vermilion. Men ploughing with teams of oxen after the rain. Wretched ploughs, with no wheel, which only stir the soil.

D

30.10.38: Fine, not very hot. One egg.

D

31.10.38: Ditto. One egg. Inside bad again.

Fruit on sale here much resembling a strawberry, but full of pips & has an unpleasant sour taste.

Put paraffin on the water in the fountain yesterday. About 30 square feet, & about a cupful of paraffin covered it. Mosquito larvae all dead by this morning.

The plough used here has a crossbar which passes under the bellies of the two draft animals, & to this are attached the yokes – wooden for oxen & sackcloth for horses etc. Oxen, mules, horses & even donkeys used for ploughing. Two different animals sometimes yoked together.

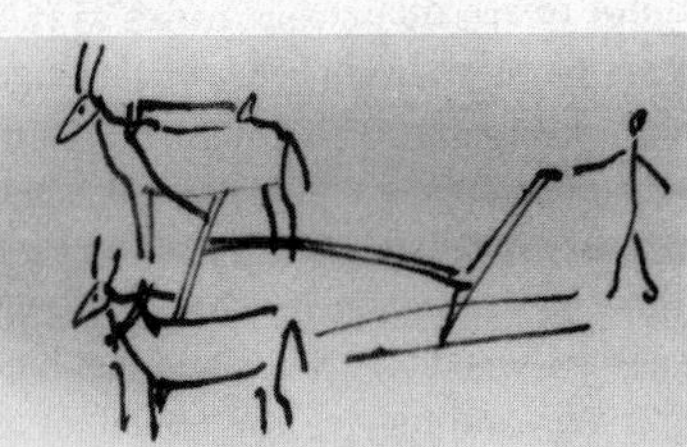

The ploughman walks on the already ploughed side & holds the handle with one hand, changing at each furrow. The share is only a sort of hollow iron point fitted over a wooden rod. The whole structure can be easily carried over the shoulder. Absence of wheel makes it far harder to guide.

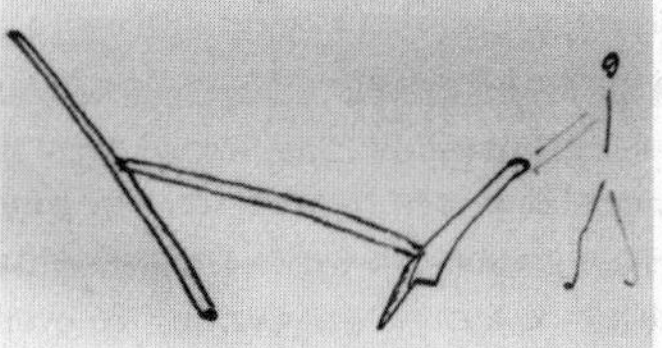

D

1.11.38: Fine, not at all hot. People ploughing everywhere. The plough stirs the soil about 4″ to 6″ deep. The soil varies greatly & some of it looks rather good. Large patches which were perhaps cultivated a few years ago have been eroded till the rock is sticking through. After the rain some kind of weed (dicotyledon) is springing up everywhere very rapidly & will no doubt give a lot of pasture soon. The fallen olives are quite black. Pomegranates now about over. The pomegranate tree is small & very unimpressive, much like a hawthorn bush. Some wheat (or some other grain) just coming up, evidently winter wheat sown about the same time as in England.

Passing a flock of sheep & goats today, a goat had just given birth to a kid. The shepherd picked the kid up & carried it & the mother hobbled after them, crying to the kid, with the placenta still hanging out of her. Goats will eat leaves of prickly pear. Others grazing at thorn bushes go down on all fours & creep under the thorns almost like a cat, to get at a few green leaves.

The nasturtium & marigold seeds germinating, the others not yet. Inside still very bad.

Another kind of orange coming into season, but still not completely ripe. A largish sour kind, rather thick skin & lots of pith, but good flavour.

M

VILLA SIMONT, ROUTE DE CASABLANCA 1.11.38: Cannot yet get any definite idea as to the land system here. All the land round here is either cultivated or what passes as cultivable, except for a few spurs of hills. We are just within the edge of the huge palm plantation which runs round the northern side of Marrakech and must be thousands of acres. The land between the palm trees is mostly cultivated the same as the fields. But there are no or very few boundaries and I cannot find out whether the peasants own their own plots or rent it, whether everyone owns a plot, and whether any land is owned communally. I suspect that some must be, as the fields lying fallow count as pasture for the sake of the few patches of weeds growing on them, and the flocks of sheep and goats are grazed everywhere. Possibly there are private plots for cultivation but common grazing rights. The palms grow in a completely haphazard way and it is difficult to believe that they can be privately owned. Immediately round our house it is an area mainly of vegetable and fruit gardens. There appear to be some peasants who cultivate fairly considerable plots and keep them in fairly good order. There are also large and well-ordered market gardens, generally walled off and owned by Europeans or rich Arabs – generally the latter, I think. Contrasting their ground with that of the ordinary peasants, one sees the enormous difference made here by having the capital to run water conduits.

Ploughing is now going on everywhere after the recent heavy rain.

From the size of the plots evidently for some cereal crop. Here and there a little wheat or some other grain coming up, presumably winter wheat sown at much the same time as in England. The local plough is a wretched thing made entirely of wood except for the share, which is merely a kind of iron point fitted over a wooden bar. The whole apparatus can easily be carried on one's shoulder. The share stirs the ground about 4″ to 6″ deep, and presumably most of the soil is never cultivated deeper than this. Nevertheless some of it does not look bad, and in places, eg. the orange grove round our house, it is extremely deep, about 4 feet (ie. the top-soil.) The lack of a wheel on the plough makes it much harder for the men and beasts and almost impossible to plough straight furrows. Oxen are mostly used, but also all the other beasts except camels, and an ox and a donkey sometimes yoked together. Should say a yoke of oxen could plough about half an acre in a day.

Chief crops round here: palms, olives, pomegranates, maize, chillis, lucerne, most of the European vegetables (beans, cabbages, tomatoes, marrows, pumpkins, peas, radishes[19]), brinjals, oranges, and some cereals, I do not yet know which. Oranges seem chiefly grown by Europeans, also lemons. Pomegranates are about over, dates coming to an end. I fancy that lucerne, which grows quickly and is cropped when about a foot high, is grown all the year round. It is the principal fodder here and is sold at 10 c. for a bundle about 3″ thick. Maize, used for fodder, probably also grown all the year round, and most of the vegetables. Quality of most of the plants very poor, owing no doubt to poor soil and still more to lack of capital for equipment. Eg. tomatoes are grown without sticks and are wretched plants. Of the animals, the sheep seem to do best on the miserable pasture, and besides making quite good mutton have excellent fleeces. Most of the other animals wretched, and no milk-yielding animals have udders of any size on them. A good class Spanish goat costs almost the same as a cow, which gives one a hint of the latter's milking qualities. Fowls are like the Indian fowl. All animals abominably treated but astonishingly docile. Tools are extremely primitive. No spades or European forks, only hoes of the Indian style. Cultivation is made much more laborious by the lack of water, because every field has to be partitioned off into tiny plots with earth banks between, to conserve water. Not only small children but very old women work in the fields, women who must be at least 60, probably 70, clearing roots etc. with pick-axes. The typical Arab village is a large enclosure with high mud walls, which looks like one huge house. Inside are the usual miserable huts, mostly of straw or palm thatch, shaped like beehives, about eight feet wide and seven high. All the people round here seem to fear robbers and like to feel themselves shut in at night. Except in the temporary field huts used for watching ripe crops, no one sleeps outside the enclosure of the village. Have not yet got to the bottom of the reason for the very high price of cereals. Eg. in the market a decalitre of wheat, weighing about 40 lb. costs Frs. 30 or over 1d a pound even in English money. Bread is correspondingly expensive. (Last month price of wheat officially fixed at Frs. 158 the quintal. See cutting *V.M.*[20] 9.10.38.)

Ramadan has begun. The Arabs here seem fairly strict about their observances, but I gather they sometimes eat forbidden things, eg. I suspect they will sometimes eat an animal that has died a natural death. Our servant and M. S[imont]'s caretaker thought it all right to eat a fowl pecked to death by the others. They appear to be strict about not drinking.[21]

Troops often passing on their way to the rifle range nearby. They look pretty good, spirits very good and marching style better than I had expected, better than ordinary French conscripts. Harold Maral, who did his military service in the Zouaves, says the latter are largely Algerian Jews and greatly looked down on by other regiments. I gather that in Morocco proper Jews are not recruited. One meets everywhere here with signs of hostility to Jews, not only among Arabs but also Europeans. Jews are said to undercut, cheat, take other people's jobs etc., etc. (See cutting *P.M.*[22] 18.10.38).

19. In the margin is a note in Orwell's hand, with no indication of where it fits: *potatoes (poor).*
20. *V.M.: La Vigie Marocaine,* a local newspaper.
21. Marginal note in Orwell's hand (though not precisely related to this paragraph): *M. also eats left-over scraps from our table.* Eating such scraps is forbidden during Ramadan. M. stands for Mahdjoub Mahommed, *our servant* see Moroccan Diary, 22.11.38. Mahjoub is illustrated helping Orwell milk a goat in *The Lost Orwell,* plate 11.
22. *Le Petit Marocain:* a Casablanca daily morning newspaper.

D

3.11.38: Yesterday one egg. Fine sunset, with green sky.

The nasturtiums & marigolds well up.

Inside terribly bad in the night.

Fairly warm. On silver poplar tree found puss-moth caterpillar about 1″ long. Found shell of dead tortoise. Some time in life it had had some kind of injury which had crushed in a portion of the shell, forming a dent, & had set & grown in that position.

The half-starved donkey which I think was bought recently by M. Simont has discovered that the goats are given barley & comes across to rob them of it.

The pool where I saw the wild duck has already largely dried up.

One egg today.

The barley about at an end. There was about 20–25 lbs, & it has lasted 3 weeks, ie. each goat gets about ½lb. a day.

D

4.11.38: One egg.

D

5.11.38: One egg.

D

6.11.38: Two eggs.

Fairly considerable rain recently at nights. In the daytime fine & rather warm. This afternoon some raindrops out of a completely clear sky, then a thunderstorm & fairly heavy rain.

After the recent rain the streams in the fields are much swollen, & water tortoises are everywhere. Today saw 10–20 of them, & often 3 or 4 at a time. They are generally sitting on the mud & leap into the water when one approaches. After a while they come to the surface & remain with eyes & nose just out of the water, like the frogs in Spain, diving at once at any alarm. They seem able to move very rapidly.

The goats almost out of milk, possibly because they have had no barley for a couple of days, though pending the arrival of the barley I have given them other things, eg. boiled maize.

The nasturtiums now quite large. 1 sweet pea showing. No phlox or pansies (about a fortnight), so evidently dud seed.

Some of the local dates quite good, very shiny & sticky, & roundish shape, about size & shape of large walnuts.

Inside better.

D

7.11.38: No rain today. A little cooler. Very yellow moon.

Today in among the orange trees they were ploughing with 1 donkey. They have a small light plough, no wheel but share as in Europe & quite sharp, made in Czechoslovakia & probably costing £1–£2. It is hard work but evidently not too much for a strong donkey, & he can plough up a fair-sized patch (this was about 25 yards by 5 yards of ground that had more or less gone back to grass) at one go.

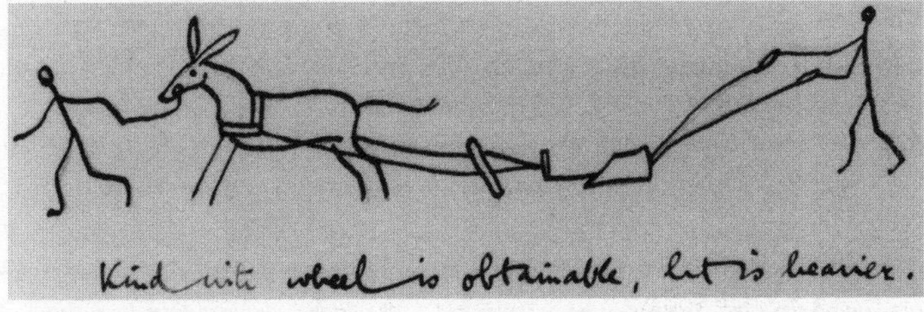

Kind with wheel is obtainable, but is heavier.

The oranges practically ripe now. We had a few of them (tangerine type) the other day.

Fresh barley today, about 30lb. for Frs. 17.50 or a little less than 1d a lb. This is less than I paid before.

In an old stone tank near the house found the decayed head of what may be a dog but I think is a jackal. There are said to be some in this country. In either case a very complete skull, so have put it up on a stick for the insects to get it clean.

D

8.11.38: Fine, rather warm. Some rain last night. A few sweet peas up.

One egg.

Footmarks of tortoises in the mud could easily be mistaken for those of a rabbit.

D

9.11.38: Sowed sweet peas (only about ½ dozen of the others have come up) carnations & violas.

D

10.11.38: Sowed pinks, godetias & clarkia.

Rainy & overcast all day, but fairly warm. Fine sunset. Green sky. Large flocks of starlings flying everywhere.

D

12.11.38: One egg.

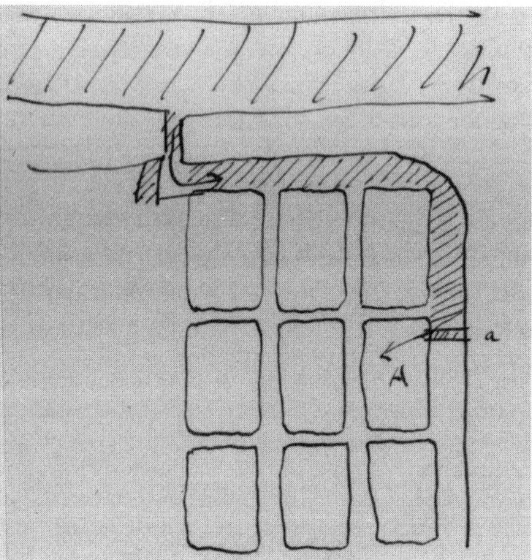

Method of irrigation used here. The soil in any field growing crops that require irrigation is divided into small beds about 4 yds–3 yds. The irrigation ditch which can be connected up with the stream, runs round the edge. If it is desired to water bed A, the ditch is damned then & a chunk cut out of A's surrounding bank. The water runs into A, & when enough has run in the bank is closed again, the dam across the ditch removed, & the water can be run to any other place required.

D

13.11.38: One egg.

The striped goat now completely out of milk.

On the whole very hot in the daytime lately. Fire at nights but not really necessary. Immense flocks of starlings, probably as many as 3000 in a flock, all the while attacking the olives, which are now ripe on the trees. Arabs out all day in the olive groves, shouting to scare the starlings away. E[ileen] compares the sound of the starlings' twittering to the rustle of a silk dress.

In an irrigation tank the other day saw quantities of tortoises, ranging from 3″ long to nearly a foot. Caught a small one. These cannot swim fast enough to get away if you wade after them. Compared with land tortoises they are not very retractile, keep their heads & limbs out even when you are holding them, & have no power to withdraw the tail. They draw their head into a kind of cylinder of skin like a muffler. They do not seem able to stay under water long without coming up for air.[23] In the same tank, underneath a stone, found some tiny leeches about ¼″ long. The first I have seen in this country.

Last night found a huge toad in the flower bed. The first I have seen here. Nearly twice the size of an English toad, very warty & able to leap a considerable way.

Shallots in the fields almost ripe. Peasant brought us some young leeks.

Today saw a dead dog by the roadside. I am afraid the same one as came asking for food a few days back, & I am afraid probably dead of starvation.

The peasants here evidently use no harrows or cultivators, merely plough the soil & then sow on the rough ridges. Curiously enough the result is to give the impression that the grain is sown in rows, though of course actually broadcast. A good deal of wheat coming up now. Broad beans about 6′ high.

23. *without coming up for air:* compare this with George Bowling in *Coming Up for Air* (which Orwell wrote whilst in Morocco): 'You know the feeling I had. Coming up for air! Like the big sea-turtles when they come paddling up to the surface, stick their noses out and fill their lungs with a great gulp before they sink down again among the seaweed and the octopuses. We're all stifling at the bottom of a dustbin, but I'd found the way to the top' (*CW*, VII, *Coming Up for Air*, p. 177). Orwell does not mention a title for this novel before its publication, 12 June 1939.

D

14.11.38: Planted out nasturtiums.

D

16.11.38: One egg.

D

17.11.38: One egg.

D

19.11.38: Two eggs.

D

21.11.38: Two eggs.

D

22.11.38: One egg.

M

VILLA SIMONT 22.11.38:

Some days back visiting the British consul. The latter (name Robert Parr) is man of about 40, cultivated, very hospitable, married, appears to be in easy circumstances. Speaks French, very careful and grammatically very correct, but very strong English accent and manner while speaking of mentally going over grammar rules. The Assistant Consul or Vice Consul is young Englishman son of missionary, who has apparently been brought up in Morocco. Nevertheless has more characteristically English manner and accent than, eg. an Englishman brought up in India.

Parr considers I was wrong about the local French attitude to the crisis. Thinks they really believed war was coming and were prepared to go through with it though thoroughly fed up. Their apparent indifference was mere surface stolidity. He believes that there will be no general election for sometime to come. Says the scandals about the Air Ministry were very bad and known to everybody,[24] and the Government would prefer to make this good before risking an election. Says he has been struck by the number of more or less ordinary Conservatives he has met who are becoming perturbed by the Government's foreign policy. Thinks a likely development in the near future would be an attempt to revive the old Liberal Party. His own opinions seem to be moderately conservative. Could not be sure, whether, as a Government servant, he has any inside knowledge of what is going on, but gather not.

Ref. note on wheat prices above, a quintal equals about 2 cwt. Recently paid Frs. 31.50 for a measure, a decalitre I think, which appears to weigh about 40 lbs. This works out at nearly the same price, ie. about 10 centimes a pound. Seventy centimes equals about a penny in English money, so that the price of wheat here is at about the English price-level. Have not yet been able to secure full price lists, but it would appear that the things cheaper here (ie. when the franc is taken as being equal to its exchange value) are meat, certain fruits and vegetables, most of the products of the local hand-workers (leather, earthenware, certain kinds of metal work and heavy-quality woollen cloth) and, of course, rent. Imported goods, especially manufactures, are all expensive. Oil of all descriptions notably expensive.

It appears that the negroes in Senegal are French citizens, the Arabs in Morocco not, this province being still called by a fiction the Cherifien Empire. *All* negroes are liable for military service just the same as Frenchmen. In Morocco only French subjects, ie. mostly Europeans, do compulsory service. The Arab troops are voluntarily engaged men and enlist for long periods. They appear to get a (by local standards) respectable pension for long service. Eg. our servant Mahdjoub Mahommed, who served about 15 years in an Arab line regiment, gets a pension of about Frs. 5 a day. Forgot to mention earlier that at the entrance to Marrakech there is a toll-station where all incoming lorries etc. have to unload and pay a tax on any goods being brought in for sale. This applies to all the vegetables taken in to market by the peasants. Do not know amount of tax, but it makes an appreciable difference to the price if one buys vegetables etc. outside the town.

24. *scandals about the Air Ministry:* this might refer to a demand by MPs on 12 May 1938 for an inquiry into the state of Britain's air defences. Sir Hugh Dowding (1882–1970), who commanded Fighter Command in the Battle of Britain, is reported to have expressed relief when Neville Chamberlain returned from Munich after the deal made with Hitler (however shabby it was) because the supply of Spitfires was not yet coming fully on stream.

D

23.11.38: One egg.

Weather fine & warm, not particularly hot. Fires some evenings. When it is reasonably clear the snow peaks of the Atlas now seem so close that one would think them only a few miles away (actually 50-100 miles I suppose.) Nearly all the seeds, except marigolds, sweet peas & nasturtiums have done very badly & most have failed to germinate, no doubt owing to having been kept for years in stock. It seems very difficult here to grow any small flowers, which are easily killed by the heat & drought. Gardens mostly specialise in shrubs.

Paid Frs. 31.50 for a measure of wheat (roundabout 40 lb. = about 1d a lb.)

Have been ill (chest) since 16th. Got up yesterday & somewhat better today.

D

24.11.38: One egg.

Cylinder of Butagaz gave out yesterday. That makes 5 weeks. It has supplied pretty regularly 3 gas-jets (one of them higher candle-power – I think 60 – than the others) & a fourth occasionally.

D

25.11.38: Two eggs.

D

27.11.38: One egg.

D

28.11.38: Two eggs.

D

29.11.38: One egg.

D

30.11.38: Two eggs.

D

1.12.38: Two eggs. (This makes 30 since 26.10.38.)

D

2.12.38: The weather has been much cooler, some days clear & fine, much like English spring, sometimes heavy mist. The day before yesterday fairly heavy rain. On clear days the Atlas mountains look extremely close, so that you can distinguish every contour, on other days completely invisible.

Very poor success with the flower seeds. Only nasturtiums, sweet peas, marigolds, carnations & a very few pinks & clarkia germinated. Phlox, pansies, violas, godetias, poppies & sunflowers failed entirely to come up, though soil conditions etc. were all right. Presumably due to seed having been in stock for years.

Find that the weaker of the two catapults will throw a stone (less satisfactory than buckshot) 90 yards at most. So a powerful catapult[25] ought to throw a buckshot about 150 yards.

Three eggs.

25. In *The Lost Orwell,* Plate 10 illustrates Orwell firing a catapult in Morocco.

D

3.12.38: Two eggs.

The tallest palms are about 25 yards high (to the base of the leaves.)

D

4.12.38: Two eggs.

D

5.12.38: Three eggs.

On a patch which I saw being ploughed 30th October or a day or two earlier, the grain is now 4–6″ high.

Oranges now ripe & on sale everywhere. Pomegranates now on sale are over-ripe & quite a different colour, brown instead of red.

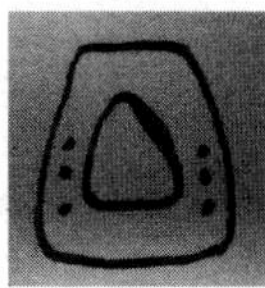

Form of donkey shoe used here.

D

6.12.38: Two eggs. Nights now are distinctly chilly.

D

7.12.38: Two eggs.

Yesterday afternoon much hotter.

Looking at the beds of streams here, it is evident that the streams have shrunk very greatly, though whether recently or not I do not know. The stream along which we walked yesterday had in effect three beds. The bed in which it was actually running; perhaps 6′ wide & 1′ deep, a bed about 10′ wide into which it evidently swells at the wettest season of the year, & outside this a wide bed channelled out of the chalk which showed that at some time in the past what is now a tiny stream was a considerable river.

Many more small birds about now. I suppose some of them migrants. Leaves of the pomegranate trees yellowing.

D

8.12.38: Two eggs.

In the morning dust-storms, then fairly heavy rain. The afternoon cold & misty, just like England.

D

9.12.38: Two eggs.

Notice that ibises always collect round a man digging & are very tame then. Presumably after worms etc. They did not do this in Burma. Probably there is next to no food in the streams here.

D

10.12.38: One egg.

M

VILLA SIMONT 10.12.38:

Cannot get any definite idea of the system of land tenure here, whether the peasants own their plots, whether they rent them etc. Land appears to be held in plots of two or three acres upwards. Evidently there are common grazing grounds, and there must obviously be some communal arrangement for the distribution of water. The small streams are diverted in different directions according as they are wanted, and by means of the channels and small dykes which exist in the fields water can be run to almost any spot. Nevertheless there is an obvious great difference in the water supply between peasants' plots and the plantations of Europeans and wealthy Arabs. The difficulty about water makes an immense amount of work. The soil in parts here is a sort of soft chalk which has streams running through it about twenty feet down. In order to get at this – often a stream of a few inches deep – wells are sunk at intervals. One sometimes finds such wells all along the edge of a field a few yards apart –

why so many I do not know, but I have seen this in a number of fields, eg. one field had 12 wells along its edge. There is evidence of great shrinkage in the water supply in recent years. Some streams have three beds, ie. one they run in now, a wider one they presumably run in after the rainiest season, and a much larger one they ran in at some time in the past. Some recently cultivated fields seem to have gone out of cultivation. It seems very difficult to get small seeds to germinate without constantly watering the soil.

The peasants here evidently do not use harrows, but they appear to plough it over several times in different directions. At the end of course it is still in furrows. This has the advantage that it gives the seed (broadcast) a certain tendency to lie in straight lines. Also perhaps conserves water better.

The winter grain (I suppose barley) is now about 4–6″ high. Trees seem to do better here than small crops, eg. the olives (black and known for their bitterness) are good. Nevertheless there are practically no trees except cultivated ones, palms, olives etc. Firewood,* ready chopped and good quality, costs about 70–80 frs. (about 8/–) for 1000 kilos (about 1 ton). The only fuel here wood and charcoal. Near here a large new plantation of olives etc. run by Frenchmen. A sort of cooly barracks for the Arab workers. Quite good, very much better than the corresponding kind of thing would be in India. Except for a few wealthy ones the Arabs in their villages almost all live in tiny straw or palm-thatch huts, like beehives, about 8–10 feet wide. A few wild-looking people living in tiny tents which are simply a piece of cloth stretched over a pole, no walls or flaps. Evidently more or less permanent, as they had built little enclosures round. Normally a village is surrounded by a mud wall about 10 feet high with thorns on top. As in Burma, only men plough but women do all other jobs in the fields, especially tiresome jobs like weeding. Children working, usually at herding animals, when they are almost too young to speak. They are extraordinarily good, never stray away from work and seem to understand exactly what they have to do. Many of the peasants one sees come out and beg as one passes. With some of them this seems to be a reflex action on sight of a European. Generally quite satisfied with 20c. None of the peasant women, at least those one sees working, are veiled.

Examining the *Petit Marocain*, find its make-up is as follows. 10 pages (some days 12) ie. 60 columns. Of this just over one third is filled with advertisements. Back page and last page but one entirely advertisements. Principal adverts are Persil and other Lever products (note it is always

* Always olive-wood, mostly roots [Orwell's note].

stated on the packet that Lever's stuff is French product), Nestlé's milk, various shipping companies, several eye-tonics and other patent medicines. Special pages are set aside for Moroccan news, which does not as a rule figure on the front page. No book reviews, and though get-up etc. is good the general tone of writing is dull compared with ordinary French papers.

All the papers here heavily patriotic. Eg. when Marshal Lyautey's[26] statue was being brought to Casablanca, both *Petit* and *Presse* for over three weeks gave never less than a column and often most of a page to the subject, ie. to adulations of Lyautey. On the actual day of the installation the *Presse* gave its entire front page to this. *La Presse* frequently demands the suppression of the Communist Party, the *Petit* not, tho' Daladier [*see above,* n. 13] is its hero and it reports de la Rocque[27] sympathetically. The most widely-read French paper in Marrakech seems to be the weekly *Candide,* which is sold on the streets everywhere. On buying it find it is virtually Fascist. Left-wing French papers seem unobtainable here.

M. Simont has sacked Hussein, evidently on the ground that he was lazy. The job here (for one man) is to look after about 2 acres planted with orange and lemon trees, and part of the ground between the trees, perhaps 20–30 rods, down under marrows etc. Also to look after a few sheep. By European standards it would be said that Hussein worked hard. M. Simont complaining that Hussein (who evidently also had some negro blood) is a Cleuh.[28] They are said to be stupid, shiftless etc. Arabs also accuse them of avarice. Apparently Europeans share the prejudice. Do not know what the pay for this job would be, but probably not more than 10 frs. a day and quarters.

26. *Marshall Louis-Hubert-Gonzalve Lyautey* (1854–1934): was, as French Resident-General of Morocco, largely responsible for the development of the country. He was French Minister of War, 1916–17, and organised the Colonial Exhibition in Paris in 1931.
27. *Colonel François de la Rocque* (1885–1946): leading figure of the extreme right who led the Croix de Feu, an anti-Marxist and anti-capitalist group. It was banned but reconstituted as the Parti Social Français (1936–40). He was anti-German and did not become a collaborator. See also 'Diary of Events', 6.8.39.
28. *Cleuh:* (also spelt Chleuh by Orwell; sometimes spelt as Shleuh and Shluh. Orwell's different spellings are reproduced here); a Berber ethnic group living chiefly in the Atlas Mountains of Morocco. See Orwell's reference to their speaking 'their own Berber dialect' and that they 'all speak Arabic' in his Moroccan Diary for 27 January 1939.

D

11.12.38: Two eggs.

Chilly & overcast, rain in afternoon.

D

12.12.38: Heavy rain all night. Cold & overcast, much like November weather in England. E[ileen] has neuralgia, probably owing to going out in the rain yesterday.

Raining most of the day.

Two eggs. (3 since 26.10.38, 23 since 1.12.38. One hen is now broody.)

D

13.12.38: Two eggs.

D

14.12.38: Three eggs.

Chilly & fine. Very heavy dew these days.

D

15.12.38: Two eggs.

Clear, fine & not hot.

D

16.12.38: Two eggs.

Fine & cool. Domestic animals here eat almost anything. Donkey eating old dried-up vegetable marrow leaves off a rubbish heap. Cows, goats & sheep being fed on waste leaves from crown artichokes. Notice that when goats & sheep are herded together, the goats fight among themselves but do not go for the sheep.

Picked up pellet of some fairly large hawk. Only wing-cases etc. of insects, mostly woodlice. Have not yet seen a snake in Morocco, though recently we picked up a fresh slough of one.

Oranges when ripe enough to pick can apparently be left on the trees for some time without falling. Wholesale price of oranges (at any rate locally) Frs. 2.30 or 3 a dozen.

Saw a dead donkey the other day – the first I have seen. The wretched brute had simply dropped & died beside one of the tracks leading from Marrakech to the Oued, & was left lying there by the owner. A few dogs hanging round waiting to start on it, but with a guilty air.

D

17.12.38: One egg.

Very heavy rain in the night. Cold during morning, about ½ hour's sun in the afternoon, then more rain. Everything flooded, the Oued Tensift swollen to considerable size – bed is 50 yards wide in places.

The donkey (actually seen dead on 11.12.38.) now an almost completely clean skeleton. Notice that they leave the head till last.

D

18.12.38: Two eggs.

D

19.12.38: Three eggs.

Heavy rain in the night. Today cold & cloudy, with heavy showers & violent wind.

D

20.12.38: Two eggs.

Heavy rain at night, raining on & off all day. The little stream we followed up some time back, then a tiny trickle of water, is now a rushing torrent about 10 yards wide. Today saw two rainbows parallel in the sky, a thing I have not seen before.

D

21.12.38: Two eggs.

Finer, cool, a few spots of rain.

One of the pigeons is dead – cause unknown.

D

22.12.38: Three eggs.

Finer in the morning, rain in the afternoon.

The surviving pigeon (presumably the hen) is sitting on a nest. Do not know whether it can survive, but possibly we may be able to get another cock for it.

The Oued Tensift has now filled up the whole of the valley it runs in, so that at the bridge it is about 300 yards wide (previously about 10 yards). Judging from the vegetation in the valley I should say this is unusual.

M

VILLA SIMONT 22.12.38:

After heavy rain such as that of the last few days the rivers swell enormously. The Oued Tensift, normally about 10 yards wide, has filled the whole valley it runs in, about 300 yards wide. But judging from the vegetation in the valley this does not happen most years.

The Arab funerals here are the wretchedest I have seen. The dead man is carried by friends and relatives on a rough wooden bier, wrapped in a cloth. Don't know whether this is due to poverty, or whether Mahomedans are supposed not to have coffins. A hole not more than two feet deep is hacked in the ground and the body dumped in it with nothing over it except a mound of earth and usually either a brick or a broken pot at one end, presumably the head. The burial places as a rule are not walled in in any way and except when there happens to be the tomb of some rich person there one would never know them for burial-places – they merely look like a rather hummocky piece of ground. No sort of identifying mark over the graves. On one, presumably of a scribe, I found a pen and inkhorn, otherwise only the broken pots etc. On one an enamel tin mug. A few vacant graves always waiting, including little ones for children. Women apparently never attend funerals.

The other widely-read French weekly paper is *Gringoire*.* Used to be a sort of gossipy literary paper, but now much as *Candide*. I notice that these papers, though evidently prosperous and having a lot of advertisements, are not above inserting pornographic advertisements. Also that in spite of their politics they publish serial stories etc. by writers who are more or less "left". On a wall in a café lavatory, "A mort Blum"[29] in very small letters. The first political inscription I have seen in French Morocco.

29. Leon Blum (1872–1950) was the first Socialist premier of France, 1936–37, 1938, presiding over a popular front government. He was imprisoned in France and Germany from 1942 until the end of World War II, and was again premier, 1946–47.

D

23.12.38: The pigeon has laid two eggs & is sitting on them.

Cold & fine. The Oued Tensift has shrunk to about twice its original size. Three eggs.

D

24.12.38: Four eggs.

Both the pigeons eggs broken – do not know how, possibly a cat tried to get up to the nest & scared the bird off. Evidently fertile eggs, as they were streaked with blood.

Clear & fine.

D

25.12.38: Quite a heavy frost in the night, everything white this morning, & a little cat-ice on the pools. Curious sight of oranges & lemons on the trees frosted over, & lemon blossom frozen stiff. Do not yet know whether it has done much damage. Bourgainvillea° blossoms look all right. Should not think frosts can be common here, but at the moment there is a wave of cold all over the world. The mountains have for sometime past been covered with snow even on the lower slopes.

Four eggs.

D

26.12.38:
27:
28: } Have been ill. Not certain number of eggs, but about 9.

Weather clear & fine.

Second cylinder of Butagaz ended 27.12.38. Exactly 3 weeks (same as last time.)[30]

30. The previous cylinder lasted five weeks; see 24.11.38

* "Gringoire" claims circulation of ½ million, evidently truthfully [Orwell's note].

D

29.12.38: Two eggs.

Clear & fine. We have got a cock-pigeon (Frs. 4.50) & put him in the cage with the hen to get acquainted. She started pecking his head gently, I think picking out lice.

D

30.12.38: Large flight (about 200) of storks or cranes passing over. Large white birds, apparently with black edges to their wings. Flying northward, but probably merely circling round to find a place to settle, as they must be migrants from Europe.

Very fine, clear & chilly. No wind.

Two eggs.

D

31.12.38: Three eggs. (102 eggs since 26.10.38 or nearly 12 a week).

1939

D

1.1.39: Three eggs.

The cock pigeon, which at first was rather sorry for himself, no doubt owing to having been confined in a cage & having had his wings bound, is better & trying to fly a little. The female at first courting him, walking round him & bowing.

Another dead donkey, with two dogs tearing its entrails out. The third I have seen. They never seem to bury them when they die.

The pepper trees, whose peppercorns were ripening about September, have now got a fresh crop on them. The nasturtiums which were nipped by the frost are mostly dead. Ditto the vegetable marrows, & the foliage of the brinjals is all withered off.

Clear & fine, not particularly cold, nice sun & no wind. E[ileen] saw four more storks.

The oranges etc., & even apparently the lemon blossom, not in the least damaged by the frost.

D

2.1.39: Two eggs.

D

3.1.39: Three eggs.

D

4.1.39: Three eggs.

Clear, fine & generally rather cold (wearing light undervest, cotton shirt, pullover, coat, light pants & grey flannel bags), & do not find this too much. Night before last the cock pigeon, which was only just regaining its power of flight, disappeared, evidently destroyed by one of the Arabs' dogs. Bought another yesterday (Frs. 6.). This one's wings are all right. Put him for the night in the cage, in the morning found the hen outside. Opened the door & they flew off together.

D

5.1.39: Two eggs.

D

6.1.39: Three eggs.

D

7.1.39: Three eggs. There are now 3 hens broody. The pigeons are all right.

Yesterday saw some men fishing in the Oued Tensift. Miserable little fish about the size of sardines. The bait is a kind of small earthworm which is found in the mud beside the river.

Day before yesterday came on some men waiting with a she-camel which had fallen in the middle of the bridge over the Oued. It was apparently about to have a calf. Belly greatly swollen up, sexual organs bleeding slightly. The creature lay on its side, its head in the air, sniffing, with a kind of air of astonishment, but evidently not in pain. An hour or so later just the same. Today passed that way. Big pool of blood on the ground, & the marks of something bloody being dragged away. Calf probably born dead.

Clear, very fine, cold in the shade, warm in the sun. We now have a hot water bottle every night, & 3 blankets & a rug on the bed.

D

8.1.39: Three eggs.

M

VILLA SIMONT 8.1.39:

Cost of sending four rather heavy parcels to England, about Frs. 400.[31] Two others not quite so heavy about Frs. 100 the two. The red tape in post offices here even worse than in France. The two which E[ileen] and I despatched personally took us over two hours. First about half an hour's wait to get a place at the counter. This not due to Xmas, as it is always much the same. Then endless filling up of forms and the usual search by the officials through large books to find out which forms should be used. Then the usual complaint that the parcels were insufficiently secure. One had not thick enough string, the other which was enveloped in cloth had to be sewn up. Went out and bought string, needles and thread and did the sewing up. Then a complaint because the parcels were not sealed. Fresh journey to buy sealing wax. This kind of thing seems inseparable from French post offices. Notice that most of the minor officials here, of the type who in India would be Indians, are French. Eg. all the post-office clerks and clerks in the other offices, and even most of the traffic policemen.

Supply of native clerks evidently does not exist. Most Arabs who are in contact with Europeans speak a little French, but have not yet met an Arab whose French seemed to be perfect.

31. *Frs. 400:* approximately £2.35 at the time (say £90 at today's values).

On Xmas Eve there was a very heavy frost here, which did a good deal of damage. From the type of vegetation and what the Arabs say I do not think this can be usual. Notice, however, that oranges and lemons were quite unaffected by it.

The French here seem to take even less notice of Xmas than in France. They celebrate New Year. Arabs all acquainted with New Year and use it as a pretext for begging. There are said to be less tourists than usual this year.

People gathering lucerne draw it up with their hands instead of cutting with the sickle, thus saving an inch or two on each plant. The people in the little walled village near the house give the impression of owning their land communally, as they all turn out and do the same jobs, weeding, ploughing etc., together.

Examined recently the grave of what was evidently a fairly rich man, in a little mud enclosure. A concrete grave of the usual pattern, with a sort of little oven evidently for burnt offerings at the head. No name on the grave. On a tree over the grave various little charms, bunches of wool etc., hanging. Stole one of the charms, a sort of little leather purse. Inside it a bunch of wool and a paper with writing.

D

9.1.39: Two eggs. Saw large flock of green plover, apparently the same as in England. Clear & fine, afternoons fairly warm.

D

10.1.39: Three eggs.

D

11.1.39: One egg.

D

12.1.39: Three eggs.

D

13.1.39: Two eggs. (135 since 26.10.38.)

In the cleft of the rock on the N. side of one of the little hills near hear° are growing a plant like angelica, a fleshy plant with round leaves & quantities of moss. Evidently these can only grow in places where the sun does not reach them at any time.

D

14.1.39: to 17.1.39: Four eggs (about 4 of the hens now broody.)

Saw a stork standing among the ibises the other day. It is enormous – English heron would look small beside it.

Greenfinch evidently exists here as well as the goldfinch, both as in Europe. Broad beans grown round here are very good, no black fly at all. It seems tangerines are damaged by frost though ordinary oranges are not.

M

VILLA SIMONT 27.1.39:

Have just returned after spending a week at Taddert in the Atlas, about 95 km. from Marrakech. T. is at 1650 metres elevation, ie. about 5000 ft. When one gets about 2000 feet above the plain (itself about 1000 feet above sea level) one gets to a different type of vegetation, oaks and firs, more or less stunted, fairly good grass, of the downland type, and above about 4000 feet walnut trees, which grow profusely and very well, but evidently don't grow wild. The fig tree does grow at about 5000, but evidently doesn't do well. Almonds seem to do well. On the whole the mountain slopes are exceedingly bare and only begin to be well forested when one gets about 1000 feet above the valleys through which the main road runs. The lower slopes for about 500 feet above a village are often completely bare, mere chipped-up limestone like a slag-heap. Probably this is partly due to goats. The French Gov.t is now apparently beginning to do something about reafforestation, and is going to prohibit grazing on some of the hills. Evidently this area, even round the motor-road, is only in process of being accurately surveyed, as the landmarks for the survey people have only been newly set up. Road is good though not too wide. The bus does the journey from Marrakech to Taddert in 3 hours and the return in about 2½. There is a great deal of what appears to be iron ore in the mountains, but evidently quite unexploited. In the inhabited valleys there does not seem to be so much shortage of water as down here.

If one looks round from a high peak one sees that only about one valley in twenty, even round the motor road, is inhabited. Most of the valleys are mere clefts, and evidently the soil is only cultivable in those into which the sun gets for a good deal of the day. At this time of year there is frost every night, which hangs on in shady places for most of the day. Snow drifts everywhere, but nowhere below about 6000 ft. where the hills are impassable because of snow. Cultivation is of the terrace type, much as in the hills in Burma. The terraces are very skilfully done, walled up with limestone, as in Spain, and the soil appears to be deep, 4 feet or so, though of course it is artificially made up.

In moderately shady valleys and along banks of streams there are small but quite good pastures for the cows, the goats being grazed right on the tops of the hills. Goats are as down here, the sheep mostly of a quite different breed, with exceedingly silky wool. From what people say locally and from general appearances it appears that all the villagers own a small piece of land, and of course grazing is free, though evidently each village has its recognized beat. Could not make an accurate judgement, but I should not say that more than one acre is cultivated per head of population. It appears that barley is grown in winter-spring (the barley is coming up now, though not so advanced as down here), this is cut in June and then maize is sown. The local French consider that the Chleuh are good cultivators, and they evidently use plenty of manure. Ploughing is done with a cow and donkey, as here. The people have plenty of animals, and no doubt their staple food is barley and goats' milk.

The villages are quite different from those in the plains, as they are not walled in. The houses are of mud, very occasionally limestone, and square, with flat roofs. These are thatched over with wild broom and then covered with earth, which is possible owing to the dryness. When one looks down at a village from above one sees that as a rule all the houses on the same level have a common roof, though inside they are separate. This points to a certain amount of communal life. Practically none have glass windows. What woodwork there is is mostly crude.

The Chleuh seem to be rather remarkable people. The men are not greatly different in appearance from Arabs, but the women are exceedingly striking. In general they are rather fair, sometimes fair enough to have red in their cheeks, with black hair and remarkable eyes. None are veiled, and all wear a cloth round their heads tied with blue or black cords, the dominant colours of their dress being red and blue. All the women have tattooing on their chins and sometimes down each cheek. Their manner is much less timid than that of most Arab women. Virtually the whole population is ragged and there is no evidence of any being much richer than the others. The children for the most part have nothing on but a ragged blanket. Begging is almost universal, and the women have discovered that their jewellery (amber and rough silver, some of it exceedingly well worked) is liked by Europeans and will sell it for prices that cannot be much above the value of the silver. The children beg as soon as they can walk and will follow for miles over mountain tracks in hopes of a sou. Tobacco is greatly appreciated by those who do smoke, but I notice that a great many do not, and none of the women. Children beg for bread and are glad to get it. Nevertheless it is difficult to be certain about the real amount of poverty. Probably there is no actual destitution, at any rate no one is homeless or quite propertyless. I notice under the walnut trees quantities of nuts which have been left to rot, which does not suggest serious hunger. But evidently everyone's life is at a low level.

In some parts of the mountains carpets, leatherwork etc. are made. Near Taddert the chief trade apart from agriculture seems to be charcoal-burning. The people can of course get good wood (mostly oak) free, though possibly the Gov.t will interfere with this later, and they cook it in exceedingly primitive earth ovens and sell it at Frs. 12 for a large sack (about Frs. 35 in Marrakech.) Local physique is pretty good, though the people are not particularly large or very athletic in appearance. All walk well, and the women easily walk up steep hillsides carrying a huge bundle of wood or a three-gallon stone jar of water. Apart from their own Berber dialect all speak Arabic, but few or none French. A few have reddish hair. There seems to be a Jew or two in most of the villages, not easily distinguishable from the rest of the population.

Graveyards not quite the same as the Arab ones, though the people are Mahomedans. The graveyard is generally a patch of good grass and the cattle browse among the graves. Owing to plentiful stone the graves are generally covered with a cairn, not a mere mound of earth, as here, but they have no names or other indications of individuals. Judging from a few that had fallen in, it seems usual to make the grave as a kind of cave with flat slabs of rock, and then cover this over, originally perhaps as a protection against wild animals. Some of the graves are immensely long, 8 or 10 feet. I saw one funeral. It was done in the usual way by a party of friends, one of whom kept up a sort of mumbling recitative noise. The women as usual were not present, but a group sat on a rock within sight 100 yards away and kept up a rather perfunctory kind of wailing.

Talked a number of times in Taddert with a German in the Foreign Legion, who is there on some job I could not understand, something to do with some electric installation. A friendly intelligent man, who speaks French well. Has been eight years in the Legion and does not seem particularly discontented. Intends to stay his full time to get his small pension. Says they do not give you free tobacco in the French army and that you have to serve some time before your pay reaches even a franc a day, so that newcomers generally cannot smoke. No particular political opinions. Says there were 5 million unemployed when he left Germany and that he cannot go back as he is wanted for desertion. Did not express any opinion about Hitler. Seemed mildly pro-Government in the Spanish war.

Today the news of the fall of Barcelona has come. Nobody in Marrakech seems much interested, though the papers are splashing it. I note that there are at least 2 Socialist weeklies in Morocco, the *Dépêche de Fez* and another whose name I forget. Not extreme and evidently (this is really why French Socialist papers are allowed to run and Arab ones not) not anti-imperialist. But both they and the P.S.F.[32] *Presse* keep up the abusive and scurrilous tradition of French newspapers, which the more moderate papers do not. Eg. the *Dépêche de Fez* makes accusations of German corruption of the French press, naming names. This could not be done in newspapers either in England or in India without a prosecution, though the papers would probably only be fined. On the other hand, evidently no paper in Morocco can suggest that Morocco should be independent, without being suppressed. If the papers are reporting truthfully, there were demonstrations among the Spaniards in Tangier to celebrate the fall of Barcelona, without any kind of counter-demonstrations. Yet I had had the impression that the pro-Government Spaniards in Tangier slightly outnumbered the others. The hotel at Taddert exactly like a cheap Paris hotel, and ditto with the one or two cafés on the route. The people one met, also, completely [like] the ordinary lower-middle-class French, living exactly the same life as in France except that they are obliged to speak a little Arabic.

32. *P.S.F.:* Parti Social Français: see n. 27.

D

18.2.39: Spent a week at Taddert, 1650 m. up in the Atlas, about 95 km. from Marrakech, & since then have been ill for nearly 3 weeks (about 10 days in bed.)

Most essential points about Taddert are noted in the other diary.[33] Birds seen there are as follow: raven (I rather suspect that the so-called crows down here are ravens too), partridge (fairly common), hawk, some other much larger predatory bird, possibly eagle (only seen in the distance), rock dove & wood-pigeon, blue tit, other birds much as down here, but no storks or ibises. No animals. Found in the snow on a peak tracks conceivably of mouflon, but probably goat. There was some reference to some animal called blet or bilet (presumably Arab word) which was liable to come & kill chickens etc. Tame peacocks kept at the hotel seemed to do well. Breeds of domestic animals much as here, except the sheep, which are quite different with very silky wool. Camels are used, but not taken off the main roads. Donkeys seem able to ascend almost all hills.

Trees etc.: oak (smallish), very tiny dwarf oak, wild broom, kind of heather stuff, as in Spain, blackberry, wild daffodil (or some kind of wild tulip – not in flower now), species of ash, small fir tree, various plants of sedum & saxifrage type at tops of peaks, a few with very beautiful flowers, daisy. Walnuts grow profusely, but not wild. Almonds are grown & appear to do well. Fig tree will just grow at about 5000 feet, but does not do well. The spring crop is barley, which is cut in June & followed by maize. Grass in places very good, almost like England. This is only in vicinity of streams, & evidently it has to be cultivated. In the grass a kind of edible sorrel, used in salads.

The river again much swollen after the rain of two days ago. The other day the water very clear & could see the fish, small ones about 4″ long, of barbel type (grubbing along the bottom). Shall try for them when the water subsides again. Weeds have grown tremendously & the fields are fairly green. One or two of our nasturtiums in bloom, & sweet peas etc. have grown fairly well, but I have quite neglected the garden.

Owing to illness lost count of the eggs. The hens laid 19 in the week we were away. At present only about 1 is laying.

For about 10 consecutive days the cream has tasted of garlic, some days enough to make it uneatable. Evidently the cows have got hold of some wild garlic. Williams[34] says he saw the killing of the last lion in Morocco, in 1924. Panthers & gazelles said to be still fairly common south of the Atlas.

33. *in the other diary:* Orwell's Morocco Diary (it and the Domestic Diary are here intercalated).

34. *Williams:* almost certainly an American serving in the French Foreign Legion, described in the Moroccan Diary for 12 March 1939. He is probably one of the group of three illustrated in *The Lost Orwell*, plate 16.

D

20.2.39: Wallflowers (good specimens) are blooming at the café near here. Pomegranate trees just putting forth their buds, which are brilliant red. Weeds pretty thick everywhere. This is probably as green as the country ever gets, but there are still considerable dried-up patches. Yesterday saw some wheat green but in fairly good ear.

Local method of hobbling cow with grass rope (base of horn to below knee).

Saw two storks nesting today. The nest is enormous, about twice as wide as a heron's nest & also several feet deep, a huge mass of twigs filling a whole fork of a large tree. The hen was evidently in the act of laying an egg, the cock standing beside her; presently she got up & they stood side by side. Our hen pigeon laid two more eggs & sat there for some days, then both she & the cock were mysteriously destroyed & disappeared – only a few feathers left. Said to be cats but suspect humans. That makes 4 we have lost &, of course, we shall not have any more. They evidently breed readily here. Three or four of those at the café now have eggs.

It is getting noticeably hotter & flies beginning to be a nuisance again.

Forgot to mention that at Taddert the people had camel's hair ropes, very pliable & seemed strong.

D

22.2.39: Heavy mist yesterday morning. In general distinctly hotter. A lot of wild flowers now, two of marigold type, a sort of daisy, & various others.

D

24.2.39: Pretty heavy rain last night & this morning.

Found sprays of fennel, which evidently grows here. Saw very large slow-moving black & white birds, evidently of hawk tribe. Forgot to mention curious property of human shadows, noticed at Taddert. Sometimes one stands on a crag whose shadow is cast hundreds of feet below. If one stands right on the edge of it, naturally one's shadow is cast beyond that of the crag. But I notice that whereas the shadow of the rock is black & solid, that of the human body, at anything over about 50 feet, is faint & indistinct, like the shadow of a bush. At short distances this is not noticeable & the shadow seems solid, but at long distances, say 200 feet & over, one seems to have almost no shadow at all. At certain distances the body as a whole has a sort of shadow, but, eg., the arm by itself none. I do not know whether this is because, relative to rock, the human body is not opaque, or whether it is merely a question of size.

D

4.3.39: A good deal hotter. Flies not so bad again, however, perhaps owing to rain.

A boy offered me a quail which he had just caught the other day. Much the same as those in Spain.

Many wild flowers now, including some the same or almost the same as in England. Poppies, bacon & eggs,[35] a sort of small marguerite not unlike the English daisy, a very tiny flower of primula or polyanthus type, some small flowers resembling dandelions, & a purple flower with petals not unlike those of a foxglove, but smaller. Also anchusa, bird's eye.[36] Wild marigolds are much the commonest, growing in thick clumps everywhere.

Barley is now in good ear, though still green, in many fields. Where identifiable, nearly all the crops I have seen are barley. They vary, but on the whole seem good. Cherry trees everywhere in blossom. Apples coming into leaf. Pomegranate buds getting large – these evidently put forth leaves before flowers. Lemon trees have fruit at all stages from blossom to ripe fruit on them simultaneously. These apparently continue the year round. Fig buds just appearing. Broad beans about ready to pick (green), lettuces now very good, also peas, carrots & rather small turnips. Evidently some vegetables can be grown more or less continuously here. It is noticeable that there are extremely few insect pests on the vegetables. Men cutting some tall grass resembling wheat or barley, but presumably not that, used for fodder. People also everywhere cutting & carrying home donkey-loads of the weeds which have sprung up everywhere.

The other day caught a young water-tortoise about this size or perhaps a little smaller. Perfectly formed, but at this age the tail is relatively larger. Presumably it had not been long out of the egg, so this must be the breeding season. Have not seen any adult tortoises for some time past. Yesterday saw a centipede about 3–4″ long – the first seen here.

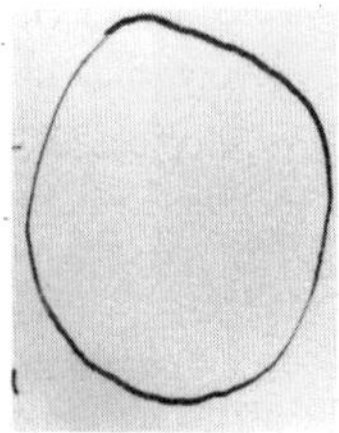

35. *bacon & eggs:* according to Geoffrey Grigson, *The Englishman's Flora*, a Somerset name for the water crowfoot (*Ranunculus fluitans*); and a Wiltshire name for toadflax (*Linaria vulgaris*). Possibly also the bulbous buttercup.
36. *anchusa, bird's eye:* Grigson gives bird's eye as a popular name for sixteen plants.

D

9.3.39: Quite hot, but today cloudy. Most of our nasturtiums in flower & everything else growing rapidly.

Mosquitoes rather bad.

M. Simont uses blood, in considerable quantities (which he can get as he is a butcher) for manuring the orange trees.

D

11.3.39: Yesterday found a dead snake, about 2′ long, the first seen in Morocco.

Very hot. It is said that this year there has been more rain than usual, so it should be a good year.

Another wildflower now common is pale yellow with deeper yellow centre, about 2″ across, & resembles a small sunflower.

M

12.3.39 VILLA SIMONT:

The section of the Morocco Diary from 12 March to 'Japanese and apart' in the fourth sentence of 28 March exists in manuscript and typed forms. Both are Orwell's work. The typed version is given here, except for obvious errors. Variants are listed in *The Complete Works*, vol XI, after each diary entry.

Troops returning from manoeuvres passed the house a few days back, to the number of about 5000 men, more than half of these Senegalese. The spahis look pretty good, general physique better than the average of the population. Horses about 14 hands, strong but not much breed, all colours, whites and greys predominating, seemingly some castrated and some not, but no mares (never ridden in this country). Notice at the rifle range all horses are well accustomed to fire. Seeing them on the march en masse, I do not now think (as I did before) that the Senegalese infantry are superior to the Arabs. They look much of a muchness. With the cavalry were some kind of small-bore quick-firing guns – could not see the mechanism as they were enveloped in canvas, but evidently the bore of the gun was 1″ or less. Rubber tyres to wheels. Transport wagons have huge all-steel disc wheels and are pulled by three mules. In addition there were pack batteries (screw guns). These guns were round about 3″, perhaps 75 mm, though, of course, different from the quick-firer 75 mm. field gun. To carry the whole gun, ammunition etc. evidently requires 6–8 mules. The breech-piece of the gun is a load for one mule. A column such as we saw could manoeuvre without difficulty anywhere in country such as this, except in the mountains. The men are sent on manoeuvre with their heavy khaki overcoats etc., but do not seem to be overloaded as they used to be. Most seemed to be carrying 40–50lb.

Five English and Americans from the Foreign Legion have been to visit us from time to time:[37]

Craig: Glasgow Irish, but Orange. Fairly superior working-class, claims that his father is well-paid office employee and to have been the same himself. Age about 25, healthy and good physique. Distinct signs of paranoia (boasting about past grandeurs etc.) as is usual with these types. Has been about 2½ years in the Legion and spent half of this in prison camps etc., having made two attempts to desert. Speaks little French. Somewhat "anti-red", showed hostility at mention of Maxton.[38] Does not like the French and would try not to fight if war came.

Williams: American, dark hair, possibly touch of dark blood. Health and physique not very good. Has nearly finished his 15 years, then gets small pension (about 500 francs a month) and expects to remain in Morocco. Is now orderly at the officers' mess. Not well-educated but well-disposed and evidently thoughtful.

Rowlands: Age about 30–35. "Superior" type and curious accent which might belong to an Eurasian. Drinks when possible. Has done 5 years in the Legion, or nearly, and thinks of leaving (they engage for 3 years and can then re-engage if they wish). Evidently has not been much in trouble. Gentle disposition, thoughtful type, but not intelligent.

Smith: American, age about 40, employed as bandsman. Some tendency to drink. Has a good many years of service. Not intelligent but evidently good-hearted.

Also a young Scotsman whom I only met once. Evidently there are only two or three other Englishmen and Americans in this lot (the 4th). It is clear that Englishmen etc. don't get on, will not put up with the rough conditions etc., and are also handicapped by inability to learn French, which the Germans are better able to do. All the above-mentioned are still privates. The Legion is predominantly German and the NCOs are usually Germans. It is clear that life in the Legion is now thoroughly dull. None of the above has seen any fighting except innocuous skirmishes. Fights occur among the men sometimes, but the duelling once prevalent has been put down. After a year or so of service a legionnaire is still only earning about 2 francs a day (3d), and it never gets much above this unless he becomes an NCO. A sergeant gets 1200 francs a month but has to pay for his food and also something for his clothes. Uniforms are badly-fitting but the men get a fair quantity of clothes. They have to launder them themselves. Each man gets ½ litre of wine a day. There is no free tobacco issue, and recruits are usually unable to smoke for their first six months.

37. The legionaries are illustrated, and also some of the women Orwell describes in his Diary, in *The Lost Orwell*, Plates 11–16 and pp. 240–1.
38. James Maxton (1885–1946), an Independent Labour MP, 1922–46; Chairman of the ILP, 1926–31, 1934–39. He approved in Parliament on 28 September 1938 Prime Minister Neville Chamberlain's announcement that Hitler had agreed to a four-power conference at Munich.

After the collapse of Catalonia the *Petit Marocain* immediately became much more pro-Franco. Every comparison of French papers with those we receive from England makes it clear that the French and British publics get their news in very different forms, and that one or other press, more probably both, is habitually lying. Eg. the local press did not mention the machine-gunning of refugees in Catalonia, alleged in the English press. To judge from the legionnaires' rumours there is still some expectation of war. Once the rumour went round that they were to be mobilised tonight. Within the last few days they have received a large consignment of machine guns and other small-arms at the depot here, as though in expectation of fresh drafts of men. Whenever a French warship touches at Casablanca numbers of the sailors are sent on voluntary-compulsory trips to Marrakech, where they fraternise with the soldiers.

Some of the crops of barley are now in ear and look fairly good. It appears that by local standards there has been a large rainfall this year and crops are expected to be good.

D

16.3.39: Yesterday not quite so hot, overcast & clouds of dust. Ditto today, probably presaging rain.

Other wild flowers here: a kind of small scabious, several vetches, one of them very pretty, with a flower about the size of that of a garden pea, in two colours, pink & magenta. Several new ones in the last few days which I cannot identify. In many places the ground is now actually covered with them, predominantly the wild marigold, a pale yellow flower which is evidently mustard, & a smallish daisy not unlike the English one. Yesterday three greenfinches, a cock & two hens, sitting on the telephone wires:

1st. greenfinch: "Little bit of bread."
2nd. " : "Little bit of bread."
1st. " : "Little bit of bread."
2nd. " : "Little bit of bread."
3rd. (the cock): "Che-e-e-e-e-e-se!"

Men still ploughing in places. Yesterday a man sowing, broadcast out of a bag. Flocks of domestic pigeons swooping down to try & steal the seed, & the men chasing them off.

Yesterday saw a very young camel cub, evidently only a few days born as it still had a bit of navel-string. Nevertheless its legs were almost as long as its mother's.

Cavalry passing yesterday. Note that all the horses seem to be stallions.

M

21.3.39 HOTEL DES NEGOCIANTS, MARRAKECH:

Yesterday the Sultan made an official visit and drove through the town, which had been previously decorated with flags etc. and several thousand troops to line the streets. Obviously this was intended partly as a loyalty-parade in connection with the present crisis. It is evident that the people, ie. Arabs, here have a great feeling of loyalty to the Sultan. There was much enthusiasm even in the Gueliz where normally there is not a large Arab population. Great numbers of the petty chiefs and their retainers, forming a sort of irregular cavalry, all armed with muzzle-loader guns. Evidently the French are not afraid to allow these guns (good up to 2 or 3 hundred yards in all probability) to be freely scattered about the countryside. The Arabs' loyalty to the Sultan, who is completely under the thumb of the French, makes things a lot easier for the French. Madame V[ellat] told me that Arabs will even make signs of obeisance when hearing the Sultan's voice over the radio.

The Sultan is a small, not very impressive-looking man of 30–40. Senegalese troops when seen in the mass look very good. Saw a detachment of the Foreign Legion march past. Contrary to my earlier impression, physique and carriage very good.

More attention being paid to the war-crisis this time. French people refer to it spontaneously, which they did not last time. Even Arabs talk about it, eg. our servant Madhjub Mahomed, who informed us that there was "going to be war" and that it was the same as last time, ie. against Germany. Madhjub evidently fought in Europe in the Great War. He cannot read any language, but has some ideas of geography, eg. he knows you have to cross the sea to get to Europe.

E[ileen] remarks that Arab children have no toys whatever. This seems to be the case. In the Arab quarters no toys of any sort are on sale, no dolls, kites, tops or what-not, and the very few toys (sometimes a ball) one sees in Arab children's hands are of European manufacture. In any case they don't seem to play much. Great numbers are working from the age of about 6 onward, and most seem to know the value of money almost as soon as they can walk. Soldiers in the Foreign Legion are not allowed into chemists' shops (because of drugs and poisons) without a special permit.

D

28.3.39: On board ss. *Yasukunimaru* (N.Y.K)[39] in Bay of Biscay.

39. *NYK:* Nippon Yusen Kaisha (Japanese Mail Steamer Co.). Yasukuni means 'peaceful country'; the Company's ships were named after shrines and this shrine is dedicated to the souls of soldiers killed in wars in and after the Meiji Restoration. As such it has attracted unwelcome attention in recent years. The ship was sunk by the US submarine *Trigger* on 31 January 1944 whilst on passage from Yokosuka to Truk. (Information provided by Professor Akihiro Yamada.)

The following was written in Marrakech on 21.3.39 to be written into the diary when the latter was unpacked: –

Until this afternoon, the last 3 or 4 days astonishingly cold. Two days ago in the midst of a rainstorm there was a few minutes' hail. At the public gardens many of the animals mating. Tortoises copulating, the male standing almost upright & the female when she moved dragging him round, so that probably he has a long flexible penis which can go round the edge of the shell. Ostriches showing signs of mating, the male chasing the female into a corner & getting astride her (not treading as with flying birds), the female when frightened hiding her head in the corner as a captured hare will do, so perhaps there is some truth in the tales about ostriches hiding their heads in the sand. Presumably these two are of the same species, but male & female very different in appearance, the male's plumage being black & the female's a kind of dirty grey. Male's neck is red, female's grey. Both have bare necks & thighs. Height of either bird something over 7′. They would not eat bread. Frogs making a great noise, though there were tadpoles about already. Male peacocks when displaying shiver their quills with a rustling sound, as though the wind were blowing through them. One monkey (tailless ground monkey of more or less baboon type) has a baby. Evidently about two days old, & making some attempts to move about on its own, which its mother does not allow. As she runs on all fours the baby clings to her under-side with its four legs, looking forward with its face upside down. Its hair is black, whereas that of its parents is yellowish-brown. Fingers, unlike those of its parents, are bare & much more manlike than those of adults. The monkey which is evidently the father, & another male, taking great interest in the baby, handling & examining it gently, & also gnashing their teeth at it as they do when angry with one another, but as the baby showed no fear it is presumably not a hostile gesture. The baby screamed with fright when it caught sight of E[ileen] & myself, on two occasions.

The tortoises have an egg. They have laid it inside their stone hutch, so it probably won't hatch.

The father monkey copulated with the mother, or began to do so, when she was carrying the baby in her arms.

We left Casablanca 4 pm on 26.3.39, passed Cape Finisterre 7 am on 28th & should pass Ushant 7 am on 29th. Run for the last 12 hours 378 miles (notes on this ship are in the other diary.) Weather after leaving Casablanca somewhat choppy, now while crossing the bay very calm, ie. not rough enough to disturb a ship of this tonnage. Of 3 passages across the bay I have made,[40] only one was rough. Have seen no life at all, except the gulls which have followed the ship from Casablanca, & some flights of ducks flying northward, some of them at least 50 miles from land. No seasickness, though the first 24 hours the ship rolled sufficiently to have made me sick if I had not taken Vasano.

The last few days in Casablanca beastly cold. Struck by the changed appearance of the country when coming from M[arrakech] to C[asablanca] by train, ie. the temporary greenness everywhere. Crops look pretty good, though great variation in different places. Wildflowers in huge patches, & the little compounds round the Arabs' huts so smothered in weeds that sometimes even the huts themselves were almost hidden. E[ileen] saw camels ploughing. I hadn't seen this before & thought it didn't happen, but evidently it is fairly usual as it was one of the things represented on the base of Lyautey's statue [*see 10.12.38 and n. 26*]. On this ship several kinds of plant, some of palm type, another of the laurel type, & some of the usual Japanese stunted fir trees, are successfully grown & look healthy.

40. Orwell crossed the Bay of Biscay on the way to Burma and then twice more on passage to and from Morocco. We know from his review of *The Civilization of France* by Ernst Robert Curtius (May 1932) that 'A few days before Sacco and Vanzetti were executed [22 August 1927] I was standing on the steps of one of the English banks in Marseilles' (*CW*, X, p. 244).

M

28.3.39 ON BOARD *SS. YASUKUNIMARU* (NYK) CROSSING BAY OF BISCAY:

Yasukuni is 11,950 tons. Do not yet know, but from vibrations judge that she is a motor-ship. Apart from the bridge, only 3 decks above water-level. Cabins and other appointments pretty good, but certain difficulties in that entire crew and personnel are Japanese and apart from the officers the majority do not speak much English. Second class fare Casablanca–London

£6.10. As the boat normally goes straight to London from Gibraltar & on this occasion went out of her way to deliver a load of tea, fare from Gibraltar would probably be the same. P.&O. tourist class is £6.10 London–Gibraltar. Food on this ship slightly better than on the P. & O. & service distinctly better, but the stewards here have the advantage that the ship is almost empty. Facilities for drinking not so good, or for deck games, owing to comparatively restricted space.

Do not know what the accommodation for passengers would be, but presumably at least 500. At present there are only 15 in the second class, about 12 in the third, & evidently not many in the 1st, though I don't know how many. One or two of the 2nd & 3rd class are Danes or other Scandinavians, one or two Dutch, the rest English, including some private soldiers who got on at Gibraltar. It appears that for its whole voyage the ship has been as empty as this. Since the Chino–Japanese war English people from the Far East will not travel on the Japanese boats. All the P. & O. boats said to be crowded out in consequence.

Run of the ship during the last 24 hours 378 miles. This was in pretty good weather conditions. Left Casablanca 4 pm on 26.3.39, & allowing for waiting for tides etc. in London river should apparently dock on evening of 30th or morning of 31st.[41]

41. *Later addition:* (morning of 30th) (in dock about 9 am = 87 hours Casa–dock.)

Ship gives out a cyclostyled sheet of news every day. Movies occasionally (have not seen them yet.)

In Casablanca went to the pictures, & saw films making it virtually certain that the French Gov.t expects war. The first a film on the life of a soldier, following up all the different branches & with some very good shots of the inner arrangements of the Maginot line. This film had evidently been hurriedly constructed & went into much greater detail than is normal in films of this kind. The other was the Pathé news gazette, in which the announcer gave what was practically a political speech denouncing Germany. Then more shots of British & French troops etc. The significant point was the attitude of the audience – utterly unenthusiastic, hardly a clap, & a few hostile comments.

This time all the French people are convinced it is war. A number began talking to us spontaneously about it, all deploring the prospect (eg. in one or two cases, "It does no good to us, it's only the rich who profit out of it", etc., etc.), though sometimes describing Hitler as a "salaud."

A.R.P. (ie F.A.P.A.C.) notices, calling for volunteer helpers, posted in Marrakech for the first time about 20th March. According to Madame M., whose son is at St Cyr, even the cadets there do not want war, though ready for it, of course.

MARRAKECH NOTEBOOK

This little notebook measures 5¼ x 3⅜ inches. Its leaves are perforated at the top and each has twenty-five faint lines. It was presumably carried by Orwell as he went about Marrakech so that he could note down prices. He numbered each page. Six pages have been filled in. There were about 175 francs to the £; 40 francs to the U.S. dollar.

* Copper tray about 2′ across, weight about 15 lb, F. 175.
* Donkey Fr. 75–150.
* Camel (small) Fr. 300. Prices probably go up to about Fr. 1000
* Mule Fr. 250–1000 (or more.)
* Cow in milk, about Fr. 600
* Horse (riding). Fr. 200 upwards.
* Lantern for candle Fr. 4–5.
* Women's soft leather slippers 10–15 Fr. (goodish quality.)
* Copper tray about 1′ 6″ across, second hand, worn & not heavy, Fr. 35.
* Couverture about 6′ by 4′, all wool, Fr. 40.

* Wheat, Frs. 30 the large measure, about a bushel & weight about 40 lb. Not certain whether overcharge (decalitre).
* Goats, young female, very poor but of about average standard, Frs. 30 & 35. Good goat (if obtainable) said to cost Frs. 60.
* Chopped lucerne 10c. a bunch about 3–4″ thick.
* Hire of a donkey about 2–3 Fr. an hour.
* Laying pullets, considered good specimens, Frs. 7.50 each (said to be rather high price.)

Hire of bicycle, Frs. 6 a day (probably overcharge, should be Frs. 4 or 5.)
Bran Frs. 1.35 a kg.
¾″ x ¾″ wood (presumably imported pine, sawn but not planed) 2 Fr. a metre.
6″ x ¾″ (ditto) Frs. 5 a m.
Plywood (poor quality) about Fr. 1.75 the square foot.
Firewood (more or less chopped) Frs. 80 for 1000 kg. (a ton.)
Hire of lorry, Frs. 125 for about 2 hours & 10 miles.

Cylinder of Butagaz (somewhat smaller than Calorgas) Frs. 85 (ie. price of gas only.)

Table waters, various, roundabout Frs. 3.50 a litre.

* "Mandarin" oranges, & lemons (October 20) about 50c. each.

* Other type of orange (Oct. 21, just coming in) Frs. 3.50 for 6

Canadian apples about Frs. 7 a kg.

* Oranges (10.11.38) 10 for Frs. 3.50

Candles (cheapest) 10 for 3.50. Better quality 8 for 6.50

Peas (13.11.38) Frs. 5 a kilo.

* All-wool (probably camel) dyed couverture, handspun & woven, about 8′ by 6′, 150 Fr.

* Copper tray, about 2′ 6″ across, weight about 25 lb. 300 Fr.

* String bottomed chairs (estimated 7 work-hours) 7 Frs. (Fr. 4 (?))

* Second-hand axe-head, about 6 lb., 7 Fr.

* Basket of type priced 2/– – 3/6 in England. 5 Fr. (overpayment.)

* Spherical unglazed earthenware-bowl with fitted lid, 4 Fr.

* 1 pint unglazed white earthenware cup, 1 Fr.

* 1½ pint red earthenware vase, roughly glazed inside 3 Fr. (probably overpayment.)

Slightly cheaper all-wool couverture, same measurements as above, 100 Fr.

† Cheaper style, part wool part cotton, 6′ by 4′, 30 Fr.

Small kettle (not tin, which apparently are not sold here) Fr. 9.50.

* Bellows (style 2/– to 3/6.) Fr. 7

Nails, 1½″ , 2Fr. kilo.

Cup of water, 5c.

† Common wine, 3–4 Fr. litre (French price about the same.)

† Common cigarettes, "Favorites", Fr. 1.50 for 20. (French price about Fr. 2.50–3.)

* Leather sandals, made to measure, (English price about 5/–), Fr. 25 (probably overcharge.)

* (native workmanship.) † (belongs to country.)

DOMESTIC DIARY VOLUME I CONTINUED

10 April 1939 – 26 May 1939

ORWELL and EILEEN had arrived in Marrakech on 14 September 1938 and two weeks later, at the Munich Conference, Germany won the agreement of Britain and France that Czechoslovakia should be sacrificed in a vain hope that peace in Europe might be maintained. It is too easy to condemn Chamberlain for this 'appeasement'. Remembrance of Mons, Gallipoli, the Somme, Ypres, and Passchendaele, must have weighed heavily on him, perhaps the more strongly because he had not been directly involved in this slaughter. He must have dreaded imposing such suffering on a new generation of young men and women. After all, even Orwell, as a member of the ILP, was a pacifist at this time, and, as Eileen memorably wrote, 'Chamberlain is our only hope . . . & certainly the man has courage' (27 September 1938; *CW*, XI, p. 206). However great were Chamberlain's limitations, it was also an uncomfortable fact that the RAF was in no state to take on the Luftwaffe had Chamberlain's government decided then on war. On 1 October, Germany occupied the Czech Sudetenland. Almost six months later, on 15 March 1939, Germany occupied the whole of Czechoslovakia and on 28 March Madrid surrendered to Franco's forces and the Spanish Civil War came to an end with triumph for the Fascists.

Whilst in Morocco Orwell had written *Coming Up for Air*. He and Eileen set sail for England from Casablanca on 26 March 1939. On the journey Orwell occupied himself by preparing a typescript of *Coming Up for Air*. As soon as he arrived in England, he submitted this to Victor Gollancz (to whom he was still contracted for this novel) and then travelled to Southwold to see his father who was seriously ill. The couple arrived back at Wallington on 11 April. The novel was published in an edition of 2,000 copies on 12 June 1939; a further 1,000 copies were run off in the same month. At the end of June Orwell's father died with Orwell by his side. At his death, Orwell's father's eyes were closed and, as was customary, weighted down with pennies. After the funeral, Orwell walked along Southwold promenade pondering on what he should do with these two pennies. He could not bring himself to spend them and eventually threw them into the sea.

D

10.4.39: *Southwold:* Have been here since 1.4.39, but spent most of the last week in bed.

A week ago, on arrival, weather mostly coldish, very still & rather misty. Thick sea mist on 2.4.39. Blackthorn flowering in places. Primroses abundant. Wild daffodils also plentiful, but for the most part not completely open. Fruit trees budding fairly strongly. Saw one of I do not know what kind (purplish flower) in blossom in a sheltered place two days ago. Roses, herbaceous plants etc. sprouting strongly. Starlings still in flocks on 2.4.39. Larks singing hard. Some asparagus heads a few inches above ground.

D

12.4.39: *Wallington:* Yesterday exceedingly warm & fine, said to have been the warmest day for that date for 70 years. Today even more so. We have now 26 hens, the youngest about 11 months. Yesterday 7 eggs (the hens have only recently started laying again.) Everything greatly neglected, full of weeds etc., ground very hard & dry, attributed to heavy falls of rain, then no rain at all for some weeks.

Although the hedges etc. are more forward when one gets a way from the sea, the spring on the whole seems backward.

Flowers now in bloom in the garden: polyanthus, aubretia, scilla, grape hyacinth, oxalis, a few narcissi. Many daffodils in the field. These are very° double & evidently not real wild daffodil but bulbs dropped there by accident. Bullaces & plums coming into blossom. Apple trees budding but no blossom yet. Pears in full blossom. Roses sprouting fairly strongly. I note that one of the standards which died is sprouting from the root, so evidently the stock can live when the scion is dead. Peonies sprouting strongly. Crocuses are just over. A few tulips in bud. A few leeks & parsnips in the garden (the latter have survived the winter without covering up & tops are still green), otherwise no vegetables. It appears that owing to severe frosts there are no winter greens locally.

Bats out everywhere. Have not found any birds' nests yet.

Wildflowers out: violets, primroses, celandine, anemones.

A little rhubarb showing. Blackcurrant bushes etc. for the most part have grown very weedy, probably for lack of hoeing round etc. Strawberries have all run & are covered with weeds but look fairly strong.

Sowed cos lettuce.

Leaf mould (beech) put down at end of 1937 is now well rotted down.

Found two thrushes' eggs under the hedge – no nest, somewhat mysterious, but perhaps left there by a child.

Today a stack being thrashed – oats, & seemingly no rats & few mice. Tried Marx[42] with a live baby mouse. He smelt & licked it but made no move to eat it.

Pigeons making their mating flight fly steeply up into the air then volplane down.

Four eggs.

42. *Marx*: the Orwells' dog – see n. 1.

D

13.4.39: Not so warm. A very light shower in the evening. Very dark night.

A few pansies & wallflowers starting to bloom. Pansies spread by self-sowing almost as much as marigolds. Red saxifrage coming into flower.

Ten eggs.

D

14.4.39: Cloudy, & a few small showers. Cold after dark.

Saw two swallows (not martins). This is rather early for this locality & a latish year. No one else has seen any.

All day cleaning out strawberries, which have not been touched since last year. It seems one plant will put out anything up to 12 or 15 runners. These seem to develop the best roots when they have rooted in very hard soil. Used some of them to fill up gaps & make another row. Doubtful whether they will take, but Titley[43] says it is not too late. Wallflowers in sheltered positions are full out. No apple blossom anywhere yet.

The 12 pullets which the Hollingsworths got from 24 of our eggs (White Leghorn x Buff Orpington – Sussex) have laid 1500 eggs since last autumn, or about 20 eggs per bird per month. They have been fed throughout on pig meal instead of ordinary laying mash. In the same period our own pullets of the same mating have not laid (ie. are only beginning now) owing to underfeeding.

Eight eggs.

For the first time M.[44] gave a quart today.

43. *Titley:* a neighbour.
44. *M:* Muriel, Orwell's goat. Crick, plate 19, shows Orwell feeding her. Muriel is, of course, the name of the goat in *Animal Farm.*

D

15.4.39: Chilly, windy in the evening, & light showers. Began clearing out rhubarb patch, otherwise busy moving hen-houses. Evidently it helps a good deal if one can induce them to eat a meal in or very near the houses immediately after moving these, otherwise they always wander back to the original site.

M[uriel] behaving as though on heat. Not certain, but shall note date (next should be 5–6 May.)

Saw another swallow. Thrush is sitting on eggs in our hedge. Dead nettle in flower. Sloe blossom quite pretty. The little tree I planted in the hedge 2 years [ago] & imagined to be a crab (because I found it under the apple tree & thought it was a sucker) turns out to be a bullace or wild plum.

Eight eggs.

D

16.4.39: Rather chilly with sunny intervals, not much wind. A very light shower in the morning.

Cowslips in flower here & there. This I think is rather early. Bluebells also beginning, a few in almost full bloom. This undoubtedly is unusually early. Wild cherries in full bloom. Sycamore leaves opening. Apple blossom almost about to open. Another thrush sitting [on] eggs in the hedge. Found a blackbird's nest with eggs. These are the only nests I have found hitherto.

The pond up by the church has become so stagnant that it no longer has duckweed, only the scummy green stuff. Nevertheless there are still a few newts in it.

Summer time began today, M's morning yield consequently small, but picked up in the evening.

Ten eggs. (Price of eggs sold yesterday 1/9 a score).

D

17.4.39: Rather chilly, some wind, occasional showers.

Buds of the walnut beginning to open. Lettuce seeds sown on 12.4.30 are germinating. A few tulips almost open.

Ten eggs. (57 this week.)

D

18.4.39: Fine but chilly.

Sowed broad beans. The ones sowed earlier are well up. Planted alyssum & antirrhinums.

Found a hatched thrush's egg – the first this year.

Five eggs.

Walnut buds opening.

D

19.4.39: Clear, sunny & rather warm.

Starlings have been courting for some days past, & flying about with straw in their beaks. One starling, presumably the male, sits on a bough erecting its neck feathers & making a rapid clicking noise with its beak, besides the usual crooning. A fair amount of swallows about. No martins yet.

Sowed peas (Notcutt's Lincoln, 1½ ft.) Sprayed about half the nettles under the walnut tree with sodium chlorate. Sitting-eggs came today but cannot obtain broody hens yet. M[uriel] restless & off her feed, possibly still on heat.

Very clear weather for the eclipse of the sun (annular), starting at 6.28 pm, which was easily visible. At the time of the greatest eclipse, 7.15 pm when nearly half the sun was covered, it became somewhat dark & cold, but not enough so for any reactions to be noticeable in birds etc. The hens did not go into the houses.

Nine eggs. (Today's price 1/8d a score.)

D

20.4.39: Fine & very warm all day.

Bluebells everywhere. White starlike single flower with many petals (Star of Bethlehem?) now in bloom. In the garden, forget-me-nots, tulips & one or two anemones in bloom.

The thrush near the bullace tree has not deserted her nest, as I had imagined. It is evident therefore that they can be off the nest a considerable time without the eggs getting cold.

Apple blossom just about bursting.

Impossible to get broody hens anywhere. Nobody seems to have any.

Ten eggs (plus another 5 laid out, since about the 14th).

D

21.4.39: Fine & warm all day. Very dry.

Believe I saw the first shoot of bindweed today. Scythed down a patch of nettles to see the result. It is said one can eradicate them if they are scythed down 3 or 4 times in the year. Those treated with the sodium chlorate are dying.

Sowed broccoli, savoys, leeks, sprouts, cos lettuce.

Thirteen eggs.

D

22.4.39: Cold & windy, with some sunny intervals & a few spots of rain.

Flag irises budding. Some apple blossom full out.

Planted early potatoes (Eclipse, about 10 lb.)

Procured two broody hens, but not putting them on the eggs till tomorrow, to make certain.

Paid for hens 3/6 each.

Water hens on the pond evidently have nest.

Twelve eggs.

[*Newspaper cutting:* 'Nettles have their Uses' – as a vegetable; to make beer]

D

23.4.39: Raining, but not hard, almost all day.

Lilacs almost out. Bindweed well up.

Great difficulties with so-called broody hens. One, after much reluctance, began to sit, but only took 8 eggs. The other evidently not broody at all, escaped & got among the other hens. This sitting of eggs probably wasted (2/6 the dozen.) Notice that when this hen went among the others they did not make hostile demonstration, as is usual. Probably owing to there being no cock. Tom Ridly[45] says that when keeping eggs awaiting a hen one should turn them daily, as in the incubator.

Put on a new cylinder of calor-gas.

Thirteen eggs. (It appears Titley is getting 2/– a score for his eggs.)

45. *Tom Ridley:* a neighbour (Orwell spells his surname 'Ridly').

D

24.4.39: Mostly fine, with rainy intervals, cold in the evening.

Applied more sodium chlorate. Nettles treated previously have blackened.

One hen refuses to sit. Took her home, as she may go broody again in familiar surroundings. The other sitting well on 11 eggs. She broke one in getting off to feed, so gave her one from the other sitting. Not certain of the effect of this – it will be 12–24 hours behind the others.

Preparing ground for turnips etc. Where the potatoes were last year there are practically no weeds.

A few strawberries beginning to blossom.

Fourteen eggs. (76 in this week – as from Sat. next shall begin ending week on Saturday.)

[*From 25 April to 9 May Diary is written in Eileen's hand.*]

D

25.4.39: Raining most of the day, & cold. 14 eggs.

D

26.4.39: Sharp frost in the night. Raining. Short fall of snow in the morning. The doubtful hen sat the eggs during the night but was finally found not to be broody. Shall still put the eggs under a hen if obtainable, & watch results.

Fifteen eggs (highest). 1/10 score.

D

27.4.39: Sharp frost during night & hens' water frozen. Snow & sleet during most of the day. Short sunny intervals. Blossom seems undamaged.

Perennial alyssum coming into flower. Scyllas & grape hyacinths coming to an end.

Starlings very busy obtaining straw for nests. Mrs. Anderson[46] heard cuckoo at 5.45. Caught a thrush in the kitchen, unhurt; a full-grown bird, very yellow inside beak.

Sixteen eggs (highest).

46. *Mrs. Anderson:* a neighbour who 'did' for the Orwells. According to Monica Bald in *Remembering Orwell*, p.115, Mrs Anderson used to say she was sure he was a writer because he got money every now and again by cheque, and then Eileen would say, 'We all got paid'.

D

28.4.39: 9 eggs.

D

29.4.39: 12 eggs.

D

30.4.39: 14 eggs. Came to Greenwich.

D

3.5.39: Outside Miller Hospital,[47] starlings & sparrows stripping bark, apparently to make nests. Some small boughs completely stripped.

47. *Greenwich; Miller Hospital:* The references to Greenwich, where Eileen's brother, Dr Laurence O'Shaughnessy lived, the Miller Hospital, and Eileen writing the Diary, may indicate that Orwell was undergoing tests under O'Shaughnessy's direction; he may even have been an in-patient for a day or two. See reference to pigeon nest 'outside hospital window' 9.5.39 and 'owing to illness', 21.5.39. Laurence, confusingly, was also referred to as 'Eric'.

D

8.5.39: Visit to Wallington. Plum blossom over, apple full out (a great quantity). First peas ½″–1″ tall. First beans 3″. Second beans not showing. Rhubarb growing but not good (? protection necessary here for good crop; Mr. A.[48] has all his in tubs). Strawberries in flower. In last three days main crop potatoes, onions, carrots, turnips, second peas & radishes sown.

Four nestlings in thrush's nest in hedge.

In flower: wallflowers, tulips, pansies, arabis (full out & decorative), yellow alyssum, aubretia, forget-me-nots & a few narcissi. Roses not in bud. Gooseberries mainly taken by frost or birds. Sowed grass seed in bare patches & scattered lawn sand.

Hens have laid 92 eggs in 8 days.

48. *Mr A.*: Probably Mr Anderson, a Wallington neighbour.

D

9.5.39: Young pigeons in nest outside hospital window.

[*From 16 May the Diary is again written in Orwell's hand.*]

D

16.5.39: *London:* Weather for the most part showery, with fine intervals. In Greenwich Park, chestnuts, pink chestnuts (but not the Spanish ones) in flower, also lilac, hawthorn. Some of the wild ducks have ducklings. Some roses in bud. Tulips & wallflowers about at their best. Noted the following named tulips, all good kinds: Venus (cerise rose), Allard Pierson (light crimson), Miss Blanche (cream), William Pitt (bright crimson), Louis XIV (brownish mauve), Pride of Harlem (bright pink), Remembrance (pale mauve), Ambrosia (*Daily Mail* rose), Bartigon (sealing wax red), Nauticus (magenta), Rev. Ewbank (very pale mauve), Sultan (very dark brown, almost black).

[*Newspaper cuttings:* Recipes using Sour Milk – 'Like Christmas Cake'; 'A Danish Recipe'; 'Yoghourt as in Jugoslavia'; 'Swedish Filmjolk'; 'Salad Dressing'; 'Scaba Putra from Latvia'; these recipes, and other hints Orwell cut out, were contributed by readers to the newspapers.]

D

21.5.39: Today & yesterday fine, but it is still not any too warm. Roses here are in full bud & almost out. Greenfly very bad. Lupins almost out. London Pride (kind of large saxifrage) is out. The gardener here[49] says that the number of varieties of roses is much exaggerated, as old varieties which have dropped out of fashion & been almost forgotten are from time to time revived under a new name. Saw yesterday a swift & a turtle dove, the first I have seen this year, owing to illness. Hawthorn is well out, especially the pink. Hay looks pretty good.

At the Zoo[50] on 19.5.39. much interested in the manatee, which I had only vaguely heard of before. An animal about the size of a large seal, with broad tail behind & two flippers of some kind in front. The head is doglike, with small eyes, the surface of the body seems like that of an elephant, but is slimy from being in the water. Movements very sluggish. The peculiar feature is the mouth, which is fringed with large hairs & acts with a kind of sucking movement to draw food in. The creature is very tame & lets itself be touched. It appears that this is the only vegetarian water-mammal. Could not be sure whether it inhabits fresh or salt water, or both.

The elephant refuses radishes, which both deer & monkeys eat readily. Marmoset refuses spring onions, which most monkeys eat. Note that some S. American monkeys can almost hang by the tail alone, ie. by the tail & one hand or foot. Mouflon, the N. African kind, have bred very freely in the Zoo & look in better condition than those in Marrakech. Two families of lion cubs at present, & evidently attempts are being made to cross a lion & a tiger.[51]

49. *The gardener here:* presumably at the O'Shaugnessy's or Greenwich Park.
50. *the Zoo*: the London Zoological Gardens, Regent's Park.
51. *to cross a lion & a tiger:* the Zoo was successful in breeding a tigon. (Tigons are found in the wild.)

D

25.5.39: Yesterday & the day before very warm. Today overcast, chilly enough to have a fire, & a few drops of rain.

Got back yesterday[52] after nearly 3 weeks' absence. Soil is very dry, weeds terrible except in kitchen garden. The field is now almost completely ruined with nettles & hemlock, but there is a small patch or two, about 200sq. yards, which may yield a little hay. Grass everywhere is lush & very green. Plenty of fruit forming on the apples. Practically no currants or gooseberries in the kitchen garden, but plenty on the odd bushes in the flower garden. First (dwarf) peas about 4″ high, the second (taller) about 2″, first broad beans 6″ or 8″ high, a few early potatoes showing. Second potatoes, French beans, carrots, onions etc. not showing (all these planted very late). Radishes showing. A lot of blossom on the strawberries, even on some of the last year's runners. Tulips & wall-flowers coming to an end. Flowers in full bloom: aubretia, yellow alyssum (very good), forget-me-nots, saxifrage, pansies. Budding: cheddar pinks, peonies, sweet williams, bush roses (not ramblers). Plenty of blossom on the loganberries.

52. *Got back yesterday:* to The Stores, Wallington.

From 9.5.39 – 23.5.39 inclusive there were 200 eggs. On 24.5.39 there were 14. Today 17. Shall start account afresh this Sunday, but I think there are none we have not recorded. Six chicks, now 10–12 days old, healthy but seem backward as to size. It appears the losses from this clutch (11 eggs) at the beginning were due to a mole which burrowed under the coop & buried some of the chicks. Eggs now are very good, much larger than a month back. Yesterday a tiny egg, about the size of a water-hen's (said locally, like a double egg, to be "always the first or the last" of a clutch). Three hens broody.

M[uriel] seems well, rather thin, appetite good. Still giving over 1½ pints (close on a year in milk now.) Yesterday planted a dozen carnations.

D

26.5.39: Warm. Ground is very dry. Fly is in the turnips. Many apples forming. Strawberries should be netted about a fortnight from now.

Titly° has potatoes already earthed up. He says Catriona do not keep well for seed but store all right if gently treated. Blue flax in bloom. Some gooseberries almost ready to pick. Of the other batch of eggs 5 chicks have hatched; expected none, as the eggs had been about 3 weeks before a hen was found, & then the hen left them after a week & another had to be put on them.

Planted antirrhinums.

14 eggs.

N.B. 12.4. – 26.5 (inc.) 550 eggs (26 hens.)

This concludes Domestic Diary Volume I.

Domestic Diary Volume II

27 May 1939 – 31 August 1939

INTERCALATED WITH

Diary of Events Leading Up to the War

2 July 1939 – 3 September 1939

Footnotes are numbered from 1 for this Volume; they are placed within or at the foot of the relevant dates.

D

27.5.39: Overcast in the morning, fine & warm in the afternoon. Blue speedwell & bugle out everywhere. Buttercups about at their tallest. Dandelions seeding. Large toadstools in the fields.

Strawed strawberries. Applied sodium chlorate to the remaining patch under the walnut tree.

Yesterday watched a thrush cracking a snail on a flat stone. Not, as I had thought, by pecking at it, but picking it up & knocking it on the stone.

15 eggs. Sold 50 eggs today, the largest batch sold hitherto. (1/10 a score).
Eggs to date (see vol. I) 565
Week starts tomorrow.

[*Newspaper cuttings:* 'Gelatine Moulds' – for plaster casting; 'A Seed-Sowing Tip' – using an old cocoa tin; 'Capturing Queen Wasps']

D

28.5.39: *(Whit Sunday):* Very chilly in early morning, the rest of the day fine & sunny. Some salvias were planted last night. *Daily Mail* rose now almost ready to open, buds on Dorothy Perkins & Albertine. Delphinium buds forming, peonies not far from opening.

13 eggs (plus 7 laid out = 20). Today starts new egg week.

29.5.39: Very fine & warm. Netted strawberries. Took M[uriel] to the billy but fear she is not on heat. Mr. N.[1] says they usually only are on autumn-spring. M. greatly afraid of a cow. The cow, on the other hand, frightened of a half-grown billy kid which was there.

16 eggs.

1. *Mr. N.:* probably Mr Nicholls, a neighbour who kept goats and who, according to Orwell, had a 'broken-down old wreck' not suitable for mating with Muriel (see *CW*, XI, p. 261).

[*Newspaper cuttings:* 'Wet Mash for Laying Period'; 'Feeding Chicks'; 'Feeding Ducklings']

D

30.5.39: Very fine & warm. Planted tomatoes (12), putting sacking over to protect them from the sun. One cheddar pink is out. A fine drizzle for a little while in the morning. Note that netting strawberries does not seem to inhibit the bees to any extent.

14 eggs

D

31.5.39: Fine & warm, but strikes very chilly as soon as the sun begins to go in. Tomatoes (protected from the sun with sacking) are O.K. A few French & runner beans showing.

M's mating no good. When bringing her back found she had not been milked since taking her there (ie. 48 hours) & her udders were very distended. Milked her & obtained a quart, which seemed not soured or otherwise unsatisfactory. Do not know whether this will put her milk-yield back.

17 eggs (sold 50 at 2/– a score).

Saw a white owl this evening.

D

1.6.39: Cold in the morning, warmed up later. Very windy. Began sticking peas, put new perches in new henhouse. Uncovered tomatoes.

11 eggs.

D

2.6.39: Very hot, very dry, a good deal of wind. Young seedlings tending to droop. Titley has peonies, columbines full out. Honeysuckle also full out. A sweet william here & there beginning to open. Apples on the grenadier about the size of marbles. Ditto T's cherries.

Stacked up some dried nettles etc. for litter. Set 10 duck eggs. Prepared ground for lettuces. Moved chicks.

M's milk has gone right back as a result of the upset. Less than a pint yesterday.

15 eggs. Weighed some eggs & found that only a very few are under 2 oz.

M. gave about 1½ pts., so perhaps is going back to normal.

D

3.6.39: Very hot & dry. Planted 1 score of T's lettuces & about a dozen (smaller) of our own. Protected with sacking, as with the tomatoes. E[ileen] planted 7 dahlias.

The hen had pushed away 4 of the duck eggs, which had become quite cold.

Put on another hen, removing one egg. Not certain whether this will have killed these eggs (which had been sat on 24 hours.)

12 eggs. Sold 40 at 2/– a score. Total this week 98 (+7 = 105).

D

4.6.39: Extremely hot & dry. Made larger runs for chicks, putting sacking over as shade. Had to take the sacking from the lettuces, which had not wilted owing to being covered. A few sweet williams coming out. The other very small dianthus is coming out. These shut up at night, the cheddar pinks do not. Many greenfly on the roses. Squirted them with soap & water. M. gave 1¾ pts. today, so is about back to normal.

14 eggs.

E[ileen] saw a white owl again last night.

D

5.6.39: Unbearably hot. Everything is drying up. A sweet william out. Ragged robin out.

Sowed peas (English wonder). Mulched tomatoes. French & runner beans have germinated very badly, so am sowing some in a box for fill-ups. New potatoes ready to be earthed up, a few of the maincrop showing.

5 eggs! (Presumably something to do with heat).

NB. that ½ pint of peas sows one of our rows (about 12 yards) thickly.

D

6.6.39: Too hot to do much in the garden. Earthed up early potatoes.

We are changing the hens on to Full-o-Pep, which is somewhat cheaper than Clarke's laying mash. Also getting corn etc. by the cwt., which effects a small saving. NB. that 1 cwt. each of Full-o-Pep & mixed corn begun today, & at 3 lb. a day of each should last till about July 12th. Great trouble with the broody hen, which at feeding time tries to rejoin the others. When caught & put into the coop, however, she goes back to her eggs.

Many turtle doves about.

11 eggs.

D

7.6.39: Extremely dry & hot, but a little wind. There is fairly heavy dew at nights.

Planted out 2 bush marrows, putting tins over them. E[ileen] cut the lawn with shears & then with the mower, which Albert H.[2] has sharpened (paid for sharpening 1/6). Continued sticking peas.

M. giving nearly a quart. Have sent for another goat, British-Alpine cross, kidded last month, £3.

9 eggs (plus 5 laid out = 14). Sold 1 score (2/–.)

2. *Albert H.*: 'H' usually signifies 'Old Hatchett', see 13.6.39, so Albert H. may be another neighbour at Wallington, perhaps Albert Hollingsworth; see 21. 8. 39.

D

8.6.39: Very dry, not quite so hot.

Prepared another marrow-bed, this time digging it less deeply & putting on 4-inch layer of lawn-clippings. Shall compare results of this style of bed with the other. Weeded & hoed the French & runner beans. Not much more than half of them are germinating. Uncovered the lettuces. Thinned out apples on the grenadier. About 60 left, but presumably not more than a dozen will stay on.

D.M.[3] rose is full out, delphiniums almost out.

M. is hardly eating any hard food, but her milk is not down.

12 eggs (plus 7 laid out = 19).

Duck eggs said to take 28 days or a month, so these are due out about June 30 – July 2.

3. *D. M.: Daily Mail;* see 16. 5. 39 and 28. 5. 39.

D

9.6.39: Very dry, less hot. No signs of rain.

Planted two more marrows & removed the covers from the others. Did more weeding. The turnips have completely disappeared & very few onions are left, & some of those wilting. Shall re-sow & plant after it has rained. Except the lettuces very little has germinated in the seed-bed. Eg. only 11 broccoli out of a packet. Maincrop potatoes now mostly up & look pretty good.

E[ileen] put six broodies in a sort of cage of wire netting, which may perhaps cure them.

The new goat arrived. Evidently had not been milked, so milked her, obtaining 1½ pints, & another ½ pint tonight. Supposed to give 3–4 pints, but this business will no doubt have put her off, as with M. a few days back. Am not stripping M. & shall gradually get her down to one milking a day, also reducing her feed. M. very jealous, butting the other goat, stealing her food etc., the other goat (name Kate) not resisting.

10 eggs.

D

10.6.39: Extremely dry & pretty hot. Began hoeing main crop potatoes, which are mostly through. Lettuces & marrows seem O.K. Many flowers in the garden drooping. The rainwater tank is now almost empty (the first time this has happened, but E[ileen] was here alone last summer).

K. wound herself up to her stake, then caught her hind leg & wound this so that it was twisted behind her neck & held there so tightly that I could only extricate her by undoing her collar. Very lame in consequence & ankle-joint swollen, but evidently nothing broken. Her yield today between 2 & 2½ pts. M. (not stripped) about 1½ pts.

8 eggs (plus 9 laid out = 17). Sold 2 score @ 2/–.

No. this week: 90.

D

11.6.39: Last night fairly heavy rain for 4–6 hours, which has freshened things up greatly. Today overcast & cooler.

Wild Flowers now out: dogrose, poppies, campion, knapweed (a few), egg & bacon, scabious (a few), elder, sanfoin.[4] A few fruits on the wild plum tree. K.'s leg better but her yield only about 2¼ pints, so am increasing her feed. 15 eggs.

4. *sanfoin:* This is the spelling of sainfoin favoured by Orwell. It means wholesome hay and is the perennial herb *Onobrychis saliva* or *viciaefolia,* a leguminous fodder plant sometimes known as everlasting grass or French grass. Orwell mentions it several times in *Coming Up for Air,* for example, 'My favourite place for reading was the loft behind the yard. . . . . There were huge piles of sacks to lie on, and a sort of plastery smell mixed up with the smell of sanfoin . . .' (*CW.* VII, p. 92).

D

12.6.39: There was evidently some rain during last night. This morning overcast & rather chilly, then from 4–6 in the afternoon heavy rain.

Finished hoeing maincrop potatoes, which are now practically all up. (There are 4 rows Epicure, 10 of Red King & 2 of King Edward. Excluding the Epicures, this ought to give about 3 cwt. of potatoes).

The hen sitting the duck eggs has twice moved them across the coop, presumably because moles burrowing below trouble her, but she seems to be sitting them all right.

E[ileen] planted out lobelia.

12 eggs.

D

13.6.39: Overcast, sunny intervals, some rain.

Took up tulips & planted out to finish their growth, also narcissi. Began putting up new hen-house (a shop-soiled one, price 17/6, which arrived uncreosoted & without roofing felt. Would accommodate 10–12 full-grown hens.) Old H.[5] planted out more lettuces. Began earthing up early potatoes for the second time. One gap in the 4 rows. Let out the broody hens, hoping that some at least will have gone off by this time. Had to throw away 1 duck egg (now only 8) as the hen had turned it out.

A jackdaw has twice been hanging round the chicken coops, obviously with designs on the chickens.

11 eggs.

5. *Old H.:* Old Hatchett, a neighbour.

D

14.6.39: Bought 8 new R.I.R.[6] pullets, 3 to 3½ months old, well forward, 4/6 each.

Finished putting up new house, which however is not creosoted or roof-felted yet, also the door needs adjustments. The old hen guarding the first lot of chicks has some sort of infection in her eye & will probably have to be destroyed.

3rd lot of peas (dwarf, sown 5.6.39) just showing. Runner & dwarf beans sown in box (6.6.39) coming up.

The broodies E[ileen] put in the cage, released yesterday, have all (seven) gone back to normal.

K[ate] now having 11 handfuls of feed at a meal, & yield rising very slightly (nearly 2½ pts.)

12 eggs. Sold 30 @ 2/– score.

6. *R.I.R.:* Rhode Island Red hens.

D

15.6.39: Windy, coldish & occasional drizzle. Put up stakes & wires upon which to stretch strings for runner beans. Fixed door of henhouse & supported it off the ground.

K.'s milk yield increasing slightly.

15 eggs.

(NB began new bottle of iron pills yesterday).

D

16.6.39: Heavy rain in the night, raining on & off most of the day, till about 5 pm when it cleared up. Too wet to do much out of doors. Placed strings for beans (much too low), began preparing a patch for turnips in place of those which failed in the drought.

Am giving the hens grit & shell – the first time they have had it, as I thought it was not necessary on a chalky soil. However, of late some of the eggshells, though not thin, have been of rather bad texture. Now that the new house is raised the pullets get out under the edges in the mornings, so it is nowhere near foxproof until floored.

A few strawberries now red. Canterbury bells well out but want sticking. Grass is a lot better after the rain. Seem to be no gaps in maincrop potatoes.

15 eggs.

[*Newspaper cutting*: 'Cream Cheese from Goat's Milk']

D

17.6.39: Fine, fairly warm.

Sowed carnations (mixed perennial). Put roofing felt on henhouse. Paid for felt 9d a yard.

Both goats' milk badly down, no doubt owing to being unable to graze yesterday. Being indoors also seems to affect their appetite for hard food.

14 eggs. Sold 30 @ 2/– score.

No. this week: 94.

[*Newspaper cutting:* making corner posts for gates and fences]

D

18.6.39: Fine in the morning, raining fairly heavily most of the afternoon.

The first ripe strawberry today. In spite of the net the birds are already getting at the partially ripe ones.

K's milk still down, only about 1 quart today.

13 eggs.

D

19.6.39: Fine most of the morning, raining most of the afternoon. Not cold. Ground now too wet to do much in garden. Put out runner beans to fill up gaps in row, sowed sweet williams & wallflowers, mended frame, substituting windolite for glass. Note that windolite tends to develop small holes & [I] do not know whether it is repairable. Began thinning carrots, which, however, are largely° gaps already, thanks to drought.

K's milk going up again (about 47 oz.)

15 eggs.

D

20.6.39: Fine in the morning, thunderstorm & fairly heavy rain in the afternoon. Earth too wet to do much. Started preparing place for a row of broccoli. Peonies almost out. Rambler (yellow) well out.

16 eggs.

[On facing page, in Orwell's hand:]

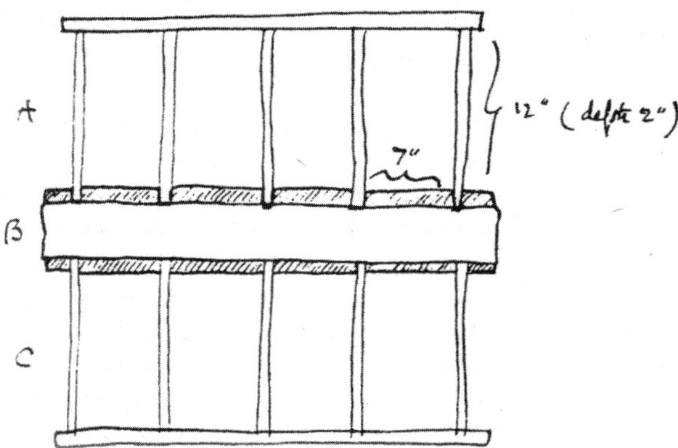

Mould° for concrete slabs. The shaded bits are nailed on (simpler than cutting tenons). A & C are each made in one piece, then jammed up against B, the ends of the sidepieces fitted into slots & weights placed against the ends. A & C can then be drawn away as the concrete begins to set. Except for B, the whole could be made of 2″ by ½″.

D

21.6.39: Cold, windy & some drizzle. Fire in the house all day. Did nothing out of doors. Did not put the goats out, owing to cold. Perennial Canterbury Bell (very poor flower) is well out.

11 eggs. Sold 40 @ 2/2 score.

D

22.6.39: Cold all day & very windy. Dense mist in the morning. Did nothing in garden.

14 eggs.

D

23.6.39: Overcast & drizzle but somewhat less cold. Did nothing in garden. Wallflowers sown 19.6.39 (in frame) beginning to show & carnations sown a day earlier also germinating. Thanks to the rain, a few carrots beginning to sprout in what were previously the gaps. Much of Innes's hay in & stacked. Peonies out. In Mrs B's garden mulleins out.

13 eggs.

[*On 24 June Orwell went to Southwold to be with his father, who was very ill. Richard Blair died of cancer of the rectum on 28 June. Orwell was by his bedside. He returned to Wallington on 30 June. From 24–30 June the Diary is written in Eileen's hand.*]

D

24.6.39: Overcast & showery all the morning but sunny periods late & less cold. Goats out all day for the first time this week. A few very fine scabious out in the hedgerows but wild flowers much scarcer than a week or two ago. Albertine rose[7] showing colour but not yet out; this & the bush roses have been in bud for a fortnight or more. Began earthing up maincrop potatoes. No gaps, though rather uneven growth.

14 eggs. Total for week: 96

7. *Albertine rose:* This is the rose that Orwell bought from Woolworth's for sixpence. He wrote about it in 'As I Please', 8, 21 January 1944 (*CW*, XVI, pp. 78 and 79. n.3). It was still flourishing some fifty years later.

D

25.vi°.39: Fine all day & fairly warm until evening. Sweet williams, two red roses & one Albertine full out. A salvia & a marigold in bud. Some stonecrop in full flower. Stonecrop appears to flower erratically as one clump has been out for two or three weeks & others (all contemporary) are still in bud.

15 eggs.

D

26.6.39: Warm sunny morning. Threats of thunderstorms in afternoon but no thunder & little rain. Potatoes earthed up. Gaps filled in french bean rows with extras sown in a box in the frame when the original rows were found to have germinated badly – i.e. after an interval of ten days or so. There is very little difference in development. Blackfly have already settled on about a quarter of the broad beans, though not in great numbers; pinched out growing points. The strings for the runner beans were tangled & stretched by rain & wind. Apparently four or five stakes are necessary for one of our rows. Weeded & hoed onions which are now three or four inches tall but with many gaps in the rows. Beans & peas have grown very rapidly, some runner bean tendrils lengthening by a couple of inches since Saturday.

12 eggs.

D

27.6.39: Very hot & sunny. Thinned carrots & hoed peas etc. Planted out 48 larkspurs, removing some poor sweet williams. Apparently sweet williams sometimes 'shoot up' for several years but cannot be made to do so.

15 eggs + 8 found in a nest.

D

28.6.39: Much cooler & occasional showers. Mr H[atchett] finished cutting the hay & collected it today. Sowed turnips & planted out a row of mixed greens from the seed bed. Both broody hens with chickens laid today, & one (the youngest) had three other eggs hidden at the back of the coop. 14 eggs + 3 in coop.

D

29.6.39: Hot & sunny most of the day. One duck had hatched this morning. Later moved the hen to new coop & left the more backward eggs with another broody. By evening 7 ducks; the eighth egg shows no sign of hatching but have put it under the hen for the night. The first ducks are fluffed up but show no disposition to walk about. Apparently ducklings are much slower to walk than chickens, being 'weak in the legs' (Mrs R.).[8] Made an awning with adjustable sacking cover & put flat dish of water in coop.

Rehoed onions which are growing at last. Marrows also growing, one strongly. White rose out.

15 eggs.

8. *Mrs R.:* Probably Mrs Ridley, a neighbour.

D

30.6.39: Ducklings still under hen this morning but in the afternoon came out to eat (brown bread crumbled with milk & dried a little with a sprinkling of chickmeal).

Thundery weather with heavy showers.

14 eggs.

D

1.7.39: Fine most of morning, very heavy showers in afternoon. Garden mostly in good condition. Some strawberries ripe, a few broad beans fit to pick, onions improving, runner beans just starting to climb strings. Hay is cut & stacked in small stack about 6' by 5', but not certain yet whether we can preserve this. M.'s milk going off considerably. Ducklings all healthy & lively, young chicks making good growth. Such currants as there are are ripening.

Marigolds (a few) in flower. Wild scabius° appearing.

10 eggs (plus 14 laid out = 24).

Sold this week 72 @ 2/2d. Total this week = 120.

D

2.7.39: Overcast most of day, a heavy shower in the afternoon, & cold enough to have a fire.

Both the hens guarding chicks have begun laying eggs the younger one showed a tendency to stray away. E[ileen] therefore put her with the other hens & put all chicks together with the other hen. This morning two of the youngest badly pecked, especially the one which for some reason is white. Have segregated these two, & we are going to wean the others at once. Three of the elder ones are already perching.

Picked about 1½ lb. of strawberries & had some broad beans (young, eaten pod & all). These are about the first produce of the garden. A few loganberries reddening. Apples on the grenadier as large as golf balls. Clarkia beginning to flower.

11 eggs.

Cylinder of Calor gas, started 8.6.39, gave out today.

Cwt. of Full-o-Pep, started 6.6.39, getting low in the bin. Should last till 12.7.39. Actually might last till about 8th or 10th, but some of it has been fed to the pullets occasionally.

DIARY OF EVENTS LEADING UP TO THE WAR

2 July 1939 – 3 September 1939

This Diary of Events Leading Up to the War is, in the main, a handwritten list of extracts from newspapers from 2 July to 1 September 1939, the day Germany invaded Poland. It concludes with a summary dated 3 September, the day Britain declared war on Germany following Germany's refusal to withdraw from Poland. No record was made for ten of the days covered by this Diary. However, items for days not specifically recorded were sometimes included later. After the break from 25th to 27th August there is a summary on the 28th. The manuscript comprises fifty-five pages each page being divided horizontally, the upper half recording events and the lower the sources of information; the pages are divided into five columns headed Foreign & General, Social, Party Politics, Miscellaneous, and Remarks. Except for 24 August (to which two pages are devoted) there is one page per day. The writing is often small and cramped. The allocation of topics and the arrangement of the information as reproduced here are sometimes arbitrary but they are Orwell's. When Orwell gives a source and date, the source is noted in square brackets but the date is given only if it differs from that at the head of the section. Orwell's remarks follow the item to which they refer and are marked '[Orwell's note]'. Some very slight corrections have been made silently. When entries from both sources are on the same date, the Domestic Diary entry precedes that for the Events Leading Up to the War.

Orwell quotes from forty-one sources for the 297 items. Of these, 138 (46.5%) are from the *Daily Telegraph*. There is a noticeable increase in references to *The Times* and the *News Chronicle* (which tended to share the stance of the Liberal Party) and a proportionate decrease in references to the *Daily Telegraph* when Orwell went to stay with L. H. Myers at Ringwood on 24 August. Orwell evidently looked to the *Daily Telegraph* for factual information during these months. Of these sources, *Socialist Correspondence* and *Revolutionary Proletarian* are worth some attention. The first was run by a 'right-wing opposition' within the left-wing ILP. Members were followers of Nikolai Bukharin, victim of a show trial in 1938 and then executed. Among its members was W.W. Sawyer, a mathematician at Manchester University and author of a popular Penguin book, *Mathematician's Delight*. *Socialist Correspondence* was an octavo of eight to sixteen pages, some of which were blank but marked 'To Let', and described itself as 'An Organ of Marxist Theory'. *Revolutionary Proletarian* was *La Révolution Prolétarienne,* founded

1 January 1925; suspended after issue 301, 25 August 1939; issue 302 was published in April 1947. Its line was anti-Stalinist. In its issue 255, 25 September 1937, it published the French translation of Orwell's 'Eye-Witness in Barcelona' on the suppression of the POUM in Barcelona which the *New Statesman* had refused to publish, but which was taken by the ILP journal, *Controversy* (see *CW*, XI, pp. 54–60). For further details, see *CW*, XI, pp. 362–3.

Entries from Orwell's Diary of Events Leading Up to the War, are intercalated with those from the Domestic Diary. 'Diary of Events' entries (as they are headed) are easily identified because they follow their sub-headings. Their footnotes immediately follow the last entry for each day. They are numbered from 1 for each day. Later references to these footnotes are by the word 'Events' plus the relevant date. These entries are marked with **E** *after the rule. Domestic Diary entries are each marked with* **D***. Their footnotes are numbered sequentially continuing from note 8 on page 154 and follow the relevant day.*

E

2.7.39:

FOREIGN & GENERAL

1. Poland states that Danzig[1] will be occupied if Danzig Senate declares for the Reich. [*Sunday Times*]
2. N.L.C.[2] of Labour Party broadcast in German in much the same terms as at September crisis. [*Observer*]

PARTY POLITICS

Sinclair,[3] Ramsay Muir,[4] Amery,[5] Eden,[6] Cripps,[7] Burgin[8] make virtually identical statements re. resistance to German agression.° [*Sunday Times*]

1. Danzig (now Gdansk, Poland), first mentioned some thousand years ago as part of Poland, has since been variously Polish and German (including Prussian). It was made a Free City by the Treaty of Versailles (1919), but became a focus of dispute between Poland and Germany, especially after the rise of the Nazis. This was the pretext for the German invasion of Poland that initiated World War II in 1939.
2. This is probably an error for NCL (National Council of Labour); see *Events, 15.7.39, Party Politics, 2.* The sense is elliptical, but seems to refer to an appeal to the German people under the heading 'Why kill each other?' made by the NCL. Summaries were broadcast by the BBC on the night of Saturday, 1 July 1939, in German, French, Italian, Portuguese, and Spanish. The NCL also arranged broadcasts to German workers from secret radio stations on the Continent and distributed printed copies of the appeal through underground organisations.
3. Archibald Sinclair (1890–1970; 1st Viscount Thurso, 1952), Liberal M.P., 1922–45, was a close friend of Winston Churchill and became political private secretary to him when the latter was Colonial Secretary, 1921–23. He served as Secretary of State for Scotland, 1931–32 but came to disapprove strongly of government policies associated with Chamberlain, and sided with Churchill and Eden. He attacked

Chamberlain's policy strongly in July 1939; and this developed into a bitter argument, centring on the refusal of *The Times* to print Sinclair's rejoinder; see *Events, 12.7.39, Social.* He was Secretary of State for Air in Churchill's wartime coalition government.

4. John Ramsay Muir (1872–1941) was Professor of Modern History at the University of Manchester, 1913–21, and politician, first as a Liberal, and from 1931, after the split within the party, as a National Liberal. He was Chairman and President successively of the National Liberal Federation, 1931–36.
5. Leopold Charles Maurice Amery (1873–1955), Conservative M.P., opposed disarmament and supported the Hoare-Laval proposals for resolving the Abyssinian crisis in 1935. In May 1940, after the fall of Norway to the Germans, he directed, at Chamberlain, Cromwell's words to the Long Parliament (1640–53): 'You have sat too long here for any good you may be doing. . . . In the name of God, go!' His *My Political Life* (1953–55) gives an account of political events of the thirties.
6. Anthony Eden, (1897–1977; Earl of Avon, 1961), Conservative M.P., was Foreign Secretary, 1935–38. He resigned to protest against Chamberlain's policy of appeasement. In 1940 he was Secretary of State for War, then Foreign Secretary in the War Cabinet, 1940–45. He was Prime Minister, 1955–57, but resigned again, as a result of Britain's disastrous involvement in the occupation of the Suez Canal Zone in 1956.
7. Sir Stafford Cripps (1889–1952), lawyer (in 1927 becoming the youngest King's Counsel) and Labour politician, entered Parliament in 1931, but was expelled from the Labour Party from 1939 to 1945. He was Ambassador to the Soviet Union, 1940–42; Minister of Aircraft Production, 1942–45, and Chancellor of the Exchequer in the Labour government, 1947–50. See Orwell's War-time Diary *8.6.40*, regarding his appointment as ambassador. See also 14.6.41 n. 184 and 14.3.42, n. 1.
8. Dr. Leslie Burgin (1887–1945), lawyer and Liberal (later National Liberal) M.P. from 1930, was Minister of Transport, 1937–39, and Minister of Supply, 1939–40. In *A Prime Minister on Prime Ministers* (1977), Harold Wilson, who worked in the Ministry of Supply for a short time in 1940, remarked that 'its organization under Burgin's ministerial direction would not have been capable of running a chip-shop' (233).

D

3.7.39: Warmer, sunny most of day.

Planted pumpkin (somewhat too late, & in a too shady position). Earthed up north side of maincrop potatoes. No gaps, but some very immature. Lifted tulip bulbs. One early potato withered up – trust not disease. Turnips (sown 28.6.39) are showing. One pullet limping.

15 eggs.

D

4.7.39: Fine & hot. A few raspberries reddening. Phloxes in bud, also bergamot. Goats escaped this morning & ate a lot of fruit tree shoots, rose shoots & some tops of phloxes. Pullet still limping badly & fear some kind of paralysis, tho' she seems otherwise in good condition. Put gate on duck run & allowed the ducklings out of the coop. Today started new cwt. of Full-o-Pep & cwt. of corn. The pullets are also having from the latter, but of course not having laying mash. On the other hand 4 old fowls sold today. The mash therefore has to do for 24 hens, the corn for

32. Mash should therefore last about 35 days, corn about the same (allowing 1½ oz. per bird.) Shall try & reach the end before ordering new stuff next time, in order to see how it lasts out. This lot ought to give out about the 8th August, which is a Tuesday. Started the hens on a course of Karswood spice today.

10 eggs.

E

4.7.39:

FOREIGN & GENERAL

1. Fighting reported on Manchukuo[1] -Mongolian border. [*Daily Telegraph*]

SOCIAL

1. Unemployment now down to about 1,350,000. [*Daily Telegraph*]
2. Egg-production of England & Wales in 1937 about 3,250 million. [*Smallholder*, 24.6.39]

1. Manchukuo was a puppet kingdom of Manchuria when occupied by the Japanese, 1932–45. It was restored to China in 1945.

D

5.7.39: Hot. A short shower in the evening. Bergamot in bud. The white chick looks bad, & the pullet which is limping no better. A few loganberries ripe enough to pick. Started creosoting henhouse. Sowed radishes, cos lettuce, parsley. E[ileen] sowed F[rench] beans.

10 eggs. Sold 2 score @ 2/6.

E

5.7.39:

FOREIGN & GENERAL

1. More fighting reported on Manchukuo border. [*Daily Telegraph*]

PARTY POLITICS

1. Conservative M.P.s to petition for Churchill's[1] entry into Cabinet. Following *D. T.'s* [2] article, many letters to this effect. [*Daily Telegraph*]

1. Sir Winston Churchill (1874–1965), politician, soldier, journalist, author, held high office in Liberal and Conservative governments over nearly half a century, but in the thirties was excluded because of his vigorous opposition to appeasement of dictators; he was branded a warmonger. He was the natural choice for prime minister after the fall of Norway following the German invasion in 1940. Despite his success as a war leader, he was not returned to office in 1945, but he did become prime minister of a peacetime government, 1951–55.
2. *Daily Telegraph's.*

D

6.7.39: Very windy, & raining lightly most of the day. Too wet to do anything outside. Nasturtiums in flower. Roses now extremely good. Another 2 lb. strawberries. (3½ lb. to date – am noting amounts in order to see what weight of fruit that space produces).

11 eggs.

E

6.7.39:

FOREIGN & GENERAL

1. Britain to grant arms credit of £100 million to Poland, Turkey & Rumania. [*Daily Telegraph*]
2. Polish, Turkish & Chinese gov.ts said to believe Stalin genuinely desires pact. [*Daily Telegraph*]

PARTY POLITICS

1. McGovern[1] again attacking L.P.[2] in Parliament. [*Daily Telegraph*]

1. John McGovern 1887–1968), Independent Labour Party M.P., 1930–47; Labour M.P., 1947–59, led a hunger march from Glasgow to London in 1934.
2. Labour Party.

D

7.7.39: Some rain in the morning, hot in the afternoon. Transplanted onions as well as possible, but there are still some gaps. New cylinder of Calor gas begun today.

9 eggs. Sold 8 @ 1½d.

E

7.7.39:

FOREIGN & GENERAL

1. Fighting on Manchukuo border reported this time from Russian sources (Tass agency). [*Daily Telegraph*]

PARTY POLITICS

1. At Zurich conference of I.F.T.U.,[1] British T.U. leaders now advocating affiliation of Russian unions. [*Manchester Guardian Weekly*]

1. The International Federation of Trade Unions, established in 1901, had failed to survive World War I. Re-established in 1919, it came into conflict with the Soviet-inspired Red International of Labour Unions. Failure to reconcile differences between Communist and non-Communist trade unions continued after World War II. British, Soviet, and U.S. unions combined briefly to establish the World Federation of Trade Unions, but in 1949 the non-Communist unions broke away to form the International Confederation of Free Trade Unions. The news item above is indicative of fundamental disagreement lasting over many decades.

D

8.7.39: Raining much of the day, a fine interval in the evening, very windy. Picked some more loganberries. One hollyhock beginning to flower. A few runner beans show buds. Tomatoes flowering, also several marrows. One or two snapdragons beginning to flower. Have evidently been overfeeding the pullets, which are leaving some of their mash. The limping one no better, though otherwise seemingly all right in health, so shall segregate her tomorrow. A few self-sown potatoes uprooted today have potatoes only about the size of marbles on them. Putting the ducklings on mash from today.

10 eggs. Sold ½ score @ 2/6. No. this week: 76

E

8.7.39:

FOREIGN & GENERAL

1. Public Information Leaflet No.1 (Civil Defence) issued by the Post Office today. Large-scale A.R.P.[1] practice to take place tonight over S. E. England. [No separate reference]

PARTY POLITICS

1. I.F.T.U. now apparently refusing Russian affiliation, France, Mexico, Norway & G.Britain voting for (the last two conditionally), U.S.A. & most European countries against. [*Daily Telegraph*]
2. Trial of Julien* Besteiro[2] begins in Madrid today. (J.B. took part in Casado[3] junta). [*Daily Telegraph*]

MISCELLANEOUS

1. Rat population of G. Britain estimated at 4–5 million. [*Smallholder*, 7.7.39]

1. Air Raid Precautions.
2. Julien Besteiro (properly Julián) (1870–1940), President of the UGT (Socialist Trade Union, Spain) to 1931, was Speaker of the Cortes (the Spanish Parliament) and temporarily President of Spain the same year. He died in prison in 1940, while serving the thirty-year sentence imposed by Franco's government (hence Orwell's asterisked note).
3. Colonel Sigismundo Casado López (1893–1968), commander of the Republican Army of the Centre, organised the campaign against Republican Prime Minister Negrín and attempted, towards the end of the civil war, to gain better terms from Franco. He failed and took refuge in Britain, though he later returned to Spain.

D

9.7.39:

Warm, no rain. The little apple tree (grenadier pippin)† so weighted down with apples that we are obliged to support the branches. Kate is unwell, refused food this evening & was sick, or threw up her cud. Muriel also somewhat off her feed. I suspect this is due to their being tethered in the hot sun without shade.

Found wild canterbury bells. Wood pigeons still sitting on nests. No crab apples on the big tree this year, though the garden apples are everywhere good. Seemingly no wild cherries. The birds have had the few red currants there were in our garden. This evening caught & brought home some newt tadpoles in varying stages of development. They get the front

* 30 years [Orwell's note].

† It seems the grenadier is a cooker, not an eater as I thought [Orwell's note].

legs first* (toads get hind legs – not certain about frogs) & have 4 fingers on each hand. Much more agile than toad tadpoles, diving into the mud when pursued. According to Edie W.[9] adult newts if put into the aquarium with tadpoles will devour them. Found a water snail whose shell was as long as the top two joints of my forefinger; have never before seen one approaching this size.

Planted a slip of rambler rose, but believe this is too early.† Picked more loganberries.

12 eggs.

9. *Edie W.*: Edie was Mrs Ridley's daughter. The 'W' stands for her husband Stanley's surname.

E

9.7.39:

FOREIGN & GENERAL

1. Madame Tabouis[1] considers chances of full Russian-French-British pact are now small & hints that Russians wish to regain position of Czarist Empire in the Baltic provinces. [*Sunday Dispatch*]

SOCIAL

1. Population of Scotland now more than 5 million. [*Sunday Times*]

PARTY POLITICS

1. I.F.T.U. rejected motion to invite Russian affiliation, but not v. large majority.§ [*Sunday Times*]

1. Genevieve Tabouis (Paris, 1892–1985) was a diplomatic and international journalist, foreign news editor of *L'Oeuvre* from 1932, and correspondent for the *Sunday Dispatch*. On 23 June 1940 that paper printed her account of her escape to England via Bordeaux after the fall of Paris. This began with a statement attributed to Hitler: 'The speech I am making to-day she knew yesterday.' She directed the weekly *Pour la Victoire*, in New York, 1941–45, and was noted for her uncanny gift for forecasting accurately the outcome of political events.

D

10.7.39: Overcast, warm & still. Some hollyhocks flowering. Madonna lilies & bergamot almost out. Did nothing in garden except weeding. K's appetite somewhat improved but bad drop in her milk today (only about 1¼ pt.) E[ileen] picked about 1½ lb. strawberries yesterday.

10 eggs.

* Not quite certain about this. They seem to have all 4 legs when still only about ½–¾ inch long [Orwell's note].

† It took all right. But died in the frost Jan. 1940 [Orwell's note].

§ Majority said to be entirely due to large vote held by Green of the A.F.L. [Orwell's note]. William Green was President of the American Federation of Labor, founded in 1886, which was split in 1935 by the formation of a faction that advocated and then organized industrial unions and in 1938 became the Congress of Industrial Organizations. The two united to form the AFL-CIO in 1955.

E

10.7.39:

FOREIGN & GENERAL

1. Germany said to be demanding entire Rumanian wheat crop, also part of what is left over from 1938 crop. [*Daily Telegraph*]
2. Large-scale practice blackout[1] on Sat. night said to have gone off successfully. [*Daily Telegraph*]

SOCIAL

1. Groups of friends entering militia are being[2] split up, sufficiently noticeably for this to call for explanation by the W.O.[3] [*Daily Telegraph*]

PARTY POLITICS

1. Papers which appealed on July 3 for inclusion of Churchill in cabinet were *D. Tel., Yorkshire Post, News-C, M. Guardian & Dy. Mirror.* It is alleged that Communist party after demanding C's inclusion for some months are becoming alarmed now that it appears likely to happen. [*Socialist Correspondence*, 8.7.39]
2. Bela Kun[4] again reported shot in Moscow. [*La Revolution Proletarienne*]

1. As part of the precautions against air attack, windows had to be completely covered to ensure no light could be seen from the street, street-lights were turned off, and essential lights (such as car headlights and traffic lights) were masked. For a brief but eloquent account of the psychological effect of the blackout, see Malcolm Muggeridge, *The Thirties*, p. 305. He notes that after two months of war the number of casualties caused by the blackout was nearly twice that of all three services combined. See Events, 10.8.39, Social, 4.
2. Orwell first wrote 'have been.'
3. War Office. The practice of separating friends, especially from the same locality, was designed to ensure that if a unit suffered heavy losses they were not all felt in the same town or city. This policy was adopted following the terrible casualties inflicted at the Battle of the Somme (July–October 1916), when units of men from the same place (e.g., the Exeter Boys) trained together, went into action together, and were then almost wiped out in a few moments, so intensifying the grief felt at home. The effect of the deaths of the five Sullivan brothers when U.S.S. *Juneau* was sunk, 13 November 1942, provides a similar Second World War example.
4. Béla Kun (1886–1939?), Communist revolutionary leader in Hungary, and briefly its Commissar for Foreign Affairs and dominant figure in the government in 1919. After fleeing from Hungary he tried, as a member of the Third International, to foment revolution in Germany and Austria. He fell out of favour and was murdered in one of Stalin's purges. For a later report of his execution, see Events, 7.8.39, Party Politics, 2.

D

11.7.39: Warm but not very sunny. Pricked out 90 wallflowers (flame). T.[10] thinks the lame pullet may have "the disease" (presumably coccidiosis) in which case it would be better to kill her. The infallible symptom is yellow dung, but apparently it usually starts with lameness in the left leg.

Started the goats on cotton cake to see whether they will eat it. K.'s milk normal again (2½ pts.) 2 lb. strawberries. Sussex hen is moulting.

12 eggs.

10. *T.*: Perhaps Mr Titley.

E

11.7.39:

FOREIGN & GENERAL

1. More reports of fighting on Manchukuo border, sufficient to indicate that fighting (prob. inconclusive) has actually taken place. [*Daily Telegraph*]
2. Chamberlain's[1] speech reiterates that we shall support Poles in case of Danzig coup, but seems to leave initiative to Poles. [*Daily Telegraph*]
3. German reports that Russian submarine fleet is larger than anticipated. Warships using Stalin canal[2] for first time. [*Daily Telegraph*]

PARTY POLITICS

1. Further letters in *D. Tel.* demanding inclusion of Churchill. These however do not imply very strong criticism of Chamberlain. *D. Tel.* prints a few against. *Times* said to be printing none for. [*Daily Telegraph*]

MISCELLANEOUS

1. Death of Havelock Ellis,[3] aged 80, gets small front page mention in *D. Tel.* [*Daily Telegraph*]

1. Prime Minister Neville Chamberlain was associated with appeasement of Hitler and Mussolini in the thirties. His stance was probably that of most British citizens, including many who were, with hindsight, to criticise him. J. L. Garvin (1868–1947), right-wing editor of *The Observer* (1908–42), argued on New Year's Day, 1939, that 'Mr. Chamberlain was a thousand times right in saving the world's peace at Munich even at the price exacted' (quoted by Robert Kee, a friend of Orwell's, *The World We Left Behind*, 1984, p. 8). Eileen Blair commented in a letter of 27 September 1938, 'It's very odd to feel that Chamberlain is our only hope, but I do believe he doesn't want war either at the moment & certainly the man has courage' (*CW*, XI, p. 206).
2. The Belomor-Baltic Canal connecting Archangel and Leningrad. It was constructed by slave labour in 1931–33 and runs for some 140 miles, saving a sea journey of 2,500 miles. It was built by a quarter of a million prisoners, nearly 200,000 of whom died or were executed.
3. Henry Havelock Ellis (1859–1939), psychologist, editor, and author, noted particularly for his work on sex in relation to society. Orwell was to review his *My Life* (1939) in May 1940; see *CW*, XII, pp. 154–6.

D

12.7.39: Hot. Madonna lilies out.

Bedstraw, mallows & knapweed in flower. Robin's pincushions on briars. Goats will not eat cake every time so shall give it them about once a week.

12 eggs. Sold 1½ score @ 2/8.

E

12.7.39:

FOREIGN & GENERAL

1. Expulsion of foreigners from Italian Tyrol does not include Americans.[1] Rumours that purpose is to cover movements of German troops into Italy. *E. Standard* correspondent declares this is a mare's nest. [*Daily Telegraph; London Evening Standard*]
2. Chamberlain's speech apparently taken seriously throughout most of world. [*Daily Herald*]

SOCIAL

1. J.A. Spender published letter in *Times* attacking Sir A. Sinclair. Sinclair's reply refused publication. Today various prominent Liberals sent joint letter to *D. Tel.* exposing this, which *D. Tel.* published.[2] [*Daily Telegraph*]
2. Labour amendment to Agricultural Development Bill, to make farm labourers' minimum wage £2 (present average 35/–) defeated by only 4 votes. [*Daily Herald*]

PARTY POLITICS

1. Catholic press as represented by the *Universe* is now strongly anti-Nazi but scarcely as yet anti-Italian & still strongly anti-red as regards Spain. [*Universe*, 7.7.39]

1. The Italian government expelled foreigners from the frontier province of Bolzano. According to Signor Giuseppe Bastiniani, Italian Under-Secretary for Foreign Affairs, foreigners of all nations were included in the decree, and the motive was 'political and military.' Those most affected were 200 to 300 Swiss, many of them hotel owners. They were forced to sell, and the lire in which they were paid could not be taken out of Italy.
2. John Alfred Spender (1862–1942), an 'old and respected Liberal' (as the joint letter referred to described him), had attacked Archibald Sinclair, leader of the Liberal Party, for 'assaulting the Prime Minister Neville Chamberlain in unmeasured terms and holding him up to odium as an incompetent man of infirm purpose.' The joint letter, signed first by Lady Violet Bonham Carter (see Events, 14.7.39, n. 1) followed by eight others, claimed that Sinclair's speech did not bear that interpretation. However, it went on, it was doubted by many (not only those in the Labour and Liberal parties) whether adequate means were being taken 'to convince the outside world that we are unanimous, and that our Government is in earnest.'

D

13.7.39: Hot. The lame hen segregated to watch developments.

14 eggs. Bergamot flowering.

E

13.7.39:

SOCIAL

1. J. A. Spender continues his attack on Sinclair. *Times* prints other letters to same effect, none contradicting.[1] [*The Times*]

PARTY POLITICS

1. Labour Party has more or less refused conditional affiliation of I.L.P.[2] I.L.P. evidently considering all-but unconditional affiliation. [*The Times; New Leader*, 14.7.39]

1. *The Times*, in a second leader defending its action, referred also to 'the now familiar clamour . . . for the instant inclusion of Mr. Churchill in the Cabinet,' clamour from which '*The Times* has steadily held aloof.' It felt 'intensely that Mr. Churchill may well be needed in a Government again' but that 'His friends have already done him infinite harm.' Orwell is correct in recording that no 'contradicting' letters were published by *The Times* on 13 July, but a number were published on other days.
2. Independent Labour Party, founded in 1893 by Keir Hardie (see Events,17.8.39. n. 3), was older than the Labour Party, which was formed by the ILP and trade unions in 1900. Orwell was a member of the ILP; see his 'Why I Join the I.L.P.,' *The New Leader*, 24 June 1938, *CW*, XI, pp. 167-9. At this time, the ILP and the Labour Party had split and were separately represented in the House of Commons. See Crick, p. 255, for some account of the character of the ILP; and Events, 10.8.39, Party Politics, 2. For subdivisions within the ILP, see *CW*, XI, pp. 362–3.

D

14.7.39: Warm, but rainy. Took nets off strawberries & began weeding, which is almost impossible owing to the growth of the bindweed.

Phloxes (perennial) beginning to flower.

12 eggs.

E

14.7.39:

FOREIGN & GENERAL

1. Public Information Leaflet No. 2 (masking windows etc.) issued today. German visitors state gas masks have not been distributed in Germany. [No reference]

SOCIAL

1. *M. G. Weekly* prints facts about the Spender letter, & letter from Bonham Carter[1] etc. [*Manchester Guardian Weekly*]

PARTY POLITICS

1. *M. G. Weekly* considers pro-Churchill move inside the Conservative party has been checkmated. [*Manchester Guardian Weekly*]
2. Communist party pamphlet against conscription withdrawn from circulation after 3 weeks. [*Left Forum*, July 1939]

1. Lady Violet Bonham Carter (1897–1969), daughter of H. H. Asquith, Liberal Prime Minister, 1908–16, and a considerable force in the Liberal Party, was a member of Churchill's group Focus on Defence of Freedom and Peace, 1936–39.

D

15.7.39: Warm. A very short light shower in the evening. Weeded out the strawberries, as well as could be done, & picked off such as were ripe. More berries forming, but doubt if we shall get any now the nets are off.* Yesterday found a late thrush's nest with one egg (bird on it). One white hen missing – possibly sitting somewhere on a nest, but afraid she is lost, as she has been gone since yesterday.

14 eggs. Sold 2 score @ 2/8. Total this week: 86.†

Butcher says hens are laying better again, so eggs will go down [in price].

E

15.7.39:

FOREIGN & GENERAL

1. Large demonstration against British Embassy in Tokio. [*Daily Telegraph*]
2. Celebration of 150th anniversary of taking of Bastille included march-past of 30,000 troops including British. [*Daily Telegraph*]
3. Conscription of all persons 18–55 ordered in Hong Kong, but evidently so phrased as to apply chiefly to Chinese & allow exemption to most of the whites. [*Daily Telegraph*]

SOCIAL

1. Cmr. Stephen King-Hall's[1] German circular letters thought to have reached 50,000 people in Germany, evading the Gestapo by different-sized envelopes & different methods of folding. [*Daily Telegraph*]
2. Beginning of what are evidently large spy-revelations in France (*cf.* U.S.A.) by arrest of various persons connected with right-wing newspapers. [*Daily Telegraph*]

PARTY POLITICS

1. Economic League accuses P.P.U.[2] of being vehicle of Nazi propaganda.[*Daily Telegraph*]
2. Individual membership of N.C.L.[3] now said to be 4,500. Affiliations: 281 Women's Co-op Guilds, 30 Trades Councils & T.U. branches, 37 Labour parties & Women's sections, 10 Co-op parties etc., 53 P.P.U. branches, & miscellaneous. Communist press accuses N.C.L. of being a Fascist body. [*No Conscription*, July–August 1939; *Daily Worker*, 13.6.39]

MISCELLANEOUS

1. Crowds at Eton-Harrow match[4] estimated at 10,000 & said to be smartest gathering for some years. [No reference]

1. Commander Stephen King-Hall (1893–1966) retired from the Royal Navy in 1929. He was elected to Parliament, as an Independent-National, in 1939. In 1936 he started the *K-H News Service Letter* (as *National News Letter* from 1941). Right-wing and outspoken, he was well regarded as a political commentator for his personal interpretation of events.

* Up to taking off nets, about 7½ lb @ 6d a lb = 3/9 [Orwell's, note].

† Improvement of 10 on last week. Hens have been on Karswood since 4.7.39 [Orwell's note].

2. Peace Pledge Union, publishers of *Peace News*, founded 1934. Max Plowman (1883–1941) was an ardent supporter and its general secretary, 1937–38. Orwell contributed a review to *Peace News*, *CW*, XI, pp. 322–4. Plowman had served in the First World War and published a memoir, *A Subaltern on the Somme*. He also wrote *An Introduction to the Study of Blake* and *The Faith Called Pacifism*. His wife, Dorothy, was one of Orwell's life-long friends.
3. No Conscription League.
4. The annual cricket game between these schools, held early in June at Lord's Cricket Ground, London. Orwell had been co-editor of a special issue of *College Days* for this match in 1920; see *CW*, X, pp. 53–4. For the outcome of this match see Events, 16.7.39, Miscellaneous. Lord's Cricket Ground had a capacity of about 25,000, achieved only on special occasions.

D

16.7.39: Sharp shower in the morning, otherwise fairly warm. The white hen has turned up, evidently having slept out somewhere. Note that Innes has coppered over some of the chains, bolts etc. in his haymaking machinery in the same way as I did experimentally with the nails, so evidently it is not so impracticable after all. The copper where I attempted it crusted the threads of bolts so that they would not turn.

All the small pools in the woods have dried up. Note that on one a waterhen had built a nest & then had to clear out when the pool dried up.

Seeds formed on bluebells, hips forming on briars.

12 eggs.

[*On facing page, in Orwell's hand*]

To drill holes in Glass (according to *Smallholder*): Use small twist drill. Mark spot with glass-cutter, give a turn or two of the drill, then smear on grease, sprinkle with emery or carborundum powder & drill gently, not pressing.

E

16.7.39:

FOREIGN & GENERAL

1. 12,000 naval reservists to be called up July 31 for about 7 weeks. [*Sunday Times*]
2. General impression that Anglo-Russian pact is going to fall through. [*Sunday Times; Sunday Express*]
3. *Sunday Express* states that move to include Churchill in Cabinet is really move to get rid of Chamberlain. [*Sunday Express*]

SOCIAL

1. No mention of dissentients among 30,000 militiamen called up yesterday. [No reference]
2. More or less scaremongering article (submarine menace) by Liddell Hart[1] in *Sunday Express*. [*Sunday Express*]

PARTY POLITICS

1. Liberal retains N. Cornwall seat, slightly increasing previous small majority. Both candidates' polls rose largely. [*Daily Telegraph*, 15.7.39]
2. Beaverbrook press[2] accuses P.P.U. of being pro-Nazi, misquoting article. [*Peace News*, 14.7.39]

MISCELLANEOUS

1. Eton Harrow match ends in a fight, the first time since 1919?[3] [*Sunday Express*]

1. Captain Sir Basil Henry Liddell Hart (1895–1970) was a writer of more than thirty books, including *History of the Second World War* (1970). He had been military correspondent to the *Daily Telegraph*, 1925–35, and to *The Times*, 1935–39, and military editor of the *Encyclopaedia Britannica*, 14th edition, 1929. In 1937 he was personal adviser to the Minister of War. He then wrote infantry training manuals and edited the series *The Next War*, 6 vols. (1938). Orwell wrote of him, 'The two military critics most favoured by the intelligentsia are Captain Liddell Hart and Major-General Fuller, the first of whom teaches that the defence is stronger than the attack, and the second that the attack is stronger than the defence. This contradiction has not prevented both of them from being accepted as authorities by the same public. The secret reason for their vogue in left-wing circles is that both of them are at odds with the War Office'; see 'Notes on Nationalism,' [October] 1945, *CW*, XVII, pp. 141–57.
2. Right-wing newspapers owned by Lord Beaverbrook, which included the *Daily Express, Sunday Express,* and *Evening Standard*. See Orwell's 'London Letter' of 15 April 1941, *CW*, XII, pp. 470–9.
3. In the annual cricket match between Eton and Harrow, the latter had a notable victory, winning by eight wickets (Harrow 294 and 131 for two; Eton 268 and 156). The front page of the *Sunday Express* carried a story prominently displayed and headed: 'Worst Hat-Bashing for Years / Our 'Gentlemen' enjoy themselves.' It states, 'Top hats were torn to shreds, umbrellas broken in pieces, ties torn up – and even trousers taken off.' It concludes: 'There have not been such scenes since the 1919 match' (when Orwell was at Eton), 'which resulted in a warning that the fixture would be cancelled if fighting occurred again.'

D

17.7.39: Warmish in morning, thunderstorms & heavy rain most of afternoon.

Picked first peas, about 1 lb. Thinned out turnips, which are very good & untouched by the fly. Began digging patch for greens, but too wet to do much.

Hens which have made nests outside will apparently continue to sit there in the middle of pouring rain. Very small newt tadpoles put into aquarium seem to disappear. Fear the large ones may be eating them, but if so this must only occur at night. Note that the water-snail is able in some way to elevate himself to the top of the water & remain floating there – or possibly is naturally buoyant & only remains down when using suction.*

11 eggs. (1 double egg – the first for some time).

E

17.7.39:

FOREIGN & GENERAL

1. British send cruiser & thus prevent threatened anti-British demonstration at Tsingtao.[1] Tokyo conversations evidently not getting anywhere. [*Daily Telegraph*]
2. Anglo-Russian pact only just makes front page of *D. Tel.* [Daily Telegraph]

SOCIAL

1. Definitely stated in *D. Tel.* that Saturday's militia draft (34,000 men) turned up with not one absentee (except cases of illness etc). [*Daily Telegraph*]

PARTY POLITICS

1. Left wing of Indian Congress party (as judged by *Congress Socialist*) more vigorously anti-war than before. Publishes vicious attack on C.P.[2] from Trotskyist angle, but another article demands democratic bloc. [*Congress Socialist*; no date given]
2. Serious trouble in I.L.P. on pacifist-revolutionary controversy & long statement from I.L.P.'ers (London group) published in *Socialist Correspondence*, which also takes other opportunities of attacking McGovern. [*Socialist Correspondence*]

1. Tsingtao (now Qingdao), port in northern China, built to rival Tientsin (Tianjin) in 1930s, occupied by the Japanese, 1938–45. See Events, 24.7.39, n. 1.
2. Communist Party.

D

18.7.39: Raining almost the whole day. Too wet to do much outside.

Female flowers coming on first marrow.

11 eggs.

D

19.7.39: Showers, but mostly fine. Everything now growing very fast. Many peas. A few tomatoes about the size of marbles. One or two marrows about size of peanuts.

Not certain whether a pullet has begun laying prematurely or whether the mother hen which is still in the youngsters' run (& which lays a small egg) had laid out, but found an egg in that run today.

Sowed canterbury bells (prob. too late, but they do very well if treated as triennials.)

13 eggs (2 very small). Sold 35 for 4/3 (2/6 a score – should have been 4/4½).

* Can also rise to surface when he wants to, or can remain on bottom without holding on [Orwell's note].

E

19.7.39:

FOREIGN & GENERAL

1. Gov.t advising all householders to lay in supply of non-perishable food. Leaflet on the subject to be issued shortly. [*Daily Telegraph*]
2. *D. Tel.* gives over 2 pages to scale pictures of entire British battle fleet. [*Daily Telegraph*]
3. German economic mission in Moscow said to be making no more progress than Anglo-Russian pact, with implication that 3-cornered bargaining is going on. [No reference]

PARTY POLITICS

1. First appearance of People's Party in Hythe by-election. [*Daily Telegraph*]
2. Appears that Lidell° Hart's book *Defence of Britain*[1] boosts Hore Belisha.° [*Daily Telegraph*, 18.7.39]

MISCELLANEOUS

1. General estimation that harvest this year will be good, not (as last year) wheat only. [No reference]

1. B. H. Liddell Hart's *Defence of Britain* was published in 1939. Leslie Hore-Belisha (1893–1957), politician, barrister, and journalist (especially for the Beaverbrook press), was a Liberal M.P., 1923–45, and was instrumental in 1931 in organising the National Liberal Party to support the 'National Government' led by Stanley Baldwin (Conservative) and Ramsay MacDonald (Labour). He served as Secretary to the Board of Trade and then as Minister of Transport, 1934–37. In 1937, Chamberlain appointed him Secretary of State for War, charging him with the task of modernising the armed forces; he served until 1940; see Events, 29.7.39, Miscellaneous, n. 3.

D

20.7.39: Some sun in the morning, otherwise almost continuous rain all day. Impossible to do anything outside. Notice that hens always eat less in this weather. Top of the hay under a few sacks is still dry in spite of the constant rain. Goats show slight tendency to diarrhea from eating wet grass. Stated today in letter in *D. Tel.* that for 1 person using electricity for all purposes, except a periodical coal fire for warming, 1800–2000 units is annual minimum consumption.

12 eggs (1 v. small – it is the mother hen that lays these).

E

20.7.39:

FOREIGN & GENERAL

1. Public Information Leaflet no. 3 (evacuation[1]) issued today. Never less than 4 searchlights visible at night from this village. [No reference]
2. News from Danzig seems to indicate that all there expect Danzig to fall into German hands in near future. [*Daily Telegraph*]

3. France said to be in favour of acceptance of Russian terms for Anglo-Russian pact, which have not been altered re. the Baltic States. [*Daily Telegraph*]

SOCIAL

1. One of the editors of *Humanité* [2] questioned by the Paris police with ref. to spy revelations, but no indication from report whether merely in advisory capacity or under suspicion of complicity. [*Daily Telegraph*]
2. Recent W.O.[3] regulation has forbidden army officers to resign their commissions & seemingly steps are being taken to prevent N.C.Os buying out from the service (present cost £35).[4] [*Daily Telegraph*]

1. Large numbers of children were dispersed from cities to country areas for safety from air attack. Many stayed in their adopted homes for the duration of the war. See also Events, 29.8.39, Foreign & General, 3; 31.8.39, Foreign & General; 1.9.39, Foreign & General, 2.
2. Leading French Communist daily newspaper.
3. War Office.
4. A serviceman could, with permission, reduce the time he had agreed to serve at his enlistment by buying his release. The practice continues today.

D

21.7.39: Fine part of the day, but overcast & damp in the morning, & a thunderstorm in the afternoon. Wheat yellowing. Planted out leeks (38 make a row). Weeds very bad everywhere. This morning a female flower on a marrow opened; shut again this evening so presumably fertilised. Goats' yield down, owing to yesterday. Gooseberries almost ripe.

13 eggs.

E

21.7.39:

FOREIGN & GENERAL

1. Polish official assassinated on Danzig frontier & consequent "tension."[1] [*Daily Telegraph*]

SOCIAL

1. *Times* has leading article explaining (not very satisfactorily) the business of the Spender letter. [*The Times*, 20.7.39]
2. *M. G. Weekly* prints long letter extolling the Italian regime in Abyssinia & another answering this. [*Manchester Guardian Weekly*]

PARTY POLITICS

1. Conservatives hold Hythe with reduced majority. Only 37% of electorate voted. People's Party candidate polled 5–600 votes. [*Daily Telegraph*]
2. Internal row in London I.L.P. still obscure, but evidently reduces to a quarrel between the E.C.[2] who wish to attract pacifists into the party & the London Divisional Council who are more or less Trotskyist. Apparently some hope of getting rid of the latter. [*New Leader*]

3. Parliamentary debate on Palestine, illegal immigration etc., passed off with less row than had been anticipated. [*Daily Telegraph*]

1. Witold Budziewicz, a Polish customs officer, was shot dead shortly after being challenged by a Danzig customs officer accompanied by two Nazis. At the time, it was not known who fired the shot. This was one of a number of incidents designed to increase tension in the area in order to provide Hitler with a pretext for intervention.
2. Executive Committee; for divisions within the ILP, see headnote to Events.

D

22.7.39: Overcast & oppressive. A good deal of rain for about an hour in the evening. E[ileen] raised 3 roots of early potatoes (only 3 months sown). Few potatoes, about 1 lb. on the 3, but many young ones coming.

12 eggs. Sold 1½ score @ 2/6. Total this week: 84.

E

22.7.39:

FOREIGN & GENERAL

1. Rumours of impending Anglo-American deal with Germany, which is said to be connected with Herr Wohltat's visit but not as yet sponsored by the Cabinet.[1] Conditions to be loan of £1000 million & access to raw materials, in return for disarmament under international surveyance.° [*Daily Telegraph*]
2. Russian fleet exercises evidently designed to impress Baltic States. [*Daily Telegraph*]

SOCIAL

1. *D. Tel.* gossip column notes that nearly 100 Conservative MPs. are officers in the territorials, R.A.F. voluntary reserve etc. [*Daily Telegraph*]

PARTY POLITICS

1. Queipo de Llano[2] relieved of his post. [*Daily Telegraph*]
2. Friendly review of my novel in *"Daily Worker."*[3] [*Daily Worker*, 19.7.39]

1. Dr. Helmut Wohltat, Economic Adviser to Hermann Goering, was visiting Britain for a conference on whaling. He undoubtedly also had discussions with R. S. Hudson of the Department of Overseas Trade. It is now known that each was acting on his own initiative, but suspicions were aroused. Prime Minister Chamberlain categorically denied to the House of Commons on 24 July that anything more was involved than informal discussion on matters of joint interest, and assured the House that no proposal for a loan had been made.
2. General Gonzalo Queipo de Llano y Serra (1875–1951) had commanded Franco's Army of the South. Though a Republican, he accepted the title of marquis in 1947. See also Events, 23.7.39, Party Politics, 1, for the reason for his dismissal from his post as Inspector-General of the Carabineros.
3. *Coming Up for Air.* Orwell's surprise was occasioned by the way the *Daily Worker* had attacked him in 1937; see letter to Victor Gollancz, 20 August 1937, *CW*, XI, pp. 72–4

D

23.7.39: A little rain in the evening, otherwise dry, but overcast & not very warm. Many harebells. Found the first ripe dewberry. Oats almost ripe in some fields, wheat grains still milky. Seagulls about – one does not usually see them here. The Ridleys have a dahlia in bloom.

12 eggs.

E

23.7.39:

FOREIGN & GENERAL

1. Appears from today's press that the offer referred to in this column yesterday has actually been talked of, but only unofficially. Cabinet disclaim knowledge but evidently know all about it. Presumption is that it has been allowed to leak out to see how the public take it. Terms were: loan (amount not stated) to Germany, raw materials & possible condominium in certain African possessions, against partial disarmament & withdrawal from Czechoslovakia. [*Sunday Times*; *Sunday Express*]
2. Now evident that Russian pact will fall through. [*Sunday Express*]
3. Calling up of territorials & naval reservists suggests that danger moment will be first week in August. [*Sunday Times*]

PARTY POLITICS

1. Cause of Queipo de Llano's dismissal said to be that he protested against tying Spain to the Axis & threatened to declare independence of Andalusia.[1] [*Sunday Express*]
2. Nat. Liberals intend to split Gov.t vote in Brecon by-election.[2] [*Sunday Express*]
3. Editor (Grey)[3] of pro-Fascist *Aeroplane* has resigned for unexplained reasons.[4] [*Sunday Express*]
4. Beaverbrook press now more openly against the Russian pact & for isolationism than for some months past. [No reference]

1. Queipo had been a member of Spain's National Council in 1937 but was left out of Franco's cabinet early in 1938. See Thomas, pp. 750, 752–54, and 948, n. 2.
2. The National Liberals were close allies of the Conservatives in Baldwin's and Chamberlain's governments. By standing in an election against a Conservative candidate, the National Liberals would split the pro-government vote. See Events, 4.8.39, Party Politics, 1.
3. Charles Grey (1875–?), a journalist with a special interest in aeronautical matters, founded *The Aeroplane* in 1911 and edited it until 1939, when he became air correspondent for several newspapers. He wrote a number of books on aircraft and edited *All the World's Aircraft*, 1916–41.
4. Claud Cockburn, in his pro-Communist journal, *The Week*, described *The Aeroplane* as 'frankly pro-Nazi.' See Events, 4.8.39, n. 1.

D

24.7.39: Fine in morning, cold & miserable in afternoon. Wildflowers now in bloom: agrimony, perforated St. John's Wort, red dead nettle, wild mignonette, self-heal, woody nightshade, stitchwort. Found nest of wild bees in grass in churchyard. Nest of moss rather like that made by dormouse. Dahlias budding. Picked first of our own lettuces today, & first ripe gooseberries yesterday. Many peas.

14 eggs (1 small). A little rain this evening.

E

24.7.39:

FOREIGN & GENERAL

1. The conversation with Wohltat was held by R. S. Hudson (Overseas Trade) who reported to the P.M. following day. Obviously the affair has been allowed to leak out intentionally. Italian press reported as suggesting that this (tie-up with Germany) is a threat aimed at impressing U.S.S.R. Anglo-Russian pact back on front page with suggestion that Stalin really wants it. German trade talks are also being resumed, this presumably a threat aimed at England. [*Daily Telegraph*]
2. Fighting on Mongolia border evidently genuine. [*Daily Telegraph*]
3. Japanese press giving advance forecast of terms to Britain over Tientsin[1] which would clearly not be accepted. [*Daily Telegraph*]

1. Tientsin (Tianjin) was a port in northern China where Britain and France had been granted Concessions by a treaty of 1858, which were extended later to Germany and Japan. It was occupied by the Japanese, 1937–45, but guerrilla and 'terrorist' resistance continued. In one incident, when the Chinese manager of the Japanese-sponsored Federal Reserve Bank was killed, and the Japanese were looking for four Chinese believed to be responsible for this, the Chinese took refuge in the British Concession. When the British refused to hand them over, the Japanese blockaded the British and French Concessions, starting on 14 June 1939. Supplies were admitted only after careful search. It was reported in *The Times*, 15 July 1939, that milk was at last being allowed into the Concession. See Events, 1.8.39, Foreign & General, 3, and 18.8.39, Social, 1.

D

25.7.39: Fine & fairly hot. Endeavouring to stack the hay. 12 eggs (1 small).

About 26 July 1939 Orwell wrote to the Scientific Poultry Breeders' Association about the Food Purchase Scheme it ran for members. His letter has not survived, but one from S. R. Harvey, General Manager and Secretary of S.P.B.A. Supplies, Ltd., dated 28 July, gives details of discounts allowed on poultry feedstuffs, and also encloses details of association membership.

E

25.7.39:

FOREIGN & GENERAL

1. Brit-Japanese agreement very vaguely worded but amounts to climbing

down on Britain's part as in effect it amounts to a promise not to help Chinese. Chamberlain denies any alteration in British policy. [*Daily Telegraph*]

2. Anglo-Soviet pact back on front page & appears more probable. [*Daily Telegraph*]

SOCIAL

1. Bill to deal with I.R.A. provides for power to prohibit entry of aliens, deportation of aliens, & compulsory registration of aliens. Also emergency power to Sup.ts of Police to search without warrant. Bill said to be for 2 years only. Not seriously opposed (passed 218–17.) [*Daily Telegraph*]

D

26.7.39: Fine & warm. Finished thatching hay, as well as it can be done, which is not very well. However this is practice for another occasion when there is more hay. Stack is about 8′ x 6′ by 5′ at highest point. Hoed out cabbages & turnips, both doing well.

11 eggs (1 small). Sold 35 @ 2/6 score (4/3 – ought to have been 4/4½).

E

26.7.39:

FOREIGN & GENERAL

1. General impression in world press that Gt. Britain has climbed down in Tokyo agreement. [*Daily Telegraph*]
2. Another demonstration flight of 240 aeroplanes over France. Joint French-British aeroplane production now claimed to equal German. [*Daily Telegraph*]

SOCIAL

1. Proposal to affiliate N.U.J.[1] to T.U.C.[2] lost by very narrow margin (ballot showed actual majority for but not ⅔ majority). [*Daily Telegraph*]

PARTY POLITICS

1. Franco evidently standing by his Axis commitments & seems about due for his June purge against de Llano, Yague[3] & others. [*Daily Telegraph*]
2. Litvinoff [4] apparently in disgrace. [*Daily Telegraph*]

1. National Union of Journalists.
2. Trades Union Congress. It was founded in 1868, to represent all unions that chose to be affiliated to it.
3. Colonel Blanco de Yagüe (1891–1952) was a successful Nationalist commander. Thomas reports that at a Falangist banquet on 19 April 1938 he praised the fighting qualities of the Republicans, and described the allies of the Nationalists, the Germans and Italians, as 'beasts of prey' (p. 819).
4. Maxim Litvinov (1876–1951) represented the Soviet Union abroad in many capacities from 1917, when he was unacknowledged Ambassador to Britain, to 1941–43, when he served as Ambassador to the United States. A Jew and a prominent anti-Nazi, who had recommended collective action against Hitler, he was dismissed as Commissar of Foreign Affairs on 3 May 1939.

D

27.7.39: Hot. A very few drops of rain in the evening.

Red mite is bad in the henhouses, partly no doubt owing to one or two hot days. Dealt with them with boiling water & sulphur afterwards, hoping this will be effective. NB. that plumber's blowlamp would be the best thing. Hen's° appetite is off as usual in hot weather. Planted out a few cos lettuce, otherwise nothing except weeding. The pumpkin has now taken hold but is still a small plant. The watersnail has laid some eggs. Don't [know] whether these creatures are bisexual or not.

NB. that for storage purposes in tanks etc., 20 gallons* space will about hold 1 cwt. of meal, or more of grain (say 1¼ cwt.)

14 eggs (2 small – believe 1 pullet is now laying).

E

27.7.39:

FOREIGN & GENERAL

1. More fighting on Manchukuo border. Japanese said to be contemplating blockade of Russian half of Sakhalin. [*Daily Telegraph*]
2. French-British-Russian staff talks being arranged for. Question of Baltic states apparently unsettled. [*Daily Telegraph*]
3. Public Information leaflet No. 4 (food storage) issued today. [No reference]

PARTY POLITICS

1. Conservatives held Monmouth div.n with reduced majority. Both polls dropped. [*Daily Telegraph*]
2. Queipo de Llano appointed ambassador to Argentine.[1] [*Daily Telegraph*]
3. Summary of efforts of the various anti-war groups to be found in *New English Weekly* 20 & 27.7.39 [*New English Weekly*, 20,27.7.39]
4. The M.P.s (19) who voted against the I.R.A. bill included Gallacher, Pritt,[2] Cripps. [*New Leader*, 28.7.39]

1. But see Events, 1.8.39, Party Politics, 1.
2. William Gallacher (1881–1965), Communist M.P. 1935–50. Dennis Noel Pritt (1887–1972), lawyer, author, and Labour M.P., 1935–40. Following policy disagreements, Pritt was expelled from the Labour Party, and was an Independent Socialist M.P. until 1950. A fervent supporter of left-wing causes and of the Soviet Union, in 1954 he was awarded the Lenin Peace Prize. Orwell had little love for Pritt; see his letter to Humphry House, 11 April 1940, *CW*, XII, pp.139–42 and Vol. XX, p. 253).

D

28.7.39: Some rain during last night. Hot. Nothing except weeding, mowing down thistles etc.

9 eggs.

* NB. That apparently 20 galls, equals almost exactly 3 cubic ft. [Orwell's note].

E

28.7.39:

FOREIGN & GENERAL

1. Americans evidently deciding to denounce commercial treaty with Japan. [*Daily Telegraph*]

SOCIAL

1. Gov.t apparently considering raising of old age pension, no doubt with an eye to general election. [*Daily Telegraph*]
2. Rich gold deposits said to have been found near Great Slave Lake in Canada. [*Daily Telegraph*]
3. Smallholders & small farmers evidently being incommoded by conscription. First special tribunal under M.T. act[1] had 20 objectors to deal with, none apparently on political grounds. [*Smallholder; Daily Telegraph*]

PARTY POLITICS

1. Fresh purge in Moscow, including Tarioff, Soviet Minister to Outer Mongolia. [*Daily Telegraph*]
2. French handing over £8 millions of Spanish gold to Franco. [*Daily Telegraph*]
3. P.P.U., N.C.L, Friends & Fellowship of Reconciliation were able to be represented at first tribunal under M.T. Act. [*Daily Telegraph*]

1. The Military Training Act permitted the call-up of men for military service and allowed for conscientious objection.

D

29.7.39: Apparently a few spots of rain in the night. Hot today. Mowed nettles. 6 eggs! (possibly something to do with heat.) Sold 25 @ 2/6 score. Total this week: 78

E

29.7.39:

FOREIGN & GENERAL

1. French general election to be postponed by decree for 2 years (ie. until 1942). [*Daily Telegraph*]
2. Evidently° that fairly severe struggle is going on in Spain between Axis supporters (Suñer[1]) & Traditionalists (esp. the generals, Yague etc.) & that there is likelihood of Franco remaining neutral in case of war. [*Manchester Guardian Weekly; Daily Telegraph*]

SOCIAL

1. Editor of *Humanité* who was tried in test case for printing various allegations about German espionage in France, acquitted. Order of arrest issued against another journalist for writing anti-Semitic article.* [*Daily Telegraph*]

* Sentence of imprisonment [Orwell's note].

PARTY POLITICS

1. Labour held Colne Valley constituency with increased majority. (Labour vote rose about 1000, Liberal & Cons, each dropped 2–3 thousand.) [*Daily Telegraph*]
2. According to figures given in *MG.*, 3–300 people a week (Republicans) have been being° shot in Catalonia from May onwards.[2] [*Manchester Guardian Weekly*]

MISCELLANEOUS

1. Guards trooped the colours in 3's[3] for the first time yesterday. [*Daily Telegraph*]

1. Ramon Serrano Suñer (1901–2003), brother-in-law of Franco and, as Minister of the Interior, second in importance to him, until dismissed in 1942. His experiences as a prisoner of the Republicans embittered him for life. As Thomas puts it, they were such 'as to make him close his eyes to pity' (p. 924, and see pp. 633–34).
2. Count Galeazzo Ciano (1903–1944), Italian Foreign Minister, visited Spain in July 1939 and reported (as quoted by Thomas, p. 924): 'trials going on every day at a speed which I would call almost summary. . . . There are still a great number of shootings. In Madrid alone, between 200 and 250 a day, in Barcelona 150, in Seville 80.' Thomas comments, 'Seville had been in nationalist Spain throughout the war: how could there be still enough people to shoot at this rate?' In 1944 it was reported that 193,000 people had been executed, but Thomas suggests this might be the number of death sentences, some of which were commuted, or that it includes those executed during the war (p. 925).
3. Infantry regiments formed up in four ranks until the 1937 reforms instituted by Secretary of State for War, Hore-Belisha (see Events, 19.7.39, Party Politics, 1.) Among them were changes in army drill to simplify the often complicated movements and so speed the process of training. The change Orwell notes here is forming up in three ranks, a practice still followed. Hore-Belisha's reforms also included the introduction of battle dress and the abolition of puttees.

D

30.7.39: A little rain during last night. Today hot. Canterbury bell seeds germinating. Pulled first carrots today. Earwigs now very troublesome.
10 eggs (2 small).

E

30.7.39:

FOREIGN & GENERAL

1. Seems clear that Parliament will adjourn as usual with no previous arrangements for recall before October.[1] [*Sunday Times*]
2. There are now 60,000 German troops (ie. including police, storm troopers etc.) in Danzig. [*Sunday Times*]
3. Seemingly authoritative article in *S. Times* states that in case of war Jugoslavia will certainly be neutral but more likely to be pro-ally if the

Russian pact goes through & the Croats are given the degree of autonomy they want. Population of 14 m. includes 5 m. Serbs, 5 m. Croats, ½m. Hungarians, ½m. Germans, the rest presumably Slovenes. Pan-Slav feeling strong among the poorer classes. [*Sunday Times*]

SOCIAL

1. One of Daladier's[2] decrees sets up separate propaganda dep.t under P.M.'s control. Working hours of civil service raised from 40 to 45.

   France's gold reserve now said to be second only to that of U.S.A. Gold holding of Bank of France is £560m. [*Sunday Times*]
2. I.R.A. suspects already being deported in fairly large numbers (about 20 hitherto). [*Sunday Times; Daily Telegraph*, 29.7.39]

1. See Events, 30.8.39, Social, 1. for adjournment of Parliament.
2. Edouard Daladier (1884–1970), Socialist Prime Minister of France, 1938–40; see Morocco Diary, n. 13.

D

31.7.39: Most of day overcast, heavy showers & thunder about mid-day. Weeded onions. Pricked out 35 carnations. The wallflowers planted on 11.7.39 about 3″ to 4″ high. One hollyhock which is coming into flower is white. There are therefore 4 colours (dark red, light red, pale pink, white) from the original dark seed. Peas are very good, much more than we can eat. Last cwt. of corn finished this morning. Begun on 4.7.39, should by calculation have lasted to about August 10th, but the 8 pullets have been fed on it for the last 3 weeks, also to some extent the 6 next chicks. Full-o-pep bought at same time only about ⅔ gone.

11 eggs (3 pullets? Evidently at least 1 pullet is now laying.)

D

1.8.39: Warm. A few drops of rain. Pricked out wallflowers (yellow) & sweet williams. Calculate roughly that each row of peas (about 12 yards) will yield 15–20 lb. Started new cwt. of wheat & kibbled maize today. This has to do for 23 adult fowls & 8 pullets (almost full grown). At 1½ oz per bird per day should last till about September 8th.

10 eggs (3 small – 3 pullets laying now.)

E

1.8.39:

FOREIGN & GENERAL

1. Military mission probably leaving for Moscow this week. Leader (Admiral Plunkett-Ernle-Erle-Drax[1]) took part in mission to Tsarist Russia just before Great War. [*Daily Telegraph*]
2. Polish Gov.t taking economic sanctions against Danzig amounting to refusal to import products of certain factories. [*Daily Telegraph*]
3. British authorities apparently agreeing to hand over the 4 Chinese alleged terrorists hiding in the Tientsin concession.[2] [*Daily Telegraph*]

SOCIAL

1. Number of unemployed for July about 1¼ millions, *½ million less than same period in 1938. Total number in insured employment close on 13 million, more than ½ million more than a year ago. [*Daily Telegraph*]
2. In first 34,000 militia men called up only 58 absented themselves without leave. [*Daily Telegraph*]
3. Prohibition inaugurated in Bombay Presidency.[3] [*Daily Telegraph*]

PARTY POLITICS

1. Queipo de Llano appointed chief of Spanish military mission to Italy. [*Daily Telegraph*]
2. *Socialist Correspondence* claims that Labour Members who voted against I.R.A. bill are being threatened with discipline by Parliamentary Group. [*Socialist Correspondence*, 29.7.39]
3. P.O U.M.[4] Youth Group managing to issue leaflets. [*Socialist Correspondence*, 29.7.39]

MISCELLANEOUS

1. New method of bracken destruction by mowing plus sodium chlorate successfully extirpates bracken using only 20 lb. of s.c. per acre. [*Daily Telegraph; Farmer & Stockbreeder*]
2. This year's European wheat production, excluding U.S.S.R., estimated at 44 million metric tons, slightly above average but 14% less than last year's [*Daily Telegraph*]

1. Admiral Sir Reginald Aylmer Ranfurley Plunkett-Ernle-Erle-Drax (1880–1967), Commander-in-Chief, The Nore, 1939–41, was accompanied by a representative of the Army and one of the Royal Air Force. Although a talented man, he was ill-briefed for this mission and was subjected to ridicule in Moscow, Voroshilov pointedly referring to his being a Knight Commander of the 'Bath'. He signed himself simply as 'Drax' (William Wilson). He was the author of the *Handbook of Solar Heating* (J. Looker, Poole, 1965; three editions).
2. See Events, 24.7.39, Foreign & General, 3, and 18.8.39, Social, 1.
3. One of the three divisions of India when administered by the East India Company; the others were Bengal and Madras. The titles were continued after the East India Company was superseded.
4. Partido Obrero de Unificatión Marxista was the Revolutionary Communist Party of Spain, anti-Stalinist. Orwell fought with it in Spain. See *Homage to Catalonia*, *CW*, VI, especially Appendix II, for the attempt by the Communist Party to eradicate the POUM.

D

2.8.39: Most of day overcast & rather chilly. Only weeding etc.
12 eggs. (2 pullets?). Sold 30 @ 2/6 score.

* 100,000 less than estimate of a month previously [Orwell's note].

E

2.8.39:

FOREIGN & GENERAL

1. Announced today that ration cards are already printed & ready. [*Daily Telegraph*]
2. Chamberlain's speech broadcast throughout U.S.S.R.[1] [*Daily Telegraph*]
3. Number of Ukrainian leaders arrested in Poland. [*Daily Telegraph*]

SOCIAL

1. Labour MPs' complaints in Parliament about conditions in militia turn upon such things as militiamen sleeping 8 in a tent. [*Daily Telegraph*]
2. Appears that German Jewish refugees are settling in great numbers in certain parts of London, eg. Golders Green, & buying houses which they have plenty of money to do. [Private (C.W.)[2]]

PARTY POLITICS

1. Rumour of quarrels among Spanish refugee higher-ups in Paris over money & disagreement between Negrín & Prieto.[3] [Private (R.R.)[4]]
2. Col. Wedgwood's [5] Catholic Constituents (to number of 5000, mostly working-class) in Newcastle under Lyne,° have memorialised stating that they will vote against him. [Private (C.W.)]

1. This speech, in the House of Commons, 31 July, announced that a mission was to go to Moscow for discussions with Soviet authorities on military matters. It reiterated the government's aim, summarised in *The Times*, 1 August, as 'peace with justice; its method . . . the formation of the "Peace Front."'
2. *C. W.*: Probably from Cyril Wright. He and his girl-friend, Mikeal Smith, were friends of Orwell's and they frequently drove over from Bedford, where he lived, to Wallington to discuss books. Wright worked as a salesman for his father, a sweet manufacturer, from 1937–39. He later became a salesman for Dean's, the manufacturer of shop blinds. It is possible that Orwell gained some knowledge of a salesman's life from Wright which was helpful to him when writing *Coming Up for Air* as well as from John Sceats. He was not a member of the ILP and once canvassed for the Labour Party.
3. Dr. Juan Negrín (1889–1956) was Socialist Prime Minister of the Republic of Spain, September 1936–March 1938. He fled to France, where he died in exile. Indalecio Prieto y Tuero (1883–1962), Socialist Minister of National Defence in Negrín's cabinet, died in exile in Mexico.
4. Either Orwell's friend Richard Rees or Reginald Reynolds (1905–1958), journalist and author, Quaker and pacifist, who supported the non-Communist Republicans in Spain and was a brilliant speaker for the ILP.
5. Josiah Clement Wedgwood (1872–1943; Baron, 1942), M.P. for Newcastle-under-Lyme, 1906–42, first as a Liberal, later for Labour; was Vice-Chairman of the Labour Party, 1921–24.

D

3.8.39: Unbroken rain from early this morning till about 8 pm. One or two dahlias now in flower. Examining yesterday one of the large black slugs common at this time of year (about 4″ long when extended) noticed that the curious hole they have a little way behind the head opens & shuts more or less rhythmically, & has inside whitish tissue like sago pudding. Possibly this is their breathing hole?

Some oats cut, barley mostly ripe & looks very good, no wheat ripe. Toadflax in flower. Only one or two plums on the wild plum tree.

Gave M[uriel] her worm powder, with great difficulty, having kept her more or less without food all day.

12 eggs (1 small – 1 pullet is now laying larger eggs.)

D

4.8.39: Raining most of day, with sunny intervals, windy. Ground now very sodden, everything growing very fast. Lifted some more early potatoes (about 3½ months). Not many on each root. Saw the lost hen again this morning. Mrs A[nderson] says she has seen her several mornings & thinks she is in the thick bushes up the west end of the field. She occasionally comes out to eat, usually in the very early morning. The trouble is that a fox or dog may get her before she has finished brooding.

13 eggs (3 small.)

E

4.8.39:

FOREIGN & GENERAL

1. French-Brit, military mission leaving tomorrow on slow liner which will take a week to reach Leningrad. *The Week*[1] suggests that the move is not intended seriously. Quotations from Finnish papers & Swedish Foreign Minister's speech suggest that Baltic States are genuinely nervous. [*Daily Telegraph; Manchester Guardian Weekly; The Week*, 2.8.39]
2. Germany said to be considering transference of Slovakia from Hungary in order to detach the latter from Poland.[2] Said also to be systematically depleting Slovakia of timber, foodstuffs & machinery. [*Manchester Guardian Weekly.*]

SOCIAL

1. Mander M.P. (Lib.)[3] declares Anglo-German Fellowship[4] a pro-German organisation & asks whether Home Sec. can suppress it. Hoare[5] replies unable to do anything unless an organisation breaks the law. [*Daily Telegraph*]

PARTY POLITICS

1. Labour won Brecon & Radnor by 2500 majority.[6] Labour vote rose about 750, Gov.t vote dropped about 4000, & total poll dropped. [*Daily Telegraph*]

MISCELLANEOUS

1. Albatross Press[7] arranging for publication of my last book require excision of certain (though not all) unfriendly references to Hitler. Say they are obliged to do this as their books circulate largely in Germany. Also

excision of a passage of about a page suggesting that war is imminent. [F.[8] Personal]

1. *The Week* was a private-circulation, ostensibly independent but pro-Communist newsletter edited by Claud Cockburn (Frank Pitcairn; 1904–81), Communist journalist. In March 1938 he helped fabricate a news story that there had been a military uprising against Franco in Tetuán in Northern Morocco. This Communist propaganda was designed to give the impression that Franco might still be defeated and so persuade the French to open their border: see Thomas, p. 805, n. 3. He was implacably opposed to the POUM, with whom Orwell had fought in Spain. In a posthumously broadcast TV interview for *Arena* in 1984, he said, 'Any damage I could do them I would do. Certainly. No bones about it at all. In the same way after all you are prepared to shoot people with a gun. Well then – as in my case, the typewriter was somewhat more mighty than the rifle'. See his *Reporter in Spain*, 1936, and *Crossing the Line*, 1956 (which refers to the Teután fraud, pp. 27–8). *The Week* was published from 29 March 1933 to 15 January 1941, when it was suppressed by government order. A new series was allowed from October 1942, and it ran until December 1946. See his *The Years of The Week* (1968), pp. 262–64.
2. This opaque summary refers to side-effects of the Munich pact. For sense, it should read 'to Hungary.' As Churchill summarised it, after Munich, 'A formal division of the spoils was made by Germany at the beginning of November. Poland was not disturbed in her occupation of Teschen [an area of Silesia opportunely seized by Poland]. The Slovaks, who had been used as a pawn by Germany, obtained a precarious autonomy. Hungary received a piece of flesh at the expense of Slovakia' (*The Second World War*, I, p. 298).
3. Geoffrey Mander (1882–1962; Kt., 1945) was a Liberal M.P., 1929–45.
4. "The Link": see Events, 6.8.39, Party Politics, n. 6.
5. Sir Samuel Hoare (1880–1959; Viscount Templewood, 1944) Conservative, was appointed foreign secretary in June 1935, but resigned in December because of opposition to his plan to settle the Abyssinian crisis. In June 1936 he became First Lord of the Admiralty and later Home Secretary. A supporter of the Munich pact, he fell with Chamberlain in May 1940. Later, as Ambassador to Spain, he negotiated the release from Spanish gaols of some 30,000 Allied prisoners and refugees.
6. See Events, 23.7.39, Party Politics, 2 and n. 2.
7. The Albatross Continental Library was a German publishing house which circulated books in English in paperback on the Continent. Although Albatross was a German firm, Orwell's contract for the publication of *Coming Up for Air* was drawn up in Paris. The contract stipulated that the book was to be issued before August 1940. See War-time Diary, 15.6.40.
8. Unidentified.

D

5.8.39: Raining almost continuously until about 6.30 pm. Parts of the day rain extremely heavy. Baldock high street said to have been flooded. Marrows swelling very rapidly. French & runner beans 3″ or 4″ long. Apples growing very fast.

Cylinder of calor gas, started 7.7.39, gave out yesterday (27 days). Started new cylinder today.

9 eggs (2 small). Sold 30 @ 2/6 score. Total this week: 77 of which 15 small.

D

6.8.39: No rain, fairly warm. The big crab tree in the lane has failed to produce any apples, but found others with fruit. Blackberries still only in flower. Hazel nuts still solid inside. Innes's cows due to calve shortly. Waterhens still have quite small chicks. Many young rabbits. Found dead cat in lane. Notice that hens will eat the large black slugs. Forgot to mention that on Thursday saw what I think must be a hawfinch. Greenfinches in the hen run from time to time, but goldfinches uncommon here.

11 eggs (3 small).

E

6.8.39:

FOREIGN & GENERAL

1. Purge of Sudeten[1] leaders taking place, evidently as result of Czech pressure & as prelude to milder methods. [*Sunday Times*)
2. Polish gov.t evidently now ready to allow Russians to use Polish air bases. [*Sunday Times*]
3. *S. Express* considers Franco has definitely come down on the side of the Axis, but hints that French & Swiss banks who have hitherto lent him £5m. are putting pressure on him by withholding further loans. [No reference given, but evidently *Sunday Express*]

SOCIAL

1. Evidently there has been trouble about the food in the militia. Number of first draft who declared themselves conscientious objectors stated at 2%. [*Sunday Times*]
2. Earnings throughout life from cabinet posts etc. of various politicians estimated by Peter Howard[2] thus: Runciman £71, Lloyd George £94, Baldwin £70, Hoare £79, Simon £78, Churchill £92 (all in thousands).[3] [*SundayExpress*]

PARTY POLITICS

1. Peter Howard considers Sir A. Wilson[4] is becoming unpopular in Hitchin Div.n owing to pro-German sentiments.* [*Sunday Express*]
2. Mosley's[5] Earls Court Stadium meeting said to have been attended by 25,000. M. said to have lost some of his East End working-class support but gained following among small business men etc. [*Left Forum*, August]
3. 'The Link' [6] said to be actively pro-Nazi & also recommended by P.P.U. [*Left Forum*, August]
4. Evidently the French spy scandals are being officially hushed up to some extent. La Rocque[7] asks Daladier[8] to pass decree – law making receipt of

* *Herts Pictorial* (15.8.39) repeats this without comment [Orwell's note].

foreign money for other than commercial purpose a criminal offence. [*Observer*]

5. *Sunday Express* prints friendly article about Japan (gossip article). [*Sunday Express*]

1. The Sudetenland, parts of Moravia and Bohemia incorporated into Czechoslovakia by the Treaty of Versailles, led by the Sudeten German Party, under Konrad Henlein (1898–1945, by suicide) wanted to reunite with Germany. It was aided and abetted by Hitler. The Munich pact of 30 September 1938 required Czechoslovakia to cede the area to Germany by 10 October 1938.
2. Peter Howard (1908–1965), author, journalist, dramatist, and farmer, was political columnist for Express Newspapers (Beaverbrook group), 1933–41.
3. Walter Runciman (1870–1949; Viscount, 1937), a Liberal M.P., 1899–1931, then a National Liberal, held many offices, including President of the Board of Trade, 1914–16, 1931–37. He led a mission to Czechoslovakia in 1938. David Lloyd George (1863–1945; Earl Lloyd George of Dwyfor, 1944), elected M.P. for Caernarfon, 1890; Chancellor of the Exchequer 1908–15; Minister for Munitions, 1915; Secretary of State for War 1916; and Prime Minister 1916–22. He had, like Pétain, been cast as a heroic leader during World War I when he proved an effective Prime Minister. He was responsible for persuading the Royal Navy to adopt the convoy system to help protect ships from German U-boats in the Atlantic. He was in a minority in seeking a conciliatory peace treaty with Germany after the war. When Chancellor of the Exchequer he introduced old-age pensions and national insurance, precursors to the welfare state. Many pensioners between the wars would speak of 'collecting their Lloyd George' – their old-age pension. Stanley Baldwin (1867–1947; Earl Baldwin, 1937), was Conservative Prime Minister three times, 1923–24,1924–29,1935–37. He successfully negotiated the crisis occasioned by the abdication of King Edward VIII, but is generally blamed for Britain's failure to prepare adequately for the impending war. For Samuel Hoare, see Events, 4.8.39, n. 5. Sir John Simon (1873–1954; Viscount, 1940) entered the House of Commons as a Liberal in 1906, and was instrumental in forming the National Liberal Party in 1931. He was Foreign Secretary, 1931–35; served at the Home Office, 1935–37, was Chancellor of the Exchequer, 1937–40, and Lord Chancellor, 1940–45. He wanted to avoid entanglements on the Continent. For Winston Churchill, see Events, 5.7.39, n. 1.
4. Sir Arnold Wilson (1884–1940) was Conservative M.P. for Hitchin, 1933–40, and Chairman of the Home Office Committee on Structural Precautions against Air Attack, 1936–38.
5. Oswald Mosley was head of the British Union of Fascists; see Wigan Pier Diary, n. 37.
6. 'The Link' was avowedly an Anglo-German cultural and friendship association. See Events, 4.8.39, Social; 7.8.39, Party Politics.
7. Colonel Francois de la Rocque: *see* Morocco Diary, n. 27.
8. Edouard Daladier: *see* Morocco Diary, n. 13.

D

7.8.39: Finer. In the morning rather cold & a little rain, afternoon overcast & warm. Finished preparing ground for winter greens. Put slugs in prepared box to test what kinds of foodstuff they go after most. Yesterday found dead newt in the road, so they must be leaving the water now. A certain number of this year's frogs about, about the size of runner beans.

9 eggs (1 small).

E

7.8.39:

SOCIAL

1. *Soc. Corresp.* repeats complaints about food etc. in militia camps with implication that the men are being treated rough more or less wilfully. [*Socialist Correspondence*]
2. 57 people reported shot in connection with recent political murders in Madrid (number of people murdered was apparently 3). [*Daily Telegraph*]

PARTY POLITICS

1. Members of the P.S.O.P.[1] arrested in France in connection with anti-war activities. C.P. making accusations of Nazi agency etc. [*Socialist Correspondence; The Week*, 2.8.39]
2. Bela Kun[2] again reported shot (from Vienna source this time). [*Daily Telegraph*]
3. Adm.l Sir Barry Domville[3] chairman of "The Link", describes statement of Hoare & Mander as a lie[4] & hopes they will repeat it outside Parliament.[5] [*Daily Telegraph*][6]

1. Parti Socialiste Ouvriers et Paysans, a left-wing splinter group of the Socialist Party (SFIO, Section Française de l'International Ouvrière); see Events, 11.8.39, n. 3.
2. See Events, 10.7.39, n. 4.
3. Admiral Sir Barry Edward Domvile (1878–1971) retired from the Navy in 1936.
4. See Events, 4.8.39, Social.
5. A statement made inside the House of Commons is privileged, and an action for slander or libel cannot be prosecuted.
6. A headline in Lord Beaverbrook's newspaper, the *Daily Express*, for 7 August boldly proclaimed, 'No War this Year.'

D

8.8.39: Some rain & thunder, but most of day fairly fine though not hot.

Goats' milk is badly off, less than a quart from the two, no doubt owing to the several days without grazing. Evenings now drawing in noticeably.

12 eggs (3 small).

E

8.8.39:

FOREIGN & GENERAL

1. Chinese dollar has now dropped below 4d. [*Daily Telegraph*]
2. Danzig senate appears to have climbed down in dispute over Polish customs officials. [*Daily Telegraph*]
3. Again reported that largish number of Asturian soldiers are still holding out in the mountains.[1] [*Daily Telegraph*]

SOCIAL

1. Complete column given in *D. Tel.* to "The Link", besides extra piece on front page. Statement by organisers that they are not propaganda agents etc. Statement that Prof. Laurie received £150 for *The Case for Germany* from German publishing firm, British firms having refused to publish book which was "pro-German". Statement that Leeds branch of "The Link" was voluntarily dissolved as organisers considered the German end was under Nazi control. [*Daily Telegraph*]
2. *D. Tel.* gives a column (in news section) to summarising "Germany's War Chances",[2] the Gollancz book translated from the Hungarian, for publication of which the author is being persecuted in Hungary. [*Daily Telegraph*]

MISCELLANEOUS

1. Death of Leonard Merrick[3] makes front page (just) of *D. Tel.* [*Daily Telegraph*]

1. Miners in Asturia, in the north of Spain, had organised revolution in 1934 (see Thomas, pp. 136ff). A feature there during the Spanish civil war, in September and October 1937, was Germany's practice of 'carpet bombing,' regardless of civilians below. Although Franco's forces were successful in obtaining for the Nationalists the coal resources of the region, *guerrilleros* continued to fight there until 1948 (Thomas, pp. 728–33).
2. The full title of the book, by Ivan Lajos, published by Gollancz in August 1939, was *Germany's War Chances: As Pictured in German Official Literature*.
3. Leonard Merrick (1864–1939), born Miller, was a novelist, now almost forgotten, but in 1918 a collected edition of his novels was published in which each was introduced by a distinguished author. He was described by Sir James Barrie as 'the novelist's novelist,' and William Dean Howells put him next in stature to Jane Austen. *The Position of Peggy Harper* (1911) was to be reissued in the Century Library series, and Orwell wrote an introduction to it. A page proof survives, dated 1948, though Orwell probably wrote the introduction in 1945; see *CW*, XVIII, pp. 216–19. The volume was never issued. See Crick, p. 500.

D

9.8.39: Some rain in the evening, otherwise warm, but overcast. Planted out 60 broccoli, rather late & all rather leggy & unpromising, but hope they may take. Impossible to get any kale etc., for which of course it is rather late.

10 eggs (2 small). Sold 30 @ 2/6 score.

D

10.8.39: Rain during much of the day. Cut side-shoots out of tomatoes (this should have been done much earlier), began preparing another patch for greens, put up another coop for the ducks, as the 7 of them can hardly crowd into one coop now. Note that fresh goat manure when piled sets up a certain amount of heat, though seemingly not so much as horse manure.

10 eggs (2 small).

E

10.8.39:

FOREIGN & GENERAL

1. Franco assumes more or less full powers of dictator. [*Daily Telegraph*]
2. The King inspects Reserve Fleet of 133 warships. [*Daily Telegraph*]

SOCIAL

1. Complaints (not very important) at militia camp in Devon reveal that reservists in large numbers have been called up as instructors. [*Daily Telegraph*]
2. 14 C[onscientious] O[bjector]s tried by tribunals, not harshly treated but work of national importance insisted on. Questions much as in Great War. No report of C.Os on other than religious-moral grounds. Secretary of S. Wales Miners' Federation on the tribunal. [*Daily Telegraph*]
3. Anti-Hitler jokes in *Eggs*.[1] [*Eggs*, 8.8.39]
4. Interior lamps of London buses now fitted with removable blue cowls for use in air-raids. [*Daily Telegraph*, 9.8.39]

PARTY POLITICS

1. After 6 weeks of no gov.t, Dutch national gov.t formed of several parties including two social-democrats. [*Daily Telegraph*]
2. Reported that at September conference I.L.P. National Council will advocate unconditional affiliation to L.P.[2] [*Daily Telegraph*]

1. *Eggs*, the official organ of the Scientific Poultry Breeders' Association, as a weekly founded in 1919. Orwell had been corresponding with the Association about feed for his hens around 26–27 July 1939.
2. See Events, 13.7.39, Party Politics, for the Labour Party's refusal of conditional affiliation.

D

11.8.39: Warm & fine. In the reservoir came upon waterhen with one very small chick. This was in close to the side & remained absolutely still, on my prodding it & turning it over with a stalk of hemlock it still made no move, so that I thought it was dead, then suddenly dived & remained under water for several minutes.

The watersnail's eggs appear to have hatched & the creatures are moving about, but they are still jellified & in some kind of embryonic state, not, as I had thought, fully developed before they come out.

Cut first marrow today. Fair amount of beans now.

11 eggs (3 small).

E

11.8.39:

FOREIGN & GENERAL

1. Chinese dollar reaches about 3½d. [*Daily Telegraph*]
2. Twenty Bulgarian MPs. received in Moscow. [*Daily Telegraph*]
3. British-French military delegation arrives Leningrad. [*Daily Telegraph*]

SOCIAL

1. Fresh reports of trials of objectors by tribunals do not in any case indicate objection on political lines (normally members of Christadelphian etc. churches). [*Daily Telegraph*]
2. Attack on "The Link" in *Time & Tide*, with implication that it should be suppressed. [*Daily Telegraph*]
3. Again denied that banning of *Time* by Federation of Wholesalers has political motive, though evidently it has. [*Daily Telegraph*]

PARTY POLITICS

1. I.L.P. Nat. Council again speaks of unconditional affiliation, but in referring to intentions within L.P. suggests activities which would amount to flatly opposing L.P.'s present line on rearmament etc. & presumably will not be accepted. [*New Leader*]
2. Those present at House of C. reception to Menna Schocat,[1] representing League for Jewish-Arab Unity included H.W. Nevinson, Chalmers Mitchell, Lord Faringdon, Wilson (Cecil), Lansbury, A. Maclaren, M.Ps.[2] [*New Leader*]
3. Various arrests in France in connection with anti-war & anti-imperialist activities include Lucien Weitz[3] & R. Louzon [4] (18 months). [*New Leader*]

1. Menna Schocat was a pioneer revolutionary in tsarist Russia who suffered imprisonment and exile. She escaped in 1905 and went to Palestine, where she was active in various workers' movements. She insisted on Jewish-Arab workers' unity and championed the cause of Arab peasants. The ILP had proposed to work for the unity of Jewish and Arab masses against British imperialism, in the hope of setting up a workers' state federated with neighbouring Arab states. It also championed the right of persecuted Jewish workers in Europe to enter not only Palestine, but all countries, including Britain and the Dominions.
2. Henry Woodd° Nevinson (1856–1941), prolific author, journalist, and foreign correspondent, was President of the Council for the Defence of Civil Liberties in 1939. Sir Peter Chalmers Mitchell (1864–1945; Kt., 1929), an eminent zoologist, was responsible for rebuilding much of the London Zoo and for the creation of the 'open' zoological garden at Whipsnade. He retired to Málaga, but the civil war forced his return to England. Orwell reviewed his translation of *The Forge*, by Arturo Barea, in *Time and Tide*, 28 June 1941 (see *CW*, XII, pp. 518–19) and in *Horizon*, September 1941 (see *CW*, XIII, pp. 33–5). During World War II, Mitchell was Treasurer to the joint committee for Soviet aid. Alexander Gavin Henderson, 2nd Baron Faringdon (1902–1977), a contemporary of Orwell at Eton, was Treasurer of the Committee of Inquiry into Non-Intervention in Spain, 1936, and Treasurer of the National Council for Civil Liberties, 1940–45. Cecil Henry Wilson (1862–1945) was a Labour M.P., 1922–31, 1935–44. George Lansbury (1859–1940), Leader of the Labour Party, 1931–35, was a pacifist and resigned as leader on that issue. Andrew MacLaren (1883–1975) was an ILP M.P., 1922–23, 1924–31, 1935–45.
3. Lucien Weitz, editor of *Independent News*, published in Paris, was also associated with the journal of Solidaridad Internacional Antifascista, of which Orwell

was a sponsor. Weitz and a number of others associated with that journal and with the ILP's brother organisation in France, Parti Socialiste Ouvriers et Paysans (see Events, 7.8.39, n. I) and its journal, *Juin 36*, were imprisoned as a result of publishing articles exposing clandestine sales by French motor manufacturers to Germany, and antimilitarist tracts.

4. Robert Louzon was imprisoned with Lucien Weitz and others. Of the nine people named in *The New Leader* as being arrested, Orwell picks out these two names presumably because they were known to him personally or by their writings: Weitz in *Independent News*, and Louzon in *La Revolution Prolétarienne* or his book *L'Economie Capitaliste.*

D

12.8.39: Warm & fine. Some carnations now well out.

10 eggs (2 small). Sold 25 @ 2/6 score & 10 (pullets) @ 2/2 score. Total this week: 73 (16 small).

E

12.8.39:

FOREIGN & GENERAL

1. *M. G.* correspondent reports that German mobilization will be at full strength halfway through August & that some attempt to terrorise Poland will be made. War stated to be likeliest issue (as also in yesterday's *Time & Tide*). The striking thing is the perfunctory air with which these statements are made in all papers, as though with an inner certainty that nothing of the kind can happen. [*Manchester Guardian Weekly*, 11.8.39; Orwell incorrectly dates this as 12.8.39]
2. Appearances seem to show that fighting on Manchurian border from Changkufeng incident[1] onwards has been fairly heavy but inconclusive. [*Manchester Guardian Weekly*, 11.8.39; misdated as 12.8.39; *La Révolution Prolétarienne*, undated]

SOCIAL

1. Refugee problem stated to be becoming serious in London especially East End. Mosley said to have not greatly increased his following however. [Private]
2. It appears that the P[ost] O[ffice] authorities are now able to read a letter, sufficient to determine nature of its contents, without opening it. [Private]

MISCELLANEOUS

1. All my books from the Obelisk Press[2] this morning seized by the police, with warning from Public Prosecutor that I am liable to be prosecuted if importing such things again. They had opened my letter addressed to Obelisk Press[3] evidently at Hitchin. Do not know yet whether because of the address or because my own mail is now scutinised. [No reference]
2. Potato & tomato said to have been successfully crossed in U.S.S.R. [*Smallholder*]

1. On 29 July 1939 some 3,000 Soviet troops with 100 tanks attacked on a four-mile front centred on Changkufeng, about a hundred miles southwest of Vladivostock. They were forced back, losing approximately 400 men to about 120 lost by the Japanese. On 6 August the German and Italian ambassadors in Tokyo intervened to urge moderation by the Japanese to settle the dispute peacefully so the 'Anti-Comintern Triangle' would not become embroiled with Russia (*The Times*, 9 August 1939).
2. Obelisk Press, Paris, published books in English for sale on the Continent, some of which British authorities regarded as obscene. Their importation into England was liable to legal proceedings. See Jack Kahane's *Memoirs of a Booklegger* (1939) and Neil Pearson, *Obelisk: A History of Jack Kahane and the Obelisk Press*, 2007.
3. Not traced. See Shelden, pp. 345–47; Bowker, p. 255.

D

13.8.39: Warm & fine.

10 eggs (2 small).

D

14.8.39: Warm & fine. Damsons (such as there are) almost ripe. Finished getting ground ready for greens. At last found the lost hen, which was sitting on 13 eggs. She has been gone just a month. Altogether 6 broodies now (out of 23 hens). Put them all in E[ileen]'s cage this afternoon. Yesterday with great difficulty we weighed a duck, &, if we were not wrong, it was about 3¾ lb (6½ weeks). So we are going to send the 2 biggest to market tomorrow to see what they fetch.

10 eggs (3 small).

Cwt. of Full-o-Pep gave out today. Started on 4.7.39 – about 40 days. Should have been 35, so perhaps have been underfeeding them a bit. On the other hand in warm weather they often don't eat all they are given.

Saw a cuckoo this morning. They have been silent for some time & are about due to leave. Found a dead shrew mouse on the road. I do not know why, one always finds them dead about this time of year.

E

14.8.39:

FOREIGN & GENERAL

1. German-Italian "compromise" scheme for Polish problem alleged to have been formulated, in a form that would obviously not be accepted by Poland. [*Daily Telegraph*]
2. Staff talks in Moscow have begun. [*Daily Telegraph*]

SOCIAL

1. Yesterday's *Sunday Express* had scare article on the illegal Jewish immigration into Palestine which was in effect anti-Jew propaganda. [*Sunday Express*, 13.8.39]

2. It appears that the opening of letters to persons connected with leftwing° parties is now so normal as to excite no remark. [E. H.[1]]
3. G. K.[2] claims that the C.P. are so strongly entrenched in the French police & other public services that the gov.t can do nothing against them. [File S.P. 1]

PARTY POLITICS

1. According to G. K., membership of the PSOP is now only 4000. [File S.P.1]
2. According to E. H., the Bermondsey anti-war conference was prevented from arriving at anything definite by the action of a few Trotskyists who will have no truck with pacifists & said so so violently as to antagonise the latter. [E. H.]
3. According to E. H., the older members of the I.L.P. are on the whole opposed to affiliation, the newer members in favour, but the only leading I.L.P.'er who is uncompromisingly against is C. A. Smith[3] [E. H.]

1. Unidentified; possibly someone in the ILP.
2. Probably George Kopp, Orwell's commander in Spain.
3. C. A. Smith was editor of *Controversy*, later *Left Forum* and then *Left*, a socialist monthly dedicated to the realisation of a classless society. He, with Orwell and others, urged that Rudolf Hess be interrogated at Nuremberg in 1946 regarding an alleged meeting with Trotsky; see *Forward*, 25 February 1946.

D

15.8.39: Hot. Had some damsons stewed (rather sour.) Ground dries up very rapidly. A few larkspurs coming into flower, roses coming into second bloom (most of them not good owing to the species of blight they have this year). The pumpkin's largest shoot now about a yard long & 1 female flower. Not certain whether it can make its growth in time, ie. in the next 6–8 weeks. Found another dead shrew. Wasps beginning to be troublesome. The new snail has laid a lot of eggs. Now that the white broody is off her nest, something finds & eats the eggs. Suspect cat, but might be rats, jackdaws or other hens.

Only 2/11 each (ie. 2/8 without commission) for 7-week ducklings weighing 4½lb. At this rate there is only a few pence profit on each bird, but we are buying mash in small quantities at which it costs 1½ lb.[II] At the price of Full-o-Pep (1⅒d per lb) there would be more.

11 eggs (2 small).

II. *1½ lb:* that is, one and a halfpence per pound.

D

16.8.39: Hot. Ground again very dried up. Hoed onions & flowers in nursery beds, watered pumpkin & tomatoes, cut down broad beans, which have got too big & are not worth leaving to ripen. Some turnips almost fit to pull. Cut second marrow. Grass which E[ileen] has cut is now quite good.

10 eggs (3 small). Sold 25 @ 2/6 score.

Ripe plums now only 2d lb.

D

17.8.39: Hot. Some blackberries reddening. Found a few mushrooms. Most of the corn now cut, & everyone working fast to get in the remainder while the good weather lasts. Coveys of partridges are mostly large (8–12 birds) but the young birds seem rather small. Saw bird which I cannot identify. In size colour & type by flight it resembled a waterhen, but apparently was not a waterhen, as it flew too well & took to the wing too readily, & also it was nowhere near water. It got up together with a hen pheasant, but was certainly not a pheasant at any stage of development. When Marx put up a covey of partridges the mother did the well known trick (it is sometimes denied that this really happens) of leading M. off by flying rather slowly & squawking, while the young ones flew away in a different direction. Saw what I believe was a fieldfare, though this seems very early. Cock goldfinch calling to mate makes sound rather like "chee-wa" (less like "cheese" than that of greenfinch).

8 eggs (3 small).

E

17.8.39:

FOREIGN & GENERAL

1. Announced that full scheme for national register is now ready.[1] [*Daily Telegraph*]

PARTY POLITICS

1. I.L.P. dissociating itself from P.P.U.'s friendly attitude towards "The Link." [*New Leader*, 18.8.39]
2. More evidences° of struggle going on between Negrín & Prieto,[2] cf. 2.8.39. [File S.P. 1 (as 'i')]
3. Speakers at Keir Hardie[3] memorial to be: Maxton, Dallas (L.P.E.C.),[4] Ebby Edwards (T.U.C.), Jas. Barr MP., Duncan Graham MP. [*New Leader*, 18.8.39]

1. This involved production of identity cards (without photographs for most people), to be carried at all times. The individual identification numbers are still in use in the 1990s for certain government purposes, although the cards disappeared long ago.
2. For Negrín and Prieto, see Events, 2.8.39, n. 3.
3. James Keir Hardie (1856–1915) was the first Socialist to be elected a Member of Parliament (1892). He led the Labour Party in the House of Commons, 1906–15.
4. Labour Party Executive Committee.

D

18.8.39: Hot. Refitted door to henhouse.

10 eggs (3 small).

E

18.8.39:

FOREIGN & GENERAL

1. *M.G.* diplomatic correspondent considers Spain will almost certainly remain neutral in case of war. The new cabinet balances the soldiers fairly evenly against the Falangists. [*Manchester Guardian Weekly*]

SOCIAL

1. Appears now fairly certain that the 4 Chinese alleged terrorists will be handed over to Japanese, in spite of plea in London for writ of habeas corpus.[1] [*Manchester Guardian Weekly*]
2. Details of national register now worked out, but announced that actual registration will not take place except on outbreak of war or possibly at 1941 census. [*Manchester Guardian Weekly*]
3. Spanish immigration into Mexico said to be proving very successful. [File S.P.i]

1. See Events, 24.7.39, n. 1. It was reported on 12 August that the government had decided that the four Chinese would be handed over to be tried by a Japanese-controlled court. It had been convinced by new evidence the Japanese had produced in Tokyo, after having refused to make it available in Tientsin. This entry and several thereafter are numbered in small roman numerals, as is 'S.P. 1' on occasion. These variations are not here recorded.

D

19.8.39: Hot. Planted out 1 score each Brussels, savoys & purple sprouting broccoli. Paid 3d per score. Not very good plants & very dry, but fairly good roots, so they should take. Suspicion of club-root (which we have never had here) in one plant which I got rid of. Some white turnips (sown 28.6.39) ready to pull.

Smallholder claims wireworm in carrot beds etc. can be dealt with by 2 oz. per sq. yard of mixed napthaline° & freshly slaked lime.

9 eggs (3 small). Sold 20 @ 2/6 score & 10 @ 2/– score.

Total this week: 68 (19 small).

E

19.8.39:

FOREIGN & GENERAL

1. Germans are buying heavily in copper & rubber for immediate delivery, & price of rubber rising rapidly. [*Daily Telegraph*]
2. Indications that difference of some kind has arisen in Moscow staff talks (stated by Tass agency not to be connected with Far East). [*Daily Telegraph*]
3. Stated more or less officially in Madrid that Spain will remain neutral. [No reference]

SOCIAL

1. Inquiries into the activities of the Bund[1] in U. S.A., rather as into those of "The Link" here. Evident that *i.* all these associations have been used for Nazi propaganda & *ii.* that attempts will be progressively made to break down cultural relations between Germany & the democracies. [*Daily Telegraph*]
2. The police are getting wise to the marriage of convenience (as a way of obtaining Brit. nationality for German women) & are going to recommend deportation in these cases. [*Daily Telegraph*]
3. Number of I.R.A. suspects expelled up to date is about 90. [*Daily Telegraph*]
4. Numbers of militiamen said to have been found to be completely illiterate. [*News Chronicle*]

MISCELLANEOUS

1. Ministry of Agric. returns for first ½ of 1939 indicate following developments: total acreage under crops & grass about 24¾ mill., decrease of about 80,000 acres, but arable land increased by about 50,000 acres & permanent grass decreased by 130,000 acres. (Change said to have taken place *before* gov.t's subsidy for ploughing-up took effect.)

   Area under wheat decreased by 150,000 acres, potatoes by about 20,000 acres, peas & cabbages also decreased, field beans increased & oats & barley increased by 56,000 & 25,000 acres resp.

   Most stock increased largely, except pigs & work horses, which decreased by about 50,000 & 14,000 resp. Fowls increased by 200,000 head. [*Smallholder*]

1. The German-American Bund was a Nazi front organization. Its leader, Fritz Kuhn, was imprisoned later in the year, having been found guilty in New York of embezzling the association's funds.

D

20.8.39: Hot in the morning. Then thunder & heavy showers. Raining hard tonight. Goats greatly terrified by the thunder, & M[uriel] managed to break loose from her chain.

Pinched out growing point of pumpkin. Gave onions their final thinning out. First peas about finished. Larkspurs flowering. Side shoots of tomatoes grow so fast that it is impossible to keep pace with them.

8 eggs (4 small – evidently another pullet laying.)

E

20.8.39:

FOREIGN & GENERAL

1. Lloyd George predicts the Danzig crisis coming to a head very shortly. Also hints (*S. Express* puts this in leaded type) that if the Poles deliberately back down we are under no obligation to act. [*Sunday Express*]
2. Tokyo conversations suspended, owing to G. Britain declaring necessity of consulting other nations on Chinese currency question. [*Sunday Times*]

SOCIAL

1. Row over Spender's articles still reverberating in *Sunday Times*. [*Sunday Times*]

PARTY POLITICS

1. Peter Howard[1] speaks of general election more or less as a certainty & predicts that increased old age pensions will be one of the gov.t's bribes. [*Sunday Express*]
2. In case of general election happening this autumn, a bill will be passed to keep the existing gov.t in being during the election period,[2] owing to the crisis. [*Sunday Times*]

1. See Events, 6.8.39, n. 2.
2. Orwell originally wrote 'crisis' for 'period.'

D

21.8.39: Hot till evening, then heavy thunder & rain. Cut side-shoots out of tomatoes, dug in a little ash from bonfire round their roots, cleared & burnt first lot of dwarf peas & began digging over this patch of ground, which will do for leeks. Planted some of those yellow flowers (sort of summer chrysanthemum) which Mrs Hollingsworth gave us, though do not know whether they will take, as some are already in flower. Gave liquid manure to some of the larkspurs. A good many self-sown antirrhinums about.

Weighed the remaining 5 ducks, which go to market tomorrow. The 5 weigh just on 24 lb., the heaviest about 5¼lb. They are just 7½ weeks old.

8 eggs (2 small).

E

21.8.39:

FOREIGN & GENERAL

1. Fresh enquiries by American I.P.O.[1] indicates that number of people believing U.S.A. would be involved in world war has greatly increased (to about 75%). Number thinking U.S.A. would send troops to Europe still only 25%. [*Daily Telegraph*]
2. Japanese preparing blockade of Hong Kong, obviously in order to put pressure on London over the silver & currency question. [*Daily Telegraph*]
3. £10m. 2 year trade agreement signed between Germany & U.S.S.R. for exchange of German manufactured goods versus Russian raw materials. [*Daily Telegraph*]
4. Strategic bridge from Danzig into E. Prussia completed. [*Daily Telegraph*]

SOCIAL

1. Railway strike for 50/– minimum wage[2] likely within the next week or two. [*Daily Telegraph*]
2. Stated that England can now supply herself with optical glass in case of war. [*Daily Telegraph*]

1. American Institute of Public Opinion, which conducted polls popularly known as Gallup polls, after its founder, statistician George Gallup (1901–1984), beginning in 1935.
2. *50/–*: Fifty shillings – £2. 10s; roughly equivalent in 2009 to £100 per week at current purchasing power.

D

22.8.39: Drizzle in the morning, rest of day fine & hot. The mist is now very thick in the early mornings. Dug some more of the patch for the leeks, gave liquid manure to larkspurs etc. E[ileen] planted some more godetias. Only 11/– for 5 ducks weighing 24 lb. Complete account is in the egg book, but worth noting here that, putting aside the bread & milk of their first week, 91 lb. of mash (actually more – say 95 lb – as they occasionally had some of the other birds' food) equals 32 lb. of meat, or about (allowing for everything) 3¼lb. of feed for 1 lb of meat.

One of the newts is now mature. Its gill formations are gone & it lies on top of the water with its head in the air much of the time. The water-snail was yesterday sucking at the piece of raw meat we put in for the newts.

Marx discovered to be very lousy, ears full of nits, no doubt partly owing to the hot weather. E[ileen] treating him with antiseptic soap, flea powder & also vinegar, which loosens the nits, allowing them to be combed out.

11 eggs (4 small). Cwt. of corn begun today.

E

22.8.39:

FOREIGN & GENERAL

1. Officially stated in Berlin that Ribbentropp°[1] flies to Moscow tomorrow to sign non-agression° pact with U.S.S.R. News later confirmed from Moscow by Tass Agency, in a way that seems to make it clear that pact will go through. Little comment in any of the papers, the news having evidently arrived in the small hours of this morning & the Russian confirmation only in time for the stop press. Reported suggestion from Washington that it may be a Russian manoeuvre (ie. to bring England & France to heel) but everyone else seems to take it at face-value. Shares on the whole have dropped. Germans still buying shellac etc. heavily. The military talks were still proceeding yesterday. [*Daily Telegraph; Daily Mail; News Chronicle; Daily Mirror*]

SOCIAL

1. Illegal radio, somewhat on the lines of German Freiheit movement's radio,[2] has been broadcasting anti-conscription propaganda. Secretary of P.P.U. (Rowntree?)* denies knowledge but does not dissociate himself from

* Palmer [Orwell's note].

the talks. P.O. engineers state that they have tracked down location of radio to within a few houses & will soon run it to earth. Indication is that it takes at least some days to locate an illegal radio. [*Daily Telegraph*]

PARTY POLITICS

1. *Letchworth Citizen*[3] reprints long article on Sir A. Wilson[4] from *Sunday Pictorial* with evident approval. [*Letchworth Citizen*, no date]
2. *Soc. Corresp*. prints long statement on war issue by Comm. Opp.[5] setting forth hopelessly complicated programme of supporting anti-Fascist war & at same time disillusioning the working class etc., etc. But makes statement (probably true as Thalheimer[6] & others would have knowledge of Russian conditions of at any rate a few years ago) that tho' the Red Army is now more or less as other armies, the reserves still receive more or less the training of a revolutionary army. Also violent attack on I.L.P. signed by 3 sets of initials one Audrey Brockway's,[7] launching slogan of 4th International.[8] [*Socialist Correspondence*]

1. Joachim von Ribbentrop (1893–1946) was German Minister of Foreign Affairs, 1938–45. He negotiated the Russo-German Non-Aggression Pact in 1939 with Molotov (see Events, 28.8.39, n. 4). He was hanged as a war criminal after being found guilty by the International Military Tribunal at Nuremberg.
2. See Events, 2.7.39, n. 2. Three months after note above, 'German Freedom Radio' was reported to be still broadcasting appeals to Germans to liberate themselves from Hitler's regime.
3. The *Letchworth Citizen* was Orwell's local paper at Wallington.
4. See Events, 6.8.39, n. 4.
5. International Communist Opposition, headquartered in Paris. The decline of the ICO was the subject of the July Supplement of *Socialist Correspondence*.
6. August Thalheimer (1884–1948) was one of the leaders of the International Communist Opposition, and was described in the *New Leader*, 20 August 1937 (to which issue he contributed an article, 'A Call for Revolutionary Socialist Unity'), as 'one of the authors of the thesis which formed the basis of the Communist International at its establishment. For many years he was the leader of the Communist Party in Germany, but was deposed from that position by the C. I. Executive because he opposed its disastrous policy of dividing the Trade Union Movement by the formation of rival Red Trade Unions.' The *New Leader* welcomed the chance to publish his views 'because it indicates that there is scope for close co-operation between the parties (including the I.L.P.) attached to the International Bureau for Revolutionary Socialist Unity and the Communist International Opposition.'
7. Audrey Brockway (1916–1974) was Secretary to the I.L.P. Guild of Youth, and was married to Jim Wood, a member of the Trotskyist group in the I.L.P.
8. The Fourth International was formed in 1938 by followers of Trotsky. They hoped the impending war would create conditions favourable for world revolution. It was reported that as Trotsky lay dying in Mexico City in 1940, victim of an assassin, he said 'I am sure of victory of the Fourth International. Go forward!'

D

23.8.39: Hot. Dug some more of the patch for leeks, transferred the cockerels (5) to the small pen, deloused the hen-houses. Great trouble getting rid of the red mite, which multiplies very fast in this weather. They have to be burned out, but even so it is hard to make sure of them. A plumber's blowlamp is what one needs. When a house is infested badly the hens will not go into it. Found nest of 14 (Rhode) eggs laid out, evidently not very new, so shall not sell them or enter them in the account, though the one I tried was not bad.

8 eggs (4 small). Sold 20 @ 2/6, & 10 @ 1/– score.

E

23.8.39:

FOREIGN & GENERAL

1. Parliament meeting tomorrow. Emergency Powers Act will be passed. Certain classes of reservists called up. The King returning to London. Reservists being called up in France & Germany. Legislation to be hurried through in Parliament to prevent further buying of nickle,° copper etc. by Germany. Almost all shares have dropped, no doubt in anticipation of this. World press comments as quoted by *D. Tel.* are very non-committal but the Axis powers evidently greatly pleased by the Russian demarche. [*Daily Telegraph*]

SOCIAL

1. Railway strike now arranged to begin in a few days' time. [*Daily Telegraph*]

PARTY POLITICS

1. Communist Party membership stated as 17,000,* which is increase of 2000 over last year. C.P. again applying for application to L.P.[1] [*Daily Telegraph*]

1. Labour Party.

D

24.8.39: Hot. Planted 2 rows leeks (about 75 plants). There are 5 different colours of larkspurs coming out.

9 eggs (4 small).

E

24.8.39:

FOREIGN & GENERAL

1. Russo-German Pact signed. Terms given in Berlin (File War etc).[1] suggest close pact & no "escape" clause. This evening's radio news gives confirmation in Moscow in same terms. Official statement from Moscow that "enemies of both countries" have tried to drive Russia & Germany into

* 40% of this in London, & membership in industrial areas negligible (C.P. pamphlet) [Orwell's note].

enmity. Brit. Ambassador calls on Hitler & is told no action of ours can influence German decision. Japanese opinion evidently seriously angered by what amounts to German desertion of anti-Comintern pact, & Spanish (Franco) opinion evidently similarly affected. Rumania said to have declared neutrality. Chamberlain's speech as reported on wireless very strong & hardly seems to allow loophole for escape from aiding Poles.

E[ileen] on visiting W.O.[2] today derived impression that war is almost certain. Police arrived this morning to arrange for billeting of soldiers. Some people (foreigners) arrived in afternoon looking for rooms – the second lot in 3 days. In spite of careful listening, impossible in pubs etc. to overhear any spontaneous comment or sign of slightest interest in the situation, in spite of fact that almost everyone when questioned believes it will be war. [*The Times; Daily Telegraph; News Chronicle; Manchester Guardian; Daily Express; Daily Herald; Daily Mail; London Evening News*]

SOCIAL

1. Emergency Powers Act passed evidently without much trouble. Contains clauses allowing preventive arrest, search without warrant & trial in camera. But not industrial conscription as yet. [Wireless 6 pm][3]
2. Moscow airport was decorated with swastikas for Ribbentrop's arrival. *M. Guardian* adds that they were screened so as to hide them from the rest of Moscow. [*Manchester Guardian*]

PARTY POLITICS

1. C.P. putting good face on Russo-German pact which is declared to be move for peace. Signature of Anglo-Soviet pact demanded as before. *D. Worker* does not print terms of pact but reprints portions of an earlier Russo-Polish pact containing an "escape" clause, in order to convey impression that this pact must contain the same. [*Daily Worker*]
2. In today's debate Sinclair & Greenwood[4] spoke strongly in support of Gov.t. Mander[5] spoke demanding "strengthening of Cabinet". Maxton[6] declared I.L.P. would not support Gov.t in war. [Wireless 6 pm]

1. Presumably a file Orwell kept on this subject. Possibly related to his reference 'File S.P. 1.'
2. Eileen was working at the War Office in the Censorship Department.
3. National news was broadcast by BBC at 6.00 p.m.
4. Archibald Sinclair; see Events, 2.7.39, n. 3. Arthur Greenwood (1880–1954) was a Labour M.P., 1922–31, 1932–54; Deputy Leader of the party, 1935; Secretary to the party research department, 1920–43. His opposition to totalitarian regimes led to his being singled out for attack by Hitler in 1938.
5. Geoffrey Mander; see Events, 4.8.39, n. 3.
6. James Maxton (1885–1946), Independent Labour MP, 1922–46; Chairman of I.L.P., 1926–31, 1934–39. See also Morocco Diary, 12.3.39, n. 38.

E

28.8.39:

[No section headings]

Have been travelling[1] etc. during the past days & therefore unable to keep up the diary in the ordinary way.

The main developments have been as follow:

Hitler has proposed some or other kind of plan which was flown across by N. Henderson[2] & has been discussed at several Cabinet meetings including one yesterday (Sunday) afternoon, but no statement has been made by the gov.t as to the Nature° of Hitler's communication. H. is to fly back today with the Brit. gov.t's reply, but even so there is no sure indication that either H.'s[3] proposal or the gov.t's reply will be communicated to the public. Various papers have published statements, all of which are officially declared to be unfounded.

No clear indication of the meaning of the Russian-German pact as yet. Papers of left tendency continue to suggest that it does not amount to very much, but it seems to be generally taken for granted that Russia will supply Germany with raw materials, & possibly that there has been a large-scale bargain which amounts to handing Europe over to Germany & Asia to Russia. Molotov[4] is to make an announcement shortly. It is clear that the Russian explanation will be, at any rate at first, that the British were playing double & did not really wish for the Anglo-French-Russian pact. Public opinion in U.S.S.R. said to be still somewhat taken aback by the change of front, & ditto left wing opinion in the West. Left wing papers continue to blame Chamberlain while making some attempt to exhonorate° Stalin, but are clearly dismayed. In France there has evidently been a swing of opinion against the Communist Party, from which there are said to be large-scale resignations (*D. Tel.* repeating Reuter). *Humanité* has been temporarily suspended. The Anglo-French military mission is already returning.

Germany & Poland now more or less fully mobilised. France has called up several more classes of reservists & is said to have 4,000,000* men under arms. No more reservists yet called up in Britain. Admiralty has taken over control of all shipping. Sale of foreign shares is being controlled by gov.t. Main buildings in London being sandbagged. Practice evacuation of children in evacuation areas today. Little or no excitement in London. For the last day or two it is possible to overhear people in the street discussing the situation, but only in terms of "is there going to be war?" Yesterday afternoon during the Cabinet meeting about 1000 people in Downing St., mostly rubbernecks, & no banners etc. No demonstrations in Hyde Park. The only political speaker there a Trotskyist[5] who

* Today (29.8.39) given as 3,000,000 [Orwell's note].

was getting a good hearing (about 200 people).* No mass-exodus from the railway stations, but immense quantities of luggage waiting to leave, by the look of it the luggage of fairly well-to-do people.

L.M.[6] is of opinion that if we do not involve Italy in the war she will sit tight until we are in difficulties & have alienated the smaller European countries & will then come in on the German side. He is of the opinion that virtually the whole of the wealthy class are entirely treacherous & quite ready to do a deal with Germany, either without war or after a short sham war, which could be presented as an honourable peace, & would allow for the imposition of fascism in England.† Spain is at present making declarations of neutrality, & Turkey still declaring she will stand by France & England.

The price of gold has risen to record heights (about 155/– per ounce).[7] Price of wheat still extremely low (price in wholesale markets recently quoted at less than 4/– the cwt.)

P.P.U. evidently completely quiescent & not intending to do anything. I.L.P. has issued official declaration that they will not support the government in war.

The Emergency Powers Act passed by over 400 votes to 4. Dissentients were Maxton (the other 2 I.L.P. MPs acted as tellers), Lansbury, Cecil Wilson & an Independent[8]. Gallacher abstained.[9] Some of the extremists, eg. Ellen Wilkinson[10] & A. Bevan[11] voted for the bill.

[*Daily Telegraph; News Chronicle; Daily Mirror; Daily Express; New Statesman; Sunday Times; Observer; Reynolds's News*°; *Empire News*; no dates given]

1. On 24 August Orwell travelled to Ringwood in Hampshire, where he stayed with novelist L. H. Myers (1891–1944). For Myers, see also Events, 29. 8. 39, n. 2. He was at Ringwood until 31 August at least. On 3 September he was in Greenwich, where the O'Shaugnessys lived. It is not possible to be sure where he was on 1 and 2 September.
2. Sir Neville Henderson (1882–1942) was British Ambassador in Berlin, 1937–39. See his *Failure of a Mission* (1940).
3. Hitler's.
4. Vyacheslav Molotov (1890–1986) was President of the USSR's Council of People's Commisars, 1930–41, and Commissar of Foreign Affairs, 1939–49, 1953–56. He negotiated the Russo-German Non-Aggression Pact in August 1939, with Ribbentrop. He was later a delegate to the United Nations General Assembly.
5. Orwell originally wrote 'Communist.'
6. This must be L. H. Myers, with whom Orwell was staying. Myers was a

* See Events, 31.8.39 (Party politics) [Orwell's note].

† NB. That L. M. says he derived this opinion from Geoffrey Pike, a Communist [Orwell's note; Myers's assessment of Italy's intentions proved accurate].

Communist, as was the source of his information. See G. H. Bantock, *L. H. Myers*, p. 152.

7. In January 1939 the price of gold was 150s 5d (£7.52). By June it had dropped to 148s 6d. In January 1940 it was 168s (£8.40). An official price was in effect from June 1945 (172s 3d) until the free market reopened in March 1954, when the price was 248s (£12.40); see R.L. Bidwell, *Currency Conversion Tables* (1970). There were $4.63 to the pound in January 1939; from January 1940 to September 1949 the rate was $4.03. The pound was then devalued and was worth about $2.80 until 1967.
8. James Maxton; see Morocco Diary, 12.3.39, n. 38; George Lansbury and Cecil Wilson; see Events, 11.8.39, n. 2.
9. William Gallacher; see Events, 27.7.39, n. 2.
10. Ellen Wilkinson (1891–1947), founder member of the Communist Party, 1920; elected Labour MP, 1924–31. Re-elected for Jarrow in 1933 and in 1936 organised the march of the unemployed from Jarrow to London. With Clement Attlee she witnessed the German bombing of Valencia during the Spanish Civil War. See also Thomas, p. 792, n.2. She served in the Coalition Wartime Government and was appointed Minister of Education in the Labour Government of 1945. She wrote two novels and *The Town that Was Murdered*, an account of the Jarrow March. She was also famed for flaming red hair.
11. Aneurin (Nye) Bevan (1897–1960), a collier from Tredegar, was a Labour M.P. representing the Ebbw Vale constituency, South Wales, from 1927 until his death. An impassioned orator, he was the idol of much of the left and was disliked, even feared, by many Conservatives. As Minister of Health, 1945–50, he was responsible for the creation of the National Health Service. He resigned from the second post-war Labour government in 1951 in disagreement over disarmament, and was defeated as leader of the party in 1955. He was a director of *Tribune* when Orwell wrote for that journal, and allowed Orwell complete freedom to say what he wished even against current party policy. His *In Place of Fear* (1952) sets out his philosophy. See also Second Wartime Diary, 27.3.42, n. 13.

E

29.8.39:

FOREIGN & GENERAL

1. N. Henderson has returned to Berlin with Brit. gov.t's reply & Parliament meets this afternoon when presumably the affair will be elucidated.
2. E. P. Act[1] coming into force. Admiralty has not only assumed control of shipping but ordered all British shipping out of the Mediterranean & the Baltic.
3. Practice evacuation of school children said to have gone off successfully. Children to stand by in schools though this is not term time.
4. Japanese Cabinet has resigned as result of Russo-German pact. Evident that Japanese policy will now become pro-British.

[Items 1, 2, 3, and 4 are bracketed and next to them *The Times, News Chronicle* – both 29.8.39 – and *Bournemouth Echo*,[2] 28.9.39; separate: *Daily Telegraph*, 29.8.39; and Radio, no date]

SOCIAL

1. Private motorists for some days past have been buying up large quantities of petrol. [No reference]

PARTY POLITICS

1. Labour Party still declaring against accepting office. Said that in case of war a Labour representative would accept office but only on terms defined by the party & so stringent as to be probably unacceptable to the Nat. gov.t. [*News Chronicle*]

MISCELLANEOUS

1. It appears from reliable private information that Sir O. Mosley is a masochist of the extreme type in his sexual life. [Private]

1. Emergency Powers Act; see 28.8.39, last paragraph.
2. The local paper for Ringwood, where Orwell was staying with L. H. Myers, from at least 24 to 31 August. As his diary shows, he was not back at Wallington until 5 September, two days after Britain's declaration of war following Germany's invasion of Poland on 1 September. He may have gone to Greenwich on 1 or 2 September, and was certainly there on 3 September; see Events, 28.8.39, n. 1. It was Myers who had provided the loan (intended as a gift) that enabled the Orwells to spend the winter of 1938–39 in French Morocco. Orwell did not know who his benefactor was until 1946, two years after Myers's death, when he made the first instalment on repaying what he took to be a debt. He sent this to Dorothy Plowman, who had acted as intermediary; see his letter to her, 19 February 1946 (*CW*, XVIII, pp. 115–16).

E

30.8.39:

FOREIGN & GENERAL

Virtually no news. Communications are passing to & fro but the Cabinet are revealing nothing. Parliament adjurned° for a week. King of the Belgians offering to mediate, which Poles have accepted & Germans express themselves sympathetic to, but meanwhile troop movements & frontier outrages continue. Rumania is fortifying her Russian frontier. 2–300,000 Russian troops said to be moving to Western frontier.

Soviet Parliament will not ratify the pact till the end of the week, obviously in order to give a different interpretation to it according to the then circumstances. If necessary it is still open to them to refuse ratification which could be used as demonstration of Soviet democracy.

Harold Nicolson[1] claims that U.S.S.R. cannot supply Germany with much oil in case of war. Third-hand information via the Stock Exchange* indicates that 3 days back the Cabinet were confident Hitler could not move. On the other hand L. M[yers] says that a few weeks back W. Churchill expressed very pessimistic views to him, based on talks with German generals. [*The Times; News Chronicle; Daily Mirror*; undated, Radio; *Private]

SOCIAL

1. Adjurnment° of Parliament for a week passed without a division. [*The Times*]

1. Harold Nicolson (1886–1968; Kt., 1953), diplomat (to 1929), biographer, and novelist, was an M.P., 1935–45. His *Diaries and Letters* (edited by his son Nigel Nicolson, 3 vols., 1966–68) give insight into the political life of the thirties. In his *English History 1914–1945*, A.J.P. Taylor records the wild scene that followed Chamberlain's announcement in the House on 28 September 1938 that Hitler had agreed to a four-power conference at Munich: 'Members rose to their feet, cheering and sobbing. Attlee [the Labour leader], Sinclair the Liberal leader, and Maxton of the I.L.P. blessed Chamberlain's mission. Only Gallacher, the Communist, spoke harshly against it.' In a footnote he asks, 'Who remained seated?' Certainly Gallacher and, quoting R. W. Seton-Watson, he adds Churchill, Eden, and Amery. Another source, J. W. Wheeler-Bennett, is quoted as saying that 'Harold Nicolson, despite the threats of those surrounding him, remained seated.' Taylor says that Nicolson remembered only being rebuked the next day by a Conservative M.P. for not rising. Nicolson, who had joined Mosley's New Party in 1931, leaving the following year when the British Union of Fascists was formed, was a National Labour member of the government. (Revised Pelican edition, 1970, p. 525.)

D

31.8.39: Ringwood (Hants). *24–29.8.39.* Hot, yesterday & today fairly heavy rain. Blackberries are ripening in this district. Finches beginning to flock. Very heavy mists in the early mornings.

E

31.8.39:

FOREIGN & GENERAL

1. No definite news. Poland has called up more reserves but this does not yet amount to full mobilisation. German occupation of Slovakia continues & 300,000 men said to be now at strategic points on Polish frontier. Hitler has set up inner cabinet of 6 not including Ribbentrop.

   16,000 children already evacuated from Paris. Evacuation of London children thought to be likely before long. No news one way or the other about ratification of Russo-German pact. Such slight indications as exist suggest pact will be ratified. German persecution of Jews said to be slightly diminished, anti-German film withdrawn from Soviet pavilion at New York world fair. Voroshilov[1] reported as stating that U.S.S.R. would supply Poland with arms. [*Daily Telegraph; News Chronicle; Daily Mirror*]

SOCIAL

1. Sir J. Anderson[2] requests the public not to buy extra stores of food & to conserve those they have, & states that there is no food shortage. [*Daily Telegraph*]
2. A.E.U.[3] is now agreeing to dilution of labour. [*Daily Telegraph*]

PARTY POLITICS

1. E[ileen]'s report of speeches in Hyde Park suggest that Communist Party are taking more left wing line but not anxious to thrash out question of Russo-German pact. Speaker (Ted Bramley) claimed that MPs who voted against E.P.Act were Gallacher, Wilkinson & A. Bevan & 1 other.[4] (Actually Maxton, Lansbury, C. Wilson & 1 other). [Private]

1. Kliment Voroshilov (1881–1969), Marshal of the Soviet Union, was People's Commissar for Defence, 1925–40, and President of the USSR, 1953–60. He was one of those responsible for organising the defence of Leningrad during the 900-day siege, September 1941–January 1944.
2. John Anderson (1882–1958; Viscount, 1952) was an MP. representing Scottish universities, 1938–50. (At the time, a few MPs were elected directly by universities.) Appointed Lord Privy Seal by Chamberlain in November 1938, with special responsibility for manpower and civil defence. He was responsible for what came to be called the 'Anderson' air-raid shelter. These were sited in back gardens. At the outbreak of war, he was made Home Secretary and Minister of Home Security; later, Lord President of the Council, 1940–43, and Chancellor of the Exchequer, 1943–45. In *The Lion and the Unicorn*, Orwell remarked that it took 'the unnecessary suffering of scores of thousands of people in the East End [sheltering in Andersons] to get rid or partially rid of Sir John Anderson' (*CW*, XII, p. 416). The shelters could be extremely uncomfortable and were prone to flooding. On 3 September 1940 Churchill wrote to Anderson to say that 'a great effort should be made to help people to drain their Anderson shelters, which reflect so much credit on your name . . .' (*The Second World War*, I, p. 313).
3. Amalgamated Engineering Union.
4. See Events, 28.8.39, last paragraph.

E

1.9.39:

Invasion of Poland began this morning. Warsaw bombed. General mobilisation proclaimed in England, ditto in France plus martial law. [Radio]

FOREIGN & GENERAL

1. Hitler's terms to Poland boil down to return of Danzig & plebiscite in the corridor,[1] to be held 1 year hence & based on 1918 census. There is some hanky panky about time the terms were presented, & as they were to be answered by night of 30.8.39., H.[2] claims that they are already refused. [*Daily Telegraph*]
2. Naval reservists and rest of army and R.A.F. reservists called up. Evacuation of children etc. begins today, involving 3 m. people & expected to take 3 days. [Radio; undated]
3. Russo-German pact ratified. Russian armed forces to be further increased. Voroshilov's speech taken as meaning that Russo-German alliance is not contemplated. [*Daily Express*]

4. Berlin report states Russian military mission is expected to arrive there shortly. [*Daily Telegraph*]

1. The Polish Corridor, which gave Poland an outlet to the Baltic Sea between 1919 and 1939; it separated East Prussia from the rest of Germany and, with Danzig, was a source of friction and an ostensible cause of the outbreak of war.
2. Hitler.

E

3.9.39 (Greenwich).:

Have again been travelling etc. Shall close this diary today, & it will as it stands serve as a diary of events leading up to the war.

We have apparently been in a state of war since 11 am. this morning. No reply was received from the German gov.t to the demand to evacuate Polish territory. The Italian gov.t made some kind of last-minute appeal for a conference to settle differences peacefully, which made some of the papers as late as this morning show a faint doubt as to whether war would actually break out. Daladier made grateful reference to the "noble effort" of Italy which may be taken as meaning that Italy's neutrality is to be respected.

No definite news yet as to what military operations are actually taking place. The Germans have taken Danzig & are attacking the corridor from 4 points north & south. Otherwise only the usual claims & counterclaims about air raids, number of aeroplanes shot down etc. From reports in *Sunday Express* & elsewhere it seems clear that the first attempted raid on Warsaw failed to get as far as the town itself. It is rumoured that there is already a British force in France. Bodies of troops with full kits constantly leaving from Waterloo, but not in enormous numbers at any one moment. Air-raid practice this morning immediately after the proclamation of state of war. Seems to have gone off satisfactorily though believed by many people to be real raid. There are now great numbers of public air-raid shelters, though most of them will take another day or two to complete. Gasmasks° being handed out free, & the public appears to take them seriously. Voluntary fire-brigades etc. all active & look quite efficient. Police from now on wear steel helmets. No panic, on the other hand no enthusiasm, & in fact not much interest. Balloon barrage[1] completely covers London & would evidently make low-flying quite impossible. Blackout at nights fairly complete but they are instituting very stringent penalties for infringement. Evacuation involving 3 m. people (over 1 m. from London alone) going on rapidly. Train services somewhat disorganised in consequence.

Churchill & Eden are coming into the cabinet. Labour are refusing office for the time being. Labour MPs. in the house make violent protestations of loyalty but tone of the left press very sour as they evidently realise the wind has been taken out of their sails. Controversy about the Russo-German pact continues to some extent. All the letters printed in *Reynolds's*[2] extol the pact but have shifted the emphasis from this being a "peace move" to its being a self-protecting move by U.S.S.R.. *Action* of 2.9.39. still agitating against the war. No atrocity stories or violent propaganda posters as yet. M.T. Act[3] extended to all men between 18–41. It is however clear that they do not as yet want large numbers of men but are passing the act in order to be able to pick on anyone they choose, & for purpose of later enforcing industrial conscription.

1. Part of the air defence system was provided by barrage balloons. These were flown, unmanned, at a height that made dive-bombing to a low level impracticable owing to the cables anchoring the balloons in position.
2. *Reynold's News* was founded 5 May 1850. It was a popular, Socialist-inclined Sunday newspaper. It was amalgamated with the *Sunday Citizen* under that name on 20 August 1944; the *Citizen* ceased publication on 18 June 1967.
3. Military Training Act.

This concludes Orwell's record of events leading up to the war.
The continuation of the Domestic Diary now follows.

DOMESTIC DIARY VOLUME II CONTINUED

5 September 1939 – 29 April 1940

Footnote numbering continues from that which began at the start of this diary volume, 27 May 1939.

D

5.9.39: Have not been able to keep up the diary owing to travelling to & fro, dislocation caused by the war etc. The weather has been mainly hot & still. On the night of 2.9.39 a tremendous thunderstorm which went on almost continuously all night.

On returning to Wallington after 10 days absence find weeds are terrible. Turnips good & some carrots have now reached a very large size. Runner beans fairly good. The last lot of peas did not come to much. A number of marrows. One pumpkin about the size of a billiard ball. Apples on the grenadier almost ripe. Damsons & bullaces ripe. All the winter vegetables have taken all right. Early potatoes rather poor, only about 5–6 potatoes to a plant, but the later ones look as if they would be good. Onions fair. Lettuces have all gone to seed. Flowers in nursery beds (wallflowers 2 kinds, sweet williams & carnations) doing all right. Hollyhocks & marigolds almost over. Roses (not ramblers) blooming again. Larkspurs quite good. Bergamot over, & phloxes almost over. Dahlias full out. Some michaelmas daisies out. Grass has grown very tall in 10 days.

It seems that since 24.8.39 (ie. 12 days) the hens have laid only 85 eggs, mostly big ones. All the older hens are moulting. Goats have been a week on grass only owing to Clarke's failing to deliver grain last week but in good condition & still giving a reasonable amount of milk.

D

6.9.39: Very hot. Rooted up first lot of French beans & dug over that patch, which will do for spring cabbage. Cut side shoots out of tomatoes. These have not done at all well. All leaf & stalk, the plants growing so huge that it is almost impossible to get them to stand upright, & few & poor tomatoes (one or two now ripening.) Probable cause too much animal manure & not enough light.

10 eggs.

D

7.9.39: Very hot. Weeded out first lot of broccoli & dug between. Cut down nettles under the apple tree & applied 1 lb. sodium chlorate. A lot of apples but they are not very good or big, & many windfalls. Made 2–3 lb. apple jelly out of the windfalls.

8 eggs (1 small).

Forgot to mention that at Ringwood I several times saw large flocks of goldfinches, in one case over 30 in the flock.

NB. to count eggs for earlier days of this week at 7 a day, as during our absence they laid 85 in 12 days.

D

8.9.39: Hot. Blackberries not ripe yet. Have lifted the remainder of the early potatoes, which are very poor, only about 5 potatoes to a root.

8 eggs.

[*Newspaper cuttings:* 'Curing a Goat Skin';[12] 'For Gathering Out-of-Reach Fruit']

12. *'Curing a Goat Skin':* Orwell may have had a particular interest in this subject in the light of his account of Flory's disastrous attempt to have a leopard skin cured for Elizabeth Lackersteen in *Burmese Days* (*CW*, II, pp. 226–7). He would later cure skins successfuly on Jura.

D

9.9.39: Very hot. Dug up 3rd batch of peas & dug over that piece of ground. Red mite again very bad. Most of the leghorns now moulting but not so many of the Rhodes. Notice that the birds' appetites always drop off in this weather, ditto the goats, though they don't drink much.

11 eggs. Sold 35 @ 3/– score. Total this week: 58

[*Newspaper cutting:* 'Feeding all Home-Grown Foods']

D

10.9.39: Warmish, but overcast. Dug the 2 rows of King Edward potatoes (actually most of them are not K.E. but another larger kind, perhaps Great Scott). Again very poor though better than the earlies. The best had 16 sizeable potatoes to the root, average about 8. A great many I had to throw away as they were squashy. Everyone here is making the same complaint, so evidently we have some disease about. The first bush marrow has produced a great number of marrows. We had already cut 2 or 3 off it & now it has 4 more sizeable ones & others coming. The pumpkin has at last got hold & is swelling rapidly, so should have time to reach a fair size before the frosts.

8 eggs.

NB. that M[uriel] was showing signs of heat about 8th & 9th, so should come on again about the 30th.

D

11.9.39: Somewhat less warm, overcast, a very few drops of rain about dark. Last night's rain had made no difference to the soil.

Weeded out the onions. These will be ready to pick in 2–3 weeks, but are not good. Applied sodium chlorate to the nettles beyond the walnut tree. Picked 1 lb. of damsons & 3¼ of bullaces. The damsons made almost

2 lb. jam, so the bullaces should make 5 or 6. The 2 rows of potatoes made 3 small sacks, I should say 50 or at most 60 lb. so if the main crop are equally bad we shall have at most another 300 lb., which is not nearly enough.

Picked out 2 boiling fowls (the old light Sussex & the one which mothered the 2nd lot of chicks) to go to market tomorrow.

Swallows beginning to gather on the telegraph wires.

9 eggs.

D

12.9.39: Chilly (enough to have a fire), overcast & windy. Some light rain in the evening. Began cleaning out the maincrop potatoes & cutting the haulm preparatory to digging. They may as well however stay in the ground another fortnight to let the skins harden. Titley's spring cabbages are too young to plant out yet, but will be ready in a fortnight, so about 25.9.39[13] will be the date for this. There should be room for 6 or 7 rows, ie. 100–150 plants. The bullaces only made 4 lb. of jam.

Sold the two old boiling fowls, 6/6 for the two, ie. about 7/6 but commission comes off this.

This morning saw what I am virtually certain was a flight of woodcock. Possibly they flock together for migration. About 8.30 a flight of about a dozen birds went over, & by their long beaks & general shape I thought for a moment they were curlews, which are never seen round here. However they were just a little too small for curlews & their flight a little too fast. At a little distance past me they made the characteristic sideways dip, & I realised they were woodcock. The thing that still makes me slightly uncertain is not there being a dozen of them together, but their being so early. Others I have seen just arriving on the Suffolk coast came in October.

NB. to save seed (about 28 lb.) when digging the maincrop potatoes.

9 eggs. (Not listing the pullets' eggs separately now as they are somewhat larger & sell for the same price. Titley says he is getting 3/4 a score from Moss's.)

13. *25.9.39:* presumably the date is underlined as a reminder. Orwell was away for the ten days before his diary entry for 28 September when he records planting sixty spring cabbages.

D

13.9.39: Overcast in the morning, a sunny patch in the afternoon, then some drizzle. Finished cleaning out potato patch, began digging the bit next to the tomatoes. One or two cockerels almost big enough for market.

7 eggs. Sold 30 @ 3/– score.

D

14.9.39: Overcast, a little drizzling rain, but fairly warm. Finished digging the patch next the tomatoes. Lifted the first row of Red King as the whole of that patch needs liming & it is simpler to lift the potatoes at once.

They are poor, but a little better than the K. Edwards, & only one or two rotten ones among them. Am going to scrap the tomatoes as they will come to nothing. Arranged to sell off all the fowls, as it is evident that we shall only be able to come down here at weekends & it is impossible to continue with any livestock. Shall probably make Mr N.[14] a present of the goats.

8 eggs.

14. *Mr N.:* perhaps Mr Nicholls, the owner of the 'broken-down old wreck' of a male goat referred to by Orwell: see Diary, Volume II, n. 1 above.

D

15.9.39: Rainy, with sunny & windy intervals.

Lifted the remainder of the Red King. Very poor. As well as I can estimate, I should say 300 lbs at most (10 rows – 200 plants). Scrapped the tomatoes. Cut down the nearer row of raspberries, which are perhaps worth keeping, very drastically, & shall manure them heavily later, as I think it possible that row may do something. Shall probably scrap the other one. Began digging patch next the raspberries. Made 2 lb. blackberry jelly out of about 2 lb. blackberries (garden) bought from Mrs Hollingsworth for 6d. Forgot to mention that I picked the apples off the grenadier, which is I think 5 years old. 22 apples, weighing 7½ lb. The apples on the big tree are mostly rotting but some will be all right.

8 eggs.

D

16.9.39: Chilly & misty in the morning, sunny but not too warm in the day, a shower in the afternoon.

Took up & burnt the final lot of peas, & dug over that patch. Arranged to sell off the 8 March pullets @ 5/6 a bird (paid 4/6 for them).

11 eggs. Sold 1 score @ 3/–. Total this week: 60.

D

17.9.39: Windy. Sacked the potatoes, evidently about 300 lb. Gave the sprouting broccoli some wood ash. Arranged to dispose of the goats. Picked about 2 lb. blackberries.

6 eggs.

D

28.9.39: Have not been able to keep up the diary, as I have been away.[15] The eggs are, however, entered in the hen book, though I think a certain number were not recorded.

Typical autumn weather, except that of late the mornings have not been misty. Nights very clear, & the moon, which is a little past full, very fine. A certain amount of leaves yellowing.

Today planted out 60 spring cabbage. Paid 2d score for plants. Continued clearing front flower bed. The chief difficulty is the loganberry against the fence, which is now presumably too old to move. Some of the stems have grown to 15 or 20 feet. Michaelmas daisies in flower, chrysanthemums not yet. The pumpkin is about the size of a football, but I am afraid is going to ripen at that size, as the leaves are turning a little. Most of the young broccoli etc. doing well. E[ileen] gave them superphosphate last week. Made another 3½ lb. apple jelly.

Decided after all not to get rid of the older hens. Shall reduce the size of the run the young ones are in now & use it for a breeding pen (Leghorn x Rhode) in the spring if we are here. The other part can be dug over for potatoes. If actually here we might also go in for rabbits & bees. Rabbits are not to be rationed. The butcher says that people will not as a rule buy tame rabbits for eating but their ideas change when meat gets short. Titley says he made a lot of money out of rabbits at the end of the last war.

4 eggs! (To date this week, including today 36).

Field & others are still getting in hay which has only just been cut, & say it still has some nutritive value in it.

15. *I have been away:* it is not known where Orwell was, nor what he had been doing. However, in his letter to Leonard Moore of 6 October 1939, he writes that Eileen had found a job in a government office (the Censorship Department in Whitehall), but 'I have so far failed to do so' (see *CW*, XI, p. 411). On 9 September he had offered his services to aid the war effort so perhaps he was seeking such work (see *CW*, XI, p. 410).

D

29.9.39: Cloudy but not cold. The nights & early mornings are reasonably warm at present. Finished cleaning out main flower bed & cleaned out the one in front of the kitchen. *Smallholder* advises sowing broad beans now & planting shallots, so shall do so if I get time.

6 eggs.

Put apples to soak for apple wine.

D

30.9.39: Fine, still & fairly warm. Continued clearing & got nearly to the trellis. Note that the white rambler rose has layered itself here & there. Gave all the broccoli nitrate of potash. Picked more apples. There is still 10–15 lb. on the tree, but how many will keep I do not know. I am only trying to keep the larger ones.

5 eggs. Sold 15 @ 3/– score. (Also sold 15 on Wed.) Total for week: 47. This must be low record for this year.

D

1.10.39: Fine but rather chilly. Made another 2 lb. apple jelly. Picked a few blackberries but had not time to go to the good places. Picked some more apples. There are not many large ones left now. Have put about 10–15 lb.

on shelf behind a sack to keep the light out, hoping they may keep at any rate for a month or two.

Five eggs.

D

2.10.39: Fine, rather cold. Beech nuts are now ripe. Yesterday saw good number of young pheasants, fairly well grown.

Selected two cockerels for market tomorrow, about 10 lb. the two.

Continued clearing out beds & got as far as the shed. Can finish tomorrow, then shall spread manure & leave it for a few days before turning in.

4 eggs.

Made a pound or two of blackberry jam, but it has come rather thick.

D

3.10.39: Fine & chilly. A very few drops of rain in the afternoon. Finished clearing out the garden & transplanted a few small plants which were in the way, so tomorrow the manure can be spread.

5 eggs. Got 6/6 for the two cockerels (ie. 7/– less commission). This works out at about 8d lb.

[*Newspaper cutting:* 'Making Coal Briquettes'[16]]

16. Coal was often in short supply during – and for long after – the war. Orwell attempted to make briquettes – see Diary, 6.10.39. It was possible to buy a mould to assist in doing this but the briquettes, though they glowed red quite comfortingly, gave out much less heat than even the poor quality coal distributed.

D

4.10.39: Rather cold, violent wind. Picked up the first ripe walnut today. There are very few, however. Spread the manure. Hoed leeks. Spring cabbages have not taken root very well, owing to the drought. Uprooted the onions, which are very poor.

6 eggs. Sold 14 @ 3/– score.

Made about 3 lb. apple ginger, which I am afraid is a little too gingery.

D

5.10.39: Some rain in the night, the day overcast & rather muggy. A light shower or two in the afternoon. The ground is still very dry a few inches under the surface. Dug over all the flower garden except the small beds. After the earth has settled the new flowers can go in.

6 eggs.

D

6.10.39: Some more rain in the night & a little this morning. Some sunny periods, & not cold.

Finished the flower garden. Planted 2 rows cabbage (36 plants). Cleared the place where the gooseberries are to go (it is too early to move them yet). Made experimentally a few briquettes of coal dust & clay. If successful will make a mould & sieve for making them on a larger scale. Evidently it is important to use only fine dust, also one must have a large metal receptacle for mixing in.

Tonight found a kind of phosphorescent worm or millipede, a thing I have never seen or heard of before. Going out on the lawn I noticed some phosphorescence, & noticed that this made a streak which constantly grew larger. I thought it must be a glowworm, except that I had never seen a glowworm which left its phosphorescence behind. After searching with an electric torch found it was a long very slender wormlike creature with many thin legs down each side & two sort° of antennae on the head. The whole length about 1¼″. Managed to catch him in a test-tube & bring him in, but his phosphorescence soon faded.

5 eggs.

On facing page:

pale yellow, very wriggly (legs relatively thinner than this.)

D

7.10.39: Misty & still. A very few drops of rain. Beech nuts now ripe. Skinned & took the pith out of a largish marrow (about 18″ long), & note that after doing this there is only about 2½ lb. of flesh. Bought Adco, 2/3 for 7ib, which is said to be enough to make 7 cwt. of compost. It appears however that you must not put woody material among the rubbish, nor very large roots. Began digging shallow pit for compost. The briquettes burn fairly well when used together with coal, so shall make arrangements for making some more. Evidently the method is to mix clay & water till it is sloppy, then mix in with your coal dust, using only so much clay as is needed to bind the dust to a very stiff paste. Moulds must be very strong, as the stuff has to be tamped down forcibly.

7 eggs. Sold 15 @ 3/– score. Total this week 38. (NB. started cylinder of calor gas today).

D

8.10.39: Picked about 2½ lb. blackberries. Finished making the pit for rubbish & treated the first two layers with Adco. Weather misty, still & rather cold.

6 eggs

D

9.10.39: Continuous & mostly heavy rain till about 4 pm. Violent wind, strong enough to loosen some of the rose bushes & lift some broccoli plants almost out of the ground. Staked some of the latter, otherwise too wet to do anything out of doors.

5 eggs.

D

10.10.39: Very still, warm & fairly sunny. A very few spots of rain in the evening. Ground greatly sodden, & a lot of chrysanthemums loosened by the wind. Dug trench for broad beans but cannot yet get the ground into sowing condition. That piece (beyond the runner beans) is full of lumps of fine clay. Took out some of the worst & dug in some sand & wood ash. Changed the manure into a larger container as I want the other for leaf mould. Moved the henhouse. Brought in the onions, which are extremely poor, & hung them up to dry. Only 10 large bunches, of which only 3 or 4 will really keep. Picked up a few walnuts but there are very few this year.

Yesterday made 2 lb. blackberry jelly. Note that 2½ lb. blackberries = 2 pints juice = 2 lb. jelly (actually a little over).

5 eggs.

D

11.10.39: Still, sunny & fairly warm. Ground a good deal dryer. Planted out 10 Canterbury bells, about 20 sweet williams, 20 carnations, 25 wall-flowers (flame). Continue tomorrow if not raining. Added some more to compost heap. Staked some of the crysanthemums° etc. T[itley] has not got the stakes yet so cannot finish off hen-run. Yesterday snapped the handle of the spade, but it seems one can get a new handle without having to buy a whole spade. Made a little apple jam, experimentally, but does not seem great success. Have made about 25 lb. of jam altogether.

8 eggs. Sold 25 @ 3/– score.

D

12.10.39: Fine autumn weather, as yesterday. Planted out about 25 more wallflowers, a few hollyhock seedlings, 20 bought tulip bulbs (2 black) & about 15 of our own, & about 30 daffodils, some bought, some of our own. Cut leaves off marrows to let them ripen. I have left one on each plant, one of them a very large one.

8 eggs.

D

13.10.39: Misty but not cold. Some swallows still about, flying very high. Mowed the lawn. Could not make much impression on it, as it has got long again, but this will probably have to be its last cut this year. Nothing more now to be done in the flower garden except the little patch up by the trellis & to trim off edges of the grass & make up paths, but I cannot do all this until the spade is mended. Cleared out the patch where the rhubarb is, preparatory to digging. Gave all the broccoli etc. superphosphate. This will be their last feed. Some savoys ready to cut & a few sprouts almost ready, but all that first lot are very poor. Planted 2 doz.

snowdrop bulbs. Put some hen-manure in the shed to dry. Tried mixture of coal-dust & tea leaves in a paper bag, which will burn more or less, so shall keep sugar cartons for this purpose.

5 eggs (1 double egg.)

D

14.10.39: Extremely heavy rain all night & in the morning. Cleared up a little in the afternoon. Began digging patch by rhubarb, otherwise impossible to do much out of doors.

5 eggs. Sold 15 @ 3/– score. Total this week 42.

D

15.10.39: Continuous & mostly heavy rain all day. Impossible to do anything out of doors.

8 eggs.

D

16.10.39: Sunny, very still, fairly warm. I believe there was a slight frost last night. Saw the white owl again yesterday evening. Limed part of the vacant patch, the part nearest the raspberries. That bit is not to be manured as I want it for root-crops. Dug a little more of the patch by the rhubarb. Soil here rather sour & must be limed when dug. Cut down the runner beans & added a layer to the compost heap. Made up a little more of the garden path.

Sold 4 cockerels for 9/– – poor price but they were very small.

3 eggs!

D

17.10.39: Still, fairly fine, not cold. Went into Baldock & bought mattock, 6/–. Also a little napthaline°, said to be good weed-killer when mixed in equal quantities with lime. Cleared out place where the blackberries are to go. Elm trees are all yellowing, beech trees not so much.

6 eggs.

D

18.10.39: Rather cold, with some sharp showers. Could not do much out of doors. Cleaned up some of the path, & put in some stakes for the blackberries. Two more stakes are needed.

7 eggs. Sold 20 @ 3/– score.

D

19.10.39: Raining almost continuously till late evening. Impossible to do much out of doors. Dug a very little more of the rhubarb bed, cleaned up the remaining bit of the path, which however cannot be re-gravelled till I have got some more cinders (no coal delivered for the past 10 days). Tried experimentally some of the lime & napthalene° mixture,* also

* T[itley] thinks it would actually encourage weeds in the long run. However this mixture is also said to be good for expelling wire-worms [Orwell's note].

crushed rock salt, both said to be good weed-killers. Tits are common about the house now. In the elm trees in the field some kind of bird makes a sawing noise every night. Don't know whether this can be the owls.

If possible the following things have to be done before the end of November:[17]

Move wire of hen-run.

Clear all the grass off the new patch & the bit joining it to the old garden.

Heap turf so as to rot.

Rough-dig the new patch.

Transplant all the fruit bushes.

Clean out & dig the patch where the fruit bushes have been.

Lime the vacant piece, the empty part of the rhubarb bed, & the place where the fruit bushes have been.

Clear out the remaining patch under the hedge & prepare bed for rambler.

Remove most of the chrysanthemums when they have withered back.

Take up & store dahlia roots.

Plant shallots.

Sow broad beans.

Plant phloxes, michaelmas daisies (if not too early.)

Plant roses, rambler & polyantha. Transplant peonies.

Transplant apple tree.

Procure and plant blackberries.

Collect several sacks dead leaves.

Clean out strawberry bed.

Possibly also:[18]

Make up paths in kitchen garden.

Make new bed by gate.

5 eggs.

17. *before the end of November:* all items have been ticked except 'Clean out & dig the patch where the fruit bushes have been' and 'Sow broad beans', which are marked with a cross, '& the place where the fruit bushes have been' and 'Plant phloxes . .' which are not marked at all.

18. *Possibly also:* the following two items are not marked with either a tick or cross.

D

20.10.39: Fine, still, sunny but not particularly warm. Finished digging the rhubarb bed, prepared the frame for dead leaves, made up a little more of the path, grubbed up the last lot of French beans. T[itley] cannot get any stakes so shall have to buy some iron ones.

5 eggs.

D

21.10.39: Very fine, clear, still autumn weather, with a touch of mist. Distinctly chilly morning & evening. E[ileen], Lydia[19] & self picked 4½ lb. blackberries. Nuts seem to be already ripened & fallen. Oak trees now mostly yellow, hawthorn & ash leaves falling.

7 eggs. Sold 15 @ 3/– score. Total this week: 41.

19. Lydia Jackson (née Jiburtovitch, 1899–1983) was educated at Leningrad University, worked for the Society of Friends in Moscow, then came to England in 1925. She did not intend to stay permanently but in 1929 she married Meredith Jackson, a lecturer in law at Cambridge University; they divorced in 1935. She started studying psychology at University College London (where she and Eileen met in 1934 and became friends); she graduated in 1942 and was awarded a D.Phil by Oxford University in 1949. She then lectured in psychology and under her pen-name, Elisaveta Fen, translated Chekhov's plays, 1951–54, published in a single Penguin volume in 1959. See her *A Russian's England* (1976) for good accounts of Eileen, Wallington, and Eileen and Orwell's relationship. Eileen was working in London and coming down at weekends, on this occasion obviously with Lydia. The 21st October was a Saturday.

D

22.10.39: Very misty, not cold, a short spell of sun in the afternoon. No wind. Turned out & examined some of the bags of potatoes. Found that some K. Edwards had gone bad, but no Red Kings, or very few. Threw away the bad ones, changed into fresh bags & scattered a little lime on the heap. Hope this will be enough to prevent serious damage. Planted out a few clumps of aubretia. Cut the pumpkin which was ripening. Only about 10 lb. T[itley] is selling first-rate cooking apples (called locally Meetrop or some such name – have not seen this apple before) at 1d lb., eating apples (Blenheims) @ 1½ lb. Cut the first savoy today. Arranged to let the milkman have our eggs @ 3/6 score instead of the 3/– the butcher has been paying. T. says you can get 3/8 at the market, but in that case there are commissions to come off.

6 eggs.

D

23.10.39: Not cold & fairly fine, but a few drops of drizzling rain in the evening. Cleaned out the piece between the rockery & the trellis, made a bed of sorts, planted 20 forget-me-nots in it, made a bed ready for the rambler. There is now nothing to be done in the flower garden except to plant the flowers (phlox etc.) when they are ready, make up paths & perhaps cut the grass once again. Made 2 lb. apple jelly yesterday. Found some eggs of either worm or snail, about the size of match-heads, whitish, translucent.

6 eggs.

D

24.10.39: Evidently a good deal of rain last night. Today overcast, not cold, a few spots of rain in the afternoon. Leaves coming down pretty fast now.

Today went into Baldock. Bought small sieve (2/–). Impossible to get iron stakes for wire netting. Timber also almost unprocurable. Managed to get 2 very poor 6 ft. stakes for gate-posts of hen-run. Put them up this evening, & shall shift wire tomorrow if not raining. Tried to mow grass, but the machine in its present state makes no impression. Shall have to leave it till the spring, then get it scythed. Mr K[20] mended the spade by using the handle of the broken fork. Quite a good mend but leaves the spade a bit short. Paid 1/–. Impossible to sow broad beans yet as the ground will not get fine. Clarke's[21] sent shallots today & shall plant them by way of experiment when I get time. NB. that 2 lb. shallots = about 60 bulbs (say 2 rows). There are now 2 barn owls which live in the stumpy elm tree, & evidently it is they that make the sawing noise. I suppose these are the ones that used to be called screech-owls, & the ordinary brown owl is the one that makes the to-whoo noise.

6 eggs. Started hens on course of Karswood today.* Also giving them more shell grit.

20. *Mr K.:* unidentified neighbour.
21. *Clarke's:* seedsmen and producers of food for fowls.

D

25.10.39: Fine, sunny, cold wind. Began clearing the vacant ground between the old garden & the new patch. Burnt a little of the rubbish. Limed another strip, also the rhubarb patch, but have not turned the lime in here. Collected the first sack of dead leaves (beech). Had noticed for 2 days that a brown hen was sitting out somewhere. Tonight found her nest – 10 eggs, 1 broken. Took the eggs, which may possibly be good, being unfertilised. Tonight she had gone back to the empty nest. Put her in the house, & hope she may be cured in a few days. This morning shifted the wire of the run. Posts are not long enough for gate posts, but can have an extra piece fitted on if I can get hold of some timber. Yesterday when sinking holes for the posts found that the chalk is only about 6″ beneath the surface, but possibly it isn't so all over the patch.

4 eggs. Sold 20 @ 3/6 (to milkman).

D

26.10.39: A very sharp white frost last night, the first severe frost of the year. The day overcast with a short sunny interval, & rather cold. Water in the

* Lasted till 14.11.39 (26 hens) [Orwell's note].

hens' basin frozen solid this morning. Turned it, & this evening there was still a little ice left. The dahlias blackened immediately, & I am afraid the marrows I had left to ripen are done for, as they had gone a funny colour. Brought them in & added the haulm to the compost-heap, which is now completed except for the old straw which is still in the flower garden. Finished clearing the waste patch, piled the turf in a heap & marked out where the path is to go. This leaves another yard width of soil. Began digging this as it will do for the shallots. Collected another sack of dead leaves & sprinkled a little saltpetre (advised in *Smallholder*) among them. Shall try & note the number of sacks collected so as to see what amount of mould they make. The turves old H[atchett] stacked earlier in the year have rotted down into beautiful fine loam, but I think I had first killed the grass on these with sodium chlorate, so presumably what I am stacking now will not rot so rapidly or completely. Put some wood-ash on the place for the broad beans. If I can't get that bit fine I must try & find space elsewhere & simply give the bad clayey patch a good liming. The broody hen goes to her nest every night. Last night she would have frozen to death if I had not happened to find her. Considerable number of goldfinches in the garden today.

7 eggs.

D

27.10.39: I think there must have been a slight frost again last night. Today about midday heavy rumbling sound which may have been either thunder or gunfire, & soon afterwards heavy sleety rain. More showers in the afternoon. Ground is very soggy again. Could not do much out of doors owing to the rain. Dug a little of the patch for the shallots.

6 eggs.

D

28.10.39: Frost again last night (not so hard as before). All today raining almost continuously. Impossible to do anything out of doors. One double egg today.

6 eggs Total this week 41.

D

3.11.39: Have been away since last Sunday (28th),[22] only returning this evening. Everything is extremely sodden. Planted a few more crocus bulbs & took up dahlia roots, which maybe worth keeping. In this time the hens have apparently only laid 28 eggs, less than 5 a day. Had not noted that before leaving on Sunday sold 1 score @ 4/–.

22. *Sunday (28th):* Sunday was actually the 29th.

D

4.11.39: Damp, but not raining to any great extent. Finished digging the ground for the shallots (still very sodden & will need several fine days to dry it), manured the rhubarb, began clearing the new patch of thistles etc. Saw the white owl in the daytime. Very beautiful toadstools in the field now, pale bluey-green, slender stalk of same colour, mauve gills, the whole toadstool coated with sort of slimy stuff. Added another ½ sack of dead leaves to heap.

5 eggs. Total this week 33 (Mrs A[nderson] has obviously underfed them).

D

5.11.39: Some wind in the morning, then nice sunny weather. Ground has dried up somewhat. In the evening violent wind & a few drops of rain. The wind actually blew the roof off the small henhouse. Enormous flocks of starlings, some tens of thousands at a time, going over with a noise that sounds like heavy rain. The leaves are mostly down now. Elder leaves just coming down. As I remember it, the elms are being stripped much earlier this year than most.

Transplanted the gooseberry bushes. Trust I haven't damaged them. One or two still had green or greenish leaves, & others were so deep in the ground I had to damage their roots considerably getting them up. The soil there (this end of garden) is in places pure clay at only 1 foot below the surface. Dug some of this out & lightened the ground as well as possible with sand & turf-mould. Then limed the ground between the bushes & dug in, also pruned the bushes a little. Hope this wind will not blow them all loose again. Added another sack of leaves.

9 eggs (probably some of these laid yesterday). Sold 30 @ 4/– score.

[Total sacks of leaves on facing page: 3½.]

D

6.11.39: Evidently it rained very heavily during last night. Today windy, a few showers but most of the day sunny. Transplanted the peonies. They are said not to stand this well, but they had withered back & I took a good ball of soil with each. Planted the little rambler cutting, the one that was in a pot. This has rooted well but is of course a very tiny plant. Dug & manured a trench to plant the first lot of currants, but don't like to plant them till the ground is a little less sodden. Limed another small patch of ground. Forgot to mention that one of the gooseberry bushes I moved yesterday had layered itself. Evidently they do this spontaneously sometimes.

5 eggs.

D

7.11.39: Rather wet, too much so to do much out of doors: Considerable rain this evening. Planted first row of currants (ie. 6 red, 5 black). Have started using chaff instead of straw for nesting-boxes. Do not know whether it will prove too expensive, but should be easier to clean out & to rot down.

6 eggs.

There was a nest of field mice at the roots of one of the currant bushes, & they came running out, 5 in all, as I levered the plant up. Fatter & lighter-coloured than the house-mouse, with a long tail (I had always had an idea they had short ones) & rather slow-moving, with a sort of hopping movement, though they all managed to get away from me.

D

8.11.39: Dry, windy, sunny, not cold. Many goldfinches about. Took the remaining nettles, or most of them, out of the new patch. Put in 2 more stakes for blackberries. Limed another patch. Added 1 sack dead leaves. [Total on facing page: 4½.]

6 eggs. Sold 20 @ 4/4.

D

9.11.39: Sunny & still. Everything still seems very wet, but evidently there was no rain last night. Made up some more of the path. Unable to do much else, as the wheelbarrow is about at its last & I was trying to repair it.

5 eggs.

D

10.11.39: Very fine, sunny, still weather. Dug the first trench of the new patch, planted shallots (not quite enough to make up the 2 rows), transplanted 3 rambler rose cuttings, 1 Albertine, one of the yellowy-white kind, the other I don't know what kind. Made up path as far as trellis. Titley says in storing dahlia bulbs the important thing is to suspend them for a while stalk downwards, as the reason they rot is that moisture runs down the hole in the stalk into the roots. Bought some more apples (Blenheims) still 1½. lb. T. says he is getting 4/6 score for eggs.

9 eggs.

D

11.11.39: Very fine weather, as yesterday. Birds all singing almost as though it were spring. Notice that horse dung of some mares & their foals out in the fields is extremely dark, almost black, presumably from being out at grass with no corn. Added another sackful of leaves. [Total on facing page: 6.]

5 eggs. Sold 1 score @ 4/4. Total this week 45.

D

12.11.39: Windless, misty, sun just visible, rather chilly. Many fungi in the woods, including one which at a certain stage gets a sort of white fluffy mildew on it & smells rather like bad meat. Immense quantities of wood pigeons & large flights of starlings. Came on a field of what appeared to be weeds but think it may possibly be buckwheat, which is sometimes grown about here for the sake of the partridges. Small black three-cornered seed like a miniature beech nut. Brought home a patch of a kind of rough moss & stuck it on the rockery, hoping it will grow. Today at 3 pm hung out a lump of fat for the tits. They had found it at before 5 pm.

5 eggs.

D

13.11.39: Beautiful still, sunny day. Last night not at all cold. Cannot make sure whether when shallots spring out of the ground it is of their own accord or partly done by the pigeons. Sometimes they are about 1′ from where they were planted. Dug 2 rows of the new patch, turned the compost heap, limed another patch, added one more sackful dead leaves. [Total on facing page: 7.] One hen is definitely broody.

6 eggs.

D

14.11.39: Rather windy, looked like rain in middle of day but actually did not rain. Dug 2 more trenches in new patch. Cannot get on faster than this owing to chalky stony streak in the middle which is hard to break into. Dug trench for remaining blackcurrants.

6 eggs.

D

15.11.39: Last night a little rain, today fine, still & mild. Dug 2 more trenches. Cut down some of the herbaceous plants. Some of the phloxes will have to be split up. Another double egg. By the look of them all the double eggs I have had recently come from the same bird, tho' it is always said locally that a double egg means the beginning or ending of a clutch.

9 eggs. Sold 1 score @ 4/4.

D

16.11.39: Some rain last night & almost continuous light rain all today. Impossible to do much out of doors. Limed another strip (lime now running short), transplanted a couple of currant bushes. Most of the trees are now completely bare. A few leaves still on the elms. Of the deciduous trees the ashes seem the last to go.

4 eggs.

D

17.11.39: Still, overcast but not more than a few spots of rain. Transplanted the remaining currant bushes except 2, which still have their leaves rather green. One of the bushes had layered itself. Cut the layer off & planted it experimentally. Limed another strip. There will be just enough lime for the remainder of the vacant patch but not for where the bushes have been. To do the whole garden would need a cwt. or somewhat over. Collected another sack of dead leaves. [Total on facing page: 8.] Added a little to compost heap.

7 eggs (actually 8 but one broken).

D

18.11.39: Rather rainy. Went into Baldock but failed to get any rose bushes. Bought a peony root which perhaps I can plant at the corner instead of a rose. Clarke's say the shortage of grains, or difficulty of sending them to & fro, is actually much greater than the papers make out. Saw a bird which I think must have been a golden plover, though so far as I know they are not found round here. Slightly larger than a snipe (it was certainly not a snipe), redshank type of flight, but its back was brownish. Too far away to see its beak. The only thing that makes me doubtful is that its belly was almost white.

9 eggs. Sold 1 score @ 4/4. (According to Clarke's the Gov.t are controlling the price at 4/–). Total this week 46.

D

19.11.39: Some rain last night. Today still, fairly fine. Winter time (deferred 2 months owing to the war) starts today so have to give the hens their evening meal about 3 pm. Dug one trench, transplanted the little rose (the one that was overgrown by the lavender) & planted peony (price of root 6d). These don't generally bloom the following year. Afraid I may have put the 3 peonies too close together.

5 eggs. (Notice nearly always a bad lay after a wet day, as yesterday).

D

20.11.39: Fine, still, reasonably warm. Planted 6 lupins (paid 9d), said to be mixed colours. NB. that T[itley] says that with lupins one should spread their roots out & not insert them too deep. Limed & began digging the final strip. This will need more doing than the rest as the ground is very sour & full of weeds. Cut down the remaining phloxes, tied up some of the chrysanthemums which had been blown over. Difficult to do much these afternoons now it is winter-time. The chrysanths now in full flower, mostly dark reddy-brown, & few ugly purple & white ones which I shan't keep. Roses still attempting to flower, otherwise no flowers in the garden now. Michaelmas daisies are over & I have cut some of them down. The 2nd lot of Brussels sprouts (planted as little plants 19.8.39) sprouting up, also some of the savoys planted at the same time beginning to hearten up a little. All that lot are small kinds. None of my broccoli yet heading to any extent, though the plants have grown well. T. says oak leaves make the best mould, & then beech.

8 eggs. Sold 8 @ 2d each (a mistake – price miscalculated).

D

21.11.39: Still, overcast, rather chilly. Did nothing out of doors. New cwt. Full-o-Pep begun today. Clarke's say the grain-shortage, such as there is, is of maize & dari (weatings).[23] The former comes from the Argentine. The latter was usually imported ready ground, & at present the English mills are not turning it out fast enough, though there is no shortage of wheat.

8 eggs.

23. *dari (weatings):* dari or durra is Indian millet. 'Wheatings' is a proprietary name for the residue of milled wheat; the word dates from 1931.

D

22.11.39: Much as yesterday. Dug some more of the limed patch, planted out the remaining black currants. A double egg again & also an egg of the type the *Smallholder* describes as pimpled. Tom R[idley] says he saw a rat come out of our garden yesterday.

9 eggs.

D

23.11.39: Rain last night, light rain all day. Cold. Impossible to do much out of doors. Dug some more of the limed patch.

8 eggs.

D

24.11.39: Fine, still, rather cold. Finished digging limed patch. Transplanted apple tree. Had great difficulty uprooting it & fear I damaged its roots seriously. Cut down remaining michaelmas daisies & transplanted one clump. Found nest of 11 eggs, not sat on & seemingly O. K., so will do for the house, but shall not enter them in book.

4 eggs.

D

25.11.39: Hard frost last night, which started about 4 pm. Thawed this morning about 10 am, cold & miserable all day. Lumps of ice turned out of hens' basins were still frozen in the evening. Made bonfire, added some of the hay which had rotted to the compost-heap. This uses up the Adco, which will not have made the 7 cwt. of manure as specified, but perhaps I used it too liberally.

7 eggs. Sold 20 @ 4/4. Total this week: 49. + 11 laid out = 60.

D

26.11.39: Cold & windy, rain some of the day. Stuck a root of wild briar in, experimentally, but not certain whether it will take as it had not much root. Shall plant some more as I want to try budding next year.

10 eggs. Sold 4 @ 2d each & 5 at 5 for 1/–.

D

27.11.39: Heavy rain in the night & all this morning. Finer & windless this afternoon. Everything very sodden. Dug another trench. Have now almost finished the amount I intend doing of the new bit. Stuck in 2 more briar roots. Shall plant about 6 of different heights & see how they do. Collected another sack of dead leaves. This amount (about 10 sacks) fills the frame. Covered over with fine soil & shall not disturb till next year.

7 eggs.

D

28.11.39: Still not too warm. Some frost in the night. Finished the new patch. This will take 5 or 6 rows of potatoes. Showed the briar stocks to T[itley], who explained that one must cut the side shoots off & bud onto those which appear in spring.

7 eggs.

D

29.11.39: Rained in the night, fine today & reasonably warm. Started digging the patch where the bushes were. This is in a terrible state & will take a long time to do, also is poor chalky soil & needs a lot of enriching. Began making path for henhouses, as the mud is very bad.

6 eggs. Sold 1 score @ 4/4.

D

30.11.39: Very mild & still. A very few light spots of rain. Bats were out (noticed midges flying about the other day, in spite of the recent frosts). Dug a little more of the weedy patch. Made up the front part of the path. Pruned the white rambler, I hope correctly. Have not seen or heard the owls for some time past.

8 eggs.

D

1.12.39: A little windier & colder than yesterday. Did some more weeding, turned the compost heap, planted another root of briar, this time a much older one.

9 eggs.

D

2.12.39: Fine, still, not very warm.

9 eggs. Sold 20 @ 4/4. Total this week: 56.

D

3.12.39: Frost last night. Today fine, windy, coldish. The common lane water-logged almost knee-deep in parts. Planted another briar root. Note that on post hammered in on 18.10.39 fungi are growing (the horizontal hard kind that look like ears) about 1″ broad, so evidently these things grow fairly rapidly.

7 eggs.

D

4.12.39: Heavy rain in the early part of last night, then frost. A little rain this morning. Windy & cold.

10 eggs. Sold 1 score @ 4/4.

D

5.12.39: Windy, overcast & decidedly cold. Some sloes still on the bushes. Plovers sitting on the ground & crying.

10 eggs.

D

6.12.39: Cold last night but no frost. Today fine & cold.

5 eggs. Sold 1 score @ 4/2.

D

7.12.39: Very hard frost last night, which did not begin to thaw till afternoon. Thick mist in the evening. Mr R[idley] turns over the frosted ground, digging the frost in, which he says kills the wireworms etc.

9 eggs.

D

8.12.39: Raining all day.

10 eggs.

D

9.12.39: Fine & rather cold. A little rain in the evening.

8 eggs. Total this week: 59.

D

10.12.39: Sunny in the morning, overcast in the afternoon, not cold. Transplanted another root of wild rose. Transferred the 4 young pullets to the main houses.

8 eggs.

D

11.12.39: Raw, chilly, thick mist most of day.

7 eggs.

D

12.12.39: (In London) Cold & overcast.

D

13.12.39: Cold, overcast, not windy.

D

28.12.39: Back at Wallington. Very cold, but no wind. In London there were a few frosts &, round about Xmas, extremely dense mists, making traffic almost impossible. Here freezing hard since yesterday, & snowing all today. Extremely light dry snow, which clings to everything, even wire netting. One of the plants that carries the snow most beautifully is lavender. Even corrugated iron looks attractive with snow on it. White Leghorn hens on the snow look quite dark yellow.

In the time we have been away, ie. since 12.12.39 there have apparently been 101 eggs – a falling off but not so bad as I expected. Shall have to make the weeks up by guesswork but can get the actual numbers right.

Mice have been very bad in the house during my absence, tearing up newspaper etc., etc. Must try poisoning them.

4 eggs (no doubt owing to cold.)

[NB. As to egg account: – the total number of eggs, including those laid on the 2 (unentered) days before we went away, & today's, is 120. I have entered the last two weeks @ 45 a week, which leaves 30 to be added to those of Friday–Sat. of this week: ie. this week's eggs will equal Friday. Sat's eggs + 30. This will make the total right even if the weeks are incorrect.][24]

24. The square brackets are Orwell's.

D

29.12.39: Freezing hard all day, but no fresh snow. Water pipes frozen this morning. Saw a rabbit run across a pool on the ice. Oat stack being thrashed at the farm.

4 eggs.

D

30.12.39: No thaw. A few light spots of snow.

5 eggs. Total this week (see above): 39. Yesterday sold 5 @ 1/–.

D

31.12.39: Considerably warmer, & thawing this afternoon, but appears to be freezing again tonight.

5 eggs.

1940

D

1.1.40: Freezing again last night. Today thawing in the sun but freezing in the shade. Some children able to slide on the ice of one of the ponds. They are ploughing in places, which the earth is not too hard for with a tractor plough. Frost turned into the soil said to be good for it, but snow is bad (ie. presumably bad for a heavy soil). The £2 an acre subsidy for ploughing up grassland said to cover the costs of ploughing including labour. Tractor said to use about 10 galls. paraffin to plough an acre.

3 eggs!

D

2.1.40: No thaw. Fallen ash-boughs all stripped & gnawed by rabbits. Pan of water left out all day is thickly frozen by evening.

6 eggs.

D

9.1.40: Back home again after nearly a week in London. The frost has now broken but it is still cold, generally damp & misty, & there is still a good deal of ice left on the pools. W.C. has at last unfrozen but there was still ice in the cistern. Chrysanthemums have now withered back, so shall cut them down & remove those that are of bad colours. The others ought also to be removed & divided in the spring, but probably there won't be time.

In 7 days the hens appear to have laid only 25 eggs. This is far worse than they were doing before & evidently Mrs A[nderson] has again underfed them. Mrs. A. sold 1 score @ 3/4

[*On facing page:*]

To even the eggs up: to end of week: 27.

New week up to & including 9.1.39[8]: 12.

(This includes those laid before I went away + 25).

D

10.1.40: Freezing very hard again. Water left outside has ice on it in only an hour or two. The pond by the church will bear my weight, but not that in the field called the Warren. The reservoir is not frozen at all. Turned up 2 rabbits in the field. They have a hole there, but whether used I am not quite certain. On the church wall found a jay & a grey squirrel, presumably shot by somebody & thrown there. Did not know the grey squirrel was found round here or that they came out of hibernation in this weather. Cut down the chrysanthemums. Made several attempts to start a bonfire, but things in frosty weather are not so dry as they look. One or two of the shallots (planted 10.11.39) beginning to show buds. One of the pullets (hatched May) has come into lay.

7 eggs.

D

11.1.40: No thaw. It would be possible to skate on the church pond, but unfortunately I have no skates here. The other ponds not bearing. Water beetles (the kind whose legs look like oars) can be seen moving about under the ice. When a brick lies on the bottom in shallow water, there appears in the ice above it a curious formation the size & shape of the brick itself, presumably something to do with the temperature of the brick when thrown in being higher than that of the water. Turned up a woodcock in the common lane. No rabbits in the field today. Birds very bold & hungry. Rooks in the vegetable garden, where they do not usually come. One or two primroses & polyanthi budding, in spite of the frost upon them. One of the elm trees apparently bleeds a brown-coloured stuff, sap or something, & large icicles of this hanging down, looking like toffee. Milk when frozen goes into a curious flaky stuff like flaky pastry.

7 eggs.

D

12.1.40: Appeared to stop freezing for about an hour in the afternoon, otherwise no thaw. Still & sunny. Poultry manure frozen hard & easy to break up, so scattered a patch with this, which can be dug in later. This patch (next the unmanured patch this side of the raspberries) will do for onions.

9 eggs.

D

13.1.40: Thawed a little in the sun in the afternoon, then freezing again.

4 eggs. Sold 1 score (presumably $3/4^{d}$). Total this week: 39.

D

14.1.40: No thaw. Thickish mist. Extremely still, no sun visible but not particularly cold.

D

15.1.40: Some sun today, & for a little while in the afternoon a little thaw in the sun, everywhere else freezing hard. Evidently the frost has been harder the last night or two, as the indoor water pipes are frozen again. Dishes of water left in the kitchen sink now freeze almost solid. This must be the longest cold snap since 1916–17, when we had very similar weather (about end of February 1917).

9 eggs.

The rime everywhere is almost like snow. Today an egg rolled out of one of the houses & got frozen. On breaking it find that the white goes to a substance like jelly with bubbles in it, & the yoke° goes to a consistency like that of stiff putty.

D

16.1.40: No thaw. In the afternoon violent & very cold wind & a little snow.

6 eggs.

D

17.1.40: No thaw. A little snow in the night, making about 1 inch depth. Last night seemingly the hardest frost of all, as even the village pump was frozen. Snow very dry & crunchy. Dung in the hen houses frozen quite hard, so broke this up & scattered on another strip, which will do for beans or peas.

5 eggs. Sold 25 @ 3/6 score.

D

18.1.40: No thaw. Unable to unfreeze pipes etc. Saw a little owl today – have not previously seen any of these round here.

11 eggs.

D

19.1.40: No thaw. A little more snow last night. Cannot unfreeze kitchen tap but unfroze the waste pipe by pouring boiling water down the straight part & hanging a hot water bottle over the bend. Tried to dig a hole to bury some refuse but found it impossible even with the pick. Even at 6″ depth the ground is like a stone.

9 eggs.

D

20.1.40: No thaw. They are now skating on the pool in the Warren. Potatoes brought in from the shed are frozen right through, with thick crust of ice under the skin. These were ones that were not covered up. Have not looked at those that are.

7 eggs. Total this week: 57. Sold 1 score @ 3/6.

D

21.1.40: Colder, more wind, & a good deal of light & rather damp snow. Tom Ridley says best way of thawing out pipes is to run a blowlamp along them.

12 eggs. (best for some months past)

Said to have been 21° frost yesterday.[25]

25. *21° frost:* approximately 11° F or -12°C. The Thames froze for the first time since 1888.

D

22.1.40: Some more snow last night, making about 4″. A little also today. Not actually thawing today, but definitely less cold. Put oilstove in the kitchen, whereupon the pipes unfroze, disclosing the fact that one is burst. Kitchen & small room flooded 1″ deep before I discovered what was happening.

Wood pigeon walking about in kitchen garden & unable to fly, presumably from hunger & cold. Did not care to molest it, though it was pecking at cabbages etc.

8 eggs. Sold 1 score @ 3/6.

D

23.1.40: Evidently a little more snow in the night. Milder, but no thaw.

6 eggs. Am not counting one that was laid on the floor of the pullets' house & was broken. There were 3 there altogether, so at any rate 2 pullets are laying.

[*Newspaper cutting*: 'How to make Macon', i.e., how to cure mutton as a substitute for bacon; bacon was then in short supply.]

D

24.1.40: No thaw. Rather windy.

6 eggs (not counting 1 broken one). Sold 1 score @ 3/6.

D

25.1.40: No thaw. Still & not cold.

11 eggs. (3 pullets definitely laying).

D

26.1.40: No thaw. In the afternoon considerable wind & some very cold rain which froze as soon as it fell, leaving a thin skin of ice over everything. Then some heavy & rather squashy snow.

4 eggs.

D

27.1.40: No thaw. Last night distinctly milder, then heavy sloshy snow. Freezing very hard again this evening. Birds very hungry. A thrush hanging round the shed today, seemingly weak with hunger.

9 eggs. Total this week: 56. Sold 1 score @ 3/6.

D

28.1.40: Very cold. Heavy snow last night, making about one foot deep. A little snow most of the day.

8 eggs.

D

29.1.40: The coldest weather hitherto. Heavy snow last night, everything snowed up, drifts 4–6′ deep in places, roads more or less impassable, so that there has been no traffic of any kind all day. Violent wind. In spite of all this the tap of the village pump is not frozen, though almost completely buried in snow this morning. Some days back after being thawed out with boiling water it was muffled in sacking, after which it has remained unfrozen.

5 eggs.

There is a break in keeping the Diary until 13 March 1940.

On 11 March 1940 Victor Gollancz published *Inside the Whale and Other Essays*. Only 1,000 copies were printed and some were destroyed by bombing. Orwell received £20 on publication

D

13.3.40: Re-opening this diary after a long absence due to 'flu etc.

The day we left, 30.1.40, the roads were so completely snowed up that of the 3½ miles to Baldock we were only able to do about ½ mile on the road. For the rest we had to strike across the fields, where the snow was frozen hard & there were not so many drifts. In the road they were at least 6′ deep in places. It was sometimes impossible to see where the road lay, as the snow covered the tops of the banks on either side. Flocks of hares, sometimes about 20 together, were wandering over the fields.

As a result of the frost all kinds of cabbages, except a few Brussels sprouts, are completely destroyed. The spring cabbages have not only died but entirely disappeared, no doubt eaten off by the birds. The leeks have survived, though rather sorry for themselves. Most of the wallflowers have survived. Some 2-years old ones which I had left in are all dead. The older carnations are also dead, but the young ones are all right. All the rose cuttings have survived except one. Snowdrops are out & some yellow crocuses, a few polyanthi trying to flower, tulips & daffodils showing, rhubarb just sprouting, ditto peonies, black currants budding, red currants not, gooseberries budding. The compost I made with Adco has not rotted down very completely. Grass everywhere very brown & sickly-looking. The soil is very fine & friable as a result of the frost.

Have now lost accurate count of the eggs & shall have to close the egg-account book, which however gives an accurate account stretching over 7 months, useful for future reference. From the milkman's account it appears the hens have laid 270 eggs since 29.1.40 (6 weeks about). Yesterday 10. It is now difficult to sell eggs, as there is a glut, so shall put some in water-glass. The last few days fine spring-like weather. Today colder & this afternoon raining hard.

Did a little digging. Hoed leeks.

14 eggs.

D

14.3.40: Heavy snow in the night & during a good deal of the day. Nasty slushy snow which will not lie long, but makes everything very nasty. Impossible to do anything out of doors.

Began water-glassing some eggs, experimentally. It appears you should use eggs 5–12 hours old, as if they have been laid a day or two it takes several months off the time they will stay good. Put 20–30 older eggs (laid about 6 days) in a glass jar, & these can be used first. Am using a large enamelled pan for newer eggs, & shall put in none more than 24 hours old.

16 eggs.

D

15.3.40: Hard frost in the night & roads very slippery this morning. Today fairly sunny & warm. Thawing fast, but most of the grass still covered with snow. A few blue crocuses appearing.

16 eggs.

D

16.3.40: Fairly fine day. The snow has now almost gone.

19 eggs. Total this week (5 days): 75.

D

17.3.40: Raining much of the day. Everything now very sodden. Roses are budding well. Alfred H[atchett] says it is not too late to plant blackberry runners, though they will do no good this year.

16 eggs.

D

18.3.40: Somewhat drier. A few drops of rain. Forked over the ground for the onion bed & applied superphosphate. A few wallflowers just beginning to bud. But there are very few that are really undamaged by the frost.

15 eggs.

D

19.3.40: Violent wind, & raining slightly on & off.

Prepared a row for broad beans & another for cauliflowers, but impossible to get the surface soil fine yet.

16 eggs.

D

20.3.40: Somewhat drier, but a few showers. Dug a little more & prepared place for blackberries.

9 eggs.

D

21.3.40: It is drying, but very slowly. Again a few showers. Sorted out potatoes, of which at least a third have rotted owing to frost. However if the remaining ones don't rot there are enough to last several months at present rate of consumption. Dug a little more. A little aubretia beginning to flower. A few scillas also. Perennials all budding pretty strongly. No. of eggs in waterglass about 100.

16 eggs.

D

22.3.40: Somewhat drier but a few drops of rain. Planted 3 blackberries (runners) & 2 roots of rhubarb. Began clearing out the strawberry bed. Blue & white crocuses now out.

13 eggs.

D

23.3.40: About the first nice spring weather, except for a shower or two in the afternoon. Buds on bullace trees.

13 eggs. Total this week: 98.

D

24.3.40: Nice spring weather most of the day. Blackthorn just budding. Catkins & female flowers on the hawthorn. Found some frogs mating. In most places they have already spawned & some of the spawn is beginning to develop. Brought a few bits home. A primrose out in the garden (also polyanthi) but could find none in the woods, though Mrs Nicholls, whom we met,[26] had found a very few, also violets. Anemones not out.

18 eggs.

26. *we met:* presumably Eileen was down for the weekend – the 24th was a Sunday.

D

25.3.40: Most of day nice weather, turning damper at night. Cleaned out a little of strawberry bed.

15 eggs. (Sold 30 for 2/–).

D

26.3.40: Raining almost without cease all day, & decidedly cold. Tadpoles I brought home are already more or less formed & working their way out of the spawn.

15 eggs.

D

27.3.40: Finer. Still impossible to sow seeds. Dug a little more, applied wood-ash to bed for onions. Tadpoles now almost fully formed & beginning to wriggle their tails.

16 eggs. Sold 1 score @ 2/10.

D

28.3.40: Sharp frost in the night, which does not appear to have done any damage, however. Today fine but rather cold. Cleared out some more of the strawberry bed, prepared the onion bed, which may be fit to sow tomorrow. Some of the tadpoles swimming about. The first daffodil in the field out. None yet in the garden, though some in other people's gardens. Five of the six briar stocks I planted budding.

20 eggs.

D

29.3.40: Sowed onions (3 rows Jas. Keeping). 2 oz. seed supposed to do 200 feet but only did about 100, no doubt because I sowed too thick. Today cold, overcast & windy, with some rain in the afternoon.

17 eggs.

D

30.3.40: Nice spring weather. Sowed 1 row carrots. Finished weeding strawberries, & applied a little manure. Place for broad beans now about fit to sow.

One or two daffodils opening in garden. Except for Innes' meadow beyond the Lodge, it is now ploughed up all the way from Wallington to Baldock, thanks to the subsidy.

19 eggs. Total this week: 120 (25 hens – probably our record lay.)

D

31.3.40: Rather cold, & violent wind all day. A certain number of primroses out, also white & blue violets, & celandine. No other wild flowers. Saw a sheep with two newborn lambs, the first I have seen this year. Notice that the spawn in the pond, from which I took a little a week ago, is still at about the same stage, whereas the bit I brought home has developed & tadpoles swimming about. No doubt due to difference in temperature.

18 eggs.

D

1.4.40: Strong wind, which has dried the soil greatly, but beautiful spring weather in the morning. In the evening overcast, but no rain. Violets out in great numbers everywhere. Larks singing, the first I have heard this year, though most years one hears them much earlier than this. Partridges pairing, rooks & seagulls not yet. A few tulips forming heads. Arabis well out. Note that a few of the carrots I left in the ground were not destroyed by the frost, though most went to mush.

Sowed broad beans, & some in box to fill up gaps. Cleared the ground where peas & parsnips are to go. Dug a little more.

17 eggs.

D

2.4.40: Most of day nice weather, but a heavy shower lasting about half an hour in the evening, & a light shower at midday. A few grape hyacinths forming heads. Some wallflowers almost in flower. Saw a bat, the first I have seen this year. Fruit trees budding fairly strongly.

Prepared the patch for artichokes, which can be sowed tomorrow if fine. Weeded large flower bed.

15 eggs. Sold 3 score @ 2/7 (7/– less commission).

D

3.4.40: Seems to have rained fairly heavily during last night. Light drizzle all this morning. Fine most of the afternoon. Sowed artichokes on the new patch, which is very stony but probably good enough for this purpose. This used 7 lb., so still have 7 lb. left. Weeded out the turf heap under the bullace tree, which will do for a marrow-bed. Pigeons are cooing.

16 eggs. Sold 1 score @ 2/6.

D

4.4.40: Thin drizzle early this morning, then sunny & windy, rain for about 2 hours in the middle of the day, then again sunny & windy. Dug some more. Soil is again extremely soggy. Applied nitrate of potash to leeks & such shallotts° as there are. Walnut tree shows things like tiny fir-cones which are presumably male flowers. Planted some roots of perennial sunflower, given me by Mr Hatchett.

15 eggs. Sold 1 score @ 2/6 (? Milkman).

D

5.4.40: Overcast but not actually raining. Dug some more, hoed strawberries, planted some more roots of sunflower.

15 eggs.

D

6.4.40: Sharp frost last night. Beautiful still sunny day, turning rather cold again this evening. Dug some more. Frost has improved the soil considerably. Weeded the patch between the currants & the strawberries, & applied lime. (Paid Titley 6d for about 7–10 lb lime). After this has been turned in the patch can lie fallow till June, when it will do for winter greens. Sowed marrows & pumpkins in pots. NB. that marrows are in the pots nearest the road.

19 eggs. 1 double egg. Sold 2 score @ 2/– (reduced price). Total this week: 115.

D

7.4.40: Fine & most of day reasonably warm. Ground has dried up a good deal. Apple trees are budding well. Finished digging the potato patch & the place for the peas. Nothing to be dug now except the limed patch. Picked up an owl's pellet in the field, very large, so perhaps the barn owls are back again. Arabis well out.

13 eggs.

D

8.4.40: Cold, overcast & a very little light drizzle. Ground has not dried up, so cannot sow peas yet. Dug the limed patch, leaving it very rough. It can remain thus for about 2 months. No more digging now remains to be done. A great deal of bindweed root in the soil, but none coming up yet. It seems to come up later than most perennial weeds. Weeded the forget-me-nots.

17 eggs.

D

9.4.40: Fine but rather cold. Hares are mating. Saw sparrow-hawks courting in the air. Sowed carrots (short-horn) & parsnips, 1 row each. Can sow peas tomorrow.

16 eggs.

D

10.4.40: A very few drops of rain last night. Today cold & windy. Sowed peas (next lot to be sown about 25th).

17 eggs. Sold 1 score @ 2/–, 1 score @ 2/6 (? milkman).

D

11.4.40: Sharp frost last night. Today clear, still & sunny, but not particularly warm. Ground now decidedly dry. Cut grass as best I could. Weeded flower bed by the shed. Gave manure mulch to hollyhocks etc. Planted 3 dwarf michaelmas daisies (pd. 2d each).

17 eggs. Dropped them & broke every one. Did not suppose they could all have broken without excepion, but so it was.

Forgot to mention 2 days back that Peter Hollingsworth had found magpie's nest with 3 eggs, & one of the farm men a robin's nest with eggs. These are the first nests I have heard of this year, & have found none. The magpie's eggs like a blackbird's but somewhat darker, ie. like a rook's, & hardly larger than a blackbird's but very pointed.

D

12.4.40: Evidently a little rain in the night, but it had dried up by the afternoon. Gathered sticks for dwarf m. daisies. Prepared a place to sow canary creeper (about 10 days hence), burnt up a little rubbish, gave wallflowers liquid manure, roughly raked the potato ground. This is still in rather poor state but probably good enough to sow. There seems to be room for about 250–300 plants. Have only ordered 2 stone seed, so better to order another stone.[27]

Saw blackbird sitting on nest. Wood pigeons evidently have nests. Still no wildflowers except primroses, violets & celandines. Buds shooting pretty well. Bluebells are out in some gardens.

15 eggs. Sold 1 score @ 2/–.

27. 1 stone = 14 pounds weight.

D

13.4.40: Still, not very warm, overcast but no rain. Sowed kale, savoys, sprouts, lettuce (cos), radishes. (Not broccoli, as the seed I have is of a late kind, to be sowed about May–June). Also leeks, 10-week stocks, foxgloves. Planted out 1 score cos lettuce. (Paid 4^{d}). Don't know whether they will survive – probably not if there is a sharp frost. Put awning of sacking over the plants. Applied a little fertiliser (Woolworths, 6^{d}) to the grass. Ground could now do with a spot of rain.

19 eggs. Total this week: 114 (of which 17 broken).

[*On facing page:*] Order in seedbed (starting from rose cuttings): kale, stocks, sprouts, lettuces, savoys, leeks, foxgloves, radishes, clarkia.

D

14.4.40: Fine, dry, not particularly warm. Raked the bare patches of the lawn & sowed some grass seed. Put up the wires for the blackberries. Sowed clarkia (in seed bed). Did some weeding.

17 eggs. Sold 44 @ 2/6 score.

D

15.4.40: Seems to have been a little rain last night. Today very variable weather. Most of day windy, some sunshine but not very warm, a few spots of rain. Then in the afternoon a few flakes of sleet & afterwards about 6 pm a sharp shower of hail. Rolled the grass, gave liquid manure to cottage tulips which are budding, prepared 3 marrow beds.

17 eggs.

D

16.4.40: Frost again last night. Most of day sunny but not too warm. Some falls of snow or sleet in the afternoon. Grape hyacinths, what there are of them, now well out. Some of the shallots branching. Planted 28 lb potatoes (Majestic). This did 12 rows, or about 225 plants. Room for another 4 rows, so shall get about another 10 lb. of seed. Had to halve a good many of the potatoes, which I don't like doing, & they were not sprouted to speak of. A few bad ones among them. Soil is not in very good heart, so, what with one thing & another, probably a long time before anything will show. Got place ready for turnips (room for 2 rows).

18 eggs.

D

17.4.40: Frost last night. Today still, sunny & fairly warm. Cut the grass, took out some of the worst of the dandelions etc., sowed a few seeds of canary creeper, got places ready to sow clarkia etc. Notice that tobacco powder does not seem very successful in keeping the sparrows off the seeds. A thrush with a white patch on top of its head is always in & out of the garden. When one has some means of identifying a bird one realises that each bird has its beat & the same individual is always to be seen about the same spot.

16 eggs. Sold 50 @ 3/– score.

D

18.4.40: Violent wind & horribly cold most of day. In the afternoon about an hour's heavy rain, after which it is warmer & more still. Narcissi are out. Wild thyme out. Daffs beginning to go off a little. Sowed sweet peas, clarkia, phlox, sunflowers (dwarf), all where they are to flower. Resticked some of the roses, & put sticks for Canterbury bells. Too cold & wet to do much out of doors.

17 eggs.

D

19.4.40: Evidently fairly heavy rain again last night. This morning overcast, the afternoon still, sunny, & fairly warm. This evening rain again, but more like April showers than the previous rain. Saw the first swallow this afternoon (two. The one I saw close to was swallow, not martin. I usually see sand martins first of all.) This is a little later than usual, but not as much as a week later. Sowed a few more sunflower seeds. Rolled the grass.

19 eggs.

D

20.4.40: Overcast but not particularly cold. Some people heard the cuckoo this morning, but I did not. Some rain about midday. Hedges are still decidedly bare. Winter wheat looks good in most places. Tulips are out in some gardens. Black currants forming their flowers. Planted 3 lupin roots (may possibly take but not flower this year). Purchased another 10 lb seed potatoes (K. Edward, $2/3^{d}$ stone). This morning some time after 9 heard an explosion. In this evening's paper it is reported that a munition works in London blew up at about that time, so this must have been the bang. Distance of round about 45 miles, & not much less as the crow flies.

14 eggs. Total this week: 118.

Onions (sown 29.3.40) are coming up thickly, also a few carrots (sown 30.3.40).

D

21.4.40: Sunny & warm. The first real spring day. Cowslips starting. Periwinkles out. Blossom forming on forget-me-nots. Still no cuckoo. E[ileen] sowed godetias & cornflowers.[28] One or two of the peas (sown 10.4.40) are showing, but no broad beans.

18 eggs. Sold 68 @ 3/3 score. (Actually 50 @ 3/3 score & 18 for 2/9).

28. The 21st April was a Sunday so Eileen would have been down at the cottage for the weekend.

D

22.10°.40: Sunny & quite warm, but very windy. On a day like this the opening of a tulip can be watched & a distinct difference noted every few hours. Sowed turnips (2 rows, white), peas (English wonder – a bit early after the others, but these were not soaked, which will set them back a day or two), & the remaining potatoes (K. Edward). This makes 16 rows of 20–25 plants a row, ie. about 350 plants. If they do reasonably well this should yield about 5 cwt.

Blackthorn almost out in some places. A few blossoms on the wild plum.

18 eggs.

D

23.4.40: Still, overcast & warm. A very few drops of rain in the afternoon. Tulips, forgetmenots° & wallflowers coming out. Fruits forming on currants & gooseberries. Plums & pear blossom full out (very late – about 3 weeks later than ordinary years). Rooks sitting on nests. Field beans well up. Planted 1 score cauliflowers (small kind I think.)

13 eggs (collected about 3 pm).

D

24.4.40: Almost continuous drizzling rain from dusk yesterday to this evening. Various seeds sown 10–15th are coming up. Clarkia sown only about a week ago coming up.

20 eggs (some presumably laid yesterday.)

D

25.4.40: Beautiful spring weather. Heard the cuckoo (first time). Many midges about now. Bullace blossom pretty well out. Cut the grass, dug a trench for 3rd row of peas, gave the strawberries a little more manure. These are now free of weeds. If they have one more good weeding after the bindweed has shown itself & the annual weeds have begun, they can then be strawed & netted up. A few broad beans up.

16 eggs. Sold 1 score @ 3/3 (? milkman).

D

26.4.40: Beautiful day again. 1 pumpkin seed coming up (sown 6.4.40). Carrots sown 9.4.40 are up, but not parsnips. Took up all but one row of the leeks, which were not very good anyway, & dug trench for runner beans. Hoed strawberries. There seem to be very few fruits on the gooseberries, perhaps because of their move. Currants are somewhat better.

14 eggs.

D

27.4.40: Rain during last night, fine & fairly warm during the morning, some showers this evening. Wild plum tree has plenty of blossom on it. Saw large flock, about 100, of what appeared to be turtle doves, sitting on telephone wires. Presumably migrants which had just arrived. Planted out 2 doz. antirrhinums (dark red & flame) & 1 doz. stocks (mixed). Paid 8^d a doz. – very expensive, but it is rather early. Price of sodium chlorate now $10½^d$ lb (before the war 8^d).

18 eggs. Sold ½ score @ 2/6. Total this week: 117.

Dandelions flowering, also dead nettle.

D

28.4.40: Some rain during last night. Today fine, warm & still. One or two nasturtiums up (self sown.) Turnips sown 22.4.40 are just up. The fly is already at these & at the seedlings of sprouts etc. A few parsnips (sown 9.4.40) are showing. One or two artichokes (sown 3.4.40) just showing. Applied sodium chlorate to waste patch by the walnut tree. Began putting up the strings for beans, but not enough time to complete the row. Planted out 1 doz. of the very tiny lettuces, putting sack° for protection. Tried to thin the clarkia, which, however, is too small to handle.

17 eggs.

D

29.4.40: I think a little rain in the night. All day overcast, with sometimes fine mist almost amounting to rain, but not exactly cold. Mended the fence, which cannot be done completely as there are not enough stakes. Planted out 1 doz. largish lettuces got from T[itley] (2^d dozen). Uncovered the little ones. Let the tadpoles go, as not certain how many days I shall be away. Gave the grass a quick cut. Leeks are just showing. Some apple blossom showing in some gardens. Find it is held locally there is always frost at the full moon (ie. in May) & people sow their runners with reference to this.

15 eggs.

This concludes Domestic Diary Volume II.

War-time Diary

28 May 1940 – 28 August 1941

Following Germany's invasion of Poland on 1 September, Britain declared war on Germany on the 3rd. On the 9th September, Orwell offered his services to aid the war effort. His letter has disappeared but that he did so is known from a reply that has survived from the Ministry of Labour and National Service telling him that he had been entered on a Central Register devoted to authors and writers. It does not seem that his services were ever called upon. Eileen worked (ironically) in a Censorship Department in Whitehall, living during the week at her brother's house in Greenwich and joining Orwell at the weekends at Wallington. Orwell spent his time at Wallington, tending his allotment, reviewing, and writing the essays that would be gathered together in *Inside the Whale*, published by Gollancz, 11 March 1940. These include 'Charles Dickens', 'Boys' Weeklies', and the title essay (see *CW*, XII, pp. 20–115). He toyed with the idea of writing a long novel to be published in three parts and from 30 January 1940 he spent six weeks at Greenwich during which time he was ill with influenza. He continued to review but felt increasingly frustrated that he was not involved in worthwhile war service. On 1 May 1940 he and Eileen moved to 18 Dorset Gardens near Regent's Park. On 10th May, the Germans invaded Holland, Belgium and Luxembourg which led to the Fall of France and the evacuation from Dunkirk.

Both the War-time Diaries were initially handwritten but seem to have been typed later (in September 1942) possibly by Eileen. In the course of typing, cuts were made and these are indicated by from four to half a dozen ellipses – Orwell's usual practice. The handwritten version of the first War-time Diary has not survived. He and Inez Holden (1906–1974; author and journalist) had a project for publishing his and her diaries jointly as a record of the times. The joint project came to nothing because she wanted to change what she did not agree with or thought inaccurate in Orwell's diary. Her diary was published in 1943 as *It Was Different at the Time*. She recalled that Gollancz turned down Orwell's War-time Diary because he feared offending people. Inez Holden supplied notes enabling certain identifications to be made for the *Complete Works* and hence for this volume. The title – 'War-time Diary' – is as Orwell wrote it.

Orwell started this diary a week before he began his short career as a theatre and film critic and two days after the evacuation began of 338,226 British and Allied servicemen from the beaches of Dunkirk. This operation was concluded on 4 June 1940. German troops entered Paris on 14 June and the French surrender was accepted on 22 June.

Notes are placed at the end of the item to which they refer. There are a number of cross-references to notes to Orwell's 'Diary of Events Leading Up to the War'. Those are indicated by the word 'Events' *plus the relevant date.*

28.5.40: This is the first day on which newspaper posters are definitely discontinued . . . Half of the front page of the early *Star*[1] devoted to news of the Belgian surrender, the other half to news to the effect that the Belgians are holding out and the King is with them. This is presumably due to paper shortage. Nevertheless of the early *Star*'s eight pages, six are devoted to racing.

For days past there has been no real news and little possibility of inferring what is really happening. The seeming possibilities were: i. That the French were really about to counterattack from the south. ii. That they hoped to do so but that the German bombers were making it impossible to concentrate an army. iii. That the forces in the north were confident of being able to hold on and it was thought better not to counterattack till the German attack had spent itself, or iv. that the position in the north was in reality hopeless and the forces there could only fight their way south, capitulate, be destroyed entirely or escape by sea, probably losing very heavily in the process. Now only the fourth alternative seems possible. The French communiqués speak of stabilising the line along the Somme and Aisne, as though the forces cut off in the north did not exist. Horrible though it is, I hope the B.E.F.[2] is cut to pieces sooner than capitulate.

People talk a little more of the war, but very little. As always hitherto, it is impossible to overhear any comments on it in pubs, etc. Last night, E[ileen] and I went to the pub to hear the 9 o'c news. The barmaid was not going to have turned it on if we had not asked her, and to all appearances nobody listened.[3]

1. There were at this time three London evening papers: *Star, Evening News,* and *Evening Standard;* only the last has survived; it is still published.
2. British Expeditionary Force, the troops in France at the time of that country's fall to the Germans.
3. In his entry for 15 April 1941 Orwell says he and Eileen went to the pub to hear the 9. o'clock news – so they evidently did not have a radio. They arrived a few minutes late and asked the barmaid what the news had been. She didn't know saying they never switched on the radio because no one listened.

29.5.40: One has to gather any major news nowadays by means of hints and allusions. The chief sensation last night was that the 9 o'c news was preceded by a cheer-up talk (quite good) by Duff-Cooper,[4] to sugar the pill, and that Churchill said in his speech that he would report again on the situation some time at the beginning of next week, and that the House must prepare itself for "dark and heavy tidings." This presumably means that they are going to attempt a withdrawal, but whether the "dark tidings" means enormous casualties, a surrender of part of the B.E.F., or what, nobody knows. Heard the news between acts at a more or less highbrow play at the Torch Theatre.[5] The audience listened a good deal more attentively than would have been the case in a pub.

E[ileen] says the people in the Censorship Department where she works lump all "red" papers together and look on the *Tribune*[6] as being in exactly the same class as the *Daily Worker*.[7] Recently when the *Daily Worker* and *Action*[8] were prohibited from export, one of her fellow-workers asked her, "Do you know this paper, the *Daily Worker and Action*?"

Current rumours: That Beaverbrook[9] since his appointment has got 2,000 extra aeroplanes into the air by cutting through bottle-necks. That the air raids, possibly on London, are due to begin in 2 days' time. That Hitler's plan for invading England is to use thousands of speed-boats which can ride over the minefields. That there is a terrible shortage of rifles (this from several sources). That the morale of the ordinary German infantry of the line is pitiably low. That at the time of the Norway business the War office° were so ill-informed as not even to know that the Norwegian nights are short, and imagined that troops which had to disembark in broad daylight would have the cover of darkness.

4. Alfred Duff Cooper (1890–1954; Viscount Norwich, 1952) was a Conservative politician, diplomat, and author. After he resigned as First Lord of the Admiralty, through disagreement with Chamberlain over Munich, he became the figurehead of the patriotic right. Churchill made him Minister of Information in May 1940. For his later career, see Second War-time Diary, 22.3.42, n. 7.
5. Orwell reviewed *Portrait of Helen* by Audrey Lucas in *Time and Tide* on the 8th June. Amongst his comments were 'the play has some good lines, but the stage management is extraordinarily bad'. See *CW*, XII, p. 181.
6. A Socialist weekly, then edited by Raymond Postgate to which Orwell contributed many reviews and essays.
7. The Communist Party's daily newspaper in Britain.
8. The journal of the British Union of Fascists.
9. In May, Max Aitken, first Baron Beaverbrook (1879–1964), the Canadian newspaper proprietor, had been made Minister of Aircraft Production by Churchill. He was effective, if controversial. Later he was Minister for War Production. In 1918 he had served as Minister of Information.

30.5.40: The B.E.F. are falling back on Dunkirk. Impossible not only to guess how many may get away, but how many are there. Last night a talk on the radio by a colonel who had come back from Belgium, which unfortunately I did not hear, but which from Eileen's account of it contained interpolations put in by the broadcaster himself to let the public know the army had been let down (a) by the French (not counterattacking), and (b) by the military authorities at home, by equipping them badly. No word anywhere in the press of recriminations against the French, and Duff-Cooper's broadcast of two nights ago especially warned against this . . . Today's map looks as if the French contingent in Belgium are sacrificing themselves to let the B.E.F. get away.

Borkenau[10] says England is now definitely in the first stage of revolution. Commenting on this, Connolly[11] related that recently a ship was coming away from northern France with refugees on board and a few ordinary passengers. The refugees were mostly children who were in a terrible state after having been machine-gunned etc., etc. Among the passengers was Lady --------,[12] who tried to push herself to the head of the queue to get on the boat, and when ordered back said indignantly, "Do you know who I am?" The steward answered, "I don't care who you are, you bloody bitch. You can take your turn in the queue." Interesting if true.

Still no evidences of any interest in the war. Yet the by-elections, responses to appeals for men, etc., show what people's feelings are. It is seemingly quite impossible for them to grasp that they are in danger, although there is good reason to think that the invasion of England may be attempted within a few days, and all the papers are saying this. They will grasp nothing until the bombs are dropping. Connolly says they will then panic, but I don't think so.

10. Dr. Franz Borkenau (1900–1957), Austrian sociologist and political writer, born in Vienna, was from 1921 to 1929 a member of the German Communist Party. His *Zur Soziologie des Faschismus* was published in Tübingen, in 1933, the year he emigrated because of the coming to power of the Nazis. He published *Pareto* (1936) in the Modern Sociologists Series. Orwell reviewed his *The Spanish Cockpit* (see *CW*, XI, pp. 51–2), *The Communist International* (*CW*, XI, 202–4) and *The Totalitarian Enemy* (*CW*, XII, pp. 158–60). Borkenau died in Zürich. For his conversations with Orwell at the time of Dunkirk, see below, 6.6.40.
11. Cyril Connolly (1903–1974) was with Orwell at St Cyprian's Preparatory School and Eton. They met again in 1935 after Connolly had reviewed *Burmese Days* and were associated in a number of literary activities particularly the journal, *Horizon*, which Connolly edited and for which Orwell wrote. Orwell's second wife, Sonia Brownell, worked for *Horizon* and they were introduced to each other by Connolly. Extracts from his *Enemies of Promise* (1938) relevant to Orwell are included in *Orwell Remembered* (pp. 32–4).
12. Unidentified. The number of hyphens Orwell used may not always represent the number of letters of the original name; the number in the diary is given here.

31.5.40: Last night to see Denis Ogden's play *The Peaceful Inn*. The most fearful tripe. The interesting point was that though the play was cast in 1940, it contained no reference direct or indirect to the war.[13]

Struck by the fewness of the men who even now have been called up. As a rule, looking round the street, it is impossible to see a uniform . . .

Barbed wire entanglements are being put up at many strategic points, eg. beside the Charles I statue in Trafalgar Square . . . Have heard on so many sides of the shortage of rifles that I believe it must be true.

13. Published with Orwell's review of *Portrait of Helen, CW,* XII, p. 180. Orwell found it impossible to take the characters' problems seriously.

1.6.40: Last night to Waterloo and Victoria to see whether I could get any news of [Eric].[14] Quite impossible, of course. The men who have been repatriated have orders not to speak to civilians and are in any case removed from the railway stations as promptly as possible. Actually I saw very few British soldiers, ie. from the B.E.F., but great numbers of Belgian or French refugees, a few Belgian or French soldiers, and some sailors, including a few naval men. The refugees seemed mostly middling people of the shop-keeper-clerk type, and were in quite good trim, with a certain amount of personal belongings. One family had a parrot in a huge cage. One refugee woman was crying, or nearly so, but most seemed only bewildered by the crowds and the general strangeness. A considerable crowd was watching at Victoria and had to be held back by the police to let the refugees and others get to the street. The refugees were greeted in silence but all sailors of any description enthusiastically cheered. A naval officer in a uniform that had been in the water and parts of a soldier's equipment hurried towards a bus, smiling and touching his tin hat to either side as the women shouted at him and clapped him on the shoulder.

Saw a company of Marines marching through the station to entrain for Chatham. Was amazed by their splendid physique and bearing, the tremendous stamp of boots and the superb carriage of the officers, all taking me back to 1914, when all soldiers seemed like giants to me.

This morning's papers claim variously four-fifths and three-quarters of the B.E.F. already removed. Photos, probably selected or faked, show the men in good trim with their equipment fairly intact.

14. 'Eric,' abbreviated from his second name, was the name by which Eileen Blair's much-loved brother, Laurence Frederick O'Shaughnessy, was known. Orwell does not type his name in his diary, representing it by four short dashes. He was a distinguished chest and heart surgeon, having won four scholarships and studied medicine at Durham and in Berlin. He was Hunterian Professor at the Royal College of Surgeons, 1933–35. In 1937 he won the Hunter Medal Triennial Prize for research work in surgery of the thorax, and the following year he received an honorarium and certificate of honourable mention for a dissertation on surgery of the heart. He produced an adaptation of Sauerbruch's *Thoracic Surgery* (1937) and in 1939 collaborated with two others in work on pulmonary tuberculosis. He joined the Royal Army Medical Corps at the outbreak of war and was killed tending the wounded on the beaches of Dunkirk. He was by then a major and only thirty-six years old

(from obituary in *The Times*, 8 June 1940). His wife, Gwen, was also a doctor. Her brother's death greatly affected Eileen; see Tosco Fyvel, *George Orwell: A Personal Memoir*, pp.105–06, 136.

2.6.40: Impossible to tell how many men of the B.E.F. have really been repatriated, but statements appearing in various papers suggest that it is about 150,000 and that the number that originally advanced into Belgium was about 300,000. No indication as to how many French troops were with them. There are hints in several papers that it may be intended to hang onto Dunkirk instead of evacuating it completely. This would seem quite impossible without tying down a great number of aeroplanes to that one spot. But if 150,000 have really been removed, it will presumably be possible to remove large numbers more. Italy's entry into the war is now predicted at any time after June 4th, presumably with some kind of peace offer to give it a pretext. . . . . . General expectation that some attempt will now be made to invade England, if only as a diversion while Germany and Italy endeavour to polish off France . . . . The possibility of a landing in Ireland is evidently believed in by many people including de Valera.[15] This idea has barely been mentioned until the last few days, although it was an obvious one from the start.

The usual Sunday crowds drifting to and fro, perambulators, cycling clubs, people exercising dogs, knots of young men loitering at street corners, with not an indication in any face or in anything that one can overhear that these people grasp that they are likely to be invaded within a few weeks, though today all the Sunday papers are telling them so. The response to renewed appeals for evacuation of children from London has been very poor. Evidently the reasoning is, "The air raids didn't happen last time, so they won't happen this time." Yet these people will behave bravely enough when the time comes, if only they are told what to do.

Rough analysis of advertisements in today's issue of the *People*[16] –

Paper consists of 12 pages[17] – 84 columns. Of this, just about 26½ columns (over ¼) is advertisements. These are divided up as follows:

Food and drink: 5¾ columns.

Patent medicines: 9 and a third.

Tobacco: 1.

Gambling: 2 and a third.

Clothes: 1½.

Miscellaneous: 6¾.

Of 9 food and drink adverts., 6 are for unnecessary luxuries. Of 29 adverts, for medicines, 19 are for things which are either fraudulent (baldness cured etc.), more or less deleterious (Kruschen Salts, Bile Beans etc.), or of the blackmail type ("Your child's stomach needs magnesia"). Benefit of doubt has been allowed in the case of a few medicines. Of

14 miscellaneous adverts., 4 are for soap, 1 for cosmetics, 1 for a holiday resort and 2 are government advertisements, including a large one for national savings. Only 3 adverts, in all classes are cashing in on the war.

15. Eamon de Valera (1882–1975), Irish political leader, was at this time Prime Minister of the Irish Free State. He became its president in 1959.
16. A popular Sunday newspaper.
17. The number of pages was reduced to six on 1 July; see below 1.7.40.

3.6.40: From a letter from Lady Oxford[18] to the *Daily Telegraph*, on the subject of war economies:

"Since most London houses are deserted there is little entertaining . . . in any case, most people have to part with their cooks and live in hotels."

Apparently nothing will ever teach these people that the other 99 % of the population exist.

18. Margot Asquith (1864–1945) was the widow of Herbert Henry Asquith, Earl of Oxford and Asquith, Prime Minister, 1906–16.

6.6.40: Both Borkenau and I considered that Hitler was likely to make his next attack on France, not England, and as it turns out we were right. Borkenau considers that the Dunkirk business has proved once for all that aeroplanes cannot defeat warships if the latter have planes of their own. The figures given out were 6 destroyers and about 25 boats of other kinds lost in the evacuation of nearly 330,000 men. The number of men evacuated is presumably truthful, and even if one doubled the number of ships lost[19] it would not be a great loss for such a large undertaking, considering that the circumstances were about as favourable to the aeroplanes as they could well be.

Borkenau thinks Hitler's plan is to knock out France and demand the French fleet as part of the peace terms. After that the invasion of England with sea-borne troops might be feasible.

Huge advert. on the side of a bus: "FIRST AID IN WARTIME, FOR HEALTH, STRENGTH AND FORTITUDE. WRIGLEY'S CHEWING GUM."

19. These figures were correct. Although most of their equipment was lost, 198,000 British and 140,000 mainly French and Belgian soldiers were evacuated. Of the forty-one naval vessels involved, six were sunk and nineteen damaged. In addition, about 220,000 servicemen were evacuated from ports in Normandy and Brittany.

7.6.40: Although newspaper posters are now suppressed,[20] one fairly frequently sees the paper-sellers displaying a poster. It appears that old ones are resuscitated and used, and ones with captions like "R.A.F. raids on Germany" or "Enormous German losses" can be used at almost all times.

20. 'Suppressed' implies censorship; such posters (that is, newspaper-sellers placards) were forbidden simply to conserve raw materials and economise on imports, thereby saving shipping space.

8.6.40: In the middle of a fearful battle in which, I suppose, thousands of men are being killed every day, one has the impression that there is no news. The evening papers are the same as the morning ones, the morning ones are the same as those of the night before, and the radio repeats what is in the papers. As to truthfulness of news, however, there is probably more suppression than downright lying. Borkenau considers that the effect of the radio has been to make war comparatively truthful, and that the only large-scale lying hitherto has been the German claims of British ships sunk. These have certainly been fantastic. Recently one of the evening papers which had made a note of the German announcements pointed out that in about 10 days the Germans claimed to have sunk 25 capital ships, ie. 10 more than we ever possessed.

Stephen Spender said to me recently, "Don't you feel that any time during the past ten years you have been able to foretell events better than, say, the Cabinet?" I had to agree to this. Partly it is a question of not being blinded by class interests etc., eg. anyone not financially interested could see at a glance the strategic danger to England of letting Germany and Italy dominate Spain, whereas many rightwingers, even professional soldiers, simply could not grasp this most obvious fact. But where I feel that people like us understand the situation better than so-called experts is not in any power to foretell specific events, but in the power to grasp what *kind* of world we are living in. At any rate I have known since about 1931 (Spender says he has known since 1929) that the future must be catastrophic. I could not say exactly what wars and revolutions would happen, but they never surprised me when they came. Since 1934 I have known war between England and Germany was coming, and since 1936 I have known it with complete certainty.[21] I could feel it in my belly, and the chatter of the pacifists on the one hand, and the Popular Front people who pretended to fear that Britain was preparing for war against Russia on the other, never deceived me. Similarly such horrors as the Russian purges never surprised me, because I had always felt that – not *exactly* that, but something *like* that – was implicit in Bolshevik rule. I could feel it in their literature.

. . . . Who would have believed seven years ago that Winston Churchill had any kind of political future before him? A year ago Cripps[22] was the naughty boy of the Labour Party, who expelled him and refused even to hear his defence. On the other hand, from the Conservative point of view he was a dangerous Red. Now he is ambassador in Moscow, the Beaverbrook press having led the cry for his appointment. Impossible to say yet whether he is the right man. If the Russians are disposed to come round to our side, he probably is, but if they are still hostile, it would have been better to send a man who does not admire the Russian regime.

21. See 'My Country Right or Left,' *CW*, XII, pp. 269–72. The title of the essay adapts Stephen Decatur's 'My country right or wrong', 1816.

22. Sir Stafford Cripps; see Events, 2.7.39, n. 7.

10.6.40: Have just heard, though it is not in the papers, that Italy has declared war. . . . The allied troops are withdrawing from Norway, the reason given being that they can be used elsewhere and Narvik after its capture was rendered useless to the Germans. But in fact Narvik will not be necessary to them till the winter, it wouldn't have been much use anyway when Norway had ceased to be neutral, and I shouldn't have thought the allies had enough troops in Norway to make much difference. The real reason is probably so as not to have to waste warships.

This afternoon I remembered very vividly that incident with the taxi-driver in Paris in 1936, and was going to have written something about it in this diary. But now I feel so saddened that I can't write it. Everything is disintegrating. It makes me writhe to be writing book-reviews etc. at such a time, and even angers me that such time-wasting should still be permitted. The interview at the War Office on Saturday *may* come to something, if I am clever at faking my way past the doctor. If once in the army, I know by the analogy of the Spanish war that I shall cease to care about public events. At present I feel as I felt in 1936 when the Fascists were closing in on Madrid, only far worse. But I will write about the taxi driver some time.[23]

23. Orwell wrote about the incident with the Parisian taxi driver in 'As I Please', 42, 15 September 1944. In brief, his taxi journey was so short that the driver was furious for being taken 'off the rank for a fare which in English money was about threepence' – and then more so because Orwell had no change. They had a 'sordid squabble' which 'left me at the moment violently angry, and a little later saddened and disgusted. "Why do people have to behave like that?" I thought'. For the full account see, *CW*, XVI, pp. 402–3.

12.6.40: E[ileen] and I last night walked through Soho to see whether the damage to Italian shops etc. was as reported. It seemed to have been exaggerated in the newspapers, but we did see, I think, 3 shops which had had their windows smashed. The majority had hurriedly labelled themselves "British". Gennari's, the Italian grocer's°, was plastered all over with printed placards saying "This establishment is entirely British". The Spaghetti House, a shop specialising in Italian foodstuffs, had renamed itself "British Food Shop". Another shop proclaimed itself Swiss, and even a French restaurant had labelled itself British. The interesting thing is that all these placards must evidently have been printed beforehand and kept in readiness. . . . . Disgusting though these attacks on harmless Italian shopkeepers are, they are an interesting phenomenon, because English people, ie. people of a kind who would be likely to loot shops, don't as a rule take a spontaneous interest in foreign politics. I don't think there was anything of this kind during the Abyssinian war, and the Spanish war simply did not touch the mass of the people. Nor was there any popular move against the Germans resident in England until the last month or two. The low-down cold-blooded meanness of Mussolini's declaration of war at that moment must have made an impression even on people who as rule barely read the newspapers.

13.6.40: Yesterday to a group conference of the L.D.V.,[24] held in the Committee Room at Lord's . . . Last time I was at Lord's must have been at the Eton-Harrow match in 1921. At that time I should have felt that to go into the Pavilion, not being a member of the M.C.C.,[25] was on a par with pissing on the altar, and years later would have had some vague idea that it was a legal offence for which you could be prosecuted.

I notice that one of the posters recruiting for the Pioneers, of a foot treading on a swastika with the legend "Step on it", is cribbed from a Government poster of the Spanish war, ie. cribbed as to the idea. Of course it is vulgarised and made comic, but its appearance at any rate shows that the Government are beginning to be willing to learn.

The Communist candidate in the Bow[26] by-election got about 500 votes. This is a new depth-record, though the Blackshirts have often got less (in one case about 150). The more remarkable because Bow was Lansbury's seat[27] and might be expected to contain a lot of pacifists. The whole poll was very low, however.

24. Local Defence Volunteers, later the Home Guard. Orwell joined on 12 June what became C Company, 5th County of London Battalion, and was soon promoted to sergeant, with ten men to instruct. He took his duties very seriously. See Crick, pp. 396–401.
25. Marylebone Cricket Club, the body that then controlled national and international cricket.
26. A working-class constituency in the East End of London.
27. George Lansbury, a fervent pacifist; see Events, 11.8.39, n. 2.

14.6.40: The Germans are definitely in Paris, one day ahead of schedule. It can be taken as a certainty that Hitler will go to Versailles. Why don't they mine it and blow it up while he is there? Spanish troops have occupied

Tangier, obviously with a view to letting the Italians use it as a base. To conquer Spanish Morocco from French Morocco would probably be easy at this date, and to do so, ditto the other Spanish colonies, and set up Negrin[28] or someone of his kind as an alternative government, would be a severe blow at Franco. But even the present British government would never think of doing such a thing. One has almost lost the power of imagining that the Allied governments can ever take the initiative.

Always, as I walk through the Underground stations, sickened by the advertisements, the silly staring faces and strident colours,[29] the general frantic struggle to induce people to waste labour and material by consuming useless luxuries or harmful drugs. How much rubbish this war will sweep away, if only we can hang on throughout the summer. War is simply a reversal of civilised life, its motto is "Evil be thou my good",[30] and so much of the good of modern life is actually evil that it is questionable whether on balance war does harm.

28. Juan Negrín, former Prime Minister of Spain; see Events, 2.8.39, n. 3.
29. For Orwell's hatred of such 'ad-posters,' featuring idiotic, grinning, yard-wide, ham-pink faces, see *Keep the Aspidistra Flying*, published four years earlier; for example, *CW*, IV, pp. 14,16,
30. Milton, *Paradise Lost*, iv, 110.

15.6.40: It has just occurred to me to wonder whether the fall of Paris means the end of the Albatross Library, as I suppose it does.[31] If so, I am £30 to the bad. It seems incredible that people still attach any importance to long-term contracts, stocks and shares, insurance policies etc. in such times as these. The sensible thing to do now would be to borrow money right and left and buy solid goods. A short while back E[ileen] made enquiries about the hire-purchase terms for sewing machines and found they had agreements stretching over two and a half years.

P.W.[32] related that Unity Mitford,[33] besides having tried to shoot herself while in Germany, is going to have a baby. Whereupon a little man with a creased face, whose name I forget, exclaimed, "The Fuehrer wouldn't do such a thing!"

31. *Albatross Library:* The Albatross Continental Library had undertaken to publish *Coming Up for Air* on the Continent. See Events, 4.8.39, n. 7. The contract stipulated that the book was to be issued before August 1940. After the Germans occupied Paris on 14 June a decree was promulgated forbidding the sale of British books published after 1870 and thus the edition was not published.
32. *P.W.:* Victor William (Peter) Watson (1908–1956), a rich young man who, after much travel, decided, about 1939, to devote his life to the arts, and became co-founder with his friend Cyril Connolly of the magazine *Horizon*, which he financed and also provided all the material for the art section. In 1948 he was one of the founders of the Institute of Contemporary Arts. He was always

an admirer of Orwell's writing. See Michael Shelden, *Friends of Promise: Cyril Connolly and the World of "Horizon"* (1989).

33. The Hon. Unity Valkyrie Mitford (1914–1948), fourth daughter of the second Lord Redesdale, was, from 1934, when she first met Hitler, his admirer. In January 1940 she was brought back to England from Germany suffering from self-inflicted bullet wounds in the head. Thereafter she lived in retirement. She was not pregnant.

16.6.40: This morning's papers make it reasonably clear that at any rate until after the presidential election, the U.S.A. will not do anything, ie. will not declare war, which in fact is what matters. For if the U.S.A. is not actually in the war there will never be sufficient control of either business or labour to speed up production of armaments. In the last war this was the case even when the U.S.A. was a belligerent.

It is impossible even yet to decide what to do in the case of German conquest of England. The one thing I will not do is to clear out, at any rate not further than Ireland, supposing that to be feasible. If the fleet is intact and it appears that the war is to be continued from America and the Dominions, then one must remain alive if possible, if necessary in the concentration camp. If the U.S.A. is going to submit to conquest as well, there is nothing for it but to die fighting, but one must above all die *fighting* and have the satisfaction of killing somebody else first.

Talking yesterday to M.,[34] one of the Jewish members of my L.D.V. section, I said that if and when the present crisis passed there would be a revolt in the Conservative party against Churchill and an attempt to force wages down again, etc. He said that in that case there would be revolution, "or at least he hoped so". M. is a manufacturer and I imagine fairly well off.

34. Possibly Michael, the owner of the small clothing factory mentioned in Orwell's diary entry of 3.9.40.

17.6.40: The French have surrendered. This could be foreseen from last night's broadcast and in fact should have been foreseeable when they failed to defend Paris, the one place where it might have been possible to stop the German tanks. Strategically all turns on the French fleet, of which there is no news yet. . . .

Considerable excitement today over the French surrender, and people everywhere to be heard discussing it. Usual line, "Thank God we've got a navy". A Scottish private, with medals of the last war, partly drunk, making a patriotic speech in a carriage in the Underground, which the other passengers seemed rather to like. Such a rush on evening papers that I had to make four attempts before getting one.

Nowadays, when I write a review, I sit down at the typewriter and type it straight out. Till recently, indeed till six months ago, I never did this and would have said that I could not do it. Virtually all that I wrote was written at least twice, and my books as a whole three times – individual passages as many as five or ten times. It is not really that I have gained in facility, merely that I have ceased to care, so long as the work will pass inspection and bring in a little money. It is a deterioration directly due to the war.

Considerable throng at Canada House, where I went to make enquiries, as G.[35] contemplates sending her child to Canada. Apart from mothers, they are not allowing anyone between 16 and 60 to leave, evidently fearing a panic rush.

35. *G.*: Gwen O'Shaughnessy, Eileen's sister-in-law. In the early stages of the war, there was a government-sponsored scheme to evacuate children to Canada and the United States. Gwen's son, Laurence, nineteen months old in June 1940, went to Canada on one of the last ships to take evacuees before the evacuee-ship *City of Benares* was sunk in the Atlantic. See below, 25.7.40.

20.6.40: Went to the office of the [*New Statesman*][36] to see what line they are taking about home defence. C.,[37] who is now in reality the big noise there, was rather against the "arm the people" line and said that its dangers outweighed its possible advantages. If a German invading force finds civilians armed it may commit such barbarities as will cow the people altogether and make everyone anxious to surrender. He said it was dangerous to count on ordinary people being courageous and instanced the case of some riot in Glasgow when a tank was driven round the town and everyone fled in the most cowardly way. The circumstances were different, however, because the people in that case were unarmed and, as always in internal strife, conscious of fighting with ropes round their necks. . . . C. said that he thought Churchill, though a good man up to a point, was incapable of doing the necessary thing and turning this into a revolutionary war, and for that reason shielded Chamberlain and Co. and hesitated to bring the whole nation into the struggle. I don't of course think Churchill sees it in quite the same colours as we do, but I don't think he would jib at any step (eg. equalisation of incomes, independence for India) which he thought necessary for winning the war. Of course it's possible that today's secret session *may* achieve enough to get Chamberlain and Co. out for good. I asked C. what hope he thought there was of this, and he said none at all. But I remember that the day the British began to evacuate Namsos[38] I asked Bevan and Strauss,[39] who had just come from the House, what hope there was of this business unseating Chamberlain, and they also said none at all. Yet a week or so later the new government was formed.[40]

The belief in direct treachery in the higher command is now widespread, enough so to be dangerous. . . . Personally I believe that such conscious treachery as exists is only in the pro-Fascist element of the aristocracy and perhaps in the Army command. Of course the unconscious sabotage and stupidity which have got us into this situation, eg. the idiotic handling of Italy and Spain, is a different matter. R. H.[41] says that private soldiers back from Dunkirk whom he has spoken to all complain of the conduct of their officers, saying that the latter cleared off in cars and left them in the soup, etc., etc. This sort of thing is always said after a defeat and may or may not be true. One could verify it by studying the lists of casualties, if and when they are published in full. But it is not altogether bad that that sort of thing should be said, provided it doesn't lead to sudden panic, because of the absolute need for getting the whole thing onto a new class basis. In the new armies middle-class people are bound to predominate as officers, they did so even, for instance, in the Spanish militias, but it is a question of umblimping. Ditto with the L.D.V. Under the stress of emergency we shall umblimp if we have time, but time is all.[42]

A thought that occurred to me yesterday: how is it that England, with one of the smallest armies in the world, has so many retired colonels?

I notice that all the "left" intellectuals I meet believe that Hitler if he gets here will take the trouble to shoot people like ourselves and will have very extensive lists of undesirables. C.[43] says there is a move on foot to get our police records (no doubt we all have them) at Scotland Yard destroyed.[44] Some hope! The police are the very people who would go over to Hitler once they were certain he had won. Well, if only we can hold out for a few months, in a year's time we shall see red militia billeted in the Ritz,[45] and it would not particularly surprise me to see Churchill or Lloyd George at the head of them.

Thinking always of my island in the Hebrides,[46] which I suppose I shall never possess nor even see. Compton Mackenzie says even now most of the islands are uninhabited (there are 500 of them, only 10 per cent inhabited at normal times), and most have water and a little cultivable land, and goats will live on them. According to R.H., a woman who rented an island in the Hebrides in order to avoid air raids was the first air raid casualty of the war, the R.A.F. dropping a bomb there by mistake. Good if true.

The first air raid of any consequence on Great Britain the night before last. Fourteen killed, seven German aeroplanes claimed shot down. The papers have photos of three wrecked German planes, so possibly the claim is true.

36. *New Statesman* seems probable here, though the diary has five hyphens.
37. Probably Richard Crossman (1907–1974), scholar, intellectual, journalist, and left-wing politician, who was assistant editor of *The New Statesman*, 1938–55, and editor, 1970–72. He was also a Labour M.P., 1945–70; Minister of Housing and Local Government, 1964–66, and Minister of Health and Social Security, 1964–70.
38. The British 146th Infantry Brigade landed at Namsos, Norway, on the coast

some 300 miles north of Oslo, on 16–17 April 1940. They withdrew 2–3 May. The last Allied forces left Norway on 9 June.

39. For Aneurin Bevan, Labour M.P., see Events, 28.8.39, n. 11. In 1949 Orwell said to a friend, 'If only I could become Nye's *éminence grise* we'd soon have this country on its feet.' G. R. Strauss (1901–1993, Life Peer, 1979) was a Labour M.P. and co-director of *Tribune*.
40. Neville Chamberlain's government fell on 10 May 1940, and a coalition government under Winston Churchill was formed. Magnanimously, Churchill included Chamberlain in his Cabinet.
41. *R.H.:* Rayner Heppenstall (1911–1981), novelist, critic, crime historian and BBC radio producer. He produced Orwell's radio adaptation of *Animal Farm* and commissioned his radio play *The Voyage of the Beagle*, 29 March 1946 (see *CW*, XVIII, pp. 179–201). He and Orwell shared a flat in 1935 (not wholly amicably) but they remained lifelong friends. His *Four Absentees* (1960) has reminiscences of Orwell (reproduced in *Orwell Remembered*, pp. 106–15).
42. 'Unblimping' was a frequent concern of Orwell's. See, for example: 'War-time Diary,' 23.8.40; 'The Home Guard and You' *CW*, XII, pp. 309–12; 'Don't Let Colonel Blimp Ruin the Home Guard' , *CW*, XII, pp. 362–5; review of *Home Guard for Victory!*, *CW*, XII, pp. 387–9; 'London Letter,' *CW*, XII, pp. 474–5.
43. Not certainly identified. Possibly Richard Crossman again (see n. 37 above) or Cyril Connolly. Inez Holden suggested either Christopher Hollis or a mysterious man known as Carter, whom Orwell's friends never met.
44. See 'London Letter,' *CW*, XII, p. 355.
45. See 'My Country Right or Left,' *CW*, XII, pp. 269–72.
46. This is the first reference to Orwell's dream of living in the Hebrides, to be realised in 1945 when he rented Barnhill, on Jura. Compare Winston Smith's vision of the Golden Country in *Nineteen Eighty-Four*, *CW*, IX, pp. 129–130; see also Orwell's review of *Priest Island*, *CW*, XII, pp. 190–1.

21.6.40: No real news. I see from yesterday's paper that Chiappe[47] has been elected president of the Paris Municipal Council, presumably under German pressure. So much for the claim that Hitler is the friend of the working classes, enemy of plutocracy, etc.

Yesterday the first drill of our platoon of the L.D.V. They were really admirable, only 3 or 4 in the whole lot (about 60 men) who were not old soldiers. Some officers who were there and had, I think, come to scoff were quite impressed.

47. Jean Chiappe (1878–1940), Corsican head of the Paris police, 1927–34, was pro-Fascist and responsible for severely repressive measures against the left. Elliot Paul, referring to his dismissal on 2 February 1934, described him as 'one of the ringleaders of Pétain's Cagoulards, the hooded order conspiring for a fascist dictatorship' *(A Narrow Street*, 1942, chap. 24). For Orwell on Chiappe's death, see War-time Diary, 1.12.40.

22.6.40: No real news yet of the German terms to France. They are said to be "so complicated" as to need long discussion. I suppose one may assume that what is really happening is that the Germans on the one side and Pétain[48] and Co. on the other are trying to hammer out a formula that will induce the French commanders in the colonies and the navy to surrender. Hitler has in reality no power over these except through the French government. . . . I think we have all been rather hasty in assuming that Hitler will now invade England, indeed it has been so generally expected that one might almost infer from this that he wouldn't do it. . . . If I were him I should march across Spain, seize Gibraltar and then clean up North Africa and Egypt. If the British have a fluid force of say ¼ million men, the proper course would be to transfer it to French Morocco, then suddenly seize Spanish Morocco and hoist the Republican flag. The other Spanish colonies could be mopped up without much trouble. Alas, no hope of any such thing happening.

The Communists are apparently swinging back to an anti-Nazi position. This morning picked up a leaflet denouncing the "betrayal" of France by Pétain and Co., although till a week or two ago these people were almost openly pro-German.

48. Henri Philippe Pétain (1856–1951), successful defender of Verdun in 1916, which led to his being regarded as a national hero, was created a Marshal of France in 1918. He became premier in 1940, presided over the defeat and dismemberment of France by the Germans, and led the occupied zone's Vichy government until war's end. He was tried for collaboration with the Nazis and sentenced to death. President de Gaulle commuted his sentence to solitary confinement for life.

24.6.40: The German armistice terms are much as expected. . . . What is interesting about the whole thing is the extent to which the traditional pattern of loyalties and honour is breaking down. Pétain, ironically enough, is the originator (at Verdun) of the phrase "ils ne passeront pas", so long an anti-Fascist slogan. Twenty years ago any Frenchman who would have signed such an armistice would have had to be either an extreme leftwinger or an extreme pacifist, and even then there would have been misgivings. Now the people who are virtually changing sides in the middle of the war are the professional patriots. To Pétain, Laval,[49] Flandin[50] and Co. the whole war must have seemed like a lunatic internecine struggle at the moment when your real enemy is waiting to slosh you. . . . . . It is therefore practically certain that high-up influences in England are preparing for a similar sell-out, and while eg. --- is ---- there is no certainty that they won't succeed even without the invasion of England. The one good thing about the whole business is that the bottom is being knocked out of Hitler's pretence of being the poor man's friend. The people actually willing to do a deal with him are bankers, generals, bishops, kings, big industrialists, etc., etc. . . . . . . Hitler is the leader of a tremendous counter-attack of the capitalist class, which is forming itself into a vast corporation, losing its privileges to some extent in doing so, but still retaining its power over the working class. When it comes to resisting such an attack as this, anyone who is of the capitalist class must be treacherous or half-treacherous, and will swallow the most fearful indignities rather than put up a real fight. . . . Whichever way one looks, whether it is at the wider strategic aspects or the most petty details of local defence, one sees that any real struggle means revolution. Churchill evidently can't see or won't accept this, so he will have to go. But whether he goes in time to save England from conquest depends on how quickly the people at large can grasp the essentials. What I fear is that they will never move until it is too late.

Strategically, all turns upon hanging on until the winter. . . . By that time, with huge armies of occupation everywhere, food almost certainly running short and the difficulty of forcing the conquered populations to work, Hitler must be in an awkward position. It will be interesting to see whether he rehabilitates the suppressed French Communist party and tries to use it against the working class in northern France as he has used Pétain against the Blimp class.

If the invasion happens and fails, all is well, and we shall have a definitely leftwing government and a conscious movement against the governing class. I think, though, people are in error in imagining that Russia would be more friendly towards us if we had a revolutionary government. After Spain, I cannot help feeling that Russia, i.e. Stalin, must be hostile to any country that is genuinely undergoing revolution. They would be moving in opposite directions. A revolution starts off with wide diffusion of the ideas of liberty, equality, etc. Then comes the growth of an oligarchy which is as much interested in holding onto its privileges as any other governing class. Such an oligarchy must necessarily be hostile to revolutions elsewhere, which inevitably re-awaken the ideas of liberty and equality. This morning's *News Chronicle* announces that saluting of superior ranks has been re-instituted in the Red Army. A revolutionary army would *start* by abolishing saluting, and this tiny point is symptomatic of the whole situation. Not that saluting and such things are not probably necessary.

Orders to the L.D.V. that *all* revolvers are to be handed over to the police, as they are needed for the army. Clinging to useless weapons like revolvers, when the Germans have submachine guns, is typical of the British army, but I believe the real reason for the order is to prevent weapons getting into "the wrong" hands.

Both E[ileen] and G.[51] insistent that I should go to Canada if the worst comes to the worst, in order to stay alive and keep up propaganda. I will go if I have some function, e.g., if the government were transferred to

Canada and I had some kind of job, but not as a refugee, nor as an expatriate journalist squealing from a safe distance. There are too many of these exiled "antifascists" already. Better to die if necessary, and maybe even as propaganda one's death might achieve more than going abroad and living more or less unwanted on other people's charity. Not that I want to die; I have so much to live for, in spite of poor health and having no children.

Another government leaflet this morning, on treatment of air-raid casualties. The leaflets are getting much better in tone and language, and the broadcasts are also better, especially Duff-Cooper's, which in fact are ideal for anyone down to the £5-a-week level. But there is still nothing in really demotic speech, nothing that will move the poorer working class or even be quite certainly intelligible. Most educated people simply don't realise how little impression abstract words make on the average man. When Acland was sending round his asinine "Manifesto of Plain Men" (written by himself and signed on the dotted line by "plain men" whom he selected) he told me he had the first draft vetted by the Mass Observers, who tried it on working men, and found that the most fantastic misunderstandings arose. . . . . . The first sign that things are really happening in England will be the disappearance of that horrible plummy voice from the radio. Watching in public bars, I have noticed that working men only pay attention to the broadcasts when some bit of demotic speech creeps in. E[ileen] however claims, with some truth I think, that uneducated people are often moved by a speech in solemn language which they don't actually understand but feel to be impressive. E.g. Mrs. A.[52] is impressed by Churchill's speeches, though not understanding them word for word.

49. Pierre Laval (1883–1945) served at various times as French Minister of Public Works, Justice, Labour, Colonies, and Foreign Affairs, and was Premier, 1931–32, 1935–36. He left the Socialist Party in 1920 and gradually moved to the extreme right. On 7 January 1935, as Foreign Minister, he signed an agreement with Mussolini that backed Italian claims to areas of Abyssinia (Ethiopia) in return for Italian support against German intervention in Austria. Italy invaded Abyssinia on 3 October 1935, and on 18 December the British Foreign Secretary, Sir Samuel Hoare, was forced to resign when it was revealed that he had entered into a pact with Laval appeasing Mussolini. After the fall of France, Laval came to represent treacherous collaboration. He even provided Frenchmen for work in German industry. Tried in 1945, he was executed after failing in a suicide attempt. For Hoare, see Events, 2.7.39, n. 5 and 4.8.39, n. 5. He was at this time British Ambassador in Spain.

50. Pierre-Étienne Flandin (1889–1958) held numerous offices in French governments. He was Premier, 1934–35, and Foreign Minister in Pétain's government in 1940, but attempted to resist German demands and was replaced by Laval. He was forbidden to participate in public life after the war.

51. Eileen Blair and Gwen O'Shaughnessy, her sister-in-law, the wife of Eileen's brother, Eric O'Shaughnessy killed at Dunkirk (see War-time Diary, 1.6.40, n. 14).

52. Probably Mrs. Anderson, who cleaned for the Orwells in Wallington. Although Orwell had, by the time this was written, been living in London for five or six weeks, he still visited Wallington. The Stores was not given up completely until 1947.

25.6.40: Last night an air raid warning about 1a.m. It was a false alarm as regards London, but evidently there was a real raid somewhere. We got up and dressed, but did not go to the shelter. This is what everyone did, i.e. got up and then simply stood about talking, which seems very foolish. But it seems natural to get up when one hears the siren, and then in the absence of gunfire or other excitement one is ashamed to go to the shelter.

I saw in one of yesterday's papers that gas masks are being issued in America, though people have to pay for them. Gas masks are probably useless to the civilian population in England and almost certainly so in America. The issue of them is simply a symbol of national solidarity, the first step towards wearing a uniform As soon as war started the carrying or not carrying of a gas mask assumed social and political implications. In the first few days people like myself who refused to carry one were stared at and it was generally assumed that the non-carriers were "left". Then the habit wore off, and the assumption was that a person who carried a gas mask was of the ultra-cautious type, the suburban rate-payer type. With the bad news the habit has revived and I should think 20 per cent now carry them. But you are still a little stared at if you carry one without being in uniform. Until the big raids have happened and it is grasped that the Germans don't, in fact, use gas, the extent to which masks are carried will probably be a pretty good index of the impression the war news is making on the public.

Went this afternoon to the recruiting office to put my name down for the Home Service Battalions. Have to go again on Friday to be medically examined, but as it is for men from 30 to 50 I suppose the standards are low. The man who took my name, etc., was the usual imbecile, an old soldier with medals of the last war, who could barely write. In writing capital letters he more than once actually wrote them upside down.

27.6.40: It appears that the night before last, during the air-raid alarm, many people all over London were woken by the All Clear signal, took that for the warning and went to the shelters and stayed there till morning, waiting for the All Clear. This after ten months of war and God knows how many explanations of the air-raid precautions.

The fact that the government hasn't this time had to do a recruiting campaign has had a deadening effect on propaganda. . . . A striking thing is the absence of any propaganda posters of a general kind, dealing with the struggle against Fascism, etc. If only someone would show the M.O.I.[53] the posters used in the Spanish war, even the Franco ones for that matter. But how can these people possibly rouse the nation *against Fascism* when they themselves are subjectively pro-Fascist and were buttering up Mussolini till almost the moment when Italy entered the war? Butler,[54] answering questions about the Spanish occupation of Tangier, says H.M. Government has "accepted the word" of the Spanish government that the Spaniards are only doing so in order to preserve Tangier's neutrality – this after Falangist demonstrations in Madrid to celebrate the "conquest" of Tangier. . . . This morning's papers publish a "denial" that Hoare in Madrid is asking questions about an armistice. In other words he *is* doing so. Only question – can we get rid of these people in the next few weeks, before it is too late?

The unconscious treacherousness of the British ruling class in what is in effect a class war is too obvious to be worth mentioning. The difficult question is how much *deliberate* treachery exists. . . . . L.M.,[55] who knows or at least has met all these people, says that with individual exceptions like Churchill the entire British aristocracy is utterly corrupt and lacking in the most ordinary patriotism, caring in fact for nothing except preserving their own standards of life. He says that they are also intensely class-conscious and recognise clearly the community of their interests with those of rich people elsewhere. The idea that Mussolini might fall has always been a nightmare to them, he says. Up to date L.M's predictions about the war, made the day it began, have been very correct. He said nothing would happen all the winter, Italy would be treated with great respect and then suddenly come in against us, and the German aim would be to force on England a puppet government through which Hitler could rule Britain without the mass of the public grasping what was happening. . . . . . The only point where L.M. proved wrong is that like myself he assumed Russia would continue to collaborate with Germany, which now looks as if it may not happen. But then the Russians probably did not expect France to collapse so suddenly. If they can bring it off, Pétain and Co. are working towards the same kind of doublecross against Russia as Russia previously worked against England. It was interesting that at the time of the Russo-German pact nearly everyone assumed that the pact was all to Russia's advantage and that Stalin had in some way "stopped" Hitler, though one had only to look at the map in order to see that this was not so. In western Europe Communism and left extremism generally are now almost entirely a form of masturbation. People who are in fact without power over events console themselves by pretending that they are in some way controlling events. From the Communist point of view, nothing matters so long as they can persuade themselves that Russia is on top. It now seems doubtful whether the Russians gained much more from the pact than a breathing-space, though they did this much better than we did at Munich. Perhaps England and the U.S.S.R. will be forced into alliance after all, an interesting instance of real interests overriding the most hearty ideological hatred.

The New Leader[56] is now talking about the "betrayal" by Pétain and Co. and the "workers' struggle" against Hitler. Presumably they would be in favour of a "workers" resistance if Hitler invaded England. And what will the workers fight with? With weapons. Yet the I.L.P. clamour simultaneously for sabotage in the arms factories. These people live almost entirely in a masturbation fantasy, conditioned by the fact that nothing they say or do will ever influence events, not even the turning-out of a single shell.

53. Ministry of Information, which was responsible for wartime propaganda. It had offices in the Senate House of the University of London, the city's tallest new building of the interwar years. It suggested to Orwell Minitrue of *Nineteen Eighty-Four*.
54. R. A. Butler (1902–1984; Life Peer, 1965) was Under-Secretary of State for Foreign Affairs, 1938–41, Chancellor of the Exchequer, and later Foreign Secretary in the Conservative government of 1951–64.
55. L. H. Myers was a novelist and good friend to Orwell. He underwrote (unknowingly to Orwell) his and Eileen's stay in Morocco in 1938–39.
56. Weekly newspaper of the Independent Labour Party, which Orwell had joined in June 1938, having fought with the ILP contingent in Spain. He left the party at the beginning of the war because it maintained a pacifist stance.

28.6.40: Horribly depressed by the way things are turning out. Went this morning for my medical board and was turned down, my grade being C., in which they aren't at present taking any men in any corps. . . . . . What is appalling is the unimaginativeness of a system which can find *no* use for a man who is below the average level of fitness but at least is not an invalid. An army needs an immense amount of clerical work, most of which is done by people who are perfectly healthy and only half-literate. . . . One could forgive the government for failing to employ the intelligentsia, who on the whole are politically unreliable, if they were making any attempt to mobilise the manpower of the nation and change people over from the luxury trades to productive work. This simply isn't happening, as one can see by looking down any street.

The Russians entered Bessarabia to-day. Practically no interest aroused, and the few remarks I could overhear were mildly approving or at least not hostile. Cf. the intense popular anger over the invasion of Finland. I don't think the difference is due to a perception that Finland and Rumania are different propositions. It is probably because of our own desperate straits and the notion that this move may embarrass Hitler – as I believe it must, though evidently sanctioned by him.

29.6.40: The British government has recognised de Gaulle,[57] but apparently in some equivocal manner, i.e. it has not stated that it will not recognise the Pétain government.

One very hopeful thing is that the press is on our side and retains its independence. . . . . But contained in this is the difficulty that the "freedom" of the press really means that it depends on vested interests and largely (through its advertisements) on the luxury trades. Newspapers which would resist direct treachery can't take a strong line about cutting down luxuries when they live by advertising chocolates and silk stockings.

57. Charles de Gaulle (1890–1970) was at this time leader of the Free French and the inspiration for continuing French resistance to Germany after the fall of France. His national pride, coupled with the humiliation he felt at France's collapse and his determination to free his country, made it difficult at times for the Allies to work with him. After the war, he was interim President 1945–46. He returned to power in 1958 as a result of the crisis in Algeria, and, as architect and President of the Fifth Republic, 1959–69, maintained France's military and strategic independence.

30.6.40: This afternoon a parade in Regent's Park[58] of the L.D.V. of the whole "zone", i.e. 12 platoons of theoretically about 60 men each (actually a little under strength at present.) Predominantly old soldiers and, allowing for the dreadful appearance that men drilling in mufti always present, not a bad lot. Perhaps 25 per cent are working class. If that percentage exists in the Regent's Park area, it must be much higher in some others. What I do not yet know is whether there has been any tendency to avoid raising L.D.V. contingents in very poor districts where the whole direction would have to be in working-class hands. At present the whole organisation is in an anomalous and confused state which has many different possibilities. Already people are spontaneously forming local defence squads and hand-grenades are probably being manufactured by amateurs. The higher-ups are no doubt thoroughly frightened by these tendencies. . . . The general inspecting the parade was the usual senile imbecile, actually decrepit, and made one of the most uninspiring speeches I ever heard. The men, however, very ready to be inspired. Loud cheering at the news that rifles have arrived at last.

Yesterday the news of Balbo's[59] death was on the posters as C.[60] and the M.'s[61] and I walked down the street. C. and I thoroughly pleased, C. relating how Balbo and his friends had taken the chief of the Senussi up in an aeroplane and thrown him out, and even the M.'s (all but pure pacifists) were not ill-pleased, I think. E[ileen] also delighted. Later in the evening (I spent the night at Crooms Hill[62]) we found a mouse which had slipped down into the sink and could not get up the sides. We went to great pains to make a sort of staircase of boxes of soap flakes, etc., by which it could climb out, but by this time it was so terrified that it fled under the lead strip at the edge of the sink and would not move, even when we left it alone for half an hour or so. In the end E[ileen] gently took it out with her fingers and let it go. This sort of thing does not matter. . . . . but when I remember how the *Thetis*[63] disaster upset me, actually to the point of interfering with my appetite, I do think it a dreadful effect of war that one is actually pleased to hear of an enemy submarine going to the bottom.

58. Orwell was then living at 18 Dorset Chambers, Chagford Street, NW1; illustrated in Thompson, 54. This was about 150 yards from the south-east boundary of Regent's Park.
59. Italo Balbo (1896–1940), head of the Italian Air Force, was responsible for the bombing of Ethiopians during the Italo-Ethiopian War, 1935–36.
60. Cyril Connolly.
61. Unidentified. Probably not L. H. Myers and his wife, for whom the description 'all but pure pacifists' is inappropriate.
62. The home of Gwen O'Shaughnessy in Greenwich.
63. In June 1939 the British submarine *Thetis* failed to surface on its trials. Only four of the complement of 103 were saved, owing to faulty escape apparatus. The painfully slow progress, and virtual failure, of the rescue attempts were followed with horror by many radio listeners. The submarine was recovered and entered active service as HMS *Thunderbolt* in November 1940. All the crew were told of the submarine's history and given the opportunity to decline to serve in her. After a successful career, she was depth-charged and lost with all hands in March 1943. The *non sequitur* stems from Orwell's cut.

1.7.40: Newspapers now reduced to 6 pages, i.e., 3 sheets.[64] Print reduced in size. Rough analysis of to-day's *News Chronicle*: 6 pages = 48 columns. Of these (excluding small adverts, besides headlines on front page) 15 columns or nearly one third are adverts. About 1½ columns of this are taken up in notices of situations vacant, etc., but the greater part of the ad.s are for more or less useless consumption goods. The financial columns also overlap with the advertisements, some of the reports of directors' meetings, etc., probably being paid for by the companies themselves.

To-day's *Express* consists of 6 pages = 42 columns, of which 12 are taken up in advertisements.

Rumours in all to-day's papers that Balbo was actually bumped off by his own side, as in the case of General von Fritsch.[65] Nowadays when any eminent person is killed in battle this suggestion inevitably arises. Cases in the Spanish war were Durruti and General Mola.[66] The rumour about Balbo is based on a statement by the R.A.F. that they know nothing about the air-fight in which Balbo is alleged to have been killed. If this is a lie, as it well may be, it is one of the first really good strokes the British propaganda has brought off.

64. See War-time Diary, 2.6.40, when *People* was twelve pages, for analysis of its contents.
65. Werner von Fritsch (1880–1939), an old-guard general on the German Army General Staff, never concealed his contempt for Hitler. His death in action in 1939 was always thought to have been engineered by the Führer.
66. Buenaventura Durruti, a gunman who became a general and popular leader. He was killed in the defence of Madrid, possibly by Communists. His funeral gave rise to a great popular demonstration in Barcelona. Emilio Mola Vidal (1887–1937), an equal colleague of Franco, was killed in the early stages of the civil war, before the question of primacy with Franco could arise.

3.7.40: Everywhere a feeling of something near despair among thinking people because of the failure of the government to act and the continuance of dead minds and pro-Fascists in positions of command. Growing recognition that the only thing that would certainly right the situation is an unsuccessful invasion; and coupled with this a growing fear that Hitler won't after all attempt the invasion but will go for Africa and the Near East.

5.7.40: The almost complete lack of British casualties in the action against the French warships at Oran[67] makes it pretty clear that the French seamen must have refused to serve the guns, or at any rate did so without much enthusiasm. . . . In spite of the to-do in the papers about "French fleet out of action", etc., etc., it appears from the list of ships actually given that about half the French navy is not accounted for, and no doubt more than half the submarines. But how many have actually fallen into German or Italian hands, and how many are still on the oceans, there is nothing in the papers to show. . . . . . The frightful outburst of fury by the German radio (if rightly reported, actually calling on the English people to hang Churchill in Trafalgar Square) shows how right it was to make this move.

67. On 3 July, the Royal Navy under the command of Vice-Admiral Sir John Somerville attacked French warships at Oran and Mers el-Kébir, Algeria. Among the French ships sunk or damaged were the battleships *Provence* and *Bretagne* and the fast battlecruiser *Dunkerque;* 1,300 French seamen were killed. Several ships, including the battlecruiser *Strasbourg* and the aircraft carrier *Commandant Teste,* escaped to Toulon. French ships at Portsmouth and Plymouth were also seized, including 2 battleships, 2 cruisers, 8 destroyers, some 200 small craft, and a number of submarines. Crews had the option of joining the Allies or being repatriated.

10.7.40: They have disabled the French battleship *Richelieu*, which was in Dakar harbour.[68] But no move to seize any of the French West African ports, which no doubt are not strongly held. . . . . According to Vernon Bartlett,[69] the Germans are going to make a peace offer, along the lines I foresaw earlier, i.e. England to keep out of Europe but retain the Empire, and the Churchill government to go out and be replaced by one acceptable to Hitler. The presumption is that a faction anxious to agree to this exists in England, and no doubt a shadow cabinet has been formed. It seems almost incredible that anyone should imagine that the mass of the people would tolerate such an arrangement, unless they had been fought to a standstill first . . . The Duke of Windsor[70] has been shipped off as Governor of the Bahamas, virtually a sentence of exile. . . . . . The book Gollancz has brought out, *Guilty Men*, the usual "indictment" of the Munich crowd, is selling like hot cakes. According to *Time*, the American Communists are working hand in glove with the local Nazis to prevent American arms getting to England. One can't be sure how much local freedom of action the various Communists have. Till very recently it appeared that they had none. Of late however they have sometimes pursued contradictory policies in different countries. It is possible that they are allowed to abandon the "line" when strict clinging to it would mean extinction.

68. On 8 July 1940, Royal Navy torpedo-boats attacked and seriously damaged the *Richelieu* at Dakar and the *Jean Bart* at Casablanca.
69. Vernon Bartlett (1894–1983), author of many books of political affairs, was at this time a leading liberal political journalist. He worked for the *News Chronicle* (which tended to favour the Liberal Party's approach) and reported on world crises, especially those associated with Hitler, Mussolini, and the Far East. Won a sensational by-election in 1938 as an Independent MP opposing the Munich Agreement.
70. Edward, Duke of Windsor (1894–1972), had, as Prince of Wales, been extremely popular, expressing sympathy with the unemployed and those living in depressed areas. He ascended the throne, as Edward VIII, on 20 January 1936, but his decision to marry a twice-divorced woman, Mrs. Wallis Simpson, caused a crisis that led to his abdication on 10 December 1936. He and Mrs. Simpson married and lived in France thereafter except for the war years, when he acted as governor of the Bahamas. Ill-feeling and controversy, about 'the Abdication Crisis' and his association with Nazi Germany have not entirely evaporated.

16.7.40: No real news for some days, except the British government's semi-surrender to Japan, i.e. the agreement to stop sending war supplies along the Burma Road for a stated period. This however is not so definite that it could not be revoked by a subsequent government. F.[71] thinks it is the British government's last effort (i.e. the last effort of those with investments in Hong Kong, etc.) to appease Japan, after which they will be driven into definitely supporting China. It may be so. But what a way to do things – never to perform a decent action until you are kicked into it and the rest of the world has ceased to believe that your motives can possibly be honest.

W.[72] says that the London "left" intelligentsia are now completely defeatist, look on the situation as hopeless and all but wish for surrender. How easy it ought to have been to foresee, under their Popular Front bawlings, that they would collapse when the real show began.

71. Unidentified; possibly Tosco Fyvel (1907–1985). He was Jewish; his parents had emigrated from Vienna to what was then Palestine, where he was associated with the Zionist movement and had worked with Golda Meir. Orwell and he met in January 1940, with Fredric Warburg and others. The outcome of a series of further meetings was Searchlight Books, of which Orwell's *The Lion and the Unicorn* (1941) was the first. See also T. R. Fyvel, *George Orwell: A Personal Memoir* (1982), 91–102.
72. Unidentified; possibly Fredric Warburg.

22.7.40: No real news for days past. The principal event of the moment is the pan-American conference, now just beginning, and the Russian absorption of the Baltic states, which must be directed against Germany. Cripps's wife and daughters are going to Moscow, so evidently he expects a long stay there. Spain is said to be importing oil in large quantities, obviously for German use, and we are not stopping it. Much hooey in the *News Chronicle* this morning about Franco desiring to keep out of war, trying to counter German influence, etc., etc. . . . . . It will be just as I said. Franco will play up his pretence of being pro-British, this will be used as a reason for handling Spain gently and allowing imports in any quantity, and ultimately Franco will come in on the German side.

25.7.40: No news, really. . . . . . Various people who have sent their children to Canada are already regretting it.[73] Casualties, i.e. fatal ones, from air-raids for last month were given out as about 340. If true, this is substantially less than the number of road deaths in the same period. . . . The L.D.V, now said to be 1,300,000 strong, is stopping recruiting and is to be renamed the Home Guard. There are rumours also that those acting as N.C.O's are to be replaced by men from the regular army. This seems to indicate either that the authorities are beginning to take the L.D.V. seriously as a fighting force, or that they are afraid of it.

There are now rumours that Lloyd George[74] is the potential Pétain of England. . . . . . The Italian press makes the same claim and says that L.G's silence proves it true. It is of course fairly easy to imagine L. G. playing this part out of sheer spite and jealousy because he has not been given a job, but much less easy to imagine him collaborating with the Tory clique who would in fact be in favour of such a course.

Constantly, as I walk down the street, I find myself looking up at the windows to see which of them would make good machine-gun nests. D.[75] says it is the same with him.[76]

73. See War-time Diary, 17.6.40 regarding evacuation of children to Canada.

74. David Lloyd George had, like Pétain, been cast as a heroic leader during World War I, when he proved an effective prime minister. He was in a minority in seeking a conciliatory peace treaty with Germany after the war. For Lloyd George see also Events, 6.8.39, n. 3.
75. Unidentified.
76. On 16 July 1940, Hitler had said, in his Directive 16: 'I have decided to prepare a landing operation against England, and, if necessary, to carry it out. The aim . . . will be to eliminate the English homeland . . . and, if necessary, to occupy it completely' *(Hitler's War Directives* 1939–45, edited by Hugh Trevor-Roper, 1964).

28.7.40: This evening I saw a heron flying over Baker Street. But this is not so improbable as the thing I saw a week or two ago, i.e., a kestrel killing a sparrow in the middle of Lord's cricket ground. I suppose it is possible that the war, i.e. the diminution of traffic, tends to increase bird life in inner London.

The little man whose name I always forget used to know Joyce,[77] of the split-off Fascist party, commonly credited with being Lord Haw-Haw. He says that Joyce hated Mosley[78] passionately and talked about him in the most unprintable language. Mosley being Hitler's chief supporter in England, it is interesting that he should employ Joyce and not one of Mosley's men. This bears out what Borkenau said, that Hitler does not want a too-strong Fascist party to exist in England.[79] Evidently the motive is always to split, and even to split the splitters. The German press is attacking the Pétain government, with what motive is not absolutely certain, and so also are elements of the French press under German control. Doriot[80] is of course to the fore here. It was a shock to me when the *Sunday Times* also stated that the Germans in Paris are making use of Bergery.[81] But I accept this with caution, knowing how these small dissident Left parties are habitually lied about by the Right and the official Left alike.

77. William Joyce (1908–1946), known as Lord Haw-Haw supposedly from his way of speaking, was an American citizen who never acquired British nationality, although he spent most of his life in England and was a rabid nationalist. He became a Fascist for whom Oswald Mosley's line was too mild. In August 1939 he went to Germany and in 1940 became a naturalized German. Throughout the early part of the war he broadcast propaganda to England. He was hanged by the British, 3 January 1946.
78. Oswald Mosley, head of the British Union of Fascists; see Wigan Pier Diary, 16.3.36, n. 37.
79. See Orwell's 'London Letter,' *CW*, XII, pp. 353–4, .
80. Jacques Doriot (1898–1945), a Communist who had turned to Fascism, was leader of the Parti Populaire François, which was financed by the Germans. On 25 March 1943, he wrote to Hitler: 'L'armée allemande et ses allies ne combattant pas seulement pour l'Allemagne, mais pour Europe et par consequent pour France.' He was behind the formation of La Légion des volontaires français contre bolchevisme (the LVF) – a first step in military

collaboration with Germany during the occupation. Some 10,000 volunteers served in the Wehrmacht on the Eastern Front. (Information from Memorial Museum, Caen.)

81. Gaston Bergery, a French deputy and intellectual, moved from the extreme right to the extreme left, and after the fall of France collaborated with the Germans.

8.8.40: The Italian attack on Egypt, or rather on British Somaliland, has begun. No real news yet, but the papers hint that Somaliland can't be held with the troops we have there. The important point is Perim, loss of which would practically close the Red Sea.

H. G. Wells[82] knows Churchill well and says that he is a good man, not mercenary and not even a careerist. He has always lived "like a Russian commissar", "requisitions" his motor cars, etc., but cares nothing about money. But [H. G. Wells] says Churchill has a certain power of shutting his eyes to facts and has the weakness of never wanting to let down a personal friend, which accounts for the non-sacking of various people. [Wells] has already made a considerable row about the persecution of refugees. He considers that the centre of all the sabotage is the War Office. He believes that the jailing of anti-Fascist refugees is a perfectly conscious piece of sabotage based on the knowledge that some of these people are in touch with underground movements in Europe and might at some moment be able to bring about a "Bolshevik" revolution, which from the point of view of the governing class is much worse than defeat. He says that Lord Swinton[83] is the man most to blame. I asked him did he think it was a conscious action on Lord [Swinton]'s part, this being always the hardest thing to decide. He said he believed Lord [Swinton] knows perfectly well what he is doing.

To-night to a lecture with lantern slides by an officer who had been in the Dunkirk campaign. Very bad lecture. He said the Belgians fought well and it was not true that they surrendered without warning (actually they gave three days' warning), but spoke badly of the French. He had one photograph of a regiment of Zouaves in full flight after looting houses, one man being dead drunk on the pavement.

82. When the diary was typed, five hyphens were shown here, but Orwell wrote 'H. G. Wells' above them; so his name has been given here without square brackets. The second use of his name and initials, in square brackets, had seven hyphens; the third had five hyphens, so the initials have been dropped. The word 'careerist' would be Orwell's, not Wells's. It was one of the most damning characteristics Orwell attributed to those of whom he disapproved.

83. Orwell wrote 'Swinton' over the seven hyphens originally typed, so his name is given here without square brackets. The next appearance of 'Swinton,' in square brackets, replaces seven hyphens; the third use replaces six. The six must, in this context, stand for 'Swinton' so it is apparent that the number of hyphens cannot be wholly relied upon. Philip Cunliffe-Lister, Viscount Swinton

(1884–1972; Earl, 1955), entered Parliament as a Unionist (allied closely with the Conservatives) in 1918. He was Secretary of State for the Colonies, 1931–35; Secretary of State for Air, 1935–38; Chairman of the United Kingdom Commercial Corporation, 1940–42; Cabinet Minister Resident in West Africa, 1942–44; and Minister of Civil Aviation, 1944–45.

9.8.40: The money situation is becoming completely unbearable. . . . . . Wrote a long letter to the Income Tax people[84] pointing out that the war had practically put an end to my livelihood while at the same time the government refused to give me any kind of job. The fact which is really relevant to a writer's position, the impossibility of writing books with this nightmare going on, would have no weight officially. . . . Towards the government I feel no scruples and would dodge paying the tax if I could. Yet I would give my life for England readily enough, if I thought it necessary. No one is patriotic about taxes.

No real news for days past. Only air battles, in which, if the reports are true, the British always score heavily. I wish I could talk to some R.A.F. officer and get some kind of idea whether these reports are truthful.[85]

84. The fact that Orwell was being pressed for income tax is of interest in the light of his near-poverty in the thirties. In 1939 only some twenty per cent of the population paid income tax (see Dearden Farrow, 19.2.85). Orwell's difficulties, common to writers, actors, and others, may have been caused by higher earnings in an earlier year (for example, royalties for *The Road to Wigan Pier)* and because Eileen's earnings would then, for tax, be treated as his.

85. Fewer planes were actually shot down than British and German air forces claimed at the time. On 14 August the Royal Air Force claimed to have shot down 144 German planes; this was revised to 71 after the war, when German records could be examined. On that day the RAF lost 16 planes, but eight pilots were saved. On 15 September 185 German planes were claimed; this proved to be 56; 26 RAF planes were lost, but half the pilots were rescued. This was the largest number claimed for any day of the Battle of Britain. From July to the end of October, the claim was 2,698 German planes shot down; the correct number was 1,733. The Germans claimed 3,058 RAF planes, but losses were 915 planes. To what extent this was deliberate official exaggeration and to what degree overenthusiastic reporting by pilots is difficult to assess.

16.8.40: Things are evidently going badly in Somaliland, which is the flanking operation in the attack on Egypt. Enormous air battles over the Channel, with, if the reports are anywhere near the truth, stupendous German losses. E.g. about 145 were reported shot down yesterday. . . . . . The people in Inner London could do with one real raid to teach them how to behave. At present everyone's behaviour is foolish in the extreme, everything except transport being held up but no precautions taken. For the first 15 seconds there is great alarm, blowing of whistles and shouts to children to go indoors, then people begin to congregate on the streets and gaze expectantly at the sky. In the daytime people are apparently ashamed to go into the shelters till they hear the bombs.

On Tuesday and Wednesday had two glorious days at Wallington. No newspapers and no mention of the war. They were cutting the oats and we took Marx out both days to help course the rabbits, at which Marx showed unexpected speed. The whole thing took me straight back to my childhood, perhaps the last bit of that kind of life that I shall ever have.

19.8.40: A feature of the air raids is the extreme credulity of almost everyone about damage done to distant places. George M.[86] arrived recently from Newcastle, which is generally believed here to have been seriously smashed about, and told us that the damage there was nothing to signify. On the other hand he arrived expecting to find London knocked to pieces and his first question on arrival was "whether we had had a very bad time." It is easy to see how people as far away as America can believe that London is in flames, England starving, etc., etc. And at the same time all this raises the presumption that our own raids on western Germany are much less damaging than is reported.

86. This is probably George Mason, a medical consultant and close friend of Laurence O'Shaughnessy. Eileen saw him professionally early in 1945, and in a letter remarked that he and her brother thought well of Harvey Evers, the surgeon who operated on her on 29 March 1945. See Crick, p. 478.

20.8.40: The papers are putting as good a face as possible upon the withdrawal from Somaliland, which is nevertheless a serious defeat, the first loss of British territory for centuries . . . It's a pity that the papers (at any rate the *News Chronicle*, the only one I have seen to-day) are so resolute in treating the news as good. This might have been made the start of another agitation which would have got some more of the duds out of the government.

Complaints among the Home Guards, now that air raids are getting commoner, because sentries have no tin hats. Explanation from Gen. Macnamara, who tells us that the regular army is still short of 300,000 tin hats – this after nearly a year of war.

22.8.40: The Beaverbrook press, compared with the headlines I saw on other papers, seems to be playing down the suggestions that Trotsky's murder[87] was carried out by the G.P.U. In fact today's *Evening Standard*, with several separate items about Trotsky, didn't mention this suggestion. No doubt they still have their eye on Russia and want to placate the Russians at all costs, in spite of Low's cartoons,[88] but under this there may lie a much subtler manoeuvre. The men responsible for the *Standard's* present pro-Russian policy are no doubt shrewd enough to know that a Popular Front "line" is not really the way to secure a Russian alliance. But they also know that the mass of leftish opinion in England still takes it for granted that a full anti-fascist policy is the way to line up Russia on our side. To crack up Russia is therefore a way of pushing public opinion leftward. It is curious that I always attribute these devious motives to other people, being anything but cunning myself and finding it hard to use indirect methods even when I see the need for them.

Today in Portman Square saw a four-wheeler cab, in quite good trim, with a good horse and a cabman quite of the pre-1914 type.

87. Leon Trotsky (1879–1940), a leader of the October 1917 revolution in Russia, and Commissar for Foreign Affairs and for War, 1917–24, was instrumental in the creation of the Red Army. In the power struggle that followed the death of Lenin in 1924 he lost to Stalin and was exiled. He was assassinated in Mexico because he and those who followed him continued to oppose Stalin. His death was attributed to the Soviet secret police, the OGPU.
88. David Low (1891–1963) was a fine political cartoonist of left-wing views who worked for the *Evening Standard* and later for the *Manchester Guardian*.

23.8.40: This morning an air-raid warning about 3 a.m. Got up, looked at the time, then felt unable to do anything and promptly went to sleep again. They are talking of rearranging the alarm system, and they will have to do so if they are to prevent every alarm from costing thousands of pounds in wasted time, lost sleep, etc. The fact that at present the alarm sounds all over a wide area when the German planes are only operating in one part of it, means not only that people are unnecessarily woken up or taken away from work, but that an impression is spread that an air-raid alarm will *always* be false, which is obviously dangerous.

Have got my Home Guard uniform, after 2½ months.

Last night to a lecture by General--------,[89] who is in command of about a quarter of a million men. He said he had been 41 years in the army. Was through the Flanders campaign, and no doubt *limogé* [90] for incompetence. Dilating on the Home Guard being a static defensive force, he said contemptuously and in a rather marked way that he saw no use in our practising taking cover, "crawling about on our stomachs", etc., etc., evidently as a hit at the Osterley Park training school.[91] Our job, he said, was to die at our posts. Was also great on bayonet practice, and hinted that regular army ranks, saluting, etc., were to be introduced shortly. . . . . These wretched old blimps, so obviously silly and senile, and so degenerate in everything except physical courage, are merely pathetic in themselves, and one would feel rather sorry for them if they were not hanging round our necks like millstones. The attitude of the rank and file at these would-be pep-talks – so anxious to be enthusiastic, so ready to cheer and laugh at the jokes, and yet all the time half feeling that there is something wrong – always strikes me as pathetic. The time has almost arrived when one will only have to jump up on the platform and tell them how they are being wasted and how the war is being lost, and by whom, for them to rise up and shovel the blimps into the dustbin. When I watch them listening to one of these asinine talks, I always remember that passage in Samuel Butler's *Notebook* about a young calf he once saw eating dung.[92] It could not quite make up its mind whether it liked the stuff or not, and all it needed was some experienced cow to give it a prod with her horn, after which it would have remembered for life that dung is not good to eat.

It occurred to me yesterday, how will the Russian state get on without Trotsky? Or the Communists elsewhere? Probably they will be forced to invent a substitute.

89. Unidentified. Tom Hopkinson, one of the founders of the unofficial Home Guard Training School at Osterley Park, tells how a Brigadier Whitehead attempted to have the school stopped in the autumn of 1940 because it did not have a licence; see his *Of This Our Time* (1982), p. 180. Orwell cannot be referring to Lieutenant-General Sir T. R. Eastwood, who took command of the Home Guard in the autumn of 1940; he was under fifty.

90. Passed over for promotion.

91. Osterley Park training school was run by Tom Wintringham (1898–1949) and Hugh (Humphrey) Slater (1905–1958). They taught guerrilla tactics and street-fighting based on their experience with the International Brigade in the Spanish Civil War. Orwell's Lecture Notes for Instructing the Home Guard survive. They deal in considerable detail with street fighting, field fortifications, and smoke mortars (see *CW*, XII, 328–40).

Wintringham had served with the Royal Flying Corps in World War I and edited *Left Review*, 1934–36. He commanded the British Battalion of the International Brigade near Madrid in 1937. He was a founder member of the Communist Party of Great Britain but left after seventeen years following his service in Spain. He was the author of a Penguin Special, *New Ways of War* (1940).

Slater was a painter and author. He was at one time a Communist and was involved in anti-Nazi politics in Berlin in the early thirties. He fought for the Republicans in Spain (1936–38), becoming Chief of Operations in the International Brigade. His manual, *Home Guard for Victory! An Essay in Strategy, Tactics and Training* (1941) was reviewed by Orwell (*CW*, XII, pp. 387–89, and pp. 439–41). Also in 1941 he published *War into Europe: Attack in Depth*.

92. 'Art of Knowing What Gives One Pleasure,' *Further Extracts from the Note-Books of Samuel Butler*, chosen and edited by A. T. Bartholomew (1934), pp. 165–66. This book was reviewed by Orwell in 1934, *CW*, X, pp. 339–40.

26.8.40: (Greenwich). The raid which occurred on the 24th was the first real raid on London so far as I am concerned, i.e. the first in which I could hear the bombs. We were watching at the front door when the East India docks were hit. No mention of the docks being hit in Sunday's papers, so evidently they do conceal it when important objectives are hit. . . . . It was a loudish bang but not alarming and gave no impression of making the earth tremble, so evidently these are not very large bombs that they are dropping. I remember the two big bombs that dropped near Huesca when I was in the hospital at Monflorite. The first, quite 4 kilometres away, made a terrific roar that shook the houses and sent us all fleeing out of our beds in alarm. Perhaps that was a 2000 lb. bomb[93] and the ones at present being dropped are 500 lb. ones.

They will have to do something very soon about localising alarms. At present millions of people are kept awake or kept away from work every time an aeroplane appears over any part of London.

93. In this raid the first bombs fell on central London; St Giles's Church, Cripplegate, was hit. Although eleven-ton blockbuster bombs were later dropped by the RAF, at this stage of the war 2,000-pound bombs were not available. In the attack on Woolwich Arsenal and the London docks on 7 September 1940, some 300 German bombers dropped 337 tons of bombs – an average of 2,500 pounds per plane. Orwell may have had parachute mines, or their effect, in mind here. Churchill wrote General Ismay a memorandum on 19 September 1940 noting that the Germans had dropped 36 parachute mines. He wanted an appropriate response – 1,000-pound bombs if parachute mines were not available. The disadvantage of the parachute mine, except as a weapon of terror, was that, released at 5,000 feet and subject to the vagaries of the wind, it could not find a specific target. See Winston Churchill, *The Second World War,* II, pp. 321–22.

29.8.40: Air-raid alarms during the last 3 nights have totalled about 16–18 hours for the three nights. . . . . It is perfectly clear that these night raids are intended chiefly as a nuisance, and as long as it is taken for granted that at the sound of the siren everyone must dive for the shelter, Hitler only needs to send his planes over half-a-dozen at a time to hold up work and rob people of sleep to an indefinite extent. However, this idea is already wearing off. . . . For the first time in 20 years I have overheard bus conductors losing their tempers and being rude to passengers. E.g. the other night, a voice out of the darkness: "'Oo's conducting this bus, lady, me or you?" It took me straight back to the end of the last war.

. . . . . . E[ileen] and I have paid the minimum of attention to raids and I was honestly under the impression that they did not worry me at all except because of the disorganisation, etc., that they cause.[94] This morning, however, putting in a couple of hours' sleep as I always do when returning from guard duty, I had a very disagreeable dream of a bomb dropping near me and frightening me out of my wits. Cf. the dream I used to have towards the end of our time in Spain, of being on a grass bank with no cover and mortar shells dropping round me.

94. See Orwell's 'London Letter,' *CW,* XII, pp. 356–7

31.8.40: Air-raid warnings, of which there are now half a dozen or thereabouts every 24 hours, becoming a great bore. Opinion spreading rapidly that one ought simply to disregard the raids except when they are known to be big-scale ones and in one's own area. Of the people strolling in Regent's Park, I should say at least half pay no attention to a raid-warning . . . . . Last night just as we were going to bed, a pretty heavy explosion. Later in the night woken up by a tremendous crash, said to be caused by a bomb in Maida Vale.[95] E[ileen] and I merely remarked on the loudness and fell asleep again. Falling asleep, with a vague impression of anti-aircraft guns firing, found myself mentally back in the Spanish war, on one of those nights when you had good straw to sleep on, dry feet, several hours rest ahead of you, and the sound of distant gunfire, which acts as a soporific provided it is distant.

95. A suburb of London straddling NW8 and W9, about a mile from where the Orwells were living in Chagford Street.

1.9.40: Recently bought a forage cap. . . . . It seems that forage caps over size 7 are a great rarity. Evidently they expect all soldiers to have small heads. This tallies with the remark made by some higher-up to R.R.[96] in Paris when he tried to join the army – "Good God, you don't suppose we want intelligent men in the front line, do you?" All the Home Guard uniforms are made with 20-inch necks. . . . . Shops everywhere are beginning to cash in on the Home Guard, khaki shirts, etc., being displayed at fantastic prices with notices "suitable for the Home Guard." Just as in Barcelona, in the early days when it was fashionable to be in the militia.

96. *R.R.*: Sir Richard Rees, Bt. (1900–1970), was a long-time friend and benefactor of Orwell, especially when Orwell was trying to establish himself. Ravelston of *Keep the Aspidistra Flying* owes something to his generous nature. He was a painter and, from 1930–37, editor of *The Adelphi*. He was Orwell's partner in his farm on Jura and became (with Sonia Orwell) his joint literary executor. See his *George Orwell: Fugitive from the Camp of Victory* (1961) and extracts therefrom in *Orwell Remembered*, with part of a BBC interview (pp. 115–26). See also note on Rees, *CW*, X, pp. 181–2.

3.9.40: Yesterday talking with Mrs. C.,[97] who had recently come back from Cardiff. Raids there have been almost continuous, and finally it was decided that work in the docks must continue, raids or no raids. Almost immediately afterwards a German plane managed to drop a bomb straight into the hold of a ship, and according to Mrs. C. the remains of seven men working there "had to be brought up in pails". Immediately there was a dock strike, after which they had to go back to the practice of taking cover. This is the sort of thing that does not get into the papers. It is now stated on all sides that the casualties in the most recent raids, e.g. at Ramsgate, have been officially minimised, which greatly incenses the locals, who do not like to read about "negligible damage" when 100 people have been killed, etc., etc. Shall be interested to see the figures for casualities for this month, i.e. August. I should say that up to about 2000 a month they would tell the truth, but would cover it up for figures over that.[98]

Michael[99] estimates that in his clothing factory, evidently a small individually-owned affair, time lost in air-raids cost £50 last week.

97. Unidentified.
98. The number killed in air raids in September was 6,954; 10,615 were seriously injured. The figures during the ensuing winter throughout Britain were:

	Killed	*Injured*
October 1940	6,334	8,695
November	4,588	6,202
December	3,793	5,244
January 1941	1,500	2,012
February	789	1,068
March	4,259	5,557

In the devastation of Coventry on 16 November (code-named 'Moonlight Sonata' by the Germans), 554 people were killed of a population of a quarter of a million; only one German plane was shot down. Throughout the war, 60,595 civilians were killed by enemy action. This stands in contrast to 30,248 members of the Merchant Marine; 50,758 Royal Navy; 69,606 RAF; and 144,079 Army. Of some 36,500 civilians killed in air raids to the end of 1941, more than 20,000 died in London, more than 4,000 in Liverpool, over 2,000 in Birmingham, and nearly 2,000 in Glasgow.
99. Probably the 'M' mentioned in diary entry of 16.6.40. £50 would be about a week's wages for 10–12 people.

7.9.40: Air-raid alarms now frequent enough, and lasting long enough, for people habitually to forget whether the alarm is on at the moment, or whether the All Clear has sounded. Noise of bombs and gunfire, except when very close (which probably means within two miles) now accepted as a normal background to sleep or conversation. I have still not heard a bomb go off with the sort of bang that makes you feel you are personally involved.

In Churchill's speech, number killed in air-raids during August given as 1075. Even if truthful, probably a large understatement as it includes only civilian casualties The secretiveness officially practised about raids is extraordinary. To-day's papers report that a bomb fell in a square "in central London". Impossible to find out which square it was, though thousands of people must know.

10.9.40: Can't write much of the insanities of the last few days. It is not so much that the bombing is worrying in itself as that the disorganisation of traffic, frequent difficulty of telephoning, shutting of shops whenever there is a raid on, etc., etc., combined with the necessity of getting on with one's ordinary work, wear one out and turn life into a constant scramble to catch up lost time. Herewith a few notes on bombs, etc.: –

I have seen no bomb crater deeper than about 12 feet. One opposite the house at Greenwich was only (interrupted by air raid: continued 11.9.40) about the size of those made in Spain by 15 cm. shells. In general the noises are formidable but not absolutely shattering like those of the huge bombs I saw dropped at Huesca. Putting "screaming" bombs aside, I have frequently heard the whistle of a bomb – to hear which one must I assume be within at most a mile of it – and then a not overwhelmingly loud explosion. On the whole I conclude that they are using small bombs. Those which did most of the damage in the Old Kent Road had a curiously limited effect. Often a small house would be reduced to a pile of bricks and the house next door to it barely chipped. Ditto with the incendiary bombs, which will sometimes burn the inner part of a house completely out while leaving the front almost intact.

The delayed-action bombs are a great nuisance, but they appear to be successful in locating most of them and getting all the neighbouring people out until the bomb shall have exploded. All over South London, little groups of disconsolate-looking people wandering about with suitcases and bundles, either people who have been rendered homeless or, in more cases, who have been turned out by the authorities because of an unexploded bomb.

Notable bits of damage so far: Tremendous fires in the docks on 7 and 8.9.40, Cheapside on 9.9.40. Bank of England just chipped (bomb crater about 15 feet from wall). Naval college at Greenwich also chipped. Much damage in Holborn. Bomb in Marylebone goods yard.[100] Cinema at Madame Tussauds destroyed. Several other large fires, many gas mains and electric cables burst, much diversion of road traffic, London Bridge and Westminster Bridge being out of use for several days, and enough damage to railway lines to slow down rail traffic for a day or two. Power station somewhere in South London hit, stopping trams for about half a day. Said to be very heavy damage in Woolwich,[101] and, to judge by the column of flame and smoke, one or more of the big oil drums in the estuary of the Thames was hit on 7.9.40. Deliveries of milk and letters delayed to some extent, newspapers mostly coming out a few hours late, all theatres (except the Criterion,[102] which is underground) closed on 10.9.40, and I think all cinemas as well.

Most of last night in the public shelter, having been driven there by recurrent whistle and crash of bombs not very far away at intervals of about a quarter of an hour. Frightful discomfort owing to overcrowding, though the place was well-appointed, with electric light and fans. People, mostly elderly working class, grousing bitterly about the hardness of the seats and the longness of the night, but no defeatist talk. . . . . . People are now to be seen every night about dusk queuing up at the doors of the Shelters with their bedding. Those who come in first grab places on the floor and probably pass a reasonably good night. Day raids apart, the raiding hours are pretty regularly 8 p.m. to 4.30 a.m., i.e. dusk to just before dawn.

I should think 3 months of continuous raids at the same intensity as the last 4 nights would break down everyone's morale. But it is doubtful whether anyone could keep up the attack on such a scale for 3 months, especially when he is suffering much the same himself.

100. Holborn is in the City of London; Marylebone Railway Station, a London terminus, was some 200–300 yards from where Orwell was living in Chagford Street.

101. Woolwich, two to three miles east of Greenwich, where the O'Shaughnessys lived, was the location of a Royal Artillery depot, the Royal Military Academy, and the Royal Arsenal.

102. The Criterion is in Piccadilly Circus. The Windmill Theatre, as it proudly boasted, also 'never closed'; it was a little to the northeast of Piccadilly Circus.

12.9.40: As soon as the air-raids began seriously it was noticeable that people were much readier than before to talk to strangers in the street. . . . . This morning met a youth of about 20, in dirty overalls, perhaps a garage hand. Very embittered and defeatist about the war, and horrified by the destruction he had seen in South London. He said that Churchill had visited the bombed area near the Elephant[103] and at a spot where 20 out of 22 houses had been destroyed, remarked that it was "not so bad". The youth: "I'd have wrung his bloody neck if he'd said it to me." He was pessimistic about the war, considered Hitler was sure to win and would reduce London to much the same state as Warsaw. He spoke bitterly about the people rendered homeless in South London and eagerly took up my point when I said the empty houses in the West End should be requisitioned for them. He considered that all wars were fought for the profit of the rich, but agreed with me that this one would probably end in revolution. With all this he was not unpatriotic. Part of his grouch was that he had tried to join the Air Force 4 times in the last 6 months, and always been put off.

To-night and last night they have been trying the new device of keeping up a continuous A.A. barrage, apparently firing blind or merely by sound, though I suppose there is some kind of sound-detector which estimates the height at which they must make the shells burst. . . . . . The noise is tremendous and almost continuous, but I don't mind it, feeling it to be on my side. Spent last night at S's place[104] with a battery firing in the square at short intervals throughout the night. Slept through it easily enough, no bombs being audible in that place.

The havoc in the East End and South London is terrible, by all accounts. . . . . . . Churchill's speech last night referred very seriously to danger of imminent invasion. If invasion is actually attempted and this is not a feint, the idea is presumably either to knock out our air bases along the South Coast, after which the ground defences can be well bombed, at the same time causing all possible confusion in London and its southward communications, or to draw as much as possible of our defensive forces south before delivering the attack on Scotland or possibly Ireland.

Meanwhile our platoon of Home Guards, after 3½ months, have about 1 rifle for 6 men, no other weapons except incendiary bombs, and perhaps 1 uniform for 4 men. After all, they have stood out against letting the rifles be taken home by individual men.[105] They are all parked in one place, where a bomb may destroy the whole lot of them any night.

103. The Elephant and Castle, a public house, gave its name to this major working-class residential area, shopping centre, and meeting point of several important roads.

104. Stephen Spender's flat, and the *Horizon* office, in Lansdowne Terrace, WC1. Orwell originally typed 'S.S's place' but the first S was crossed out.

105. On 22 September 1940, Churchill wrote to President Roosevelt saying that 250,000 rifles 'are most urgently needed, as I have 250,000 trained and uniformed men [the Home Guard] into whose hands they can be put.' If they could be made available, it would 'enable us to take 250,000 .303 rifles from the Home Guard and transfer them to the Regular Army, leaving the Home Guard armed with about 800,000 American rifles' *(The Second World War,* II, p. 596).

14.9.40: On the first night of the barrage,[106] which was the heaviest, they are said to have fired 500,000 shells, i.e. at an average cost of £5 per shell, £2½ millions worth. But well worth it, for the effect on morale.

106. When the Germans first bombed London, there appeared to be no anti-aircraft defence. Sometimes a single enemy plane would be cruising above and people could only wait anxiously, often for seemingly long periods, for a bomb to be dropped. At other times there would be a concentrated attack of incendiary bombs, high explosives, or both. After all the anti-aircraft guns available had been regrouped around London, quite unexpectedly they all opened up on the night of 10 September. Orwell is absolutely correct about the effect on morale.

15.9.40: This morning, for the first time, saw an aeroplane shot down. It fell slowly out of the clouds, nose foremost, just like a snipe that has been shot high overhead. Terrific jubilation among the people watching, punctuated every now and then by the question, "Are you sure it's a German?"

So puzzling are the directions given, and so many the types of aeroplane, that no one even knows which are German planes and which are our own. My only test is that if a bomber is seen over London it must be a German, whereas a fighter is likelier to be ours.

17.9.40: Heavy bombing in this area last night till about 11 p.m. . . . . . I was talking in the hallway of this house to two young men and a girl who was with them. Psychological attitude of all 3 was interesting. They were quite openly and unashamedly frightened, talking about how their knees were knocking together, etc., and yet at the same time excited and interested, dodging out of doors between bombs to see what was happening and pick up shrapnel splinters. Afterwards in Mrs. C's little reinforced room downstairs, with Mrs. C. and her daughter, the maid, and three young girls who are also lodgers here. All the women, except the maid, screaming in unison, clasping each other and hiding their faces, every time a bomb went past, but betweenwhiles quite happy and normal, with animated conversation proceeding, The dog subdued and obviously frightened, knowing something to be wrong. Marx is also like this during raids, i.e. subdued and uneasy. Some dogs, however, go wild and savage during a raid and have had to be shot. They allege here, and E[ileen] says the same thing about Greenwich, that all the dogs in the park now bolt for home when they hear the siren.

Yesterday when having my hair cut in the City, asked the barber if he carried on during raids. He said he did. And even if he was shaving someone? I said. Oh, yes, he carried on just the same. And one day a bomb will drop near enough to make him jump, and he will slice half somebody's face off.

Later, accosted by a man, I should think some kind of commercial traveller, with a bad type of face, while I was waiting for a bus. He began a rambling talk about how he was getting himself and his wife out of London, how his nerves were giving way and he suffered from stomach trouble, etc., etc. I don't know how much of this kind of thing there is. . . . . There has of course been a big exodus from the East End, and every night what amount to mass migrations to places where there is sufficient shelter accommodation. The practice of taking a 2d ticket and spending the night in one of the deep Tube stations, e.g. Piccadilly, is growing. . . . . . . Everyone I have talked to agrees that the empty furnished houses in the West End should be used for the homeless; but I suppose the rich swine still have enough pull to prevent this from happening. The other day 50 people from the East End, headed by some of the Borough Councillors, marched into the Savoy and demanded to use the air-raid shelter. The management didn't succeed in ejecting them till the raid was over, when they went voluntarily. When you see how the wealthy are *still* behaving, in what is manifestly developing into a revolutionary war, you think of St. Petersburg in 1916.

(Evening). Almost impossible to write in this infernal racket. (Electric lights have just gone off. Luckily I have some candles.) So many streets in (lights on again) the quarter roped off because of unexploded bombs, that to get home from Baker Street, say 300 yards, is like trying to find your way to the heart of a maze.

21.9.40: Have been unable for some days to buy another volume to continue this diary because of the three or 4 stationers' shops in the immediate neighbourhood, all but one are cordoned off because of unexploded bombs.

Regular features of the time: neatly swept-up piles of glass, litter of stone and splinters of flint, smell of escaping gas, knots of sightseers waiting at the cordons.

Yesterday, at the entry to a street near here, a little crowd waiting with an A.R.P. man in a black tin hat among them. A devastating roar, with a huge cloud of dust, etc. The man with the black hat comes running towards the A.R.P. headquarters, where another with a white hat is emerging, munching at a mouthful of bread and butter.

The man with the black hat: "Dorset Square, sir."

The man with the white hat: "O.K." (Makes a tick in his note-book.)

Nondescript people wandering about, having been evacuated from their houses because of delayed-action bombs. Yesterday two girls stopping me in the street, very elegant in appearance except that their faces were filthily dirty: "Please, sir, can you tell us where we are?"

Withal, huge areas of London almost normal, and everyone quite happy in the daytime, never seeming to think about the coming night, like animals which are unable to foresee the future so long as they have a bit of food and a place in the sun.

24.9.40: Oxford Street yesterday, from Oxford Circus up to the Marble Arch, completely empty of traffic, and only a few pedestrians, with the late afternoon sun shining straight down the empty roadway and glittering on innumerable fragments of broken glass. Outside John Lewis's,[107] a pile of plaster dress models, very pink and realistic, looking so like a pile of corpses that one could have mistaken them for that at a little distance. Just the same sight in Barcelona, only there it was plaster saints from desecrated churches.

Much discussion as to whether you would hear a bomb (i.e. its whistle) which was coming straight at you. All turns upon whether the bomb travels faster than sound. . . . . . One thing I have worked out, I think satisfactorily, is that the further away from you a bomb falls, the longer the whistle you will hear. The short whizz is therefore the sound that should make you dive for cover. I think this is really the principle one goes on in dodging a shell, but there one seems to know by a kind of instinct.

The aeroplanes come back and come back, every few minutes. It is just like in an eastern country, when you keep thinking you have killed the last mosquito inside your net, and every time, as soon as you have turned the light out, another starts droning.

107. A leading department store, organized as a staff partnership, which still thrives.

27.9.40: The *News Chronicle* to-day is markedly defeatist, as well it may be after yesterday's news about Dakar.[108] But I have a feeling that the *News Chronicle* is bound to become defeatist anyway and will be promptly to the fore when plausible peace terms come forward. These people have no definable policy and no sense of responsibility, nothing except a traditional dislike of the British ruling class, based ultimately on the Nonconformist conscience. They are only noise-makers, like the *New Statesman*, etc. All these people can be counted on to collapse when the conditions of war become intolerable.

Many bombs last night, though I think none dropped within half a mile of this house. The commotion made by the mere passage of the bomb through the air is astonishing. The whole house shakes, enough to rattle objects on the table. Of course they are dropping very large bombs now. The unexploded one in Regent's Park is said to be "the size of a pillar box." Almost every night the lights go out at least once, not suddenly flicking off as when a connection is broken, but gradually fading out, and usually coming on again in about five minutes. Why it is that the lights dip when a bomb passes close by, nobody seems to know.

108. In September 1940 a British expedition, co-operating with Free French forces under General de Gaulle, made an attempt to recapture the port of Dakar, West Africa, from the Vichy government. The expedition was a failure.

15.10.40: Writing this at Wallington, having been more or less ill for about a fortnight with a poisoned arm. Not much news – i.e. only events of worldwide importance; nothing that has much affected me personally.

There are now 11 evacuee children in Wallington (12 arrived, but one ran away and had to be sent home). They come from the East End. One little girl, from Stepney, said that her grand-father had been bombed out seven times. They seem nice children and to be settling down quite well. Nevertheless there are the usual complaints against them in some quarters. E.g. of the little boy who is with Mrs.------, aged seven: "He's a dirty little devil, he is. He wets his bed and dirties his breeches. I'd rub his nose in it if I had charge of him, the dirty, little devil."

Some murmurings about the number of Jews in Baldock. ----[109] declares that Jews greatly predominate among the people sheltering in the Tubes. Must try and verify this.

Potato crop very good this year, in spite of the dry weather, which is just as well.

109. Both names unidentified.

19.10.40: The unspeakable depression of lighting the fires every morning with papers of a year ago, and getting glimpses of optimistic headlines as they go up in smoke.

21.10.40: With reference to the advertisements in the Tube stations, "Be a Man" etc. (asking able-bodied men not to shelter there but to leave the space for women and children), D[110] says the joke going round London is that it was a mistake to print these notices in English.

Priestley,[111] whose Sunday night broadcasts were by implication Socialist propaganda, has been shoved off the air, evidently at the instance of the Conservative party . . . . . . It looks rather as though the Margesson[112] crew are now about to stage a come-back.

110. Unidentified.

111. J. B. Priestley (1894–1984), a prolific popular novelist, dramatist, and man of letters. During 1940 and 1941 he gave a series of weekly radio talks urging the nation to take a united and determined stand against Hitler, hoping to make the country more democratic and egalitarian.

112. David R. Margesson (1890–1965; Viscount, 1942), Conservative M.P. for Rugby, 1924–42; Government Chief Whip, 1931–40, was loyal to each prime minister he served. Under Churchill he continued as Joint Government Whip, and after six months was Secretary of State for War.

25.10.40: The other night examined the crowds sheltering in Chancery Lane, Oxford Circus and Baker Street stations. *Not* all Jews, but, I think, a higher proportion of Jews than one would normally see in a crowd of this size. What is bad about Jews is that they are not only conspicuous, but go out of their way to make themselves so. A fearful Jewish woman, a regular comic-paper cartoon of a Jewess, fought her way off the train at Oxford Circus, landing blows on anyone who stood in her way. It took me back to old days on the Paris Metro.

Surprised to find that D., who is distinctly Left in his views, is inclined to share the current feeling against the Jews. He says that the Jews in business circles are turning pro-Hitler, or preparing to do so. This sounds almost incredible, but according to D. they will always admire anyone who kicks them. What I do feel is that any Jew, i.e. European Jew, would prefer Hitler's kind of social system to ours, if it were not that he happens to persecute them. Ditto with almost any Central European, e.g. the refugees. They make use of England as a sanctuary, but they cannot help feeling the profoundest contempt for it. You can see this in their eyes, even when they don't say it outright. The fact is that the insular outlook and the continental outlook are completely incompatible.

According to F.,[113] it is quite true that foreigners are more frightened than English people during the raids. It is not their war, and therefore they have nothing to sustain them. I think this might also account for the fact – I am virtually sure it is a fact, though one mustn't mention it – that working-class people are more frightened than middle-class.

The same feeling of despair over impending events in France, Africa, Syria, Spain – the sense of foreseeing what must happen and being powerless to prevent it, and feeling with absolute certainty that a British government *cannot* act in such a way as to get its blow in first. Air raids much milder the last few days.

113. Probably Tosco Fyvel, with whom Orwell was then working; see n. 71 above. 'D' not identified.

16.11.40: I never thought I should live to grow blasé about the sound of gunfire, but so I have.

23.11.40: The day before yesterday lunching with H. P., editor of -------.[114] H. P. rather pessimistic about the war. Thinks there is no answer to the New Order,[115] i.e. this government is incapable of framing any answer, and people here and in America could easily be brought to accept it. I queried whether people would not for certain see any peace offer along these lines as a trap. H. P.: "Hell's bells, I could dress it up so that they'd think it was the greatest victory in the history of the world. I could make them eat it." That is true, of course. All depends on the form in which it is put to people. So long as our own newspapers don't do the dirty they will be quite indifferent to appeals from Europe. H.P., however, is certain that -----[116] and Co. are working for a sell-out. It appears that though ------[117] is not submitted for censorship, all papers are now warned not to publish interpretations of the government's policy towards Spain. A few weeks back Duff-Cooper[118] had the press correspondents up and assured them "on his word of honour" that "things were going very well indeed in Spain." The most one can say is that Duff-Cooper's word of honour is worth more than Hoare's.

H. P. says that when France collapsed there was a Cabinet meeting to decide whether to continue the war or whether to seek terms. The vote was actually 50-50 except for one casting vote, and according to H. P. this was *Chamberlain's*. If true, I wonder whether this will ever be made public. It was poor old Chamberlain's last public act, as one might say, poor old man.

Characteristic war-time sound, in winter: the musical tinkle of rain-drops on your tin hat.

114. Editor and journal not identified.
115. Hitler's New Order for Europe – Nazism.
116. It is possible that Orwell's animosity towards Sir Samuel Hoare (see last sentence of the paragraph) may have led him to retail H.P.'s assertion. In *The Second World War*, Churchill, discussing the formation of his War Cabinet, in May 1940, defends Hoare, Halifax, and Simon against charges of responsibility for shortcomings in the period leading to the war (II, p. 10). Although he included the two lords in his Cabinet, he had Hoare appointed ambassador to Spain on 17 May. He later comments that 'no one could have carried out better this wearing, delicate, and cardinal five years' mission' (II, p. 459). For Hoare, see Events, 4.8.39, n. 5.
117. Unidentified; its six hyphens may be an error for the seven of H. P.'s journal.
118. Alfred Duff Cooper, Minister of Information; see War-time Diary, 29.5.40 n. 4.

28.11.40: Lunching yesterday with C.,[119] editor of *France*. . . . To my surprise he was in good spirits and had no grievances. I would have expected a French refugee to be grumbling endlessly about the food, etc. However, C. knows England well and has lived here before.

He says there is much more resistance both in occupied and unoccupied France than people here realise. The press is playing it down, no doubt because of our continued relations with Vichy. He says that at the time of the French collapse no European looked on it as conceivable that England would go on fighting, and generally speaking Americans did not either. He is evidently somewhat of an Anglophile and considers the monarchy a great advantage to England. According to him it has been a main factor in preventing the establishment of Fascism here. He considers that the abdication of Edward VIII was brought about because of Mrs. S.'s[120] known Fascist connections. . . . It is a fact that, on the whole, anti-Fascist opinion in England was pro-Edward, but C. is evidently repeating what was current on the continent.

C. was head of the press department during Laval's government.[121] Laval said to him in 1935 that England was now "only an appearance" and Italy was a really strong country, so that France must break with England and go in with Italy. On returning from signing the Franco-Russian pact he said that Stalin was the most powerful man in Europe. On the whole Laval's prophecies seem to have been falsified, clever though he is.

Completely conflicting accounts, from eye witnesses, about the damage to Coventry.[122] It seems impossible to learn the truth about bombing at a distance. When we have a quiet night here, I find that many people are faintly uneasy, because feeling certain that they are getting it badly in the industrial towns. What every one feels at the back of his mind is that we are now hardened to it and the morale elsewhere is less reliable.

119. Pierre Comert, French journalist and former diplomat, came to England after the fall of France.
120. Mrs. Wallis Simpson, by this time married to the Duke of Windsor; see War-time Diary, 10.7.40, n. 70.
121. For Pierre Laval, see War-time Diary, 24.6.40, n. 49.
122. Coventry was attacked during the night of 14 November 1940. The *Daily Herald* headlines for 16 November read 'Midlands City Is Now Like A Bombarded French Town,' 'Coventry Homeless Slept by Roadside This Morning,' 'Not a Mortal Blow – Work will Restart.' It reported that 500 planes were involved, that the Germans claimed 30,000 fire bombs fell in a dusk-to-dawn raid, and that the Ministry of Home Security said there were a thousand casualties (*War Papers*; *The War Papers* is a reprinted series of newspapers, in 74 parts, 1977–78.). *2194 Days of War* states that 449 German planes carried out 'carpet bombing' of the centre of Coventry, destroying many historic buildings, including the fourteenth-century cathedral. There were 550 dead and many more wounded; 21 factories were destroyed, but the city's productive capacity was not seriously affected. It concludes: 'After this the Germans coined the word *Coventrisieren* meaning "annihilate, raze to the ground"' (pp. 78–79). Churchill gives a figure of 400 killed and many more seriously injured and adds, 'The German radio proclaimed that our other cities would be similarly "Coventrated"' (*The Second World War*, II, p. 332). See also Tom Harrisson, *Living Through the Blitz* (1976), especially chap. VI, 'Coventration.'

1.12.40: That bastard Chiappe[123] is cold meat. Everyone delighted, as when Balbo[124] died. This war is at any rate killing off a few Fascists.

123. See War-time Diary, 21.6.40, n. 47.
124. See War-time Diary, 30.6.40, n. 59.

8.12.40: Broadcasting the night before last[125]. . . . . . Met there a Pole who has only recently escaped from Poland by some underground route he would not disclose. . . . . He said that in the siege of Warsaw 95 per cent of the houses were damaged and about 25 per cent demolished. All services, electricity, water, etc., broke down, and towards the end people had no defence whatever against the aeroplanes and, what was worse, the artillery. He described people rushing out to cut bits off a horse killed by shell-fire, then being driven back by fresh shells, then rushing out again. When Warsaw was completely cut off the people were upheld by the belief that the English were coming to help them, rumours all the while of an English army in Danzig, etc. etc . . .

The story going round about a week back was that the report in the papers to the effect that the Italian commander in Albania had shot himself was due to a misprint.

During the bad period of the bombing, when everyone was semi-insane, not so much from the bombing itself as from broken sleep, interrupted telephone calls, the difficulty of communications, etc., etc., I found that scraps of nonsense poetry were constantly coming into my mind. They never got beyond a line or two and the tendency stopped when the bombing slacked off, but examples were: –

An old Rumanian peasant
Who lived at Mornington Crescent

and

And the key doesn't fit and the bell doesn't ring,
But we all stand up for God save the King[126]

and

When the Borough Surveyor has gone to roost
On his rod, his pole or his perch.

125. This was a discussion programme with Desmond Hawkins on 'The Proletarian Writer'. Reprinted in *CW*, XII, pp. 244–9.

126. See the reference in 'My Country Right or Left' to people being mildly shocked at ridiculing royalty, *CW*, XII, p. 272.

29.12.40: From a newspaper account of a raid (not ironical): "Bombs were falling like manna".

1941

2.1.41: The rightwing reaction is now in full swing, and Margesson's entry into the Cabinet is no doubt a deliberate cash-in on Wavell's victory in Egypt. Comically enough a review of Wavell's life of Allenby which I wrote some months ago was printed in *Horizon* just at the time when the news of Sidi Barrani came through. I said in the review that as Wavell held so important a command the chief interest of the book was the light that it threw on his own intellect, and left it to be inferred that I didn't think much of this. So the laugh was on me – though, God knows, I am glad enough to have been wrong.[127]

The word "blitz" now used everywhere to mean any kind of attack on anything. Cf. "strafe" in the last war. "Blitz" is not yet used as a verb, a development I am expecting.[128]

127. For Orwell's review, published in December 1940, see *CW*, XII, pp. 292–3. General Wavell's forces broke through the Italian lines commanded by General Graziani at Sidi Barrani on 9 December 1940. In the March issue of *Horizon*, the Editorial Comment concluded with this paragraph: 'To the *Spectator*, and the many *Horizon* readers who have objected to Orwell's review of Wavell's *Allenby*, the Editor would like to point out that the review was written in the early summer, at a time when, after France, the title of general was

unreassuring, and when Orwell had no inkling that the biographer of Allenby was to prove greater than his subject. It was several months before space could be found for it, and Mr. Orwell states that he was mistaken about General Wavell, and is glad he was mistaken, sorry to have made the mistake'.

128. For Orwell's recording of its use as a verb, see below 22.1.41.

22.1.41: ------[129] is convinced, perhaps rightly, that the danger of the People's Convention[130] racket is much underestimated and that one must fight back and not ignore it. He says that thousands of simple-minded people are taken in by the appealing programme of the People's Convention and do not realise that it is a defeatist manoeuvre intended to help Hitler. He quoted a letter from the Dean of Canterbury[131] who said "I want you to understand that I am wholeheartedly for winning the war, and that I believe Winston Churchill to be the only possible leader for us till the war is over" (or words to that effect), and nevertheless supported the People's Convention. It appears that there are thousands like this.

Apropos of what ---- says, it is at any rate a fact that the People's Convention crew have raised a lot of money from somewhere. Their posters are everywhere, also a lot of new ones from the *Daily Worker*. The space has not been paid for, but even so the printing, etc., would cost a good deal. Yesterday I ripped down a number of these posters, the first time I have ever done such a thing. Cf. in the summer when I chalked up "Sack Chamberlain", etc., and in Barcelona, after the suppression of the POUM, when I chalked up "Visca POUM".[132] At any normal time it is against my instincts to write on a wall or to interfere with what anyone else has written.

The onion shortage has made everyone intensely sensitive to the smell of onions. A quarter of an onion shredded into a stew seems exceedingly strong. E[ileen] the other day knew as soon as I kissed her that I had eaten onions some 6 hours earlier.

An instance of the sort of racketeering that goes on when any article whose price is not controlled becomes scarce – the price of alarm clocks. The cheapest now obtainable are 15/ ---- these the sort of rubbishy German-made clocks which used to sell for 3/6d. The little tin French ones which used to be 5/– are now 18/6d, and all others at corresponding prices.

The *Daily Express* has used "blitz" as a verb.[133]

This morning's news – the defences of Tobruk pierced,[134] and the *Daily Worker* suppressed.[135] Only very doubtfully pleased about the latter.

129. Unidentified.

130. The People's Convention was organised in January 1941 by the Communists, ostensibly to fight for public rights, higher wages, better air-raid precautions, and friendship with the USSR, but some historians have said its true purpose was to agitate against the war effort. In July 1941, after Russia's entry into the war, it immediately called for a second front. By 1942 its active work had ceased.

131. The Very Reverend Hewlett Johnson (1874–1966), Dean of Canterbury, 1931–63, became known as 'the Red Dean' for his pro-Russian sympathies. Among the books he wrote were *The Socialist Sixth of the World, Soviet Strength,* and *Christians and Communism.*
132. See *Homage to Catalonia, CW,* VI, p. 181.
133. See n. 128 above.
134. Tobruk fell to the British on 22 January 1941. It was retaken, on 21 June 1942, by German forces under General Erwin Rommel (1891–1944), the brilliant commander of the Afrika Korps, 1941–43, and in northern France at the time of the Allied landings in 1944.
135. Suppression lasted from 22 January 1941 to 6 September 1942.

26.1.41: Allocation of space in this week's *New Statesman*:

Fall of Tobruk (with 20,000 prisoners) – 2 lines.

Suppression of the *Daily Worker* and *The Week*[136] – 108 lines.

. . . . . . All thinking people uneasy about the lull at this end of the war, feeling sure that some new devilry is being prepared. But popular optimism is probably growing again and the cessation of raids for even a few days has its dangers. Listening in the other day[137] to somebody else's telephone conversation, as one is always doing nowadays owing to the crossing of wires, I heard two women talking to the effect of "it won't be long now", etc., etc. The next morning, going into Mrs. J.'s shop, I happened to remark that the war would probably last 3 years. Mrs. J. amazed and horrified. "Oh, you don't think so! Oh, it couldn't! Why, we've properly got them on the run now. We've got Bardia, and from there we can march on into Italy, and that's the way into Germany, isn't it?" Mrs. J. is, I should say, an exceptionally sharp, level-headed woman. Nevertheless she is unaware that Africa is on the other side of the Mediterranean.

136. A Communist newsletter for private subscribers edited by Claud Cockburn (also as Frank Pitcairn; 1904–81). *The Week*, which he edited from 1933–46, was a Communist newsletter for private subscribers.
137. This conversation must have been overheard shortly after 5 January 1941, when Bardia fell, to which the unidentified Mrs. J. referred on the next day. The fall of Tobruk was not complete until 22 January, when the Italian garrison surrendered. Some 30,000 prisoners were taken (as compared to 40–45,000 at Bardia), for the loss of some 1,000 British and Allied killed and wounded. Mrs. J.'s confidence was not, therefore, quite as misplaced as later events proved. That *The New Statesman* allocated only two lines to the fall of Tobruk was partly a result of this being last-minute (and premature) news.

7.2.41: There is now more and more division of opinion – the question is implicit from the start but people have only recently become aware of it – as to whether we are fighting the Nazis or the German people. This is bound up with the question of whether England should declare her war aims, or, indeed, have any war aims. All of what one might call respectable opinion is against giving the war any meaning whatever ("Our job is to beat the Boche – that's the only war aim worth talking about"), and this is probably bound to become official policy as well. Vansittart's "hate Germany" pamphlet[138] is said to be selling like hot cakes.

No definite news from France. It is obvious that Pétain will give in about taking Laval into the Cabinet. Then there will be a fresh to-do about the passage of troops through unoccupied France, bases in Africa, etc., another "firm stand", and then more giving in. All depends on the time factor, i.e. whether the Germans can obtain a footing in Africa before the Italian armies there finally collapse. Perhaps next the guns will be turned against Spain, and we shall be told that Franco is making a "firm stand" and that that shows how right the British government were to take a conciliatory attitude towards Spain, until Franco gives in and attacks Gibraltar or allows the German armies to cross his territory. Or perhaps Laval, when in power, will for a short time resist the more extreme German demands, and then Laval will suddenly turn from a villain into a patriot who is making a "firm stand", like Pétain now. The thing that British Conservatives *will not* understand is that the forces of the right have no strength in them and exist only to be knocked down.

138. Robert Vansittart (1881–1957; Kt., 1929; Baron Vansittart of Denham, 1941), diplomat and writer, Permanent Under-Secretary of State for Foreign Affairs, 1930–38, chief diplomatic adviser to the Foreign Secretary, 1938–41, was well known before and during the early part of the war for his outspoken criticism of Germany and the Germans. The pamphlet referred to here was *Black Record: Germans Past and Present* (1941). Peter Vansittart (1920–2008), novelist and friend of Orwell's, was a distant cousin.

12.2.41: Arthur Koestler[139] is being called up this week and will be drafted into the Pioneers,[140] other sections of the forces being barred to him, as a German. What appalling stupidity, when you have a youngish gifted man who speaks I do not know how many languages and really knows something about Europe, especially the European political movements, to be unable to make any use of him except for shovelling bricks.

Appalled today by the havoc all round St. Paul's, which I had not seen before. St. Paul's, barely chipped, standing out like a rock. It struck me for the first time that it is a pity the cross on top of the dome is such an ornate one. It should be a plain cross, sticking up like the hilt of a sword.

Curiously enough, there don't seem to have been any repercussions to speak of about that old fool Ironside taking the title of "Lord Ironside of Archangel".[141] It really was an atrocious piece of impudence, a thing to protest against whatever one's opinion of the Russian regime.

139. Arthur Koestler (1905–1983), novelist and essayist born in Budapest, joined the Communist Party in 1931 (from which he withdrew in the late 1930s) and spent a year in the USSR. He worked as a reporter during the Spanish civil war, was captured and condemned to death; he escaped when included in an exchange of prisoners. He was interned in France in 1940 and imprisoned by the British as an alien. *Spanish Testament* (1937) describes his experiences in Spain, and *Scum of the Earth* (1941; his first book written in English) his later experiences. Orwell reviewed his *Darkness at Noon* in 1941, and they became close friends. See Orwell's 'Arthur Koestler,' written in 1944 and included in *Critical Essays* (1946); Arthur and Cynthia Koestler, *Stranger on the Square*, edited by Harold Harris (1984); and *Living with Koestler, Mamaine Koestler's Letters 1945–51*, edited by Celia Goodman (1985).

140. The Pioneer Corps was the equivalent of the Construction Battalions in the United States Navy. It was in part recruited from those whom the authorities deemed to be politically uncertain – though frequently they were Jewish refugees from Germany and elsewhere who had the strongest grounds for opposing the Nazis. Later some such Pioneers were transferred to more dangerous and politically sensitive units, where their special knowledge and intelligence could be put to more useful and dangerous service.

141. William Edmund Ironside, first Baron of Archangel and Ironside (1880–1959), had been commander of Allied forces sent to fight the Bolsheviks at Archangel in 1918. He was later Chief of the Imperial General Staff, 1939–40, and head of Home Defence forces, May–July 1940. He was promoted a field marshal before he retired in 1940.

1.3.41: The B.s, who only came up to London a few weeks ago and have seen nothing of the blitz, say that they find Londoners very much changed, everyone very hysterical, talking in much louder tones, etc., etc. If this is so, it is something that happens gradually and that one does not notice while in the middle of it, as with the growth of a child. The only change I have definitely noticed since the air-raids began is that people are much more ready to speak to strangers in the street. . . . The Tube stations don't now stink to any extent, the new metal bunks are quite good,[142] and the people one sees there are reasonably well found as to bedding and seem contented and normal in all ways – but this is just what disquiets me. What is one to think of people who go on living this subhuman life night after night for months, including periods of 3 week or more when no aeroplane has come near London? . . . It is appalling to see children still in all the Tube stations, taking it all for granted and having great fun riding round and round the Inner Circle. A little while back D.J.[143] was coming to London from Cheltenham, and in the train was a young woman with her two children who had been evacuated to somewhere in the West Country and whom she was now bringing back. As the train neared London an air-raid began and the woman spent the rest of the journey in tears. What had decided her to come back was the fact that at that time there had been no raid on London for a week or more, and so she had concluded that "it was all right now". What is one to think of the mentality of such people?

142. Tiers of metal bunks were provided so that people could sleep in Underground stations (used as air-raid shelters) in safety and relative comfort. For the effect of sheltering in this manner, see Henry Moore's drawings: these express more than photographs. Moore suggests sleepers 'doomed and haunted,' suffering 'an "unease" that is profoundly disturbing' (Dennis Rudder, quoted by Eric Newton in his introduction to *War Through Artists' Eyes*, 1945, p. 9. Moore is represented on pp. 62, 63, 65).

143. Denzil Jacobs, who was returning from Cheltenham where he had been conducting an audit (letter to editor, 23 May 1997). With his uncle and guardian, Victor Jacobs, a manufacturer of pianos (for whom he worked), he joined the Home Guard (then the Local Defence Volunteers) at Lord's Cricket Ground on 12 June 1940. He served in Orwell's platoon until he joined the RAF as a navigator in 1941. Mr Jacobs described the composition of the platoon to the editor on 22 August 1996. It was made up of very different men from wealthy wholesale grocers, to Victor Gollancz (who had fought as a Lieutenant at Passchendaele in 1917), to a van driver working for Selfridge's in Oxford Street. The wealthy would play poker in quiet moments. Orwell joined in on one occasion but having lost ten shillings (50p in metric currency, roughly £20 today) he stopped, finding the stakes too high. Orwell, he said, was a fine section leader and particularly good on street fighting. He also built up a large (and very dangerous) stock of petrol bombs which he stored in a disused shed. Both men visited Orwell on a number of occasions in University College Hospital. Orwell, with some of his Home Guard section (including Fredric Warburg) are illustrated in Plate 18 of *The Lost Orwell*.

3.3.41: Last night with G.[144] to see the shelter in the crypt under Greenwich church. The usual wooden and sacking bunks, dirty (no doubt also lousy when it gets warmer), ill-lighted and smelly, but not on this particular night very crowded. The crypt is simply a system of narrow passages running between vaults on which are the names of the families buried in them, the most recent being about 1800. . . . G. and the others insisted that I had not seen it at its worst, because on nights when it is crowded (about 250 people) the stench is said to be almost insupportable. I stuck to it, however, though none of the others would agree with me, that it is far worse for children to be playing about among vaults full of corpses than that they should have to put up with a certain amount of living human smell.

144. Gwen O'Shaughnessy, Eileen's sister-in-law.

4.3.41: At Wallington. Crocuses out everywhere, a few wallflowers budding, snowdrops just at their best. Couples of hares sitting about in the winter wheat and gazing at one another. Now and again in this war, at intervals of months, you get your nose above water for a few moments and notice that the earth is still going round the sun.

14.3.41: For the last few days there have been rumours everywhere, also hints in the papers, that "something is going to happen" in the Balkans, i.e. that we are going to send an expeditionary force to Greece. If so, it must presumably be the army now in Libya, or the bulk of it.[145] I had heard a month back that Metaxas[146] before he died asked us for 10 divisions and we offered him 4. It seems a terribly dangerous thing to risk an army anywhere west of the Straits. To have any worthwhile ideas about the strategy of such a campaign, one would have to know how many men Wavell disposes of and how many are needed to hold Libya, how the shipping position stands, what the communications from Bulgaria into Greece are like, how much of their mechanised stuff the Germans have managed to bring across Europe, and who effectively controls the sea between Sicily and Tripoli. It would be an appalling disaster if while our main force was bogged in Salonika the Germans managed to cross the sea from Sicily and win back all the Italians have lost. Everyone who thinks of the matter is torn both ways. To place an army in Greece is a tremendous risk and doesn't offer much *positive* gain, except that once Turkey is involved our warships can enter the Black Sea: on the other hand if we let Greece down we have demonstrated once and for all that we can't and won't help any European nation to keep its independence. The thing I fear most is half-hearted intervention and a ghastly failure, as in Norway. I am in favour of putting all our eggs in one basket and risking a big defeat, because I don't think any defeat or victory in the narrow military sense matters so much as demonstrating that we are on the side of the weak against the strong.

The trouble is that it becomes harder and harder to understand the reactions of European peoples, just as they seem incapable of understanding ours. Numbers of Germans I have spoken to have exclaimed on our appalling mistake at the beginning of the war in not bombing Berlin promptly but merely scattering fatuous leaflets.[147] Yet I believe *all* English people were delighted at this gesture (we should still have been so if we had known at the time what drivel the leaflets were), because we saw it as a demonstration that we had no quarrel with the common people of Germany. On the other hand, in his book which we have just published, Haffner[148] exclaims that it is folly on our part to let the Irish withhold vitally important bases and that we should simply take these bases without more ado. He says that the spectacle of our allowing a sham-independent country like Ireland to defy us simply makes all Europe laugh at us. There you have the European outlook, with its non-understanding of the English-speaking peoples. Actually, if we took the Irish bases by force, without a long course of propaganda beforehand, the effect on public opinion, not only in the U.S.A. but *in England*, would be disastrous.

I don't like the tone of official utterances about Abyssinia. They are mumbling about having a British "resident", as at the courts of Indian rajahs, when the Emperor is restored. The effect may be appalling if we let it be even plausibly *said* that we are swiping Abyssinia for ourselves. If the Italians are driven right out[149] we have the chance to make the most tremendous gesture, demonstrating beyond argument that we are not simply fighting for our own hand. It would echo all round the world. But will they have the guts or decency to make it? One can't feel certain. One can foresee the specious arguments that will be put forward for grabbing Abyssinia for ourselves, the rot about slavery, etc., etc.

A considerable number of German planes shot down in the last few nights, probably because they have been clear nights and favourable to the fighters, but there is much excitement about some "secret weapon" that is said to be in use. The popular rumour is that it is a net made of wire which is shot into the air and in which the aeroplane becomes entangled.[150]

145. On 12 February, Churchill, in the same telegram in which he congratulated General Wavell on the capture of Benghazi, ordered him to leave a minimum force to hold Cyrenaica, and send the largest force he could to Greece. The outcome proved Orwell's worst fears to be correct.

146. General Ioannis Metaxas (1871–1941), Prime Minister of Greece since 1935, had established a form of dictatorship despite being a strong supporter of the monarchy. He successfully organised the defence when Italy invaded in 1940, but declined the offer of British tank and artillery units, foreseeing that Churchill could offer only limited aid, which could provoke a German invasion. Following his death, on 29 January, Churchill renewed the offer, which was accepted. A British Expeditionary Force landed at Piraeus on 7 March, the Germans invaded on 6 April, and had conquered Greece by 28 April.

147. At the beginning of the war, the RAF was required to drop leaflets over Germany, instead of bombs, in a vain hope of persuading the German people of the folly of their leaders' ways. It was not an action that commended itself to the ordinary man-in-the-street at the time. Nevil Shute's popular novel *Landfall* gave a fair indication of the response to this policy: pilots flying such a mission in January 1940 'were amused and scornful of the job they had to do. "Hitler doesn't give a . . . for the stuff," was the general opinion. . . . They expressed the view that the Fuhrer welcomed the paper for sanitary reasons' (chapter V).

148. Sebastian Haffner (1907–1999) had arrived in England from Germany in 1938. He was not Jewish, but his wife was, and he was strongly opposed to Nazism. Although Secker & Warburg had published his 'brilliant analysis of Nazism, *Germany – Jekyll and Hyde*' (Fyvel, p. 99), which came out the day Paris fell, 14 June 1940, the British authorities interned him, and it took all Warburg's persuasive powers to have him released. He became a correspondent on German affairs for *The Observer* and wrote for Fyvel and Orwell the Searchlight Book *Offensive Against Germany,* to which Orwell here refers. The book, which attempted to distinguish between 'Germany' and 'Nazism,' came out in late February or early March 1941. Haffner returned to work in Germany in 1954. His real name was Raimund Pretzel; the pseudonym was adopted from the title of a Mozart symphony. See Frederic Warburg, *All Authors are Equal,* pp. 6–8.

149. The liberation of Eritrea and Abyssinia (as Ethiopia was then called) from the Italians was rapidly and efficiently carried out. The exiled emperor, Haile Selassie, was escorted back to Ethiopia on 20 January 1941 and re-entered his capital on 5 May accompanied by General Orde Wingate. The Duke of Aosta, Italian Viceroy of Ethiopia, surrendered on 19 May. Forces under General Wavell had, with this surrender, taken some 230,000 Italians prisoner in North and East Africa. Mopping up lasted until October; by then the British commander, General Alan Cunningham, had left to command the 8th Army. Despite Orwell's fears, Britain recognised an independent Ethiopia on 31 January 1942.

150. Rumours abound in wartime, and this sounds particularly fanciful. It may, however, refer to the use of radar (then called radiolocation in Britain), which the RAF announced on 17 June 1941 as having been instrumental in defeating the Luftwaffe, and possibly to IFF – the Identification Friend or Foe system – a revised form of which had been installed in all Fighter Command's planes after the fall of France. This might suggest an 'electronic net' (information from RAF Museum).

20.3.41: Fairly heavy raids last night, but only 1 plane brought down, so no doubt the rumours about a "secret weapon" are all baloney.

A lot of bombs at Greenwich, one of them while I was talking to E[ileen] over the 'phone. A sudden pause in the conversation and a tinkling sound:

I. 'What's that?'

B. 'Only the windows falling in.'[151]

The bomb had dropped in the park opposite the house, broke the cable of the barrage balloon and wounded one of the balloon barrage men and a Home Guard. Greenwich church was on fire and the people still sheltering in the crypt with the fire burning overhead and water flowing down, making no move to get out till made to do so by the wardens.

German consul in Tangier (the first time since 1914). It appears that in deference to American opinion we are going to let more food into France. Even if some kind of neutral commission is set up to supervise this it will do no good to the French. The Germans will simply allow them to keep such wheat, etc., as we send in and withhold a corresponding quantity elsewhere. Even while we make ready to allow the food ships in, there is no sign of the government extorting anything in return – e.g., expulsion of German agents from North Africa. The proper course would be to wait till France is on the verge of starvation and the Pétain government consequently rocking, and then hand over a really large supply of food in return for some substantial concession, e.g. surrender of important units of the French fleet. Any such policy totally unthinkable at present, of course. If only one could be sure whether ----- , ----- and all their kind are really traitors, or only fools.

Looking back through this diary, I see that of late I have written in it at much longer intervals and much less about public events than when I started it. The feeling of helplessness is growing in everyone. One feels that the necessary swing of opinion cannot now happen except at the price of another disaster, which we cannot afford and which therefore one dare not hope for. The worst is that the crisis now coming is going to be a crisis of hunger, which the English people have no real experience of. Quite soon it is going to be a question of whether to import arms or food. It is a mercy that the worst period will come in the summer months, but it will be devilish difficult to get the people to face hunger when, so far as they can see, there is no purpose in the war whatever, and when the rich are still carrying on just as before, as they will be, of course, unless dealt with forcibly. It doesn't matter having no war aims when it is a question of repelling invasion, because from the point of view of ordinary people keeping foreigners out of England is quite a sufficient war aim. But how can you ask them to starve their children in order to build tanks to fight in Africa, when in all that they are told at present there is nothing to make clear that fighting in Africa, or in Europe, has anything to do with the defence of England?

On a wall in South London some Communist or Blackshirt had chalked "Cheese, not Churchill". What a silly slogan. It sums up the psychological ignorance of these people who even now have not grasped that whereas some people would die for Churchill, nobody will die for cheese.

151. The laconic humour is typical of Eileen.

23.3.41: Yesterday attended a more or less compulsory Home Guard church parade, to take part in the national day of prayer. There were also contingents of the A.F.S.,[152] Air Force cadets, W.A.A.F's,[153] etc., etc. Appalled by the jingoism and self-righteousness of the whole thing. . . . I am not shocked by the Church condoning war, as many people profess to be – nearly always people who are not religious believers themselves, I notice. If you accept government you accept war, and if you accept war you must in most cases desire one side or the other to win. I can never work up any disgust over bishops blessing the colours of regiments, etc. All that kind of thing is founded on a sentimental idea that fighting is incompatible with loving your enemies. Actually you can only love your enemies if you are willing to kill them in certain circumstances. But what is disgusting about services like these is the absence of any kind of self-criticism. Apparently God is expected to help us on the ground that we are *better* than the Germans. In the set prayer composed for the occasion God is asked "to turn the hearts of our enemies, and to help us to forgive them; to give them repentance for their misdoings, and a readiness to make amends." Nothing about our enemies forgiving us. It seems to me that the Christian attitude would be that we are no better than our enemies, we are all miserable sinners, but that it so happens that it would be better if our cause prevailed and therefore that it is legitimate to pray for this. . . . . . . I suppose the idea is that it would be bad for morale to let people realise that the enemy has a case, though even that is a psychological error, in my opinion. But perhaps they aren't thinking primarily about the effect on the people taking part in the service but are simply looking for direct results from their nation-wide praying campaign, a sort of box barrage fired at the angels.

152. Auxiliary Fire Service.
153. Women's Auxiliary Air Force.

24.3.41: The reports of German heavy cruisers in the Atlantic somehow have the appearance of being a false rumour to draw British capital ships away.[154] That might conceivably be a prelude to invasion. Expectation of invasion has much faded away, because it is generally felt that Hitler could not now conquer England with any force he would be able to bring here, unless British sea and air power had been greatly worn down beforehand. I think this is probably so and that Hitler will not attempt invasion until he has had a spectacular success elsewhere, because the invasion itself would appear as a failure and would need something to offset it. But I think that an unsuccessful invasion meaning the loss of, say, 100,000 or even 500,000 men, might well do his job for him, because of the utter paralysis of industry and internal food-supply it might cause. If a few hundred thousand men could be landed and could hold out for even three weeks they would have done more damage than thousands of air-raids could do. But the effects of this would not be apparent immediately, and therefore Hitler is only likely to try it when things are going conspicuously well for him.

Evidently there is very serious shortage of Home Guard equipment, i.e. weapons On the other hand, the captures of arms in Africa are said to be so enormous that experts are being sent out to inventory them. Drawings will then be made and fresh weapons manufactured to these specifications, the captured ones being sufficient as the nucleus for a whole new range of armaments.

154. It was no false rumour. The pocket-battleship *Scheer* and the battlecruisers *Scharnhorst* and *Gneisenau* sank or captured seventeen ships about this time (long-range bombers sank 41; U-boats, 41). The battlecruisers reached Brest on 22 March but were then immobilized following British air attacks on the port.

7.4.41: Belgrade bombed yesterday, and the first official announcement this morning that there is a British army in Greece – 150,000 men, so they say. So the mystery of where the British army in Libya has gone to is at last cleared up, though this had been obvious enough when the British retreated from Benghazi. Impossible to say yet whether the treaty of friendship between Jugo-Slavia and the U.S.S.R. means anything or nothing, but it is difficult to believe that it doesn't point to a worsening of Russo-German relations. One will get another indication of the Russian attitude when and if the Emperor of Abyssinia is restored – i.e., whether the Russian government recognizes him and sends an ambassador to his court.

... Shortage of labour more and more apparent and prices of such things as textiles and furniture rising to a frightening extent ... The secondhand furniture trade, after years of depression, is booming ... It is evident that calling-up is now being consciously used as a way of silencing undesirables. The reserved age for journalists has been raised to 41 – this won't bring them in more than a few hundred men, but can be used against individuals whenever desired. It would be comic if after having been turned down for the army on health grounds ten months ago it were suddenly found that my health had improved to just the point at which I was fit to be a private in the Pioneers.[155]

... Thinking always of our army in Greece and the desperate risk it runs of being driven into the sea. One can imagine how the strategists of the Liddell Hart[156] type must be wringing their hands over this rash move. Politically it is right, however, if one looks 2–3 years ahead. The best one can say is that even in the narrow strategic sense it must offer some hope of success, or the generals concerned would have refused to undertake it. It is difficult to feel that Hitler has not mistimed his stroke by a month or thereabouts. Abyssinia at any rate is gone, and the Italian naval disaster can hardly have been intended.[157] Also if war in the Balkans lasts even three months the effects on Germany's food supply in the autumn must be serious.

155. The Pioneer Corps; see War-time Diary, 12.2.41, n. 140.
156. Captain Sir Basil Liddell Hart; see Events, 16.7.39, n. 1. His *The British Way in Warfare* was reviewed by Orwell in *The New Statesman and Nation,* 21 November 1942, *CW,* XIV, pp. 188–90. Though critical, Orwell also wrote, 'No military writer in our time has done more to enlighten public opinion.'
157. The defeat at the Battle of Cape Matapan. The British sank without loss to themselves the Italian cruisers *Zara, Fiume,* and *Pola* and the destroyers *Alfieri* and *Carducci*. The battleship *Vittorio Veneto* was crippled.

8.4.41: Have just read *The Battle of Britain*, the M.O.I.'s best-seller (there was so great a run on it that copies were unprocurable for some days). It is said to have been compiled by Francis Beeding, the writer of thrillers. I suppose it is not as bad as it might be, but seeing that it is being translated into many languages and will undoubtedly be read all over the world – it is the first official account, at any rate in English, of the first great air battle in history – it is a pity that they did not have the sense to avoid the propagandist note altogether. The pamphlet is full of "heroic", "glorious exploits", etc., and the Germans are spoken of more or less slightingly. Why couldn't they simply give a cold accurate account of the facts, which after all are favourable enough? For the sake of the bit of cheer-up that this pamphlet will accomplish in England, they throw away the chance of producing something that would be accepted all over the world as a standard authority and used to counteract German lies.

But what chiefly impresses me when reading *The Battle of Britain* and looking up the corresponding dates in this diary, is the way in which "epic" events never seem very important at the time. Actually I have a number of vivid memories of the day the Germans broke through and fired the docks (I think it must have been the 7th September), but mostly of trivial things. First of all riding down in the bus to have tea with Connolly, and two women in front of me insisting that shell-bursts in the sky were parachutes, till I had a hard job of it not to chip in and correct them. Then sheltering in a doorway in Piccadilly from falling shrapnel, just as one might shelter from a cloudburst. Then a long line of German planes filing across the sky, and some very young R.A.F. and naval officers running out of one of the hotels and passing a pair of field glasses from hand to hand. Then sitting in Connolly's top-floor flat[158] and watching the enormous fires beyond St. Paul's, and the great plume of smoke from an oil drum somewhere down the river, and Hugh Slater sitting in the window and saying, "It's just like Madrid – quite nostalgic." The only person suitably impressed was Connolly, who took us up to the roof and after gazing for some time at the fires, said "It's the end of capitalism. It's a judgment on us". I didn't feel this to be so, but was chiefly struck by the size and beauty of the flames. That night I was woken up by the explosions and actually went out into the street to see if the fires were still alight – as a matter of fact it was almost as bright as day, even in the N.W. quarter – but still didn't feel as though any important historical event were happening. Afterwards, when the attempt to conquer England by air bombardment had evidently been abandoned, I said to Fyvel, "That was Trafalgar. Now there's Austerlitz",[159] but I hadn't seen this analogy at the time.

The *News Chronicle* very defeatist again, making a great outcry about the abandonment of Benghazi, with the implication that we ought to have gone for Tripoli while the going was good instead of withdrawing troops to use in Greece.[160] And these are exactly the people who would have raised the loudest squeal if we had gone on with the conquest of the Italian empire and left the Greeks in the soup.

158. Cyril Connolly then had a furnished flat on the top floor of Athenaeum Court, Piccadilly, partly paid for by Peter Watson, sponsor of *Horizon*. For watching the raid from the roof-top on 7 September 1940, see Michael Shelden, *Friends of Promise*, p. 62. For Hugh Slater, see War-time Diary, 23.8.40, n. 91.

159. Admiral Nelson defeated the French fleet at the Battle of Trafalgar, but Napoleon nevertheless went on to victory at Austerlitz later that year, defeating the combined forces of Russia and Austria and forcing Austria out of the war. Hitler may have lost the Battle of London, Orwell was saying, but it must be expected that he would have subsequent victories elsewhere.

160. See War-time Diary, 14.3.41, nn. 145 and 146.

9.4.41: The budget has almost knocked the Balkan campaign out of the news. It is the former and not the latter that I overhear people everywhere discussing.[161]

This evening's news has the appearance of being very bad. The Greek C. in C. has issued a statement that the Serbs have retreated and uncovered his left flank. The significance of this is that people don't officially say things like that – practically a statement that the Serbs have let the Greeks down – unless they feel things to be going very badly.

The Home Guard now have tommy guns, at any rate two per company. It seems a far cry from the time when we were going to be armed with shotguns – only there weren't any shotguns – and my question as to whether we might hope for some machine guns was laughed off as an absurdity.

161. The budget raised the basic rate of income tax to ten shillings in the pound (50%).

11.4.41: Reported in yesterday's papers that Britain is arranging to lend £2,500,000 to Spain – as a reward for seizing Tangier, I suppose. This is a very bad symptom. Throughout the war it has always been when we were in exceptionally desperate straits that we have begun making concessions to the minor totalitarian powers.

12.4.41: The idea that the German troops in Libya, or some of them, got there via French ships and French African territory, is readily accepted by everyone that one suggests it to. Absolutely no mention of any such possibility in the press, however. Perhaps they are still being instructed to pipe down on criticisms of Vichy France.

The day before yesterday saw fresh-water fish (perch) for sale in a fishmonger's shop. A year ago English people, i.e. town people, wouldn't have touched such a thing.

13.4.41: No real news at all about either Greece or Libya. . . . Of the two papers I was able to procure today, the *Sunday Pictorial* was blackly defeatist and the *Sunday Express* not much less so. Yesterday's *Evening Standard* has an article by "Our Military Correspondent" . . . which was even more so.

All this suggests that the newspapers may be receiving bad news which they are not allowed to pass on. . . . God knows it is all a ghastly mess. The one thing that is perhaps encouraging is that all the military experts are convinced that our intervention in Greece is disastrous, and the military experts are always wrong.

When the campaign in the Near East is settled one way or the other, and the situation is in some way stabilised, I shall discontinue this diary. It covers the period between Hitler's spring campaigns of 1940 and 1941. Some time within the next month or two a new military and political phase must begin. The first six months of this diary covered the quasi-revolutionary period following on the disaster in France. Now we are evidently in for another period of disaster, but of a different kind, less intelligible to ordinary people and not necessarily producing any corresponding political improvement. Looking back to the early part of this diary, I see how my political predictions have been falsified, and yet, as it were, the revolutionary changes that I expected are happening, but in slow motion. I made an entry, I see, implying that private advertisements would have disappeared from the walls within a year. They haven't, of course – that disgusting Famel Cough Syrup advert, is still plastered all over the place, also He's Twice the Man on Worthington and Somebody's Mother isn't Using Persil – but they are far fewer, and the government posters far more numerous. Connolly said once that intellectuals tend to be right about the direction of events but wrong about their tempo, which is very true.[162]

Registering on Saturday, with the 38 group, I was appalled to see what a scrubby-looking lot they were. A thing that strikes one when one sees a group like this, picked out simply by date of birth, is how much more rapidly the working classes age. They don't, however, live less long, or only a few years less long, than the middle class. But they have an enormous middle age, stretching from thirty to sixty.

162. Connolly not only said but wrote this: 'For the weak point in the judgment of intellectuals is that they tend to be right about the course of events, but wrong about their tempo' (Comment, *Horizon*, September 1940, p. 83).

14.4.41: The news today is appalling. The Germans are at the Egyptian frontier and a British force in Tobruk has the appearance of being cut off, though this is denied from Cairo.[163] Opinion is divided as to whether the Germans really have an overwhelming army in Libya, or whether they have only a comparatively small force while we have practically nothing, most of the troops and fighting vehicles having been withdrawn to other fronts as soon as we had taken Benghazi. In my opinion the latter is the likelier, and also the probability is that we sent only European troops to Greece and have chiefly Indians and Negroes in Egypt. D., speaking from a knowledge of South Africa, thinks that after Benghazi was taken the army was removed not so much for use in Greece as to polish off the Abyssinian campaign, and that the motive for this was political, to give the South Africans, who are more or less hostile to us, a victory to keep them in a good temper. If we can hang on to Egypt the whole thing will have been worth while for the sake of clearing the Red Sea and opening that route to American ships. But the necessary complement to this is the French West African ports, which we could have seized a year ago almost without fighting.

Non-aggression pact between Russia and Japan, the published terms of which are vague in the extreme. But there must presumably be a secret clause by which Russia agrees to abandon China, no doubt gradually and without admitting what is happening, as in the case of Spain. Otherwise it is difficult to see what meaning the pact can have.

From Greece no real news whatever. One silly story about a British armoured-car patrol surprising a party of Germans has now been repeated three days running.

163. General Rommel's troops encircled Tobruk on 12 April. The British forces had been swept out of Cyrenaica very rapidly (their strength having been depleted to send a force to Greece). However, Tobruk held out until relieved on 4 December 1941.

15.4.41: Last night went to the pub to listen to the 9 o'clock news, and arriving there a few minutes late, asked the landlady what the news had been. "Oh, we never turn it on. Nobody listens to it, you see. And they've got the piano playing in the other bar, and they won't turn it off just for the news." This at a moment when there is a most deadly threat to the Suez canal°. Cf. during the worst moment of the Dunkirk campaign, when the barmaid would not have turned on the news unless I had asked her. . . .[164] Cf. also the time in 1936 when the Germans re-occupied the Rhineland. I was in Barnsley at the time. I went into a pub just after the news had come through and remarked at random, "The German army has crossed the Rhine". With a vague air of remembering something someone murmured "Parley-voo".[165] No more response than that . . . So also at every moment of crisis from 1931 onwards. You have all the time the sensation of kicking against an impenetrable wall of stupidity. But of course at times their stupidity has stood them in good stead. Any European nation situated as we are would have been squealing for peace long ago.

164. See War-time Diary, 28.5.40 and 24.6.40.

165. Refrain from World War I song 'Mademoiselle from Armentières,' or 'Armenteers,' as it was sung.

17.4.41: Very heavy raid last night, probably the heaviest in many months, so far as London is concerned . . . Bomb in Lord's cricket ground (schoolboys having their exercise at the nets as usual this morning, a few yards from the crater) and another in St. John's Wood churchyard. This one luckily didn't land among the graves, a thing I have been dreading will happen. . . . Passed this morning a side-street somewhere in Hampstead with one house in it reduced to a pile of rubbish by a bomb – a sight so usual that one hardly notices it. The street is cordoned off, however, digging squads at work, and a line of ambulances waiting. Underneath that huge pile of bricks there are mangled bodies, some of them perhaps alive.

The guns kept up their racket nearly all night. . . . Today I can find no one who admits to having slept last night, and E[ileen] says the same. The formula is: "I never closed my eyes for an instant". I believe this is all nonsense. Certainly it is hard to sleep in such a din, but E[ileen] and I must have slept quite half the night.

22.4.41: Have been 2 or 3 days at Wallington. Saturday night's blitz could easily be heard there – 45 miles distant.

Sowed while at Wallington 40 or 50 lb. of potatoes, which might give 200 to 600 lbs. according to the season, etc. It would be queer – I hope it won't be so, but it quite well may – if when this autumn comes those potatoes seem a more important achievement than all the articles, broadcasts, etc. I shall have done this year.

The Greek-British line seems to have swung south, hingeing on Janina, to a position not far north of Athens. If the newspaper reports are truthful, they got across the plain of Thessaly without being too much damaged. The thing that disturbs everyone and is evidently going to raise a storm in Australia, is the lack of real news. Churchill in his speech said that even the government had difficulty in getting news from Greece. The thing that most disturbs me is the repeated statement that we are inflicting enormous casualties, the Germans advance in close formation and are mown down in swathes, etc., etc.[166] Just the same as was said during the battle of France. . . . Attack on Gibraltar, or at any rate some adverse move in Spain, evidently timed to happen soon. Churchill's speeches begin to sound like Chamberlain's – evading questions, etc., etc.

British troops entered Irak° a couple of days ago. No news yet as to whether they are doing the proper thing, wiping up German agents, etc. People on all sides saying, "Mosul will be no good to Hitler even if he gets there. The British will blow up the wells long before." Will they, I wonder? Did they blow up the Rumanian wells when the opportunity existed? The most depressing thing in this war is not the disasters we are bound to suffer at this stage, but the knowledge that we are being led by weaklings. . . . It is as though your life depended on a game of chess, and you had to sit watching it, seeing the most idiotic moves being made and being powerless to prevent them.

166. Orwell's suspicion that German troops had not been 'mown down in swathes' was well founded. For details of losses, see War-time Diary, 3.5.41.

23.4.41: The Greeks appear to be packing up. Evidently there is going to be hell to pay in Australia.[167] So long as it merely leads to an inquest on the Greek campaign, and a general row in which the position of Australia in the Empire will be defined and perhaps the conduct of the war democratised somewhat, this is all to the good.

167. The anxiety felt by Australians and New Zealanders that their troops had been lost pointlessly was, perhaps, the reason for Churchill's giving, in his history of the war, the total losses as percentages: 55.8% for United Kingdom troops, 25.1 for Australians, and 19.1 for New Zealanders. (*The Second World War*, III, p. 206). The percentage lost of those in Greece at the time of the attack (which Churchill does not calculate) were 34% UK troops lost; 17.33% Australians; and 13.55% New Zealanders. See also below, 3.5.41, n. 170. A New Zealander, General Bernard Freyburg, VC, took command in Crete.

24.4.41: No definite news from Greece. All one knows is that a Greek army, or part of a Greek army, or possibly the whole Greek army, has capitulated. No indication as to how many men we have there, what sort of position they are left in, whether it will be possible to hang on, and if so, where, etc., etc. Hints thrown out in the *Daily Express* suggest that we have practically no aeroplanes there. Armistice terms drawn up by the Italians evidently aim at later using Greek prisoners as hostages, with a view to blackmailing the British into giving up Crete and other islands.

No indication of the Russian attitude. The Germans are now close to the Dardanelles and attack on Turkey evidently imminent. The Russians will then have to decide definitely whether to make a stand against Germany, put pressure on Turkey not to resist and perhaps get Iran as the price of this, or sit still and watch the whole southern shore of the Black Sea pass into German hands. In my opinion they will do the second, or less probably the third, in either case with public orgies of self-righteousness.

25.4.41: C, of my section of the Home Guard, a poulterer by trade but at present dealing in meat of all kinds, yesterday bought 20 zebras which are being sold off by the Zoo. Only for dog meat, presumably, not human consumption.[168] It seems rather a waste. . . . There are said to be still 2,000 racehorses in England, each of which will be eating 10–15 lb. of grain a day. I.e. these brutes are devouring *every day* the equivalent of the bread ration of a division of troops.

168. The London Zoo's animals were sold because of the shortage of food to feed them.

28.4.41: Churchill's speech last night very good, as a speech. But impossible to dig any information out of it. The sole solid fact I could extract was that at the time of his offensive in Libya Wavell could never concentrate more than 2 divisions, say 30,000 men. Heard the speech at the Home Guard post. The men impressed by it, in fact moved. But I think only two of the ones there were men below the £5-a-week level. Churchill's oratory is really good, in an old-fashioned way, though I don't like his delivery. What a pity that he either can't, or doesn't want, or isn't allowed ever to say anything definite!

2.5.41: A man came from ------'s[169] yesterday morning to cut out the cover for our armchair. The usual draper type, smallish, neat, with something feminine about him and nests of pins all over his person. He informed me that this was the only domestic job he was doing today. Nearly all the time he is cutting out covers for guns, which it seems have to be made in the same way as chair covers. ------'s are keeping going largely on this, he said.

169. Unidentified.

3.5.41: The number evacuated from Greece is now estimated at 41–43,000, but it is stated that we had less men there than had been supposed, probably about 55,000. Casualties supposed to be 3,000, and prisoners presumably 7 or 8 thousand, which would tally with the German figures.[170] 8000 vehicles said to have been lost, I suppose vehicles of all kinds. No mention of ships lost, though they must have lost some. Spender, one of the Australian ministers,[171] states publicly that "rifles are as useless against tanks as bows and arrows". That at any rate is a step forward.

Apparently there is what amounts to war in Irak°. At the very best this is a disaster. . . . In all probability we shan't even deal properly with the so-called army of Irak, which could no doubt be bombed to pieces in a few hours. Either some sort of agreement will be signed in which we shall give away everything and leave the stage set for the same thing to happen again; or you will hear that the Irak government is in control of the oil wells, but this doesn't matter, as they have agreed to give us all necessary facilities, etc., etc., and then presently you will hear that German experts are arriving by plane or via Turkey; or we shall stand on the defensive and do nothing until the Germans have managed to transport an army by air, when we shall fight at a disadvantage. Whenever you contemplate the British government's policy, and this has been true without a single break since 1931, you have the same feeling as when pressing on the accelerator of a car that is only firing on one cylinder, a feeling of deadly weakness. One doesn't know in advance exactly what they will do, but one does know that in no case can they possibly succeed, or possibly act before it is too late. . . . It is curious how comparatively confident one feels when it is a question of mere *fighting* and how helpless when it is a question of strategy or diplomacy. One knows in advance that the strategy of a British Conservative Government *must* fail, because the will to make it succeed is not there. Their scruples about attacking neutrals – and that is the chief strategic difference between us and Germany in the present war – are merely the sign of a subconscious desire to fail. People don't have scruples when they are fighting for a cause they believe in.

170. According to Liddell Hart, 'On March 7, . . . the first contingent of a British force of 50,000 troops landed in Greece. . . . They narrowly escaped complete disaster . . . leaving all their tanks, most of their other equipment, and 12,000 men behind in German hands' *(History of the Second World War,* 1970, p. 125). Churchill gives the 'losses' as: United Kingdom, 6,606 (presumably including Polish forces), Australian, 2,968, New Zealand, 2,266, or, 11,840 of the 53,051 in Greece at the time of the German attack. Of the survivors, 18,850 were evacuated to Crete; 7,000 went to Crete and later to Egypt; 15,361, including the wounded, went directly to Egypt; some 9,451 others, not army, were also evacuated – a total of 50,662 *(The Second World War,* III, pp. 205–06). *2194 Days of War* states that the expeditionary force lost 12,712 men, of whom 9,000 were taken prisoner; Italian losses in the six months of the campaign were 13,755 dead, 50,000 wounded, 12,368 severely frostbitten, 25,067 missing; German losses in Greece *and* Yugoslavia were 1,684 dead, 3,752 wounded, 548 missing (hardly 'mown down in swathes;' see above 22.4.41); the Greeks lost 15,700 dead and missing. The evacuation, conducted mainly by the Royal Navy, but with the help of Allied ships, was successful (*2194 Days of War*, p. 120).

171. Sir Percy Spender (1897–1985), lawyer and politician, was at this time Minister for the Army in the Australian War Cabinet. At the 1950 Commonwealth Conference he proposed a scheme for the economic development of south and south-east Asia, which came to be known as the Colombo Plan. He was a judge at the International Court of Justice, The Hague, 1958–64, and President of the Court, 1964–67.

6.5.41: The Turks have offered to mediate in Irak, probably a bad sign. Mobilisation in Iran. The American government stops shipments of war materials to the U.S.S.R., a good thing in itself but probably another bad sign.

Astonishing sights in the Tube stations when one goes through late at night. What is most striking is the cleanly, normal, domesticated air that everything now has. Especially the young married couples, the sort of homely cautious types that would probably be buying their houses from a building society, tucked up together under pink counterpanes. And the large families one sees here and there, father, mother and several children all laid out in a row like rabbits on the slab. They all seem so peacefully asleep in the bright lamplight. The children lying on their backs, with their little pink cheeks like wax dolls, and all fast asleep.

11.5.41: The most important news of the last few days, which was tucked away on a back page of the newspapers, was the Russian announcement that they could not any longer recognize the governments of Norway and Belgium. Ditto with Jugo-Slavia, according to yesterday's papers. This is the first diplomatic move since Stalin made himself premier, and amounts to an announcement that Russia will now acquiesce in any act of aggression whatever. It must have been done under German pressure, and coming together with Molotov's removal[172] must indicate a definite orientation of Russian policy on the German side, which needs Stalin's personal authority to enforce it. Before long they must make some hostile move against Turkey or Iran, or both.

Heavy air-raid last night. A bomb slightly damaged this building, the first time this has happened to any house I have been in. About 2 a.m., in the middle of the usual gunfire and distant bombs, a devastating crash, which woke us up but did not break the windows or noticeably shake the room. E[ileen] got up and went to the window, where she heard someone shouting that it was this house that had been hit. A little later we went out into the passage and found much smoke and a smell of burning rubber. Going up on the roof, saw enormous fires at most points of the compass, one over to the west, several miles away, with huge leaping flames, which must have been a warehouse full of some inflammable material. Smoke was drifting over the roof, but we finally decided that it was not this block of flats that had been hit. Going downstairs again we were told that it *was* this block, but that everyone was to stay in his flat. By this time the smoke was thick enough to make it difficult to see down the passage. Presently we heard shouts of "Yes! Yes! There's still someone in Number 111",[173] and the wardens shouting to us to get out. We slipped on some clothes, grabbed up a few things and went out, at this time imagining that the house might be seriously on fire and it might be impossible to get back. At such times one takes what one feels to be important, and I noticed afterwards that what I had taken was not my typewriter or any documents but my firearms and a haversack containing food, etc., which was always kept ready. Actually all that had happened was that the bomb had set fire to the garage and burned out the cars that were in it.

We went in to the D.s, who gave us tea, and ate a slab of chocolate we had been saving for months. Later I remarked on E[ileen]'s blackened face, and she said "What do you think your own is like?" I looked in the glass and saw that my face was quite black. It had not occurred to me till then that this would be so.

172. Vyacheslav Molotov (see Events, 28.8.39, n. 4) had been Chairman of the Council of People's Commissars (later Council of Ministers) from 1930, but was replaced in May 1941; he remained Deputy Chairman.

173. Number 111 was the Orwell's flat in Langford Court, Abbey Road, NW8. It was not a house, as Orwell describes it a line or two later, but a block of flats.

13.5.41: I have absolutely no theory about the reason for Hess's arrival.[174] It is completely mysterious. The one thing I know is that if a possibility exists of missing this propaganda opportunity, the British government will find it.

174. Rudolf Hess (1894–1987), Nazi Deputy Führer and close friend of Hitler, flew a Messerschmitt-110 to Scotland on 10 May 1941. He baled out, was captured by the Home Guard, and, giving his name as Alfred Horn, asked to see the Duke of Hamilton; he hoped, through him, to negotiate a peace settlement. Churchill, not wanting peace discussed when affairs were going so badly, had Hess's arrival kept quiet, but the Germans broke the news on 13 May and declared that Hess was insane. He was sentenced in 1946, at the Nuremberg war crimes trials, to life imprisonment and was incarcerated in Spandau prison until his death, in controversial circumstances. Allegations have been made that the man who flew to Britain and who died in Spandau was an impostor.

18.5.41: Irak, Syria, Morocco, Spain, Darlan,[175] Stalin, Raschid Ali,[176] Franco – sensation of utter helplessness.[177] If there is a wrong thing to do, it will be done, infallibly. One has come to believe in that as if it were a law of nature.

Yesterday or the day before on the newspaper placards, "Nazis using Syrian air bases", and reports in the paper that when this fact was announced in Parliament there were cries of "Shame!" Apparently there are people capable of being surprised when the armistice terms are broken and the French empire made use of by the Nazis. And yet any mere outsider like myself could see on the day France went out of the war that this would happen.

Evidently all chance of winning the war in any decent way is lost. The plan of Churchill and Co. is apparently to give everything away and then win it all back with American aeroplanes and rivers of blood. Of course they can't succeed. The whole world would swing against them, America probably included. Within two years we shall either be conquered or we shall be a Socialist republic fighting for its life, with a secret police force and half the population starving. The British ruling class condemned themselves to death when they failed to walk into Dakar, the Canaries, Tangier and Syria while the opportunity existed.

175. Admiral François Darlan (1881–1942) was Commander-in-Chief of the French Navy from 1939; Vice-Premier and Foreign Minister in the Vichy government, February 1941–April 1942. He was assassinated on 24 December 1942; see Second War-time Diary, 30.5.42.
176. Rashid Ali al-Gailani (1892–1965), pro-Nazi Prime Minister of Iraq, on 19 April 1941 refused permission for British forces to move through his country on the basis of a 1930 treaty. After a brief struggle, an armistice was agreed and a pro-British government installed. Rashid Ali fled to Iran on 30 May 1941.
177. Orwell's 'sensation of utter helplessness' seems to be expressed by his running together the names of Nazi and Communist leaders opposed to Britain and territories which might be vulnerable to attack and which might provide the means of encircling Germany and Italy. However, Britain's resources in men, ships, and planes were severely strained, making takeovers of Dakar, the Canaries, Tangier, Syria, Morocco, and Iraq impracticable. Nevertheless, the troops already in Iraq were reinforced from 24 April, Baghdad was occupied on 1 June, and a pro-British Iraqi cabinet was appointed on 5 June. On 8 June, British and Free French troops entered Syria, and French troops loyal to Vichy accepted an armistice on 11 July. Given these operations, the fighting in North Africa, a spring bombing campaign against Britain, the disasters in Greece and unfolding in Crete, to take such a plum as Dakar, with its Vichy warships, was beyond Allied hopes. An attempted assault on Dakar on 24–25 September 1940 had not been continued when it was realized how effective and determined the defences were.

21.5.41: All eyes on Crete. Everyone saying the same thing – that this will demonstrate one way or the other the possibility of invading England. This might be so if we were told the one relevant fact, i.e., how many men we have there, and how equipped. If we have only 10–20,000 men,[178] and those infantry, the Germans may overwhelm them with mere numbers, even if unable to land tanks, etc. On balance, the circumstances in Crete are much more favourable to the Germans than they could be in England. In so far as the attack on Crete is a try-out, it is much more likely to be a try-out for the attack on Gibraltar.

178. There were in all some 42,500 troops in Crete: 17,960 British; 10,300 Greek; 7,700 New Zealanders; 6,540 Australians. (Liddell Hart gives 28,600 British, Australian, and New Zealand troops and 'almost as many Greeks.') Only recently escaped from Greece, they were ill-organised and had little air protection. They had only sixty-eight anti-aircraft guns to cover an island nearly 160 miles in length. The German air force attacked early in the morning of 20 May with great effect, and troops were then dropped by parachute and flown in by plane. The officer commanding, General Freyburg, had told Churchill on 5 May that he was 'not in the least anxious about airborne attack . . . can cope adequately with the troops at my disposal' *(The Second World War,* III,

p. 246). Despite the success of the German paratroopers, Hitler was disinclined to attempt another attack by his airborne forces.

24.5.41: News from Crete ostensibly fairly good, but a note of pessimism visible everywhere under the surface. No news at all from Syria or Irak, and that is the worst indication. Darlan announces that he is not going to hand over the French fleet. More punches will be pulled, no doubt, on the strength of this palpable lie.

25.5.41: I hear privately that we have lost three cruisers in the operations off Crete.[179] Much excuse-making in the papers about our having no fighter planes there.[180] No explanation of why such landing grounds as exist in Crete had not previously been made impossible for the German troop-carriers, nor of why we failed to arm the Cretan population until it was too late.

179. Of the more than fifty warships engaged, many in attempting to protect troops from air attack, three cruisers and eight destroyers were sunk; three battleships, an aircraft carrier, seven cruisers, nine destroyers, and some smaller ships were damaged; the Navy lost 2,261 men (*The War Papers,* No. 15; Liddell Hart gives slightly different figures, p. 142).

180. It was no empty excuse. British Middle East Command lost some 200 planes in Greece. The RAF had only 21 serviceable Hurricanes to defend Libya and 14 to protect Suez and Alexandria. Hence the burden placed on the Royal Navy, and the cruel naval ditty: 'Roll out the *Nelson,* the *Rodney,* the *Hood,* / Since the whole bloody air force is no bloody good.' *Hood,* alas, was there only for the rhyme; it was sunk by *Bismark* on 24 May 1941, on the day before this Diary entry (*The War Papers,* No. 15).

31.5.41: Still not quite happy about Abyssinia. Saw to-day the news-reel of the South African troops marching into Addis Ababa. At the Emperor's palace (or whatever the building was) the Union Jack was hauled up first and only afterwards the Abyssinian flag.

1.6.41: We are clearing out of Crete. Mention of 13,000 men being evacuated.[181] No mention yet of the total number involved. The most frightful impression will be created if we remove the British troops and leave the Greeks behind, though from a cold-blooded military point of view it might be the right thing to do.

The British are in Bagdad°. It would be even better to hear they were in Damascus. One knows in advance that we shall not make sufficiently harsh terms with the Irakis, i.e. shall not make possession of the oil wells a condition of granting them an armistice. Hess has simply dropped out of the news for some days past. The evasive answers to questions about him in Parliament, denial that the Duke of Hamilton had ever received a letter from him, statement that M.O.I, had been "misinformed" when it issued this piece of news, failure apparently by the whole House to ask who had misinformed M.O.I., and why, were so disgraceful that I am tempted to look the debate up in Hansard and find out whether it was not censored in the newspaper reports.

The sirens have just sounded, after a period of 3 weeks in which there has not been a single air-raid.

181. Of the 42,500 servicemen on Crete, 16,500 were rescued, of whom some 2,000 were Greek soldiers (Liddell Hart, p. 14).

3.6.41: Now that the evacuation of Crete is completed, there is talk of 20,000 men having been removed. Obviously, therefore, they must have begun clearing out long before this was admitted in the press, and the ships sunk were probably lost in that operation. Total losses will presumably be about 10,000 men, 7 warships (3 cruisers, 4 destroyers),[182] probably some merchant ships as well, a good many AA guns, and a few tanks and aeroplanes. And all this for absolutely nothing . . . The newspapers criticise more boldly than they have ever done hitherto. One of the Australian papers says openly that it is no use trying to defend Cyprus unless we are taking action against Syria. No sign of this, apparently. Reports this morning that the Germans have already landed armoured units at Latakia.[183] Together with this, vague hints that the British "may" invade Syria. Within a few days it may be too late, if it is not six months too late already.

182. The cruisers *Calcutta, Fiji,* and *Gloucester* were sunk, as were the destroyers *Greyhound, Hereward, Imperial,* and *Juno,* with the loss of 2,011 sailors on these ships and others hit but not sunk. The Allied forces lost 16,583 men (of which 8,200 were British, 3,376 Australian, 2,996 New Zealanders). The Germans lost 3,714 killed and missing and some 2,500 wounded *(2194 Days of War,* 2 June 1941).

183. Latakia in Syria. The report was not correct. The British expected the Germans to 'pounce upon Cyprus, Syria, Suez, or Malta' after taking Crete. After the war, General K. Student, Commander-in-Chief of the German Airborne Forces, revealed that Hitler was reluctant to risk the attack on Crete. After the heavy losses suffered in taking Crete (though the Allied losses were much greater), he refused 'a further jump from Cyprus to capture the Suez Canal' (Liddell Hart, pp.144–45).

8.6.41: The British entered Syria this morning.

14.6.41: Complete mystery, about which no one has any real news, surrounds the state of affairs between Russia and Germany. Cannot yet make contact with anyone who has seen Cripps since his return.[184] One can only judge by general probabilities, and it seems to me that the two governing facts are (i) Stalin will not go to war with Germany if there is any way short of suicide of avoiding it, and (ii) it is not to Hitler's advantage to make Stalin lose face at this stage, as he is all the while using him against the working class of the world. Much likelier than any direct attack on Russia, therefore, or any agreement that is manifestly to Russia's disadvantage, is a concession masked as an alliance, perhaps covered up by an attack on Iran or Turkey. Then you will hear that there has been an "exchange of technicians", etc., etc., and that there seem to be rather a lot of German engineers at Baku. But the possibility that the whole seeming manoeuvre is simply a bluff to cover some approaching move elsewhere, possibly the invasion of England, has to be kept sight of.

184. Stafford Cripps (1889–1952), then Britain's Ambassador in Moscow, had returned to London on 11 June. On 13 June, Count Friedrich von Schulenburg, German Ambassador in Moscow, telegraphed the German Foreign Office: '... Even before the return of the English Ambassador Cripps to London, but especially since his return, there have been widespread rumours of an impending war between the U.S.S.R. and Germany in the English and foreign press.' He described these rumours as obviously absurd, but had thought it necessary in responsible circles in Moscow 'to state they are a clumsy propaganda manoeuvre' (Churchill, *The Second World War*, III, pp. 326–37). See also Events, 2.7.39, n. 7.

19.6.41: Non-aggression pact between Germany and Turkey. This is our reward for not mopping up Syria quickly. From now on the Turkish press will be turned against us, and this will have its effect on the Arab peoples.

The Derby was run yesterday, at Newmarket, and apparently attended by enormous crowds. Even the *Daily Express* was derisive about this. The *Evening Standard* has been declaring that Hitler must invade Britain within 80 days and suggesting that the manoeuvres in Eastern Europe are probably a mask for this – but this, I think, with the idea of frightening people into working harder.

The British government has ceased issuing navicerts[185] to Petsamo and stopped three Finnish ships, on the ground that Finland is now for all purposes enemy-occupied territory. This is the most definite indication yet that something is really happening between Russia and Germany.

185. Ships of neutral countries (such as Finland) could be issued with certificates by consular officials stating that the ship and its cargo should be allowed free passage without being boarded and searched.

20.6.41: We have all been in a semi-melting condition for some days past. It struck me that one minor benefit of this war is that it has broken the newspapers of their idiotic habit of making headline news out of yesterday's weather.

22.6.41: The Germans invaded the U.S.S.R. this morning.

Everyone greatly excited. It is universally assumed that this development is to our advantage. It is only so, however, if the Russians actually intend to fight back and can put up a serious resistance, if not enough to halt the Germans, at any rate enough to wear down their air force and navy. Evidently the immediate German objective is not either territory or oil, but simply to wipe out the Russian air force and thus remove a danger from their rear while they deal finally with England. Impossible to guess what kind of show the Russians can put up. The worst omen is that the Germans would probably not have attempted this unless certain that they can bring it off, and quite rapidly at that.

23.6.41: Churchill's speech in my opinion very good. It will not please the Left, but they forget that he has to speak to the whole world, e.g. to middle-western Americans, airmen and naval officers, disgruntled shopkeepers and farmers, and also the Russians themselves, as well as to the leftwing political parties. His hostile references to Communism were entirely right and simply emphasised the fact that this offer of help was sincere. One can imagine the squeal that will be raised over these by correspondents in the *New Statesman*, etc. What sort of impression do they think it would make if Stalin stood up and announced "I have always been a convinced supporter of capitalism"?

Impossible to guess what impression this move of Hitler's will make in the U.S.A. The idea that it will promptly bring into being a strong pro-Nazi party in England is a complete error. There are no doubt wealthy people who would like to see Hitler destroy the Soviet regime, but they will be a small minority. The Catholics will certainly be among them, but will probably be too acute to show their hands until Russian resistance begins to break down. Talking to people in the Home Guard, including Blimps and quite wealthy businessmen, I find everyone completely pro-Russian, though much divided in opinion about the Russian capacity to resist. Typical conversation, recorded as well as I can remember it: –

Wholesale poulterer: "Well, I hope the Russians give them a bloody good hiding."

Clothing manufacturer (Jewish): "They won't. They'll go to pieces, just like last time. You'll see."

Doctor (some kind of foreigner, perhaps refugee): "You're absolutely wrong. Everyone's underrated the strength of Russia. They'll wipe the floor with the Nazis."

Wholesale grocer: "Damn it, there's two hundred bloody millions of them".

Clothing manufacturer: "Yes, but they're not organised", etc., etc., etc.

All spoken in ignorance, but showing what people's sentiments are. Three years ago the great majority of people above £1000 a year, or even about £6 a week, would have sided with the Germans as against the Russians. By this time, however, hatred of Germany has made them forget everything else.

All really depends on whether Russia and Britain are ready really to cooperate, with no *arrière-pensée* and no attempt to shove the brunt of the fighting on to one another. No doubt a strong pro-Nazi party exists in Russia, and I dare say Stalin is at the head of it. If Russia changes sides again and Stalin plays the part of Pétain, no doubt the Communists here will follow him and go pro-Nazi again. If the Soviet régime is simply wiped out and Stalin killed or taken prisoner, many Communists would in my opinion transfer their loyalty to Hitler. At present the British Communists have issued some kind of manifesto calling for a "People's Government", etc. etc. They will change their tune as soon as the hand-out from Moscow comes. If the Russians are really resisting it is not in their interest to have a weak government in Britain, or subversive influences at work here. The Communists will no doubt be super-patriotic within ten days – the slogan will probably be "All power to Churchill" – and completely disregarded. But if the alliance between the two countries is genuine, with a certain amount of give-and-take, the internal political effects on both sides must be all for the best. The special circumstances which made the Russian military assistance a bad influence in Spain don't exist here.

Everyone is remarking in anticipation what a bore the Free Russians will be. It is forecast that they will be just like the White Russians. People have visions of Stalin in a little shop in Putney, selling samovars and doing Caucasian dances, etc., etc.

30.6.41: No real news of the Russo-German campaign. Extravagant claims by both sides, all through the week, about the number of enemy tanks, etc., destroyed. All one can really believe in is captures of towns, etc., and the German claims so far are not large. They have taken Lemberg and appear to have occupied Lithuania, and claim also to have by-passed Minsk, though the Russians claim that their advance has been stopped. At any rate there has been no break-through. Everyone already over-optimistic. "The Germans have bitten off more than they can chew. If Hitler doesn't break through in the next week he is finished", etc., etc. Few people reflect that the Germans are good soldiers and would not have undertaken this campaign without weighing the chances beforehand. More sober estimates put it thus: "If by October there is still a Russian army in being and fighting against Hitler, he is done for, probably this winter." Uncertain what to make of the Russian government's action in confiscating all private wirelesses. It is capable of several explanations.

Nothing definite about the nature of our alliance with the U.S.S.R. Last night everyone waited with much amusement to hear whether the Internationale was played after the national anthems of the other allies.[186] No such thing, of course. However, it was a long time before the Abyssinian national anthem was added to the others. They will ultimately have to play some tune to represent the U.S.S.R., but to choose it will be a delicate business.

186. It was the custom of the BBC to play the national anthems of all Allied nations each Sunday evening.

3.7.41: Stalin's broadcast speech is a direct return to the Popular Front, defence of democracy line, and in effect a complete contradiction of all that he and his followers have been saying for the past two years. It was nevertheless a magnificent fighting speech, just the right counterpart to Churchill's, and made it clear that no compromise is intended, at any rate at this moment. Passages in it seemed to imply that a big retreat is contemplated, however. Britain and the U.S.A. referred to in friendly terms and more or less as allies,[187] though apparently no formal alliance exists as yet. Ribbentrop and Co. spoken of as "cannibals", which *Pravda* has also been calling them. Apparently one reason for the queer phraseology that translated Russian speeches often have is that Russian contains so large a vocabulary of abusive words that English equivalents do not exist.

One could not have a better example of the moral and emotional shallowness of our time, than the fact that we are now all more or less proStalin.° This disgusting murderer is temporarily on our side, and so the purges, etc., are suddenly forgotten. So also with Franco, Mussolini, etc., should they ultimately come over to us. The most one can truly say for Stalin is that probably he is individually sincere, as his followers cannot be, for his endless changes of front are at any rate his own decision. It is a case of "when Father turns we all turn",[188] and Father presumably turns because the spirit moves him.

187. The direct avoidance of the word 'allies' at this stage was significant. On 12 July, an Anglo-Russian agreement was signed in Moscow by Sir Stafford Cripps and Vyacheslav Molotov. This declared that each party would support the other 'in the present war against Hitlerite Germany' and would not sign a separate armistice or peace agreement. The distinction between being an ally and being a 'co-belligerent' was pointedly made in commentaries. Thus, Vernon Bartlett, *News Chronicle* political correspondent, wrote, on 14 July (the day the agreement was announced), under the heading 'Moscow Not an Ally But a "Co-Belligerent"': 'People were asking yesterday whether the Soviet Union is now to be looked upon as an allied or an associate Power. Such questions are . . . foolish.' As to the phrase 'Hitlerite Germany,' he said it suggested that 'the Russians still hope to split public opinion inside Germany.'

188. Perhaps more commonly known as 'There were ten in the bed and the little one said, "Roll over"' (from a popular song).

6.7.41: Several of the papers are growing very restive because we are not doing more to help the U.S.S.R. I do not know whether any action, other than air-raids, is really intended, but if nothing is attempted, quite apart from the military and political consequences this may have, it is a disquieting symptom. For if we can't make a land offensive now, when the Germans have 150 divisions busy in Russia, when the devil shall we be able to? I hear no rumours whatever about movements of troops, so apparently no expedition is being prepared at any rate from England.[189] The only new development is the beginning of Beaverbrook's big drive for tanks, similar to his drive for planes last year. But this can't bear fruit for some months, and where these tanks are to be used there is no hint. I can't believe they want them for use against a German invasion. If the Germans were in a position to bring large numbers of armoured units here, i.e. if they had complete command of the sea and air, we should have lost the war already.

No talk of any formal alliance with Russia, nor indeed anything clarifying our relationship, in spite of more or less friendly utterances on either side. We can't, of course, take any big risk until it is certain that they are in firm alliance with us, i.e. will go on fighting even if they have succeeded in beating back the invasion.

No reliable news from the fronts. The Germans are across the Pruth, but it seems to be disputed whether they are across the Beresina. The destruction claimed by both sides is obviously untruthful. The Russians claim that German casualties are already 700,000, i.e. about 10 per cent of Hitler's whole army.

Examined a number of Catholic papers, also several copies of *Truth*,[190] to see what their attitude is to our quasi-alliance with the U.S.S.R. The Catholic papers have not gone pro-Nazi, and perhaps will not do so. The "line" apparently is that Russia is objectively on our side and must be supported, but that there must be no definite alliance. *Truth*, which hates Churchill, takes much the same line but is a shade more anti-Russian, perhaps. Some of the Irish Catholic papers have now gone frankly pro-Nazi, it appears. If that is so there will have been similar repercussions in the U.S.A. It will be interesting to see whether the "neutrality" that has been imposed on the Irish press, forbidding it to make any comment on any belligerent, will be enforced in the case of Russia, now that Russia is in the war.

The People's Convention have voted full support for the government and demand "vigorous prosecution of the war" – this only a fortnight after they were demanding a "people's peace". The story is going round that when the news of Hitler's invasion of Russia reached a New York café where some Communists were talking, one of them who had gone out to the lavatory returned to find that the "party line" had changed in his absence.

189. From the moment the Soviet Union entered the war on the same side as Britain there was constant agitation for the opening of a second front. Much of this was promoted by Communists and Communist sympathisers.

190. A journal of the extreme right.

28.8.41: I am now definitely an employee of the B.B.C.

The line on the eastern front, in so far as there is a line, now runs roughly Tallinn, Gomel, Smolensk, Kiev, Dnepropetrovsk, Kherson. The Germans have occupied an area which must be larger than Germany, but have not destroyed the Russian Armies. The British and Russians invaded Iran 3 days ago and the Iranians have already packed up. No rumours that one can take hold of about movements of troops in this country. They have only about a month now in which to start something on the continent, and I don't believe they intend anything of the kind. Beneath the terms of the Churchill-Roosevelt declaration one can read that American anti-Hitler feeling has cooled off as a result of the invasion of the U.S.S.R. On the other hand there is no sign that willingness to endure sacrifices etc. in this country has increased because of it. There are still popular complaints because we are not doing enough to help the U.S.S.R. but their whole volume is tiny. I think the Russian campaign can be taken as settled in the sense that Hitler cannot break through to the Caucasus and the Middle East this winter, but that he is not going to collapse and that he has inflicted more damage than he has received. There is no victory in sight at present. We are in for a long, dreary, exhausting war, with everyone growing poorer all the time. The new phase which I foresaw earlier has now started, and the quasi-revolutionary period which began with Dunkirk is finished. I therefore bring this diary to an end, as I intended to do when the new phase started.

This was the last entry in Orwell's War-time Diary until 14 March 1942.

Second War-time Diary

14 March 1942 – 15 November 1942

On 18 August 1941 Orwell was appointed a Talks Assistant in the Overseas Service of the BBC at a salary of £640 a year – perhaps about £22,000 at today's values. He attended an induction course of two 5½-day weeks, held at Bedford College, University of London in Regent's Park. The course was called, sardonically, by the poet and scholar, William Empson, 'the Liars' School'. In fact, the schedule of talks and classes (which has survived) suggested a sensible, if basic, introduction to broadcasting given the short time available. (See *CW*, XIII, pp. 3–21 and 82–92.) Orwell then joined the Eastern Overseas Service and worked broadcasting to India, Malaya and Indonesia until 24 November 1943 when he became Literary Editor of *Tribune*. Orwell first worked at 55 Portland Place, the source of his 'Room 101'. This was a committee room where Orwell suffered meetings of the Eastern Services Committee. Although in *Nineteen Eighty-Four* Room 101 is a place of physical torture, it should be borne in mind that O'Brien describes Room 101 as varying from individual to individual: 'It may be burial alive, or death by drowning, or by impalement, or fifty other deaths. There are cases where it is some quite trivial thing, not even fatal'. For Orwell it was the deadly boredom of meetings; for Winston Smith it was rats – and rats, of course had caused Orwell problems at various times, notably in the Spanish front line. Early in June 1942 the department moved to 200 Oxford Street. The late Eric Robertson, who worked there and knew Orwell, told me that it was familiarly known as not 200 but ZOO – and that, he thought, had a link with *Animal Farm*. Orwell produced and wrote an enormous number of programmes. For example, he wrote 104 or 105 newsletters in English and 115 or 116 for translation in vernacular languages. Fifty scripts of broadcasts made to India have survived. Orwell's idea of propaganda was very much slanted in the direction of literature and culture. One important series was 'Let's Act it Out' in which its participants learnt techniques which they introduced into travelling drama productions on their return to India. He also initiated what would now be called 'Open University' courses on literature, science, and psychology. For these he was able to recruit outstanding writers and scholars, such as T.S. Eliot, Herbert Reed, E.M. Forster, Joseph Needham, and C.D. Darlington. Orwell, in a typical self-denigrating tone, described his time at the BBC as 'two wasted years'. Certainly the broadcasts were heard by few people but that was not because of the quality of what he produced, and was no reflection on his laudable intentions, but because there were few radios, poor reception, many time shifts, and a multitude of languages. A full record of Orwell at the BBC will be found in *The Complete Works*, volumes XIII, XIV, and XV.

For much time covered by these diary entries, Orwell was also a very active member of the Home Guard. He was a sergeant in command of a section, one of whom was his publisher, Fredric Warburg (who had served as a Second Lieutenant at Passchendaele); see also War-time Diary, 12.2.41, n. 143. He still found time to write articles, notably his 'London Letter' for the American journal, *Partisan Review*.

This Diary exists in two versions: manuscript (without a heading) and typewritten by Orwell headed 'WAR DIARY (continued)'. The manuscript has words and passages omitted from the typescript (which notes where cuts have been made). Orwell probably intended the shorter typed version to be published jointly with Inez Holden's diary (see headnote to War-time Diary, 28 May 1940 – 28 August 1941) but the diary was not published in Orwell's lifetime. Here, passages appearing only in manuscript are printed in italics within square brackets; they follow the typed version. Titles (e.g. of journals) that would be italicized within roman setting are left in italic in the passages in italic but are underlined. If a name is given only by initials in the typescript but is spelt out in the manuscript the full name is incorporated in roman type. Only a few significant verbal differences between typed and handwritten versions are footnoted. Full details are recorded in *Complete Works*.

Footnotes are numbered from 1.

14.3.42: I reopen this diary after an interval of about 6 months, the war being once again in a new phase.

The actual date of Cripps's departure for India was not given out,[1] but presumably he has gone by this time. Ordinary public opinion here seems gloomy about his departure. A frequent comment – "They've done it to get him out of the way" (which is also one of the reasons alleged on the German wireless). This is very silly and reflects the provincialism of English people who can't grasp that India is of any importance. Better-informed people are pessimistic because the non-publication of the Government's terms to India indicates almost certainly that they are not good terms. Impossible to discover what powers Cripps has got. Those who may know will disclose nothing and one can draw hints out of them only by indirect means. Eg. I propose in my newsletters,[2] having been instructed to give Cripps a buildup, to build him up as a political extremist. This draws the warning, "Don't go too far in that direction", which raises the presumption that the higher-ups haven't much hope of full independence being granted to India.

Rumours of all descriptions flying round. Many people appear to suspect that Russia and Germany will conclude a separate peace this year. From studying the German and Russian wireless I have long come to the conclusion that the reports of Russian victories are largely phony, though, of course, the campaign has not gone according to the German plan, [*I think the Russians have merely won the kind of victory that we did in the Battle of Britain – ie., staving off defeat for the time being but deciding nothing.*] I don't believe in a separate peace unless Russia is definitely knocked out, because I don't see how either Russia or Germany can agree to relinquish the Ukraine. [*On the other hand some people think (I had this, eg. from Abrams, a Baltic Russian of strong Stalinist sympathies though probably not a C.P. member) that if the Russians could get the Germans off their soil they would make a sort of undeclared peace and thereafter only keep up a sham fight.*]

Rumours about Beaverbrook's departure:[3]

a. Cripps insisted on this as a condition of entering the Government.
b. Beaverbrook was got rid of because he is known to be in contact with Goering with a view to a compromise peace.
c. The army insisted on Beaverbrook's removal because he was sending all the aeroplanes etc. to Russia instead of to Libya and the Far East.

I have now been in the BBC about 6 months. Shall remain in it if the political changes I foresee come off, otherwise probably not. Its atmosphere is something halfway between a girls' school and a lunatic asylum, and all we are doing at present is useless, or slightly worse than useless. Our radio strategy is even more hopeless than our military strategy. Nevertheless one rapidly becomes propaganda-minded and develops a cunning one did not previously have. Eg. I am regularly alleging in my newsletters that the Japanese are plotting to attack Russia. I don't believe this to be so, but the calculation is:

a. If the Japanese do attack Russia, we can then say "I told you so".
b. If the Russians attack first, we can, having built up the picture of a Japanese plot beforehand, pretend that it was the Japanese who started it.
c. If no war breaks out at all, we can claim that it is because the Japanese are too frightened of Russia.

All propaganda is lies, even when one is telling the truth. I don't think this matters so long as one knows what one is doing, and why.

[*Current story:*

An A.T.[4] *stops a Home Guard: "Excuse me, but your front door is open".*

H.G. "Oh. And did you by any chance see a tall strong sentry guarding the door?"

A.T. "No, all I saw was an old Home Guard lying on a pair of sandbags."

On 11.3.42 I started the rumour that beer is to be rationed, and told it to 3 different people. I shall be interested to see at what date this rumour comes back to me.] *30.5.42:* Never came back. So this casts no light on the way in which rumours come into being.

Talked for a little while the other day to William Hickey,[5] just back from the USA. He says morale there is appalling. Production is not getting under way and anti-British feeling of all kinds is rampant, also anti-Russian feeling, stimulated by the Catholics.

1. Sir Stafford Cripps (see Events, 2.7.39, n. 7 and 14.6.41, n.184) flew to India on 22 March, to arrange a compromise settlement with the Indian Congress Party, the party of Indian independence. He hoped to obtain Indian cooperation during the war and agreement to gradual transition to independence when it was over. Nehru and the Congress Party would accept nothing less than complete independence and the talks broke down on 10 April.
2. One of Orwell's duties for the BBC Service to India was writing newsletters. In all, he wrote in English 55 or 56 for India,30 for Malaya, and 19 for Indonesia. He also wrote 115 or 116 for translation into Gujarati, Marathi, Bengali, Tamil and Hindustani. For these references, see Newsletter in Marathi, No. 3, 19 March 1942, *CW*, XIII, pp. 234–5 and his Weekly News Review in English, No. 15, 21 March 1942, *CW*, XIII, pp. 236–9.
3. Lord Beaverbrook (see War-time Diary, 29.5.40, n. 9) had, under Churchill, been Minister of Aircraft Production, 1940–41, and Minister of Supply, 1941–42. His contribution was controversial but his boundless energy inspired confidence and the supply of planes increased.
4. A member of the (women's) Auxiliary Territorial Service, later WRAC – Women's Royal Army Corps
5. 'William Hickey' wrote a social-diary column in the *Daily Express* for more than fifty years; it was edited by various journalists. At this time, its originator, Tom Driberg (1905–1976), a left-wing politician who later became a Labour M.P., was its editor. Orwell added a handwritten footnote to the typescript identifying 'William Hickey' as Tom Driberg. Despite serving as Chairman of the Labour Party (1957–58), Driberg earlier worked for the KGB. His code name was 'Lepage' (see Christopher Andrew and Vasili Mitrokhin, *The Mitrokhin Archive*, 1999, pp. 522–6). Orwell suspected him of treachery and included him in his 'List of Crypto-Communists and Fellow Travellers' (see *CW*, XX, pp. 242 and 246).

15.3.42: Short air raid alert about 11.30 this morning. No bombs or guns. The first time in 10 months that I had heard this sound. Inwardly rather frightened, and everyone else evidently the same, though studiously taking no notice and indeed not referring to the fact of there being a raid on until the All Clear had sounded.

22.3.42: Empson tells me that there is a strict ban by the Foreign Office on any suggestion that Japan is going to attack the USSR. So this subject is being studiously avoided in the Far Eastern broadcasts while being pushed all the time in the India broadcasts. They haven't yet got onto the fact that we are saying this, we haven't been warned and don't officially know about the ban, and are making the best of our opportunity while it lasts. The same chaos everywhere on the propaganda front. [*Eg. Horizon was nearly stopped from getting its extra paper to print copies for export on the strength of my article on Kipling (all well at the last moment because Harold Nicolson*[6] *and Duff Cooper*[7] *intervened), at the same time as the BBC asked me to write a "feature" based on the article.*]

German propaganda is inconsistent in quite a different way – ie, deliberately so, with an utter unscrupulousness in offering everything to everybody, freedom to India and a colonial empire to Spain, emancipation to the Kaffirs and stricter race laws to the Boers, etc., etc. All quite sound from a propaganda point of view in my opinion, seeing how politically ignorant the majority of people are, how uninterested in anything outside their immediate affairs, and how little impressed by inconsistency. A few weeks back the NBBS[8] was actually attacking the Workers' Challenge [*Station*],[9] warning people not to listen to it as it was "financed from Moscow."

The Communists in Mexico are again chasing Victor Serge[10] and other Trotskyist refugees who got there from France, urging their expulsion, etc., etc. Just the same tactics as in Spain. Horribly depressed to see these ancient intrigues coming up again, not so much because they are morally disgusting as from this reflection: for 20 years the Comintern has used these methods and the Comintern has always and everywhere been defeated by the Fascists; therefore we, being tied to them in a species of alliance, shall be defeated with them.

Suspicion that Russia intends making a separate peace now seems widespread. Of the two, it would be easier for Russia to surrender the Ukraine, both on geographical and psychological grounds, but they obviously couldn't give up the Caucasus oilfields without a fight. One possible development is a secret agreement between Hitler and Stalin, Hitler to keep what Russian territory he has overrun, or parts of it, but thereafter to make no further attacks but to direct his offensive southward towards the oilfields of Irak and Iran, Russia and Germany keeping up a sham war meanwhile. It appears to me that a separate peace is distinctly likelier if we do make a continental invasion this year, because if we succeed in embarrassing the Germans and drawing off a large part of their armies, Russia is immediately in a much better position both to win back the occupied territories, and to bargain. I nevertheless think we ought to invade Europe if the shipping will run to it. The one thing that might stop this kind of filthy doublecrossing is a firm alliance between ourselves and the USSR, with war aims declared in detail. Impossible while this government rules us, and probably also while Stalin remains in power:

[*at least only possible if we could get a different kind of government and then find some way of speaking over Stalin's head to the Russian people*].

The same feeling as one had during the Battle of France – that there is no news. This arises principally from endless newspaper-reading. [*In connection with my newsletters I now read four or five morning newspapers every day and several editions of the evening ones, besides the daily monitoring report.*] The amount of new matter in each piece of print one reads is so small that one gets a general impression that nothing is happening. Besides, when things are going badly one can foresee everything. The only event that has surprised me for weeks past was Cripps's mission to India.

6. For Harold Nicolson (1886–1968; Kt. 1953) critic, biographer, and M.P., see Events, 30.8.39, n. 1. Among his biographies were those of Tennyson, Byron, Swinburne, Lord Curzon, King George V, and Sainte-Beuve.
7. For Alfred Duff Cooper (1890–1954; Viscount Norwich, 1952), diplomat, biographer of Talleyrand and Earl Haig; see War-time Diary, 29.5.40 n. 4. He had served briefly as War Cabinet representative in Singapore, and responsibility was partly, if hardly fairly, laid at his door for its fall. He was British representative with the French Committee of National Liberation in North Africa (headed by General de Gaulle), and for three years from September 1944 was British Ambassador in Paris. His autobiography is *Old Men Forget* (1953).
8. New British Broadcasting Station broadcast propaganda in English from Germany. For Orwell's description of its policy, see his 'London Letter,' 1 January 1942, *CW*, XIII, pp. 110–111. W.J. West devotes a chapter of his *Truth Betrayed* (1987) to the New British Broadcasting Station. He also discusses two other German stations which broadcast to Britain, the Workers Challenge Station and the Christian Peace Movement [station]; he prints three of their broadcasts in an Appendix.
9. This was another station broadcasting propaganda in English from Germany.
10. Victor Serge (Kilbat'chiche; 1890–1947), author and journalist, born in Brussels of exiled Russian intellectuals, was French by adoption. He was associated with the anarchist movement in Paris. After the Russian Revolution, he transferred his activities to Moscow, Leningrad, and Berlin (where he ran a newspaper, the *Communist International*). His close association with Trotsky led to his deportation to Siberia in 1933. After his release, he was Paris correspondent for the POUM during the Spanish civil war. In 1941 he settled in Mexico, where he died, impoverished. Among his many books are *From Lenin to Stalin* (1937; translated from French); *Vie et mort de Trotsky* (Paris, 1951), and *Memoires d'un révolutionnaire 1901–1941* (Paris, 1951; English translation, *Memoirs of a Revolutionary*, 1963). He wrote an introduction to *Revolution et contre-revolution en Espagne* by Joaquin Maurin (1896–1973) co-founder of the POUM (1937).

27.3.42: News of the terms Cripps took to India supposed to be bursting tomorrow. Meanwhile only rumours, all plausible but completely incompatible with one another. The best-supported – that India is to be offered a treaty similar to the Egyptian one. K.S.S.[11] who is our fairly embittered enemy, considers this would be accepted if Indians were given the

Ministries of Defence, Finance and Internal Affairs. All the Indians here, after a week or two of gloom, much more optimistic, seeming to have smelt out somehow (perhaps by studying long faces in the India Office) that the terms are not so bad after all.

[*Terrific debate in the House over the affaire Daily Mirror.*[12] *A. Bevan*[13] *reading numerous extracts from Morrison's*[14] *own articles in the D.M., written since war started, to the amusement of Conservatives who are anti-D.M. but can never resist the spectacle of two Socialists slamming one another. Cassandra*[15] *announces he is resigning to join the army. Prophecy he will be back in journalism within 3 months. But where shall we all be within 3 months any way?*]

Government candidate defeated (very small majority) in the Grantham by-election. The first time since the war started that this has happened, I think.

Surprise call-out of our Company of Home Guard a week or two back. It took 4½ hours to assemble the Company and dish out ammunition, and would have taken them another hour to get them into their battle positions. This mainly due to the bottleneck caused by refusing to distribute ammunition but making each man come to HQ to be issued with it there. Sent a memo on this to Dr Tom Jones,[16] who has forwarded it direct to Sir Jas. Grigg.[17] In my own unit I could not get such a memo even as far as the Company Commander – or at least, could not get it attended to.

Crocuses now full out. One seems to catch glimpses of them dimly through a haze of war news.

[*Abusive letter from H. G. Wells, who addresses me as "You shit", among other things.*[18]

The Vatican is exchanging diplomatic representatives with Tokio. The Vatican now has diplomatic relations with all the Axis powers and – I think – with none of the Allies. A bad sign and yet in a sense a good one, in that this last step means that they have now definitely decided that the Axis and not we stand for the more reactionary policy.]

11. Dr. Krishna S. Shelvankar (1906–1996), Indian writer and journalist. He was in England during the war as a correspondent for Indian newspapers. His book, *The Problem of India* (Penguin Special, 1940), was banned in India. Orwell's superior at the BBC, Z. A. Bokhari, wrote to the Eastern Service Director to say he was strongly opposed to Shelvankar being allowed to broadcast: 'Call me a die-hard if you like, but in my opinion the time has not come for us to make such advances towards the truculent damsel – "Miss Nationalism"' (*CW*, XIII, p. 242). Despite Orwell's reference to Shelvankar as 'our fairly embittered enemy', he did broadcast to India under Orwell's aegis. When Pakistan became independent, Bokhari was appointed Director-General of Pakistan Radio.
12. The *Daily Mirror*, a popular leftist daily newspaper, had been called to order by Churchill for taking what he called a defeatist line, that is, critical of the government's handling of the war. After the debate in the House of Commons the affair fizzled out.

13. Aneurin (Nye) Bevan (see Events, 28.8.39, n. 11), Labour M.P., had been, for most of 1939, in conflict with his party and he was expelled for supporting Sir Stafford's Cripps's Popular Front campaign though his integrity was never in doubt. He edited *Tribune*, 1942–45 (a remarkable achievement for someone who could barely read when he left school at the age of thirteen), and gave Orwell support even when he disagreed with him. His great achievement was the creation of the National Health Service out of a variety of earlier proposals. His *In Place of Fear* (1952) sets out his philosophy.
14. Herbert Morrison (1888–1965; Baron Morrison of Lambeth), Labour MP from 1923, Leader of the London County Council, 1933–40; Home Secretary and Minister of Home Security, 1940–45. He was Leader of the House of Commons and Deputy Prime Minister, in Clement Attlee's two administrations, 1945–51. In the debate to which Orwell refers, his subversive writings from World War I, when he was a conscientious objector, were also quoted (see Hugh Cudlipp, *Publish and be Damned*, pp. 195–6).
15. This was the pseudonym of William Connor (1900–1967; Kt., 1966), a well-known radical journalist who wrote this personal column in the *Daily Mirror*. His *English at War* (April 1941) was the most popular of the Searchlight Books edited by T. R. Fyvel and Orwell; it was reprinted three times.
16. Dr Tom Jones (1870–1955; CH), Cabinet Secretary to Lloyd George. In 1939 he was instrumental in the establishment of CEMA – the Council for the Encouragement of Music and the Arts – which later became the Arts Council of Great Britain.
17. Sir James Grigg (1890–1964; KCB), Permanent Under-Secretary for War, 1939–42, and Secretary of State for War, 1942–45. He had served as Finance Member on the Viceroy of India's Council and when Churchill set up the India Committee on 25 February 1942 he was selected to advise on Indian affairs. Churchill wanted him to accept a peerage but he declined. His wife, Lady Grigg, who was involved in the radio series, 'Women Generally Speaking', for the BBC's Eastern Service, was a thorn in Orwell's flesh.
18. This stemmed initially from Orwell's article 'Wells, Hitler and the World State,' *Horizon*, August 1941 (*CW*, XII, pp. 536–41) and was further stimulated by his broadcast talk 'The Re-discovery of Europe,' about which Wells wrote to *The Listener*. Inez Holden was present at a 'God-awful row' between Wells and Orwell arising from the *Horizon* article. Orwell thought Wells's belief that the Germans might be defeated quite soon was a disservice to the general public; Wells accused Orwell of being defeatist, though he withdrew that. This outburst passed over reasonably amicably, but was revived when Orwell's broadcast was printed in *The Listener*, leading to the abusive letter mentioned here. Holden wrote to Ian Angus, 21 May 1967, that Orwell very much regretted the *Horizon* article and was sorry he had upset Wells, whom he had always greatly admired. See also Crick, pp. 427–31.

1.4.42: Greatly depressed by the apparent failure of the Cripps mission. Most of the Indians seem down in the mouth about it too. Even the ones who hate England want a solution, I think. [*I believe, however, that in spite of the "take it or leave it" with which our government started off, the terms will actually be modified, perhaps in response to pressure at this end.*] Some think the

Russians are behind the Cripps plan and that this accounts for Cripps's confidence in putting forward something so apparently uninviting. Since they are not in the war against Japan the Russians cannot have any official attitude about the Indian affair, but they may serve out a directive to their followers, from whom it will get round to other pro-Russians. But then not many Indians are reliably pro-Russian. No sign yet from the English Communist party, whose behaviour might give a clue to the Russian attitude. It is on this kind of guesswork that we have to frame our propaganda, no clear or useful directive ever being handed out from above.

Connolly wanted yesterday to quote a passage from *Homage to Catalonia* in his broadcast. I opened the book and came on these sentences:

"One of the most horrible features of war is that all the war-propaganda, all the screaming and lies and hatred, comes invariably from people who are not fighting. . . . It is the same in all wars; the soldiers do the fighting, the journalists do the shouting, and no true patriot ever gets near a front-line trench, except on the briefest of propaganda tours. Sometimes it is a comfort to me to think that the aeroplane is altering the conditions of war. Perhaps when the next great war comes we may see that sight unprecedented in all history, a jingo with a bullet-hole in him."[19]

Here I am in the BBC, less than 5 years after writing that. I suppose sooner or later we all write our own epitaphs.

19. *Homage to Catalonia, CW,* VI, Appendix I, pp. 208 and 209.

3.4.42: Cripps's decision to stay an extra week in India is taken as a good omen. Otherwise not much to be hopeful about. Gandhi is deliberately making trouble, [*sending telegrams of condolence to Bose's* [20] *family on the report of his death, then telegrams of congratulation when it turned out that the report was untrue. Also urging Indians not to adopt the scorched earth policy if India is invaded*]. Impossible to be quite sure what his game is. Those who are anti-Gandhi allege that he has the worst kind of (Indian) capitalist interests behind him, and it is a fact that he usually seems to be staying at the mansion of some kind of millionaire [*or other. This is not necessarily incompatible with his alleged saintliness. His pacifism may be genuine, however. In the bad period of 1940 he also urged non-resistance in England, should England be invaded*]. I do not know whether Gandhi or Buchman[21] is the nearest equivalent to Rasputin in our time.

Anand[22] says the morale among the exile Indians here is very low. They are still inclined to think that Japan has no evil designs on India and are all talking of a separate peace with Japan. So much for their declarations of loyalty towards Russia and China. I said to A[nand] that the basic fact about nearly all Indian intellectuals is that they don't expect independence, can't imagine it and at heart don't want it. They want to be permanently in opposition, suffering a painless martyrdom, and are foolish enough to imagine that they could play the same schoolboy games with Japan or Germany as they can with Britain. Somewhat to my surprise he agreed. He says that "opposition mentality" is general among them, especially among the Communists, and that Krishna Menon[23] is "longing for the moment when negotiations will break down". At the same moment as they are coolly talking of betraying China by making a separate peace, they are shouting that the Chinese troops in Burma are not getting proper air support. I remarked that this was childish. A: "You cannot overestimate their childishness, George. It is fathomless". [*The question is how far the Indians here reflect the viewpoint of the intellectuals in India. They are further from the danger and have probably, like the rest of us, been infected by the peaceful atmosphere of the last 10 months, but on the other hand nearly all who remain here long become tinged with a western Socialist outlook, so that the Indian intellectuals proper are probably far worse. A. himself has not got these vices. He is genuinely anti-Fascist, and has done violence to his feelings, and probably to his reputation, by backing Britain up because he recognizes that Britain is objectively on the anti-Fascist side.*]

20. Subhas Chandra Bose (1897–1945) was an Indian nationalist leader and left-wing member of the Indian National Congress. Fiercely anti-British, he organised an Indian National Army to support the Japanese. This he led, unsuccessfully, against the British. He believed that when the INA faced Indian troops led by the British, the latter would not fight but be converted. 'Instead, the revolutionary had reverted to his comfortable mercenary status. INA soldiers took to looting from local tribes' (Mihir Bose, *The Lost Hero* [1982], p. 236). His followers long believed him to be still alive (despite two Indian government inquiries), but it seems certain he died following a plane crash on 19 August 1945 (*The Lost Hero*, pp. 251–52). Documents released by the War Office in November 1993 show that a substantial number of Indian prisoners of war defected to the Italians, the first 3,000 arriving in Italy in August 1942. A British Intelligence report stated, 'We have by our policy towards India, bred up a new class of officer who may be loyal to India, and perhaps to Congress, but is not necessarily loyal to us' (*Daily Telegraph*, 5 December 1993).
21. Frank Nathan Daniel Buchman (1878–1961), evangelist and propagandist, founded, in 1921, the Moral Re-Armament movement, also known, from its place of foundation, as the Oxford Group Movement, and sometimes as Buchmanism.
22. Mulk Raj Anand (1905–2004), novelist, story-writer, essayist, and critic. He was born in India, fought in the Spanish Civil War (though he did not meet Orwell there), and taught literature and philosophy to London County Council adult education classes. He wrote scripts for the BBC, 1939–45. After the war he returned to India and lectured at various universities and was made Professor of Fine Arts, University of Punjab, in 1963. Orwell reviewed his *The Sword*

and the Sickle in *Horizon*, July 1942 (*CW*, XIII, pp. 379–81). In a letter of 29 September 1983 Anand wrote this of Orwell: 'In his life his voice was restrained. He talked in furtive whispers. Often he dismissed the ugly realities with cynical good humour. And I seldom saw him show anger in his face, though the two deep lines on his cheeks and the furrowed brow signified permanent despair. He smiled at tea time and he was a good companion in a pub. But he delivered his shafts in a very mellow voice, something peculiarly English deriving from the Cockney sense of humour'. See Abha Sharma Rodrigues, 'George Orwell, the BBC, and India: A Critical Study' (Edinburgh University, PhD, 1994).

23. V. K. Krishna Menon (1897–1974), Indian statesman, lawyer, author, and journalist, was then living in England. He was active in British left-wing politics and was spokesman of the Indian Congress Party in England in the struggle for independence. In 1947, when India had become independent, he was High Commissioner for India and he represented India at the United Nations, 1952–61. On 31 January 1943, he was one of six speakers at the 'India Demonstration' at the London Coliseum (*Tribune*, 29 January 1943, p. 20).

6.4.42: [*Yesterday had a look at the bit of the by-pass road which is being built between Uxbridge and Denham. Amazed at the enormous scale of the undertaking. West of Uxbridge is the valley of the Colne, and over this the road runs on a viaduct of brick and concrete pillars, the viaduct being I suppose ¼ mile long. After that it runs on a raised embankment. Each of these pillars is 20 feet high or thereabouts, about 15 by 10 feet thick, and there are two of them every fifteen yards or so. I should say each pillar would use 40,000 bricks, exclusive of foundations, and exclusive of the concrete running above, which must use up tons of steel and concrete for every yard of road. Stupendous quantities of steel (for reinforcing) lying about, also huge slabs of granite. Building this viaduct alone must be a job comparable, in the amount of labour it uses up, to building a good-sized warship. And the by-pass is very unlikely to be of any use till after the war, even if finished by that time. Meanwhile there is a labour shortage everywhere. Apparently the people who sell bricks are all-powerful. (Cf. the useless surface-shelters, which even when they were being put up were pronounced to be useless by everyone who knew anything about building, and the unnecessary repairs to uninhabited private houses which are going on all over London). Evidently when a scandal passes a certain magnitude it becomes invisible.*]

Saw in Denham someone driving a dog-cart, in quite good trim.

10.4.42: British naval losses in the last 3 or 4 days: 2 cruisers and an aircraft carrier sunk, 1 destroyer wrecked.[24] Axis losses: 1 cruiser sunk.

From Nehru's speech today: "Who dies if India live?" How impressed the pinks will be – and how they would snigger at "Who dies if England live?"[25]

24. On 5 April, the heavy cruisers *Dorsetshire* and *Cornwall*, the destroyer *Tenedos*, and the armed merchant-ship *Hector* were sunk by Japanese aircraft operating from carriers in the Indian Ocean. On 9 April (the day 64,000 Filipinos and 12,000 Americans surrendered at Bataan) the aircraft carrier *Hermes* and the destroyer *Vampire* were among a further group of ships sunk by the Japanese in the Indian Ocean, including 135,000 tons of merchant and troop ships.
25. 'Who dies if England live?' comes from Kipling's 'For All We Have and Are' (1914) and was quoted by Orwell in 'Notes on the Way', 30 March and 6 April 1940 (*CW*, XII, p. 126); it also has the line, 'The Hun is at the gate! Although 'Hun' had been used derogatively for a German in the nineteenth century, its twentieth-century usage was introduced by Kaiser Wilhelm II in a widely reported speech when addressing his troops on 27 July 1900 before their departure for China.

11.4.42: It[26] has flopped after all. I don't regard this as final, however.

Listened-in to Cripps's speech coming from Delhi, which we were re-broadcasting for England etc. These transmissions which we occasionally listen-in to from Delhi are our only clue as to how our own broadcasts sound in India. Always very bad quality and a great deal of background noise which it is impossible to take out in recordings. [*The speech good in the earlier part and plain-speaking enough to cause, I should think, a lot of offence. In the later part it rather moved off into the breezy uplands vein.*] It is a curious fact that in the more exalted passages in his speeches Cripps seems to have caught certain inflexions of voice from Churchill. This may point to the fact – which would explain his having undertaken this mission when only having such bad terms to offer – that he is at present much under Churchill's personal influence.

26. Sir Stafford Cripps's mission to India.

18.4.42: No question that Cripps's speeches etc. have caused a lot of offence, ie. in India. Outside India I doubt whether many people blame the British government for the breakdown. One trouble at the moment is the tactless utterances of Americans who for years have been blahing about "Indian freedom" and British imperialism, and have suddenly had their eyes opened to the fact that the Indian intelligentsia don't want independence, ie. responsibility. Nehru is making provocative speeches to the effect that all the English are the same, of whatever political party, and also trying to make trouble between Britain and the USA by alleging that the USA has done all the real fighting. At the same time he reiterates at intervals that he is not pro-Japanese and Congress will defend India to the last. The BBC thereupon picks out these passages from his speeches and broadcasts them without mentioning the anti-British passages, whereat Nehru complains (quite justly) that he has been misrepresented.

[A recent directive tells us that when one of his speeches contains both anti-British and anti-Japanese passages, we had better ignore it altogether. What a mess it all is. But I think on balance the Cripps mission has done good, because without discrediting Cripps in this country (as it so easily might have done) it has clarified the issue. Whatever is said officially, the inference the whole world will draw is that (a) the British ruling class doesn't intend to abdicate and (b) India doesn't want independence and therefore won't get it, whatever the outcome of the war.

Talking to Wintringham[27] about the possible Russian attitude towards the Cripps negotiations (of course, not being in the war against Japan, they can't have an official attitude) I said it might make things easier if as many as possible of the military instructors etc. who will later have to be sent to India were Russians. One possible outcome is that India will ultimately be taken over by the USSR, and though I have never believed that the Russians would behave better in India than ourselves, they might behave differently, owing to the different economic set-up. Wintringham said that even in Spain some of the Russian delegates tended to treat the Spaniards as "natives", and would no doubt do likewise in India. It's very hard not to, seeing that in practice the majority of Indians are inferior to Europeans and one can't help feeling this and, after a little while, acting accordingly.]

American opinion will soon swing back and begin putting all the blame for the Indian situation on the British, as before. It is clear from what American papers one can get hold of that anti-British feeling is in full cry and that all the Isolationists, after a momentary retirement, have re-emerged with the same slogans as before. [*Father Coughlin's paper,[28] however, has just been excluded from the mails.*] What always horrifies me about American anti-British sentiment is its appalling ignorance. Ditto presumably with anti-American feeling in England.

27. Thomas Henry (Tom) Wintringham, writer and soldier, had commanded the British Battalion of the International Brigade in the Spanish civil war. He later founded Osterley Park Training Centre for the Home Guard. His books include *New Ways of War, Politics of Victory,* and *People's War.* See See War-time Diary, 23. 8. 40, n. 91 and David Fernbach, 'Tom Wintringham and Socialist Defense Strategy' *History Workshop,* 14 (1982), 63–91.
28. Father Charles E. Coughlin (1891–1979), born and educated in Canada, became a Roman Catholic priest and achieved prominence through use of the radio in the United States in the 1930s. As early as 1934, when he founded the National Union for Social Justice, he argued that the United States was being manipulated by Britain into involvement in a new European war; 'I raise my voice,' he said, 'to keep America out of war.' Orwell refers to his magazine, *Social Justice,* in which he expressed near-Fascist views. Its circulation through the mail was forbidden in the United States because it contravened the Espionage Act. It ceased publication in 1942, the year Coughlin was silenced by his ecclesiastical superiors.

19.4.42: Tokio bombed, or supposed to have been bombed, yesterday.[29] Hitherto this comes only from Japanese and German sources. Nowadays one takes it so much for granted that everyone is lying that a report of this kind is never believed until confirmed by both sides. Even an admission by the enemy that his capital had been bombed might for some reason or other be a lie.

[E[ileen] says that Anand remarked to her yesterday, as though it were a matter of course, that Britain would make a separate peace this year, and seemed surprised when she demurred. Of course Indians have to say this, and have been saying it ever since 1940, because it furnishes them if necessary with an excuse for being anti-war, and also because if they could allow themselves to think any good of Britain whatever their mental framework would be destroyed. Fyvel told me how in 1940, at the time when Chamberlain was still in the government, he was at a meeting at which Pritt and various Indians were present. The Indians were remarking in their pseudo-Marxist way "Of course the Churchill-Chamberlain government is about to make a compromise peace", whereat Pritt told them that Churchill would never make peace and that the only difference (then) existing in Britain was the difference between Churchill and Chamberlain.]

More and more talk about an invasion of Europe – so much so as to make one think something of the kind must be afoot, otherwise the newspapers would not risk causing disappointment by talking so much about it. Amazed by the unrealism of much of this talk. Nearly everyone seems still to think that gratitude is a factor in power politics. Two assumptions which are habitually made throughout the Left press are a. that opening up a second front is the way to stop Russia making a separate peace, and b. that the more fighting we do the more say we shall have in the final peace settlement. Few people seem to reflect that if an invasion of Europe succeeded to the point of drawing the German armies away from Russia, Stalin would have no strong motive for going on fighting *[and that a sell-out of this kind would be quite in line with the Russo-German pact and the agreement which the USSR has evidently entered into with Japan]*. As to the other assumption, many people talk as though the power to decide policy when a war has been won were a sort of reward for having fought well in it. Of course the people actually able to dominate affairs are those who have the most military power, cf. America at the end of the last war.

Meanwhile the two steps which could right the situation, a. a clear agreement with the USSR and a joint (and fairly detailed) declaration of war aims, and b. an invasion of Spain, are politically quite impossible under the present government.

29. On 18 April 1942, sixteen B-25 bombers, led by Colonel James H. Doolittle, flew from the carrier *Hornet* and bombed Tokyo. The effect was psychological

rather than military. Because the planes had insufficient fuel to make the return flight, they flew on to China. Bad weather forced several crash-landings; one plane landed near Vladivostok and the crew was interned; two landed in Japanese-held territory and some airmen were executed on 15 October 1942. Of the 80 crew members, 71 survived.

25.4.42: U.S. airmen making a forced landing on Russian soil after bombing Tokio have been interned. According to the Japanese wireless the Russians are expediting the movement of Japanese agents across Russia from Sweden (and hence from Germany) to Japan. [*If true, this is a new development, this traffic having been stopped at the time when Germany attacked the USSR.*]

The mystery of Subhas Chandra Bose's whereabouts remains impenetrable. [*The leading facts are: –*

i. *At the time of his disappearance, the British government declared that he had gone to Berlin.*
ii. *A voice, identified as his, broadcasts on the Free India radio (Germany).*
iii. *The Italian radio has claimed at least once that Bose is in Japanese territory.*
iv. *Indians here seem on the whole to think that he is in Japanese territory.*
v. *Escape to Japanese territory would have been physically easier than escape in the other direction, though the latter would not be impossible.*
vi. *The Vichy report of his death in a plane accident between Bangkok and Tokio, though almost certainly mistaken, seemed to suggest that Vichy quarters took it for granted that he was in Japanese territory.*
vii. *According to engineers it would not be impossible to broadcast his voice scrambled from Tokio to Berlin and there unscramble and rebroadcast it.*

There are innumerable other considerations and endless rumours.] The two questions hardest to answer are: If Bose is in Japanese territory, why this elaborate effort to make it appear that he is in Berlin, where he is comparatively ineffectual? If Bose is in German territory, how did he get there? Of course it is quite reasonably likely that he got there with Russian connivance. Then the question arises, if the Russians had previously passed Bose through, did they afterwards tip us off when they came into the war on our side? To know the answer to that would give one a useful clue to their attitude towards ourselves. Of course one can get no information about questions of that type here. One has to do one's propaganda in the dark, discreetly sabotaging the policy directives when they seem more than usually silly.[30]

To judge from their wireless, the Germans believe in a forthcoming invasion, either of France or Norway. What a chance to have a go at Spain! As, however, they have fixed a date for it (May 1st) they may merely be discussing the possibility of invasion in order to jeer when it does not come off. No sign here of any invasion preparations – no rumours about assembly of troops or boats, re-arrangement of railway schedules etc. The most positive sign is Beaverbrook's pro-invasion speech in the USA.

[*There seems to be no news whatever. It must be months since the papers were so empty.*]

Struck by the mediocre physique and poor general appearance of the American soldiers one sees from time to time in the street. The officers usually better than the men, however.

30. Bose escaped from India, with German help, via Afghanistan, in the winter of 1940–41 When he reached Moscow, the Russians 'were extremely hospitable but determinedly evasive about helping him. In Berlin the Germans were more receptive' (Mihir Bose, *The Lost Hero*, p. 162). He was in Germany until 8 February 1943, when he sailed from Kiel in a U-boat (p. 205).

27.4.42: [*Much speculation about the meaning of Hitler's speech yesterday. In general it gives an impression of pessimism. Beaverbrook's invasion speech is variously interpreted, at its face value, as a pep talk for the Americans, as something to persuade the Russians that we are not leaving them in the lurch, and as the beginning of an attack on Churchill (who may be forced into opposing offensive action). Nowadays, whatever is said or done, one looks instantly for hidden motives and assumes that words mean anything except what they appear to mean.*]

From the Italian radio, describing life in London:

"Five shillings were given for one egg yesterday, and one pound sterling for a kilogram of potatoes. Rice has disappeared, even from the Black Market, and peas have become the prerogative of millionaires. There is no sugar on the market, although small quantities are still to be found at prohibitive prices".

One would say that this is stupid propaganda, because if such conditions really existed England would stop fighting in a few weeks, and when this fails to happen the listener is bound to see that he has been deceived. But in fact there is no such reaction. You can go on and on telling lies, and the most palpable lies at that, and even if they are not actually believed, there is no strong revulsion either.

We are all drowning in filth. When I talk to anyone or read the writings of anyone who has any axe to grind, I feel that intellectual honesty and balanced judgement have simply disappeared from the face of the earth. Everyone's thought is forensic, everyone is simply putting a "case" with deliberate suppression of his opponent's point of view, and, what is more, with complete insensitiveness to any sufferings except those of himself and his friends. The Indian nationalist is sunken in self-pity and hatred of Britain and utterly indifferent to the miseries of China, the English pacifist works himself up into frenzies about the concentration camps in the Isle of Man and forgets about those in Germany, etc., etc. One notices this in the case of people one disagrees with, such as Fascists or pacifists but in fact everyone is the same, at least everyone who has definite opinions. Everyone is dishonest, and everyone is utterly heartless towards people who are outside the immediate range of his own interests. What is most striking of all is the way sympathy can be turned on and off like a tap according to political expediency. [*All the pinks, or most of them, who flung themselves to and fro in their rage against Nazi atrocities before the war, forgot all about these atrocities and obviously lost their sympathy with the Jews etc. as soon as the war began to bore them. Ditto with people who hated Russia like poison up to June 22 1941 and then suddenly forgot about the purges, the G.P.U. etc. the moment Russia came into the war. I am not thinking of lying for political ends, but of actual changes in subjective feeling.*] But is there no one who has both firm opinions and a balanced outlook? Actually there are plenty, but they are powerless. All power is in the hands of paranoiacs.

29.4.42: Yesterday to the House to hear the India debate. A poor show except for Cripps's speech. They are now sitting in the House of Lords.[31] During Cripps's speech one had the impression that the house was full, but on counting I found only about 200–250 members, which is enough to fill most of the seats. Everything had a somewhat mangy look. Red rexine cushions on the benches – I could swear they used to be red plush at one time. The ushers' shirt fronts were very dingy. When I see this dreary rubbish going on, or when I read about the later days of the League of Nations or the antics of Indian politicians, with their endless changes of front, line-ups, *demarches*, denunciations, protests and gestures generally, I always remember that the Roman Senate still existed under the later Empire. [*This is the twilight of Parliamentary democracy and*] these creatures are simply ghosts gibbering in some corner while the real events happen elsewhere.

31. The chamber of the House of Commons was severely damaged in an air raid on 10 May 1941. The Commons sat in the Lords' chamber, which had been only slightly damaged. The Lords sat in their robing room.

6.5.42: People do not seem pleased about Madagascar[32] as they did about Syria,[33] perhaps not grasping equally well its strategical significance, but more, I think, for want of a suitable propaganda buildup beforehand. [*In the case of Syria the obviousness of the danger, the continual stories about German infiltration, and the long uncertainty as to whether the Government would act, gave people the impression that it was public opinion which had forced the decision. For all I know it may even have done so, to some extent. No similar preparation in this case.*] As soon as it became clear that Singapore was in danger I pointed out that we might have to seize Madagascar and had better begin the buildup in our Indian newsletters. I was somewhat choked off even then, and some weeks back a directive came, I suppose from the Foreign Office, that Madagascar was not to be mentioned. Reason given (after the British troops had landed) "So as not to give the show away". Result, the seizure of Madagascar can be represented all over Asia as a piece of imperialist grabbing.

Saw two women driving in an old-fashioned governess cart today. A week or two back saw two men in a carriage and pair, and one of the men actually wearing a grey bowler hat.

[*Much speculation as to the authorship of articles in the Tribune, violently attacking Churchill and signed "Thomas Rainsborough".*[34] *Considered by some to be Frank Owen,*[35] *which I do not believe.*]

32. Allied forces landed at Diego-Suarez, Madagascar, on 5 May and by September had taken over the island, strategically important in the light of naval losses in the Indian Ocean. It had supported the Vichy government under Pétain.
33. It was rumoured that the Germans would move east from Crete in June 1941. Allied forces therefore invaded Syria, wresting it from Vichy French troops.
34. The original Thomas Rainsborough, or Rainborow, was a republican who fought for the Commonwealth in the Civil War. He commanded the warship *Swallow* in 1643 and two years later a regiment in the New Model Army. In 1646 he became an M.P. and led republicans in Parliament but was eventually reconciled with Cromwell. He was fatally wounded in battle in 1648. The name was adopted in *Tribune* to exemplify extreme radical, Leveller-type views. The pseudonym *was* being used by Frank Owen.
35. Frank Owen (1905–1979; OBE, military), journalist, author, and broadcaster, was a Liberal M.P., 1929–31; edited the *Daily Express,* 1931–37 and the *Evening Standard,* 1938–41 (both right-wing Beaverbrook newspapers). With Michael Foot (acting editor, *Evening Standard,* 1942; later, Deputy Leader and Leader of the Labour Party, 1976–83) and Peter Howard, he wrote *Guilty Men* (Gollancz 1940), under the pseudonym Cato, which attacked Chamberlain, Halifax, and other Conservative leaders for appeasing Hitler. In *Beaverbrook: A Study in Power and Frustration* (1956), Tom Driberg writes of Owen, 'who had lately been called up but was writing in *Tribune,* under the pseudonym Thomas Rainsborough, articles severely critical of Churchill and his war strategy' (p. 287). He served in the Royal Armoured Corps and South East Asia Command, 1942–46, and was promoted from trooper to lieutenant colonel by Lord Louis Mountbatten with instructions to produce a daily paper for the command from 1943 despite the strenuous opposition of Sir James Grigg. He reprinted in *SEAC* seven of the occasional pieces Orwell wrote for the *Evening Standard,* 1945–46. He edited the *Daily Mail,* 1947–50, and wrote, among other books, *The Three Dictators* (1940) and *The Fall of Singapore* (1960).

8.5.42: According to W.[36] a real Anglo-Russian alliance is to be signed up and the Russian delegates are already in London. I don't believe this.

The Turkish radio (for some time past I think this has been one of the most reliable sources of information) alleges that both Germans and Russians are preparing to use poison gas in the forthcoming battle.

[*Great naval battle in progress in the Coral Sea.*[37] *Sinkings claimed by both sides so vast that one does not know what to believe. But from the willingness of the Japanese radio to talk about the battle (they have already named it the Battle of the Coral Sea) the presumption is that they count on making their objective.*

My guess as to the identity of 'Thomas Rainsboro': Tom Wintringham. (Right!)

(30.5.42. Wintringham denies authorship of these articles, but I still think he wrote them.) [38]]

36. Fredric Warburg (1898–1980), managing director of Secker & Warburg and Orwell's publisher.
37. The Battle of the Coral Sea, 4–8 May, was the first naval engagement fought entirely by aircraft, the ships involved never coming into each other's sight. The Americans lost the aircraft carrier *Lexington*, a tanker, a destroyer, 74 planes, and 543 men; the Japanese lost the light carrier *Shoho*, a destroyer, over 80 planes and more than 1,000 men. (Liddell Hart, *History of the Second World War*, pp. 361–63).
38. Entry in parentheses, dated 30 May, was added by Orwell to the manuscript version only.

11.5.42: Another gas warning (in Churchill's speech) last night. I suppose we shall be using it before many weeks are over.

From a Japanese broadcast: "In order to do justice to the patriotic spirit of the Koreans, the Japanese Government have decided to introduce compulsory military service in Korea".

Rumoured date for the German invasion of Britain: May 25th.

15.5.42: I saw Cripps on Wednesday, the first time I had actually spoken to him. Rather well impressed. He was more approachable and easy-going than I had expected, and quite ready to answer questions. Though aged 53 some of his movements are almost boyish. On the other hand he has decidedly a red nose. [I *saw him in one of the reception rooms, or whatever they are called, off the House of Lords. Some interesting old prints on the walls, coronets on the chairs and on the ashtrays, but everything with the vaguely decayed look that all Parliamentary institutions now have. A string of non-descript people waiting to see Cripps. As I waited trying to talk to his secretary, a phrase I always remember on these occasions came into my mind – "shivering in ante-rooms". In eighteenth-century biographies you always read about people waiting on their* *patrons and "shivering in anterooms". It is one of those ready made phrases like "leave no stone unturned", and yet how true it is as soon as you get anywhere near politics, or even the more expensive kinds of journalism.*]

Cripps considers that Bose is definitely in German territory. He says it is known that he got out through Afghanistan. I asked him what he thought of Bose, whom he used to know well, and he described him as "a thoroughly bad egg". I said there seemed little doubt that he is subjectively pro-Fascist. Cripps: "He's pro-Subhas. That is all he really cares about. He will do anything that he thinks will help his career along".

I am not certain, on the evidence of Bose's broadcasts, that this is so. I said I thought very few Indians were reliably anti-Fascist. Cripps disagreed so far as the younger generation go. He said the young Communists and left wing Socialists are wholeheartedly anti-Fascist and have a western conception of Socialism and internationalism. Let's hope it's so.

19.5.42: Attlee reminds me of nothing so much as a recently dead fish, before it has had time to stiffen.

21.5.42: Molotov is said to be in London. I don't believe this.

22.5.42: It is said that Molotov is not only in London but that the new Anglo-Russian treaty is already signed.[39] This however comes from Warburg, who is alternately over-optimistic and over-pessimistic – at any rate, always believes in the imminence of enormous and dramatic changes. If true it would be a godsend for the filling-up of my [BBC] newsletters. It is getting harder and harder to find anything to put into these, with nothing happening except on the Russian front, and the news from there, whether from Russian or German sources, growing more and more phony. I wish I could spare a week to go through the Russian and German broadcasts of the past year and tot up their various claims. I should say the Germans would have killed 10 million men and the Russians would have advanced to somewhere well out in the Atlantic Ocean.

39. A twenty-year treaty of collaboration between Russia and Britain was signed in London on 26 May 1942.

27.5.42: Cutting from the *D. Express* of 26.5.42:

CAIRO, Monday. – General Auchinleck, in a drive against red tape hindering the war effort in the Middle East, has sent this letter "to all officers and headquarters of this command": –

"An extract from a letter written by Wellington from Spain about 1810 to the Secretary for War, Lord Bradford:

"'My lord, if I attempted to answer the mass of futile correspondence that surrounds me, I should be debarred from all serious business of campaigning.

"'So long as I retain an independent position I shall see to it that no officer under my command is debarred, by attending to the futile drivelling of mere quill driving in your lordship's office, from attending to his first duty – which is, as always, to train the private men under his command.'"

General Auchinleck[40] adds: "I know that this does not apply to you; but please see to it that it can never be applied to you or to anyone working under you." – A.P.

This is printed in the papers and even given out over the air, but, after all, the operative fact is that no one does or can talk like that to the War Office nowadays.

More rumours that Molotov is in London. Also cryptic paras in the papers suggesting that this may be so (no mention of names, of course).

40. General (later Field Marshal) Sir Claude Auchinleck (familiarly known as 'The Auk') (1884–1981), served in World War 1 in the Mesopotamian campaign. In World War 2 he took part in the failed Norwegian campaign in 1940. In July 1941 took over the Eighth Army from Field Marshal Wavell in North Africa. Despite some success, he lost the confidence of Winston Churchill and was transferred to India. There he organized with considerable success the training of forces for the Burma Campaign and the supply of materials for the Fourteenth Army.

30.5.42: Almost every day in the neighbourhood of Upper Regent Street one can see a tiny, elderly, very yellow Japanese, with a face like a suffering monkey's, walking slowly along with an enormous policeman walking beside him. On some days they are holding a solemn conversation. I suppose he is one of the Embassy staff. But whether the policeman is there to prevent him from committing acts of sabotage, or to protect him from the infuriated mob, there is no knowing.

The Molotov rumour seems to have faded out. Warburg, who accepted the Molotov story without question, has now forgotten it and is full of the inner story of why Garvin[41] was sacked from the *Observer*. It was because he refused to attack Churchill. The Astors are determined to get rid of Churchill because he is pro-Russian and the transformation of the *Observer* is part of this manoeuvre. The *Observer* is to lead the attack on Churchill and at the same time canalise the gifted young journalists who are liable to give the war a revolutionary meaning, making them use their energies on futilities until they can be dispensed with. All inherently probable. On the other hand I don't believe that David Astor,[42] who acts as the decoy elephant, is consciously taking part in any such thing.* It is amusing to see not only the Beaverbrook press, which is now *plus royaliste que le roi* so far as Russia is concerned, but the T.U.[43] Weekly *Labour's Northern Voice*, suddenly discovering Garvin as a well-known anti-Fascist who has been sacked for his radical opinions. One thing that strikes me about nearly everyone nowadays is the shortness of their memories. Desmond Hawkins[44] told me a little while back that he recently bought some fried fish wrapped up in a sheet of newspaper dating from 1940. On one side was an article proving that the Red Army was no good, and on the other a write-up of that gallant sailor and well-known Anglophile, Admiral Darlan.[45]

Pasted into the Diary is 'That Monstrous Man', a poem by Nicholas Moore[46] (for which see *CW*, XIII, p. 341). This is followed by Orwell's comment:

Cf. Alexander Comfort's letter in the last *Horizon*[47]

41. J. L. Garvin, right-wing journalist, was the editor of *The Observer*, 1908 to 28 February 1942. At the beginning of the war, he disagreed with Viscount Astor, the proprietor of the paper, who questioned the advisability of Churchill's being Prime Minister and Minister of Defence at the same time.
42. The Honourable David Astor (1912–2001), served in the Royal Marines, 1940–45 (Croix de Guerre, 1944) and was foreign editor, 1946–48, editor, 1948–75, and Director, 1976–81 of the *Observer*. He made the *Observer* a paper of ideas so that it overtook the circulation of the *Sunday Times* in 1946. He believed in clear English prose and would circulate Orwell's 'Politics and the English Language' (*CW*, XVII, pp. 421–32) to new members of staff as a guide to clear thinking and precise writing. Astor and Orwell became good friends and he told the editor that whenever he needed cheering up he would arrange to meet Orwell in a pub in order to enjoy his sense of humour. Astor arranged for Orwell to be buried, as Orwell wished, according to the rites of the Church of England. See *Remembering Orwell*, pp. 218–20.
43. Trades Union.
44. Desmond Hawkins (1908–1999; OBE, 1963), novelist, literary critic and broadcaster. He did much free-lance work for the BBC during the war. He wrote the London Letter for *Partisan Review* before Orwell and recommended that Orwell succeed him.

* Mentioned this to Tom Harrisson, who has better opportunities of judging than I have. He considers it has a base in reality. He says the Astors, especially Lady A, are exceedingly intelligent in their way and realise that all they consider worth having will be lost if we do not make a compromise peace They are, of course, anti-Russian, and therefore necessarily anti-Churchill. At one time they were actually scheming to make Trenchard Prime Minister. The man who would be ideal for their purpose would be Lloyd George, "if he could walk". I agree here, but was somewhat surprised to find Harrisson saying it – would have rather expected him to be pro-Lloyd George. He also said he thought it quite possible that Beaverbrook is financing the Communist Party. [Orwell's footnote added to typed version]

45. Admiral Francois Darlan, (1881–1942), Commander-in-Chief of the French Navy, and Vice-Premier and Foreign Minister in the Vichy Government from February 1941 to April 1942. When the Allies invaded Morocco and Tunisia (then French territories) in November 1942, a deal, much criticised in Britain and America, was negotiated with him, in order to reduce casualties in completing the occupation of both countries, whereby he became high commissioner and commander-in-chief of naval forces. He was assassinated on 24 December 1942, by Bonnier de la Chapelle. His twenty-year-old assassin was tried by court-martial and executed two days later. As Churchill wrote, this 'relieved the Allies of their embarrassment in working with him' (*The Second World War*, IV, pp. 577–78). Churchill accords Darlan a critical but generous obituary: 'Few men have paid more heavily for errors of judgment and failure of character than Admiral Darlan. . . . His life's work had been to recreate the French Navy, and he had raised it to a position it had never held since the days of the French kings. . . . Let him rest in peace, and let us all be thankful we have never had to face the trials under which he broke' (IV, pp. 579–80).
46. Nicholas Moore (1918–1986) was editor of *Spleen*, 1938–40 (the title also of a book of his verse, 1973), and assistant to Tambimuttu on *Poetry (London)* in the 1940s. He produced nine volumes of poetry before 1949; thereafter, *Spleen* and three posthumously published collections. For his letter to *Partisan Review* about Orwell's 'London Letter' of 15 April 1941 (*CW*, XII, pp. 470–9).
47. Alexander Comfort, (1920–2000) poet, novelist and medical biologist. His *The Joy of Sex* (1972) sold over ten million copies. *Horizon* printed (May 1942, pp. 358–62) his long letter on the alleged absence of war poetry and the reasons for it arguing that three campaigns had been waged against poets. In his contribution to 'Pacifism and War: A Controversy' (see *CW*, XIII, pp. 396-9), Orwell quotes several lines from Comfort's letter to *Horizon*.

4.6.42: Very hot weather. Struck by the normality of everything – lack of hurry, fewness of uniforms, general unwarlike appearance of the crowds who drift slowly through the streets, pushing prams or loitering in the squares to look at the hawthorn bushes. It is already noticeable that there are much fewer cars, however. Here and there a car with a fuel converter at the back, having slightly the appearance of an old-fashioned milkcart. Evidently there is not so much bootleg petrol about after all.

6.6.42: The Molotov rumour still persists. He was here to negotiate the treaty, and has gone back, so it is said. No hint of this in any newspaper, however.

There is said to be much disagreement on the staff of the *New Statesman* over the question of the Second Front.[48] Having squealed for a year that we must open a second front immediately, Kingsley Martin[49] now has cold feet. He says they now say that the army cannot be trusted, the soldiers will shoot their officers in the back etc. – this after endeavouring throughout the war to make the soldiers mistrust their officers. Meanwhile

I think now that a second front is definitely projected, at any rate if enough shipping can be scraped together.

48. At this time the opening of a second front was almost daily expected. When Dwight D. Eisenhower's arrival in England was reported in the *Daily Express* on 26 June 1942, his photograph was headlined: 'U.S. Second Front general is here.' Although, in response to Stalin's demand that a Second Front be opened, consideration was given to a cross-Channel landing in August or September 1942, the first new front (not regarded by most people as a Second Front) was not opened until 8 November 1942, and then in North Africa.
49. Kingsley Martin (1897–1969) left-wing journalist and editor of *The New Statesman* (1931–60), caused the Indian Section considerable trouble, from what he said and from his squabbling about fees. He was regarded as unreliable by the BBC for not sticking to censored scripts, and was, in effect, barred by the Home Office and Ministry of Information because of his contribution to 'Answering You,' broadcast to North America in December 1941.

7.6.42: The *Sunday Express* has also gone cold on the second front. The official line now appears to be that our air raids are a second front. Obviously there has been some kind of government handout to the papers, telling them to pipe down on this subject. [*If the government merely wishes to stop them spreading misleading rumours, the puzzle is why they weren't silenced earlier.*] It is just possible that the invasion has now been definitely decided on and the papers have been told to go anti-second front in order to throw the enemy off the scent. In this labyrinth of lies in which we are living the one explanation one never believes is the obvious one. [*Cf. David Astor's story about the two German Jews meeting in the train:*

First Jew. Where are you going to?

Second Jew. Berlin.

First Jew. Liar! You just say that to deceive me. You know that if you say you are going to Berlin I shall think you are going to Leipzig, and all the time, you dirty crook, you really are going to Berlin!']

Last Tuesday [2 June 1942] spent a long evening with Cripps (who had expressed a desire to meet some literary people) together with Empson, Jack Common, David Owen, Norman Cameron, Guy Burgess[50] and another man (an official) whose name I didn't get. About 2½ hours of it, with nothing to drink. The usual inconclusive discussion. Cripps, however, very human and willing to listen. The person who stood up to him most successfully was Jack Common. Cripps said several things that amazed and slightly horrified me. One was that many people whose opinion was worth considering believed that the war would be over by October – ie. that Germany would be flat out by that time. When I said that I should look on that as a disaster pure and simple (because if the war were won as easily as that there would have been no real upheaval here and the American millionaires would still be in situ) he appeared not to understand. He said that once the war was won the surviving great powers would in any case have to administer the world as a unit, and seemed not to feel that it made much difference whether the great powers were capitalist or socialist.* [*Both David Owen and the man whose name I don't know supported him.*] I saw that I was up against the official mind, which sees everything as a problem in administration and does not grasp that at a certain point, ie. when certain economic interests are menaced, public spirit ceases to function. [The *basic assumption of such people is that everyone wants the world to function properly and will do his best to keep the wheels running. They don't realise that most of those who have the power don't care a damn about the world as a whole and are only intent on feathering their own nests.*] I can't help feeling a strong impression that Cripps has already been got at. Not with money or anything of that kind of course, nor even by flattery and the sense of power, which in all probability he genuinely doesn't care about: but simply by responsibility, which automatically makes a man timid. Besides, as soon as you are in power your perspectives are foreshortened. Perhaps a bird's eye view is as distorted as a worm's eye view.

[*Wintringham denies being "Thomas Rainboro'", I think perhaps with truth. If not Wintringham, it might perhaps be Lord Winster (Commander Fletcher).*[51]]

50. William Empson (1906–83; Kt., 1979), poet, critic, and, before the war, Professor of English, Tokyo and Peking. Like Orwell, he worked for the BBC's Eastern Service but broadcast to China. He was Professor of English Literature, Sheffield University, 1953–71. He had already achieved scholarly recognition with *Seven Types of Ambiguity* (1930), and *Some Versions of Pastoral* (1935); among later writings was *The Structure of Complex Words* (1951). His obituary in *The Times* described him as 'the most famously over-sophisticated man of his time who revolutionized our ways of reading a poem'.

Jack Common (1903–68), a worker from Tyneside employed by *The Adelphi*, first as a circulation pusher from June 1930, then as assistant editor, from 1932. He and Orwell became friends and he stayed in the Orwells' cottage at Wallington when they were in Marrakech. He achieved success with *The Freedom of the Streets*, which Orwell reviewed on 16 June 1938 (*CW*, X, pp. 162–3). See also *Orwell Remembered*, pp. 139–43.

Arthur David Kemp Owen (1904–70) personal assistant to Sir Stafford Cripps, 19 February to 21 November 1942.

Norman Cameron (1905–53) was a friend and disciple of Robert Graves, with whom he and Alan Hodge edited *Work in Hand* (1942). His *The Winter House and Other Poems* was published in 1935. He also translated from French and German.

Guy Burgess (1911–63), educated at Eton and Trinity College, Cambridge, was a good talker and a man of considerable gifts, which he used to proselytise the cause of Communism. He worked for the British security services and the BBC (as a Home Service talks producer) and then joined the Foreign Office.

* *Very interesting but perhaps rather hard on Cripps to report an impression like this from a private interview* [Orwell's handwritten footnote on typescript].

His pro-Soviet activities were not suspected until, in May 1951, he suddenly left with Donald Maclean for Moscow remaining there until his death.

51. Lord Winster (Commander R. T. H. Fletcher, 1885–1961), Liberal M.P., 1923–24; Labour M.P., 1935–42, was Parliamentary Private Secretary to the First Lord of the Admiralty, May 1940–December 1941. The pseudonym 'Rainsborough' was then being used by Frank Owen.

10.6.42: The only time when one hears people singing in the BBC is in the early morning, between 6 and 8. That is the time when the charwomen are at work. A huge army of them arrives all at the same time, they sit in the reception hall waiting for their brooms to be issued to them and making as much noise as a parrot house, and then they have wonderful choruses, all singing together as they sweep the passages. The place has a quite different atmosphere at this time from what it has later in the day.

11.6.42: [*The Germans announce over the wireless that as the inhabitants of a Czech village called Ladice° (about 1200 inhabitants) were guilty of harbouring the assassins of Heydrich they have shot all the males in the village, sent all the women to concentration camps, sent all the children to be "re-educated", razed the whole village to the ground and changed its name. I am keeping a copy of the announcement, as recorded in the BBC monitoring report.*]

From the BBC monitoring report: –

PRAGUE (CZECH HOME STATIONS). IN GERMAN FOR PROTECTORATE. 10.6.42

Heydrich Revenge: Village Wiped Out: All Men Shot: ANNOUNCEMENT

It is officially announced: The search and investigation for the murderers of S.S. Obergruppenfuehrer Gen. Heydrich[52] has established unimpeachable indications (*sic*) that the population of the locality of Lidice, near Kladno, supported and gave assistance to the circle (*sic*) of perpetrators in question. In spite of the interrogation of the local inhabitants, the pertinent means of evidence were secured without the help of the population. The attitude of the inhabitants to the outrage thus manifested, is manifested also by other acts hostile to the Reich, by the discoveries of printed matter hostile to the Reich, of dumps of arms and ammunition, of an illegal wireless transmitter, of huge quantities of controlled goods, as well as by the fact that inhabitants of the locality are in active enemy service abroad. Since the inhabitants of this village (*sic*) have flagrantly violated the laws which have been issued, by their activity and by the support given to the murderers of S.S. Obergruppenfuehrer Heydrich, the male adults have been shot, the women have been sent to a concentration camp and the children have been handed over to the appropriate educational authorities. The buildings of the locality have been levelled to the ground, and the name of the community has been obliterated.

(Note: This is an identical repetition, in German, of an announcement made in Czech, from Prague at 19.00, when reception was very bad).

It does not particularly surprise me that people do this kind of thing, nor even that they announce that they are doing them. What does impress me, however, is that other people's reaction to such happenings is governed solely by the political fashion of the moment. Thus before the war the pinks believed any and every horror story that came out of Germany or China. Now the pinks no longer believe in German or Japanese atrocities and automatically write off all horror stories as "propaganda". In a little while you will be jeered at if you suggest that the story of Lidice could possibly be true. And yet there the facts are, announced by the Germans themselves and recorded on gramophone discs which no doubt will still be available. Cf. the long list of atrocities from 1914 onwards [*German atrocities in Belgium, Bolshevik atrocities, Turkish atrocities, British atrocities in India, American atrocities in Nicaragua, Nazi atrocities, Italian atrocities in Abyssinia and Cyrenaica, red and white atrocities in Spain, Japanese atrocities in China*[53]----] in every case believed in or disbelieved in according to political predilection, with utter non-interest in the facts and with complete willingness to alter one's beliefs as soon as the political scene alters.

Atrocities (post 1918)

Date	Believed in by the Right	Believed in by the Left
1920	Turkish atrocities (Smyrna)	Turkish atrocities (Smyrna)
1920	Sinn Fein atrocities	Black and Tan atrocities
(circa)	Bolshevik atrocities	British atrocities in India (Amritsar)
1923		French atrocities (the Ruhr)
1928		American atrocities (Nicaragua)
1933	Bolshevik atrocities (White Sea canal etc.)	
1934–9		German atrocities
1935		Italian atrocities (Abyssinia)
1936–9	Red atrocities in Spain	Fascist atrocities in Spain
1937	Bolshevik atrocities (the purges)	Japanese atrocities [53]
1939	German atrocities et seq.	British atrocities (Isle of Man etc.) [54]
1941	Japanese atrocities et seq.	

52. Reinhard Heydrich (1904–1942), head of the Reich Main Security Office (the Gestapo, criminal police, and SS Security Service), deputy to Heinrich Himmler, leading organizer of the Nazi 'final solution,' was appointed 'Protector of Bohemia and Moravia' in September 1941. On 27 May 1942, he was wounded by Czech patriots trained in England and died on 4 June. In reprisal, the village of Lidice was 'exterminated.' The population had been about 2,000; very few survived. Humphrey Jennings made a deeply moving film of the incident, as if it had occurred in the Welsh village of Ystradgynlais (*The Silent Village*, 1943), as part of the British government's propaganda towards the defeat of Nazism. A copy of the pamphlet describing the film is in Orwell's collection of pamphlets, now in the British Library. Throughout his manuscript, Orwell spells the village 'Ladice.'
53. Orwell had written to Hsiao Ch'ien on 14 January 1942 asking for 'one talk on the ordinary atrocity lines' in connection with the Japanese invasion of China. This was broadcast on 26 February 1942.
54. The manuscript and typewritten versions differ slightly. Thus, as well as the White Sea Canal, Orwell includes the Ukraine famine, and as well as Abyssinia he includes Cyrenaica, and Nanking is specifically listed as a Japanese atrocity. Against British atrocities he includes the *SS Dunera*.

Under the Government Regulation 18B, because of exaggerated fears that amongst those who had come to Britain as refugees, especially from Nazi Germany, there were concealed spies and saboteurs, thousands of innocent people were interned on the Isle of Man. Although bitterly ironic, this hardly amounted to an atrocity in the grim scale of such horrors. The deporting of Jews on the S.S *Dunera* to Australia on similar grounds was also misconceived, and led to treatment that was cruel as well as stupid.

13.6.42: The most impressive fact about the Molotov visit is that the Germans knew nothing about it. Not a word on the radio about Molotov's presence in London till the signature of the treaty was officially announced, although all the while the German radio was shouting about the bolshevisation of Britain. Obviously they would have spilt the beans if they had known. Taken in conjunction with certain other things (eg. the capture last year of two very amateurish spies dropped by parachute, with portable wireless transmitters and actually with chunks of German sausage in their suitcases) this suggests that the German spy system in this country cannot be up to much.

A sequence of four newspaper cuttings is pasted into the manuscript Diary at this point. For full details see *Complete Works*, XIII, pp. 362–3.:

1. From editorial in *Tribune* of 12.6.42, on the death of Wm. Mellor.[55] Their idea of "Vigorous style".

2. From Hitler's speeches, quoted *in Reynolds's*[56] of 21.6.42.

3. *Tribune* of 12.6.42. (article by Wilfred Macartney). Cf. prewar references to Axis censorship, radio hypnosis etc. Cf. also German official statements in the Cologne raid.

4. How we live in 1942 (cutting from *E. Standard*: Illustration of five women, captioned 'Russia's Tommy-Gun Girls are Ready to Fight.'

55. William Mellor (1888–1942), left-wing journalist and author, edited the *Daily Herald*, which he had joined in 1903, from 1926 to 1930. He was then Assistant Managing Editor of Odhams Press until he became editor of *Tribune*, 1 January 1937. He wrote *Direct Action* (1920) and, with G.D.H. Cole, *The Meaning of Industrial Freedom* (1918). He was a member of the National Council of the Socialist League.
56. *Reynold's News* was a Labour-inclined Sunday newspaper: see Diary of Events Leading up to the War, 3.9.39, n. 2

15.6.42: No question now that the second front has been decided on. All the papers talk of it as a certainty and Moscow is publicising it widely. Whether it is really feasible remains to be seen, of course.

Cutting from BBC monitoring report. Typical of many similar German announcements.

Pasted sideways in the manuscript is the BBC monitoring report and his own typed report of the liquidation of Lidice. The texts are verbally the same. (See *CW*, XIII, p. 364).

21.6.42: The thing that strikes one in the BBC – and it is evidently the same in various of the other departments – is not so much the moral squalor and the ultimate futility of what we are doing, as the feeling of frustration, the impossibility of getting anything done, even any successful piece of scoundrelism. Our policy is so ill-defined, the disorganisation is so great [*there are so many changes of plan*] and the fear and hatred of intelligence are so all-pervading, that one cannot plan any sort of wireless campaign whatever. [*When one plans some series of talks, with some more or less definite propaganda line behind it, one is first told to go ahead, then choked off on the ground that this or that is "injudicious" or "premature", then told again to go ahead, then told to water everything down and cut out any plain statements that may have crept in here and there, then told to "modify" the series in some way that removes its original meaning; and then at the last moment the whole thing is suddenly cancelled by some mysterious edict from above and one is told to improvise some different series which one feels no interest in and which in any case has no definite idea behind it.*] One is constantly putting sheer rubbish on the air because of having talks which sounded too intelligent cancelled at the last moment. In addition the organisation is so overstaffed that numbers of people have almost literally nothing to do. But even when one manages to get something fairly good on the air one is weighed down by the knowledge that hardly anybody is listening. Except, I suppose, in Europe the BBC simply isn't listened to overseas, a fact known to everyone concerned with overseas broadcasting. [*Some listener research has been done in America and it is known that in the whole of the USA about 300,000 people listen to the BBC. In India or Australia the number would not be anywhere near that.*] It has come out recently that (two years after the Empire service was started) plenty of Indians with shortwave sets don't even know that the BBC broadcasts to India.

It is the same with the only other public activity I take part in, the Home Guard. After two years no real training has been done, no specialised tactics worked out, no battle positions fixed upon, no fortifications built – all this owing to endless changes of plan and complete vagueness as to what we are supposed to be aiming at. Details of organisation, battle positions etc. have been changed so frequently that hardly anyone knows at any given moment what the current arrangements are supposed to be. To give just one example, for well over a year our company has been trying to dig a system of trenches in Regents Park, in case airborne troops land there. Though dug over and over again these trenches have never once been in a completed state, because when they are half done there is always a change of plan and fresh orders. Ditto with everything. Whatever one undertakes, one starts with the knowledge that presently there will come a sudden change of orders, and then another change, and so on indefinitely. Nothing ever happens except continuous dithering, resulting in progressive disillusionment all round. The best one can hope is that it is much the same on the other side.

24.6.42: Listened-in last night to Lord Haw Haw – not Joyce,[57] who apparently has been off the air for some time, but a man who sounded to me like a South African, followed by another with more of a cockney voice. There was a good deal about the Congress of the Free India movement in Bangkok. Was amazed to notice that all the Indian names were mispronounced, and grossly mispronounced – eg. Ras Behari Bose[58] rendered as Rash Beery Bose. Yet after all the Indians who are broadcasting from Germany are available for advice on these points. They probably go in and out of the same building as Lord Haw Haw every day. It is rather encouraging to see this kind of slovenliness happening on the other side as well.

57. For William Joyce, who broadcast from Berlin as 'Lord Haw Haw,' see Wartime Diary, 28.7.40, n. 77

58. Ras Behari Bose (1880?–1945) was no relation of Subhas Chandra Bose. He had worked for Indian independence since 1911. After the failure of the Cripps Mission, he was asked by the Japanese to make way for Subhas. He agreed and on 17 April 1942 the Japanese Cabinet decided to use Subhas to 'present policy' (Mihir Bose, *The Lost Hero*, pp. 191, 197–8; he spells the name Rash Behari Bose).

26.6.42: Everyone very defeatist after the Libya business.[59] Some of the papers going cold on the Second Front again. Tom Driberg ("William Hickey") wins the Malden by-election, scoring twice as many votes as the Conservative candidate. That makes 4 out of the last 6 elections that the Government has lost.

59. The sudden fall of Tobruk to Rommel's forces on 21 June 1942, despite its having held out for eight months in 1941 before being relieved in December of that year. The loss was a blow to morale second only to the fall of Singapore. Twenty-five thousand troops were taken prisoner. For a brief account of what led to the splitting of the Eighth Army in a vain attempt to keep Tobruk, and Churchill's part in this, see Liddell Hart, *History of the Second World War*, p. 287; for the retreat to El Alamein, fifty-five miles from Alexandria, see pp. 287–303). Much blame fell on General Sir Claude Auchinleck (and see 27.5.42 n. 40), who was relieved of his command after Churchill visited Cairo, 4 August. He was held in high esteem by Rommel, who thought he had handled his forces with considerable skill (Liddell Hart, pp. 301–02). After the war he was given the thankless task of dividing the Indian Army between newly independent India and Pakistan. He did this so well that he was appointed commander of each army by the newly independent governments.

1.7.42: At Callow End, Worcs. (staying on a farm).[60] No noise except aeroplanes, birds and the mowers cutting the hay. No mention of the war except with reference to the Italian prisoners, who are working on some of the farms. They seem to be considered good workers and for fruit-picking are preferred to the town people who come out from Worcester and are described as "artful". In spite of the feeding difficulties, plenty of pigs, poultry, geese and turkeys about. Cream for every meal at this place.[61]

[*Huge bombers flying overhead all day. Also aeroplanes doing extraordinary things, eg. towing other planes by a wire (perhaps gliders?) or carrying smaller planes perched on their backs.*]

60. This was Orwell's only break of any length whilst working for the BBC. He stayed at Callow End, Worcestershire and spent much of the time fishing from Sunday 28 June to Saturday 11 July. He was passionately keen on fishing even though, on this occasion, fish, and the beer, were in short supply. He listed what he caught on the penultimate page of Volume 3 of this War-time Diary. It amounted to eighteen dace (though one might have been a roach), two eels and one perch. On five days he caught nothing.

61. Although some cream-making was permitted for sale locally, production on the normal scale and general distribution had been stopped to conserve resources.

3.7.42: Vote of censure defeated 475–25. This figure means that there were very few abstentions. The same trick as usual – the debate twisted into a demand for a vote of confidence in Churchill himself, which has to be given, since there is no one to take Churchill's place. Things are made much easier for the government by the obvious bad motives of some of its chief attackers, eg. Hore-Belisha.[62] I don't know how much longer this comedy can go on, but not much longer.

No reference to the second front in Churchill's speech.

The Japanese are evidently going to attack Russia fairly soon. They appear to be firmly lodged in the outer Aleutians, which can't have any meaning except as a move to cut communications between Russia and the USA.

The pinks are panicking to an extent they haven't equalled since Dunkirk. The *New Statesman's* leading article is headed "Facing the Spectre". They take the loss of Egypt for granted. Heaven knows whether this will actually happen, but these people have prophecied° the loss of Egypt so often before that their doing so again is almost enough to persuade one that it won't happen. It is curious how they always do what the Germans want them to do – eg., for some time past, demanding that we stop the raids on Germany and send our bombers to Egypt. A little earlier we were to send our bombers to India. In each case the same move as was being demanded by the German "freedom" stations. A thing that strikes one also is the airy disdain with which all the pinks talk of our air raids on Germany – air raids make very little impression, etc., etc. And these are the people who squealed loudest during the blitz on London.

62. Leslie Hore-Belisha was Secretary of State for War, 1937–40; an Independent M.P., 1942–45. Chamberlain appointed him Secretary for War in 1937, but dismissed him in 1940. Churchill did not give him a place in his government, and he remained out of office throughout the war. For his earlier career, see Events, 19.7.39, n. 1.

4.7.42: Everyone seems stupefied by Wardlaw-Milne's[63] suggestion [*in the speech moving the vote of censure,*] that the Duke of Gloucester should be made Commander-in-Chief. The most likely explanation is that Gloucester was intended to act as dummy for somebody else [*(Possibly Mountbatten?)*] *Even so one could hardly imagine a worse figurehead than this fat mental defective.*

Pubs in this village shut quite a lot of the time for lack of beer. Possibly only due to the recent spell of hot weather. This is a hop area and I find the farmers have been asked not to cut down their acreage of hops, indeed some have increased it. All these hops go for beer, at least all the high-grade ones.

63. Sir John Wardlaw-Milne (1879–1967) was Unionist M.P. for Kidderminster, 1922–45; Chairman of House of Commons Select Committee on National Expenditure, and author of pamphlets on financial matters. He was strongly

opposed to Churchill and moved the vote of censure in which he made this proposal. As Churchill put it, 'This proved injurious to his case.' See *The Second World War*, IV, pp. 356–66, for the debate and Wardlaw-Milne's proposal in particular.

10.7.42: A day or two ago a couple of lorries belonging to the Navy arrived with a party of Wrens[64] and sailors who put in several hours work weeding out the turnips in Mr. Phillips's[65] field. All the village women delighted by the appearance of the sailors in their blue trousers and white singlets. "Don't they look clean, like! I like sailors. They always look so clean". [*The sailors and Wrens also seemed to enjoy their outing and drinks in the pub afterwards. It appeared that they belonged to some volunteer organisation which sends workers out as they are needed*] Mrs Phillips explains it:. "It's the voluntary organization from Malvern.[66] Sometimes it's A.Ts [67] they send and sometimes sailors. Of course we like having them. Well, it makes you a bit independent of your own work-people, you see. The work-people, they're awful nowadays. Just do so much and no more. [*They know you can't do without them, you see. And you can't get a woman to do a bit indoors nowadays. The girls won't stay here, with no picture-house in the village. I do have a woman who comes in, but I can't get any work out of her.*] It helps a bit when you get a few voluntary workers. Makes you more independent, like".

How right and proper it all is [*when you consider how necessary it is that agricultural work should not be neglected, and how right and proper also that town people should get a bit of contact with the soil.*] Yet these voluntary organisations, plus the work done by soldiers in the hay-making etc., and the Italian prisoners, are simply blackleg labour.

The Government wins at Salisbury. Hipwell,[68] the editor of *Reveille*, was the Independent candidate. Wherever this mountebank stands the Government wins automatically. How grateful they must be to him, if indeed they aren't actually paying him to do it.

The "Blue Bell" again shut for lack of beer. Quite serious boozing for 4 or 5 days of the week, then drought. [*Sometimes, however, when they are shut the local officers are to be seen drinking in a private room, the common soldiers as well as the labourers being shut out. The "Red Lion" in the next village, goes on a different system which the proprietor explains to me: "I don't hold with giving it all to the summer visitors. If beer's short, let the locals come first, I say. A lot of days I keep the pub door shut, and then only the locals know the way in at the back. A man that's working in the fields needs his beer, 'specially with the food they got to eat nowadays. But I rations 'em. I says to 'em, 'Now look here, you want your beer regular, don't you? Wouldn't you rather have a pint with your dinner every day than four pints one day and three the next?' Same with the soldiers. I don't like to refuse beer to a soldier, but I only lets 'em have a pint their first drink. After that it's 'Half pints only, boys'. Like that it gets shared out a bit."*].

64. Women's Royal Naval Service.
65. Presumably the farmer at whose farm Orwell was staying. There is no indication as to whether Eileen was able to get leave at the same time as her husband.
66. Malvern, far inland, might seem an unlikely setting for a naval establishment, but a radar research base and an initial training unit were sited there.
67. Auxiliary Territorial Service, the women's army service, now the WRAC, Women's Royal Army Corps.
68. W. R. Hipwell.

22.7.42: From Ahmed Ali's[69] last letter from India:

"Here is a little bit of old Delhi which might interest you.

"In a busy street a newsboy was shouting in Urdu: 'Pandit Jawaharlal[70] saying his rosary the other way round'. What he meant was that he had changed his attitude towards the Government. Questioned he said: 'You can never be sure of him, today he says side with the Government and help in the war effort, tomorrow just the opposite'. He turned away from me and began shouting his cry, adding: 'Jawaharlal has given a challenge to the Government'. I could not find this 'challenge' in the papers.

"Other newsboys selling Urdu papers: 'Germany has smashed Russia in the very first attack'. Needless to say I read just the opposite in my English papers the next morning. Obviously the Urdu papers had repeated what Berlin had said. No one stops the newsboys shouting what they like.

"One day going in a tonga I heard the driver shout to his horse as he shied: 'Why do you get back like our Sarkar! Go forward like Hitler!' and he swore".

[*"Its rather fun going out to the bazars and markets and listening to the loud gossip – provided, of course, it is not unbearably hot. I shall tell you more from time to time, if you are interested."*]

69. Ahmed Ali (1910–1994), Pakistani writer and Professor of English, Bengal. Served as Listener Research Director for the BBC in New Delhi, 1942–45. Worked for the Government of Pakistan, 1949–60. He was co-editor of *Indian Writing* (London, 1940–45) and *Tomorrow Bombay* (India, 1942–44). He published in Urdu and English and works in the latter language include *Twilight in Delhi* (1940) and *Ocean of Night* (1964), which reflect on the Muslim heritage in India. A critical work, *Mr Eliot's Penny-World of Dreams,* was published in 1941.
70. Pandit Jawaharlal Nehru (1889–1964), General Secretary and then President of the Indian National Congress, was educated at Harrow and Cambridge. After the massacre at Amritsar in 1919, he joined the fight for independence and was particularly associated with Gandhi, although at times they opposed one another's policies. Frequently imprisoned by the British, he became India's first prime minister when independence was achieved in 1947.

23.7.42: I now make entries in this diary much more seldom than I used to, for the reason that I literally have not any spare time. And yet I am doing nothing that is not futility and have less and less to show for the time I waste. It seems to be the same with everyone – the most fearful feeling of frustration, of just footling round doing imbecile things, not imbecile because they are a part of the war and war is inherently foolish, but things which in fact don't help or in any way affect the war effort, but are considered necessary by the huge bureaucratic machine in which we are all caught up. Much of the stuff that goes out from the BBC is just shot into the stratosphere, not listened to by anybody and known by those responsible for it to be not listened to by anybody. And round this futile stuff hundreds of skilled workers are grouped [, *costing the country tens of thousands per annum*,] and tagging on to them are thousands of others who in effect have no real job but have found themselves a quiet niche and are sitting in it pretending to work. The same everywhere, especially in the Ministries.

[*However, the bread one casts on the waters sometimes fetches up in strange places. We did a series of 6 talks on modern English literature, very highbrow and, I believe, completely un-listened to in India. Hsiao Chi'en, the Chinese student, reads the talks in the "Listener" and is so impressed that he begins writing a book in Chinese on modern Western literature, drawing largely on our talks. So the propaganda aimed at India misses India and accidentally hits China. Perhaps the best way to influence India would be by broadcasting to China.*]

The Indian Communist party, and its press, legalised again. I should say after this they will have to take the ban off the *Daily Worker*, otherwise the position is too absurd.

This reminds me of the story David Owen* told me and which I believe I didn't enter in this diary. Cripps on his arrival in India asked the Viceroy to release the interned Communists. The Viceroy consented (I believe most of them have been released since), but at the last moment got cold feet and said nervously: "But how can you be sure they're really Communists?"

We are going to have to increase our consumption of potatoes by 20 percent, so it is said. Partly to save bread, and partly to dispose of this year's potato crop, which is enormous.[71]

71. The Ministry of Food (where Eileen worked) promoted a cartoon character, Potato Pete, in a campaign to persuade people to eat a pound of potatoes a day.

* *Then secretary to Stafford Cripps* [Orwell's handwritten footnote in typescript]

26.7.42: Yesterday and today, on the Home Guard manoeuvres, passing various small camps of soldiers in the woods, radiolocation [= *radar*] stations etc. Struck by the appearance of the soldiers, their magnificent health and the brutalized look in their faces. All young and fresh, with round fat limbs and rosy faces with beautiful clear skins. But sullen brutish expressions – not fierce or wicked in any way, but simply stupefied by boredom, loneliness, discontent, endless tiredness and mere physical health.

27.7.42: Talking today with Sultana, one of the Maltese broadcasters. He says he is able to keep in fairly good touch with Malta and conditions are very bad there. "The last letter I get this morning was like a – how you say? (much gesticulation) – like a sieve. All the pieces what the censor cut out, you understand. But I make something out of it, all the same." He went on to tell me, among other things, that 5 lbs of potatoes now cost the equivalent of 8 shillings. [*He considers that of the two convoys which recently endeavoured to reach Malta the one from England, which succeeded in getting there, carried munitions, and the one from Egypt, which failed to get there, carried food.*] I said, "Why can't they send dehydrated food by plane?" He shrugged his shoulders, seeming to feel instinctively that the British government would never go to that much trouble over Malta. Yet it seems that the Maltese are solidly pro-British, thanks to Mussolini, no doubt.

[*The German broadcasts are claiming that Voroshilov*[72] *is in London, which is not very likely and has not been rumoured here. Probably a shot in the dark to offset their recent failure over Molotov,*[73] *and made on the calculation that some high-up Russian military delegate is likely to be here at this moment. If the story should turn out to be true, I shall have to revise my ideas about the German secret service in this country.*]

The crowd at the Second Front meeting in Trafalgar Square estimated at 40,000 in the rightwing papers and 60,000 in the leftwing. Perhaps 50,000 in reality. My spy reports that in spite of the present Communist line of "all power to Churchill", the Communist speakers in fact attacked the Government very bitterly.

72. For General Kliment Voroshilov, see Events, 31.8.39, n.1. Churchill was to meet him, on 12 August 1942, but in Moscow (see Winston Churchill, *The Second World War*, IV, p. 429).
73. For Vyacheslav Molotov, see Events, 28.8.39, n. 4. Churchill gives an account of a private talk with him at this time in *The Second World War* (IV, pp. 436–37). A principal issue at stake was the opening of a Second Front.

28.7.42: Today I have read less newspapers than usual, but the ones I have seen have gone cold on the Second Front, except for the *News Chronicle*. [*The* <u>Evening News</u> *published an anti-Second Front article (by General Brownrigg*[74]*) on its front page.*] I remarked on this to Herbert Read[75] who said gloomily "The Government has told them to shut up about it". [*It* *is true of course that if they are intending to start something they must still seem to deny it.*] Read said he thought the position in Russia was desperate and seemed very upset about it, though in the past he has been even more anti-Stalin than I. I said to him, "Don't you feel quite differently towards the Russians now they are in a jam?" and he agreed. For that matter I felt quite differently towards England when I saw that England was in a jam. Looking back I see that I was anti-Russian (or more exactly anti-Stalin) during the years when Russia appeared to be powerful, militarily and politically, ie. 1933 to 1941. Before and after those dates I was pro-Russian. One could interpret this in several different ways.

A small raid on the outskirts of London last night. The new rocket guns, some of which are [now] manned by Home Guards,[76] were in action [*and are said to have brought down some planes (8 planes down altogether).*]

This is the first time the Home Guard can properly be said to have been in action, a little over 2 years after its formation.

The Germans never admit damage to military objectives, but they acknowledge civilian casualties after our bigger raids. After the Hamburg raid of 2 nights ago they described the casualties as heavy. The papers here reproduce this with pride. Two years ago we would all have been aghast at the idea of killing civilians. I remember saying to someone during the blitz, when the RAF were hitting back as best they could, "In a year's time you'll see headlines in the *Daily Express*: 'Successful Raid on Berlin Orphanage. Babies Set on Fire'." It hasn't come to that yet, but that is the direction we are going in.

74. Lieutenant-General Sir W. Douglas S. Brownrigg (1886–1946) was Adjutant-General to the British Expeditionary Force, 1939–40. He retired in 1940 but was appointed Zone and Sector Commander of the Home Guard, 1941.
75. Herbert Read (1893–1968; Kt. 1953), poet, critic, educator and interpreter of modern art. Served in World War 1 (DSO, MC) and was particularly influential in the thirties and forties. He was assistant keeper at the Victoria & Albert Museum, and taught at Edinburgh University, 1931–2. Edited the *Burlington Magazine*, 1933–39. His *Education through Art* was an important influence after the war. He was an influential supporter of anarchism after World War 1 at least until he was knighted.
76. The anti-aircraft branch of the Home Guard, under General Sir Frederick Pile (1884–1976, Bt.), was equipped with rocket launchers. These were each capable of firing two one-hundredweight rockets and were massed in batteries of sixty-four. Not all the rockets would necessarily be fired at once. The rockets were not particularly accurate, but they created a 'box' of shrapnel capable of damaging and bringing down planes. In my experience on rocket battery 101 at Iver, near Slough, they were not used against low-flying planes in built-up areas because they were liable to sheer off the roofs of houses surrounding the battery. Orwell probably dropped 'now' from the typescript because these guns, though to a small extent manned by full-time servicemen, were, like the spigot mortar, chiefly Home Guard weapons.

1.8.42: If the figures given are correct, the Germans have lost about 10 per cent of their strength in each of the last raids. According to Peter Masefield this isn't anything to do with the new guns but has all been done by the night fighters. He also told me that the new FW 190 fighter is much better than any fighter we now have in actual service. [*An aircraft construction man named Bowyer who was broadcasting together with him agreed with this.*] Oliver Stewart considers that the recent German raids are reconnaissance raids and that they intend starting the big blitz again soon, at any rate if they can get their hands free in Russia.[77]

Not much to do over the bank holiday weekend.[78] Busy at every odd moment making a hen-house. This kind of thing now needs great ingenuity owing to the extreme difficulty of getting hold of timber. No sense of guilt or time-wasting when I do anything of this type – on the contrary, a vague feeling that any sane occupation must be useful, or at any rate justifiable.

77. Peter Masefield (1914–2006; Kt. 1972), was war correspondent with the RAF and US Eighth Air Force, 1939–43. Became Chief Executive of British European Airways, 1949–52. He was scheduled to discuss Aviation in one of Orwell's broadcasts to India on 31 July 1942 with Oliver Stewart (1895–1976, editor of *Aeronautics*, 1939–62), but when he had to drop out, Orwell engaged E.C. Bowyer who was on the staff of the Society of British Aircraft Constructors.
78. The weekend would have been spent at the Orwells' cottage at Wallington.

3.8.42: D[avid] A[stor] says Churchill is in Moscow.[79] He also says there isn't going to be any second front. However, if a second front is intended, the Government must do all it can to spread the contrary impression beforehand, [*and D.A. might be one of the people used to plant the rumour.*

D.A. says that when the commandos land the Germans never fight but always clear out immediately. No doubt they have orders to do so. This fact is not allowed to be published – presumable reason, to prevent the public from becoming over-confident.]

According to D.A., Cripps *does* intend to resign from the Government[80] and has his alternative policy ready. He can't, of course, speak of this in public but will do so in private. However, I hear that Macmurray[81] when staying with Cripps recently could get nothing whatever out of him as to his political intentions.

79. Churchill arrived in Cairo on this day, then, via Teheran, reached Moscow on 12 August. He and Stalin did discuss the opening of a second front (see *The Second World War*, IV, pp. 411, 430–33).
80. Cripps came near to resignation but did not leave the War Cabinet until 22 November 1942, the day he was appointed Minister of Aircraft Production, a post he held until the end of the war in Europe.
81. John Macmurray (1891–1976) was Grote Professor of the Philosophy of Mind and Logic, University of London.

4.8.42: The Turkish radio (among others) also says Churchill is in Moscow.

5.8.42: General dismay over the Government of India's rash act in publishing the documents seized in the police raid on Congress headquarters.[82] [*As usual the crucial document is capable of more than one interpretation and the resulting squabble will simply turn wavering elements in Congress more anti-British.*] The anti-Indian feeling which the publication has aroused in America, and perhaps Russia and China, is not in the long run any good to us. The Russian government announces discovery of a Tsarist plot, quite in the old style. I can't help a vague feeling that this is somehow linked up with the simultaneous discovery of Gandhi's plot with the Japanese.

82. After the failure of Cripps's mission to India, Congress had become increasingly intransigent. At the beginning of August Gandhi inaugurated a campaign of civil disobedience. In attempting to ensure order, the government of India raided Congress headquarters and seized the text of the original draft of the Resolution on Indian Independence submitted to the Congress Working Committee and published it.

7.8.42: [*Hugh Slater is very despondent about the war. He says that at the rate at which the Russians have been retreating it is not possible that Timoshenko has really got his army away intact, as reported. He also says that the tone of the Moscow press and wireless shows that morale in Russia must be very bad.*] Like almost everyone I know, except Warburg, Hugh Slater considers that there isn't going to be any Second Front. This is the inference everyone draws from Churchill's visit to Moscow.[83] People say, "Why should he go to Moscow to tell them we're going to[84] open a second front? He must have gone there to tell them we can't do it". Everyone agrees with my suggestion that it would be a good job if Churchill were sunk on the way back, like Kitchener.[85] [*Of course the possibility remains that Churchill isn't in Moscow.*]

Last night for the first time took a Sten gun to pieces.[86] There is almost nothing to learn in it. [*No spare parts. If the gun goes seriously wrong you simply chuck it away and get another.*] Weight of the gun without magazine is 5½ pounds – [*weight of the Tommy gun would be 12–15 lb. Estimated price is not 50/– as I had imagined, but 18/–.*] I can see a million or two million of these things, each with 500 cartridges and a book of instructions, floating down all over Europe on little parachutes. If the Government had the guts to do that they would really have burned their boats.

83. The following passage is crossed through in the manuscript: 'The question asked on every side is, "If the Second Front is going to be opened, what point is there in Churchill going to Moscow? He must have gone there to tell them we can't do it."'

84. The manuscript originally had 'we can't,' but this is crossed through and altered to read as in typescript.
85. Field Marshal Horatio Herbert Kitchener (1850–1916; 1st Earl Kitchener), who had reconquered the Sudan (1896–98) and was successful against the Boers in the South African War (1900–02), was regarded as a hero by the British populace. At the outbreak of World War I he was appointed Secretary of State for War. He was drowned when HMS *Hampshire*, taking him on a mission to Russia, struck a mine. He realized earlier than most the need to raise a large army and rapidly increased the strength of 'Kitchener's Army,' as it was called, from twenty to seventy divisions. He found co-operative work difficult and was less popular with Cabinet colleagues than with the general public. Orwell's second published work, when still at preparatory school, was a poem on the subject of the loss of Kitchener: see *CW*, X, p. 24.
86. In 1940 the only sub-machine-gun available to the British army was the American Thompson, but at least 100,0000 were lost at sea on the way from the USA causing an urgent need for a cheap home-produced automatic. The Sten, named after its designers, Major R. Vernon Sheppard and Harold J. Turpin, and the place of manufacture, Enfield, cost only £2 10s. It did not rely on machined parts and had no wooden stock. The magazine, based on the German 9mm MP 40, had a tendency to jam or fire single shots unexpectedly. But the Sten proved highly successful and was much favoured by resistance fighters.

9.8.42: Fired the Sten gun for the first time today. No kick, no vibration, very little noise, and reasonable accuracy. Out of about 2500 rounds fired, 2 stoppages, in each case due to a dud cartridge – treatment, simply to work the bolt by hand.

10.8.42: Nehru, Gandhi, Azad[87] and many others in jail. Rioting over most of India, a number of deaths, countless arrests. Ghastly speech by Amery,[88] speaking of Nehru and Co. as "wicked men", "saboteurs" etc. This of course broadcast on the Empire service and rebroadcast by AIR.[89] The best joke of all was that the Germans did their best to jam it, unfortunately without success.

Terrible feeling of depression among the Indians and everyone sympathetic to India. [*Even Bokhari, a Moslem League*[90] *man, almost in tears and talking about resigning from the BBC.*] It is strange, but quite truly the way the British Government is now behaving upsets me more than a military defeat.

87. Abdul Kalam Azad (1888–1958), Indian Nationalist Moslem leader, was spokesman for the Indian National Congress in the 1945 independence negotiations. His *India Wins Freedom* was published in 1959.
88. Leo Amery, Conservative M.P., was Secretary of State for India, 1940–45; see Events, 2.7.39, n. 5.
89. All-India Radio.

90. The Moslem League was founded as a religious organisation to protect the interests of Moslems in British India. It supported the Indian National Congress until 1935, when Hindu interests dominated the Congress Party and the League was developed into a political organisation. It was led by Mohammed Ali Jinnah and demanded the partition of India. When Pakistan was created in 1947, the League secured control of its first Constituent Assembly.

12.8.42: Appalling policy handout this morning about affairs in India. The riots are of no significance – situation is well in hand – after all the number of deaths is not large, etc., etc. As to the participation of students in the riots, this is explained along "boys will be boys" lines. "We all know that students everywhere are only too glad to join in any kind of rag", etc., etc. Almost everyone utterly disgusted. Some of the Indians when they hear this kind of stuff turn quite pale, a strange sight.

Most of the press taking a tough line, the Rothermere press disgustingly so. If these repressive measures in India are seemingly successful for the time being, the effects in this country will be very bad. All seems set for a big come-back of the reactionaries, and it almost begins to appear as though leaving Russia in the lurch were part of the manoeuvre. [*This afternoon shown in strict confidence by David Owen Amery's statement [on] postwar policy towards Burma, based on Dorman-Smith's*[91] *report. It envisages a return to "direct rule" for a period of 5–7 years, Burma's reconstruction to be financed by Britain and the big British firms to be re-established on much the same terms as before. Please God no document of this kind gets into enemy hands. I did however get from Owen and from the confidential document one useful piece of information – that, so far as is known, the scorched earth policy was really carried out with extreme thoroughness.*]

91. Sir Reginald Hugh Dorman-Smith (1899–1977) was Governor of Burma in 1941 and during the British withdrawal in 1942.

14.8.42: Horrabin was broadcasting today, and as always we introduced him as the man who drew the maps for Wells's *Outline of History* and Nehru's *Glimpses of World History*.[92] This had been extensively trailed and advertised beforehand, Horrabin's connection with Nehru being naturally a draw for India. Today the reference to Nehru was cut out from the announcement – N. being in prison and therefore having become Bad.

92. Properly, *Glimpses of World History: Being Further Letters to His Daughter, written in Prison, and containing a Rambling Account of History for Young People* (Allahabad, 1934); revised edition printed, with fifty maps by J. F. Horrabin in 1939 by Lindsay Drummond. According to Inez Holden, in a private communication, Orwell thought of asking Drummond to publish his and her war diaries.

18.8.42: From Georges Kopp's[93] last letter from Marseilles (after some rigmarole about the engineering work he has been doing): ". . . I am about to start production on an industrial scale. But I am not at all certain that I shall actually do so, because I have definite contracts with my firm, which has, I am afraid, developed lately connections which reduce considerably its independence and it is possible that another firm would eventually profit by my work, which I should hate since I have no arrangements at all with the latter and will not, for the time being, be prepared to sign any. If I am compelled to stop, I really don't know what I am going to do; I wish some of my very dear friends to whom I have written repeatedly would not be as slow and as passive as they seem to be. If no prospects open in this field, I contemplate to make use of another process of mine, related to bridge-building [*, which, you may remember, I have put into successful operation at San Mateo before the war."*]

Translated: "I am afraid France is going into full alliance with Germany. If the Second Front is not opened soon I shall do my best to escape to England".

93. Georges Kopp (1902–51), presented himself in many fictional forms but there is no doubt that he was Orwell's commandant in Spain, a brave man who worked for the French secret service and then MI5. One remarkable irony was that one of those involved in recruiting him for MI5 was the traitor, Anthony Blunt (1907–83). Orwell and he were friends and, despite Orwell's perspicacity in seeing through those such as Peter Smollett, he went along with Kopp's stories of himself. Bert Govaerts of Antwerp has uncovered a great deal of Kopp's life and fictions: see *The Lost Orwell*, pp. 83–91.

19.8.42: Big Commando raid on Dieppe today. Raid was still continuing this evening. Just conceivably the first step in an invasion, or a try-out for the first step, though I don't think so. The warning that was broadcast to the French people that this was only a raid and they were not to join in would in that case be a bluff.

22.8.42: D[avid] A[stor] very damping about the Dieppe raid, which he saw at more or less close quarters and which he says was an almost complete failure except for the very heavy destruction of German fighter planes, which was not part of the plan. He says that the affair was definitely misrepresented in the press[94] and is now being misrepresented in the reports to the P.M., and that the main facts were: – Something over 5000 men were engaged, of whom at least 2000 were killed or prisoners. It was not intended to stay longer on shore than was actually done (ie. till about 4 pm), but the idea was to destroy all the defences of Dieppe, and the attempt to do this was an utter failure. In fact only comparatively trivial damage was done, a few batteries of guns knocked out etc., and only one of the three main parties really made its objective. The others did not get far and many were massacred on the beach by artillery fire. The defences were formidable and would have been difficult to deal with even if there had been artillery support, as the guns were sunk in the face of the cliffs or under enormous concrete coverings. More tank-landing craft were sunk than got ashore. About 20 or 30 tanks were landed but none got off again. The newspaper photos which showed tanks apparently being brought back to England were intentionally misleading. The general impression was that the Germans knew of the raid beforehand.[95] Almost as soon as it was begun they had a man broadcasting a spurious "eye-witness" account from somewhere further up the coast, and another man broadcasting false orders in English. On the other hand the Germans were evidently surprised by the strength of the air support. Whereas normally they have kept their fighters on the ground so as to conserve their strength, they sent them into the air as soon as they heard that tanks were landing, and lost a number of planes variously estimated, but considered by some RAF officers to be as high as 270. Owing to the British strength in the air the destroyers were able to lie outside Dieppe all day. One was sunk, but this was by a shore battery. When a request came to attack some objective on shore, the destroyers formed in line and raced inshore firing their guns while the fighter planes supported them overhead.

David Astor considers that this definitely proves that an invasion of Europe is impossible. [*Of course we can't feel sure that he hasn't been planted to say this, considering who his parents are.*] I can't help feeling that to get ashore at all at such a strongly defended spot, without either bomber support, artillery support except for the guns of the destroyers (4.9 guns I suppose) or airborne troops, was a considerable achievement.

94. The Dieppe raid proved, at least in the short term, a sad waste except in so far as it brought home to senior servicemen the lessons to be learned for future landings. More than 6,000 men, mainly Canadian, were involved and well over half were killed, wounded, or captured. Churchill states that of 5,000 Canadians, 18% were killed and nearly 2,000 were captured (*The Second World War*, IV, p. 459). All 27 tanks landed were almost immediately destroyed; the RAF lost 70 planes, and 34 ships were sunk. The Germans admitted losing 297 killed and 294 wounded or captured, and 48 planes. The newspapers claimed in headlines at the time, 'Big Hun Losses' (*Daily Mirror*, 20 August 1942), but as *The War Papers*, 22 (1977) put it, 'they might have added, "Even Bigger Allied Losses".' David Astor served in the Royal Marines, 1940–45, and was decorated with the Croix de Guerre.

95. It was alleged that the Germans had cracked British codes and so had advance notice of the raid, but it seems that the first warning was given by German trawlers just as the Allied flotilla approached the coast. The failure of the raid was publicly put down to 'careless talk' or even to an advertisement for soap flakes which showed a woman pruning a tree dressed in what was headlined as 'BEACH COAT from DIEPPE.' A newspaper cutting of this advertisement,

which appeared in the *Daily Telegraph*, 15.8.42, was annotated by Orwell, 'Advert, popularly believed to have given the Germans advance warning of the Dieppe raid.' (The cutting is in Box 39 of Orwell's pamphlet collection in the British Library.) The film *Next of Kin* (1942), made to drive home the lesson that careless talk could endanger such enterprises, began its life as a shorter services training film. Churchill maintains, 'Our postwar examination of their records shows that the Germans did not receive, through leakages of information, any special warning of our attention to attack' *(The Second World War*, IV, p. 458).

25.8.42: One of the many rumours circulating among Indians here is that Nehru, Gandhi and others have been deported to South Africa. This is the kind of thing that results from press censorship and suppressing newspapers.

27.8.42: Ban on the *Daily Worker* lifted.[96] [*It is to reappear on Sept. 7th (same day as Churchill makes his statement to Parliament.*]

[*German radio again alleging S. C. Bose is in Penang. But the indications are that this was a slip of the tongue for R. B. Bose.*]

96. The *Daily Worker* had been suppressed on 22 January 1941.

29.8.42: Advert in pub for pick-me-up tablets – phenacetin or something of the kind: –

BLITZ
Thoroughly recommended by the
Medical Profession
The
"LIGHTNING"
Marvellous discovery
Millions take this remedy
for
Hangover
War Nerves
Influenza
Headache
Toothache
Neuralgia
Sleeplessness
Rheumatism
Depression, etc., etc.
Contains no Aspirin.

Another rumour among the Indians about Nehru – this time that he has escaped.

7.9.42: There is evidently trouble in Syria. Handout this morning to the effect that – most unfortunately and much against H.M. Government's will – General de Gaulle is insisting that Syria is still under a French mandate and it is impossible yet to make a treaty, as in the case of Irak. General de Gaulle's attitude is considered most deplorable, but as he is, after all, the accredited leader of the Free French and the whole legal position is very obscure (the matter should be decided upon by the League of Nations which unfortunately no longer exists) H.M. Government is unable, etc. etc. In other words the Syrians will get no treaty, the blame for this is placed on our puppet de Gaulle, and if possible we shall swipe Syria for ourselves. When I heard this hollow rubbish trotted out by Rushbrooke-Williams[97] this morning and we all had to listen and keep straight faces, there came into my head, I don't quite know why, the lines from Hardy's *Dynasts* about the crowning of Napoleon in Rome:

> Do not the prelate's accents falter thin,
> His lips with inheld laughter grow deformed,
> In blessing one whose aim is but to win
> The golden seat that other bums have warmed?[98]

The *Daily Worker* reappeared today – very mild, but they are urging (a) a second front (b) all help to Russia in the way of arms etc., and (c) a demagogic programme of higher wages all round which would be utterly incompatible with (a) and (b).

97. Laurence Frederic Rushbrook Williams (1890–1978; CBE, 1923; Orwell sometimes hyphenated his name, as here), had been Professor of Modern Indian History, Allahabad University, 1914–19, and Director of the Indian Central Bureau of Information, 1920–26. He was Director of the BBC's Eastern Service from 1941 to November 1944. He then joined *The Times* (to 1955). His attitude to India was enlightened and is well expressed in his *India* (Oxford Pamphlets on World Affairs, 1940). He also wrote *The State of Pakistan*, 1962, and *The East Pakistan Tragedy*, 1972.
98. In *The Dynasts*, Napoleon places the crown on his own head in Milan Cathedral, not in Rome (Complete Edition, 1910, 35; Part I, Act I, Scene 6). Orwell discussed *The Dynasts* in *Tribune*, 18 September 1942 (*CW*, XIV, pp. 42–5).

10.9.42: Lecturing last night at Morley College, Lambeth. Small hall, about 100 people, working-class intelligentsia (same sort of audience as Left Book Club branch[99]). During the questions afterwards, no less than 6 people asked "Does not the lecturer think it was a great mistake to lift the ban from the *Daily Worker*" – reasons given, that the *D.W's* loyalty is not reliable and it is a waste of paper. [*Only one woman stood up for the D. W, evidently a Communist at whom one or two of the others expressed impatience ("Oh, she's always saying that"!)*] This after a year during which there has been a ceaseless clamour for the lifting of the ban. One is constantly being thrown out in one's calculations because one listens to the articulate minority and forgets the other 99 per cent. Cf. Munich, when the mass of the people were almost certainly behind Chamberlain's policy, though to read the *New Statesman* etc. you wouldn't have thought so.

99. The Left Book Club, founded by Victor Gollancz in 1936, still published a book a month on anti-Fascist or Socialist topics. Local group meetings had been revived in the middle of 1942, and some fifty branches were formed. *The Road to Wigan Pier* was published under its auspices.

15.9.42: Ghastly feeling of impotence over the India business, Churchill's speeches, the evident intention of the blimps to have one more try at being what they consider tough, and the impudent way in which the newspapers can misrepresent the whole issue, well knowing that the public will never know enough or take enough interest to verify the facts. This last is the worst symptom of all – though actually our own apathy about India is not worse than the non-interest of Indian intellectuals in the struggle against Fascism in Europe.

21.9.42: Yesterday met Liddell Hart for the first time. Very defeatist and even, in my judgement, somewhat inclined to be pro-German subjectively. [*In a great stew about the barbarism of bombing Lübeck. Considered that during the wars of recent centuries the British have the worst record of all for atrocities and destructiveness.*] Although, of course, strongly opposed to the Second Front, also anxious for us to call off the bombing. There is no point in doing it, as it can achieve nothing and does not weaken Germany. On the other hand we ought not to have started the bombing in the first place (he stuck to it that it was we who started it), as it merely brought heavier reprisals on ourselves.

Osbert Sitwell[100] was also there. [*He was at one time connected with Mosley's movement, but probably somewhat less inclined to go pro-German than L-H.*] Both of them professed to be disgusted by our seizure of the Vichy colonies. Sitwell said that our motto was "When things look bad, retake Madagascar". He said that in Cornwall in case of invasion the Home Guard have orders to shoot all artists. I said that in Cornwall this might be all for the best. Sitwell: "Some instinct would lead them to the good ones".

100. Sir Osbert Sitwell (1892–1969) was educated at Eton and served in the Grenadier Guards, 1912–19. In 1916 his poetry, with his sister Edith's, was published as *Twentieth-Century Harlequinade*. He also wrote short stories (*Triple Fugue*, 1924;

Open the Door, 1941), a number of novels, including *Before the Bombardment* (1926), *The Man Who Lost Himself* (1929), *Those Were the Days* (1938), *A Place of One's Own* (1941), many essays and some critical studies (particularly on Dickens). He selected and arranged the text of William Walton's *Belshazzar's Feast* (1931). Orwell described his *Left Hand, Right Hand!, The Scarlet Tree,* and *Great Morning!* (1944–47) as 'among the best autobiographies of our time'; see *CW*, XIX, pp. 385–8.

22.9.42: Most of the ammunition for our Sten guns is Italian, or rather made in Germany for Italy. I fancy this must be the first weapon the British army has had whose bore was measured in millimetres instead of inches. They were going to make a new cheap automatic weapon, and having the vast stocks of ammunition captured in Abyssinia handy, manufactured the guns to fit the cartridges instead of the other way about. The advantage is that the ammunition of almost any continental submachine gun will fit it. It will be interesting to see whether the Germans or Japanese come out with a .303 weapon to fit captured British ammunition.

28.9.42: Open-air church parade in Regents Park yesterday. How touching the scene ought to be – the battalion in hollow square, band of the Coldstream Guards, the men standing bareheaded (beautiful autumn day, faint mist and not a leaf stirring, dogs gambolling round) and singing the hymns as best they could. But unfortunately there was a sermon with the jingoistic muck which is usual on these occasions and which makes me go pro-German for as long as I listen to it. Also a special prayer "for the people of Stalingrad" – the Judas kiss. [*A detail that gets me down on these occasions is the clergyman's white surplice, which looks all wrong against a background of military uniforms. Struck by the professionalism of the band, especially the bandmaster (an officer in the black peaked cap of the Guards). As each prayer drew to its close, a stirring in the band, the trombones come out of their leather suitcases, the bandmaster's baton comes up, and they are ready to snap into the Amen just as the priest reaches "through Jesus Christ our Lord".*]

5.10.42: New viceroy of India to be appointed shortly. No clue as to who he will be. Some say General Auchinleck – who, it is said, gets on well with leftwing Indians.

Long talk with Brander, who is back after his 6 months tour in India.[101] His conclusions so depressing that I can hardly bring myself to write them down. Briefly – affairs are much worse in India than anyone here is allowed to realise, the situation is in fact retrievable but won't be retrieved because the government is determined to make no real concessions, hell will break loose when and if there is a Japanese invasion, and our broadcasts are utterly useless because nobody listens to them. Brander did say, however, that the Indians listen to BBC news, because they regard it as more truthful than that given out by Tokio or Berlin. He considers that we should broadcast news and music and nothing else. This is what I have been saying for some time past.

101. Laurence Brander (1903–?) author and lecturer in English literature in India for twelve years before the war, was employed by the BBC as Intelligence Officer, Eastern Service, 1941–44. In 1954 his study *George Orwell* was published. Pages 8–9 give a succinct insight to Orwell at the BBC:

"Everyone liked and respected him and he was the inspiration of that rudimentary Third Programme which was sent out to the Indian student. He soon sensed that the audience for the programme was not so large as was thought by the senior officials and, before I went to India early in 1942 to find out, he gave a great deal of time to discussing the problems with me. I found that our programmes were at a time of day when nobody was listening and that they could hardly be heard because the signal was so weak. Very few students had access to wireless sets. . . .

I was always grateful to Orwell while we worked together in the B.B.C. He laughed very readily at the nonsense that went on, and made it tolerable. This did not interfere with his sense of responsibility, for he knew how important radio propaganda could be, if intelligently organized, and he worked very hard on his own talks, which were always good and usually brilliant. His voice was a great handicap. Thin and flat, it did not go over well on short-wave broadcasting". [The quality of Orwell's voice had been badly affected by his being shot through the throat when fighting in Spain.]

Brander goes on to refer to the proposal to put into print the good talks that were not being heard, and it was he who suggested that Blair broadcast under the name Orwell (see *CW*, XIV, pp. 89 and 100–2). After the war, he was Director of Publications for the British Council.

10.10.42: Today in honour of the anniversary of the Chinese Revolution the Chinese flag was hoisted over Broadcasting House. Unfortunately it was upside down.

[*According to D[avid] A[stor], Cripps is going to resign shortly – pretext, that the War Cabinet is a sham, Churchill being in reality the sole power in it.*]

11.10.42: The authorities in Canada have now chained up a number of German prisoners equal to the number of British prisoners chained up in Germany. What the devil are we coming to?[102]

102. The Germans chained some 2,500 Allied prisoners (mainly Canadian) taken at Dieppe because they claimed that British Commandos had chained their German prisoners. The British War Office denied this. Canada then manacled 1,376 German prisoners. On 15 October, the Swiss Red Cross offered to mediate. See Orwell's (unpublished) letter to the *Times*, 12 October 1942, in which he argues that by such retaliation we 'descend . . . to the level of our enemies' (*CW*, XIV, pp. 97–8). On 18 October, Hitler ordered German troops to shoot all captured Allied Commandos 'to the last man.'

15.10.42: A little bit of India transplanted to England. For some weeks our Marathi newsletters were translated and broadcast by a little man named Kothari, completely spherical but quite intelligent and, so far as I could judge, genuinely anti-Fascist. Suddenly one of the mysterious bodies which control recruitment for the BBC (in this case I think MI5)[103] got onto the fact that Kothari was or had been a Communist, active in the students' movement, and had been in jail, so the order came to get rid of him. A youth named Jatha, working at India House and politically OK, was engaged in his place. Translators in this language are not easy to find and Indians who speak it as their native tongue seem to tend to forget it while in England. After a few weeks my assistant, Miss Chitale, came to me with great secrecy and confided that the newsletters were still in fact being written by Kothari. Jatha, though still able to read the language, was no longer equal to writing it and Kothari was ghosting for him. No doubt the fee was being split between them. We can't find another competent translator, so Kothari is to continue and we officially know nothing about it. Wherever Indians are to be found, this kind of thing will be happening.

103. This is presumably a reference to the mysterious and unexplained 'College' to which Orwell refers from time to time.

17.10.42: Heard a "Jew joke" on the stage at the Players' theatre last night – a mild one, and told by a Jew, but still slightly anti-Jew in tendency.[104] More Second Front rumours. The date this time is given as October 20th, an unlikely date, being a Tuesday. It seems pretty clear that something is going to happen in West or North-west Africa however.

104. Orwell traced the telling of 'Jew-jokes' as an example of anti-Semitism.

15.11.42: Church bells rung this morning – in celebration for the victory in Egypt.[105] The first time that I have heard them in over two years.

105. Following the attack launched at El Alamein on 23 October 1942, the Eighth Army cleared Egypt by 11 November 1942; Tobruk, in Libya, was retaken on 12 November. Allied forces landed in Morocco and Algeria on 8 November, and by 12 November were close to the western Tunisian border. Final victory in North Africa, however, was not to come until mid-May 1943.

This concludes Orwell's War-time Diaries.

The Jura Diaries

DOMESTIC DIARY VOLUME III

7 May 1946 – 5 January 1947

When Orwell left the BBC on 23 November 1943 he also resigned, on medical grounds, from the Home Guard. Its chief offensive work in 1943 and 1944 was manning Anti-Aircraft Batteries (especially the 'Z' or rocket batteries for which he was ill-suited). On 3 December 1943 he wrote the first of eighty personal columns, 'As I Please', for *Tribune* and later that month began reviewing for *The Manchester Evening News*. During the winter of 1943–44 he wrote *Animal Farm*. By the end of May 1944 he had finished *The English People,* although it would not be published until August 1947. In June 1944, the Orwells adopted a son, Richard. The following month, on the 28th, their flat was bombed destroying many of his books and leaving his typescript of *Animal Farm,* as he explained to T. S. Eliot, in a 'slightly crumpled condition'. Eliot rejected it (as he had *Down and Out in Paris and London*) on behalf of Faber. Orwell's friend, Inez Holden, wrote that the flat was no longer habitable, but Orwell 'goes each day to rummage in the rubble to recover as many books as possible and wheel them away in a wheel-barrow. He makes this journey from Fleet Street during his lunch hour'. That summer Orwell visited Jura for the first time and in October he and Eileen moved into a flat in Canonbury Square, Islington. That would be his last London home.

From 15 February to 24 May 1945 Orwell worked as a war correspondent in France, Germany and Austria writing articles for *The Manchester Evening News* and *The Observer.* Eileen had been ill intermittently for a number of years and in March 1945 it was decided she should undergo an operation. Unfortunately she died under the anaesthetic on the 29th. Their exchanges of letters at this time are particularly touching; Eileen's last letter was left unfinished as she was wheeled off for the operation. After arranging for his little son to be cared for, Orwell completed his tour of duty as a war correspondent.

Although Orwell told Fredric Warburg that he had first thought of *Nineteen Eighty-Four* in 1943, we now know that Orwell was specifically motivated to start writing the novel after hearing John Baker speak on the falsification of science in the USSR at the PEN Conference in London, 22–26 August 1944 (see *The Lost Orwell,* pp. 128–33). Progress was slow. On 25th June 1945, Fredric Warburg reported that Orwell 'has written the first twelve pages of his new novel' (*Nineteen Eighty-Four*) and on 26 September 1946 (in the mid-period of this Diary) he wrote to Humphrey Slater that 'I have at last started my novel about the future, but I've only done about 50 pages'. The novel would be completed in December 1948. In the meantime, on 17 August 1945, after many rejections, *Animal Farm* was published by Secker & Warburg. It was published in the USA in 1946 and made American Book-of-the-Month Club choice. On 14 February 1946 his volume, *Critical Essays,* was published by Secker & Warburg.

When staying in a fisherman's cottage on Jura in September 1945, he visited Barnhill at the north of the island and decided to rent it from 23 May to 13 October 1946.

Orwell's third Domestic Diary, which he called 'Vol. III,' was written in a hundred-leaf exercise book, 8x7 inches (Denbigh Commercial Books, D.34/100). The diary is written almost entirely on recto pages (1 to 182, as numbered by the editor). Following it are garden plans (reproduced here) and lists of metaphors, clichés, and so on. These are not given here but can be found in *CW*, XVII, pp. 432–8. The entries cover the period 7 May to 8 October 1946. Orwell left Jura for London on 9 October. He went back to Jura early in January 1947 and made two more entries, for 4 and 5 January 1947. The diary is in manuscript only, in Orwell's hand, and he did not, as he did for earlier diaries, type it up. Assistance in identifying some of the people mentioned was provided by a list prepared by Avril Dunn.

Jura, an island of the Inner Hebrides, lies roughly in line with Edinburgh and Glasgow. It is approximately twenty-six miles in length and varies in width from about eight miles to some three miles at Barnhill, which is about three miles south of the northern tip of the island. Its population in 1946 was about 250, but over the next thirty years it increased to about 400. The Sound of Jura, which separates the island from the mainland, is about four miles wide at Barnhill; the crossing, which can be affected by severe Atlantic swells, takes longer farther south. From Tarbert, on the mainland (actually West Tarbert), to Craighouse is about thirty miles, and the crossing then took about two to two-and-a-half hours. Craighouse, where Orwell collected his rations, had the island's only shop and doctor; there was also a telephone there. As the crow flies, it is twenty-three miles south of Barnhill, but with 'declivities' (see 2.6.46) it is, perhaps, twenty-seven miles. The road, often not much more than a track then, was in poor condition and caused many a puncture. Further, journeys were much longer than a direct measurement on the map indicates. When Orwell lived at Barnhill, a ship called at Jura from the mainland three times a week. From Barnhill to Ardlussa is about seven miles. He gives Kinuachdrachd (which he always spelt without the final 'd') as one and a half miles to the north of Barnhill, but it is slightly less as the crow flies. A made-up road, the A846, runs round the southern tip of the island, then north via Craighouse and Tarbert to a little south of Ardlussa, whence it declines to a track. Ordnance Survey Landranger Map 61, 'Jura & Colonsay,' 1987, marks Barnhill.

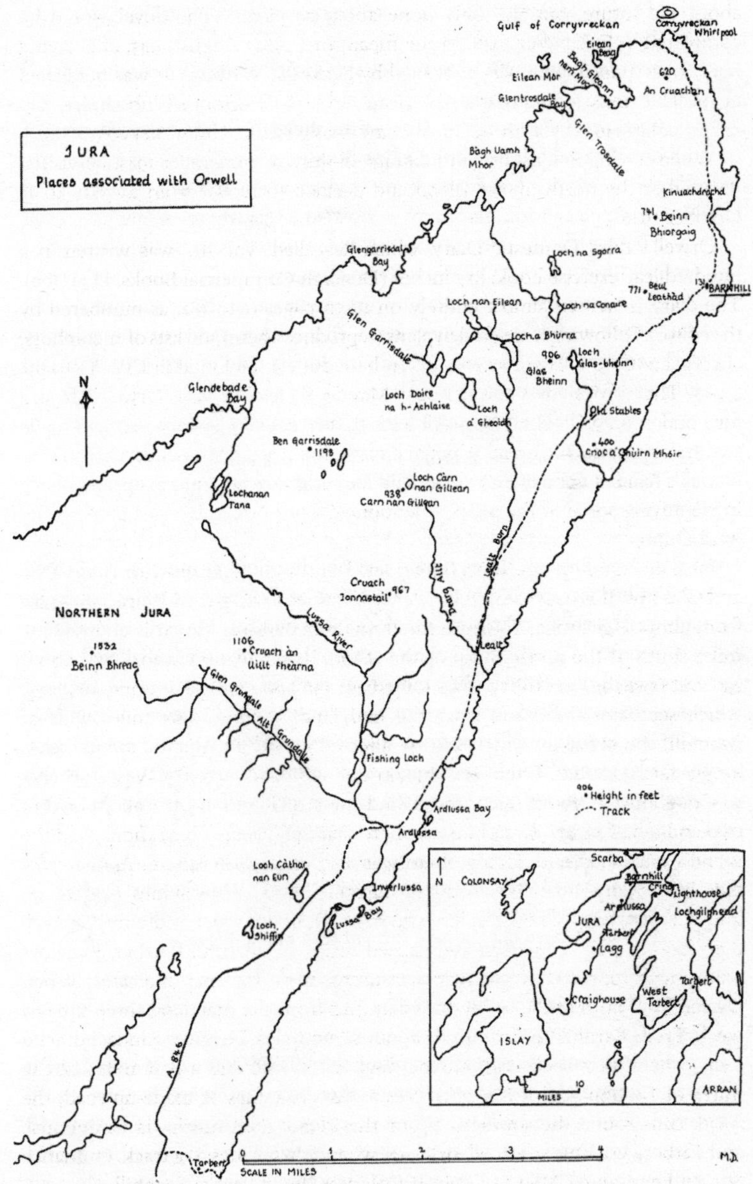
JURA
Places associated with Orwell
Gulf of Corryvreckan
Corryvreckan Whirlpool
Eilean Beag
Eilean Mòr
Bàgh Gleann nam Muc
620
An Cruachan
Glentrosdale Bay
Glen Trosdale
Bàgh Uamh Mhor
Kinuachdrachd
741 Beinn Bhiorgaig
Glengarrisdale Bay
Loch na Sgorra
771 Beul Leathàd
131 BARNHILL
Loch nan Eilean
Loch na Conaire
Glen Garrisdale
Loch a Bhùrra
906 Glas Bheinn
Loch Glas-bheinn
N
Glendebade Bay
Loch Doire na h-Achlaise
Loch a' Gheoidh
Old Stables
400 Cnoc a' Chùirn Mhòir
Ben Garrisdale 1198
Loch Càrn nan Gillean
938 Carn nan Gillean
Lochanan Tana
Leatt Burn
Dubh Allt
Cruach Ionnastail 967
Lussa River
NORTHERN JURA
1532 Beinn Bhreac
1106 Cruach àn Uillt Fhearna
Glen Grundale
Alt Grundale
Lealt
Fishing Loch
906 Height in feet
Track
Ardlussa Bay
Ardlussa
Loch Càthar nan Eun
Inverlussa
Lussa Bay
Loch Shiffin
A 846
Tarbert
0 1 2 3 4
SCALE IN MILES
M.D.
N
Scarba
COLONSAY
Barnhill
Crinan
Lighthouse
Lochgilphead
Ardlussa
JURA
Tarbert
Lagg
Tarbert
Craighouse
West Tarbert
ISLAY
10
MILES
ARRAN

7.5.46: *London:* Making notes now for purposes of comparison later with Edinburgh & Jura.

Last two days spent in neighbourhood of Newark,[1] returning by car Nottingham – Amersham.

Vegetation in Nottinghamshire seems ahead of London area. Most trees full out. Oaks about half out. Leaves of latter are yellowish, as in autumn. Leaves of copper beech much paler than when full out. Chestnuts in bloom. Apples in full bloom, or almost so, everywhere. A few have even shed their blossom. Hawthorn well out – some bushes almost covered with it. Bluebells in full bloom. Ditto Honesty (? tall purplish-red weed.) Tulips at their best, ditto wallflowers, aubretia, arabis. Lilac pretty well out. Stone crop not blooming yet. General appearance of the countryside very green & forward, in spite of beastly cold of last few days. Did not see a swallow or hear a cuckoo.

Grass on chalk areas appears paler than on clay soil.

1. Orwell attended the funeral of his sister Marjorie, Humphrey Dakin's wife. The funeral probably took place on 6 May 1946. See his letter to Dakin, 8 May 1946, *CW*, XVIII, p. 309.

14.5.46: *Nr. Edinburgh:* Trees pretty well out, but flowers much behind those of Nottingham area & London. Those now at their best are tulips, saxifrage, aubretia, bluebells, wild forget-me-nots. Lilacs budding, but no colour in them yet. Peonies in green bud. Apples barely in blossom, except sheltered spots. Gorse well out. Rabbits very numerous here, in contrast to s. of England since the war. Black geese seem fairly numerous. Curlews mating have warbling cry quite different from what they make in winter. Drought here has been greater than in s. of England, & pools etc. very low & clear. In this area[2] "corn" means oats. Estimated average yield of oats, 12 cwt. per acre.

2. 'This area' was Biggar, some thirty miles southwest of Edinburgh and thirty-five miles southeast of Glasgow. Georges and Doreen Kopp had taken a farm there, and Orwell stayed with them for a week. (Doreen was Gwen O'Shaughnessy's half-sister; for George Kopp, see Second War-time Diary, 18.8.42, n. 93). Orwell did not have Richard with him at Biggar.

16.5.46: Shot a black rabbit yesterday (young one.)[3] Very black, under side grey. They seem to be common about here.

Field of oats (1¾ acres) was ploughed, disced & sown in two days. It was a grass field & still very rough after being ploughed & then disced twice. Seed was broadcast, which it seems is still usual here with small plots. The sower has what is called a "sowing sheet", consisting of a kidney-shaped basket of canvas on a wooden frame. This fits against his belly & is slung to his shoulders with straps. He marches up & down, spraying the seed in both directions with either hand alternately. It is scattered pretty evenly, the grains being generally about 3 inches apart. He sowed the 1¾ acres in a short afternoon. At least one other person is required, however, to follow him up & down with a bucket & keep him supplied with seed. Also someone with a gun to keep the rooks off. Amount of seed supplied was 3 bags containing (I think) 12 bushels in all, but the field took only 2½ bags. Today the ground was rolled. The discing, which was due for the second time after sowing, covers the seed up fairly well.

The goat which kidded 3 days ago is giving so much milk that her two kids are overfed & have bad diarrhea.° She has to be milked fairly strenuously – about 3 pints a day in addition to what the kids are taking.

Note the variation in feeding habits of goats. These two are in a grass paddock with no access to foliage. They graze peacefully, making no attempt to get out, though the fence is a low one. Snow on nearby hill (2700 feet)[4] this afternoon.

3. Orwell more than once refers to himself as being 'a bad shot' but that was typical of his self-denigration.
4. The 'nearby hill' was presumably either Broad Law, 2,723 feet, or Dollar Law, 2,681 feet, both about a dozen miles southeast of Biggar. The hills close to Biggar are 1,200 to 1,400 feet in height.

22.5.46: May only about half out in most places.

Made a scarecrow on Saturday (18th). Rooks frightened of it at first, but by Monday night already feeding within 20 yards of it.

Polyantha roses on E[ileen]'s grave[5] have all rooted well. Planted aubretia, miniature phlox, saxifrage, a kind of dwarf broom, a house-leek of some kind, & a miniature dianthus. Plants not in very good condition, but it was rainy weather, so they should strike.

Weather wetter, but no really heavy rain. Today fine but not very warm.

Crossing Gourroch – Craighouse.

Left Gourroch about 9.30 am (Glasgow 8 am)

Dunoon about 10.

Rothesay 10.35

Colintraive 11.10

Tigh-na-bruaich 11.30

Tarbert East 12.30 (v. late).

Tarbert East – Tarbert West 5 miles of road

Left Tarbert W. 1.40 (50 mins. late)

5. Orwell visited Eileen's grave in St. Andrew's and Jesmond Cemetery, two or three miles north of Newcastle upon Tyne, whilst at Biggar. The return journey by road would be a little over two hundred miles.

23.5.46: *Jura:* Still very dry & hot. Owing to the prolonged drought, streams which are normally quite considerable torrents have dried up. Not only bush fruits but apples seem to do quite well here if they get a little shelter. Azaleas do well, rhododendras° become almost a weed, fuchsias grow into huge woody bushes & also (I think) grow wild. Plenty of trees here but very gnarled & not large. Deer very tame. Rabbits very numerous but the grown-up ones rather timid. Too busy settling house to do much outside, but shot a rabbit in the garden (young one). No vegetables except haricot beans. Shall try the experiment of stewing him with pickled onions.

Bluebells in profusion everywhere. Primroses still full out, also thrift (on rocks almost in the sea.) Wild iris just coming into flower. These grow within a few yards of the high-tide mark. In spite of the drought, grass very green where it is not overwhelmed by rushes, which are about the worst weed here, worse even than bracken. Hoodie crows[6] here all summer, not merely in winter as in East Anglia. Oyster catcher fairly common.

Fishing, ie. in the sea, has been very poor so far this year. Said to be due to the dry weather & east wind.

6. The hooded crow *(Corvus cornix).*

24.5.46: Started digging garden, ie. breaking in the turf. Back-breaking work. Soil not only as dry as a bone, but very stony. Nevertheless there was a little rain last night. As soon as I have a fair patch dug, shall stick in salad vegetables. This autumn shall put in bushes, rhubarb & fruit trees if possible, but it will need a very high & strong fence to keep the deer off them. Shot at a rabbit in the dusk & missed him. Keep seeing at the end of the garden a young very light-coloured rabbit, a sort of fawn colour so light as to be almost white in some lights. Have never seen one of this colour before. As always when one sees an animal with some peculiarity like this, one is made aware of how often one sees the same animal over & over again.

Saw a seal close inshore. Slowly rising up & sinking down, with nose almost perpendicular, like a periscope.

Donald Darroch[7] tells me last month two heifers died of bracken poisoning – this was the vet's diagnosis. One would think that if bracken is poisonous to them, either they would have the sense to let it alone, or no cattle could survive in such a place.

7. Donald Darroch and his sister Katie had a croft a mile or so from Barnhill, at Kinuachdrachd. Orwell went there every day for milk until he bought a cow. He and Donald, who worked on a profit-sharing basis with Orwell's laird, Robin Fletcher, were very friendly. Often referred to by Orwell as 'D.D.' and 'K.D.'

26.5.46: Weather more overcast the last two days, but still very hot & dry. When digging in garden it is more comfortable to be half naked. Sowed lettuces, radishes, spring onions, cress. Will do nothing until there is rain. Ground is dry as a bone down to 8 inches.

Today came on a fully-gorged tick which I suppose had just dropped off a cow. It was slightly larger than a pea, but of oval shape, about the size of a small dried haricot bean. Skin grey, shiny & fairly tough. Cut it open & found it full of dark viscous blood.

27.5.46: Some rain in the night & this morning, but it has not gone even an inch into the soil. All today very blowy, & generally overcast. Wind shifting round to all quarters. Clouds extremely low at times, but still not raining.

Dug some more. Only a small part of the garden can be broken in straight off, the rest will have to be sodium chlorated to kill the rushes, & then preferably ploughed.

Saw what I think was an eagle, but it was some way off & I am not very familiar with the large birds of prey, so perhaps it was some kind of buzzard. Rock doves here as well as wood pigeons.

28.5.46: Rain, heavier than yesterday, for about an hour & a half this evening. This time it has gone in a little way. Rain always seems to have the effect of calming the sea.

Yesterday made a trestle for sawing logs. Making anything out of timber one cuts in the woods is a curious job because the trees are so gnarled that it is hard to get a straight piece. Today made a sledge – primitive substitute for wheelbarrow – out of driftwood & some old matchboarding. One can drag quite a load if one steers for the smooth places. They use sledges here for dragging things up steep hills, but probably quite a different pattern. Started building incinerator out of stone. Very tedious job because of the difficulty of finding flat pieces of stone. Found the peat beds & shall try digging some tomorrow if the weather is fine. It is usual to dig it in May or not later than the first week in June – reason, that in middle summer the grass gets long & the peat does not get a chance to dry. It is usual to lay the blocks out in rows, then, when the top side is dry, build them up into little pyramids for further drying, then cart them home. In exceptionally dry weather they will dry in 3 weeks. If an average family depends wholly on peat, it means roughly a month's work a year.

The highland cattle are definitely a small breed. The herd I saw here & took for half-grown heifers are 3 years old. Their milk is said to be rich, but not large in quantity. A few are black. This is a reversion to the original breed, which used to be called the "black cattle."

"Corn" is habitually sown broadcast here. It nevertheless tends to come up in rows, because the furrows from the ploughing persist even after harrowing, & the grains tend to roll down into the furrows. Ditto in Morocco, where they not only sow broadcast, but don't even harrow, merely ploughing the ground over & over.

29.5.46: Late last night distinctly cold. All today very blowy & mostly overcast. Wind changing round to all quarters. Black-backed gulls coming inland, & at times a bit of a sea getting up in the straits. Still no rain, however. Last night's rain did temporarily fill the ditch full enough for some water to come through into the tank, but today it is almost dry again.

Finished digging patch under window. Cleared out a few thistles, put up shelves. Did not do much else as I felt very tired & slept for 2 or 3 hours in the afternoon.

This evening missed a large rabbit, sitting, at 35 yards! Partly because this gun has a harder pull than I am accustomed to.

30.5.46: Very hot, dry & still all day. Sea like glass. Late this evening literally a few drops of rain for about 5 minutes.

Saw 3 of the fawn-coloured rabbits – of different sizes & in different places, so there must be a breed of them about here.

Started digging the patch by the railing. Soil here is deeper & less stony. Dug out about 100 blocks of peat & set them out in rows. Surprised by the easiness of the operation: to dig 100 blocks or more took me less than an hour. Notice that the peat does not necessarily lie in very deep beds. Up to 1 spit down it was pure peat, then I came on some paler stuff which looked like sandy soil, rather sodden.

Put up more shelves, covered stool.

Tits evidently have a nest in the gatepost (iron), as I see them coming out of the hole occasionally. Two days ago one got momentarily stuck in the hole when I was approaching & shrieked with terror.

31.5.46: A light shower in the afternoon.

Shot one of the fawn-coloured rabbits (a doe.) A quite striking, almost reddish fawn pelt. Shall try to cure it.

1.6.46: Treated the rabbit skin according to the recipe in the other diary,[8] but uncertain whether I got the fat off completely enough. NB. to examine it about 15.6.46.

Overcast, & a little drizzling rain, but not cold.

Came on a raven on the cliff which must have been asleep or something of the kind – at any rate it had difficulty in struggling through the bracken before it could get on the wing.

Large hovering hawk of some kind – in style of flight somewhat like a larger edition of a kestrel, but flaps its wings more slowly – always about behind the house. Presumably some kind of buzzard. Turned up medium-sized brown-coloured bird in the wood, which had all the appearance of being a woodcock. I thought they did not stay the summer here. Black game fairly numerous. When one sees them in pairs, both seem the same colour – thought the hen (called "grey hen") would be lighter.

The stonecrop with reddish leaves, so common on the rocks here, is out. Pinky-white flowers. Tried transplanting a small piece of it, tho' it is probably rather late to do so.

8. Some of Orwell's diaries have not been traced, including the one referred to here.

2.6.46: All day very hot and dry, until the evening, when a light drizzle. Crossed over from Kinuachdrach to Glentrosdale[9] – about 3½ miles as the crow flies, but about 5 allowing for declivities. Time going, 2 hours: returning, 1¾ hours.

Killed a snake. Brown colour, about 18″ long, some kind of zigzag marking on its back. Again uncertain whether an adder, but resolved to kill all snakes close to the house, to be on safe side with R[ichard]. In killing it, cut it in half. Then picked up, as I thought, the safe end to examine it, but it was the head, which promptly tried to bite me. Had previously seen another snake, but only momentarily.

Saw 3 wild goats. They were about 400 yards away, & at that distance looked definitely black. Somewhat heavy movements, compared with the deer.

Saw (I think) a gold-crested wren.

9. Glentrosdale is on the west coast of Jura; it is about two miles as the crow flies from Kinuachdrachd (Orwell always omitted the final 'd').

3.6.46: This morning overcast & a little drizzle, rest of day dry but windy. Said to have been some rain in the night.

Sowed cress, radishes, spring onions, lettuces. Cress & another seed (I think lettuce) both sowed 26.5.46, now showing.

Two young cuckoos, not yet quite firm on the wing, sitting on the fence. Swallow has nest in the big byre.

4.6.46: Quite heavy rain all day until about 5.30 pm, after which fine. Pleasant mild weather in evening, with some sun. Sea roughish in morning, calming down rapidly in evening.

Radishes (sown 26.5.46) are up. Put soot round all seeds showing. Slugs awful.

5.6.46: Very blustery all day. Wind from west. Rain occasionally stopped, but wind continues. Considerable sea running.

Too wet to do much out of doors. Cleared up the big barn to make room for coal etc. Floor deeply covered with very dry dung which was coated with a white deposit, I suppose nitre. Got about half a load of manure thus.

Two enormous birds of hawk tribe, which I think must have been eagles, circling quite close to house, sometimes only 20 or 30 yards from the ground. Crows hawking at them, sometimes almost perching on their backs. Went out for walk & only saw one rabbit. Perhaps they do not venture out in very windy weather. Again turned up a woodcock.

6.6.46: Fine all day, with only one or two very light showers of a few minutes. Sea fairly calm.

Last night late shot another fawn-coloured rabbit. Cured skin. NB. to examine about 20.6.46. Quite a high proportion, perhaps as many as one in ten, of the rabbits round here are of this colour. Nevertheless it must have a poor survival value as they are much more conspicuous. Could see this one in almost complete darkness when I could not have seen an ordinary rabbit.

Mattock arrived, so started digging the rushes out of the back yard. Comparatively easy job with this tool.

Broached 40 gallon drum of paraffin. If we use 2 gallons a week (shall test this accurately later), should last us till nearly end of October.

7.6.46: Fine all day. Walked to Glengarrisdale[10] & back. Exactly 3 hours each way, but probably increased if not choosing the best ground. Distance as crow flies about 10 miles, but by the route one has to take, about 14 (ie. in all.) Saw flock of wild goats. They are definitely shyer than the deer. Most of them quite black, but some have white patches. At the distance at which one can see them, ie. about 300 yards, they appear very large, so that one could almost mistake them for cattle. Probably due to shagginess of coats.

Old human skull, with some other bones, lying on beach at

Glengarrisdale. Said to be survivor from massacre of the McCleans° by the Campbells,[11] & probably at any rate 200 years old. Two teeth (back) still in it. Quite undecayed.

Although lobsters round here are numerous & good, crabs are seldom large & not considered worth sending away. Two lobsters fairly frequently taken in one creel. Current market price of lobsters 2/11½ a lb. Yesterday cooked two lobsters by boiling them alive – only practicable way of killing them. They appeared to remain alive (at any rate struggling) for some seconds after being put in the boiling water. Nevertheless parts of their shells begin to turn red the instant they are put in.

Half gallon of paraffin fills Aladdin lamp, standard lamp & 1 wall lamp pretty full, & another wall lamp about ½ full. This should be lighting for about 2 days. Allowing the oil stove to use ½ gallon a week, paraffin consumption should be about 2½ galls a week, or say 3 gallons if another small stove is used for drying. So that 40 galls of paraffin should last till end of August.

10. Glengarrisdale Bay is on the western side of Jura, about four miles from the north tip of the island and 3½ miles as the crow flies due west of Barnhill.
11. This is one of a number of less well-known massacres perpetrated by the Campbells, not that of the Macdonalds at Glencoe, some fifty miles to the north, in 1692.

8.6.46: Fine all day. Warm but not very sunny. Sea calm. Elder coming into flower (late, I think?). Rowan trees have been well in flower for some time. Cress sown on 3.6.46 already germinating. No sign of first lot of onions. Wagtail has nest in barn. Very busy carrying tufts of moss to & fro. Have noticed that one does not see thrushes or blackbirds round here. Also finches, even sparrows, very scarce – in fact I do not think we have seen a sparrow since coming here. Ditto starlings. Larks are to be seen, but not very common. Field mice are common. No house mice or rats round this house as yet.

Price of some goslings aged (I think) 6 weeks, 25/– each. Actually not very expensive for nowadays, if one considers that during most of their life they will feed chiefly on grass.

9.6.46: Fine but overcast till about 5 pm, then rain. Sea calm. Deer have trampled on a good deal of the peat we laid out to dry. Probably due to laying it out not on the grass but in the peat-bed itself, which the deer use as a stamping ground.

A[vril][12] found what was evidently a young rat dead near gate. Hitherto no rats or mice (ie. other than field mice) round this house.

12. Avril (usually as 'A.'), was Orwell's younger sister. It was Avril who would care for Orwell's son, Richard Blair, after Orwell's death.

10.6.46: Raining all morning, fine all afternoon. Strongish wind from west some of afternoon, & not particularly warm. Sea calm.

Sowed lettuces. Second lot (sown 3.6.46) are up. Onions sown 26.5.46 are just showing. Put soot round the seeds that are up.

Outboard motor boat (ie. small rowing boat with outboard) makes the journey from Ardlussa to Glengarrisdale (said to be 15m. but I should have said more)[13] in 2–3 hours, sometimes as little as 2 hours, on 1½ gallons of petrol. Consumption would be about 8m. to the gallon. Outboard can be put on to any boat, even flat-bottomed.

Evidently the fish referred to as "lithe" is a pollack, but sometimes this is referred to as though it were a variety of "saythe" (the phrase "rock saythe" is used), the "saythe's" other name being, I think, cole-fish.* It is some time since I have seen either but I do not believe these fish are of the same family.

13. About fifteen miles is correct.

15.6.46: Have been away at Biggar & Glasgow for several days.

Today warm & overcast. A little drizzling rain this afternoon.

Sowed carrots, beetroot, spinach, French beans, turnips, swedes, cress – small quantities of most of these. Lettuces sown 10.6.46 already showing. Radish seedlings had been eaten by something. Suspected slugs & put more soot, but shortly afterwards saw a very young rabbit, one of a family which lives in the garden, browsing near the salad bed, so suppose the rabbit was to blame. Would have expected it to attack the lettuce seedlings first. Put strands of wire netting loosely over bed – hope will be enough to keep the rabbits out.

Brought home the geese. Now aged 2 months. Fully fledged &, I should say, weighing 8–10 lb each. Perhaps owing to upset of move, they have not wandered about as I expected but spent most of day huddling round the back door & not grazing much.

Three kestrels sitting on the fence together today. Presumably young birds which have recently learned to fly.

The corn sowed at Biggar has come up well, with a pretty even distribution. If anything it appears to be thickest in the corner where the rooks were the worst. So possibly the rooks are maligned & only come for insects.

* coal fish [Orwell's footnote]. The lythe (as it is usually spelt) is a dusky, green-backed fish of the cod family. It is also known as the saithe and pollack. At 22.8.46 Orwell notes that the correct spelling is 'saithe,' though his spelling still varies thereafter and has been left as he gave it. The final 'e' is sometimes dropped.

16.6.46: Overcast all day, raining pretty steadily from about 11.30 onwards.

Walked over to the W-shaped bays[14] next to Glentrosdale. About an hour & a half walking each way. Saw a snake – adder, I think. Failed to kill it, not having a suitable stick. Twelve or more seals in one of the bays. About half a dozen of them sitting out on the rocks. On seeing us, swam towards the shore, seemingly from curiosity. Have not seen a young one yet – at least, not knowingly. Young ones are said to be white.

The unidentified bird I saw last night may have been a phalarope.[15] Long beak like a snipe's, fairly stout body, shortish wings, & a cry that sounded like cheep–cheep. Size a bit bigger than a thrush.

Onions sown 3.6.46. are just showing.

Lady's bedstraw now out allover the place. Bluebells not quite over. A few primroses still blooming here & there. Foxgloves about at their best.

14. The coastline north and south of Glentrosdale Bay is indented. Orwell presumably has in mind the bay to the north of Glentrosdale, Bagh Gleann nam Muc, and that to the south, Bàgh Uamh Mhor.
15. A wading bird with coot-like feet.

17.6.46: Fine all day. Sowed leeks, lupins, delphiniums, pansies, aubretia, stonecrop, saxifrage, cheddar pinks.

18.6.46: Fine & warm. Sowed turnips.

In afternoon started cutting rushes from road. To clear 200 yards of road, ie. where the rushes are almost continuous, is about 2½ hours work. Could make no impression on them with the scythe & had to use the sickle. Note that the small heavy type of sickle, without a back, can be used back-handed as well as forehanded.

Put such peat as remains into "threes." Still very damp on under side. About 100–150 blocks, another 100 or so having been trampled by the deer. However, enough for experimental purposes. Note that one must always lay it out to dry on the grass not in the peat bed, where, apart from the deer coming & trampling it, the under side stays much wetter. It is said here one should not cut it after the first week in June, as after that the grass gets tall & it has no chance to dry.

Cured another rabbit skin (ordinary one). NB. to examine about beginning of July.

19.6.46: A couple of showers in the early morning, otherwise fine & warm all day.

In the morning walked to Ardlussa. Time exactly 2¼ hours, so the distance cannot be 9 miles as commonly said. Possibly 9 miles to Kinuachdrach, & about 7½ to Barnhill.

Swallows in the barn have evidently hatched as I found a hatched egg.

20.6.46: A bit of rain in the morning, otherwise fine & rather windy.

Lettuces sown 25.5.46 are almost ready to transplant. The geese still tend to hang round the back door, apparently liking to sit on the stones, & will go into any of the barns if these are left open. They graze a good deal but will not go far afield, & if driven out into the field behind the house seem terrified & want only to get back. They are not being given much beyond house scraps but seem well & fat. Their habit of staying in one place makes one realise what huge quantities of dung they produce. The 6 of them, judging by the amount we scrape up & put on the manure heap, must produce a pound or two every day.

Saw last night one unidentified bird of prey hawking over the sea shore. It was whitish & its flight was that of an owl, but so far as I could see (2–300 yards away) it had a black & white colouring on head & neck such as I have never seen on an owl.

21.6.46: Fine but overcast all day till about 9 pm, after which there was a thick "Scotch mist", enough to drench one to the skin.

Planted out about a dozen lettuces. Very small, so put sacking to protect them. Cured another rabbit skin (to be opened about 5.7.46).

22.6.46: Fine & warm from about noon onwards. At the same time dense mists rolling off the sea very suddenly. Sea like glass. Sowed carrots. Planted another row of lettuce. Turnips sown 15.6.46 are up, & swedes sown the same day just showing.

23.6.46: Drizzling rain most of the day. In the evening it cleared up, but dense mists kept rolling up & down, sometimes lying very low, so that the coast of the mainland was invisible while higher ground many miles inland stood out quite clearly.

Too wet to do much out of doors. Took sacking off lettuces, which look as if they will do all right if I can keep the slugs & rabbits off them. Turnips sown 18.6.46 are up.

The common wild rose of these parts is now coming into blossom. A white flower with tendency to pink at the edges. Bud large & very beautiful, with bright pink tip. Leaves have a faint sweetbriar smell. Evidently this is the "Scotch" or "burnet" rose (*rosa spinosissima*). Some of the stems are very spiny, but they vary. Do not know whether one can bud onto this rose.

Geese getting somewhat more enterprising. Today enjoying the rain & bathing themselves in puddles. As a result they look draggled & filthy, the opposite of what one would expect.

24.6.46: Fine & warm most of the day. Beetroots (sown 15.6.46) just showing.

In the evening spent about 2 hours trying to get a cow out of a bog. She had fallen into a narrow ditch beside the road & was sunk in the mud about up to her neck. Would probably have sunk altogether if the ditch had not been very narrow, so that the sides held her up. Another man & myself made efforts to drag her out & lever her out with lengths of board, but it would evidently need 5 or 6 men at least to do this. She was ultimately dragged out by the lorry. I heard she was none the worse for it, though she must have been there for at least 5 hours.

The electric fence, supposed to keep the herds of cattle separate, is evidently not working. They have not only broken through it & jumped over it, but D[onald] D[arroch] states that he saw one of the Highland cattle scratching its back against the wire.

25.6.46: Fine till evening, when rain started. Boat arrived this morning, but too wet & sea too rough to fish. Varnished boat & prepared rollers. It is extremely difficult to find straight pieces of timber here. Even when cutting pieces for stool legs, I find that any sizeable & strong branch has a kink in it.

Another rose, this time a pink one, is out. I suppose this is the dog rose, but it looks a bit different from the English kind – much more stunted, & stems more spiny – & seems to have a faint sweetbriarish scent in both flowers & leaves. I don't think it can be the sweetbriar, which so far as I know never has a flower.[16]

There is catmint or peppermint all over the place down by the sea. Foxgloves now almost past their best. Today found a mushroom – a "true" mushroom, I think.

Thinned out radishes & lettuces. All lettuces doing well so long as I can keep the rabbits & slugs off them. Set some more peat into "threes." Total amount we have cut would not be more than 2 cwt.

[*On facing page*]

Fuchsia cuttings. July–August. 4″ long, from side shoots. Cut with a heel, remove lower leaves, trim heel. Plant in sandy soil. Keep moist & shelter from midday sun, but do not shade all the time.

Escallonia ditto, but in late summer.

16. The sweetbriar (or eglantine), *rosa rubiginosa*, does have single pink flowers, strong thorns, and a pleasant scent. The word 'briar' (or 'brier') can also be given to the wild, or dog, rose (*rosa canina*), which also has a single pink flower.

26.6.46: Fine most of the day but very windy. Sea roughish but calm in the bay. Went fishing about 10pm. 2 saythe, taken on the red reel. Might have had more, but had to come in as boat was taking in water. About 11 pm, a shoal of fish jumping out of the water like dace.

27.6.46: Very stormy & heavy rain till about 8 pm. Sea very rough, but calmed down somewhat in the evening. Too wet to do much out of doors. Wind S.E.

Carrots (sown 13.6.46) now showing. Spinach sown same day just showing. Rabbits again eating lettuces etc. Put more wire over them.

Have ordered one dozen each red currants, black currants, gooseberries, 1 dozen roots rhubarb, 2 dozen raspberry canes, 4 dozen strawberries, 6 apple trees; but probably shall not get all of them.

Shot 2 rabbits – the first time I have got two in one day, in spite of the enormous numbers of them. Spots in the corn which rabbits most frequent are nibbled down almost like mown grass.

Saw another mushroom. A[vril] found two ripe whortleberries (very early?)

28.6.46: Very blowy all day (wind SW), but not much rain after about 2 pm. Sea still rough. Roads not as mucky as I would have expected.

Cured rabbit skin (white one). To be opened about July 12th. Started breaking in new patch. This one to be manured, so that it will be suitable for planting strawberries or raspberries. Am using the dung scraped off the floor of the big barn, which is literally years old, mixed into a little goose dung & ashes. Soil here probably needs lime.

Got drum of petrol, 40 galls. Unless we get extra allotment, this should last until about end of October (allowance for the 2 vehicles[17] is 8½ galls a month, but there is only ½ gall due for the motor bike in June). Shall note all amounts taken out of drum. Today took 1 gallon.

French beans coming up.

M. McKechnie[18] says rabbit wire has to be 4 ft. high. They can get over anything lower than that.

17. The two vehicles were, presumably, the lorry bought from Kopp and the motor-bike. In his entry for 7 July, Orwell seems to refer to a car – the word is not clear – but he had no car. Fuel, like much else, was severely rationed.
18. Malcolm M'Kechnie, headman at Ardlussa; he had ten children. Orwell sometimes spells his name, as here, 'McKechnie.'

29.6.46: Stormy, but part of the day fine. Sea still rather rough. Re-varnished boat & caulked what looked like two bad seams. Planted a few more lettuces. Shortened oars of boat 6″ each.

30.6.46: Fine but still blowy. Breakers on sea most of day. Sowed swedes. Spinach showing but not very well up. Soil near fence much deeper than near house. Am manuring it & shall put strawberries at that end of second patch, if plants obtainable. Just room in that patch for 4 dozen strawberries, 2 dozen raspberries, & a bed of rhubarb which can go on the bad soil.

To make cultivated parts rabbit proof will need 100 yards of wire & about 50* stakes.

[*on facing page*]

* 25 (of which 6 thick ones)

7.7.46: Away in London for several days till day before yesterday.[19] Weather in London unbearably hot. Here it has been raining most of the time up till yesterday when it was fine though not very warm. From about Glasgow onwards hay is nearly all cut & some of it in cocks. Not cut in Jura yet.

Note that starlings, never seen up this end of the island, are quite common at Craighouse.[20] Yesterday saw a blackbird – almost a rare bird here.

Have planted out more lettuce. All seeds well up except spinach, which seems to have almost failed to germinate – presumably bad seed. Cut some cress yesterday – first fruits of the garden, which was started in virgin meadow about 20.5.46.

Having been out fishing about half a dozen times, we have never had a blank day, though one day (when we went out about 8pm) we only caught 1 fish. Best catch (twice) 15 fish, 14 saythe & 1 pollock. Last night A[vril] caught a mackerel, but in picking it off the hook it got back into the water. Mackerel fishing proper starts in August. The fish always seem to bite round about dusk, ie. now about 11 pm. There is a period of about 10 minutes when one is pulling them in for all one is worth, then they suddenly stop.

Petrol: took out 3 gallons (a bit less) for motor bike
2 gallons for car[21]
2 gallons borrowed by Ardlussa.[22]

Total amount taken hitherto 8–2 gallons (6 if the borrowed 2 are returned).

Have definitely ordered the following:

½ doz apple trees including 2 espaliers
½ doz other fruit trees including 2 espalier morellos
1 doz black currant
1 doz red currant

1 doz gooseberry
2 doz raspberry
4 doz strawberry
1 doz rhubarb.

Strawberries arrive in September. Preparing ground now; dunging it fairly heavily with old stuff from the floor of the byre. Other plants will not arrive till late November, so possible difficulty about planting. Lupins up, also pansies.

Trying to get permit for 100 yards rabbit wire.[23] Rabbits not so bad lately, no doubt because I shoot at them so frequently.

19. Orwell went to London to collect his son, Richard.
20. Craighouse is about twenty-three miles south of Barnhill.
21. This reads like 'care'; Orwell had no car, but 'care' does not make sense. Perhaps he contributed two gallons of petrol (bearing in mind that petrol was rationed) to the car owner who ferried visitors to Barnhill. He advised Sally McEwan to 'ask for the hired car at McKechnie's shop' (5 July 1946, *CW*, XVIII, p. 339). Orwell also mentions bribing the driver to carry on along a very poor road; the 'bribe' may not always have been in cash (in writing to Michael Meyer he suggests 5s 0d) but possibly in petrol.
22. Borrowed by the Fletchers; see Diary, 20.8.46. Ardlussa was seven to eight miles south of Barnhill as the crow flies. The Ardlussa Estate had been inherited by Robin Fletcher, formerly an Eton housemaster. He and his wife, Margaret, set about restoring the estate and developing crofting. Her interview for the BBC *Arena* programme of 1984 is reproduced in *Orwell Remembered*, pp. 225–9. She vividly describes how she remembered Orwell: 'how ill, how terribly ill, he looked – and drawn: a sad face he had. . . . I think he very much missed his wife . . . He was devoted to Richard.'
23. A permit was required to purchase such materials which were in short supply.

8.7.46: Fine most of day, but thick mists, & a little rain in the evening. Last night caught 25 saythe & 1 pollock.

9.7.46: Beautiful fine hot day. Turned chilly rather suddenly in the evening. Saw some hazel nuts half formed. A[vril] has found one or two more mushrooms. A certain amount of flea on the turnips. Watered them with soapy water.

Only 3 saythe.

It was on 9th July that Orwell's dramatization of *Little Red Riding Hood* was broadcast in the BBC's Children's Hour programme: for the script, see *CW*, XVIII, pp. 343–54.]

10.7.46: Cured a rabbit skin (ordinary one). To be opened about 25.7.46.

Only 4 saythe last night. Movements of these fish quite unpredictable, but presumably they are following the shoals of fry or whitebait. The things one finds in their stomachs look like tiny eels, about 1½″ long.

11.7.46: 8 saythe last night. Fish jumping all over the place.

Hot all day, striking rather chilly in the evening, & wind veering round to west, but no rain.

While stalking a rabbit, I saw a stoat playing on the big stones near the gate. It was only a few feet away from me, but it appeared almost unafraid, & sometimes simply sat on the rock & looked at me. My impression was that it was darker in colour (more chocolate-coloured) than the stoats one sees in England. I notice that the animals of this family, normally shy enough, seem to have moments when they lose all fear of man.

No result from rabbit snares hitherto (have 12 out.) Probably it needs long practice before one can get them exactly right. One or two of mine have been disturbed, however, showing that the rabbits do not in all cases actually avoid the run where a snare is. D[onald] D[arroch] says one should collect any rabbits that are caught early in the morning, otherwise the gulls have them.

Today saw a few primroses in bloom in shady places. Another spotted orchis is coming up, this time a dark mauve one. The other was light mauve, almost white. A[vril] says it is the same flower, but must surely be a sub-variety. Eggs & bacon still out all over the place. A little rather pretty flower called Eyebright out in the grass in the garden. Self Heal everywhere.

Of the flower seeds I sowed on 7.6.46, only lupins, pansies & cheddar pinks have shown yet. The spinach has definitely failed to germinate & I shall use the ground for something else.

The so-called wild cat is in fact not very wild. I have seen it quite close to on various occasions. It always gives the appearance of stalking in a very amateurish way, & in any case it is a sign of the great quantities of game here that an animal so conspicuously marked (brilliant tortoiseshell) can subsist at all.

12.7.46: 24 saythe last night. These were all caught in about 20 minutes, after which we packed up, not wanting to waste fish. We could have caught 50 if we had wanted them. The sea was alive with the creatures, jumping all round the boat. On weighing one or two, we find that the biggest we catch are about 11–12 ounces. But they are uniform in size & I should think not many are below 6 ounces. They are delicious eating.

Trying to find out exactly the method by which people here dry them for the winter.

The geese are moulting a bit, probably because of poor feeding. I don't think they ought to moult before August.

13.7.46: Very hot & dry all yesterday. Sea like glass. Horse flies awful.

In the night a few drops of rain. This morning wet & misty, wind in west. Yesterday thinned out first lot of turnips, sowed more leeks. In the evening, about 10.30, by the new stable, saw 3 otters together, running across the grass about 30 yards away. They looked almost black in the half light.

This morning for the first time caught a rabbit in a wire. Went down to get the wires in, taking the gun as I thought a rabbit or two might be out. Saw one sitting about 40 yards away & shot & killed it, to find it was already caught in the snare (round the neck.)

Notice in skinning these rabbits the great difference between old & young ones. In the young ones the skin comes off like a glove, whereas some of the older ones are quite difficult to skin. Also, when cured, the pelts of the younger ones remain much suppler. Have now cured six or seven skins; no sign of their going bad yet, but must keep them some months to test. Then must find out how to make them supple (pretty stiff at present.)[24]

Cleared up for a bit in the afternoon, rain again at night. The very low tides continue, in fact the water never seems to come within 20 yards of the high tide mark. However A. McK.[25] says the spring tides will begin soon.

In the afternoon a tremendous column of water suddenly shot up just outside the bay. A[vril] said a "whale thrasher", or granpus.[26] Know nothing about these creatures – not even quite certain whether they are mammals or not.

A[vril] bought a lobster creel which we have put out. Another to arrive next week. Think I put it too near inshore. As we had plenty of food in hand we went out intending to catch only 1 fish to bait the creel with, but they immediately started biting so fast that we found ourselves with 8 or 9 by the time we had the creel ready.

Coal almost finished (1 ton, beginning about May 25th.). I.e. a ton of coal lasts about 6 weeks. More coming shortly. Meanwhile collecting & cutting up wood, which, if one uses nothing else, means about 2 hours work a day for 2 people.

Made handle for sledge hammer out of a bough of mountain ash. Shall be interested to see whether it is strong enough. Almost impossible here to get hold of a piece of timber which is either straight or without a flaw in it. Cured a rabbit skin – to be opened at end of July.

24. Perhaps Orwell had at the back of his mind the disastrous outcome of Flory's attempt to have a leopard skin cured for Elizabeth in *Burmese Days (CW,* II, pp. 224–27).
25. Angus M'Kechnie, who lived in Ardlussa.
26. *grampus griseus:* a cetacean resembling a dolphin but lacking its beak-like snout.

14.7.46: Some rain in the night. This morning very blowy (wind from west) with alternate rain & sunny intervals.

Pulled first radishes, sown 25.5.46. Fair, but would probably have been better ones if I had sown one of the short kinds. Spring onions in a week or so, lettuces in 10 days or a fortnight.

Took up creel. A crab (usual edible kind) was in it, but he did not seem big enough to be worth keeping, so threw him back. Almost all the crabs here are smallish & only worth keeping if one has 2 or 3, so we must institute a storage box.

15.7.46: Rain in night, fairly heavy & continuous rain this morning, & decidedly cold.

Later part of day alternate rain & sun, but pretty blowy. Wind shifting round to S.E. at times.

Did not fish or inspect creel. Boat riding well at anchor, but the tides have suddenly changed, the water coming quite far in, so that she was too far out & we could not get to her at high tide. Made box for fish, but decided it was too big & clumsy so shall use it as a storage box for crabs.

Thinned first lot of swedes, ditto carrots & beetroots. Shall sow more lettuces as they grow so fast this year that if sown now they should be ready before the end of September. Have taken netting off the beds as I think I have temporarily scared the rabbits off & have wiped out the family that was living actually in the garden.

Stags now have very large horns, but still velvety. Mother wagtail sitting on fence feeding young one. This breed[27] left the nest about 3 days ago, so they evidently go on feeding them for some days after they can fly.

27. Possibly 'brood' is intended, but the double 'e' is clearly so written.

19.7.46: Diary not kept up for several days owing to pen being mislaid.

Until yesterday weather has been mostly rainy, & generally blowy as well. Yesterday evening it cleared up & is still fine. Wind generally in west. Sea calm.

Fishing has gone off. Only 2 fish, ie. saythe (we generally catch one or two pollock as well) last night, & 7 the night before last. No fish jumping now. Last night A[vril] hooked a mackerel & again lost him as he was being lifted into the boat.

Creel is lost, after only about 3 nights' use. I suppose I put it too near the channel, or else did not weight it sufficiently, & it drifted.

Tides now very much higher. Much adjustment needed to anchor the boat so that we can get to her when the water is high, without having to drag her a long distance when it is low.

Have cured 2 rabbit skins, to be opened about beginning of August.

Saw a number of the rabbits with white collars round Kinuachdrach. They are never seen here, not much more than a mile away, whereas the fawn-coloured ones, common here, are never seen up that end.

Peat has been brought in & is being used, though still rather damp. About 150 blocks.

Found blueberries ripe yesterday. Large numbers of hazel nuts round Kinuachdrach. Said to get ripe about beginning of September. Black currants now ripe, or mostly.

D. D. & his sister[28] doing terrific job thinning their turnips – about a quarter of an acre. The turnips are now 8″ high or so, & are thinned by hand. D.D. will not use a hoe as he says that if one does so one cannot single out the strongest plants. Actually one can hoe roughly first & then single [out] each clump. However, it is the custom here not to use the hoe. It takes days of work to thin this area of turnips.

The D. s will be lifting a few potatoes soon, which is just as well for us as we are running out.

28. Donald and Katie Darroch. There is in *Remembering Orwell* a brief but telling memoir of Orwell by Katie Darroch. She describes Orwell as 'cheery and happy in his own way' – and a great fan of her scones! (pp. 174–5).

20.7.46: Not much rain during the day, but overcast, blowing & decidedly cold. Thinned second lot of turnips.

Rabbit wire arrived, 100 yards of 3 ft. Shall need about 30 stakes, difficult to procure here as there is no straight wood. Sodium chlorate is coming, 1 cwt., of which, however, the F[letcher]s want to borrow half. Half cwt. should be enough to cover the whole area here in pretty strong solution, but I would like to give 2 applications.

Took out ½ gall. petrol. Up to date, 8½ – 2[29] galls, taken out.

New ton of coal started today. The first ton has therefore lasted about 8 weeks, but this is with the use of a great deal of wood & a little peat. So 6 tons a year is none too much for this house.[30]

Sowed radishes.

Shot one of the rabbits with white neck. The white marking is only round the neck & nose, & these rabbits are extremely local, only seen in two small areas.

Fishing has definitely gone off for the time being. Only 3, ie. saythe, last night, & 2 the night before that. Last night suddenly saw a creel at the point & sprang to the conclusion it was our lost one. When hauling it up found it was not ours, but it may have been the other that I. & A.[31] promised to leave for us. A sizeable crab in it, which I kept. Tremendous struggle to get him out as he clung to the netting & I had to prize° his claws apart at risk of being pinched.

The F.s have already lifted a field of potatoes & presumably somewhat prematurely as all their people have now run out of potatoes.

Tides much higher. Strong current in the sea, but surface still calm.

Cured 2 rabbit skins (open about 3.8.46).

29. The total of 8½ gallons (and on the 24th of 9½ gallons) minus two is to represent the two gallons borrowed by Ardlussa; see 7.7.46 and n. 22. Orwell's concern was not, of course, that the two gallons had not been paid back, but to estimate accurately how his ration of petrol was lasting.

30. Like much else, coal was rationed. Six tons would have been the allowance for a year.

31. Ian and Angus M'Kechnie. Ian was an estate worker at Ardlussa and lived at Inverlussa; Angus was a lobster fisherman and, unlike Ian and Malcolm M'Kechnie, was not on the Astors' payroll.

21.7.46: Miserable weather. Rain not heavy but almost continuous all day. Cold enough to make one want a fire in every room. Too wet to do much out of doors. Set creel & lengthened rope of storage box, but did not fish, as there was a nasty swell on the water.

22.7.46: Went down to Craighouse. Violent rain that end of the island, this end not quite so bad.

Notice that down that end chaffinches are quite common – they do exist up here, but one does not see them frequently.

Tried to fish, but great difficulty in landing & beaching boat. Fairly strong sea & very strong current. Caught several pollock in about 5 minutes, then they suddenly stopped biting. No saythe except a very tiny one. Nothing in creel.

23.7.46: Rain most of day, which became torrential in the evening. Streams overflow their banks & roads turn into rivers after only an hour or two of rain of this kind. Too rough to fish, but took up creel (empty), getting wetted to the waist in landing the boat. Wind shifting round to south.

Shot two rabbits in one shot, which does not often happen, ie. with adult rabbits.

24.7.46: Violent storm for part of night, calming down this morning. Some thunder.

Went down to inspect boat & found that though riding secure at her anchor she had been swamped by a heavy sea & the gratings etc. washed overboard. However recovered everything. Boat has a bad crack forward, & when putting her in the water found she was taking in water badly – not enough to make it quite impossible to use her, but badly enough to make it necessary to bale every quarter of an hour or so. Turned her over, worked plasticine into the crack, caulked up one or two seams, & varnished thickly. Shall test whether this waterproofs her sufficiently as soon as the sea is calm, but she really needs a new board forward – actually 2 boards.

Wind still in south most of day. Some rain in the morning, sunny & warm most of the afternoon.

Forgot to note, took out another gallon of petrol on 22.7.46, ie. 9½ – 2 galls.

For a week or so past terns very busy & noisy over the little island at the mouth of the harbour at Kinuachdrach. They keep making darts at the ground almost as they do over the sea when fishing. Presumably feeding families of young ones (terns lay late in the year, I think). I note some of them darting at the tree that grows on the island, so possibly there are nests in the branches as well as on the ground.

I hardly see any of the fawn-coloured rabbits now, though I have certainly not shot all that were here – I think I have shot 8, to be exact, & they were quite common in May–June. Now there is only one that I see, always round about the same place. Presumably, being so conspicuous, they are the first to fall to hawks & perhaps owls. They are almost certainly not a separate breed, ie. merely a sport tending to recur in one locality, like black rabbits, & it will be interesting to see whether they are equally common next year. The rabbits with white markings are extremely local. I see them in 3 places, & nowhere else. When one sees identifiable animals like this, one realises how restricted a rabbit's movements are.

Otters it appears catch not only sea fish, but lobsters. They are said to catch bigger lobsters than are ever caught by human beings, ie. those that are too big to get into the creel. Ditto salmon – a 40 lb. salmon partly devoured by an otter is said to have been found here, no human being ever having caught one of such a size on this island.

25.7.46: Rather rainy in morning, clearing in afternoon. Sea roughish. Walked over to Glengarrisdale. Getting there took 2¾ hours, coming back about 2 hours & 40 minutes, so the route we now use is evidently an improvement (3 hours each way last time). Sea on the Atlantic side calmer than here, to my surprise. Found some fresh mussel shells, though no mussels actually on the rocks. They seem not to exist on this side of the island.

Saw an almost white hind – white patches more or less covering back, but brown on belly. Saw no stags all day, though literally hundreds of hinds. Evidently they separate at this time of year, but it is a puzzle where the stags go to.

Saw a flock of chaffinches, so they are commoner this end of the island than I thought.

Again saw an eagle mobbed by hoodie crows.

26.7.46: Fine & warm, sea calmer, though wind has gone round to west again. Large crab in the creel, which this time was baited with rabbit. Painted entire bottom of boat with red under-paint – shall follow up with white, & paint her green inside. She does not now take in water so badly.

27.7.46: Fine all day, though not particularly hot. Lobster in creel (our first). Fixed rollers on rope to make a continuous chain of them on which the boat can be dragged up, & shall put them in place tomorrow when the tide is low. Tonight only 3 saythe – 12 last night. Last night we twice hooked a mackerel & lost it when drawing it into the boat, making 4 times that this has happened. The reason seems to be that as the mackerel is a fighter, it generally makes a last-minute dash which causes it to bang against the boat or one of the other rods. One really wants a landing net.

Rabbits have been in the garden again & done some damage. The worst seem to be the families of very young rabbits. Saw another of the whitey-coloured ones yesterday.

Ian McKechnie says that the lobster's "scissors claw" is not always on the same side: it is as though some lobsters were right-handed & some left-handed.

28.7.46: Rain almost continuous all day. In the afternoon wind in south & sea quite violent, calming down very rapidly later.

Put rollers in position, but probably have not weighted them sufficiently to prevent the tide shifting them. Too wet to fish.

29.7.46: Some rain, but finer. The tide had flung the rollers all over the place & it took me about an hour to disentangle them & put them back. In the evening, after another tide, they had not moved much. Evidently they want weighting all the way up the row. But when in place they save a great deal of labour.

In the evening 6 saythe & 1 pollock. Only a medium sized crab in the creel, which I killed & left there to serve as bait. It appears that when there is a crab in the creel, & one does not intend to keep him, one should kill him, as otherwise he will eat the remainder of the bait. A lobster, once finding himself caught, does not continue eating the bait – or so it is said.

Lifted some of D[onald] D[arroch]'s potatoes. Very poor crop, in spite of the good haulm.[32] I should say on average 5 or 6 potatoes on plant. Reason given, ground was not manured.

32. Stems, usually of straw but particularly applicable to peas, beans and potatoes.

30.7.46: Continuous driving rain till evening. About 5 pm it began to clear, with violent wind & some sun. Today & yesterday the wind has been veering about between west & south, & the sea in the bay shows the effects almost at once. The water is always reasonably calm, ie. inshore, when the wind is in the west. Did not take up creel. Too wet to do anything out of doors. Began repairing wheelbarrow.

31.7.46: Beautiful fine day, & quite hot. Sea very calm in bay, but a ground swell outside. Water very clear & blue, very low tide. Found the lost creel, which, as A[ngus] M[cKechnie] predicted, showed itself when the water was at its lowest. I had tangled the rope, shortening it by about 6 feet, which is evidently a thing to beware of when setting the creel. Painted the boat green & white. Schedule of digging for July only just finished on time. I notice that when the grass is cleared away from the various currant & gooseberry bushes which the deer have grazed down, they do not look so bad, & may bear again if protected this winter. Several of the currant bushes have layered themselves, forming small bushes which I shall transplant later.

Set one creel, not having bait for the other.

Took out 1½ galls petrol. (Altogether 11 – 2 galls).

1.8.46: Fine till about 10 pm, when a drizzle set in, turning later into heavy rain. Caught (ie. landed) the first mackerel of the year.

2.8.46: Showers, but fine most of the day. Wind all the time veering about west–south, & sea roughish. It is almost always difficult to launch the boat when the wind is in the south.

Saw a family of young pheasants, about 6 or 8 of them very forward for August & flying strongly.

Cured a rabbit skin (fawn-coloured). To be opened about middle of August.

Set both creels, baiting with rabbit.

3.8.46: Fine all day, strongish wind from west, sea fairly calm inshore.

Cut more fence posts. Rabbits have been in the garden again. Curiously enough they seem to attack the radishes before anything else.

Green blackberries forming, some rowan berries almost ripe, scabius budding.

4.8.46: Very stormy in morning, clearing up in afternoon, but wind still strong. Opened a hazel nut. Only pith inside. Evidently there is going to be a large crop of hazel nuts.

5.8.46: Less wind. Some showers, but fine on the whole. Finished wheelbarrow (very flimsy, owing to lack of suitable timber) & marked out third bed. I now have enough fence posts to start putting up the wire. Just calm enough to launch the boat. Rollers had been flung all over the place again & it is clear that each one will have to be anchored down individually. Six saythe, but we hooked & lost about as many as we caught. A large crab with no claws in one of the creels. It appears they can survive without claws. I had not noticed before that a lobster has a small claw on one of its legs just behind the main claw. It uses this chiefly for feeding, the big ones being weapons. When putting a lobster in the box after it has been out of the water for some time, one should be careful not to drown it. The way to avoid this is to dip it in water a number of times before finally dropping it in. A lobster needs a cubic foot of fresh sea water every 24 hours, so that the box must be well aerated.

6.8.46: Rain, on & off. Started new bed, prepared fence posts. Pruned bushes, which do not now look absolutely hopeless. Lettuces just ready to cut (sown 28.5.46.). Rabbits have been in the garden again & have even been scratching in the beds. Have not been able to shoot a rabbit for 2 or 3 days past. They seem to alternate between extreme shyness & the opposite. Put 2 lobsters in the box. They had been out of the water about 6 hours, so we shall see whether they drown when put back after this interval.

Nothing in the creels, which we shall put over the other side of the bay next time. Fear that this bay may have been cleared out for the time being by the lobster boats from the mainland.

Ian says when one gets a conger eel in the creel, it is important to kill it while inside & not let it out, or it will work havoc. One should kill it by cutting through its backbone.

Forgot to mention that I killed another snake (small one) the day before yesterday. Again not completely sure it was an adder, but prefer not to take chances anywhere near the house.

In tying up a lobster's claws, one should tie the "scissor" claw first.

I was stung by a wasp today – hitherto we have not seen any.

Boat again swamped by the fairly heavy sea that was running as a result of the south wind this morning. If properly tied bow & stern she does not shift from her anchor, but one cannot prevent seas breaking over her & therefore has to remove anything liable to be washed away, such as the gratings.

7.8.46: Fine & very blowy all day till evening, when some light rain fell. Put up about three quarters of rabbit wire. Most places it is sunk about 2″, which is said to be sufficient.

Sea rough, calming somewhat in the evening.

8.8.46: Rain almost continuous till evening, but not heavy, rather a succession of drizzling showers. Wind mostly south & sea quite rough in morning calming a little in evening. Too wet to do much out of doors. Killed the first of the geese. It was the one with the deformed wings – not the biggest, but not the smallest. After drawing, weight 7½ lb, so live weight would be 8 or 9 lb. Age 3½–4 months, so I suppose some will be 10 lb or more before we eat them. Struck by the enormous size & extreme toughness of the gizzard.

Today given a stag's liver. Very large, very dark & on the tough side.

9.8.46: Very heavy rain in the night. Tried to fish last night, but too rough to launch the boat. Anchor rope had broken & boat was attached only by the shore rope, but fortunately undamaged. NB. that one wants a bit of chain for the last few feet to the anchor.

Soil here evidently wants lime. The bed up against the wall has done all right (probably has had some lime from lumps of mortar), but in the bed nearest the fence the soil seems very sour & none of the seeds in it have done very well. Incidentally about half the flower seeds I had from Carters'[33] have completely failed to germinate.

Raining all this morning, & sea rough. In the afternoon it suddenly cleared up, & there was a beautiful still evening, with the sea like a mirror & a splendid moon. All afternoon busy unblocking a blocked water pipe (only partially successful.) Recovered anchor. Caught 8 saythe, some of them quite large ones. There were shoals of little ones, about 4″ long, following the baits & snapping at them, & from time to time one cannot help catching these tiny creatures, which, however, can generally be got off the hook undamaged & thrown back. Set creels in a new place.

33. A leading firm of seedsmen (as Carters Tested Seeds today).

10.8.46: Very fine day, except for a very light shower of a few minutes in the afternoon. Experimentally applied a small quantity of sodium chlorate to nettles, at the rate of 1 lb to the gallon & about 1 gallon to 10 square yards. If this kills them, I shall apply in the same strength to the rushes.

One lobster (medium-sized) in creel. Tied his claws, I hope satisfactorily, but I had no string & had to unpick a strand of rope. Tied scissor claw first, making a slip knot & pulling it tight before winding round, holding him down with my foot while doing so.

Today saw lizard (brown one) – the first time that I have seen one here. In digging, accidentally killed a toad which was buried a few inches deep in the earth. At this time of year, I think this must have been a toad which had failed to wake up for the spring. They would hardly begin hibernating again yet.

Wind in north much of day.

Ian took out (I think) about 2 galls. petrol, making 13 – 2 galls.

11.8.46: Very fine & still day, except for a sharp shower of about a quarter of an hour in the afternoon, & another lighter one later. Sea had some waves on it in the morning; in the afternoon so still that we could see the reflection of the lighthouse.

Ate the goose – good flavour but not fat (entirely grass-fed.)

Began preparing stakes for trees & bushes. Red hot pokers, of which I find there are a few here, are almost out. Nettles treated with sodium chlorate bleached & wilting. Saw a robin, not a very common bird here. Tried the "insect repellant", which seems to work but has to be renewed pretty often.

12.8.46: Not so fine as yesterday. A few showers, & looks as though it would be wet tonight. Applied sodium chlorate to some of the rushes. On one patch applied at the same rate as for the nettles, ie. 1 lb to a gallon & about 1 gallon to 10 sq. yards, & on another tried the experiment of scattering the sodium chlorate dry, trusting to the rain to wash it in.

Wind in west.

Yesterday saw another fawn-coloured rabbit (baby one.) Put away half dozen of the cured rabbit skins in a drawer, considering that they had dried sufficiently. Shall put moth balls with them, & see what they look like next year. One would, I think, only get on average an oblong of 8″ by 4″ or 5″ inches out of each pelt, so that one would need about 100 to make a good bed rug. On the other hand about 4 or perhaps 6 should make a pair of bedroom slippers.

18.8.46: Diary not filled up for some days owing to journeys etc.

Last 5 or 6 days very fine weather, sunny & windy, with an occasional brief shower but one or two days with no rain whatever. Roads dried up almost completely in this period. Today very dirty again, with south wind & rough sea.

Visited Islay for the first time. Note that jackdaws are common there – have never seen one on this island.

Yesterday travelled to Ardlussa in outboard motor boat. Time from Barnhill to Ardlussa almost exactly 1 hour. Distance by land is about 7½ miles but presumably somewhat less by sea. We had the tide with his, but on the other hand there were 4 people in the boat, & 6 dozen lobsters, which would weigh about as much as another person.

Have caught two more lobsters & one or two crabs. Have now mastered the trick of tying a lobster's claws. Much the hardest part of the operation is getting them out of the creel, especially in the case of crabs, which cling to the netting.

Concentration of sodium chlorate which kills nettles & grass makes no impression on rushes. Tried at a strength of 2 lb. to 1½ galls water – again no impression. This concentration appears to kill bracken, however. For the moment shall confine myself to killing off all the nettles, bracken & ragwort.

Sowed spring cabbage a few days ago. Planted out some cuttings of perennial cabbage. Planted out some cheddar pink seedlings, & brought in a few clumps of thrift to see whether they can be acclimatised. If so it would be a good rockery plant, but this may be the wrong time of year for transplanting.

Fishing is variable. One night we got 22 fish & could have got many more if we had not been preoccupied with baling the boat. Another night only 1 – a mackerel. There seem to be very few mackerel about this year, & we have not caught any on the spinner.

Method of salting saythe – gut them, cut their heads off, then pack them in layers in rough salt, a layer of salt & a layer of fish, & so on. Leave for several days, then in dry sunny weather, take them out & hang them on a line in pairs by their tails until thoroughly dry. After this they can be hung up indoors & will keep for months.

A[vril] procured some specimens of edible seaweed – dulse, not carragheen. She is drying it. Directions for preparing & cooking it vary somewhat, but it is said, when cooked in milk, to make a pudding rather like blancmange.

19.8.46: Very dirty weather all yesterday. Heavy seas out in the strait. Dragged up boat, which had shipped a wave again. Too wet to do much out of doors. Applied some more sodium chlorate, throwing it on dry & trusting to the rain to wash it in. Sodium chlorate applied earlier does now seem to be attacking the rushes, but more slowly than in the case of nettles etc.

The D[arroch]s are now salting & drying saythe. They should be dried till they are as hard as a board. Before using they are soaked to get the salt out.

Fine & blowy all day today. Wind in west. Sea calm in the bay, but still some breakers in the strait.

20.8.46: Beautiful day all yesterday. In the afternoon when lifting the creels saw a shoal of small fish jumping out of the water, evidently pursued by mackerel. Got out the rods & rowed through the place, without result. In the evening, however, caught 8 mackerel as well as 8 saythe, so the mackerel have started. Nothing in creels (second time running, so shall change the place.)

Started cylinder of Calor gas. If, as intended, we only use it for breakfast & for occasional odd kettles of water, it should last about 6 weeks & should therefore come to an end about the end of September. Have 2 cylinders. Time elapsing between ordering cylinders & receiving them, 17 days. Should always have at least 1 cylinder in reserve, so NB. to order more gas about *middle of September*.

Forgot to mention the F[letcher]s borrowed another 2 galls of petrol, making 15 – 4 galls taken out (ie. about 25 gallons remaining.)

21.8.46: This morning fine & warm. Showers began about 4 pm, & this evening the weather turned dirty, wind going round to south & sea getting up somewhat. Some difficulty in launching the boat to set creels.

D[onald] D[arroch] struggling to get his hay in. A good deal of the hay on the island is now in, or at any rate is in the small cocks into which it is built up before being taken indoors. D's hay very poor & short, partly owing to rain having come at the wrong times. D. says that when a field has been left unmown, like this one, for several years, it is hard to cut, because of old & young grass being mixed up.

Rushes treated with sodium chlorate turning an extraordinary yellow colour, almost pink.

Saythe should be kept in the salt a day & a night. In default of dry weather it can be dried indoors. In the days of peat fires it was usually dried indoors.

Several ravens flying overhead today. Not usually seen in this part of the island. Found a dead rabbit in the lane, newly killed, with the back of its neck torn out & backbone exposed. Probably hoodie crows. Came on the "wild" cat again today. It did not attempt to run away until I was two or three yards from it.

N.B. to remind F[letcher]s we had 2 lobsters from Ian & Angus, weight 7 lb. the two.

22.8.46: Fine & windy. Sea calm. Killed another goose (not the largest). Again 7½ lb. after drawing.

Applied more sodium chlorate, put soot round spring cabbages (just up), thinned second lot of carrots & radishes.

Only 5 saythe (N.B. it seems that the correct spelling is SAITHE.) Meanwhile at Kinuachdrach they got 200 – all saithe, no mackerel.

23.8.46: Overcast & rather cold. Intermittent rain from early afternoon onwards. Sea mostly roughish. Too wet to do much out of doors. Painted bicycle.

D[onald] D[arroch]'s turnips, sown I think about end of May, already larger than cricket halls. Devil's Bit (previously wrongly referred to as scabius) now full out.[34] It is darker than a scabius. Some bracken turning. Brown owls hooting the last few nights. One does not seem to hear them hooting earlier in the summer.

34. *Scabiosa succisa.*

24.8.46: Continuous heavy rain until about 4 pm. Evidently there had been much rain in the night, as the road to Ardlussa was simply a running stream for much of the way. Evening beautiful & still, with sea glassy. Nevertheless caught only 1 fish – a saithe.

Pricked out lupins from seedbed. 25 plants, which is enough if they all take root. Perennial cabbage cuttings look as if they are rooting all right.

25.8.46: Some rain in the morning, otherwise a beautiful warm day, with sea like glass. Many gulls & cormorants in the bay, so during the afternoon when setting the creels tried the mackerel spinner – No mackerel, but one large saythe° & a few small ones. In the evening, 5 mackerel, 4 saythe.

Planted fuchsia cuttings. Uncertain whether I have done it rightly.

Geese got into the garden for only a few minutes & ate every lettuce to the ground. Other plants mostly not damaged, fortunately.

26.8.46: A few showers in the afternoon, otherwise a beautiful day. Sea very calm. D[onald] D[arroch] struggling to get his hay in, but when the breeze drops the midges were so bad as to make it almost impossible to work. Tried to help him, but driven out of the field after about half an hour. D.D. ditto. One is actually breathing them into one's nostrils, & the irritation is maddening. Forgot to mention I was yesterday stung by a wasp – almost the first I have seen this year.[35]

Incredible quantities of slugs – black ones of enormous size. Yesterday A., I.[36] & myself, coming back from Kinuachdrach, decided to see how many slugs we could tread on without leaving the path. Between the spring & this house, ie. about a mile, the number was 102.

Last night 27 fish, including 2 mackerel & 5 pollock. A[vril] is trying the experiment of salting some saithe.

A very strange crab in one of the creels yesterday. Body round & very flat, with serrated edge in front, cross section of claws (he had only one) & legs surprisingly flat. Colour a dull reddish with green stripes on legs. Size across the body was about 4 inches.

35. Orwell records that he was stung by a wasp – 'hitherto we have not seen any' – on 6 August.
36. A and I: probably Avril and Inez Holden.

27.8.46: Beautiful day all day. Sea so still that we could see the reflection of the lighthouse. Set fire to some of the rushes which I think have been killed by the sodium chlorate. Shall try to kill & burn the whole of this patch so as to get it more or less bare before autumn. Only 4 fish this evening, all mackerel. Again lost a creel. It disappeared within a few minutes of being dropped. May be able to get it back at low tide.

28.8.46: This morning raining. A fine interval in the afternoon, then heavy rain & thunder. Evening dull & wet. Sea calmer in afternoon. Applied more sodium chlorate to the patch I am trying to clear. Otherwise all afternoon trying to mend puncture in motor bike. Transplanted a few pansies & cheddar pinks.

29.8.46: Beautiful day except for a very light shower about 1 pm. Recovered the lost creel, with a large lobster in it. Evidently the correct time to look is slack water, ie. slack water on the low, because then the rope stands upright. About half an hour beforehand A[vril] was out in the boat & saw the cork about 6 ft. below, apparently not recoverable. Yet when I arrived it was on the surface.

D[onald] D[arroch] struggling to get in the oats as well as the hay, as the former are being "laid". He has about 5 acres of oats all together.

After scything the sheaves are gathered up & bound by hand, by the process of twisting about half a dozen stalks round them & turning the ends in. One can thus only gather up a rather thin sheaf, ie. thin enough to allow for its being encircled by a stalk of oats. The sheaves are built up into cocks in eights. In the Lowlands, D.D. says, they are built up in sixes. Probably because in those parts the reaper & binder is not quite unheard of, & when used would make somewhat thicker sheaves.

Constructed a tide table up to 15.9.46, assuming (a) that it was low tide at 1.15 yesterday, & (b) that there is 1½ hours difference every day. Can test accuracy of this in about a week.

Tonight 5 mackerel, 6 saythe & a pollock.

When setting a scythe, one should so fix the blade that the blade itself, the length of handle up to the lower grip, & the space between the lower grip & the tip of the blade, form an equilateral triangle. Fix with a piece of fence wire, which should be bent in the fire to avoid hammering on the blade, & then peg the ring.

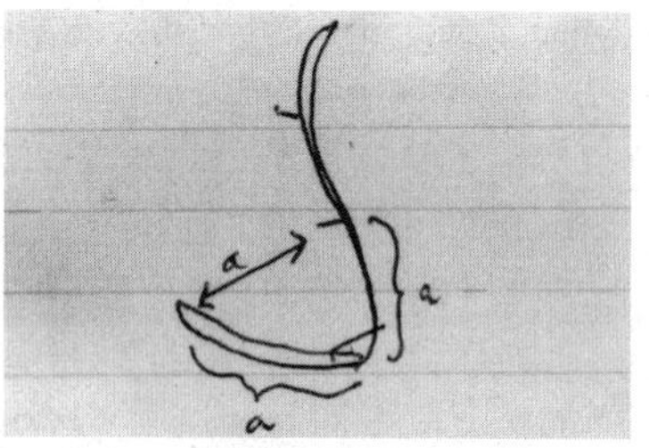

[*On facing page*]

Wrong. *See 12.9.46*

30.8.46: Beautiful day except for a light shower or two. Sowed onions (Ailsa Craig) & lettuces for next year.

In the evening 20 saythe.

31.8.46: Evidently some rain in the night, but a beautiful day. Road to Ardlussa still very bad. A good deal of the corn now in stooks. Nothing in creels. Caught 11 mackerel & 4 saithe. I am nearly certain that one catches more when one has new flies. Boat is letting [in] water badly.

5.9.46: Diary not entered up for some days.

Until yesterday very fine weather, though always with a light shower or two at some time during the day. Heavy rain during last night, & this morning raining & dark. Bracken is definitely turning. A few blackberries ripe, but not enough to be worth an expedition. Great numbers coming on. Rowan trees at their best. Some have reddish leaves, so that in the distance it looks as though the tree were entirely covered with berries.

Hazelnuts do not seem to be ripe yet. Have pulled first carrots. A few turnips almost ready to pull.

Have caught more mackerel lately, & not many saithe. Great numbers of very small saithe which are rather a nuisance as they snap at the hook all the time & deteriorate the flies. We now put on new flies about every 3 or 4 days. I am almost certain one catches more fish when one has new flies. Yesterday when rowing round to bait the creels, some large dogfish, nearly 2 feet long, swimming after the boat, a foot or so below the surface. They appeared pinkish in colour, but this must be due to their being seen through water. They would not pay any attention to the mackerel spinner, which we trailed in front of them. If one could catch them (probably on a lump of fish), they would solve the bait problem. No more lobsters recently, but one or two crabs. Some of these are as large as those one sees in the shops, but in general they run small here & are never sent to market. A[vril] now has about 2 dozen saithe salted. Mackerel are said not to be satisfactory when salted, but we intend to try smoking some like kippers.

When removing a crab from the creel, one should haul him out with the boat hook. If he is prodded with this he will often grip hold of it, & can then be dragged out. Cannot accurately test tide table yet. It appears to be wrong, but not much wrong.

Some fine intervals today, but mostly wet. Caught 21 mackerel, our largest catch hitherto, ie. of mackerel. No saithe except small ones. Lobster in one creel. Did not lift the other as it is in deep water & has to be lifted at low tide.

6.9.46: Miserable day. Road to Ardlussa is a morass. Wind mostly in south & sea rough. Saw 5 stags all together – latterly have not been seeing stags at all, other than the one that haunts the corn field. Too rough to fish.

7.9.46: Filthy weather. Sea a bit calmer. Large crab in one creel. When putting him into the box, found that the crab put in the other day had eaten one of the lobsters, although the latter's claws were not tied up. It was, however, a smallish lobster & a very large crab. Making another box so as not to put crabs & lobsters together. Trying experiment of kippering a few mackerel over a wood fire. Using oak logs as these are said to be best, though probably it does not make much difference.

Caught 7 mackerel. No saithe at all.

8.9.46: Weather better, with much wind & no rain to speak of. Went over to the W. bay. Many seals on the rocks, as usual, & others diving about in the sea a few yards from the shore, apparently in play. When they are on the rocks it is possible to get within about 30 yards of them. In the water they look black, but are quite light-coloured, & spotty, when dry. They seem to be of two distinct colours, some brownish & some greyish.

9.9.46: A light shower or two, but mostly fine & windy. Saw immense herd of deer near the new stable – probably between 50 & 100 animals, including one or two stags & some fawns. Only 3 saithe. Smoked mackerel (they had been in salt for about 36 hours, then smoked over wood fire for about 20 hours) very good.

10.9.46: Filthy day. Rain continuous. Wind mostly in south & sea rough. Planted 4 dozen strawberries (Royal Sovereign). Good plants & seemingly in good condition, though they had been 4 days travelling. Soil where they are planted not very good – rather lumpy & weedy, & appears to want lime, as moss was growing on it after lying fallow only a month or two. Too wet to do anything else out of doors. Made box for lobsters.

11.9.46: Beautiful day all day. Very hot sun in afternoon. Turned a bit coldish in evening, but no rain & no wind. Sea very smooth, & clear down to a depth of 20 or 30 ft. Wonderful harvest moon. Rollers washed away by yesterday's rough weather.

Two lobsters (small ones) in one creel. 24 mackerel. One of these succeeded in breaking a hook. New lobster box floats too high in water because too much perforated, which makes it into a mere wooden frame, & hence fairly buoyant, instead of a box. Have weighted with stones, but nb.° that these must be tied down, otherwise they will shift about & damage the lobsters.

Tobacco pouch lost. Made makeshift one of a rabbit skin, lined with inner tube. 1 small skin about large enough for a pouch. Made mustard spoon out of deer's bone.

Still large herds of deer near the old stable, mostly hinds with a few stags & fawns among them. Was within 20 yards of 2 stags. No doubt they are all over this side because they are shooting over on the Glengarrisdale side.

12.9.46: Dreadful weather. In the morning sea calm & not much wind, though it was raining a little. All afternoon violent rain & raging wind from south & southwest. Sea very heavy. Fear the boat may have been bashed about, but it would probably have been impossible to take her in even if the weather had encouraged one to go out of doors. Took up creels in morning. One crab, fair sized.

Too wet to do much out of doors. Re-set scythe according: to D[onald] D[arroch]'s instructions. NB. that these were wrongly stated in an earlier entry. The rule is that the blade of the scythe, a length of the handle equal to the blade of the scythe, & the distance between the upper extremity of this length & the tip of the blade, should form an equilateral triangle. The blade is held in place with a thick piece of wire, eg. fencing wire, which passes through the hole under the cutting edge, then curves over the other side. One has to get it red hot to hammer it into shape, otherwise one is liable to break the blade by hammering on it.

[*On facing page*]

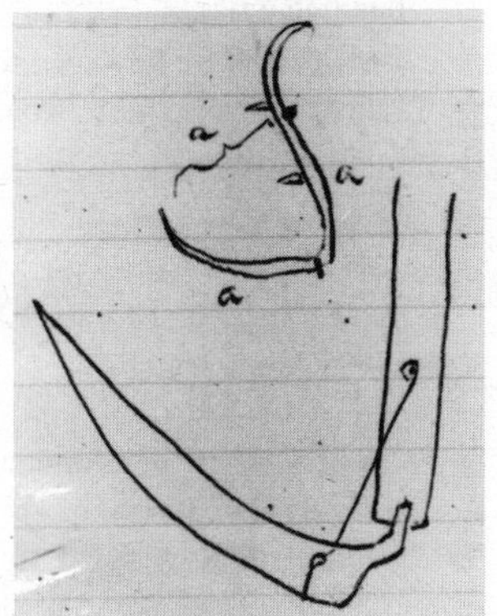

Let socket of scythe blade be A & tip of blade B. Measure AB. Mark off from bottom of handle a length AC equal to AB. Then set blade at such an angle that BC also equals AB.

Made mustard spoon out of bone & salt spoon out of deer's antler. Bone is better.

D.D. sharpens his scythe blade along the whole length, & does not give what is called a "quick sharpen" – ie. a sharpening only of the edge. He holds the stone (carborundum) almost parallel with the blade & sharpens a width of half an inch or an inch all the way up the blade.

13.9.46: Some fine intervals in the morning, but rain all afternoon, & violent wind, mostly from west. Sea calmer. Boat has been badly stove in – 3 boards gone. Possibly repairable, but not here. Evidently the anchor had shifted in the storm. One lobster box washed away. The other may be recoverable from the shore at low tide. Creels not recoverable. At present too wet & rough to fish, but when the weather improves & the wind is off-shore shall try from the point, throwing the fly with my large fly-rod. K[atie] D[arroch] says that when her father fished from the shore, he used to throw in fragments of boiled potato to attract the fish. Limpets are more usual, & they are generally boiled first – reason given, that they are then easier to get out of the shells.

Tried scythe. With it as it is now, I can get a little grass off, & might improve with practice.

A good many ravens about. Pigeons in the cornfields, but impossible to get near enough for a shot.

14.9.46: Dreadful day on the whole. A bright interval of about 20 minutes in the early evening, otherwise raining most of the time. Road to Ardlussa is a running stream most of the way. Near Ardlussa jetty the road surface has been washed right away & channels in some places two feet deep scooped out of the running water. Had to fetch the rations on push bikes. Barnhill to Ardlussa (unloaded), about 2 hours, return journey about 3 hours. It was, however, too dark to ride much for the last 2 miles of the journey, so with better conditions one could do it in about 2½ hours. D.D. does it with a bigger load in about 1½ hours.

15.9.46: Somewhat better. Very blowy, but bright, & with only one or two showers. Heavy shower of hail about 8 am this morning. Wind still in south & sea rough.

Tried some hazel nuts. Not ripe yet, though the shells are almost full. Should be ripe in about 10 days.

Thinned out spring cabbages. Turnips sown (15.6.46.) just large enough to pull. Onions sown for next year are well up. Ditto lettuces, but chaffinches had some of them as soon as they appeared.

16.9.46: Violent wind in the night. This morning even more stormy, tremendous wind from south, seas heavier than I have ever seen them. Overcast, & a few drops of rain from time to time.

About noon the Ardlussa lorry arrived with 10 or 20 people, in hopes of getting in D[onald D[arroch]'s second field of oats. Quite hopeless. Rain started by the time the reaper had been round the field about twice, & continued almost without a break all day. Terrific wind all the time, but it was all from west & south & had no drying effect even when it was not actually raining.

Watched the estate carpenter putting in a new sash cord in D.D's house. NB. that one has to start by taking out the side strips which hold the lower half of the window in place, then those which hold the upper half, but it is not necessary to take out the top & bottom pieces.

17.9.46: Somewhat better. Wind still in south & very violent, but not much rain, & some sunny intervals. Shot at a curlew, but missed him. The first time I have been near enough to one here to get a shot.

Have bought carcase of deer from the F[letchers'] as arranged. Don't know price yet, but the market price is about 10d. a lb. dead weight (ie. without guts but with hide & antlers), & this one should be 150 lb. or more, so price will probably be roundabout £6. He was left at the new stable (shot yesterday), & D.D. brought him back this morning. The usual complications. The tractor, which is remaining here until it is possible to cut the fields, had been backed into the stable in front of D.D's cart, & as he could not get it started, he could not get his cart out to fetch the stag. Had to drag it on a hurriedly-constructed sledge which broke when he was still about a quarter of a mile from home. This afternoon watched him skinning it. We shall each have a haunch, then put the rest into brine for the winter. It is important to clean out the carcase thoroughly, split it open right down the front & wedge it open, remove the windpipe & lungs, & cut off the portions of flesh along the edges of the belly, which become soiled when the animal is first gutted. After skinning it is hoisted into the air (without pulleys this needs all the strength of 4 people), & hangs for 24 hours before being cut up. There was more fat on the carcase than I would have expected to find in a wild animal. Took about half the hide, as much as I thought I had curing materials for, & shall cure it in the same manner as the rabbit skins. A whole skin would make a nice large hearth rug. D.D. cut off the ears & was careful to put them in a place where the dogs could not get at them. It is something to do with taxation – at any rate, the ears of every deer shot have to be produced for inspection at need.

Tonight raining again, on & off.

18.9.46: Some rain in night. This morning cold & overcast, but wind has dropped. Sea calmer.

Afternoon on the whole fine & sunny. A few drops of rain in the afternoon, a sharp shower about 6, & a little more rain in the night.

Tried fishing off the rock, without success, although with the wind almost in the north I could cast at least 40 feet out & into places where we sometimes catch fish. Of course if you are stationary you are dependent on the shoal happening to come that way.

The deer is to be "broken up" tonight or tomorrow, before the flies get at it. Cured about half the hide, all I had curing mixture for, in the same manner as the rabbit skins. NB. to open about 3rd. October.

D.D. very busy scything his second field & binding & stooking the sheaves with K.D's help. He is anxious to get as much as possible done before the Ardlussa party come back with the reaper. He says they made a dreadful mess of the little bit they cut 3 days ago. The sheaves were too large, & all tied round at the top. When wet they are almost too heavy to lift, & most of the stooks made that day have fallen down.

19.9.46: Some showers about breakfast time.

Most of the day blowy & coldish, but with a fair amount of sunlight & not much rain. Sea calmer, though wind shifted to the south for a bit.

D.D's field finished, ie. the cutting, by the reaper, which then came on to do the Barnhill field. Prevented by various complications. First the knife was left behind at Kinuachdrach, then the tractor would not start, then it could not be driven over the boggiest part of the field. Finally after cutting a quarter of the field or less, it was decided to come again tomorrow, cut the corn but not stook it or tie it into sheaves, but leave it in "swathes", gathering it into the barn later, like hay. Apparently it is feasible to do this if one is not going to thrash the corn. Corn extremely wet & much "laid", but where the rabbits have left it alone it does not seem a bad crop.

Recovered creels & 1 lobster box. The other had been smashed to bits. The bigger one had not actually been broken up, but had shifted its moorings, & the lobsters had got out owing to lid becoming loosened. Nothing in creels. Great difficulty in hauling them up as they were embedded in huge masses of seaweed. Vast deposits of weed on the beach after the storm. Examined boat again. Actually it is repairable, but it wants 5 boards, which of course is not a job that can be done on the beach. However, it has easily repaid its original cost (£10) in fish, & next year we will keep whatever boat we have at Kinuachdrach.

20.9.46: This morning fine & sunny, though cold. Little wind, & sea calm.

A light shower about 4 pm., otherwise fine, sunny & coldish all day. Great flocks of gulls very busy out in the sound, presumably after shoals of mackerel.

Corn in Barnhill field is cut & lying in swathes. They say that when harvested in this way it does not need turning but will get dry as it is.

The sea trout the F[letcher]s brought us yesterday was full of roe – very large globules, reddish yellow. Did not know they had it at this time of year.

A good many blackberries, but they are not full as yet. Hazel nuts definitely not ripe.

Calor gas cylinder has been running for a month today. When this gives out, it will not be quite an accurate test of how long they last, as some gas was lost owing to a leak. Forgot to mention we started 5 gall drum of paraffin (the right stuff this time) on 16.9.46. We are using it for double burner lamps, & to some extent for a Valor stove, a Beatrice stove,[37] & storm lanterns. Probably will not last more than 2 weeks, but NB. to note date when it gives out.

Some coal, about ¾ ton delivered today. It will about see us through till our departure on October 9th, leaving 2¼ tons for next year (ie. till June next year). Allowance for this house is 6 tons a year. Since about 25th May, ie. nearly 4 months, we have used almost exactly 3 tons. We have also used a good deal of wood, & no fire except the kitchen one has been burning regularly. We have also used Calor gas to some extent during the past month. So that if one was here all the year round, one would need quite 10 tons of coal yearly. Of course this heats the water & allows the kitchen to be used as a living room, besides doing the cooking.

The stag is now cut up & in the brine, less the haunches, which the D.s & ourselves are eating fresh. Paid for the stag £8.8.0. He was estimated to weigh 14 stone, of which 2 stone are deducted for the head & feet, & the market price is now 1/– a pound. After removal of the hide there would probably be 10 stone (140 lb) of meat including bone. As we are halving it with the Darrochs, we shall each have about 70 lb. of meat, of which about 30 lb. has been salted. This is almost equal to one person's meat ration for a year.[38]

37. Trade names of paraffin heaters.

38. At the end of the war the basic weekly food ration included 4 ozs bacon; 8 ozs made up of butter, margarine and lard; 3 ozs of cheese (which was three times the 1940 ration); 2 ozs tea; and 1s 2d (6 new pence, say £1.80 today) of meat some of which must be corned beef. Luxury foods such as tinned fruit, fish, and meat were rationed according to a points system and an adult could expect about three eggs a month. It was not permitted to make cream. Even after the war, ingredients for making better than basic bakery products were not available except to those taking professional bakery courses at technical schools in order to keep the techniques alive. Clothes also were rationed and at times *after the war* bread and potatoes were rationed. Petrol was rationed at five gallons per month and coal was rationed. Resentment was caused when rations were reduced to allow food to be diverted to Germany, then near starvation. It was not until July 1954 that meat was taken off ration. In some country districts (as here on Jura) some foods were more freely available.

21.9.46: Awful day. Violent wind from the south, & a good deal of rain. After about 9 pm rain grew much heavier, & wind was raging all night.

Finished mending, ie. heeling, army boots. Seems quite easy to do, but one needs a grindstone & heelball to finish off with.

Stags roaring. I think this is the first time I have heard them this year. Large flights of rooks. I did not know we had them here, & when seeing a single black bird of that family, not a hoodie, have usually set it down as a raven. These however were almost certainly rooks. Qy. where they nest, as there are no tall trees here.[39]

39. In Scotland, in places where there are no trees, rooks and hooded crows nest on the ground, usually among heather.

22.9.46: Weather a very little better. Wind blew itself out in the night & the morning was fairly fine. Afternoon raining on & off. Sea calming down. Stags roaring all over the place.

23.9.46: Better on the whole. Most of day fine, blowy & rather cold, but not much rain until about 6pm, when there was about an hour's continuous rain. Some more showers in the night. Wind from south & south west very violent, & sea still rough.

Cylinder of calor gas gave out. That is a month & 3 days – say 5 weeks, allowing for the fact that there had been some wastage. Have ordered more cylinders. The new one I have put on should well see us out till we leave in October.

Had big bonfire & burnt up much of the rubbish. Have been meaning to do this for weeks but this was the first day when it was dry enough.

24.9.46: Much better day. Fine, with a drying wind & barely a shower all day. Burnt out the patch which has been treated with sodium chlorate. It burnt well & there is hardly a rush left, though possibly the roots of some of them are still alive. Impossible to deal with the other large patch of rushes unless I can get the drum of sodium chlorate down from the stable fairly soon.

D.D. very busy stacking. One stack completed, but not thatched, today. He will have about 5. He builds small round stacks, tapered to a pretty sharp point at the top, & thatched with rushes. One stack appears to mean about 6 cartloads, or about an acre of corn. The stuff was still very damp & one has to select what sheaves one will cart, building the others up into stooks again, to get dry some more. It does not so much matter putting damp ones at the top of the stack. In tapering off, D.D. makes use of the very small sheaves, ie. very short ones, in which there is hardly any straw, generally owing to their having been rabbit-eaten. These are put aside & used last, when the stack begins to taper. He says a round stack stands up to the wind better than the other shape.

Today put on underclothes for the first time.

25.9.46: Fine & blowy till about 4 pm, after which some rain: Wind still in south & sea rough. Began clearing bed under window, transplanted seedlings of perennial cabbage (these seem to have formed roots all right) & some spring cabbage seedlings. The latter are poor plants, probably owing to their having been merely thinned out & not pricked out into a nursery bed. Soil in this bed quite different (much darker) from that in the other beds, only about 5 yards away. Turf dug in about the end of May has just about rotted down. One therefore has to allow about 4 months before one can dig at all deeply in soil where one has dug turf in.

An eagle flew over the house today. It always seems to be in very windy weather that we see them down this end. One of D[onald] D[arroch]'s dogs killed a hare (mountain hare) on the "tops" today. D.D. says they are not so very uncommon. He says definitely that this variety turns white in winter, ditto the stoats (or perhaps weasels). As there is not much snow here this may partly account for the scarcity of hares.

Dobbies[40] have no bush roses, so am ordering 6 ramblers & 12 polyanthas. Do not know whether they will be able to spare so many. Tulip bulbs not arrived yet.

40. An Edinburgh nurseryman who sold by mail order. In 2009, as Dobies of Devon, Torquay. Orwell's spelling is retained.

26.9.46: Very stormy during last night. Today a vile day. Not actually raining, though overcast, till about midday, after which it rained most of the time, sometimes very heavily. Sea rough.

Could not do much out of doors. Finished clearing bed under window & made the place for the first espalier tree. It will be difficult to fix them onto these walls as one cannot drive nails into the stone.

Trying to note how many meals we get of half a deer. Up to date we have had 7 meals (for anything from 2–6 people) off the preliminary parts, ie. the liver, heart & tongue, & the joint one eats fresh. Also about a pound of suet & a large bowl of dripping.

Dobbie's° have no lime. It will be a calamity if I cannot get some from somewhere.

27.9.46: Much better day. Very stormy last night, & this morning almost continuous rain till about 1 pm. Then it cleared up & became very warm & still, with no rain. A beautiful calm evening, with the sun showing a little. Sea calmed down very suddenly. Midges start up again the instant the wind drops.

Extended bed under the wall up to the porch, & made place for rose bush. Weeded & lightly dug over the empty portion of the strawberry patch. Soil is very sodden. Up near the porch the soil is no good, so shall transplant some wild foxgloves & primroses there. Pruned & manured the surviving fruit bushes.

This morning a large seagull, this year's bird by its plumage, hanging round the house & feeding with the geese. Probably they get especially hungry in stormy weather owing to being unable to fish.

Bracken has now almost all turned brown. Trees showing just a little sign of turning. Picked some hazel nuts. Pretty well ripe, but about half of them are rotten, no doubt owing to its being such a wet year. A lot of blackberries now but they are not really good this year, most of them looking a bit spotty.

28.9.46: Beautiful day. Slightly misty, very warm, & not a breath of wind. Sea like glass & beautiful pale blue. Road has already dried up a good deal. Getting to Ardlussa took 1 hour 55 minutes, returning, less time for lunch, 2 hours 25 minutes. This time not carrying such a heavy load as usual, however.

Two stags standing close together near the old stable, about 100 yards from the road, & roaring in a very bellicose manner, apparently at me. When not roaring they were grazing quite amicably side by side. So apparently they do not necessarily fight when they meet, though this is supposed to be the mating season.

Planted 2 roots of large plants (I forget their name) which M[argaret] F[letcher] gave me, also some wild foxgloves in the corner where the soil is poor. In a dark spot saw a foxglove still trying to flower – they were flowering in late May when I came here.

29.9.46: Beautiful day. Quite hot in early afternoon. More wind than yesterday, however, & sea rough, though the wind was in the north some of the time. Wind tonight is quite violent.

Made pit for compost heap, burned out more rushes, brought in bits of fence to put round cherry trees. A[vril] brought home some nuts which were on the ground, presumably blown off by the recent gales. They appeared ripe, but were mostly rotten. Evidently no good this year.

30.9.46: Raining this morning, but cleared up in the afternoon & was calm & still, with some sun. Sea calmer. Went down to shore. No fresh drift. D.D. went to the W. bay[41] yesterday to see what drift the gales had brought in, but apparently nothing interesting.

Cut & sharpened stakes for trees, finished 3rd patch, scythed plot for trees & put cuttings into the compost pit, & prepared places for 2 trees. They will be about 8 ft. apart each way, which is enough for dwarf trees. Manure will be just about enough for these trees, & no more.

For the first time, saw the deer that frequents the place down by the shore, just outside the deer fence. A hind. She was grazing not more than 5 yards from me, with her head down in the iris plants, & did not see or hear me till I deliberately made a noise to disturb her.

Last of the 5 gallons of oil used up tonight – will run the lamps for about 1 day more, or at least a couple of them. Started on (I think) 16.9.46, so will have run about a fortnight. If one were also using a heating stove at all frequently (we have used the heating stoves, but not much), one would have to allow for a total consumption of quite 3 galls a week, probably 3½.

41. Presumably 'the W-shaped bays next to Glentrosdale'.

Facing the entries for 30 September to 3 October on three successive verso folios are diagrams which Orwell drew to show how he planned the development of his plot. The first four words of the first line at the top of the first facing recto are also written at the top of the first drawing but crossed through. It would seem likely that Orwell began these drawings on 30 September. A fourth layout of the garden was drawn on a loose sheet of paper tucked into the diary. All four drawings are reproduced successively here for the reader's convenience. See 4.1.47 for the layout of bushes planted on his return to Barnhill on 2 January 1947. The last two pages of the book have two lists, one giving what is to be done before leaving, with '(October)' in parentheses, and the second with a list of things needed for Barnhill. As these were presumably drawn up about this time, they are placed after the drawings. The layouts are here reduced in size.

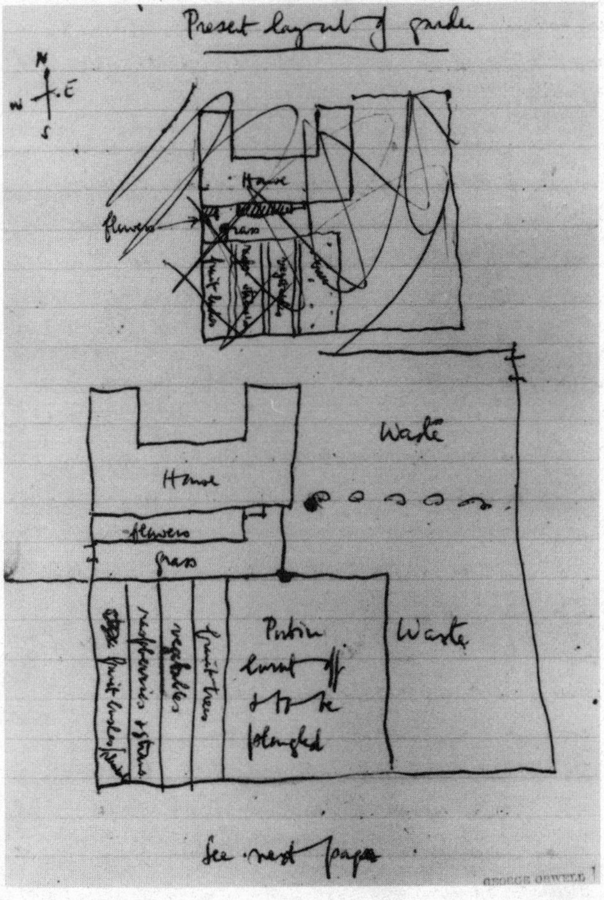

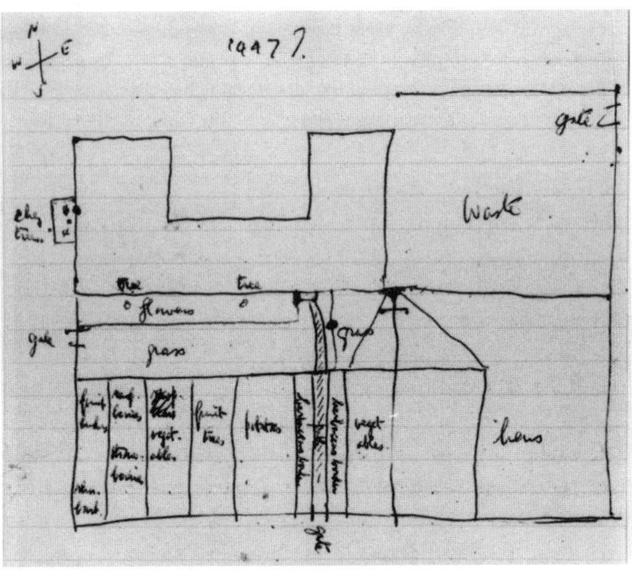
1947 ?
N
W
E
S
gate
waste
tree
flowers
gate
grass
fruit trees
potatoes
vegetables
hens
gate

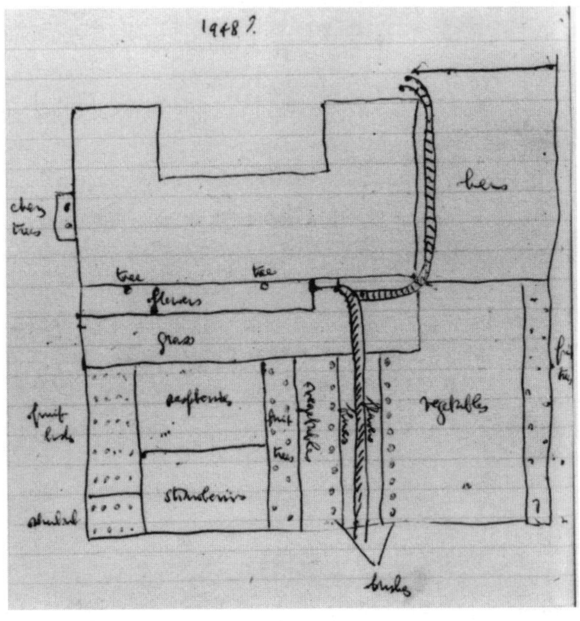
1948 ?
hens
tree
tree
flowers
grass
raspberries
fruit bushes
strawberries
fruit trees
vegetables
vegetables
bushes

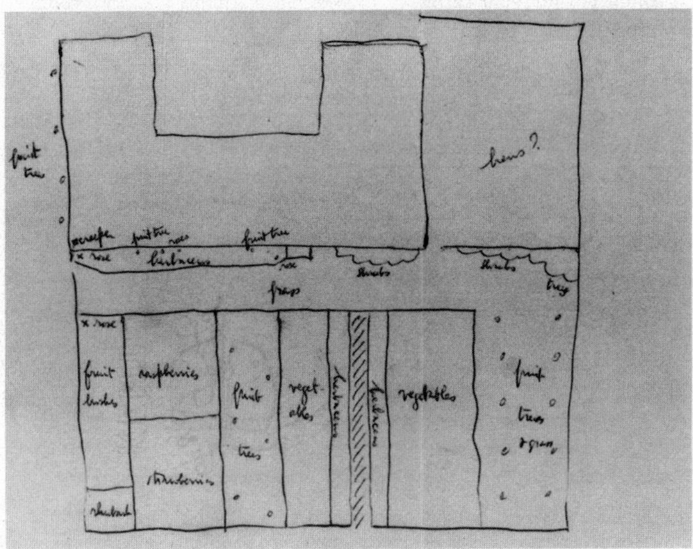

Before going away (October)[42]:

Inspect deer fence. Mend gate.

Close gap in back garden (2 beans[43] sufficient.)

Prepare places for fruit trees, ditto rose bushes.

Cut stakes (about 12 for trees, 6 or 8 for wire netting, 1 doz. small for rose bushes).

Put wire netting round bed near house.

Clear beds.

Square off edges.

Plant cabbages, lupins, pansies, cheddar pinks, primroses(?), tulips(?).

Lime as much of soil as possible.

Drag up boat.

Make cover for ditto (corrugated iron?)

Grease tools (& bring in). (bike)

Measure stairs & passage.

Put stones on lid of tank

Collect seaweed /leaf mould.

Wanted for Barnhill:[44]

4 small carpets (about 14' by 6')

1 good hearth-rug

4 small ditto (bedside mats)

About 15 yards stair carpet
About 10 yards passage matting
Piece of lino, about 12' by 6'.
5 tables, various sizes (mostly kitchen tables).
2 armchairs.
About half-dozen upright chairs.
Several fenders.
Pillow cases (1 doz.)
Cups, plates, cutlery (incl. carving knife & fork).
4 table cloths, checked.
Mincing machine. Irons. Radio. Sewing machine?

Tools. Mowing machine, hay rake, large vice, planes various, chisels various, hammers & mallets various, oil cans, paint brushes, paint, tar, cement, rope, chain. Hand cultivator. Telescope.

Outboard motor (& boat).

Hand cart.

42. All items are ticked except 'Square off edges' and 'Grease tools . . . bike),' which are unmarked; 'Lime as much of soil as possible' and 'Collect seaweed / leaf mould,' against each of which is a cross; and 'Make cover . . . iron?)' and 'Drag up boat,' which are crossed through. All the question marks are Orwell's.
43. 'beans' presumably means bean poles. Orwell makes the letter 'm' quite clearly on this page so it is unlikely that 'beams' is intended.
44. 'Radio' and 'Mowing machine' are ticked. The question mark is Orwell's.

1.10.46: Nice warm day, sometimes overcast, but mostly sunny & with not much wind. This evening about 9.30 pm a sudden torrential downpour of rain, which went on for about 5 minutes & was followed by light rain.

The Ardlussa people arrived this morning to make another attempt at getting in the corn. Raked it over, then tossed it with forks, the idea being that by the afternoon it would be dry enough to cart. Much of it was still damp, however, so it was racked up into heaps about 5 ft. high, in hopes that it could be carted tomorrow (it is to be stored in our byre). Tonight's rain will presumably have wetted it through again.

Extended bed under wall, prepared place for another fruit tree & some ramblers, planted azaleas & a root of some kind of geranium (blue I think) which M[argaret] F[letcher] gave me. In the evening went up to Kinuachdrach with the F's rifle to try & get a shot at the deer which comes into D[onald] D[arroch]'s corn. He did not turn up. A difficult job to get a shot, as he comes at night & after about 8 pm it is too dark to shoot.

D.D. has one stack thatched, another made but not thatched, & another about halfway up – ie. round about half his corn is in. It appears that he does not cut into the stacks when he wants corn, but takes them into the barn one after the other as he needs them, & serves out the corn from there. An awful double labour, caused by his not having enough barn space.

Undid the cured deer skin. Seems all right (ie. it does not smell), but very damp, & the paper it was done up in had become mildewy & stuck to the skin in places. Have no alum or saltpetre left, but rubbed it with salt again before hanging it up to dry.

2.10.46: Very damp, still & dark all day, but no rain. Light was already failing by 6.15 pm.

Cut fence posts, prepared 6 more places for trees, collected leaf mould (for the trees), brought in about a dozen wild primroses & planted them. The latter not easy to find at this time of year, as the leaves go limp & the grass covers them. Soil where some of the fruit trees are to go is very poor – very sticky & clayey, with a rock subsoil so near the surface that the stakes will not hold firm & will have to be propped.

No sign of the deer. When buying potatoes from the D's, they showed me one which D. D. had weighed, & it was just 1 lb. (Great Scott – supposed not to be a first class potato, but they are well-shaped & hence easy to peel as well as large).

Yesterday started the new (40 gall.) drum of paraffin. Shall send 5 galls to London by rail, as it is very difficult to get there. Allowing for that & for a week's consumption now & another week in November,[45] we have a reserve for about 2 months next year. Ditto of coal – ie. about 2 tons or rather over. Of Calor gas there should be 2 weeks' supply in the cylinder, & two cylinders, ie. about 9 weeks' supply, to come. So we should be O.K. for the first 2 months next year.

45. Orwell did not return until January (see Diary entries below for that month).

3.10.46: Cold & overcast all day. One or two very light showers in the evening. Sea moderately calm.

Planted out lupins (25 plants), pansies (about 50 plants) & some cheddar pinks – the latter not very good, & I doubt whether this limeless soil suits them. Put fence round the 2 places for trees outside the garden, prepared the holes, & put wire netting here & round the flower bed. Not very rabbit proof, but should deter them to some extent. Started clearing first bed. Radishes which have been left unpulled are already about 8″ long and 1″ thick. Some of the swedes sown 15.6.46 just big enough to eat.

Forgot to mention A[vril] saw a mouse in the byre yesterday. Had previously seen signs of them, ie. chewed-up paper, but had never seen one in the house & always hoped they were only field mice (qu. do these also make nests of chewed paper?) Rats, hitherto non-existent here, are bound to come when the corn is put into the byre.

4.10.46: Damp, overcast, rather windy, but not cold. A few light showers. D. D. getting in some more corn all the same, & hoping to finish the third stack today. Repaired deer fence & gate at the bottom of the field. Not very good job, but it is better than it was before. Started digging first bed. The turf has just about rotted down & the soil is in much nicer condition than when it was first broken.

5.10.46: Some rain in the night. Today overcast & blowy, but only one or two light showers.

Mowing machine ("New British" – fairly light & presumably cheap make) arrived today. Cut the grass, ie. as much of it as is in a condition to be cut. Does not look bad, & will be quite good after another good cut next spring. Planted tulips (50 mixed, but whether late or early I do not know). NB. tulips are in two clumps, one in front of espalier apple tree, the other in front of the water pipe. Must not put roses on top of them. Paid for 50 bulbs 16/3, ie. about 4d. each.

Tomorrow if possible:
Remove holly tree & re-turf the place.
Finish digging first patch. morning.[46]
Prop fruit tree stakes (1 doz. stakes)
Collect a little leaf mould
Bring in some more wild foxgloves
Dig one more place for rambler & put wire round the other.
If this is done, the garden is actually finished for this year, ie. it is up to schedule.

Today tried killing individual docks with very strong solution of sodium chlorate, dipping a spike into this & digging it into their roots.

46. 'morning' was initially bracketed against the first three tasks but it was crossed through to enclose only the first two. There are ticks beside tasks 1, 2, 5, and 6.

6.10.46: First day of G.M.T.[47]

Beautiful day. Sunny & clear, almost no wind, sea calm & a beautiful rather pale blue. It turned cold, however, as soon as the sun was behind the hill. It was dark today before 7 pm.

Removed holly bush & began re-turfing the place. Cleared out some of the undergrowth from round the fuchsia bush, & removed dead branches.

47. Greenwich Mean Time; clocks would have been put back one hour from Summer Time – hence dark before 7 p.m. instead of 8 p.m.

7.10.46: Again a beautiful day, but somewhat colder & more windy than yesterday. Wireless said there was frost in the night (not here, I think). Some mist this morning & mainland almost invisible. Wind veering about from one quarter to another & sea rather rough.

Brought in some more wild foxgloves. Nothing left to do now except prop fruit tree stakes &, if possible, collect a little manure to put on top of the compost heap & assist rotting.

D.D. has got all his corn in – this although today & yesterday he has had a bad cold & sore throat. The last load was coming in & the fifth stack was half way up when I arrived there this afternoon. Only the first stack is thatched as yet.

Four pheasants pecking about in D.D's field as I went past. The deer has never reappeared, ie. in daytime.

8.10.46: Fine & dry, but colder, & a lot of wind, mostly in south. Sea rougher. Saw a black cock close to in the wood. It looked enormous – definitely bigger than a pheasant. I thought it must be a capercailzie, but as it had white on its wings I suppose it was a black cock.

All day clearing up etc. Brought in a few roots of thrift & stuck them in, as the other root I brought in has taken. Propped fruit tree stakes, finished turfing bare patch. Garden is now finished, ie. is up to schedule.

We are leaving tomorrow & I expect to return & plant the trees about mid-November.

Orwell returned to London writing for Tribune, *etc.*
His article, 'How the Poor Die', was published in November.
He got back to Barnhill 2 January 1947

4.1.47: Have been here since 2.1.47. Was to arrive two days earlier, but missed boat on 30th & had to hang about for 2 days in Glasgow. Rough crossing from Tarbert, & was very sick. Did not take tablets until on the point of being sick – on the return journey shall take them before embarking. It took the boat about half an hour to tie up at Craighouse pier, as with the sea that was running she could not get in close. After tying up she could only keep in position for a minute or two, in spite of the cables, & the passengers had only just time to nip across the gangway.

The day I arrived here was a beautiful sunny day, like April. Yesterday raining most of the time & the wind so violent that it was difficult to stay on one's feet. Today somewhat better – cold & overcast, but not much wind.

All the small plants I put in – pansies, lupins, cheddar pinks & cabbages – have completely disappeared, evidently owing to rabbits. The rabbits had also grubbed up & eaten the few turnips that were still in the ground, but had not touched the carrots. What is worse is that they have destroyed most of the strawberries. A few are all right, but most of them have disappeared – however, if the crowns are still there they may revive in the spring. The wire round the flower bed was not pegged down & the rabbits have got under it. Am setting traps before leaving. Round the vegetable patch it is sunk a few inches & there was no sign that they had got under it, so they must have climbed over (3 ft. wire), which they are said to be able to do.

Today planted 1 doz fruit trees, 1 doz red currants, 1 doz black currants, 1 doz gooseberries, 1 doz rhubarb, 1 doz roses (6 ramblers & climbers). Shall plant raspberries tomorrow.

On the verso page facing the entry for 4 January 1947, Orwell drew a plan to show the layout of his fruit trees: see page 421. To the left of the house on the plan: two morello cherry trees. Ten trees are shown on the plan below the outline of the house, five in each of two columns. Against the first tree of the left-hand column is a question mark; the three below are Allington Pippin, Ribston Pippin, and Lord Derby; the fifth is unnamed. The right-hand column lists Golden Spire, Ellison's Orange, one unnamed, James Grieve, and Lady Sudeley.

5.1.47: Much wind in night. This morning wind still strong, & sea rough. Sunny but cold.

Planted raspberries (2 dozen, not very good plants).
Set 2 traps
Tulips fairly well up.
NB. That when returning we have in store:
About 30 galls paraffin (about 8 weeks supply).
2 cylinders Calor Gas (about 9 weeks supply).
2 tons coal (at Ardlussa) (about 2 months supply).

This completed the entries to Volume III of Orwell's Domestic Diary. At the end of the notebook are Orwell's notes for his essay 'Politics and the English Language' (*CW*, XIV, pp. 432–8). This was published in *Horizon*, April 1946, (*CW*, XVII, pp. 421–32). Volume IV begins 12 April 1947 (see page 423).

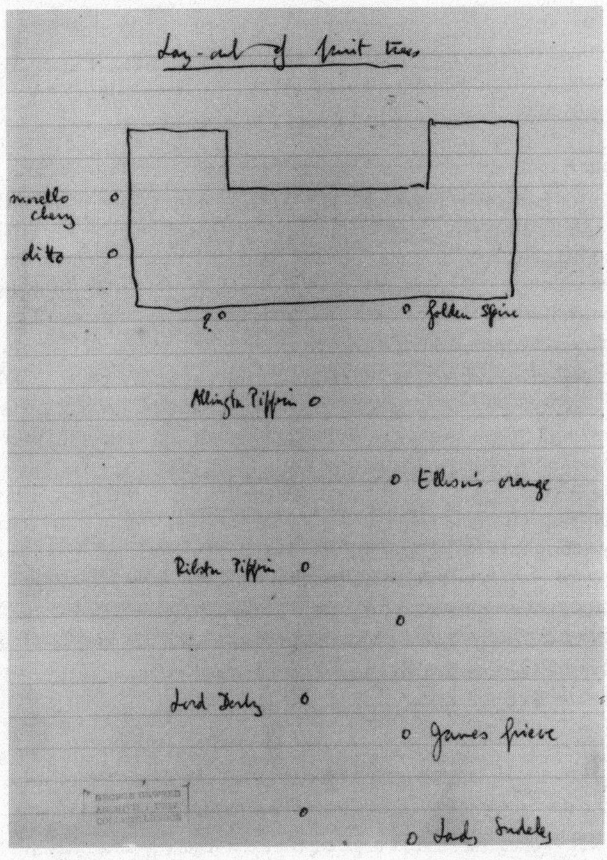

This concludes Domestic Diary Volume III.

DOMESTIC DIARY VOLUME IV

12 April 1947 – 11 September 1947

On 14 January 1947 Orwell's adaptation of *Animal Farm* was broadcast by the BBC on the Third Programme, the antecedent of Radio Three. It was repeated on 2 February. In order to emphasise what he called 'the turning-point of the story . . . when the pigs kept the milk and apples for themselves', he added four lines to the radio script. The significance of these was lost on the BBC producer, who cut them out.

His eightieth and last 'As I Please' column was published by *Tribune* on 4 April 1947 and the following week he went to Barnhill, Jura, and worked on *Nineteen Eighty-Four.* Despite often being ill and though desperate to complete his novel, he also drafted his essay, 'Such, Such Were the Joys'. He sent that to Fredric Warburg on 31 May 1947. Although he knew it could not be published in his lifetime for fear of libel actions, he continued revising the essay completing it about May 1948. In August 1947 *The English People* was published by Collins in its series *Britain in Pictures* and in September 1947 he gave up his lease of The Stores, Wallington.

By October 1947 Orwell was so ill he had to work in bed. He completed the first draft of *Nineteen Eighty-Four* on 7 November 1947.

From 20 December 1947 until 28 July 1948, he was a patient at Hairmyres Hospital, East Kilbride, near Glasgow, with tuberculosis of the left lung. Whilst he was in hospital, his sister Avril made brief entries in his diary, chiefly referring to the state of the weather. These are briefly summarised at the end of Volume V.

Orwell began the second draft of *Nineteen Eighty-Four* in May 1948 whilst still a patient in Hairmyres Hospital. He got back to Barnhill on 29th July, opening what was to be his last Diary two days later. He completed writing *Nineteen Eighty-Four* early in November 1948. No secretary could be persuaded to travel to Barnhill to undertake typing out a fair copy of the novel so, often in bed and coughing up blood, Orwell undertook this laborious task himself. He finished on 4 December 1948 and copies were immediately posted to his agent, Leonard Moore, and his publisher, Fredric Warburg. It was from a carbon copy of this typescript that the US edition of *Nineteen Eighty-Four* would be printed. Also in December – and significantly – he gave up the lease of his flat in Canonbury Square, Islington; clearly he knew he would never live there again.

Volume IV of Orwell's Domestic Diary was written on ninety-five recto pages and six verso pages of a 7½ x 6½ins. notebook with twenty-two ruled lines per page. Before the first entry Orwell wrote 'VOL. IV' and below that, 'Diary (cont. from previous volume)'. Volume V continues from 12 September in a different notebook. Orwell indicates the totals of gallons of petrol used: petrol was then rationed. He also gives a running total in parentheses of eggs collected.

Footnotes are numbered from 1.

12.4.47: Barnhill. Arrived yesterday evening. Fine yesterday & today, but coldish. Everything extremely backward. Grass has not started to grow, ditto rushes, birds on trees hardly visible. Daffodils just coming out, snowdrops barely over – a few still in bloom. Flying from Glasgow saw many streaks of snow still on high ground. There was about 6 weeks frost on Jura, then rain, & ground is still very sodden. Many lambs & calves lost during the winter. Reason given, the sheep & cows had not enough milk.

The trees & bushes I planted all seem to be alive. The two cordon trees against the south wall budding well. Onions etc. that I saved & which were well up in January have practically all disappeared in the frost. Most of the strawberries seem to have survived, but are very tiny. Rhubarb is coming up well. Tulips well up.

They have caught no sea fish yet. Rabbits said to be scarce this year.

Beautiful day all day, striking chilly about 5 pm. Saw one primrose blooming in a sheltered spot, otherwise no wild flowers. Stone crop just beginning to sprout, wild irises & bluebells coming up. Grass still completely wintry in appearance. Saw a few rabbits. Pigeons towering up with a loud rattle of wings – their courting flight, I think. Sea very calm. No seals about.

Sowed dwarf peas. NB. to sow a second batch about 25.4.47. Pruned roses drastically. Several have no buds showing at all, so cannot yet tell whether they are alive. Ground in bad state & impossible to sow small seeds. Covered rhubarb with manure. D.[1] has ploughed roughly the patch I asked him to do. Shall hoe it over enough to get some sort of tilth & then sow potatoes when I can get some. It ought to be properly dug over, but, after all, this much cultivation is all that a field crop gets.

Compost put in pit last autumn has not properly rotted down yet.

1. Donald Darroch and Katie his sister. Often as D.D. and K.D.

13.4.47: Fine all day, but colder than yesterday. A good deal of wind, from west & south. Sea rougher.

Put up sectional henhouse. Wretched workmanship, & will need a lot of strengthening & weighting down to make it stay in place. Two of the wheels arrived broken. Before the war these were easily obtainable, but probably not now. Planted 4 dozen gladiolus bulbs (pink & yellow). Soil somewhat better after the wind, so it may be possible to sow small seeds tomorrow.

14.4.47: Much rain in the night. Today fine, with fair sun, but again cold & windy. Sea moderate. Raven in the distance dancing about, evidently courting.

Put up stakes for wire round hen-run. Sowed marigolds. Could not do much outside as R.[2] fell this morning & gashed his forehead extremely badly. Hope to get him to the doctor tomorrow – impossible today, as no conveyance.

Opened bottle of brandy. With a small ration each daily, we[3] hope to make one bottle last a week.

DBST[4] started yesterday. Three different times are observed on this island.

2. R .= Richard, Orwell's two-year-old son. (usually as 'R' but that can also stand for Richard Rees). The only doctor on Jura was at Craighouse, some 25 miles to the south by poor roads.
3. Orwell and his sister Avril (usually as A.).
4. Double British Summer Time. To aid daylight saving, clocks were advanced one hour from late spring to early autumn; during the war and in the years immediately after, clocks were advanced for one hour throughout the year and for a second hour during the 'summer' period. The measure was particularly unpopular with farmers. By 'three different times', Orwell probably means DBST, Summer Time (time advanced by only one hour), and 'natural time,' that which regulated farm and stock management.

15.4.47: Raining almost all day, very windy & rather cold. Did nothing in garden etc, as was taking R. to be treated by the doctor. Two stitches put in. NB. to be removed about a week hence (not more than 10 days.)

16.4.47: Cold, overcast & rather windy. Somewhat finer in late evening, & sea calmer.

Impossible to sow seeds. Spread lime (not very well slaked), put roofing felt on hen-house.

Saw one of the whitish rabbits this evening (in the distance, but seemingly a full-grown one).

17.4.47: Much better day. Some wind, but sunny & fairly warm. Began digging the ploughed patch. Not bad – will do for potatoes. Sowed turnips, carrots, cress, lettuces (NB. next sowing about the 27th), clarkias, godetias. Also sowed a few of the potatoes we bought for eating, no seed potatoes having turned up yet. They all had eyes so should come up all right.

Tried the RAF rubber dinghy. Very buoyant, & seemingly has no tendency to turn over, but hardly navigable at all. Evidently it will only be useful for getting out to the other boat.

A dead deer down by our bay. Rather unpleasant as it is too heavy to drag away.

A few more primroses out, & one or two celandine. Brought home a root or two of primroses. It is remarkable what a difference it makes when there is no bracken – ie. the relative easiness of walking everywhere. No midges yet. Cormorants swimming in the bay, so presumably there are some fish about.

18.4.47: Cold, blowy & overcast. A little sun during the afternoon, then light rain. Sea moderate.

Dug a little more of the ploughed patch, put in posts for gate of hen-run.

While digging the ploughed patch, dug up a nest of 3 young rabbits – about 10 days' old, I should say. One appeared to be dead already, the other two I killed. The nest was only a few inches below the surface. It was evidently reached by a hole outside the garden, about 10 yards away.

Saw a number of ordinary green plovers. I do not think I remember seeing these birds here before. Brought in some frog spawn in a jar. Should be hatched out in a week or 10 days.

19.4.47: A better day. Sunny & not much wind, though not very warm. Evening blowy & cold, with some rain. Sea roughish outside the bay.

Dug some more of patch, weeded & limed strawberries. These do not now look so bad, & there are fewer gaps than I thought. Unlikely to give much fruit this year, however.

Only one of the roses is still showing no buds (an American Pillar[5]). One by the gate (Alberic Barbier[6]), which I thought dead, has a tiny bud down near the root, so I cut it down to just above the end. Made 2 cement blocks, about 1 ft. square & 2″ deep (or even less), reinforced with wire netting. Will do as part of path. NB. for 2 square feet of cement block, 5 fire shovels of sand & one of cement needed – more if it is to be at least 2″ thick, as it should be.

5. American Pillar (which Orwell spells with small 'p') is a carmine pink climbing rose with a white eye and golden stamens.

6. Albéric Barbier is a vigorous climbing rose with a creamy white flower with a yellow centre. It was introduced by the same raiser as Albertine, the rose Orwell grew so successfully at his cottage at Wallington before the war. Orwell omitted the accent.

20.4.47: Very violent gale all last night, & much rain. Today till about 5 pm blowing hard, mostly from south, cold & usually raining. Sea very rough, breaking right over the point. This evening calmer, some interludes of sunshine, but still far from warm.

Could not do much out of doors. Shot a rabbit, the first this year. I notice that when rabbits are shy the ones one succeeds in shooting are almost invariably gravid females. I never fancy eating these. I suppose it is partly because the pregnant ones are less in a hurry about running away, but last year females preponderated so greatly among the rabbits I shot as to make me wonder whether they are actually more numerous than the males.

Alastair & the D.s[7] in a great state with the sheep. They are lambing in such a state of weakness that they have no milk, sometimes actually refuse to take their lambs, & even now that the grass is coming on, some of them are too weak to graze. The D.s say the gulls & hoodies attack weak sheep, & yesterday took the eye out of one of them.

7. Alastair M'Kechnie and the Darrochs, the brother and sister Donald and Katie.

21.4.47: Awful weather. Violent gale all last night, & still more so this morning, at times so strong that one could hardly stay on one's feet. Chicken-house blown off its base – fortunately not damaged. Shall have to fix it down with guy ropes. Rain most of day. About 4 pm finer & some sun, but wind not abating. Sea rough.

Bottle of brandy lasts A[vril] & me 1 week, with a fairly good peg each (a bit less than a double) once a day.

Did nothing out of doors.

22.4.47: A better day. Wind still high, but not much rain, some interludes of sun, & somewhat warmer. Sea calming down a little.

Still not feeling well enough to do much out of doors. A[vril] finished digging the first plot in the ploughed patch. Room there for 4 rows of potatoes (about 10 lb. of seed). Am going to use some of D[onald] D[arroch]'s seed – Great Scott I think.

Took down the corrugated iron at the side of the house. Will be enough to cover hen-house, & the frame it was on will make a gate for the run. Impossible to finish this job till the wind drops. Cut sticks for dwarf peas. Began cutting bean sticks. The lone sheep in the field has lambed. Does not take much notice of the lamb, & walks on whenever the latter begins to suck. Nevertheless she made a demonstration when I picked the lamb up with the idea of taking it indoors. Lamb fairly strong, though it only seemed to me to weigh a pound or two.

Many more birds round the house owing to chaff in the yard. Still no sparrows, but flocks of chaffinches almost as numerous as sparrows. Qy. whether these also attack peas & beetroots.

Fruit bushes now mostly budding fairly well.

D.D. says the cuckoo is usually heard here earlier than this. Swallows, on the other hand, do not usually appear till about May 12th.

Cannot be sure, but I think we are using quite 4 galls of paraffin a week – if so, the current barrel will give out about the end of May (have another in stock). The reason is the cold weather & consequent use of Valor stoves. One of these uses quite ½ gall a day if burning all the time.

Some rain after about 7 pm.

To be ordered for next year (better order early this time.)

3 cooking apple trees
4 plums
1 damson
1 greengage
1 quince
6 cherries (eating)
2 doz. bush roses
1 doz peony roots (red & pink)
200 tulip bulbs
Strawberries? [*crossed through*] 3 loganberries [*written in lighter ink*]
[*On facing page*]
NB. Order also:
6 roses (2 climbing, 4 bush)
6 gooseberries.

23.4.47: Dreadful weather till about 4 pm. Violent wind, continuous rain, & very cold. After that somewhat better, mostly raining but a few intervals of sun. In the evening very still, rain still falling. Sea calms down with surprising speed.

The lamb born yesterday died this morning. A[vril] found it in a moribund condition & brought it in. It was oozing blood from the mouth, & according to Alastair had been attacked by gulls or hoodies. The mother seems quite strong & well, but she more or less ignored the lamb from the start, so presumably she has no milk.

R[ichard] very poorly with feverish cold & cough, which started last night. However his forehead is making a good job of healing. The doctor took the stitches out today, & there were no complications & does not look as if there would be much of a scar. Seed potatoes (Great Scott) arrived yesterday. Can sow as soon as ground dries a little.

Some more primroses out. Gorse well out. Otherwise no wild flowers except a very occasional celandine.

Wind today strong enough to blow off some sticks of young rhubarb. Tulips not damaged, but they are more sheltered. All roses now budding except one.

24.4.47: Morning fine, windy & cold. In the afternoon rainstorms & showers alternating with sun. Some hail about 5.30 pm. Cold all day, & wind strong until evening. Fined up the new patch with hoe & cultivator, but it will have to dry a bit before it is even possible to put potatoes in it. Began cutting bean sticks.

R[ichard] slightly better, but feverish again this evening.

Have ordered trees etc. for next year.

All apple trees now budding except the James Grieve, which looks rather as if it were dead. No buds on raspberries yet. I think all the other fruit bushes are budding. NB. the Jas. Grieve was the one with the broken root.

25.4.47: Vile weather. Very cold, rain almost continuous, & strong wind from about midday onwards. Mud worse than ever. Did nothing out of doors. R's cough still bad, & temperature high during most of day.

Saw in the distance a bird which might have been a martin.

Violent, driving rainstorms during the evening.

26.4.47: A much better day. Fine, windy & less cold. Ground drying up nicely, but still not quite fit for the potatoes. Dug a little more of the ploughed patch, sowed spring onions (White Lisbon), began cutting grass between fruit trees. Patches of this can be cut with the mower, but one has to take the clumps of old grass off with the scythe or shears. The second cutting could be done with the mower.

R[ichard] seems better – hardly any temperature at 6pm, & the rash, which was over most of him including his legs a few hours earlier, had temporarily disappeared.

A[vril] heard the cuckoo this morning.

They have now finished ploughing the field in front of the house. About 4½ acres, & yesterday & today I should say they were on it about 8 hours in all, including two occasions when the tractor was bogged. They have taken in a bit more than last year, which will mean fewer rushes.

A. saw a mountain hare, still almost white! Presumably when they change colour is determined simply by the temperature.

It is now definitely established that R. has measles. He will have to be in bed another week & stay indoors for a week after that.

27.4.47: Violent rain all night, or almost all night. Huge pools everywhere this morning.

Morning rainy & cold. Afternoon mostly sunny & windy, with some rainstorms. Net effect of day has probably been to dry the ground slightly.

Did nothing out of doors. Made frame for gate of hen-run. Very heavy, & it will be difficult to hinge it, as I not only have no hinges of that size, but the piece it will hang on is not straight. The gate will have to rest on the ground, in which case the best way to hinge it is probably with ropes or wires. Ideally one would put wheels at the bottom of the gate, but I think skids (bottom of barrel) will do if I level the ground.

R. better. Tried to make jigsaw puzzle for him, but can only cut pieces with straight edges as my only coping-saw blade is broken.

A. yesterday saw unidentified duck-like birds – probably some kind of diver.

Saw a swallow (or martin – only a glimpse.)

28.4.47: Rain in the night (& hail, according to K[atie] D[arroch]). Most of today blowy & overcast, with rain showers & fair patches alternating. Evening still & fine. Cold all day. This evening is about the first time the wind has dropped in a week or more. I do not think it has shifted away from the west all that time.

Set up gate on its skid, which seems fairly satisfactory.

Heard the cuckoo (first time). Primroses now comparatively numerous, buds getting fairly thick on the hazels, wild irises about 6″ to 1′ high. No sign of bracken growing yet.

29.4.47: Seemingly no rain during last night. Rain began about 10 am & fell almost continuously (not very heavy) till about 8 pm, when it cleared somewhat.

Everything is again a morass. There has been much less wind than yesterday.

Could not do anything out of doors. Cemented crack in larder wall.

We are using up oil very fast, owing to having two Valor stoves going all day. Impossible to get hold of dry firewood in this weather. Even in the barn, which is quite watertight, it stays damp, & I notice that cement takes days to get dry.

30.4.47: A much better day, though very cold. No rain, sun shining all day, & a raging wind from the north which has dried things up considerably.

Peas, lettuces & turnips have all just appeared, but the chaffinches have pulled up, I think, all the lettuce seedlings, & at any rate many of the turnips. They were also starting on the peas. Re-sowed lettuces & covered seeds with wire, which I should have done at the beginning. Three gooseberry bushes still not budding. Some of the raspberries budding down near the roots – I should probably have cut the canes off short when I put them in. Jas. Grieve still has no signs of buds. Weeds are now getting started.

Dug a little more, finished cutting the grass between fruit trees, staked the peas. Next time this grass can be cut entirely with the machine, & the holes where I dug out rushes can be filled & re-sown or turfed. Started new cylinder of Calor Gas today (nb. to order 2 more). Should last till first week in June. There is less paraffin than I thought (1–2 weeks supply, I should say). However we have a barrel in hand.

1.5.47: Fine day. No rain, though it looked threatening for about half an hour in the afternoon. Otherwise sunny all day. Less wind than yesterday, but still cold.

Sowed potatoes (Great Scott), 5 rows, about 15 lb. of seed, or perhaps nearer 20 lb. Rooted up old gooseberry bushes. With help of Neal McArthur & Duggie Clark,[8] got hen house on to base. Trust it will not be blown down again before I can fix bolts.

Killed a mouse in the larder. A[vril] came out to tell me there was one there behaving in a very bold way. Went in & found it eating something on the floor & paying no attention to either of us. Hit it with a barrel stave & killed it. It is curious how the tameness of animals varies from one day to another.

Gooseberries & currants forming on the old plants – however there are very few of these, & I can hardly expect my own bushes to fruit this year.

8. Duggie (Dougie?) Clark worked on the Astors' estate at Tarbert, as, probably, did Neal (Neil?) McArthur.

2.5.47: Fine all day. Warmer than yesterday & very little wind. Overcast for a while in the afternoon & literally a few drops of rain.

Put corrugated iron on chicken house. Should stay on, I think, but it still remains to anchor the house down. I cannot bolt it to the floor because I have no bolts long enough. Examined how D[onald] D[arroch]'s henhouse is wired down. Huge rocks are placed at either side of the house & a piece of fence wire wound round them double. Then a double strand of wire passed round the wire on the stones, & over the roof. This wire is then tightened up by twisting. I think this is the normal method here.

For the first time this year, saw one or two youngish rabbits. Chaffinches etc. still flocking to roost, so they cannot have nests yet. The chaffinches have evidently destroyed all the turnips, so I shall have to re-sow.

Paraffin barrel feels as if it will only last a few more days – ie. about 1 month instead of 2 as I anticipated. However there may have been less in it than I thought when we left last year.

R[ichard] came downstairs for first time today. Also had his bandage off for the first time. Scar has healed beautifully & is not very conspicuous.

3.5.47: Cold & overcast nearly all day. Light rain during much of afternoon. Evening somewhat finer, but cold. Sea rough.

Could not do much out of doors. Dug a little more, made seed-protector, re-sowed turnips. NB. that even with wire netting over them the chaffinches still go for the seeds. They are not afraid to go under the netting.

The last rose has a bud, so there are no dead ones. Some of the new currant bushes which are in fairly full leaf have currants on them, though of course not very many.

4.5.47: Fine all day, except for a very few spots of rain for a few minutes in the evening. Not very sunny, but warmer than yesterday. Sea still rough in the morning, calming down in the evening.

Dug a little more, finished cutting grass between beds of fruit bushes, sowed clarkia, marigolds, Shirley poppies, candytuft.

Frogspawn failed to hatch out, probably owing to not adding fresh water, which I did not think to be necessary before the tadpoles hatched.

A few strawberries showing flower buds.

Chaffinches still going for the turnip seed, in spite of wire & cottons. Shot one & left its body on the bed. Probably the effect of this will only last for a day or two.

Looking down towards the sea, over the wood, hardly a green leaf to be seen anywhere.

Drum of paraffin almost at an end – almost 5 weeks less than I thought. But there may have been less in it than I imagined to start with.

Sending for 2 cylinders of calor gas. (Have sent empties).

5.5.47: Mostly overcast, with a few sunny intervals & some wind. A few short showers.

Dug a little more, cut bean sticks, staked cherry trees, pegged down henhouse – very amateurish job, but probably enough for the summer winds.

Many primroses now out. Stonecrop barely visible & has not started growing. They have not heard the cuckoo at Ardlussa yet.

They sowed & harrowed the field in front of the house today. The seed was sown first on to the raw ploughed soil (broadcasting about 4½ acres only seemed to take about 2 hours), then the field was harrowed twice over afterwards. Did not know it was possible to do it this way round, & would have thought it meant burying the corn at very uneven depths & for the most part much too deeply, as where raw sods have been turned up you get a furrow quite 8″ deep. It has the advantage that the seed all rolls down into the furrows & thus comes up in rows, but it tends to do this any way, as even after harrowing a trace of the furrows remains.

Drum of paraffin gave out today.

D's trap killed an enormous rat in the byre.

6.5.47: Some rain in the morning, sunny & windy in the afternoon. Somewhat warmer.

Dug a little more, retrained cherry trees & one of the espalier apples. These last have masses of blossom coming, but not much of it is likely to stay on, also it may not get fertilised if the other apples do not blossom.

Bracken fronds now coming up.

7.5.47: Very still all day, & mostly overcast. A little very light rain in the morning. Sea calm.

Sowed peas (Daisy, 2nd early, 1½ ft) & lettuces. A few of the first lot of lettuces seem to have survived the chaffinches.

Several of the rhubarb plants have died – reason, probably, that they were young tender plants & I put too much cow manure on top of them. Raspberries are now mostly budding round the roots. Three gooseberries still not budding & I am afraid they are dead.

Began new drum of paraffin today. Should last to end of July at least, but <u>NB. to start agitating for a new drum some time in June.</u>

One or two of the primroses I transferred beginning to flower.

8.5.47: Morning still & overcast. Some rain during afternoon. Fairly warm. Began putting wire round hen-run.

9.5.47: Beautiful, warm, still day, sunny till evening. The first day since we have been here when it was pleasant to sit about out of doors. Sea very calm.

Not well enough to do much. Cut grass in front of house (a lot of ragwort etc., but this can be easily kept down by frequent cutting).

Inspected peat beds. Peat now dry enough to cut. Made tousling fork. Lit rubbish fire.

Gladioli (planted 13.4.47) showing here & there.

Saw violets in bloom (first I have seen this year, but A[vril] had seen them earlier.)

Another dead deer up not far from the ruined hut. They say a lot have died this winter.

Saw a swallow sitting on the ground, which I think is unusual.

An hour or two's rain in late evening.

12.5.47: In bed last 3 days. 8 tablets M & B[9] on 10.5.47. Very sick until this morning. Got up for some hours this afternoon. Still shaky.

A thunderstorm & heavy rain for an hour or two on the evening of 10.5.47, otherwise all these days warm & still. Vegetation jumping remarkably.

Wild cherries covered with blossom. One or two tulips out. Shirley poppies sown 4.5.47 are up. A good many gladioli now showing.

9. May and Baker, makers of sulphonamides, and the drug sulphapyridine, used to treat pneumonia, and commonly known by the manufacturer's initials.

13.5.47: Better. Went out a little, but did not do anything.

Beautiful day. Vegetation all jumping.

They sowed the field with rye-grass today. This comes up later than the oats & is not much affected by the reaping of the latter. The following year it can be harvested as hay, but in this case will be left as pasture at least the first year. The seed is sown with a "spinner," which shoots it out in all directions – being so light, it would be difficult to broadcast in the ordinary way. By operating a small lever, some of the seed comes out of the bag onto a tin disc divided into sections, which can rotate rapidly. The sower walks along slowly, with the apparatus hanging round his neck, & rotates the disk by working a bow to & fro. One sack did whole field (4½ acres.)

Outboard has arrived at Ardlussa. Can fetch boat next week, when car is running.

Have ordered hens – 8 28-week old pullets, preferably R.I.R. x W.L.[10] crosses. They have to come from Yorkshire, a long journey.

10. A cross of Rhode Island Reds with White Leghorns.

14.5.47: Blowy & overcast in morning, but fairly warm. Rain a good deal of afternoon.

Somewhat better. Put some more of the wire round the hen run. Will need a good deal of pegging down.

Cast a plug for bathroom basin out of lead. There is something in this operation that I do wrong. Although it lies quite smooth in the melting pot, the lead always boils & splutters when poured into the mould, & one does not seem to be able to get a cast free from flaws. Q. because of differences of temperature. In that case ought one to heat the mould?

R[ichard] is 3 years old today.

Cylinder of Calor gas gave out, after only a fortnight! Gas from new cylinder difficult to light because pressure appears too strong. Perhaps the filling of these things is irregular.

15.5.47: Morning blowy & rather cold. Some showers in afternoon, then fine & warm. Evening pleasant & still. Sea calm.

Went on with wire netting. Nearly finished, apart from pegging down etc. Cut sticks for gladioli (first bed are now all up.)

Went over to Kinuachdrach for first time in about 10 days. A few bluebells out. Some blackthorn just budding (I remember that we did not find any sloes last year.) Hazels barely leafing. Saw the brown flies one finds on cowdung for the first time this year. Bluebottles getting fairly common.

K[atie]D[arroch] says last night's wireless announced no poultry were to be sent from England to Scotland, to prevent spread of some disease or other. There is certainly some order about not importing poultry into the U.K. from abroad. Shall perhaps hear next mail from the dealer to whom I wrote.

Lettuces sown 7.5.46° are up, but not the onions sown a few days earlier.

16.5.47: Fine & sunny all day, but wind rather chilly at times.

Finished putting wire up (still needs pegging down.)

Cleaned strawberry bed & trimmed edges, cut down raspberries. Weeds now getting very rampant.

Onions coming up.

17.5.47: Overcast, but not very cold. Rain or drizzle all afternoon & evening.

Sowed parsley, cut more gladiolus sticks (now have enough.) Slugs getting more numerous. Trying tobacco powder round lettuces.

A[vril] saw some kind of whale crossing the bay this morning. Perhaps a grampus,[11] like last year.

Saw one of the white-collared rabbits, in the same place as usual. First time this year.

Stonecrop at last starting to grow on the rocks. Wild irises a foot or eighteen inches high.

11. A cetacean resembling a dolphin but lacking its beak-like snout. Properly Risso's dolphin, but used generally of whales of different kinds.

18.5.47: Evidently a good deal of rain in the night. This morning blowy & overcast, with some rain. Afternoon sunny, but coldish all day.

Dug a little more (still cannot dig much), cut out place for marrow bed, pegged down wire (one or two corners still a bit sketchy.)

Tulips we bought as mixed are nearly all yellow.

19.5.47: Beautiful sunny day. Sea calm.

Sowed marrows (bush) out of doors under pots, ie tins with hole in the bottom. NB. to look in about a week & see if they have germinated. Sticked gladioli, hoed turnips, began thinning second bed. Pruned roses some more, as they seem to need it.

One or two other apple trees now budding. Those on the cordon trees are now opening & probably will not get fertilised. One or two blossoms coming on the cherry trees.

20.5.47: Beautiful, hot, still day.

Prepared ground for beetroots. Cut bean sticks. Some strawberries setting fruits. A good many apple blossoms open. Corn in field in front of house well up. Large king-cups in marshy places. Primroses out everywhere.

Reflections of the lighthouses on the islands visible today, which is said locally to be a sign that rain is coming.

If weather is fine, we intend bringing the boat home on Sunday (25th).

21.5.47: Still day, overcast in morning, sunny most of afternoon. Sea very calm, rather misty.

Began cutting peat. Cut 200 blocks, which takes 2 people 2 hours, including stripping off the turf before hand. Slung a rope round them, which I hope may keep the deer & cattle off. We hope to cut not less than 1000 blocks in all.

Put tobacco dust on apple trees. NB. to wash off tomorrow. Four of the trees, ie. of those in the grass, have quite a lot of blossom coming, but it will probably not coincide with the espalier trees.

Thrift flowering.

So many cormorants always in the bay that I think there must be a colony of nests down there, as at this time of year they could not be constantly at a long distance from their nesting places.

22.5.47: Overcast, but not cold. Very little wind. Light rain most of afternoon. Sea calm.

Sowed beetroots & turnips.

Hens have arrived, ie. at Ardlussa. Will presumably get here on Saturday.

Don't yet know what kind (ordered crosses if possible, failing that pure R.I.Rs.)

23.5.47: Beautiful warm day. Sea calm.

Moved wire from round fruit patch, cut grass in front of house, began cutting among fruit trees. Applied sodium chlorate to some of the rushes & nettles.

Some of the leaves of apple trees still do not look too good.

Cow bogged last night. When dragged out, she was too weak to stand, & had to be given gruel which A[vril] made.

24.5.47: Not so warm as yesterday, & more blowy. Wind changing round to all quarters. Sea rather rough.

Brought in bits of stonecrop which I want to attempt acclimatising. Thrift stuck in last year has taken pretty well.

Hens have arrived (Rhodes). They have been waiting at Ardlussa since the 21st, during which time they laid 6 eggs. By the look of them all or most are coming into lay.

The F[letcher]s yesterday got a lot of gulls eggs, of which however a good many were already sat-on, so it is evidently now too late. Mem. that about the 15th–20th must be the proper date. But they also got a lot of good ones & gave us 16. Surprisingly large eggs, as large as hens' eggs. Perhaps of the black-backed gull or herring gull. These could not be sold as counterfeit for plovers eggs, as I think used to be done with some gulls' eggs.

Slugs are eating marigolds. Trying tobacco powder.

25.5.47: Fine, but windier than yesterday. Went over to Ardlussa with the idea of bringing the boat back, but the sea seemed too rough.

Everything at Ardlussa more forward than here.

Hens laid no eggs.

26.5.47: Fine & very blowy. Sea rough, calming somewhat towards evening.

Cut more peat (150 blocks), continued cutting grass between trees.

1 potato showing, from second lot. The others (sown 17.4.47) still not up, but they are germinating, as I uncovered one or two to see.

Some showers in late evening.

No eggs.

27.5.47: Still & fairly warm. Overcast a good deal of the time. Sea fairly calm.

Cut peat (130 blocks) & put the first lot into threes. Thinned clarkia (slugs have eaten some of them), put sodium chlorate on docks in back yard.

With A[vril] & myself working together, cutting peat seems to work out pretty regularly at 100 blocks an hour. If one doubles this, to allow for the time taken up in turning, stacking & carting, it would take about 40 hours work (for 2 people) to bring in a ton of peat. No doubt practiced° diggers can do it immensely faster, & also it would be easier if there were 3 or 4 people, which saves changing from one operation to another.

28.5.47: Fine day, mostly windy. Sea roughish till evening, when it calmed down.

Did nothing out of doors, as I was busy making a post-box.

Turnips sown 22.5.47 are up.

Still no eggs. Janet McK.[12] said the hens they got from England went off lay for a week after arriving.

12. Janet M'Kechnie; Orwell uses the forms M'Kechnie and McKechnie.

29.5.47: Some rain in night. Light rain & rolling mists a good deal of the day. Sea calmer.

Sowed alyssum (annual), thinned first lot of turnips. The Jas. Grieve apple is evidently not dead. The deaths therefore – from about 90 plants excluding the strawberries – are 3 gooseberries, 1 blackcurrant, 3 roots of rhubarb, about ½ dozen raspberries. Not bad considering late planting & very bad weather conditions.

2 eggs (the first we have had).

A good many potatoes up from first lot.

30.5.47: Still & warm.

Ian[13] brought boat round last night, as they were going round to Glengarrisdale to collect drift. Took her round to Kinuachdrach. Some trouble in starting (plug not very good.)

This afternoon landed on island at mouth of harbour to see if the terns are nesting yet. Had not started, but found one gull's egg.

A[vril] saw some more fawn-coloured rabbits.

Bluebells about in full swing.

No eggs.

13. Ian M'Kechnie. Glengarrisdale Bay is on the western side of Jura, almost directly opposite Barnhill.

31.5.47: Evidently a good deal of rain last night. Today still & warm, mostly not very sunny. Sea calm.

Finished cutting grass between trees, thinned clarkia & poppies.

Beetroots (sown 22.5.47) are up. One marrow just poking through the earth.

2 eggs. Have started the hens on Karswood.[14]

We have started on the 50 gallon drum of petrol (which has to last till end of August). A[vril] took out 9 galls.

14. A proprietary brand of poultry feed.

1.6.47: Thunder & heavy rain during the night. Today mostly fine & warm, but misty, after a sharp shower in the morning.

Went over to Scarba.[15] About ½ hour's run in the boat (3–4 miles). When we returned the engine would not start (probably defective plug) & we were obliged to row. A stiff job, taking about 2 hours. Scarba much barer than Jura. Almost no trees, good grass. While there killed a very large snake.

Sowed lettuces.

1 egg.

15. Scarba lies to the north of Jura; the islands are separated by the Gulf of Corryvreckan.

2.6.47: Beautiful warm, still day, with some mist. Sea very calm.

Cut peat (200 blocks). Applied more sodium chlorate.

2 eggs (a third hen is now in lay.)

2 roses now have buds. All except two apple trees have now blossomed. Second lot of gladioli have not come up well (only about half have appeared).

D[onald] D[arroch] gave me a load of manure.

Cuckoos all over the place. Qy. whether they really change their note in June or merely become more irritating as they cease to be a novelty.

3.6.47: Still, cloudy & warm. No rain, though it looked like rain several times. Sea very smooth. Milk sours quickly this weather.

Finished preparing ground for beans. Greased outboard motor, cut petrol feed as I[an] M'K[echnie] suggested, & put in new plug. This was taken from the Austin & appeared to me as bad as the old one – however, have sent for new ones. Could not try engine as the boat was out of reach. Shall take the RAF dinghy round to Kinuachdrach as soon as the engine is running.

A[vril] & B.D.[16] went fishing last night – again nothing. Apparently there are only tiddlers about.

Blossom on the old pear tree in the hedge. However, when I arrived here last year (& everything was weeks earlier), I had the impression it had blossomed, but it gave no fruit. Alyssum is coming up. Rowan trees coming into blossom. Oaks in full leaf.

3 eggs. (10)

16. Bill Dunn. William Dunn (1921–1992) had been an officer in the army, but after the loss of a leg had been invalided out. He came to Jura to farm in 1947. After five months he moved down from his farm above Barnhill and joined Orwell and his sister, Avril. He later entered into a partnership with Richard Rees to farm Barnhill. He married Avril in 1951 and they brought up Richard, Orwell's son. See transcript of Bill Dunn's interview by Nigel Williams in *Orwell Remembered*, pp. 231–35; also *Remembering Orwell*, pp. 182–85. In February and March 2009, Richard Blair contributed very interesting essay to the *Eric & Us* website (www.finlay-publisher.com), reproduced on the Orwell Prize website. This essay is archived.

4.6.47: A good deal of rain in the night. Rain & "Scotch mist" almost all day. Ground very sodden.

Impossible to sow beans. Began sticking peas, fixed bolt on barn door, trimmed lamps.

Found a columbine in the garden (the old-fashioned purple kind). It must have survived here from the time when the house was last inhabited, about 12 years ago. The other flowers to survive are daffodils, snowdrops (both of these in great numbers), red hot pokers, monkshood.

Paraffin consumption at present only 1–2 gallons a week.

4 eggs (I think 5 hens are laying.) (14).

5.6.47: Overcast, coldish, & raining lightly most of day. Clearing somewhat in evening. Sea calm.

Sowed beans (dibbed them, as the ground was very sticky) & sticked them. Made another attempt to get the engine started – no use. Cannot be sure till the new plugs arrive, but I am afraid the trouble may be the magneto, which I do not understand.

While with D[onald] D[arroch] in the boat he landed on the island.

No terns' eggs yet, but they appear to be making their nests (ie. scooping hollows). D.D. found a nest with two fledged chicks, dark & striped, about the size of a day-old chick. Probably oyster-catchers, as two of these are always round there.

A lot of water in the boat – however, this was probably mostly rainwater. No eggs.

6.6.47: Windy, mostly fine but some intervals of mist & light rain.

Cut more grass. B[ill] D[unn] & D[onald] D[arroch] caught one fish (small saythe) last night.

4 eggs (18).

7.6.47: Blowy, mostly fine. Coldish in morning. Sea rougher.

Last night shot a very young rabbit in the garden. Threw the corpse into the trench, whence it had disappeared this morning – presumably cats. NB. to put up the rest of the wire soon.

Put new plug in the motor-boat engine and, on the advice of Ian M'K. increased the proportion of petrol in the tank. The boat was high & dry, so I fitted the engine on the stern to try it, the propellor being clear of the ground. It started almost at once, & then would not stop, probably owing to throttle wire sticking. So it was running for about 5 minutes without water, & by the time the petrol in the carburettor gave out the grease in the gear box was sizzling. Trust no harm done. Tap of petrol barrel tends to drip.

Took out about a gallon, making 10 gallons.

3 eggs (21).

Received cwt. of maize yesterday from the F[letcher]s.

8.6.47: Blowy, coldish, raining on & off throughout the day. Wind mostly from west. Sea rough.

Another rabbit in the garden last night. Shot at him but missed him.

Sowed sweet peas (a few) & anchusas. Took up tulips & the 3 dead gooseberry bushes. From the look of the roots of one of these I thought it possible that it was not dead.

Drip from petrol drum seems to be about a pint in the 24 hours. If one lost one-tenth of this by evaporation, the loss would be about 1 gallon in 2½ months, which I suppose is not excessive.

2 eggs (23).

9.6.47: Fine warm day. Sea calm. Little wind.

Put up rest of wire netting (only gate uncovered now), cleared raspberry & rhubarb beds. Shot another young rabbit trying to get into garden.

In the evening tried to take the RAF dinghy round to Kinuachdrach, towing it behind the boat. Fearful job as the engine stopped half way (probably over-oiling) & we had to row, leaving the dinghy at old Kinuachdrach harbour until we can pick it up.

Saw an owl (first I have seen this year). It appeared to be definitely black & white.[17]

3 eggs (26).

17. That is, in its summer plumage.

10.6.47: Overcast all day, light rain most of the time. Little wind. Sea calm.

Cut grass in front. Made hens' drinking trough. 5 roses now budding.

No ramblers budding yet.

4 eggs (30).

NB. Petrol drip. This is put in a bottle & poured into car[18] from time to time. Must keep note of amount used up in this way. To date, 3 pints.

18. This could be 'can' but 'car' is clear at 3.7.47.

11.6.47: Beautiful, still, hot day, about the best day we have had this year. Sea like glass.

Thinned carrots.

Took dinghy to Kinuachdrach. One cannot satisfactorily propel oneself by poling, so the best method will be to use a rope to pull oneself out by. Tried engine with more petrol in the mixture. It started at once, so over-oiling must have been the trouble.

Parsley (sown 17.3.47) just showing.

Petrol drip 4 pints.

4 eggs (34).

12.6.47: Beautiful still day, more misty than yesterday, but about equally hot in the afternoon. Sea very calm.

Cut peat (150 blocks) & put the rest into "threes." The deer have been on it, but not seriously. Sowed parsnips.

Cotton grass out all over the place. Rowans in full bloom. Their flowers have the same smell as hawthorn or elder, but even more oppressive. Cherries forming on the wild cherry trees (also on the little morello trees, but most of these will probably drop off.) All but 2 or 3 potatoes now through.

Saw the buzzard carrying a rat or something about that size in its claws. The first time I have seen one of these birds with prey.

Five rats (2 young ones, 2 enormous) caught in the byre during about the last fortnight. These rats seem to let themselves be caught very easily. The traps are simply set in the runs, unbaited & almost unconcealed. Also no precautions taken about handling them. I hear that recently two children at Ardlussa were bitten by rats (in the face, as usual.)

Petrol drip 5 pints.

5 eggs (39).

13.6.47: Evidently a good deal of rain in the night. Overcast all day, light drizzle a good deal of the time. Very still. Sea calm. Everything very sodden.

Foxgloves budding (in garden). Last year they were full out long before this.

Think hens have lice, applied DDT. Found what appeared to be the white of an egg in one nest, but no signs of shell. Possibly some kind of accident & not egg-eating.

Petrol drip 6 pints.

5 eggs (44).

14.6.47: Fine & still, but not so warm as the day before yesterday. Sea somewhat less calm.

Hoed potatoes, thinned turnips, gave strawberries liquid manure.

This evening two rabbits not only in the garden, but actually taking refuge under the house. There is a drain or something of the kind behind one of the apple trees, which D[onald] D[arroch] warned me they went into during winter. The trouble is it probably leads out into the back yard, so that they have a way of circumventing the wire netting. Probably it is they & not slugs which have been eating down the clarkia. Closed hole with a slate jammed in place by a stone. NB. to put wire on gate.

A[vril] & B[ill] Dunn] caught 16 fish last night (smallish).

Petrol drip 7 pints. To be on safe side better call it a gallon, making 11 gallons.

Fuchsia nearly in flower (last year in flower at end of May).

3 eggs (47)

15.6.47: Some rain in the night. Today sunny & windy, not very warm. Sea fresher. No breakers.

Got both the rabbits that were sheltering in the hole under the house, by pushing a trap inside the hole & then re-blocking it. Both young ones. As they both tried to get out this way, there cannot be any outlet the other end. D.D. says the hole is only a ventilator.

Put a long rope from the shore to the anchor buoy, so that when the boat is out of reach one can get to her with the dinghy.

Took out 3 galls of petrol, making 14 galls.

Big drip, 1½ pints (drip worse after using tap.)

5 eggs (52).

Several raspberries I thought dead are sprouting.

Earthed up first lot of potatoes.

A[vril] & B[ill] D[unn] caught 31 fish last night.

16.6.47: There may perhaps have been a little rain in the night. Most of day overcast, blowy & coldish. In the late afternoon strong wind from south, & a little rain. Sea rough, with heavy breakers outside. Seemed all right in Kinuachdrach harbour, the wind being in the south.

Sowed peas (last lot).

Having reset the trap in the hole under the house, caught a rat in it, (small one). So there may be a way through to the back for rats, though there evidently is not for rabbits.

Some wild irises out. D.D is sowing turnips, 2 acres. It will be a ghastly job thinning this quantity by hand.

Petrol drip, 3 pints.

6 eggs (58).

17.6.47: Pelting rain late last evening & some rain in night. This morning overcast, then clearing up for a few hours. More rain & wind this evening. Sea rough.

Baled out boat, which was full of water. Put wire over gate. Ditto round gooseberry bushes, to prevent R[ichard] getting at them.

Eggs & bacon[19] just coming out. Some strawberries about the size of acorns.

A[vril] starts waterglassing eggs today.[20]

Petrol drip 4 pints (not quite so bad now.)

5 eggs (63).

19. Toad flax or field snapdragon.
20. In order to preserve them for use in the winter. Eggs preserved in waterglass could not be used as boiled eggs; they had to be used for cooking or, at a pinch, they might be scrambled.

18.6.47: Evidently a good deal of rain in the night. Dense mists this morning, clearing off about 2 pm. Afternoon sunny & moderately warm, with little wind.

Earthed up second lot of potatoes. Thinned beetroots. Began turfing up holes in grass among fruit trees. A[vril] applied sodium chlorate to rushes in side garden. Thinned marrows.

One rambler rose has flower buds coming. The trees have set quite a lot of apples between them, but of course not many will stay on.

Big petrol drip (better today) 3½ pints.

No. of eggs now in waterglass, 9.

4 eggs (67).

19.6.47: A little rain in the night. Today a few brief showers, but mostly fine & still, moderately warm. Sea calm.

Tried outboard engine again. Ran perfectly at first, then, after stopping, refused to re-start. Landed on island. Found 3 terns' eggs (not worth taking). Found dead tern. Struck by brilliant scarlet colour of its beak & legs. Oyster catchers which frequent the island evidently live almost exclusively on limpets. Struck by luxuriance of grass & wild flowers (thrift

& stonecrop) on the island, which is about 40 yards long by 5–10 wide. Some deer living there. Apparently a deer swam out to it when being chased.

Saw two sheld-duck in the nearer bay. Eyebright in flower. Killed a green wasp (A[vril] killed one some time ago.) D[onald] D[arroch] rolled the oats in front of the house today. They are about 6″ high, which I suppose is the right height to roll them at. Young wagtail being fed on the ground by parents. Afraid one hen is already broody.

Big petrol drip, 4 pints.

5 eggs (72).

20.6.47: (filling this in on 21.6.47).

Dense mist most of day, & a few light showers. Very still till evening, wind springing up about 6 pm & veering about. Sea calm. Went to Ardlussa by boat, car being punctured. Each way the journey Barnhill–Ardlussa took about 1¼ hours, with wind & sea against us. Hugged shore as close as possible. Engine runs all right if the mixture is exact, but still difficult starting.

Saw an eagle, sitting on ground, later taking to the wing, near the shore about halfway between the new stable & the old stable.

Big petrol drip 5½ pints (worse when it is opened up). Took out a gallon, making 15 gallons.

4 eggs (76).

Cylinder of Calor Gas giving out. It was started on 15.5.47, so has run 5 weeks as scheduled. The previous cylinder must have been defective.

Some stonecrop beginning to flower on the rocks. Sea pinks past their best.

21.6.47: Dry, sunny & windy, not very warm. Wind in north in morning, later changing to west. Sea calm inshore, breakers in strait part of day.

Cut peat (150 blocks) & set up last lot. Cows had been over it, but not much damage. That completes the 1000 blocks. If dry weather should continue, it could be put into small piles in about a week, & into a single pile about a fortnight after that.

Weeded & hoed small seedlings, which get droopy in the dry wind. Slugs have eaten one of the two marrow plants – may possibly recover.

Shot a gull (kittiwake) for the tail feathers. Not very large or stiff. A goose's wing feathers are definitely the best.

Caught another rat under the house (young one).

Started new cylinder of Calor Gas. Should run to nearly end of July.

Big petrol drip, 6 pints.

5 eggs (81).

22.6.47: Dry, warm & still. Sea calm.

A good many runner beans showing. Some sweet peas showing. Fuchsia almost out (last year out towards end of May), mallow out. A lot of roses coming on one or two of the plants.

Last night a deer (hind) in the corn. Don't know where it got in, as gate was shut.

Forgot to mention yesterday killed a very large snake in the yard. It was lying on the coal-heap.

Big petrol drip 6½ pints.

6 eggs (87).

23.6.47: Overcast all day & raining most of the time. Clearing up a little in the evening. Sea variable, but part of the day roughish in the bay.

First peas have a flower or two. Gave them liquid manure. Slugs have destroyed one of the two marrow plants. Ought not to have thinned them out so early. Last lot of peas just showing.

Big petrol drip, 7 pints.

Eggs now in waterglass, 12.

6 eggs (93).

Amount of paraffin in drum now about 20 galls (probably). NB. to order new drum soon.

24.6.47: Rain almost continuous all day. Coldish & blowy, wind mostly from SW. Sea rough.

Began clearing strawberry bed. It is time they were strawed up. There seem to be a fair number of strawberries coming, but very small.

Herd of cows came down from Lealt & have been on the peat, but hitherto not very badly.

Big petrol drip, 7¼ pints, say 1 gall, making 16 gallons.

Eggs now in waterglass, 17.

5 eggs (98). It is a month today since hens arrived, in which time they have averaged about 2 doz. a week.

25.6.47: Sunny & windy in the morning, looking like rain but not actually raining – Afternoon drier & a great deal warmer. Evening clouding over again.

Strawed strawberries (not enough straw.)

Two hens now broody, & 6 laying.

5 eggs (103).

26.6.47: Blowy & cold. A little sun in the afternoon, but not warm. No rain, but a damp feeling in the air. Evening overcast & looking like rain. Sea rough.

Sowed carrots & a few radishes.

A[vril] & B[ill] D[unn] fished last night – nothing. It was decidedly rough, & last year when it was rough we generally did not catch anything except a few pollock. However, we never had an actually blank day in the Barnhill bay.

An eagle flew over the house yesterday.

Big petrol drip (including yesterday) ½ pint.

Eggs now in waterglass, 20.

3 eggs (106).

27.6.47: Overcast, warm & close. Strongish wind during part of afternoon, but most of day still. Once or twice it looked like rain, but no rain fell.

Set out to take boat down to the beach near Lealt & collect drift. As usual, boat started well at the beginning, then would not re-start after stopping at Barnhill to take A[vril] & R[ichard] aboard. It took half an hour to get her started again, so ran back to Kinuachdrach. A. landed on island. About a dozen terns' eggs – not worth taking as they are very tiny. 3 gulls' eggs, which we took.*

[*Orwell's note on facing page.*] * All bad, with chicks quite far developed inside.

Spotted orchis out in great numbers & very fine. Really well worth acclimatising if we could identify the bulbs in autumn. A[vril] found one butterfly orchis. A good many wild irises now out.

Big petrol drip, 1 pint.

Took out ½ gall., making 16½ galls.

Parsnips still not up – perhaps bad seed.

5 eggs (111).

28.6.47: Close, warm & still. Overcast most of time, but some sun. Sea calm.

Set remaining peat up into "threes." Cows had been on it, but not very badly. Some of what is undisturbed is very dry. Could be built up into small piles if we had two or three dry days running.

A few parsnips showing, but not very good.

Balancer meal arrived today, evidently 12 lb., 1 month's ration.

An egg had been eaten in one of the boxes – no doubt accidentally broken. In addition to this, 4 eggs (115).

29.6.47: Some rain in the night. This morning close & warm, afternoon somewhat colder, with a little more wind. Overcast all day. A few drops of rain occasionally. Sea roughish in morning, calming somewhat by evening.

Cut front grass. Transplanted a few lettuces. Slugs have had the last marrow – it may survive, but they have eaten the growing point out. Found a monstrous slug at it last night, in spite of a ring of soot & sand.

Went fishing last night, – nothing, though we did see one fish jump.

5 eggs (120).

30.6.47: Very still, overcast & damp all day. Rather close, getting cooler in evening. Light drizzling rain & dense mist all afternoon. Everything very sodden. Sea like glass.

Impossible to do much out of doors. Netted strawberries. Last night tried putting out bran mixed with Meta[21] for slugs. A good many dead this morning – not certain, however, whether the net effect of this is not to attract slugs to the neighbourhood of plants one wants to protect.

Sweet peas well up, but there are only a very few of them – about 1 doz. seeds from each packet.

4 eggs (124).

21. Metaldehyde, used in solid block form as a fuel from 1924, and as a slug-killer from 1938.

1.7.47: Morning very still, with dense mists which cleared up later. Rather close. Evening cooler, with a little more wind & some light drizzling rain from about 6 pm onwards. Sea very calm.

Went down to the bay I noticed on the way to Ardlussa, & collected about 4 cwt of drift. A lot more still there, including pit props & large planks. Coming back, dropped A[vril] & R[ichard] & the wood at Barnhill, then petrol ran out about halfway to Kinuachdrach, so had to come back after a hard row. We had started out with about ¾ gall., evidently not enough for this journey, which would be about half the run to Ardlussa, ie. as a return journey about 5 miles. One must allow quite 1½ galls, for the run to Ardlussa. NB. that the engine stops when there is still about ½″ of petrol in the tank. Starting now much better.

Gave liquid manure to one or two roses about to come into flower.

Young cormorants swimming in the sea with their mother – behaviour very similar to families of ducks. Four wild ducks (mallard) flying together – qy. whether two of them this year's birds. Two small birds I could not identify in the garden, one of them quite impressive, with reddish-brown rump, black head & a white spot on top of this.* The others seemed very interested in the strawberries, in spite of the pea-guards over them – Wild rose (white, but qy. whether not ordinary briar) in bloom. A good many of first peas in bloom.

Took out ½ gall petrol, making 17 galls. Drip is now negligible.

2 eggs (126).

[*Orwell's note on facing page.*] * Redstart?

2.7.47: Dense mist in the morning, clearing somewhat in afternoon. Rain at about 5 pm. Fairly warm & very still. Sea very calm.

Some turnips (sown 17.4.47.) almost ready to pull.

Wild roses out. Took out 2 galls, petrol, making 19 galls.

A[vril] &B[ill] D[unn] fished last night – 2 fish.

R.R.,[22] crossing from Tarbert today, saw a large shark in the strait.

3 eggs (129).

22. Sir Richard Rees (1900–1970), editor, painter, and critic; he and Orwell became friends through *The Adelphi*,, and Rees was to be Orwell's literary executor. He came to Jura to paint and stayed with Orwell until September. In his *George Orwell: Fugitive from the Camp of Victory* he gives a good account of Orwell's life on Jura; and see passages reprinted in *Orwell Remembered* (pp. 115–23). One passage epitomises Orwell on Jura: 'Life on the isle of Jura revealed clearly another not unexpected characteristic, namely, his enthusiasm for heroic and desperate remedies. The district was supposed to be infested by adders [see, for example, 22.6.47] and Orwell greatly relished the idea – though I can imagine no one who would be more reluctant to apply it – of the cigar cure for snake bites. This consisted, according to him, in lighting a cigar and then stubbing it out against the wound' (p. 152; *Orwell Remembered*, p. 122).

3.7.47: Filthy day till about 8 pm. Mist & rain, sometimes only a drizzle, sometimes fairly heavy. Evening clearer. Sea calm.

A few strawberries reddening.

Afraid we have an egg-eater among the hens. If so & I can detect her, shall kill her.

Petrol dripped about ¾ gall, owing to my leaving the tap pointing downwards. Put this into the car. Call it one gallon, making 20 galls.

3 eggs (132).

4.7.47: Filthy day. Blowy, overcast, coldish & raining on & off, quite heavily at times. Sea choppy.

Lealt herd have been down again (the reason for their coming here is no doubt the Highland bull) & trampled the peat, but not badly. Set up what they had knocked over. A lot of it is fairly dry. If there were about 3 good days it could be set up into small piles.

Could not do much out of doors. Gave liquid manure to some more roses. All except 3 roses now have flower buds coming.

Wild duck with young ones (could not see what kind, but did not look like sheld-duck) swimming in bay near Kinuachdrach.

A[vril] & B[ill] D[unn] fished last night – again nothing. The lobster fishermen from Luing[23] say it is possible to catch some fish about 1 am.

2 eggs. Afraid there must be an egg-eater at work. (134)

23. Orwell writes this as 'Ling' but he must mean the island of Luing, rather than its adjacent islet of Lunga or a place on the mainland also called Lunga; all three are within about half-a-dozen miles of the northern tip of Jura. What tilts the likelihood towards Luing is the report of Orwell's escape from the whirlpool of Corryvreckan in the *Glasgow Herald*, 30 August 1947. This states that two fishermen came to the aid of Orwell's party and that they came from Toberonochy, island of Luing.' See 19.8.47, n. 35.

5.7.47: Better day. Blowy & windy all day (wind in west), & mostly sunny though coldish. No rain except for a short shower about 2 pm. Sea choppy, with breakers in the sound.

Went over to Ardlussa to return the pony. Walked most of way, as it was too tiring sitting on the pony with no saddle, D[onald] D[arroch] riding Prince. Had pony shod, then borrowed saddle & rode on to Tarbert. Only 6 miles, but somewhat sore after being on a horse for the first time in many years.[24]

Saw a mountain hare near Tarbert. Definitely smaller than the brown hare, long legs, a lot of white round the rump. Saw several lots of skuas – the first time I have seen them, though I believe they are common here.

Roses full out at Ardlussa, some lupins already seeding, a red hot poker already in bloom.

Planted out 25 broccoli* seedlings which arrived yesterday by post. Not good weather for planting, especially after they have been out of the ground for several days.

2 eggs (136).

Took out 1 gall petrol making 21 galls.

[*Orwell's note on facing page.*] * cabbage

24. The results of Orwell's examinations to enter the Indian Imperial Police in 1922 show that although he was awarded particularly high marks for Latin and Greek he came 21st of 23 candidates in the riding test receiving 104 marks out of 200 (the pass mark being 100). He would have ridden since then, especially in Burma.

6.7.47: Fine, blowy, not very warm. Some black clouds occasionally, but no rain.

A[vril] fell & dislocated her shoulder. R[ichard] R[ees] has taken her down to Craighouse to the doctor.[25]

Put new ropes on creels. Tacked down loose rib on boat & put on a small patch of paint. Thinned runner beans. Put net over "wild" red currants.

Some strawberries reddening. One rose showing colour (pink). A little honeysuckle out, including some growing on the rocks almost in the sea.

Took out 4 galls petrol, making 25 gallons. Provided we have recorded takings-out correctly, & there has been no appreciable wastage, there should be 25 galls left, which has to last till the end of August. That is, our consumption from now on should not average more than 3 galls a week. The run to Ardlussa, by either boat or car, takes about 1½ galls for the return journey, so we should manage.

5 eggs (141).

25. Rees recalls this incident in his book: 'his sister dislocated her arm in jumping over a wall. Orwell rushed back to the house and called to me: "You've done first aid, haven't you? [Rees served with an ambulance unit on the Madrid front in the Spanish civil war.] Avril's put her arm out. You'll be able to get it back? You just have to jerk it sharply upwards, isn't that it?" The remedy did not work, perhaps because I didn't summon up enough sharpness (Orwell made no attempt to summon up any) and we had to drive the twenty-five miles to the doctor, who was also unsuccessful' (his *George Orwell*, p.152; *Orwell Remembered*, p.122). See also 7.7.47.

7.7.47: Coldish, blowy, overcast, some rain. Sea roughish.

As the doctor could not set A's arm, D.D., R.R. & B.D. took her across to Crinan in the boat. They returned on the tide about 11 pm. Evidently a nasty trip. A's arm was set at Lochgilphead & is evidently now all right.[26]

Too busy with R[ichard] etc. to do anything out of doors.[27]

Took out 1¾ galls, petrol, say 2 galls, making, 27 gallons.

2 eggs (143).

26. Because the doctor at Craighouse could not set Avril's dislocated arm, Donald Darroch, Bill Dunn, and Richard Rees took her across the Sound of Jura (about six miles, direct sailing – but see 16.8.47) to the little port of Crinan on the mainland and then a further six miles by road to Lochgilphead, which lies on the shore of Loch Fyne. By the time she had her arm set, Avril had been driven some fifty miles on Jura's rough roads, sailed six miles, and then been driven a further six, before making the return trip of a dozen miles.

27. Rees, in his *George Orwell*, says that Orwell was 'certainly happy' on Jura, 'working in the garden, fishing for mackerel from a boat, being bullied by his adopted son' (p. 149; *Orwell Remembered*, 120).

8.7.47: Most of day rather cold & overcast, with showers. Some rain during last night. This evening fine & pleasant. Sea calm.

Picked literally a handful of strawberries, the first fruits of the garden, barring gooseberries. Carrots sown 26.6.47 are up.

Many lettuces* coming up among the oats in the field. This was over-sown with rye-grass, which would come up after the corn has been cut & form hay next year. Qy. whether wrong seed was used (rye-grass is very small seed) or merely impure seed.

Deer in the field again – Must stop up hole.

4 eggs (147).

[*Orwell's note on facing page.*] * Chicory. Mixed in seed intentionally as it is supposed to improve the soil.

9.7.47: Fine, sunny & blowy. Not very warm. Sea calm. Everything has dried up a great deal.

Stacked peat into small piles. A good deal of it is pretty dry, especially the small blocks (NB. to cut thinner blocks next year.) Took up tulip bulbs.

2 eggs (149).

10.7.47: Overcast nearly all day, but no rain. Not very warm. Sea calm, & this evening glassy.

Pulled first turnips.

A[vril] went fishing last night – 6 saythe, 2 lithe.

Set creels (first time this year). The netting is old & may give, but they have new ropes on, so the frame-work should not be lost.

Paraffin getting very low. Another drum is ready for us, but it is questionable when it will arrive.

Drink gave out today – just 3 months for 12 bottles.[28] No more has arrived yet.

2 eggs (151).

28. Brandy, presumably; see 14.4.47.

11.7.47: Finer. A little rain during last night. Very faint drizzle for a few minutes during the day. Not much wind. Sea calm.

Took up creels – nothing. One, I now notice, is damaged near the bottom, & a lobster could have crawled out. Put meta° round straw-berries, which slugs are eating badly.

Several roses have buds opening – no white ones, I am glad to say. Picked a bunch of wild roses this afternoon. Three definitely different kinds of rose. One pink, apparently the ordinary briar, except that it had a smell, which I thought the briar did not. One a little rather frail white rose which I think is the "white rose of Scotland." Another also white, with more robust growth & – I think – blunter leaves. Both these last have something like the sweet briar smell.

Took out 1 gall petrol, making 28 galls. Managed to get the air-hole at the top open & measured the petrol. Cask seems almost half full, so my records have probably been about correct.

2 eggs (153).

12.7.47: Overcast most of day, with a few sunny intervals. In the evening a very few spots of rain, & stronger wind. Sea calm till evening, then roughening somewhat.

R[ichard] has trampled on two of the cauliflowers. The others appear to have rooted all right. The first rose is out (salmon pink).

7 eggs (5 laid out) (160).

13.7.47: Some rain in the night, I think. Drizzle in the morning, clearing up to a beautiful, still, sunny afternoon & evening. Sea calm.

Had to put prop for bough of one apple tree, because already weighted down with fruit. Got a small picking of strawberries, less than ½ lb. More coming. Many runners. Evidently they do well here, so shall try to put in some more this autumn if I can get the ground ready.

2 eggs (162).

14.7.47: Warm, some wind from south, overcast part of the time, but no rain. Sea calm.

Went down to collect drift. Boat ran well. Great difficulty in getting her afloat again on a stony beach, the tide having gone down a little while we were collecting drift. NB. with a boat as heavy as this one should always leave her anchored in fairly deep water.

Another rose out (dark red polyantha). Thinned apples.

Petrol drip, 2 pints.

4 eggs (166).

15.7.47: Beautiful sunny day, one of the best we have had. Hardly any wind. Sea very calm.

Stacked up peat. It makes a stack 4′ by 5′. Most of it now pretty dry.

A[vril] went fishing last night – nothing. Apparently they are catching hardly anything at Ardlussa either.

Picked a very few strawberries.

3 eggs (169).

16.7.47: A filthy day. Rain almost continuous until about 7 pm. Evidently some rain during last night as well. Sea calm.

Thinned first carrots (final thinning).

3 eggs (172).

17.7.47: Warm, rather close, overcast some of the time but no rain. Sea calm.

Thinned radishes, put netting round third° peas (no more sticks). Another rose coming out. Candytuft budding, ditto poppies.

Petrol drip ¾ gall. (owing to changing taps), plus, 1 quart previously, 1 gall, making 29 galls.

2 eggs, (174).

18.7.47: Close, still day, overcast much of the time but not actually raining till 6 pm, when there was a heavy shower. Sea like glass. This morning so still that when a cormorant rose from the sea I could hear its wings flapping from my room (distance about 400 yards).

Sowed perennial alyssum. Cut front grass & scattered sand on it.

Took out 1 gall, petrol, making 30 galls. This leaves 20 galls to last us to end of August, ie. about 3 galls a week, but we have the prospect of another 7 galls.

3 eggs (177).

19.7.47: Some fairly heavy rain during last night. Today very warm & close, overcast a good deal of the time, but no rain. Sea less calm. Horseflies ("cligs") very bad.

Dug a few of the first lot of potatoes (3 months in the ground) – much too small, must be left another 3 weeks or so. Picked a few strawberries, less than ½ lb.

Began making path.

Currants changing colour. Perhaps about 1 lb. in all in this garden. The third rose to come out is apparently the same as the first one. Of the dozen roses I had last year, only about 3 are bushes, the rest all polyantha, ramblers or climbers. May get some better ones this time as they are getting less scarce.

3 eggs (180).

Cylinder of Calor gas gave out today. Only 4 weeks this time. Put on the last one. NB. to send for more as soon as possible.

20.7.47: Some rain in the night. Today warm & overcast, no rain till about 7 pm when there was a light shower. Sea not very calm.

Started removing elder trees from place where gate will come. Another rose out (dark red polyantha, like the other).

Petrol drip 1 quart.

3 eggs (183).

21.7.47: Rain almost continuous till about 5 pm, after which it cleared & a strong wind began blowing from S. or SE. Sea rough all day, increasingly so in the evening.

Could not do much out of doors. Thinned parsnips.

Some hens moulting. Today a double egg, supposed to be a bad sign, as it is said to be the last of the clutch so far as that particular hen is concerned.

4 eggs (187).

An eagle over the field today, soaring high up. It is always in windy weather that one sees them here.

22.7.47: A very few drops of rain about 10 am, otherwise dry & windy, quite warm in afternoon. Sea rough.

Finished path but could not sow it as it was too windy.

Eagle over field again today. Crows mobbing him appeared to succeed in forcing him down to the ground. Peat pretty dry in spite of yesterday's rain. Two or three more windy days, & it would be dry enough to bring in, after which a couple of weeks in the barn would finish it.

Petrol drip ½ gall (put this into car).

3 eggs (190).

23.7.47: Rain almost continuous all day. Some mist in the morning. Strongish wind, mostly from south, in afternoon. Sea calm.

Tried to set creels, but impossible to get boat out, as the tide was very low. Have set one buoy nearer to the anchor.

A[vril] & B[ill] D[unn] caught 11 fish last night.

D[onald] D[arroch] has started to mow the field behind the house, but impossible to continue in the rain.

Picked the last of the strawberries. In all about 1 to 2 lb. – perhaps not bad for first year.

3 eggs (193).

24.7.47: Rain most of morning. Afternoon fairly fine, but not much sun. Some wind most of day, dropping in the evening. Sea calm.

Sowed path (rather thin one end as there was not quite enough seed.)

A[vril] now picking second lot of turnips (sown 22.5.47). First peas ready to pick in about a week.

Mended lobster box. Transferred the wood R[ichard] R[ees] has cut to the stable. NB. to see whether it stays drier there.

I note one hen is steadily laying a pullet-sized egg. I think it must be a hen that was broody & has come off. Two hens went broody almost at once, when they can only have laid a very small clutch. One may have gone broody before she had finished her pullet eggs, & therefore is still laying the small ones.

Candytuft flowering. Two more polyantha roses almost out (lighter red than the others).

4 eggs (197.)

25.7.47: Beautiful day. Morning overcast, warm & still, afternoon sunny. Hardly a breath of wind. Sea very calm.

Removed straw from strawberry bed. Pegged down one or two runners to fill up gaps.

Hay cut in the field behind the house already in the small heaps. Not good hay, half of it rushes.

A[vril] fished last night – nothing.

Some carrots ready to pull. Currants nearly ripe.

Today saw a pair of bullfinches. The cock very striking. Only the second time I have seen them here.

Petrol drip ¾ gall.

4 eggs (201). This makes almost exactly 200 in 2 months, or 2 doz. a week. If this was an average for 8 hens it will be all right, but of course they will go off when they begin to moult.

26.7.47: Warm, very still day, but not very sunny. Sea calm.

Part of the field behind the house has hay already in the small stacks, called here ricks, about 8 ft. high. Each of these appears to use up the hay of 400 or 500 square yards, ie. where the hay is poor, as here. Apparently, given good weather, the procedure is as follows. Soon after the hay is cut, perhaps 24 hours after, it is raked up into lines. These are then raked up into heaps about 2 ft. high. Next day these are scattered again. The hay is again raked into lines. Then it is raked together into a circle containing enough hay for a rick. Two people with pitchforks stand inside the circle & build the rick, which is tapered off when it has reached 5 or 6 feet. The sides are combed with the rake to get out the loose bits. Then a rope is strained over the top & tied to a thick twist of hay at the bottom on both sides (more usually 2 ropes, & some people weight them with stones). Given good weather, this whole process need only take about 3 days, but the hay has to dry in the rick for some days more before being stacked.

Pulled first carrots today.

Killed very large snake. As soon as it saw us it showed fight, turning round & hissing. I have not seen them do this before.

4 eggs (205).

27.7.47: Beautiful hot day. No wind. Sea like glass.

Planted 3 lupins – not very suitable weather or time of year for doing so.

Took up creels. 1 lobster, 1 crab. First lobster of the year. Lobster box is unsatisfactory, as it has too many apertures in it & therefore does not submerge properly. Could not reset creels, as we had no bait.

3 eggs (208).

28.7.47: A dreadful day. About 8 am a violent thunderstorm & extremely heavy rain, going on for some hours. The burns immediately turned into large torrents & flowed across the fields. Surface of the road washed away in some places. Wooden bridge near Kinuachdrach washed away. Two drills of D[onald] D[arroch]'s turnips destroyed. In the middle of the day it cleared up slightly, but there was more thunder & heavy rain during most of the afternoon. Dense "Scotch mist" in the evening. Everything in the garden looks battered & splashed with mud.

In the afternoon tried fishing in the Lealt,[29] as we had to go to meet J.[30] Only 1 very small trout. There were more there, but without a boat it was impossible to get to the place where they were rising.

5 eggs (213).

29. Lealt Burn runs from two small lochs a little south and to the west of Barnhill down to the Sound of Jura about five miles south of Barnhill; the small hamlet of Lealt stands where the road from Barnhill to Ardlussa crosses Lealt Burn.

30. Orwell's niece, Jane Dakin. Crick notes: 'That summer Humphrey Dakin, now a widower, sent his daughters, teenage Lucy and her sister Jane, just leaving the Women's Land Army, to stay with their aunt and uncle for a longer holiday. Their elder brother Henry also turned up, then a second lieutenant in the Army on leave. They liked their uncle Eric, though for days on end they hardly saw him, just like at Leeds [their home town] when they were small children, except at mealtimes since he worked almost without interruption' (p. 527). See also Shelden, p. 461.

29.7.47: Fine sunny day, with some wind from the west. Sea calm.

Made 1 lobster box. There will have to be two, as I have no box big enough to divide into compartments.

D.D. turning hay over again, but what was lying out is too wet to be built up into ricks. Picked a few roses – the first picking. Afraid grass-seed has been washed away from the path, but it is difficult to make sure.

3 eggs (216).

1.8.47: Last 3 days at Glengarrisdale.[31] Marvellous weather all the time. Sea very calm. Journey either way 2 hours or a little under, or somewhat less than 1 gall, petrol. Going, we timed it so as to pass Kinuachdrach ½ hour before high tide, & coming back so as to leave Glengarrisdale about an hour before low tide.

Fished yesterday in Loch nan Eilean.[32] Six good-sized trout & some tiddlers. The two biggest fish were about ½ lb, the rest 5 or 6 ounces. Mostly taken on a claret-coloured fly. Lost about as many as I caught, owing to difficulty of using the landing net when single-handed.

Enormous quantities of puffins on the west side of the island – seldom seen round this side.

A small patch of the garden appears to have been struck by lightning in the storm on Monday. The day after it happened I noticed that the potatoes seemed to be withering up. Now, over a patch about 5 yards square, nearly all the potatoes, most of the runner beans, some turnips & radishes, some young peas, & even some weeds, are frizzled up & dying, as though a flame had passed over them. It must be something to do with the storm, & I do not think the rush of water can have washed any bad substance into the bed. What is impressive is that all the damaged plants are in one patch, the rest of the garden being untouched. It is true, however, that within this patch there is one row of peas that does not seem affected.

Eggs from 30th onwards (3 days) 7 (223).

31. Camping on the Atlantic side of Jura, in a shepherd's hut more or less opposite Barnhill.
32. Loch nan Eilean is about one mile inland from the west coast at Glengarrisdale and some 2½ to 3 miles as the crow flies from Barnhill.

2.8.47: Warm & overcast. A few drops of rain about midday, light drizzle in the evening. Sea calm.

Picked some peas (first picking, sown 12.4.47).

Forgot to mention, took out 3 galls. petrol before the trip to Glengarrisdale, making 33 galls. Think I have forgotten to enter some, so say 35 galls. Have secured a slightly larger allocation as from September. Hayfield now largely cut. About a dozen of the "ricks" now up. Today what was spread out had to be put in small heaps in expectation of rain.

2 eggs (225).

3.8.47: Evidently a good deal of rain in the night. This morning misty & drizzling. Afternoon warm, still & sunny. Sea calm.

Took up creels – nothing. Prepared the two new creels & took over the new lobster boxes. The lobster in the store box was dead, probably owing to the fresh water washed down by the storm. The crab all right. Thinned carrots.

The blasted patch in the garden cannot actually have been struck by lightning, but I suppose that it is imaginable that a flash of lightning may pass through a sheet of rain on its way down, so that it reaches the ground heavily charged with electricity. At any rate, as the withering-up effect appeared the day after the storm, & has affected only one patch of the garden, it must be in some way connected with the storm.

Forgot to mention A[vril] took out 1 gall, of petrol day before yesterday, making 36 galls.

Killed a small snake in the hay field yesterday. D.D. killed one there the day before. Another egg eaten today.

3 eggs. (228).

4.8.47: Beautiful sunny day till evening. A fair amount of wind. Mist coming off the hill in the evening. Sea calm.

The hayfield behind the house now cut, & about half of it in "ricks." It appears there will be 28 or 30 of these, which will make up into 3 stacks. So presumably a stack equals about 10 ricks. To build a rick, once the hay is more or less gathered together, takes 3 people about 20 minutes. One stands on top & builds up, while the others fork the hay to him.

Marigolds out. Ditto the pink flower (don't know name) which M[argaret] F[letcher] gave us.

4 eggs (232).

5.8.47: Scotch mist till about 4 pm. After that somewhat clearer, but no sun. Very close & still most of the day. Sea calm.

Put out creels (all 4). Although it was almost low tide, nearly lost one of them, as there is evidently a hole about 200 yards along to the left from the harbour.

Some young seagulls (brown plumage) flying about.

R[ichard] R[ees] began bringing in the peat, which is fairly dry but will have to dry off in the barn for some weeks.

3 eggs (235).

6.8.47: Overcast all day, but no rain, & quite warm most of day. A fair amount of wind from west & north. Sea calm.

Made nursery bed & pricked out wallflowers, sweet williams, lupins, canterbury bells & a few other flowers, which A[vril] had sown. Started clearing one of the beds. Garden now in a bad state after being almost untouched for a week.

Another rose out (pale pink). Rambler by gate just coming out (crimson).

2 eggs (237).

7.8.47: Beautiful, sunny, warm day. Little wind. Sea calm & very blue.

Took up creels. All 4 completely empty. Tried anchoring the boat in a new place. Not sure whether we can get to her there at high tide, but if so will save the misery of dragging her up & down.

Cut grass in front. Scythed down ragwort in hen-run.

4 eggs. 2 of these laid out, including one which looked as if it had been hid some days. Also another which had got broken in the house, perhaps owing to insufficient chaff in the nesting boxes. (241).

8.8.47: Beautiful sunny day. A good deal of wind from south. Sea slightly less calm.

Set creels. Place where we tried anchoring the boat is not good as one cannot get to it at high tide. Tried anchoring in front of slip, but about 5 yards further out, with a long shore rope, along which one could work the dinghy at high tide.

Took runners off strawberries, except two which I have allowed to root to fill up gaps.

A[vril], J[ane], & B[ill] D[unn] caught 30 fish last night, including 8 mackerel (first this year.)

One or two clarkia beginning to flower.

3 eggs, also another Richard broke. Shells are very thin – NB. to get more shell grit.

9.8.47: Dry, warm, windy day. Wind veering about, mostly south & east. Breakers on the sea in the morning, calm in afternoon & evening.

Weeded raspberries. Burnt some of the grass in the side patch.

Two snakes killed in the hay field yesterday. Large slowworm (about 1 ft. long) in the garden today.

Took out 2½ galls petrol, making 38½ galls (ie. about 10–12 galls left till end of August, but we have some supplementary coupons.[33])

3 eggs (247).

33. Fuel was strictly rationed, but sometimes supplementary supplies were allowed against specially issued coupons.

10.8.47: Dry & warm, somewhat less sunny, very little wind. Sea very calm.

Went down to the near bay, next beyond Barnhill, to collect driftwood. A good deal there, including a large block which would do for a small anvil.

Everything in garden very dried up. Seedlings in nursery bed have to be watered every evening, & even so I think some of the wallflowers have died. A few runner beans trying to flower (sown 5.6.47). Dug some more of the first lot of potatoes, sown nearly 4 months ago. Now quite good, but of course not good as "new" potatoes as they are not an early kind. The others will I am afraid come to nothing after their blasting.

Took out ½ gall petrol, making 39 galls.

2 eggs (249).

11.8.47: Mostly overcast, less warm than yesterday. Sea calm. Sowed turnips & a few swedes (probably not too late as a last sowing.) Gave liquid manure to runner beans, which, even apart from the blasted ones, are not very good.

Another rambler coming out (pink).

Berries on rowan trees getting red. Hazel nuts pretty large.

4 eggs (253)

12.8.47: Warm, dry, fairly sunny, some wind. Sea calm. Earth now very dried up.

A[vril] & the others fishing last night – about 30 fish, including 1 mackerel. Brought home oar to make mast for boat.

2 eggs (255).

13.8.47: Blazing hot day. Sea calm.

Made mast for boat (6½ feet high, ie. six & a half after clearing the gunwhale.)

New drum of paraffin arrived.

4 eggs (259).

14.8.47: Blazing hot day, about the hottest we have had. Sea like glass.

Tried to raise creels – no use as the tide was not low enough. After this fished, but only 2 saithe.

One or two godetias coming out.

Took out 1½ galls, petrol, making 40½ galls.

5 eggs (264).

Rats in byre very bad. Reset traps, caught one rat.

15.8.47: Similar day to yesterday.

Everything very dried up. Water in tank very low – about 2 days' supply, I should say, unless it rains.

New barrel of oil arrived yesterday, but the old one is not quite finished yet. It was started on 6.5.47. Supposing it to last 2 weeks more, as I should think it would by the weight of it, our average summer consumption (40 galls in about 14–15 weeks) is less than 3 galls a week.

Started cylinder of Calor Gas today. The last, which gave out yesterday, was started on 19.7.47, so has run less than 4 weeks.

4 eggs (268).

16.8.47: Fine hot day, little wind. Sea very calm.

Went over to Crinan to buy oatmeal. About 1 hour 10 minutes going (probably about 8 miles), more coming back, owing to aiming too far south & being swept down the sound by the tide.

Took out ¾ gall petrol, making about 41½ galls.

Last night saw the northern lights for the first time. Long streaks of white stuff, like cloud, forming an arc[34] in the sky, & every now & then an extraordinary flickering passing over them, as though a searchlight were playing upon them.

3 eggs (271).

34. 'an arc' makes sense, but the writing looks more like 'a one,' which makes no sense.

19.8.47: Since 17.8.47. at Glengarrisdale. Fine weather all the time. Sea calm. Water supply has dried up & will not begin again until it rains. Well in field fairly good water.

Time to Glengarrisdale about 1 hour 45 minutes. On return journey today ran into the whirlpool[35] & were all nearly drowned. Engine sucked off by the sea & went to the bottom. Just managed to keep the boat steady with the oars, & after going through the whirlpool twice, ran into smooth water & found ourselves only about 100 yards from Eilean Mór,[36] so ran in quickly & managed to clamber ashore. H[umphrey] D[akin] jumped ashore first with the rope, then the boat overturned spilling L[ucy] D[akin], R[ichard] & myself into the sea. R. trapped under the boat for a moment, but we managed to get him out. Most of the stuff in the boat lost including the oars. Eilean Mór is larger than it looks – I should say 2 acres at least. The whole surface completely undermined by puffins' nests. Countless wild birds, including many young cormorants learning to fly. Curiously enough it has a considerable pool of what appears to be fresh water, so there must be a spring. No wood whatever on the island, as there is no place where drift could fetch up. However we managed to get my cigarette lighter dry & made a fire of dead grass & lumps of dry peat, prised off the surface, at which we dried our clothes. We were taken off about 3 hours later by the Ling° fishermen who happened to be bringing picknickers round. We left Glengarrisdale at about 10.30, which was about 2 hours after high tide. So must have struck Corryvreckan at about 11.30, ie. when the tide had been ebbing about 3 hours. It appears this was the very worst time, & one should time it so as to pass Corryvreckan on slack water. The boat is all right. Only serious loss, the engine & 12 blankets.

Yesterday fished Loch nan Eilean & a Bhùrra.[37] 12 trout, mostly small. There are a lot of fish in a Bhùrra but I could not catch anything over about 5 ounces. It is very shallow, with a sandy or shingly bottom.

Took out 1½ galls, petrol making 43 galls.

Eggs for last 3 days 15 (286).

35. The whirlpool in the Gulf of Corryvreckan, between Jura and Scarba, was – and still is – extremely dangerous. Orwell makes light of this escapade, but they were singularly fortunate not to be drowned. Crick reproduces Henry Dakin's graphic account (pp. 527–29) and Orwell's statement that the story was reported to the *Daily Express* (in his letter to Anthony Powell, 8 September 1947). It has not been traced in the London editions of the *Daily Express* held by the British Library; a search of the *Scottish Daily Express* made on the editor's behalf by Mrs. Helen Stokes in the National Library of Scotland, Edinburgh, and by Mr. Telfer Stokes in the Mitchell Library, Glasgow, proved fruitless. No copies were held in Edinburgh; in Glasgow there were no copies of a Scottish edition for August; no mention was made in the September issues (from the second number of which the masthead name changed from *Daily Express* to *Scottish Daily Express*). It *was* reported by the *Glasgow Herald*, 30 August 1947. This stated: 'They had gone to see the whirlpool when their motor-boat was drawn into one of the smaller whirlpools and overturned. Fortunately, with Mr Blair's help, they all reached a small islet from which, after several hours, they were rescued by two fishermen from Toberonochy, island of Luing.' Luing is north of Scarba, and Toberonochy is six or seven miles from the north tip of Jura and a little further from Eilean Mór, the islet referred to. Both Donald Darroch and Ian McKechnie stoutly defended Orwell: Orwell knew well what he was doing, even though he might have taken more advice: he had simply misread the tide tables which was 'easy enough to do' (Crick, p. 529).
36. Eilean Mór is a little island some five hundred yards off the northwest tip of Jura. Orwell omits the accent.
37. Loch a Bhùrra lies a little to the southeast of Loch nan Eilean and is midway between the east and west coasts of Jura. Orwell spells it 'Bura.'

20.8.47: Weather as before. Sea very calm. The house has now had no water for about 4 days.

Caulked boat as best I could, not having either tar or proper caulking twine, & being very short of plasticine. She was not much damaged, merely a grating & one seat gone, & a little sprung near the bows, which I think I have tightened up.

Godetias now well in flower. All except one rose have now flowered. Marrow has a good many fruits coming but no flowers out yet.

Yesterday put in an L.T. battery in the wireless. They are supposed to last 2 months, the H.T. batteries 4 months, so we shall need one of each about 20th October. NB. to write about 10th October.

5 eggs (291).

21.8.47: Weather as before. Sea a little less calm.

Cleared strawberry bed. Runners still growing very fast. Some gladioli now have flower buds. One or two raspberries fruiting (only one or two berries).

5 eggs (296).

22.8.47: More overcast than yesterday, still very hot. Sea less calm.

Started trying to make new back seat for boat.

Some red hot pokers have buds. Turnips sown 11.8.47 are up in places. Honeysuckle almost over. Dead shrew on the path. Corn ripening in places. Candytuft almost over. Seedlings in nursery bed still alive in spite of drought.

8 eggs (4 laid out) (304).

Old drum of paraffin about at an end. Begun 7.5.47. Ie. 40 galls, has lasted 14–15 weeks, so that summer expenditure averages less than 3 galls. a week.

23.8.47: Warm & dry, a good deal of wind (W.) at times, no sign of rain. Sea calm.

Planted 25 sprouting broccoli on place where I had taken the peas up. Not very good weather for planting, & they had been several days in the post as well.

5 eggs (309).

24.8.47: Weather much as before. Heavy low mist late last night & early this morning, but no sign of rain. Sea very calm.

Cut grass in front. Took up the potatoes, as they had withered up – would not make any more growth. Slightly better than I had expected, as they had only been planted 3 months when blasted. About 100 lb. from 5 rows (about 25 lb. of seed), & perhaps 10–20 pounds had been dug before. The seed was Great Scott, & with normal growth I think one might expect 2¾ cwt. from this amount of seed.

4 eggs (313).

25.8.47: Weather as before. Sea less calm this morning, but glassy again in the afternoon.

Finished mending boat. Seat not good. Very difficult job putting it in unless one has good timber & a vice to shape it in.

One or two gladioli out (pink). A few rowan berries ripe.

Started new drum of paraffin. Should last at least to middle of November.

7 eggs (320).

26.8.47: Weather as before. Sea very calm.

Dug over patch where potatoes had been. Ground very dry & lumpy. Perpetual spinach to go here. Should have been sown 2–3 weeks ago. Sowed grass seed in bare patches on path.

A[vril] tried the boat last night – still letting in water badly. More caulking needed near bows.

R[ichard] R[ees] saw a grampus (or something of the kind) in the sound today.

3 eggs (323).

27.8.47: As before. A little less warm. Sea calm.

Caulked boat some more & applied a little tar. Difficult to apply as I had no brush.

Cylinder of Calor Gas gave out today. Put on new one. The last has gone only for 12 days. However we have used nothing else for cooking & heating water for over a week, as until there is water in the tanks it is dangerous to light the fire.

Runner beans & late peas very poor, no doubt owing to drought.

5 eggs (328).

28.8.47: As before. Very warm in afternoon.

Sowed perpetual spinach. Should have been sown about 3 weeks ago, but I had not the ground ready.

D[onald] D[arroch] started cutting corn. Seemingly much better than last year, with more & better straw.

Honeysuckle over, most rowan berries ripe, loosestrife about over, some blackberries red, a good many hazel nuts, but not ripe yet. A good many corn marigolds about – A[vril] says she did not see any last year. Dews now very heavy, which is the salvation of turnips in the garden.

4 eggs (332).

29.8.47: As before. Very hot in afternoon. Sea glassy.

Tried boat on water. Does not seem to take in quite as badly. Watered sprouting broccoli, which look very sorry for themselves.

Have sent for Calor Gas.

4 eggs (336).

30.8.47: As before. A little less warm. Sea calm.

Tried fishing in the Lealt again. It is dried up into a series of disconnected shallow pools in which actually there are a good many fish, but all very small. Could not catch anything even as large as ¼ lb. Also when the water is so shrunken the fish can see you & will not rise unless you hide yourself while casting.

Yellow gladioli out. One or two sweet peas beginning to flower.

4 eggs (340).

31.8.47: Somewhat less warm. Overcast & sometimes misty. Sea calm.

Most of afternoon trying to mend typewriter. Removed more strawberry runners. Started on new balancer meal.

1 egg (341).

1.9.47: Much as before. Sea calm.

They have started cutting D.D.'s field with the reaper & binder. This makes much larger sheaves, which I think are somewhat easier to build into stooks. Saw a grampus momentarily.

1 egg & 1 laid out (343).

2.9.47: Cooler, & distinctly chilly in evening. Wind from W. & heavy low cloud a good deal of the time, but still no rain. Sea calm. Fire in sitting room for first time today.

Weeded between blackcurrants etc. with help of G.,[38] & lit a bonfire in hopes of getting some ash to spread. All that patch of ground is obviously very sour & I think needs potash as well as lime. Shall try to get some Kainit.[39]

D.D's corn now all cut & stooked (binder was here today.)

2 eggs (345).

38. Probably Gwen O'Shaughnessy, Eileen's sister-in-law, who came up to Jura with her children (Crick, 527).

39. Kainit is the German name for hydrous magnesium sulphate with potassium chloride (found in salt deposits); it was used as a fertiliser.

3.9.47: Cold & overcast, with low clouds. A very few spots of rain, not enough to wet the ground. More rain coming, by appearances. Wind from S. Sea rougher.

Felt unwell, did nothing out of doors. The field in front cut & stooked today, in spite of various mishaps to binder (string breaking etc.) About half a dozen rabbits killed. Three hens now broody.

Finished up cask of petrol.

1 egg (346).

4.9.47: Evidently a very little rain in the night. Fairly persistent but very thin drizzle most of day. Stream to tank still dry, soil only wetted about 1″ deep.

Sea less calm.

New wheelbarrow arrived (rather too small.) Began manuring patch for spring cabbages. Retied one or two apple trees. At least 3 hens now broody.

1 egg (347).

5.9.47: Somewhat more rain, but clearing up again this afternoon. Stream to tank still not affected. This evening very clear, with some sun. Sea fairly calm.

Unwell (chest), hardly went outside. Turnips sown 11.8.47 want thinning.

1 egg (348).

6.9.47: Some rain, including one or two heavyish showers. Tomorrow we intend taking the top off the tank to get some water direct if it rains. Ought to have done this earlier. Little rain & midges awful. Sea calm.

Thinned carrots & turnips, weeded between gooseberries, transplanted alyssum to nursery bed, ditto one or two rooted strawberry runners. Gooseberries very poor & have hardly made any growth this year. Presumably sour soil, though it had a fairly good liming this spring. If obtainable shall apply Kainit to make up the potash, then more lime in spring. Dug in 1 lb. of Epsom salts under the apple tree which I think has magnesium deficiency.

1 egg (349).

7.9.47: Drizzle most of day. A few patches of sun. Water in taps now, but none in hot tank. Sea calm. Ground still very dry a few inches down.

Started making pen for ducklings. Am ordering 6. (3 weeks).

Cylinder of Calor Gas gave out. Cannot light kitchen fire till water in hot tank.

Ate first cabbage today (planted 5.7.47).

1 egg (350).

8.9.47: Raining on & off through the day, with sunny patches. Rain at times fairly heavy. Little wind. Sea calm. Put up place for ducklings. Sweet peas fairly well out. Soil still extremely dry.

No eggs. (350).

9.9.47: Raining all or most of last night. Violent rain during much of the day, & very violent wind from S. & W. Sea very rough till evening, when it calmed somewhat. Water in taps now normal. Spinach germinating.

1 egg (351).

10.9.47: Rain a good deal of the day. Little wind till evening. Sea fairly calm.

No eggs (351).

11.9.47: Light rain most of the morning, clearing up in evening. Little wind. Sea fairly calm.

Picked the first bunch of sweet peas. Everything very flattened out by the wind & rain. Clarkia & godetias about over.

No eggs. (351).

The last double opening of Domestic Diary IV was used by Orwell for various notes. The question marks and ticks reproduced are as in the manuscript.

On verso:

Before going away.

Take up all crops.
Weed all patches.
Spread manure.
Put wire across gap.
Get in stakes.
Put barbed wire round cherry trees.
Cut grass.
Dig patch for spring vegetables.
Mark places for fruit trees etc.
Plant tulip bulbs & peonies (?)
Plant perennial flowers (if any).
Make bottom of gate rabbit-proof
Weight down hen-house.
Drag up & cover boat.
Prune bush roses (?)
Make sure fruit trees properly tied.
Make sure wood etc. is in dry place.
Oil / calor gas.
Engine?[40]
Grease tools.
Manure fruit trees & bushes ✓

Wanted

Fence wire
Barbed wire
Wire netting[41]
Staples (large)
Stakes (for barbed wire)
Angle irons.

Wheelbarrow ✓
Tarpaulins.
On recto:

"Coming Up"	not later than	30.4.48
"Burmese Days"	..	31.10.48
"Down & Out"	..	30.4.49[42]
"Homage to Catalonia"		
"Critical Essays"		when original edit.s
"Animal Farm"		out of print

12.9.47: – lecture, Working Men's College, Crowndale Rd. NW. 1. time? (lecture 45–60 mins.)[43]

November – introduction (Borough Librarian. St. Pancras. Town Hall, Euston Rd. TER 7070)

£7,826-8-7 (19.6.47)
(£250)
(£150)[44]

40. Crossed through.
41. Crossed through; 'Barbed wire' is probably a substitution.
42. These are presumably the dates when Orwell expected his books to be published in the Uniform Edition. *Coming Up for Air* was published in May 1948; *Burmese Days,* January 1949; *Down and Out in Paris and London,* September 1949; *Homage to Catalonia,* February 1951; *Critical Essays,* 22 February 1951. *Animal Farm* appeared in a cheap edition, similar in appearance to the Uniform Edition, in June 1949, but was not re-set until October 1965 for the Collected Edition.
43. Orwell was too ill to leave Jura to give this lecture. The St Pancras Borough Librarian, Frederick Sinclair, was keen to develop cultural activities and would almost certainly have been going to introduce Orwell.
44. Presumably money received by Orwell, although whether £7,826 8s 7d was the amount received on 19 June 1947 or up until that date is not known. After the publication of *Animal Farm,* he certainly received much larger royalties and fees than those recorded for earlier years in his Payments Book.

This concludes Domestic Diary Volume IV.

DOMESTIC DIARY VOLUME V

12 September 1947 – 29 October 1947

Volume V of Orwell's Domestic Diary was written on thirty-three recto and three verso pages of a notebook measuring 9¾ x 7¾ins. with 26 lines per page. Orwell broke off the entries at 29 October 1947 and Avril continued from 27 December to 10 May 1948. Orwell re-opened the diary after seven months' absence in hospital (as he put it) on 31 July 1948 and continued until 24 December 1948 by when he had just completed *Nineteen Eighty-Four.* Avril's entries have been summarised. When the originals were printed in full in *The Complete Works* it was with the permission of her husband, William Dunn. They married in 1951. Avril died in 1978 and Bill died in 1992.

Footnote numbering continues from that of preceding Volume.

12.9.47: Raining a good deal of the day. Strong wind, mostly from S. till evening. Sea rough.

Applied chicken manure to the place for the new blackcurrants. Had to stake some of the raspberries, which were being loosened at the root. NB. to put wires next year.

9 eggs (laid out.) (360).

13.9.47: Fine but overcast most of day. Little wind. A few spots of rain in the evening. Not very warm. Breakers on sea most of day.

Planted about 50 spring cabbage.

Put on new cylinder of Calor Gas.

9 eggs (laid out.) (369).

14.9.47: Driving rain most of day till evening, when it cleared up somewhat. Violent wind from SW, dropping a little in the evening. Sea very rough most of day.

No eggs (369).

15.9.47: Rain part of day. Violent wind from S. in afternoon. Sea rough.

Took the 3 broodies out of the henhouse & let them loose in the back yard, in hopes this may cure them.

Most of afternoon opening up drain from kitchen sink, which was blocked.

15 galls petrol arrived (supposed to last to end of October.) About 2 tons of coal delivered.

1 egg (370).

16.9.47: Raining till about 5 pm.

Gave the grass path its first cut, chiefly to keep down dandelions etc.

9 eggs (laid out). (379).

17.9.47: Finer. Only a few drops of rain. Sunny most of day, but not very warm. Little wind. Sea fairly calm.

Put broodies back. Re-covered drain, provisionally. Edged off path, which now looks fairly good.

6 eggs (4 laid out). (385).

18.9.47: Only a drop or two of rain, about 5 pm. Otherwise fine autumnal weather, sunny but not very warm. Little wind sea calm.

Tarred bottom of boat, ie. as thoroughly as I could, as there was only a little tar left.

D[onald] D[arroch] is building a stack in the field behind the house. Some of his own hay already stowed away in the barn.

Picked about ½ lb. of nuts, more or less ripe. A[vril] picked about 1 lb. blackberries (the first this year). R[ichard] R[ees] found some mushrooms, not very many but large & good.

2 eggs (387).

19.9.47: Weather much as yesterday. No rain. Little or no wind. Sea fairly calm.

Applied wood ash (& peat ash) to gooseberries.

B[ill] D[unn] bought 22 lambs, presumably about 6 months old, price 43/6^{d} each.[45]

Took out 2 galls petrol. 2 galls.

3 eggs (390).

45. = £2.17½p in today's currency (value roughly 30 times higher).

20.9.47: Fairly heavy rain in the morning. Rest of day overcast, still, fairly warm. Sea calm. Little wind till evening.

Took up last lot of peas.

Took out 1 gall petrol. 3 galls.

It is now pretty dark at 8 pm.

3 eggs (393).

21.9.47: Beautiful clear day, not very warm. A very few light drops of rain. Sea calm.

2 eggs (395).

22.9.47: Violent rain & wind almost continuous all day, clearing slightly in the evening. Wind mostly from S. Sea very rough.

2 eggs (397).

23.9.47: Squally, with some sun & fairly sharp showers of rain. Sea roughish.

Went fishing in Lussa river.[46] Hooked a salmon (3–4 lb. by his appearance) but lost him almost immediately. Cast did not break so presumably he was only lightly hooked.

Took out 2½ galls petrol. 5½ galls.

4 eggs (401).

46. The Lussa River runs southeast across Jura into the sea via Ardlussa and Inverlussa.

24.9.47: Raining lightly most of morning, clearing in afternoon. Wind mostly from N. or N. W. Sea roughish in morning, calming in afternoon.

R[ichard]R[ees] picked a considerable quantity of mushrooms.

Took runners off strawberries (this must be the 4th or 5th time).

2 eggs (403).

25.9.47: Beautiful clear day, sunny most of the time. Sea calm.

Picked first marrow (the only one & very poor.)

Apples came from Rankin.[47] About 15–20 lb. of eating apples, ditto of cookers, & some pears.

3 eggs (406).

47. Rankin was a greengrocer on the mainland.

26.9.47: Beautiful clear day till late evening, when a little rain. Fairly warm. Sea calm.

Field in front "hutted," ie. put up into small stacks, today.

2 eggs (408).

27.9.47: Horrible day. Thin driving rain all day, wind from W. Sea variable, sometimes quite rough.

Worked out area of Barnhill croft as accurately as I could from the 6″ map. Exclusive of the garden & the marshy field it appears to me to be just over 16 acres.

Started sack of wheat (140 lb) today. Three hens now moulting. One broody.

3 eggs (411).

28.9.47: Alternate rain & sun all day. Rather cold. Sea fairly calm. Bracken mostly going brown. Took out 2 galls petrol. 7½ galls.

1 egg (412).

29.9.47: A nasty day. Patches of sun, but mostly thin driving rain, & decidedly cold. Wind from W. & N. Sea fairly calm in daytime.

1 egg (413).

30.9.47: Somewhat better day. Some light showers. Sea fairly calm.

3 eggs (416).

1.10.47: Overcast. Only a few drops of rain. Sea calm.

A few godetias & shirley poppies, & a good many marigolds still blooming, ditto red-hot pokers. Picked the first parsnips today – very poor.

1 egg (417).

2.10.47: Beautiful still day. Overcast part of time, but sunny & quite hot in the afternoon. Sea like glass.

D[onald] D[arroch] now has all his corn stacked.

Picked a few blackberries. Still not a great number ripe.

2 eggs (419).

3.10.47: Beautiful still day. Not very warm. Sea calm.

3 eggs (422).

4.10.47: Beautiful day. Mist from about 4 pm, thickening from then onwards. Not very warm. Sea calm.

Took up bean sticks. Cleared parsnips (very poor).

Took out about 2 galls petrol, 9½ galls. There seems to be hardly any left in the cask (supposed to be 15 gallons.)

3 eggs (425).

5.10.47: Thick mist last night. Still, overcast day with occasional sun. Not very warm. Sea calm.

Removed dandelions from grass path (already very numerous).

A[vril] picked considerable quantities of blackberries. Saw two eagles over the house.

3 eggs (428).

6.10.47: Still day, mostly overcast, but no rain. Not very warm. Sea calm.

Manured all fruit bushes (NB. I think the blackcurrant bushes could do with a bit more.)

Still some runners on strawberries, which I removed. One or two recently-ripened raspberries, so I think these must be an autumn kind.

3 eggs (431).

7.10.47: Still, overcast, light rain during much of the afternoon. Sea rougher.

The corn in the front field brought into the byre today (very damp). Window of stable mended. Sent for Calor Gas.

4 eggs (435).

8.10.47: Rough night. Sea very rough this morning, calming by evening. This morning windy & rainy, this afternoon better, with sunny intervals & drizzle.

Started clearing out shrubs for tulip bed.

4 eggs (439).

9.10.47: Nasty morning & sea rough. Clearer in afternoon, with occasional sun, & sea calmer.

Cleared out fuchsia stump.

Started new cylinder of Calor Gas. Last cylinder has gone less than a month, but has been used a good deal.

2 eggs (441).

10.10.47: Mostly fine, though overcast. A short light shower about 1 pm. Sea fairly calm.

Began preparing tulip bed.

3 eggs (444).

11.10.47: Filthy day, raining most of time, with nasty driving wind from S. in the afternoon. Sea roughish.

4 eggs (445)[48]

48. The 4 eggs added to the 444 of 10.10.47 should, of course, give a total of 448. Totals hereafter are 3 short.

12.10.47: Very stormy last night & sea rough this morning. Raining a good deal of the day, but wind dropping by afternoon. Sea fairly calm by evening.

Slight cold, did not go out of doors.

4 eggs (449).

13.10.47: Beautiful clear day. Sun quite hot for part of the morning. Sea calm.

Unwell, did not go out.

2 eggs (451).

14.10.47: Mostly fine, some showers. Sea calm.

Began digging tulip bed.

3 eggs (454)[49]

49. An entry has been crossed through between 14 and 15 October. The day of the month cannot be deciphered, but the entry reads: 'Very stormy last night & sea rough this morning. Raining a good deal of the day, but wind dropping by afternoon. Sea fairly calm by evening.' This suggests that entries were not always made at the end of the day to which they refer or, at the latest, on the following day; Orwell would otherwise have remembered what the weather was like on what must have been 15 October, especially because it was so very different from that of the fourteenth. On the other hand, it might be a by-product of his developing illness.

15.10.47: Nasty day. Overcast & rather cold, with mist & thin driving rain most of time. Wind from W. Sea calm inshore, roughish outside.

4 eggs (458).

16.10.47: Beautiful clear day, sunny but not very warm. No wind. Sea calm.

Finished tulip bed (will take about 150 bulbs), began clearing bed under window.

Two Golden Spire apples ripe, which we ate. Quite good crisp apples, lemony flavour.

Stags roaring all night. Have only been hearing them for about the last 10 days.

D[onald] D[arroch] taking in the last of his hay today (from the field behind the house). B[ill] D[unn] put his sheep up on the hill as they should be there before the frosts begin.

4 eggs, but I think 1 other had been broken & eaten. (462).

17.10.47: Nasty damp day, but not actually much rain, & no wind. Sea calm.

Paraffin running rather low (started about 6 weeks ago). Have ordered another drum.

Took out 1 gall petrol. 10½ galls. Only a little left in cask.

2 eggs (464).

18.10.47: Dull, still day. Hardly any rain. Sea calm.

Began clearing flower bed.

3 eggs (467).

19.10.47: Dull, overcast day, no rain, not cold. Some wind in afternoon. Sea roughish, especially in morning.

Went on clearing flower bed, spread a little manure (very short of this.)

New oil cooker used for first time today (Valor).

The swallows I think have gone. The last time I saw one was a week or 10 days ago. Chaffinches flocking.

4 eggs (471).

20.10.47: Fine, sunny, windy day. Chilly in morning & evening. Sea roughish.

Planted tulips (the new bulbs, about 100–150). Gave them a very little potassium sulphate. Finished clearing flower bed.

New oil cooker seems to use about 1 pint an hour for each burner (one burner works oven).

One hen still almost naked from moulting, & the others persecuting her a bit. Qy. whether to segregate her as she is probably not getting enough to eat.

3 eggs (474).

21.10.47: Fine day, sunny with some mist, rather cold. Sea fairly calm.

Planted Madonna lilies (6 I think).

3 eggs (477).

22.10.47: Fine, clear, coldish day till about 8pm, when it began raining. Sea fairly calm.

Planted more tulips (about 120) & transplanted one or two sweet williams.

3 eggs (480).

23.10.47: Evidently fairly heavy rain in the night. Today dull, overcast, still, with occasional rain & mist. Sea very calm.

Planted crocuses, supposed to be 200 but I think not so many. Very poor bulbs, & not enough of them. Must order about 100 more. NB. to order some scillas as well.

4 eggs (484).

On the facing page against 23.10.47 Orwell has written and ticked, implying he had placed the following order:

Order crocuses.

24.10.47: Clear, fine day, quite warm in the morning. Sea roughish.

Today a burst water pipe, a great nuisance but fortunately in the scullery & not upstairs. Nobody knows where the main cock is, as it is somewhere underground, near the door of the byre probably. The only way of cutting off the water is to disconnect the pipe from the tank, at the point where it crosses the stream. This soon empties the cistern & thus stops the water running, but of course while one is doing the mend the water is running out of the tank, & in dry weather it might not be easy to get it full again. NB. that one cannot disconnect the pipe without a large monkey wrench which we have not got.

3 eggs (487).

On the facing page against this date Orwell has written:

Order monkey wrench.

25.10.47: Beautiful, clear, windless day. Sea somewhat calmer.

Pruned gooseberry bushes (old ones). Applied sulphate of potash to fruit bushes & strawberries, & the two espalier apple trees.

Put new batteries in radio. NB. we shall need H.T. battery about 25.2.48 & L.-T. battery about 25.12.47. Order 10 days beforehand.

Saw a piece of honeysuckle in bloom yesterday, in a bush that had ripe berries. One or two flowers on the thrift, must be second blooming. Forgot to mention, saw some starlings about a week ago.

3 eggs (490).

Against this date on the facing page Orwell has written:

Order H.T. battery 15.2.48.
Order L.T. battery 15.12.47.[50]

50. Orwell's radio (like many others in the 1930s and 1940s) did not run on mains electricity but on two accumulators (high and low tension) which had from time to time to be recharged.

26.10.47: Still day, more overcast than yesterday, but no rain. Sea calm.

Gave manure to apple trees. The scion of the James Grieve appeared to have rooted. Cut the rootlets through – not certain whether this is the right thing to do.

5 eggs (495).

27.10.47: Fine still day, not much sun, no wind. Sea fairly calm.

New gate & tomato house have arrived. Also ½ ton hay, barrel of paraffin, calor gas. Gateposts 8½ [feet] long, must be cut down, as in this soil it would be almost impossible to sink them deep enough.

1 egg. (496).

28.10.47: Fine still day, not much sun, little wind, coldish. Sea calm.

Started clearing stable. NB. order large stiff broom.

Began new drum of paraffin. Allowing that we use 5 galls a week, this should last to 28.12.47. Important not to run out at Xmas time. Order another drum at beginning of December.

3 eggs (499).

Against this date on the facing page Orwell has written:

Order yard broom.
Order paraffin about 1.12.47.

29.10.47: Fine clear day, not very warm, with some sun. Sea roughish.

A[vril] & B[ill] D[unn] continued clearing stable. Mowed lawn (last time this year).

3 eggs (& 1 I think eaten). 502.

After this entry, Orwell ceased to write his diary, owing to becoming seriously ill. His letters from here on and well into 1948 were handwritten from bed. His sister Avril took over recording events – chiefly the weather, the number of eggs collected – and the number of punctures suffered.

SUMMARY OF AVRIL'S ENTRIES

27 December 1947 – 10 May 1948

ORWELL'S YOUNGER sister, Avril (who, after his death, would bring up Orwell's son, Richard) lived at Barnhill with Orwell and cared for him. She worked hard gardening and caring for the animals – indeed, keeping the small property going. She made brief entries in Orwell's Domestic Diary, Volume 5, from 27 December 1947 until 22 February 1948, when she went to stay in London. On her return she continued making brief entries from 9 March to 10 May 1948. Orwell took up his diary again on 31 July 1948.

Avril's entries always include, and usually start with, a description of the weather, for example, 'Mt. Scarba heavily covered' with snow, 'Tearing South East Wind', 'Still beastly weather', 'A terrible day', and, less often, 'Beautiful fine day'. In this she is following Orwell's practice. Mt. Scarba dominated the island of Scarba which lies just north of Jura some five or six miles from Barnhill. Its peak rises to 1,474 ft. Only the very last entry has no reference to the weather. Avril always records the number of eggs collected and, until her visit to London, gives, as did Orwell, a running total. Perhaps because she did not know how many eggs had been laid whilst she was away, she decided not to continue recording a total on her return. (For the record, the total number of eggs collected at the end of her entries would have been 777.) She mentions very briefly, with the names of those who helped her, especially Bill Dunn, the work done about Barnhill – sowing fertilizer, bringing hay, arrival of the rations, and the like. She clearly worked very hard. The entry for 13 February 1948 gives a fair indication of the effort she put in: 'Staked & wired the loganberries. Cleaned out the hen house & started to dig the side garden. A terrific labour as it is filled with boulders'. On 19 March: 'Spread a little dung & dug & weeded some of the garden. Manured the rhubarb'. Then, on 11 April, 'Bill & I started to plant the potatoes, a backbreaking job'. At a more mundane level she enters 'Did all the washing' and, again, 'Did all the washing & ironing' (and, of course, in those days without washing or drying machines). However, on 20 March, with the rations there arrived 'my new mangle'. There are very occasional signs of relaxation. Thus, on 7 February she writes, 'Took Rick' (Orwell's son, Richard) 'to children's party at Ardlussa & saw a white mountain hare on way home'. Ardlussa was about seven miles south of Barnhill by a very poor road. The quality (or otherwise) of that road was doubtless the source of one puncture after another which they suffered. Just three such entries tell their own story: 'Bill & I mended a puncture & had two more on the way back from Ardlussa' on 26 March; on 10 April, 'Went to Ardlussa & had a puncture as usual'; and then on 29 April, 'Puncture on the way home & had to leave the car at Lagg' – Lagg is a hamlet about fifteen miles south of Barnhill. Rabbits are reported as shot; the McDonalds (who lived at Lealt about five miles south of Barnhill) gave them a kid on 13 March and on the 18th it 'strayed away'; the mail has always to be brought or collected from Ardlussa, often with punctures en route. But there are moments of triumph. On 10 March, 'Got the tractor going' (its wheels had arrived with the seed potatoes on 17 February). And a rewarding moment: 'Fetched up a sack of wood from the beach & found a perfectly good hairbrush', followed by, 'Dug a bit more garden'. Like her brother, she took delight in the natural world around her. Thus, on 13 March 1948, 'Crocus in full bloom', on 14 April the first tulip was out and the next day she was able to pick the first rhubarb. Then, on 9 May, French beans and sweet peas were 'just showing'. And, despite all the trials of punctures and hard farm work, Avril had time to spend several days sowing 'the new herbaceous border with cornflowers, poppies, clarkia, godetia, sweet sultan, candytuft & saponaria'.

Relevant Entries from Orwell's Notebooks

c. 20 February 1948 – 21 May 1948

In this section are entries from Orwell's fifth Diary and a number of related entries from his Second and his Last Literary Notebooks.

Hairmyres Hospital Timetable, *c.* 20 February 1948
Diary Entry in Orwell's Second Literary Notebook
(*CW*, XIX, p. 274)

It is not possible to date this timetable precisely, but it must have been written after Orwell began his course of streptomycin injections on 19 or 20 February 1948. This is therefore a convenient, rather than a precise, position to place it. (Asterisks are Orwell's own.)

Time table at this hospital (times all approximate)

*12 midnight – injection
5.30 am – noise (people going to & fro, water being drawn, etc.) begins.
6.30 am – called, with hot water.
7 am – temperature taken
7.30 am – breakfast
*8 am – injection
8.15 am – cleaning begins (continues on & off for about 2 hours)
9 am – bed made
 . . . medicine
10 am – temperature taken
10.30 am – doctors come round
11–12 noon – during this time, though of course not every day, one goes to be X-rayed, "refilled", etc.
12 noon – lunch
2 pm – temperature taken
3 pm – tea
*4 pm – injection
6 pm – temperature taken
6.30 pm – supper
10 pm – temperature taken
lights out

NB. that the injections are a temporary feature.

Diary Entry in Orwell's Second Literary Notebook
(*CW*, XIX, pp. 307–8)

Handwritten: textual variations are not listed here but can be found in *Complete Works*.

30.3.48: When you are acutely ill, or recovering from acute illness, your brain frankly strikes work & you are only equal to picture papers, easy crossword puzzles etc. But when it is a case of a long illness, where you are weak & without appetite but not actually feverish or in pain, you have the impression that your brain is quite normal. Your thoughts are just as active as ever, you are interested in the same things, you seem to be able to talk normally, & you can read anything that you would read at any other time. It is only when you attempt to write, even to write the simplest & stupidest newspaper article, that you realise what a deterioration has happened inside your skull. At the start it is impossible to get anything on to paper at all. Your mind turns away to any conceivable subject rather than the one you are trying to deal with, & even the physical act of writing is unbearably irksome. Then, perhaps, you begin to be able to write a little, but whatever you write, once it is set down on paper, turns out to be stupid & obvious. You have also no command of language, or rather you can think of nothing except flat, obvious expressions: a good, lively phrase never occurs to you. And even when you begin to re-acquire the habit of writing, you seem to be incapable of preserving continuity. From time to time you may strike out a fairly good sentence, but it is extraordinarily difficult to make consecutive sentences sound as though they had anything to do with one another. The reason for this is that you cannot concentrate for more than a few seconds, & therefore cannot even remember what you said a moment ago. In all this the striking thing is the contrast between the apparent normality of your mind, & its helplessness when you attempt to get anything on to paper. Your thoughts, when you think them, seem to be just like your thoughts at any other time, but as soon as they are reduced to some kind of order they always turn out to be badly-expressed platitudes.

What I would like to know is whether enough is known about the localisation of brain functions to account for this kind of thing. It would seem natural enough if the effect of illness were simply to stop you thinking, but that is not what happens. What happens is that your mind is just as active as usual, perhaps more so, but always to no purpose. You can use words, but always inappropriate words, & you can have ideas, but you cannot fit them together. If mental activity is determined, for instance, by the supply of blood to the brain, it looks as though when you are ill there is enough blood to feed the areas that produce stupid thoughts, but not the ones that produce intelligent thoughts.

Diary Entry in Orwell's Second Literary Notebook (*CW*, XIX, pp. 310–11)

This handwritten entry is taken from Orwell's last (not his Second) Literary Notebook. Although written a year after the treatment it describes, it is placed here because Orwell started the fifty-day course of treatment with streptomycin on 19 or 20 February 1948; fifty days later would be 8 or 9 April – i.e., a few days after the description on page 481 of how he had been affected mentally by his illness.

24.3.49: Before I forget them it is worth writing down the secondary symptoms produced by streptomycin when I was treated with it last year. Streptomycin was then almost a new drug & had never been used at that hospital before. The symptoms in my case were quite different from those described in the American medical journal in which we read the subject up beforehand.

At first, though the streptomycin seemed to produce an almost immediate improvement in my health, there were no secondary symptoms, except that a sort of discoloration appeared at the base of my finger & toe nails. Then my face became noticeably redder & the skin had a tendency to flake off, & a sort of rash appeared all over my body, especially down my back. There was no itching associated with this. After abt 3 weeks I got a severe sore throat, which did not go away & was not affected by sucking penicillin lozenges. It was very painful to swallow & I had to have a special diet for some weeks. There was now ulceration with blisters in my throat & on the insides of my cheeks, & the blood kept coming up into little blisters on my lips. At night these burst & bled considerably, so that in the morning my lips were always stuck together with blood & I had to bathe them before I could open my mouth. Meanwhile my nails had disintegrated at the roots & the disintegration grew, as it were, up the nail, new nails forming beneath meanwhile. My hair began to come out, & one or two patches of quite white hair appeared at the back (previously it was only speckled with grey.)

After 50 days the streptomycin, which had been injected at the rate of 1 gramme a day, was discontinued. The lips etc. healed almost immediately & the rash went away, though not quite so promptly. My hair stopped coming out & went back to its normal colour, though I think with more grey in it than before. The old nails ended by dropping out altogether, & some months after leaving hospital I had only ragged tips, which kept splitting, to the new nails. Some of the toenails did not drop out. Even now my nails are not normal. They are much more corrugated than before, & a great deal thinner, with a constant tendency to split if I do not keep them very short.

At that time the Board of Trade would not give import permits for streptomycin, except to a few hospitals for experimental purposes. One had to get hold of it by some kind of wire-pulling. It cost £1 a gramme, plus 60% Purchase Tax.

Diary Entry in Orwell's Second Literary Notebook
(*CW*, XIX, pp. 19–20)

Handwritten: textual variations are not listed here, but can be found in *Complete Works*.

18.4.48: How memory works, or doesn't. Last night, as I was settling down after the lights had been turned out, I suddenly, for no apparent reason remembered something that had happened during the war. This was that at some time or other – when, I did not know, but it was evidently a good long time back – I was shown a document which was so secret that the Minister concerned, or his secretary (I think it was his secretary), apparently had orders not to let it pass out of his own hand. I therefore had to come round to his side of the desk & read it over his shoulder. It was a short pamphlet or memorandum printed on good quality white paper & bound with green silk thread. But the point is that though I remembered the scene vividly – especially the secretive way in which he held the page for me to read it, as though there were danger of some other unauthorised person getting a glimpse of it – I had no memory whatever as to what the document was.

This morning I thought it over, & was able to make some inferences. The only Minister I was in touch with during the war was Cripps, in 1942 & 1943, after his mission to India. The document must have had something to do with India or Burma, because it was in this connection (when I was working in the Indian Section at the BBC) that I occasionally saw Cripps. The person who showed me the document must have been David Owen, Cripps's secretary. I then remembered that after reading it I made some such comment as, "I should think you would keep a thing like that secret," which made it all the more likely that the document had something to do with India. In the afternoon I mentioned the matter to Richard Rees, & then later I remembered a little more, but in a doubtful way. I think – but I remember this much less well than I remember the style of print & paper – that the document was a memorandum on our post-war treatment of Burma, then occupied by the Japanese, saying that Burma would have to revert to "direct rule" (meaning martial law) for several years before civil government was restored. This, of course was a very different tale from what we were giving out in our propaganda. And I think (but any memory I have of this is very vague indeed) that on the strength of it I may have dropped a hint to one of the Burmese in London, warning him not to trust the British government too far.

If I did drop any such hint, this would have amounted to a breach of trust, & perhaps that was why I had preferred to forget the whole incident. But then why did I suddenly remember it again? What impresses me even more than my having remembered the scene without remembering what the document was about, is[51] that it was, so to speak, quite a new memory.[52] The moment the episode came back to me, I was aware that it had never crossed my mind for years past. It had suddenly popped up to the surface, after lying forgotten for – I think – quite five years.[53]

51. 'is' *originally followed by* the sudden reappearance of this episode in my mind after it had been forgotten for years *which was crossed through.*
52. 'memory' *originally followed by* was aware that it had never crossed my mind for years past, *which was crossed through.*
53. See 12.8.42 (p. 360) for possible origin of this memory

Diary Entry in Orwell's Second Literary Notebook
(*CW*, XIX, pp. 497–8)

Handwritten while in Hairmyers Hospital

21.5.48: *9.45 am.:* The following noises now happening simultaneously. A radio. A gramophone. Vacuum cleaner running intermittently. Orderly singing intermittently. Noise of hammering from outside. Usual clatter of boots & trolleys, whistling, cries of rooks & gulls, cackling of hens in the distance, taps running, doors opening & shutting, intermittent coughing.

Immediately below on the same page is written:

Things not foreseen in youth as part of middle age.
Perpetual tired weak feeling in legs, aching knees. Stiffness amounting to pain in small of back & down loins. Discomfort in gums. Chest more or less always constricted. Feeling in the morning of being almost unable to stand up. Sensation of cold whenever the sun is not shining. Wind on the stomach (making it difficult to think). Eyes always watering.

As painful as a grapestone under a dental plate
As noisy as a mouse in a packet of macaroni
As haughty as a fishmonger

Domestic Diary Volume V

31 July 1948 – 24 December 1948

This Diary is handwritten. Notes are numbered from 1.

31.7.48: Re-opening this diary after seven months absence in [Hairmyres] hospital. Returned here [Barnhill] on 28.7.48. Weather at present extremely hot & dry, no wind. Oats very short in the straw, presumably owing to drought in spring. Hay mostly cut & in ricks. Roses, poppies, sweet williams, marigolds full out, lupins still with some flowers, candytuft about over, clarkia coming on. Fruit bushes, other than raspberries, have not done very well & I shall move most of them. Trees fairly good. A lot of apples on some of the 1946 trees, but not much growth. Strawberries superlatively good. A[vril] says they have had about 20 lb. (50 plants), & there are more coming on, though of course getting small now. First lot of peas almost ready to pick. Lettuces good, turnips ditto, runner beans not so good. The things that always seem to fail here are anything of the onion family. Two lots of chicks coming on, 5 10-week & 10 6-week, R.I.R. x Leghorn, good chicks & very even size. Pig, born about March, very good specimen. Has been fed almost entirely on potatoes & milk, the young chicks on oatmeal & milk. Both cows still in milk. The first (Rosie) calved about February, now supposed to be in calf again (to the Highland bull.) Grass pretty good, & thistles not nearly so bad as they used to be.

Cannot for some time to come do anything in garden, except very light jobs such as pruning.

Fishing has been good. One night recently they caught 80 fish, & also 8 lobsters in a week.

Lamps in bad condition & want spare parts. Many tools missing.

At the bottom of the facing page, Orwell has written this list. All are ticked except the hammer; the third line is crossed through and ticked.

Order Tilly mantles & vapourisers.
" hammer
" washers (for taps)
" plug for bathroom basin.
" lamp chimneys.

1.8.48: A very little rain yesterday evening & in the night. Today overcast, & cooler. Sea like a sheet of lead. Midges very bad.

2.8.48: Fine but not very hot most of day. This evening mist & rain. Sea calm.

A[vril] started new cylinder of Calor Gas yesterday.

Bob[1] removed to Tarbert today. To be returned first week in October.

1. Bob was the horse.

On the facing page opposite 2.8.48, Orwell has written, and ticked:

Order Calor Gas
Order broccoli plants

3.8.48: A little rain during the night. Today very still, overcast, fairly warm, but chilly after about 8 pm. Sea very smooth & reflection of lighthouse[2] visible (supposed to be sign of rain.)

One of the R.I.R. hens is ill – comb a good colour, & eats all right, but legs as if partially paralysed.

2. This must be the lighthouse at Crinan, on the mainland, six miles east-south-east of Barnhill. From the ridge to the east of Barnhill, the coast of the mainland is easily visible; see Shelden, plate facing p. 373, and, for a grander perspective, the fine colour illustration in *Die Stern, Kultur Journal*, 1983, 'Die Insel des Grossen Bruders (wo George Orwell "1984" schrieb),' pp. 192–202, by Dorothee Kruse; photographs by Klaus Meyer-Andersen.

4.8.48: Most of day very still, misty, reasonably warm. A little rain [in] the evening. B[ill] finished cutting the other patch of hay.

Tractor does this quite satisfactorily, although it is not meant to have the reaper attached to it & has to be guided in a rather awkward manner.

Some sweet peas coming out, but not good. Forgot to mention, yesterday 3 eagles over the field in front (I think 3, though I only saw 2 at any one time). One attacked another, made it drop its prey, which looked like a rat or rabbit, & then swooped down & got it. They make a screaming noise, which I thought only the buzzards made.

5.8.48: Still & overcast, sea less calm. Some rain during the night, I think.

A[vril] & B[ill] took up the creels this morning & got 3 crabs. Angus[3] yesterday brought some dabs, which had been got by spearing them, I think at Midge bay.[4]

Montbretia flowers appearing. A few red hot pokers budding. A few flower buds on the gladioli (not good.)

On the facing page opposite 5.8.48, Orwell has written, and ticked:

Order wick for hanging lamp.
Ditto Valor

3. Angus M'Kechnie, a lobster fisherman who lived at Ardlussa (but was not on the Astors' payroll). It is not always clear whether Orwell writes McKechnie or M'Kechnie; the latter is used in this edition.
4. Presumably a family name for one of the local bays reflecting the prevalence of mosquitos there.

7.8.48: Overcast with sunny intervals. Windy & rather cold. B[ill] put the hay in the back field into coils.

On the facing page opposite 7.8.48, Orwell has written, and ticked:

Order methylated (from Glasgow)

8.8.48: Fine, rather cold. Wind in north. Sea calm. Some clarkia now out. One plum tree sending out long shoots from low down, which I presume must be cut out. A great many young rabbits about, but difficult to get a shot.

Wrote to two addresses about boats.[5]

5. Not traced.

9.8.48: Fine, not very warm. One fancies a fire in the evening nowadays. Dahlias budding well. Red hot poker shoots coming up very fast. They seem to shoot up a foot or more in 3 or 4 days. Very many rabbits about.

10.8.48: Fine, not very warm. Wind tends to be northerly. Mainland looked closer than I have ever seen it. B[ill] & his friends put the hay in the back field into ricks. Took the runners out of the strawberries, ie. the worst ones.

11.8.48: Still, overcast, fairly warm. A very few drops of rain in the afternoon. Midges very bad. Sea calm.

12.8.48: Still. Fine in morning, clouding over in afternoon, & a little rain in the evening & at night. Sea calm. Some hay brought in. Rick lifter very successful. A[vril] & B[ill] D[unn] fished & got 13 saythe.

13.8.48: Beautiful hot day. Sea calm, & glassy-smooth in afternoon. Several more ricks brought in. A[vril] cut grass in front. B[ill] & the others[6] fished in the evening & caught 70 saythe.

6. Crick, plate 30, shows Barnhill in 1948 with a tent in front of it. This, as the caption to this illustration in Bowker suggests, was used for harvest workers – which were presumably 'the others' Orwell refers to here. See 23.8.48 for a reference to the tent being blown down.

14.8.48: Less warm, & sea somewhat rougher. A few drops of rain in the evening. When B[ill] & the others went down to fish, the calf followed them down & even began to swim after them.

15.8.48: Overcast, still, not very warm. Light rain part of day. Sea less calm. A[vril] planted out broccoli. With the journey, & lying about after arrival, the plants have been out of the ground at least a week. Chaffinches seem to be flocking already.

16.8.48: Dull & damp. Sea fairly calm.

17.8.48: Overcast in morning, some sun in afternoon. Very large lobster (4½ lb.) caught this morning. Cylinder of Calor Gas gave out. Must have been leaking.

18.8.48: Fine sunny day, not much wind. Sea calm. B.D. brought in some more hay, & put some more in the back field into ricks. The barn is now full & a stack will have to be built. Tied back cherry trees & cut out dead branches. Began weeding border. Killed first queen wasp.

19.8.48: Beautiful sunny day, with a little breeze. Sea fairly calm. B[ill] & R[7] made small stack, covering with tarpaulin. Only one rick now to be brought in. Pig now put outside the gate, but does not go far afield yet. Weeded some more of the border.

Methylated running very short.

On the facing page opposite 18 and 19.8.48, Orwell has written, and ticked all but michaelmas daisies:

Order daffodil bulbs
.. crocus
.. scilla
peony roots
quince trees [crossed through]
lupins
michaelmas daisies
1 cwt lime
phloxes

7. Possibly Sir Richard Rees, but Tony Rozga, Orwell's Polish neighbour, and even his son Richard are possible (see his letter to Michael Meyer, 22 August 1948, *CW*, XIX, 423–4). In his Diary entry for 31.8.48 he refers to Rozga as 'Tony.' Avril, in her letter to Michael Kennard, 29 July 1948, said: 'Richard Rees is also here for a day or two'; his visit might have been extended or repeated. However one of the Rozgas is likely to have helped with such tasks as dipping sheep (23.8.48).

20.8.48: Beautiful sunny day. Little wind. Sea calm. B. & R. clearing up last of hay. Weeded some more.

21.8.48: Horrible day, with driving rain & violent wind, from E. part of the time. Flowers in garden much blown about. B[ill] & A[vril] caught 9 mackerel last night.

22.8.48: Very slightly better day. Strong wind in morning, but sunny. Some driving rainstorms in afternoon, but a few bright intervals. Wind still strong, mostly from W., sometimes from S. Sea rough. Much white water round the lighthouse. B[ill] brought down sheep & put them in the field with a view to dipping them.

23.8.48: Horrible day. Raging wind from all directions. Sunny in morning, driving rain showers in afternoon. Tent blown down. Some apples blown off. Sea rough, much white water. B.& R. successfully dipped the sheep in the small iron tank used for rainwater. Wind dropped somewhat towards evening.

On the facing page opposite 23.8.48, Orwell has written, and ticked:

Order paraffin.

24.8.48: Better day. Some showers about mid-day, otherwise fine & sunny, not much wind. Sea calmer. Sticked a few dahlias.

25.8.48: Misty during last night. Today mostly dry, blowy, overcast & intermittent rain. Sea less rough.

26.8.48: Fine, still, sunny day. B[ill] is putting-up wires, parallel with the ground, to lean corn sheaves against instead of stooking them. New methylated came, ie. 1 gallon, but we also got a bottle of it from M^c^Kechnie, so we have 9 pints in hand. NB. to note how long it lasts. Removed seed pods from wallflowers, which we are going to leave in the ground. People always grow them as biennials, but I think in fact they are perennials, & they might do one more fairly good flowering after the first year.[8] A[vril] cut grass.

On the facing page opposite 26.8.48, Orwell has written, but not ticked:

Order tarpaulin

8. Wallflowers, if left in the ground, will usually flower a second year, though they are inclined to become leggy.

27.8.48: Beautiful warm day. No wind. Sea very calm. B. & R.[9] started cutting corn. Very difficult because stalks are so short.

9. Again, it cannot be quite certain who is cutting corn, Richard Rees or Tony Rozga, though Rozga is more likely here.

28.8.48: Fine till evening, more wind than yesterday. Sea less calm. B. & R. continued mowing the field. They have got some of the sheaves against wires today instead of stooking them. Put the young cockerel in pen to fatten. Fine about 6pm onwards some light rain.

29.8.48: Some heavy rain in the night, & strong wind. Today damp, overcast, rather blowy, but warm. It appears the sheaves had stood up in spite of the rain in the night, so this method is justified. Retied the new fruit trees, which were becoming chafed owing to being tied with string.

Some gladioli out. They are not so good this year. The roses are really admirable. Godetias now about at their best.

On the facing page opposite 29.8.48, Orwell has written, and ticked:

Write about boat

30.8.48: Filthy day. Too wet to do anything out of doors. Sea less rough. Appears to be clearing a bit this evening.

31.8.48: Filthy day. Rain more or less continuous up to about 5 pm, then fine for two hours, then more rain. Mostly light, but quite a downpour during the night. Sea fairly calm. Tony [Rozga] saw some kind of shark or grampus in Kinuachdrach harbour, which, according to him, jumped out of the water & caught a seagull.

Peony roots now 6/– each!

On a separate page following 31.8.48, Orwell tabulates details for spraying fruit trees, etc.:

Spraying of fruit trees etc.

Apples.		Remarks.
1. Dec–mid-Feb.	Tar oil (3½–50)	
2. Early May (pink kind)	Lime sulphur (1–50)	Not in hot sun
3. Late May (petal fall)	Bordeaux Mixture	

Plums.		
1. Dec. to Mid-Jan.	Tar oil (3½–50)	
Mid-May (post blossom)	Derris (1 lb. – 50 galls)	

Cherries.

Dec. to Jan.	Tar oil (3½–50)
Mid-June	Derris (1 lb.–50)

Black Currants.

1. Dec.-Feb.	Tar oil (3½–50)
Early April	Lime sulphur (1–50)
July-August (after fruit picked)	Bordeaux Mixture (?)

Red Currants.

1. Dec–Feb.	Tar oil (3½ – 50)

Gooseberries.

1. Dec–Feb.	Tar oil (3½ – 50
June	Derris (weaker than for plums & cherries)

NB. Tar Oil. Mix with own volume of water, stir well & then add bulk of water.
Lime sulphur. All apples can stand it before blossoming.

1.9.48: Slightly better day. Some showers in morning & afternoon, also some light drizzle, but most of day fine & still. Sea calm. B. & R. cut some more corn, with difficulty, as the knife gets clogged with mud in this weather. Large slow-worm living in the peat, apparently as a permanency, as I have several times seen it. Probably this is the "snake" R[ichard] saw there. Retied cherry trees.

2.9.48: Filthy day till afternoon, when clearing up somewhat. Sea rougher, with some breakers. The second calf (2 months old) is to be bought in by the farm for £10. Apparently this is an equitable price, as it is pure-bred (a heifer) & has had about 60 galls of milk.

Rain during night.

3.9.48: Better day. A shower in the afternoon & a slight one in the morning, otherwise fine & still. Sea fairly calm. B. & R. continued cutting corn.

4.9.48: Beautiful, still, warm day. A very little breeze. Sea calm. B. & R. continued cutting. Started weeding the border under house.

5.9.48: Filthy day, wet & blowy, up to about 4 pm. After that a few showers, but finer on the whole. Sea roughish. Weeded gooseberry patch. Gooseberry bushes are still very small & poor, but do not seem diseased.

6.9.48: Filthy day, clearing partially in afternoon. Began weeding currant patch. Have now decided not to move these bushes, as they have made better growth than I had thought.

Pig keeps getting through the fence into the yard, & might find his way into the garden, which must not be allowed.

Finished the bottle of methylated started on 26.8.48. This means one bottle lasts 10–12 days, so a gallon (6 bottles?) should last at best 2 months.

On the facing page opposite 6.9.48, Orwell has written, and ticked the first two items:

Plant tulips about 20th October.
Write about petrol
.. ashes[10]
.. rubber tubing
Order garden forks (2)
.. lamp washers (pump)
.. tools for boat

10. 'ashes' is slightly uncertain; Orwell may have wanted to obtain a supply to lay on the paths.

7.9.48: Filthy day, sea rough. Did nothing out of doors.

8.9.48: Much better day, sunny & fairly warm, sea calmer. B. & R. finished cutting corn. Weeded rest of the currants.

9.9.48: Fine but not very warm. Not much wind in day-time, & sea fairly calm. Wind sprang up about 8 pm & became very violent during the night, with some rain. Weeded raspberries. A good many suckers, which can be used to fill up gaps. Some lupins still flowering.

10.9.48: Sunny, strong wind. Sea rough. Corn too wet to be stacked, so they are throwing it down on the ground again.

Started weeding the other lot of currants.

11.9.48: Vile day in the morning, blowy & rainy. Sea rough. Afternoon somewhat better, but with showers. Sea calming down.

12.9.48: Heavy rain & much wind in the night, clearing in the morning. Some showers, & not very warm, but the day fine on the whole. Sea calm. B. & R. brought the new boat back from Colonsay.[11] It appears it was rough in the Atlantic, though quite calm in the Sound. In the afternoon put wire netting along the fence to keep the pig out. He still gets in, but probably cannot do so if it is well tied down at the bottom.

11. Colonsay is a much smaller island than Jura, lying some fifteen miles to its west; the journey by boat would have been about twice that distance.

13.9.48: Filthy day, sea rough. Cleared up somewhat in the evening. B. & R. could not get the boat's engine to start, probably owing to dirty plugs. Ordered some young turkeys (3–4 months). (Unobtainable).

14.9.48: *(Hairmyres):*[12] Much better day, quite warm part of the time. Sea fairly smooth. Just a little bumpiness before reaching Gigha.[13] One child sick. Comparatively little of the hay on the mainland is gathered in.

12. Orwell had returned to Hairmyres Hospital for an examination by Mr. Dick. See his letter to David Astor at 9 October 1948 below.
13. Gigha is a small island lying southwest of Jura.

15.9.48: Tremendous rain in the night, with some thunder.

16.9.48: *(Glasgow):* Dull overcast day, but little or no rain. Evidently the tremendous rain of the other night happened all over the country. Some fields near Hairmyres were completely flooded. Very unwell, temperature about 101° each evening.

17.9.48: *(Barnhill):* Fairly fine day, but windy. Roughish crossing, but not quite enough so to be sick. Lime has arrived.

On the facing page opposite 17.9.48, Orwell has written, and ticked:

Plant peonies
Prune raspberries

18.9.48: Fine clear day, not very warm, in the morning, some rain & wind in afternoon & evening. B. & R. stacking corn, which apparently has dried up in the last two days. A[vril] picked blackberries (first this year.)

19.9.48: Alternately sunny & overcast, a few light showers, not very warm. Sea calm close in. Breakers over towards Crinan. Tried boat. Very easy to steer. Planted peonies (six, red). Very roughly planted. Pruned raspberries. Not certain whether I did it correctly.

20.9.48: One sharp shower, otherwise fine, clear & rather cold. Some wind from W. B.& R. have about finished the stack, which is to be covered with a tarpaulin. Find one of the blackcurrants (ie. those planted last year) has already sent up a small plant, presumably by layering.

21.9.48: Clear, fine day, rather cold. Little wind. Sea calm inshore. Started burning rubbish to get wood ash. A[vril] planted sweet williams in nursery bed.

22.9.48: Heavy rain in the night. From about 10 am onwards a beautiful, clear, sunny day, reasonably warm. Took boat down to the nearest bay to collect firewood. A[vril] sowed winter spinach.

23.9.48: A few small showers, but most of day simply overcast & rather cold. Wind from E. in the morning. A[vril] & B[ill] went over to Tarbert via Crinan for the cattle market. Boat ran well. B. bought 48 lambs for 24/– each. Last year's price was about 43/–. Felt very unwell, did not go out of doors.

24.9.48: Filthy day, all day, Sea rough. Unwell, stayed in bed. B[ill]'s sheep arrived.

25.9.48: Filthy night & morning, clearing slightly in the afternoon. Not much wind. Sea calmer. Got up for a little. The cats keep catching young rats, ie. what I think are young rats & not field mice. Did not know they bred so late in the year as this.

26.9.48: Horrible day. Very heavy rain in the night, & rain almost continuous throughout the day. Strong wind in the morning, mostly from S. The boat will have to be covered with a tarpaulin, as rain of this strength is liable to fill it up & sink it. Ground everywhere is a morass.

27.9.48: Rain in night, but a much better day, sunny & windy. Sea rough. Some more rain in evening.

28.9.48: Vile morning, pelting with rain, violent wind from south, sea very rough. Not cold. A few fine patches during afternoon.

29.9.48: Better day, sunny & windy. One short shower in the morning. Sea fairly calm.

30.9.48: Still, sunny & fairly warm in morning, still & overcast in afternoon. Sea calm in morning, growing slightly more choppy. Leaves beginning to fall.

1.10.48: Filthy day, all day. Boat gets a lot of water in it, evidently taking some in through the seams.

2.10.48: Nice, sunny, still day, fairly warm till evening. Sea calm. A. & B. took the boat down to Ardlussa to get the stores. The run from Barnhill to Ardlussa evidently takes about an hour. Started clearing strawberries. A curlew has adopted the fruit field & is there most of the time. Swallows seem to have flown. Bracken now brown everywhere.

3.10.48: Beautiful day, except for 1 short shower in the morning. Planted crocuses (200, yellow).

4.10.48: Beautiful day. A[vril] picked a lot of blackberries. Planted scillas (100).

A lamb died yesterday, the one that was lame. Probable reason, getting onto its back, or into a rut it could not get out of. As it was only just dead when found, the others ate it, which I did not fancy. The large calf is thought to have ringworm. Some lupins still flowering, & even new buds forming. Tremendous roaring of stags every night.

5.10.48: A little rain in the night, I think. Today a very still, overcast day, not very warm: Sea glassy. Flapping of cormorant's wings audible from the sea-shore (about 400 yards away). Today a hind & fawn got into the field, & when chased out by Bob the hind ran into the wire & broke its leg, so B[ill] had to shoot it. Transplanted a few raspberry suckers to fill up gaps in rows; the book says you should not do this.

6.10.48: Very still day, sunny in afternoon. Sea calm. A.& I.[14] made new house for the pig, making the walls of hay stuffed between two sheets of wire netting. Seems fairly wind-tight. Berries now at best on rowans. A lot of blackberries, very large.

On the facing page opposite 5 and 6.10.48, Orwell wrote, ticking the last three of the four items, and underlining 'Order hay' and 'parrafin'°:

Order Aladdin[15] chimney
Order hay.
.. parafin.°
.. other tractor

14. Avril and, presumably, Ian M'Kechnie, an estate worker at Ardlussa who lived at Inverlussa. The 'I.' cannot be Orwell himself: the full point is quite clear.
15. Trade name for a room heater fuelled by paraffin.

7.10.48: Beautiful, still day, quite warm till evening. Finished clearing the strawberries. Runners not so bad as last year. The others went out in the boat & took the creels round to the other bay. Some trouble with the petrol feed, but the engine was firing on all 4 cylinders, for almost the first time. Felt very unwell in evening (temperature 101°).

8.10.48: Strong wind all day. Sea rough. Rain in late evening. Unwell, stayed in bed (temperature 99°).

9.10.48: Dreadful day, all day. Sea rough. Impossible to fetch stores etc.

> Orwell had returned to Hairmyres Hospital for an examination by Dr Dick. In his letter to David Astor, 9 October 1948 (*CW*, XIX, pp. 450–1), Orwell wrote that 'Dr Dick seemed to be quite pleased with the results of his examination, but the journey upset me. Any kind of journey seems to do this. He told me to go on as at present, ie. spending half the day in bed, which I quite gladly do as I simply can't manage any kind of exertion. To walk a mile or pick up anything in the least heavy, or above all to get cold, promptly upsets me. Even if I go out in the evening to fetch the cows in it gives me a temperature. On the other hand so long as I live a senile sort of life I feel all right, and I seem able to work much as usual. I have got so used to writing in bed that I think I prefer it, though of course it's awkward to type there. I am just struggling with the last stages of this bloody book [*Nineteen Eighty-Four*], which is supposed to be done by early December, and will be if I don't get ill again. It would have been done by the spring if it had not been for this illness'.

10.10.48: Very heavy rain in night. Pools everywhere this morning. Today overcast, thick mist, very still, & raining lightly all morning. Rain stopped in afternoon & mist grew thicker. B[ill] & Ian [M'Kechnie] went over to Crinan, rather dangerous in this mist as they had no compass. Pig's new house gets very wet inside, but this is due to water trickling down the hillside & could be dealt with by a small trench round the wall.

11.10.48: Thick mist last night, & some rain, I think. Today blowy & overcast, but no rain till evening. Sea rough. Ian & B[ill] had some difficulty getting to Crinan, because there was so much water in the boat that it had got into the engine. All right on return journey. Ian has taken the boat to Ardlussa for Malcolm[16] to see whether there is a board loose. Eagle over the field today & yesterday. The cats keep catching shrews, which apparently are in the haystack. Yesterday we ate the first cockerel (May hatched). Quite good & made a sufficient meal for 6 people. 3 more coming on. New consignment of drink today (12 bottles). Bill's new puppy arrived (bitch). A[vril] dug trench round pig-sty.

16. Malcolm M'Kechnie, Ian's father.

12.10.48: Very blowy all day. Only a few drops of rain. Sea rough, breakers outside. Sty seems all right now that A[vril] has dug trench. Apples not quite ripe yet. Borders about due for clearing.

13.10.48: Sunny day with a number of sharp showers. A[vril] & I[an] began clearing the larger borders. Pain in side very bad. Sea calm.

16.10.48: (Some days missed out, apparently.)[17] Sunny day, with some showers. Rather chilly. Sea calm. Continued clearing the borders. Paraffin is running low. 40 gall barrel only seems to last about 6 weeks at this time of year. Picked the Golden Spire apples, three large ones. A very good-flavoured apple, though I think it is really a cooker.

Pain in side very bad on & off. Temperature (night) 100°.

17. Despite the 'apparently', this is Orwell's own entry.

17.10.48: Sunny day with a few showers. Rather chilly. Sea calm. Did not go out of doors.

18.10.48: Clear, sunny, rather cold day. No rain till night. Sea calm. A[vril] continued clearing borders.

19.10.48: Overcast day. No rain till night. Sea fairly calm, but B[ill], who returned from Crinan, said it was choppy in the middle of the Sound.

20.10.48: Overcast day, rainy in afternoon. Water supply suddenly stopped, & B[ill] & A[vril] had to go & unblock the pipe leading from the burn to the tank, which had got a lump of mud in it. A lot of potatoes are rotting this year because of the waterlogged state of the ground. We are said to have had 20'[18] of rain in the last two months. Not so bad here, but a lot lost at Ardlussa, it seems. Paraffin situation now desperate.

18. Twenty feet: Orwell must mean twenty inches (20″).

21.10.48: Overcast day, with occasional drizzle. Sea calm. A. & B. went down to Ardlussa in the boat to bring back 5 galls paraffin. Boat ran well but there is still one unlocated leak.

22.10.48: Clear, windy day, cold. Picked the apples, 4½ lb, ie. about 5½ with the others.

23.10.48: Nasty day, drizzling a good deal of the time. Sea calm till about 5 pm. The others went down in the boat to Ardlussa to fetch the stores, getting back just before the sea got up. Boat ran well but still takes in water. New drum of paraffin arrived, also Calor gas.

24.10.48: Filthy day, about the worst we have had. Rain incessant, considerable wind, sea rough. Not very cold, however. A[vril] & B[ill] baled boat, which was full of water. Leaks in roof very bad (2 places).

NB. to get Robert Shaw to deal with the tiles.

Started new Calor Gas. Ditto new drum of paraffin, which should last about 6 weeks.

On the facing page opposite 24.10.48, Orwell has written, and underlined 15.11.48:

See Robert Shaw[19] about roof.

Order paraffin about <u>15.11.48</u>

19. Robert Shaw was a building contractor who lived at Lagg, which lies on the coast road about fifteen miles south of Barnhill.

25.10.48: Better day, sunny but very cold. Wind in north. Sea fairly calm. Rabbits sitting along the bank sunning themselves.

26.10.48: Frost last night. Some short showers of hail & sleet this morning, & one short rain shower in afternoon. Otherwise clear, sunny & cold. Sea very calm. B[ill] thinks he has found the leak in the boat, which is in the shaft. Has plugged it up with grease, which is possibly all it needs. Pruned red currants (very lightly.)

27.10.48: Frost again last night, after rain in the earlier part of the night. Today a beautiful, sunny, still day, but cold. Sea less calm. A[vril] finished clearing border. Some of the leaves on the fruit trees going, after the frost. Pruned raspberries some more, cutting out all that had fruited. Deer keep getting into the field.

28.10.48: Fine, clear, sunny day, decidedly cold. There is still water in the boat, so evidently there is another leak somewhere.

29.10.48: Fine, but windy & cold. Hay arrived (1 ton, 25 bales). If possible the boat will be dragged up tomorrow, as it still takes in water. A[vril] forked the other border. Sea rough.

30.10.48: Heavy rain in the night. Today fine, and cold. The others dragged the boat up & propped it so that the stern can perhaps be caulked at low tide. B[ill] shot a rabbit which the dogs stole off the kitchen table the moment it had been skinned. Clocks go back tonight.

31.10.48: Rain in night. Violent wind all day, but not cold. Sea rough.

1.11.48: Fine & cold.

2.11.48: Filthy day, rain almost continuous. Roof dripping badly. Biro pen gave out, after only about 6 weeks.[20] Sea rough. Eagles overhead.

20. Orwell asked Julian Symons to obtain a Biro for him on 26 December 1947, enclosing £3 to pay for it. There is no other record of Biros being bought in 1948.

3.11.48: Day partly sunny, with some showers. Very heavy rain in the evening. Sea rough. Cows' yield has gone up a bit, no doubt thanks to the new hay. B[ill] has seen several more of the light-coloured rabbits.

4.11.48: Finer, but cold. A[vril] planted garden spirea, & phloxes.

5.11.48: Cold. Some fine patches & some drizzle. A little hail in the morning. Sea calm. Wind in north. A[vril] planted polyanthi.

6.11.48: Beautiful, still, windless day, warm in the sun, cold out of it. Sea calm. A[vril] & I.[21] planted tulips, about 100. A[vril] started clearing bed under window. Felt very bad in afternoon & evening, no doubt as a result of going out.[22]

21. Ian M'Kechnie.
22. It is clear from the past entries that Orwell has been able to do virtually no physical work in the garden; on 15 November he told Anthony Powell he could not so much as pull up a weed and that to walk even a few hundred yards upset him. Thus, his feeling very bad is a result of simply going outside, not going out to help with the garden. This is the period when he is typing the final version of *Nineteen Eighty-Four,* and, from the way his Biro has run out, also revising.

7.11.48: Beautiful, still, sunny day. Coldish. Sea less calm.

8.11.48: Frost in night. Clear, still, sunny day. Coldish. Sea fairly calm. B[ill] took the younger milch cow to the bull (Khilachrain). Should calve in August. A[vril] continued clearing border under house. Pruned the black-currants (a very little). Scillas showing. Qy. whether one should cover them up. Trouble with cable of tractor. Drink running low. NB. to order. Saw some blackbirds today. They are rare enough here to make one wonder what they are. A[vril] saw a flight of thrushes, possibly migrants, ie. fieldfares or redwings. One oar belonging to the dinghy in this bay has been washed away. Gladioli & dahlias over. New buds still coming on the roses.

On the facing page opposite 8.11.48, Orwell has written, and ticked:

Order gin etc.

9.11.48: Heavy wind in night. Very heavy sea. A little rain in the afternoon, after which the sea subsided somewhat.

10.11.48: Still, overcast day, mild. Sea slightly choppy.

11.11.48: Still, overcast, warm. Rain in night. Sea not very calm. The others fished in Barnhill bay & got 15. The oar which was washed away has come back. Polyanthi planted recently trying to flower.

16.11.48: Diary not filled up for some days. The last two days wet & windy, before that still & overcast. Not cold. Sea today pretty heavy. A[vril] has finished clearing the bed under the window & replanted the forget-me-nots. Pig has been lame, &c° one day would not even take any food. Now better, but still somewhat lame. Probably rheumatism, due to damp sty. He has been moved into the garage temporarily. B[ill] has got lumbago. The crossbred pullets (May hatched) look about ready to lay, but have not started yet. NB. to order paraffin & methylated.

On the facing page opposite 16.11.48, Orwell has written, and ticked the first item:

Order paraffin
Order methylated.

17.11.48: Damp & overcast, some rain. Very heavy rain in the evening. Sea rough. The new bull arrived, a young white shorthorn (beef.) Has been 15 days on the boat & is thin & in poor condition generally.

18.11.48: Beautiful day, quite warm. Sea calm. A[vril] has put up wires for the climbing roses. Pruned the plum trees. These are mostly very poor trees. Some roses still in bloom. Also a flower or two on the wallflowers which have been left in position.

19.11.48: Filthy day, rainy & very blowy. Sea rough. The first pullet started laying (May hatched). Pig active again. There are rats in the corn stack. B[ill]'s lumbago better. R.[23] caught several fish yesterday.

23. Presumably Orwell's son, Richard. In his letter to David Astor, 19 November 1948, he wrote that Richard 'goes fishing with the others and caught several fish the other day'.

20.11.48: Some sharp showers, with hail, but mostly fine. A[vril] & B[ill] brought the new van home (Chevrolet). Another pullet laying (I think). Pruned gooseberries.

21.11.48: One shower, otherwise beautiful day. Sea very calm & a wonderful colour. B[ill] trying to clean the mud from the back yard. Needs hose. Pruned the apple trees (not very hard). With the exception of one espalier tree, these have made very little growth. Qy. whether they need more manure & were grassed down too early.

On the facing page opposite 21.11.48, Orwell has written, and ticked:

Order hose (60′ ¾″)

22.11.48: Fine clear day. Sea calm. One pullet died (the one that had previously injured its breast in some way.)

23.11.48: Very dull, overcast day. Cold, but misty. Mainland invisible. Three eggs. The RIRs are still moulting badly.

24.11.48: Cold during the night. Today fine & sunny, but cold. Wind in East. Wallflowers keep trying to flower.

25.11.48: Cold. Wind E. or S.E.

26.11.48: Fairly fine, but very cold. Wind E. or S.E. Sea moderately calm. One RIR. has begun laying.

27.11.48: Still & chilly.

28.11.48: Beautiful, windless day, sea like glass. A faint mist. Mainland invisible.

29.11.48: Still, overcast day, not cold. Sea less calm. Bobbie brought back today. Rather unkempt, but seems in fairly good condition. A double egg today, apparently from one of the pullets.

30.11.48: Fine, blowy day, coldish. Sea rough. Apparently two RIRs are laying now.

1.12.48: Fine & blowy, sea rough. Some rain in the late evening. 3 or 4 eggs most days now.

2.12.48: Very violent wind in the night & throughout today. A good deal of rain. Very heavy seas. The pram dinghy[24] smashed to pieces, as the sea came up onto what is normally dry land. Trouble with the feed pipe of the lorry, the carburetter apparently not filling of its own accord.

24. A pram (or, more properly, praam) is a flat-bottomed dinghy with squared-off bow. In Orwell's phrase 'dinghy' is tautological.

3.12.48: Overcast day, some rain. Wind dropped during the course of the day. Sea still roughish, but nothing like yesterday. Most of the cattle now coming down to the byre of their own accord. Paraffin almost at an end. Lorry now apparently O.K.

4.12.48: Beautiful, still, sunny day, with a short shower in the afternoon. Two rainbows parallel to one another, one of them much fainter than the other. Qy. why this sometimes happens when there are rain & sun together. Sea calm. It appears that the bull is about 16 months old, having been born in July 1947, so he is fairly well advanced for his age, though in poor condition. Applied lime (a little) to fruit bushes.

5.12.48: Wind got up strongly in the night. Today almost incessant rain & strong wind. Sea rough. Feeling very unwell. Calor Gas cylinder about at an end. (Started 29.10.48, ie. has run 5 weeks.) Put on new cylinder.

6.12.48: Wind dropped during night. Beautiful, still, sunny day. Sea very calm. Did not feel well enough to go outside. Pig went to be slaughtered today. The others went on down to Craighouse to get paraffin, but could get only 1 gallon. Situation almost desperate till new supply reaches the island. New ram arrived today. Wireless batteries about finished (forget when put in).

7.12.48: Still, fairly sunny day. A little rain in the morning. Sea less calm. A[vril] brought back the internal fat etc. of the pig. Huge chunks of fat & meat on the cheeks. Paid for slaughtering & butchering the pig £1, & the trotters. Feeling very unwell.

Orwell made no entries until 19.12.48; that follows immediately after 7.12.48 on the same page.

19.12.48: Have not been well enough to enter up diary. Weather for the most part has been very still, overcast, not cold, sometimes almost twilight all day. Sea mostly calm. Violent wind once or twice, but little rain. A scilla trying to flower. B[ill] says grass has also grown in the last fortnight. Goose (for Xmas) brought back today. Also a young wild goat (female). Pig after removal of head & trotters weighed 2 cwt. (age about 9 months).

Started new drum of paraffin. We owe about 10 galls., so that in reality we only have about 30 galls in hand.

NB. to order more almost immediately. Cylinder of Calor gas began to give out today. There must be a leak, probably in the transformer. Started new cylinder (NB. we have only 1 this time).

On the facing page opposite 19.12.48, Orwell has written, and ticked the final item:

Order paraffin.
Order Calor gas.
Get insurance stamps.[25]
Order hay (1 ton)

25. National insurance stamps, required by law, presumably for himself as a self-employed person or for Bill Dunn as Orwell's and Richard Rees's employee.

22.12.48: Very clear, still, coldish weather the last two days. Sea very calm. One now has to light the lamps at about 3 or 3.30 pm. Today curious white streaks on the sea, presumably caused by fry milling round, but no birds taking any interest.

8½ bales of hay left, out of 25, received nearly 2 months ago. So at this time of year 1 ton (25 bales) should last nearly 3 months, ie. for 2 milch cows & a calf.

24.12.48: Sharp frosts the last two nights. The days sunny & still, sea calm. A[vril] has very bad cold. The goose for Xmas disappeared, then was found swimming in the sea round at the anchorage, about a mile from our own beach. B[ill] thinks it must have swum round. He had to follow it in a dinghy & shoot it. Weight before drawing & plucking, 10½ lbs.

Snowdrops up all over the place. A few tulips showing. Some wallflowers still trying to flower.

This concludes Orwell's Domestic Diary Volume V.

Relevant Entries from Last Literary Notebook

21 March 1949 – September 1949

Having suffered a serious relapse, Orwell was taken from Jura about 2 January 1949 to Cranham Sanatorium near Stroud in Gloucestershire.

Orwell's last Literary Notebook (see *CW*, XX, p. 200) contains a few handwritten entries relating to Cranham Sanatorium and University College Hospital. The routine is given for each hospital, as it was for Hairmyres and there are brief, dated, descriptive details. The entries for Cranham are dated 21 and 24 March and 17 April 1949. The first and last entries are given here and the second has been inserted on page 482 because it refers to Orwell's treatment with streptomycin at Hairmyres in 1948, and is therefore placed where it is relevant to the medication Orwell was then receiving. For the Cranham Sanatorium routine, see *CW*, XX, pp. 69–70.

The note numbering starts at 1.

21.3.49: The routine here (Cranham Sanatorium) is quite different from that of Hairmyres Hospital. Although everyone at Hairmyres was most kind & considerate to me – quite astonishingly so, indeed – one cannot help feeling at every moment the difference in the *texture* of life when one is paying one's own keep.

The most noticeable difference here is that it is much quieter than the hospital, & that everything is done in a more leisurely way. I live in a so-called chalet, one of a row of continuous wooden huts, with glass doors, each chalet measuring about 15' by 12'. There are hot water pipes, a washing basin, a chest of drawers & wardrobe, besides the usual bed-tables etc. Outside is a glass-roofed verandah. Everything is brought by hand – none of those abominable rattling trolleys which one is never out of the sound of in a hospital. Not much noise of radios either – all the patients have headphones. (Here these are permanently tuned in to the Home Service. At Hairmyres, usually to the Light.[1]) The most persistent sound is the song of birds.

The day's routine:–

7 am. Pulse & temperature taken. For this I don't wake up further than is necessary to put the thermometer in my mouth, & am usually too sleepy to take the reading then.

7.30. Sputum cups changed.

8.00. Breakfast. After breakfast I get up & wash. I am only allowed a bath twice a week, as it is supposed to be "weakening."

9.30. (about). Beds made.

11.00. Cup of coffee.

12.00 (about). Room swept & dusted.

12.00.–12.40. Rest hour. One is supposed to lie down during this period. Doctor generally arrives about this time.

12.40. Lunch.

2.00–2.40. Rest hour. Actually I usually sleep from about 2.30 to 3.30.

3.30. Tea.

6.00. Temperature & pulse taken.

6.00.–6.40. Rest hour.

6.40. Dinner.

9.30. (about). Cup of tea.

10.30. Lights out.

One is only weighed, screened etc. about once a month. The charge here is £12–12–0 a week, but this does not cover much more than one's board & lodging, special medicines, operations etc. being extra.

1. The Home Service would correspond to Radio 4 today and the Light programme to Radio 1 or 2. Radio 3 was then the Third Programme and more or less the same in content and style.

17.4.49: *Cranham:* Curious effect, here in the sanatorium, on Easter Sunday, when the people in this (the most expensive[2]) block of "chalets" mostly have visitors, of hearing large numbers of upper-class English voices. I have been almost out of the sound of them for two years, hearing them at most one or two at a time, my ears growing more & more used to working-class or lower-middle class Scottish voices. In the hospital at Hairmyres, for instance, I literally never heard a "cultivated" accent except when I had a visitor. It is as though I were hearing these voices for the first time. And what voices! A sort of over-fedness, a fatuous self-confidence, a constant bah-bahing of laughter about nothing, above all a sort of heaviness & richness combined with a fundamental ill-will – people who, one instinctively feels, without even being able to see them, are the enemies of anything intelligent or sensitive or beautiful. No wonder everyone hates us so.

2. The National Health Service began its 'cradle to grave' care on 5 July 1948 but there was still also private care for those who wished to pay for it.

Nineteen Eighty-Four was published by Secker & Warburg on 8 June 1949 and five days later by Harcourt, Brace in New York. Such was its impact that as early as 27 August 1949 a radio version was broadcast in the NBC University Theatre series, skilfully dramatised by Milton Wayne and with David Niven as Winston Smith; the novelist James Hilton gave an interval commentary.

On 3 September Orwell was transferred to University College Hospital, London. The following is the entry Orwell made in his last Literary Notebook, *c.* September 1949, about the daily routine at this hospital (*CW*, XX, pp.165–6). It also gives a description of his room.[3]

Daily Routine at University College Hospital (Private Wing)

7–7.30 am. Temperature taken. Routine question: "How did you sleep?"

7.30–8. Blanket bath. Bed made. Shaving water. "Back" rubbed.

8.45. (about) Breakfast. Newspaper arrives.

9.30. (about) Wing sister arrives with mail.

10. Temperature taken.

10.30. (at present) my bed is "tipped". Ward maid comes to sweep room.

11. (about) Orderly arrives to dust.

12.30. Bed taken down.

12.45 pm. Lunch.

2. Temperature taken.

2.30. Bed "tipped."

3.30. Bed taken down.

3.45. Tea.

5. Temperature taken.

5.30. (about) am washed as far as waist. "Back" rubbed.

6.45. Dinner.

10. Temperature taken; a drink of some sort.

10.30. (about) Bed "tipped" & light put out shortly after.

No fixed hour for visits of doctor. No routine daily visit.

Room has: washbasin, cupboard, bedside locker, bed table, chest of drawers, wardrobe, 2 mirrors, wireless (knobs beside bed), electric fire, radiator, armchair & 1 other chair, bedside lamp & 2 other lamps, telephone. Fees 15 guineas a week, plus extra fee for doctor, but apparently including special medicines. Does not include telephone or wireless. (Charge for wireless 3/6 a week.)

3. Orwell's room, Number 65 in the Private Wing, is illustrated in Thompson's *Orwell's London*, p. 102; the Private Wing is shown on p. 101.

Orwell's diary entries end here.

WHILST IN University College Hospital Orwell married Sonia Brownell on 13 October 1949. He hoped to be well enough to recuperate in Switzerland and friends (especially booksellers) raised funds to enable him to make the journey. Alas, before he could go, he died of a massive haemorrhage of the lungs in the early hours of Saturday, 21 January 1950. His beloved fishing rods stood in the corner of his hospital room. His funeral service was arranged by Malcolm Muggeridge at Christ Church, Albany Street, London, NW1. He had asked that he be buried, not cremated, and David Astor arranged for that to take place at All Saints, Sutton Courtney, Berkshire. His headstone is inscribed simply: 'Here Lies Eric Arthur Blair', with his dates of birth and death.

Short List of Further Reading

All Orwell's writings – and, with their accompanying notes, they take up some 9,000 pages – are to be found in *The Complete Works of George Orwell*, ed. Peter Davison, assisted by Ian Angus and Sheila Davison, 1998; second paperback edition, 2000–02. The books take up the first nine volumes and are published by Penguin with the same pagination of the texts. *The Facsimile of the Manuscript of 'Nineteen Eighty-Four'* was published in 1984; a supplementary volume, *The Lost Orwell*, was published in 2006. In 2001 Penguin Books published four collections of essays, edited by Peter Davison, which have notes additional to those in the *Complete Works*. These are:

Orwell in Spain (includes *Homage to Catalonia);* 393 pages
Orwell's England (includes *The Road to Wigan Pier*); 432 pages, with 32 pages of plates
Orwell and the Dispossessed (includes *Down and Out in Paris and London*); 424 pages
Orwell and Politics (includes *Animal Farm*); 537 pages

Footnote references: References to the *Complete Works* are given as *CW* + Volume number in roman figures + page(s), e.g. *CW*, XX, pp. 210–11. References to books listed below are given by the author's name + page number – e.g. Crick, p. 482, except for *Orwell Remembered* and *Remembering Orwell*, which are so designated + page number(s).

There are very many critical studies of George Orwell and his writings. To simplify matters, only details of recent biographies and half-a-dozen very recent critical studies are listed here. From these it will be fairly straightforward to seek out earlier biographies and studies.

Biographies:

Audrey Coppard and Bernard Crick, *Orwell Remembered,* 1984 (in the text as *Orwell Remembered*)
Stephen Wadhams, *Remembering Orwell,* 1984 (as *Remembering Orwell).*
John Thompson, *Orwell's London* (with many photographs by Philippa Scoones), 1984.

Bernard Crick, *George Orwell: A Life*, (1980), 1992 edition with important new Appendix (as Crick).

T. R. Fyvel, *George Orwell: a personal memoir*, 1982 (as Fyvel).

Michael Shelden, *Orwell: The Authorised Biography*, 1991 (UK edition) (as Shelden).

Jeffrey Meyers, *Orwell: Wintry Conscience of a Generation*, 2000.

Gordon Bowker, *George Orwell*, 2003 (as Bowker).

Scott Lucas, *Orwell*, 2003.

D. J. Taylor, *Orwell: The Life*, 2003 (as Taylor).

Jacintha Buddicom, *Eric & Us* (1974), with an important Postscript by Dione Venables, 2006.

Critical Studies:

The Cambridge Companion to George Orwell, edited by John Rodden, 2007.

Christopher Hitchens, *Orwell's Victory*, 2002 (as *Why Orwell Matters* in USA).

Douglas Kerr, *George Orwell* (in the Writers and their Work series), 2003.

Emma Larkin, *Secret Histories: Finding George Orwell in a Burmese Teashop*, 2004.

John Rodden, *Every Intellectual's Big Brother: George Orwell's Literary Siblings*, 2006. This gives a valuable account of the Centenary Conference, 'George Orwell: An Exploration of His World and Legacy', held at Wellesley College, near Boston, Massachusetts in May 2003. In many ways it takes further John Rodden's, *The Politics of Literary Reputation: The Making and Claiming of 'St. George' Orwell*, 1989.

Daniel J. Leab, *Orwell Subverted: The CIA and the Filming of 'Animal Farm'*, 2007.

Sir Richard Rees, *George Orwell: Fugitive from the Camp of Victory*, 1961 (as *George Orwell*).

Loraine Saunders, *The Unsung Artistry of George Orwell: The Novels from 'Burmese Days' to 'Nineteen Eighty-Four'*, 2008.

Hugh Thomas, *The Spanish Civil War* (1961), third edn. 1977 (as Thomas).

Internet websites:

www.finlay-publisher.com – this is the website of *Eric & Us*. This publishes essays by leading scholars every two months together with comments from readers. It is run by Dione Vennables who wrote the Postcript to the second edition to Jacintha Buddicom's book of that title (2006).

www.orwelldiaries.wordpress.com – which not only gives details of events related to the annual Orwell Prize, but also details of many other events. It reproduces some of the articles from the *Eric & Us* website and is currently reproducing Orwell's diary entries day by day seventy years on. Associated with that is Google map showing where Orwell was when he wrote his diary entries. It is run by Professor Jean Seaton and Gavin Freeguard.

Index

THIS IS AN INDEX CHIEFLY OF NAMES. No attempt is made to index the various flowers Orwell and Eileen planted, nor to index the minutiae of his concerns for his goats and hens, and the number of eggs collected, etc. In the War-time Diaries there are many, many references to, for example, the bombing of London, but only a number of entries of particular interest are indexed. Similarly, only significant entries affecting Eileen and Avril are noted. On Jura it is apparent that Orwell was closely associated with (and much helped by) Donald and Katie Darroch, and again, only selected references are indexed. To do otherwise than be selective would unhelpfully crowd this index. Specific newspapers and journals quoted in the 'Diary of Events Leading Up to the War' are *not* indexed. It is of the nature of these diaries that the phrases *et seq.* and *et passim* might be taken as read for many topics. Pages with *significant* explanatory and biographical notes are given in **bold** but by no means all references in footnotes are indexed in bold. The more interesting newspaper cuttings to which Orwell refers (e.g. curing animal skins) are indexed. Mac, Mc, and M' are indexed as if 'Mac' the order thereafter being by following letter; St is indexed as if 'Saint'. Titles are not given in the index unless there is no first name. Orwell frequently misspelt names; these are maintained in the edition, usually without comment in the diary although occasionally followed by superscript ° ; the index gives correct spellings.

ORWELL'S EARLY NOVELS

BURMESE DAYS

Based on his experiences as a policeman in Burma, George Orwell's first novel presents a devastating picture of British imperialism in a society where, 'after all, natives were natives'. When Flory, a white timber merchant, befriends Indian Dr Veraswami, he defies this orthodoxy. The doctor is in danger: U Po Kyin, a corrupt magistrate, is plotting his downfall. The only thing that can save him is membership of the all-white Club, and Flory can help. Flory's life is changed further by the arrival of beautiful Elizabeth Lackersteen from Paris, who offers an escape from the loneliness and the 'lie' of colonial life.

A CLERGYMAN'S DAUGHTER

Intimidated by her father, the Rector of Knype Hill, Dorothy performs her submissive roles of dutiful daughter and bullied housekeeper. Her thoughts are taken up with the costumes she is making for the church school play, by the hopelessness of preaching to the poor and by debts she cannot pay. Suddenly her routine shatters and Dorothy finds herself down and out in London. She is wearing silk stockings, has money in her pocket but cannot remember her name. Orwell leads us through a landscape of unemployment, poverty and hunger, where Dorothy's faith is challenged and her life changed.

ORWELL'S GREAT POLITICAL NOVELS

ANIMAL FARM

When the downtrodden animals of Manor Farm overthrow their master Mr Jones and take over the farm themselves, they imagine it is the beginning of a life of freedom and equality. But as a cunning, ruthless élite among them starts to take control, the other animals find themselves hopelessly ensnared as one form of tyranny is gradually replaced with another. Written at the end of 1943 but almost not published for its attack on Britain's wartime ally Stalin, Orwell's chilling 'fairy story' is a timeless and devastating satire of idealism betrayed by power and corruption.

NINETEEN EIGHTY-FOUR

Hidden away in the Record Department of the sprawling Ministry of Truth, Winston Smith skilfully rewrites the past to suit the needs of the Party. Yet he inwardly rebels against the totalitarian world he lives in, which demands absolute obedience and controls him through the all-seeing telescreens and the watchful eye of Big Brother. In his longing for truth and liberty, Smith begins a secret love affair with a fellow-worker, Julia, but soon discovers a nightmare world where love is hate, war is peace and the true price of freedom is betrayal.

ORWELL AMONG THE UNDERCLASS

DOWN AND OUT IN PARIS AND LONDON

'You have talked so often of going to the dogs – and well, here are the dogs, and you have reached them.'

George Orwell's vivid memoir of his time among the desperately poor and destitute in London and Paris is a moving tour of the underworld of society. Here he painstakingly documents a world of unrelenting drudgery and squalor – sleeping in bug-infested hostels and doss houses, working as a dishwasher in the vile 'Hôtel X', living alongside tramps, surviving on scraps and cigarette butts – in an unforgettable account of what being on the streets is really like.

THE ROAD TO WIGAN PIER

A searing account of George Orwell's experiences of working-class life in the bleak industrial heartlands of Yorkshire and Lancashire, *The Road to Wigan Pier* is a brilliant and bitter polemic that has lost none of its political impact over time. His graphically unforgettable descriptions of social injustice, slum housing, mining conditions, squalor, hunger and growing unemployment are written with unblinking honesty, fury and great humanity.